MR. AMERICA

Terry and Jan Todd Series on Physical Culture and Sports

MR. AMERICA

THE TRAGIC HISTORY OF A BODYBUILDING ICON

John D. Fair

University of Texas Press
Austin

Requests for permission to reproduce material from this work should be sent to:
Permissions
University of Texas Press
P.O. Box 7819
Austin, TX 78713-7819
http://utpress.utexas.edu/index.php/rp-form

♾ The paper used in this book meets the minimum requirements of
ANSI/NISO Z39.48-1992 (R1997) (Permanence of Paper).

Library of Congress Cataloging-in-Publication Data

Fair, John D.
  Mr. America : the tragic history of a bodybuilding icon / John D. Fair. — First edition.
  pages   cm. — (Terry and Jan Todd series on Physical Culture and Sports)
  Includes bibliographical references and index.
  ISBN 978-0-292-76082-0 (cloth : alk. paper)
1. Bodybuilding—Competitions—United States—History—20th century. I. Title.
II. Title: Mister America.
  GV546.5.F35 2015
  796.41—dc23   2014007953

doi:10.7560/760820

To John Hordines,
who started it all

CONTENTS

ALL HISTORY IS ABOUT BODIES AND NOTHING CAN BE WRITTEN OR UNDERSTOOD OUTSIDE OF BODILY EXPERIENCE.

= MICHAEL ANTON BUDD, *THE SCULPTURE MACHINE* =

IN 1970, JON ALEXANDER, A HISTORY PROFESSOR AT TEMPLE UNIVERSITY, complained to the editor of *Muscular Development*, a leading muscle magazine published by the York Barbell Company, that while the Philadelphia Free Library contained over five million volumes, it had only a few books on weightlifting and virtually nothing on the history of bodybuilding. He wanted to know whether any study had ever traced the history of the sport from its inception to the present. Bob Hoffman, the company's founder and the iron game's most formidable personality at the time, suggested his own *Secrets of Strength and Development*; though this rambling text was hardly a history, its author recommended the book as the "nearest thing" to the sort of study that Alexander had requested.[1] Nearly a decade later *Barbells + Beefcake*, David Webster's illustrated history of bodybuilding, filled the immense void on the subject and would no doubt have satisfied Alexander.[2] But no extensive studies delving into the historical or sociological roots of this unique activity appeared until the 1990s, when at least a half-dozen fundamental works set the tone of scholarship into the new century. They include *The Perfectible Body*, Kenneth Dutton's sweeping overview of physical culture in the context of Western civilization; Alan Klein's in-depth analysis of bodybuilding culture, *Little Big Men*; and David Chapman's landmark study of the founder of modern bodybuilding, *Sandow the Magnificent*. By the end of the decade, Pamela Moore's anthology *Building Bodies* and my *Muscletown USA*, for which this current book serves somewhat as a sequel, brought together many strands of the modern physical-culture movement.[3]

Nor have women been neglected. In *Bodymakers*, Leslie Heywood analyzes the iconography of women's bodybuilding from a feminist perspective, and Maria Lowe's *Women of Steel* reckons with the conundrum of balancing muscular development against femininity. Their appearance coincided with a burgeoning scholarly interest in the body at the end of the twentieth century. And Jan Todd's *Physical Culture and the Body Beautiful*, a study of nineteenth-century women, has provided a firm foundation for future research.[4] These scholarly works have been complemented since the 1970s by many reflections and revelations bearing such titles as *Muscle Wars*; *Muscle: Confessions of an Unlikely Bodybuilder*; *Bodybuilders, Drugs, and Sex*; *Gorilla Suit*; *Brother Iron, Sister Steel*; *Chemical Pink*; *Muscle: A Writer's Trip through a Sport with No Boundaries*; *Iron Maidens*; *Brothers of Iron*; *Heart of Steel*; and *Death, Drugs, and Muscle*—all of which suggest a turbulent and confusing cultural phenomenon.[5] It is hardly the same sport that Webster showcased a generation ago.

So extensive has the corpus of bodybuilding literature become that Emily Nussbaum recognized it as an independent field of scholarship in a 1998 *Lingua Franca* article entitled "Bodies That Matter": "Bodybuilding and weightlifting studies fit right into several current academic trends: the hot new field of sports history and sociology, body studies in general, and queer and feminist explorations of androgyny and gender bending."[6] This trend has continued since 2000 with numerous studies that treat bodybuilding as a historical and cultural phenomenon. Two of them, *Bodybuilding*, by Gordon LaVelle, and *Million Dollar Muscle*, by Adrian Tan and Doug Brignole, trace the evolution of bodybuilding through the twentieth century and place it within a larger social context. While both accounts provide many valuable insights, they are based largely on secondary sources.[7] Randy Roach's comprehensive *Muscle, Smoke, and Mirrors* also draws heavily from secondary sources but uses interviews to uncover new material on all facets of the iron game, placing bodybuilders at center stage.[8] None of these publications, however, provides more than scant coverage on the twentieth century's arguably most important physique title, Mr. America.

Mark Adams wrote a biography of Bernarr Macfadden entitled *Mr. America* (2009), yet Macfadden never held the title of Mr. America, and neither the title nor the contest is mentioned anywhere in the book.[9] The title is nevertheless somewhat appropriate for reasons of symbolism: Macfadden was a transformative figure in American life, representing the attitudes, aspirations, and foibles of many Americans who adopted his physical-culture lifestyle. But the term also has a more specific meaning, one that Macfadden promoted, for it reflected the pinnacle of manly development as drawn from ideals fostered by the ancient Greeks and epitomized in the iconic body of Charles Atlas, Macfadden's most famous protégé. Atlas was never a Mr. America, but he set the tone by focusing on the whole person and healthful living. Still, though well written and accurate, Adams's story hardly reflects its title and adds little to the two earlier biographies of Macfadden.[10]

Whatever shortcomings might exist in the present account, every effort has been made to incorporate original source material accompanied by full documentation and an interpretive focus. This is done on three levels. The basic framework is drawn from the many so-called muscle magazines — from Macfadden's *Physical Culture*, founded in 1899, to such current publications as *Iron Man*, *Muscle & Fitness*, and *MuscleMag International*. Though not without flaws of bias and omission, these magazines provide accounts of physique contests and related developments as they occurred. Supplementing these accounts is a mixture of other printed material, largely historical, biographical, and sociological, that offers access to other primary sources and viewpoints.

To fill the many gaps in printed material intended for public consumption, this study includes information from private interviews with scores of individuals associated with the iron game. Like other original sources, however, the interviews must be treated with caution. Most interviewees lived through only a portion of the period covered, and virtually none experienced the earliest decades. Furthermore, memory is a tricky medium. Subjects are often forgetful, and their recollections can be selective, misleading, or just wrong, in part because the often-irresistible opportunity to shape history to their advantage can lead them to place themselves in a favorable light and depict their adversaries as evil or misguided. Therefore, it is desirable to double- or triple-check stories with as many individuals as possible. To this end, I am indebted to the following persons, who graciously subjected themselves to my queries (asterisks indicate Mr. America title winners): Joe Abbenda★, Dale Adrian★, Jules Bacon★, John Balik, Clarence Bass, Bob Bendel, Vic Boff, Bob Bonham, Leonard Bosland, Howard Bovell, Richard Cavaler, David Chapman, Boyer Coe★, Bill Colonna, Bob Crist, Jerry Daniels★, Dave Davis, John DeCola★, Jan Dellinger, Bob Delmontique, Louis DeMarco, Wayne DeMilia, Chris Dickerson★, Mauro Di Pasquale, Dave Draper★, Alton Eliason, Neva Fickling, Kelvin Fountano, Warren Frederick★, Max Furek, Frances Gajkowski, David Gentle, Mike Graham, Bill Grant★, John Grimek★, Fairfax Hackley, Terry Hairston★, Josh Henson, Norman Hibbert, Sylvia Hibbert, John Hoffman, John Hordines, Dan Howard, Don Howorth★, Gene Jantzen, Harry Johnson★, Ted Karnezis, Bob Kennedy, Faye King, Jack King, Joan Klisanin, Steve Klisanin★, Charles Kochakian, Zabo Kozewski, Lloyd "Red" Lerille★, Jim Lorimer, Dan Lurie, Ian MacQueen, Tom Manfre, Steve Michalik★, Pete Miller, Gene Mozee, Jim Murray, David Lee Nall, Jack O'Bleness, Tommy O'Hare, Emmanuel Orlick, Jim Park★, Charlotte Parker, Joel Parker, Jimmy Payne★, Bill Pearl★, Joe Peters, Jon Rieger, Ken Rosa, Rudy Sablo, Elmo Santiago, Cliff Sawyer, Matt Shepley, Dick Smith, Harry Smith, Ken Sprague, Bill Starr, Leo Stern, Tommy Suggs, Armand Tanny★, John Terpak, Joe Tete, Terry Todd, Val Vasilieff★, Vern Weaver★, David Webster, Malcolm Whyatt, Kim Wood, Fred Yale, Chester Yorton★, and Frank Zane★. This list includes twenty-five former Mr. Americas, constituting 26 percent of the ninety-seven persons interviewed, which ensures at least some degree of authenticity.

The various extant documents, manuscripts, and photographs from the period have proved to be the most reliable source of information, but only a small fraction of such material has survived. Most people involved in the sport have thrown away items relating to their participation, perceiving them as clutter, but I nevertheless asked nearly all those I interviewed whether they had saved anything of this nature. I am particularly grateful to Dr. Jon Rieger, a professor of sociology at the University of Louisville, who had the presence of mind to save his records and donate them to me for this project. They filled a giant information void for the final two decades of the Mr. America Contest, which was no longer receiving much coverage in the muscle media. Moreover, I have been able to rely on the resources I gathered for *Muscletown* and other projects over the years, items that collectively constitute the Hoffman Papers and other collections in my possession. This study also relies heavily on the enormous archive housed in the H. J. Lutcher Stark

Center for Physical Culture and Sports at the University of Texas. For providing full access to this incomparable resource and for their invaluable counsel, support, and friendship over many years, I am indebted to Jan and Terry Todd and members of their staff.

Finally, I am grateful to my buff and beautiful wife, Sarah, for her editorial assistance, moral support, and love throughout this project.

MR. AMERICA

INTRODUCTION

WHAT A PIECE OF WORK IS A MAN! HOW NOBLE IN REASON! HOW INFINITE IN FACULTY! IN FORM, IN MOVING, HOW EXPRESS AND ADMIRABLE! IN ACTION HOW LIKE AN ANGEL! IN APPREHENSION HOW LIKE A GOD! THE BEAUTY OF THE WORLD! THE PARAGON OF ANIMALS!

= WILLIAM SHAKESPEARE, *HAMLET*, ACT 2, SCENE 2 =

IDEAL NOTIONS OF MAN AND MASCULINITY ARE DEEPLY EMBEDDED IN Western civilization. The humanistic spirit conceived by the ancient Greeks and resurrected in subsequent epochs by Italian artists, French thinkers, English scientists, and American entrepreneurs was imbued with a sense of ongoing traditions and future aspirations. Similarly, the United States, in the eyes of its citizens, is likewise bound up with founding ideals that it struggles to realize. Yet as the historians Charles Bright and Michael Geyer point out, others perceive the United States not so much according to its ideals, but rather via "Americanism," a shorthand of global brands, entertainment, and military might: "Mc-Donald's, Microsoft, pop culture, and cruise missiles." All serve as global identifiers that help define what it means to be an American.[1] The historian John Tosh maintains that such symbols and rituals "express a complex range of cultural values" reflecting "a coherence of thought

1

and behaviour which in the last resort . . . holds society together."[2] Whether any such symbol can be meaningfully attached to an ideal of American manhood is the main question addressed in this study.

Some of the most vivid and enduring images of Americans during the twentieth century were the winners of the Mr. America Contest, precedents for which can be traced to as early as 1904. In that year, Bernarr Macfadden, often dubbed the "Father of Physical Culture," staged a widely heralded bodybuilding competition in New York City. From that point until its demise in Petersburg, Virginia, in 1999, the Mr. America concept reflected a desired image of modern manhood. As societal views toward the male body and physical culture evolved, however, bodybuilders had to redefine themselves in light of the clash between revered traditions and concessions to current tastes. The Mr. America Contest, which once epitomized the aspirations of tens of thousands of weight trainees, was premised on adherence to time-honored values of health, fitness, beauty, and athleticism, while Americans—and especially bodybuilders— became obsessed with appearances and engaged in training practices and lifestyles that often subverted those ideals. By the end of the century, physique competitors and promoters seemed perplexed about what constituted a perfect specimen of manhood. Reckoning with these cultural questions became the foremost concern in modern bodybuilding not only in the United States but worldwide, since the Mr. America title, at least from the 1940s to the 1970s, was, like other aspects of American culture, a global icon.

This study endeavors to trace the history of the Mr. America concept and employ it as a benchmark for understanding the changes that occurred in bodybuilding and society during the twentieth century. Formulated by Macfadden in accordance with ancient Greek ideals, Mr. America provided a standard for U.S. masculinity through the 1950s. In its heyday, the contest was so important that several versions of it emerged, claimed by rival federations seeking to draw on the title's prestige. But it underwent a metamorphosis during the 1960s, buffeted by a host of cultural forces, including the civil rights movement, feminism, gay rights, commercialism, and drugs, set against the backdrop of other bodily displays—the Mr. Universe and Mr. Olympia contests, and the Miss America Pageant. As William Manchester observed of the sixties, "The discipline that knits a society together was weakening and at some points giving way altogether."[3] Thus, those bodybuilders for whom the sport represented a union of mind and body, and the primacy of function over form, were superseded by a new generation of baby boomers who were indifferent to those ideals. That destiny should play such a role in redefining the American male body carries overtones of a Greek tragedy.

This treatment of physique iconography is set within several larger perspectives of the body, the physical-culture movement, manliness, and a triad of gender, racial, and homosexual influences. Virtually all studies of the body go back to the Greeks and the origins of Western civilization, as distinct from societies with roots in India, China, or sub-Saharan Africa. Arnold Toynbee noted of the Western world's relationship to ancient Greece: "It is its child." Kenneth Dutton, in *The Perfectible Body*, refines this distinction by observing that while Eastern representations of the body, exemplified by the Buddha, are "turned in upon themselves, motionless and concentrating upon an interior life," the Greeks present humanity as seeking "spiritual elevation through victorious combat against the external, material world, self-mastery rather than self-abandonment to the infinite." The epitome of this is "Hercules, the 'hero of the bulging chest and contracted abdominal muscles,' . . . in search of a divinity to be attained through deeds and actions rather than by a descent into the self."[4]

For the Cambridge don G. Lowes Dickinson (1862–1932), the human form for the Greeks represented "a training in aesthetics as much as, or more than, in physical excellence." And physical development carried moral weight: "A good body was the necessary correlative of a good soul." Dickinson considered the ancient Greeks' achievement of bodily excellence to outshine even their accomplishments in science, art, and military prowess: "That sunny and frank intelligence, bathed . . . in the open air, a gracious blossom springing from the root of physical health, that unique and perfect balance of body and soul, passion and intellect, represent . . . the highest achievement of the civilization of Greece."[5] Dickinson's characterization was typical of the high regard that Victorians had for the Greeks, which helped underscore their claim, as inheritors of Hellenic traditions, to cultural superiority. This sentiment permeated the early decades of the twentieth century.

In 1912, the Oxford fellow R. W. Livingstone identified this idealistic view of the Greeks as a reflection more on modern than ancient society. It was chiefly the doing of the eighteenth-century German classicist Johann Joachim Winckelmann, whose "misconception" of the Greeks helped shape the intellectual life at Oxford and Cambridge.

> The modern interest in Hellenism really dates from Winckelmann, and Winckelmann drew his ideas of the Greeks mainly from their art....The Greeks, it appeared, were beyond all things beauty-lovers. They stripped at their sports; they gave prizes for beauty; Lais fascinated them; they spent their days in games and festivals; they studied to "observe propriety both in feature and action," so that "even a quick walk was regarded as opposed to their sense of decorum." Winckelmann had looked on the tranquil beauty of Greek art . . . till he was led almost to fancy that the serene figures of the Parthenon marbles were portraits of the ordinary Greek, and that the streets of Athens were full of well-draped statuesque men pacing reposefully through an august life....
>
> The fifth-century Athenian was no more a Mid-Victorian aesthete than he was a Cobdenite Liberal.[6]

Winckelmann had a significant impact, not only on the development of classical liberalism but also on nineteenth-century romantic writers such as Johann Wolfgang von Goethe, Gotthold Lessing, and Johann Gottfried von Herder. His view, according to Livingstone, "coloured the glasses through which Europe looked at Greece for many generations." Livingstone's own version of respect for the Greeks focused on the body's importance in their conception of man. The body was predominant "in the abiding passion for personal beauty and physical strength; in the idealization of the athlete; in the sculpture that developed its ideals as it watched in the gymnasia the naked human form." For Plato, physical beauty was "the natural expression of the beauty of the soul."[7] That it was an invented tradition and that Winckelmann drew his inspiration from the Greeks via Roman copies made the passion for Hellenic civilization no less real or acceptable, even in the highest academic circles.

Greek ideals were most vividly expressed, and most readily passed on to posterity, through art. "The great result of the working of the spirit of humanism in Greek art was the representation of the Gods in human form," wrote Percy Gardner, the Oxford Professor of Classical Archaeology, in 1921. From the rediscovery of Greek and Roman works of sculpture there emerged, after the Christian era, three neoclassical epochs. The first was the Italian Renaissance, which eventually "degenerated into the mannerism and extravagance of Bernini." The second period originated with Winckelmann, whose visit to Italy in 1755 brought about a return to "simplicity, to self-restraint, to ideality" in European art. The third Greek revival occurred in the nineteenth century, Gardner contends, when the sculptures of the Parthenon were brought to London, allowing critics to observe their infinite superiority to Roman copies and Hellenistic adaptations. From a late twentieth-century perspective, John Boardman, Gardner's successor, recognized the "Greek cult" as a contrivance, reflecting "the popular and uncritical attitude of a hundred years ago to anything classical." Yet he adheres to classical conceptions of the body: "Man was the measure of all things to the Greeks, and the artist's aim was to portray him at his ideal-ized best, indistinguishable from the gods whom he conceived in man's likeness. The heroic nudity of the gods, warriors and mortals shown by artists was a natural expression of the Greeks' open admiration for the perfectly developed male body." But it was always the male body. "What Greek art celebrates, with remarkable singleness, is masculinity," observes Margaret Walters in her study *The Nude Male* (1978). "It is the *male* body that is observed in such close and loving detail." In fact, women are depicted "less beautiful than the men."[8] The ancient Greek conception of masculinity was thus available as a role model, via Ger-many and Victorian Britain, at a critical juncture in the formation of the Mr. America concept at the outset of the twentieth century.

Complementing Winckelmann's idealization of the Greeks was the glorification of German culture after his death in 1768. According to E. M. Butler, "Winckelmann's Greece was the essential factor in the development of German poetry" from the mid-eighteenth century to the end of the nineteenth. "It was the Renaissance all over again."[9] He exhorted his countrymen to strive for the classical ideal: "The only way for us to become great . . . is to imitate the ancients."[10] This impulse co-incided with a larger national regeneration movement in which physi-cal fitness figured prominently. It was evident in the Philanthropinum, a training center founded in Dessau by J. B. Basedow in 1774. According to Horst Ueberhorst, Basedow and his educators "saw a model worthy of emulation in the Greeks and their 'Gymnastics.'" His Dessau pentathlon was intended to resemble competitions in the ancient Olympics. Also the educated German elite, while borrowing from the French Enlighten-ment, "derived their artistic and human models from Greek Antiquity."

> That was reflected in the creative achievements of German writers and thinkers whose works led to development of a strong sense of cultural self-assurance. This cultural assurance conjoined with political stirrings and developments (plans for national education, reforms in Prussia, the war of liberation, and the patriotic student movement) in the years that followed to produce intensified consciousness of state and nation.[11]

Realization of these nationalist ideals converged with the burgeoning physical-culture movement overseen by Friedrich Ludwig Jahn, often called the "Father of Gymnastics." After Napoleon's conquest of the German states, Jahn's physical regeneration ideas complemented the Prussian military reforms instigated by August von Gneisenau and Gerhard Johann von Scharnhorst as well as the romantic awakening fostered by Johann Gottfried von Herder's concept of the *Volksgeist* ("spirit of the people" or "national character").[12] In 1811, Jahn founded the first *Turnplatz* (open-air gymnasium) near Berlin to prepare young men for the war of liberation. He not only taught gymnastics and calisthenics but also initiated the use of horizontal and parallel bars as apparatuses and sponsored sports festivals. Jahn's love for Germany and purity of the *Volk* contributed to a nationalist tradition that eventually led to Germany's unification.

Jahn's legacy was felt in America. After 1815, his nationalistic exercise clubs, called turnvereins, continued to fire the spirit (and bodies) of exponents of radical political change. In the wake of unsuccessful revolutions in 1848, German immigrants took them abroad. The Cincinnati Central Turners (1848) was the first of many such societies in American cities.[13] "The significance of the German emphasis on the building of individual strength and on physical development," claims Dutton, "can hardly be overestimated."[14] Especially after Greek independence in 1829, devotion to physical training coincided in America, as in Europe, with a profound respect for the ancients. For the educator Catharine Beecher (1800–1878), the ancient Greeks, "the wisest and most powerful of all nations," exemplified health and exhibited "the most perfect forms of human beauty." Harvey Green, a historian of physical culture, recognizes that the "muscular ideal" for Americans, famously represented in Horatio Greenough's toga-clad statue of George Washington (1847), "was perhaps as much a paean to a rediscovery of that particular type of human form as it was to Greek democratic politics."[15] Later, the Greek ideal was glorified in classical motifs at the World's Columbian Exposition in Chicago in 1893, melded into the physique tableaux of Eugen Sandow, and brought to life in 1896 by a wealthy young Frenchman, Pierre, baron de Coubertin, who combined the passion of Western societies for Greek antiquity with the pursuit of bodily perfection by founding the modern Olympics in Athens.[16] Michael Budd concludes that the Victorian conception of the body, or the "sculpture machine," sought to "highlight classical ideas and imagery as popular ideals, to promote an historically based masculine ethos, rather than create an entirely new one."[17] This quest to investigate how modern meaning is derived from antiquity has coalesced broadly into the academic field of inquiry known as classical reception studies.[18] What matters is not so much whether the Greeks had exceptional bodies or how perfectly ancient artists conceived them, but the extent to which the Victorians and their successors were inspired by Greek iconography to shape their own cultural ideals.

Much of the impetus for physical improvement around 1900, however, stemmed less from satisfaction with the course of Western civilization than from deep-seated insecurities spawned by industrialism, urbanization, big business, socialism, and social Darwinism. Green perceives this pervasive anxiety as a "profound social and cultural crisis" in the making for decades. It coincided with a disorder called neurasthenia, defined by Barbara Will as "a peculiarly American condition of 'nerve deficiency' or 'nerve weakness'" afflicting those who exhausted their "'nerve energy' through tiring, reckless, or sexually profligate behavior." Although generally viewed as a crisis of masculinity, neurasthenia counted Emily Dickinson among its well-known victims, along with Theodore Roosevelt and Henry Adams.[19] This theme is developed in Michael Kimmel's work on self-made men who faced racial, gender, and ethnic challenges in the workplace. To combat the feminization of American culture, men took refuge in their bodies.

> One could replace the inner experience of manhood—a sense of manly confidence radiating outward from the virtuous self into a sturdy and muscular frame that had taken shape from years of hard physical labor—and transform it into a set of physical characteristics obtainable by persistent effort in the gymnasium. The ideal of the Self-Made Man gradually assumed increasingly physical connotations so that by the 1870s the idea of 'inner strength' was replaced by a doctrine of physicality and the body. By the turn of the century . . . he was making over his physique to *appear* powerful physically, perhaps to replace the lost real power he imagined that he—or at least his father or grandfather—once felt. If the body revealed the virtues of the man, then working on the body could demonstrate the appearance of the possession of the very virtues that one was no longer certain one possessed.[20]

This obsession with the body was fueled by a health and athletics craze that allowed men to test their manhood in the "crucible of competition." So important did the body become in defining masculinity that "the body did not contain the man; it was the man."[21] Interestingly, Kimmel's observation of fin de siècle America has been echoed by other scholars as relevant to a corresponding crisis in masculinity a century later. "One of the few attributes left, one of the few grounds on which women can never match men, is muscularity," argue the authors of *The Adonis Complex* (2000).[22]

In evaluating twentieth-century male body icons, comparisons with female body images play an important role, and the Miss America Contest shares many of the characteristics of the Mr. America Contest in celebrating an American gender ideal. The media has tended to treat them as parallel types representing what is most wholesome, healthy, and talented in American youth, with an emphasis on physical and personal appeal. As a leading gender historian observes, for "both men and women appearance is a primary mark of identification, a signal of what they consider themselves to be."[23] An examination of these contests, however, reveals that there were significant differences between the male and female versions. While the men's contest, until the late 1960s, stressed character, health, education, and athletic ability, the female version, through World War II, was mainly a beauty contest. They nearly converged in the 1950s, but by the 1980s each seemed to adopt the other's judging criteria. This divergence was due to the impact of two cultural forces—the civil rights and women's movements—on perceptions of ideal manhood and womanhood in the mid-twentieth century. Theretofore, blacks had been excluded from considerations of classic masculinity, and exemplary women were those who had been marginalized to largely decorative or auxiliary roles. By successfully challenging a value system based on white male hegemony, African Americans and women were able to advance their agendas, but developed contrasting, almost contradictory discourses while doing so.

Race and gender, curiously, constitute a relatively recent area of investigation relating to the Mr. America and Miss America competitions. George Mosse, in his classic study on the creation of modern masculinity, insists that "men cannot be seen in isolation; women are always present in men's own self-image."[24] The Mr. America Contest, despite its visibility as a masculine ritual, has attracted virtually no scholarly treatments. Two British authors, David Webster and Alan Radley, mention it only within the context of their surveys of bodybuilding and physical culture; Rick Wayne, in his polemical *Muscle Wars*, uses the contest as a basis for accusations of racism.[25] The Miss America Pageant suffers from the opposite condition, a surfeit of serious scrutiny. The studies, however, exhibit a certain sameness of approach, reiterating the same chronology of events, anecdotes, highlights, crises, and scandals. Probably the best overview is Ann-Marie Bivans's *Miss America: In Pursuit of the Crown. Live from Atlantic City: A History of the Miss America Pageant*, by A. R. Riverol, is more scholarly but far from definitive. The best-known account is *There She Is: The Life and Times of Miss America*, by the sportswriter Frank Deford. Lois Banner, in *American Beauty*, succeeds best in integrating the Miss America Pageant with changing ideals of fashion and beauty for women, and even for men.[26] The only feminist account, by Sarah Banet-Weiser, perceives the annual event as a "display of the female body as a matter of being," in which women are "judged, objectified, and fragmented" under the gaze and "power of the panoptical male." The pageant, she contends, perpetuates the notion that "women's natural 'asset' continues to be primarily located in and through the body, whereas men's natural assets include talent, intellect, and entrepreneurial ambition."[27] Such strident statements resemble Wayne's protests that the Mr. America Contest, overseen by a clique of white elders, unfairly marginalized black competitors. Unlike Banet-Weiser, however, he contends that the judging criteria, which considered attributes besides physique, favored white contestants and overlooked the superior physical assets of blacks.[28] These gender and racial critiques provide an opportunity to examine the place of the body in American iconography.[29]

While women and nonwhites are normally viewed as external to the Greek ideal, it would be difficult to gainsay the association of homosexuality with the ancients and the image of modern bodybuilding. The Greeks, notes the classical historian Charles Hupperts, uniquely viewed sexuality as an outgrowth of the ubiquitous display of both the nude male body and images that "emphasized and glorified the beauty of the male form." Sexual gratification was not considered either dirty or acceptable only in marriage. Encouraged by the gymnasia or the symposia (hours-long banquets accompanied by copious amounts of wine and conversation), sex was often a public affair and was omnipresent in the thoughts, activities, and conversations of men.

> Athenians viewed the love of a man for a girl or woman as something not altogether different from love for a boy or a man. These were two forms of sexual desire (*eros*), either of which could be more appropriate for particular individuals at certain junctures in their life. Few Greeks took the view that the man who loved a boy had a different nature from the heterosexual man. In the course of an Athenian's life, both forms of sexuality could appear together or in succession. The Greek language had not established separate terms for "heterosexuality" and "homosexuality," and so the question of sexual identity was not a pressing concern. There is

no mention in the evidence of any discrimination or of a subculture, and there is no sense of "coming out."[30]

In the Roman world, and then in the Christian era, this free-spirited attitude ended, but the body retained its erotic focus. Indeed, notes Kenneth Dutton, "one of the most important legacies of Greek artistic representation, along with that of the 'idealised' male body (the object of admiration), is that of the 'beautiful' male body (the acceptable object of sublimated erotic attention)." Notwithstanding the differences between bodybuilding display and erotic display, "it is doubtful that the element of sublimated sexual interest can ever be divorced from the appreciation of muscular development."[31] Whether the efforts of bodybuilders have been directed toward impressing females or other males is an oft-debated question, but Thomas Waugh's description of bodybuilding as "a channel and incarnation—and at the same time a camouflage—of the sexualized male body" suggests a continuing homoerotic presence.[32] That homoeroticism should focus on the image of America's most perfectly developed male is a natural assumption and worthy of note. Is it more than coincidence that Johann Winckelmann was gay?

While changes in the social roles of women, blacks, and homosexuals have greatly affected bodybuilding and the Mr. America Contest, it is equally important to recognize developments within the iron game. The most important was the addition of ergogenic aids to the bodybuilder's training regimen. The introduction of protein dietary supplements in the early 1950s by the Chicago nutritionist Irvin Johnson, and their subsequent commercialization by Bob Hoffman, Peary Rader, and Joe Weider, provided a real boost to bodybuilders and the health food industry.[33] The increased use of dietary supplements internalized thinking about physical culture and paved the way for steroids. Isolated by Charles Kochakian in 1935, anabolic-androgenic steroids were used to aid the recuperation of wounded soldiers in the 1940s and by Russian weightlifters in the 1950s.[34] John Ziegler, a Maryland physician, pioneered their use on American lifters, first in York, Pennsylvania, in the early 1960s. They then spread to virtually all sports and all forms of physical activity.[35] Greek ideals of health, symmetry, beauty, and function quickly gave way to a new standard according to which size and muscularity seemed to be all that mattered. Steroids revolutionized bodybuilding.

Closely associated with this phenomenon were the commercialization of the sport and the erosion of amateurism. Although the amateur ideal had Greek roots, it became part of the ethos of British sports in the nineteenth century through the philhellenism that prevailed among Victorian elites. It was symbolized by the "gentleman amateur," whose competitive endeavors led not to commercial gain but to enrichment of the mind, body, and spirit. "Natural grace and talent," according to Richard Holt, were its manifestations. "Gentlemen were not supposed to toil and sweat for laurels."[36] Thus, leisurely pursuits, stressing all-around talents and fair play and eschewing any incentives associated with the industrial-capitalist world, were important attributes of amateurism. In his social history of British sports, Dennis Brailsford identifies the public schools, which were in fact private schools catering to the upper middle class and the aristocracy, as primary transmitters of these values, producing men who could foster prosperity at home and administer the world's largest empire. Through sports, the schools sought to mold character by instilling "manliness, strength, loyalty, discipline and powers of leadership." The division between amateurs and professionals was more than a rejection of the notion of financial gain—"it was an assertion of the immutability of the class system."[37] Indeed the so-called Corinthian (strictly amateur) code excluded not only professional athletes but anyone earning a living from manual labor. One of the strongest adherents of amateurism was Britain's weightlifting patriarch, W. A. Pullum, who admired the Greek genius for its *balanced moderation in all things*, " most evident in architecture and statues. "Symmetry, proportion, and therefore *true artistic beauty*, these are the dominant features of these creations."[38] Oscar Heidenstam, the "Father of British Bodybuilding," was no less committed to Greek proportions and amateur ideals. He favored the traditional slender, functional physique, and was disappointed when bulk and size became the "be-all and end-all" for young bodybuilders.[39] Amateurism was also an abiding principle of the Olympic movement. Its American component, the Amateur Athletic Union (AAU), founded in 1889, nurtured this concept through the Mr. America Contest for much of the twentieth century.

While commercialism had a long tradition in the iron game, extending from Eugen Sandow through Bernarr Macfadden and Bob Hoffman, it was Joe Weider who most changed the face of bodybuilding through his moneymaking pursuits. Southern California, with its muscle beach tradition and association with Hollywood, was already in the vanguard of the physical-culture movement when Weider moved his operations from Union City, New Jersey, to Woodland Hills in 1972. Originally from Montreal, Weider built a magazine and fitness-product empire, and in 1947, with his brother Ben, founded the International

Federation of Bodybuilders (IFBB), which conducted physique contests worldwide. Eventually, their professional Mr. Olympia Contest, launched in 1965, superseded the AAU's Mr. America Contest in prestige, owing chiefly to the impact of Arnold Schwarzenegger. Effectively showcased by the Weiders, the "Austrian Oak" won an unprecedented fourteen world titles, including seven Mr. Olympias. What catapulted Schwarzenegger to fame, however, was his movie career, first in bodybuilding roles in *Stay Hungry* (1976) and *Pumping Iron* (1977), then in blockbuster thrillers such as *Conan the Barbarian* (1982) and *The Terminator* (1984). With an engaging personality, astute business sense, and a wife from one of the nation's first families, the muscular Austrian with a thick accent projected a bold American image, not unlike that conveyed by the McDonald's fast-food chain.

Physical culture thus had become a big business by the 1980s, and the Mr. America Contest, seeking to remain true to its amateur origins, became an anachronism. Its demise coincided with declining certainty about what it meant to be an American, a concept that had reached its zenith in the early twentieth century. *Americanism* is defined variously, as adherence to the traditions and ideals of the United States or as the political principles characterizing the country. According to the historians Michael Kazin and Joseph McCartin, it embodies individualism, social mobility, religious freedom, antiauthoritarianism, and "the remarkable self-confidence of most Americans, particularly white ones, that they live in a nation blessed by God that has a right, even a duty to help other nations become more like the United States."[40] Scholarship since the 1960s, however, has decentered American history from that of other nations and eroded cultural essentialism. Indeed, J. H. Elliott warns that "the besetting sin of the national historian is exceptionalism." And Janice Radway, in her 1998 presidential address to the American Studies Association, dismissed the "notion of a bounded national territory and a concomitant national identity" and questioned whether the organization should "perpetuate a specifically 'American' studies" any longer.[41] Within this cultural environment, the existence of the Mr. America title, whose existence implies meaning and identity to the word *American*, was fatally jeopardized.

A final factor that undercut the moral justification for the Mr. America Contest was a debate over the origins of Western civilization that emerged in the 1980s. A small group of scholars contended that Greek civilization had been created not so much by white Indo-Europeans (the so-called Aryan model) as by African (Egyptian) and Asiatic peoples of color. These ideas were developed by the Cornell professor Martin Bernal in *Black Athena*, which caused scholars to rethink racial and cultural paradigms. "The rise of the extreme Aryan Model," argues Bernal, "was clearly related to the triumph of European imperialism and the emergence of modern racial anti-Semitism. . . . Almost every educated European of the late nineteenth and early twentieth centuries saw Greece as the quintessence of Europe and the Aryan race." Fundamental to transmitting the Aryan model was the German romanticism promulgated by the likes of Winckelmann, Herder, Goethe, Lessing, and Jahn. According to Bernal, "German Romanticism was the mainspring of the Aryan Model and 'Classics' as we know it today."[42] Nor did Victorian Britons play a small role in constructing the framework of racial purity bequeathed to the United States. As Frank Turner notes, "Until after World War I a knowledge of Greek was required for admission to both Oxford and Cambridge." This influence was largely attributable to Winckelmann's ideas about the culture of the ancient Greeks and the conception of beauty conveyed by their sculptors.[43]

The relation of Bernal's ideas to Mr. America, though seemingly tangential, are symptomatic of the postmodern erosion of American idealism. But the new paradigm was by no means sweeping. Most scholars took exception to the Afrocentric implications of Bernal's work, and Americans' perception of the country's Western heritage remained largely conservative and positive.[44] While Bernal and other intellectuals on the left were undermining the erstwhile bases for American culture, Ronald Reagan (Reaganism) and Margaret Thatcher (Thatcherism) were reasserting traditional values and becoming iconic figures on the right. As Reagan repeatedly asserted: "With His [God's] message and with our conviction and commitment, we can still move mountains. We can work to reach our dreams and to make America a shining city on a hill."[45] The rise and fall of the Mr. America title and contest indicates both the persistence and pitfalls of this cultural consciousness.

PART 1: PRECEDENTS

1

THE GREEK IDEAL

IT IS NOT TRUE THAT A SOUND AND HEALTHY BODY IS ENOUGH TO PRODUCE A SOUND MIND, WHILE ON THE CONTRARY, THE SOUND MIND HAS POWER IN ITSELF TO MAKE THE BODILY CONDITION AS PERFECT AS IT CAN BE.

PLATO, REPUBLIC

THE MR. AMERICA CONTEST WAS BORN IN THE WANING DAYS OF PEACE in 1939, but its roots can be traced to similar endeavors at the outset of the twentieth century that mimicked the exploits of the Greeks over 2,500 years earlier. This curious conjunction of ancient and modern cultures was hardly coincidental. It followed upon a groundswell of respect for Greek values that permeated secularized European societies in the nineteenth century, culminating in the revival of the Olympic Games in 1896.[1] Greek civilization inspired a renewed preoccupation with humanity and the physical-culture ideal. In addition to depictions in Greek poetry and drama, and on Greek vases, the Hellenic aesthetic tradition that influenced Western civilization survived as damaged sculptures or Roman imitations of Greek originals. Of the works of sculpture glorifying the human body, Myron's *Discobolus* (*Discus Thrower*; c. 450 BC) is perhaps the best known.[2] The heroics of such Olympians as Milo of Crotona and the incredible feats and matchless physique of the mythical Hercules, son of Zeus, served as important representations of physical development.

The Greek ideal, however, was not limited to the body. *Arete* (goodness or excellence) meant a cultivation of the whole person, including one's mental and spiritual qualities. Harmony and balance of these components was essential, as Daniel Dombrowski points out in *Contemporary Athletics and Ancient Greek Ideals*. The Greeks believed it was possible to achieve a virtuous life by improving one's body (*askesis*), but only if done in moderation (*sophrosyne*) and with the goal of combining physical and moral excellence (*kalokagathia*). According to Dombrowski, "The Greeks tended to be hylomorphists who saw the material part of a human being (*hyle*) as integrally connected to, as informed by, the structure (*morphe*) given to it by mind (or soul). This hylomorphism was crucial in the effort to achieve the ideal of *kalokagathia*. Not only Aristotle, with his obvious hylomorphism, but also Plato would have been committed to this ideal." The concept "nothing in excess" was considered so important that it served as a motto for Greek culture in general and was inscribed on the Temple of Apollo at Delphi.[3]

The institution that epitomized the Platonic concept of a sound mind in a sound body was the gymnasia, where young men exercised, bathed, socialized, and discussed politics and philosophy. A foremost objective in these gatherings was the promotion of health. Indeed, the Greeks indulged in physical culture to prevent disease, illness, and degeneration, and to recuperate if they struck. Hippocrates, the father of medicine, believed that diet and exercise would release natural forces to promote harmonious bodily functions. According to the Oxford classicist C. M. Bowra, health was the "first of blessings" and "was inextricably connected with the Greek cult of the body." Beauty was a derivative of good health, to the extent that healthy men and women could come to resemble the gods. But health also suggested a "capacity for action," a principal reason the Greeks were so devoted to games: "Victory in the games was the realization of health and grace."[4] The Greek ideal of beauty went beyond appearances to comprehend the "harmonious relation" of bodily parts to one another, rendering a physique that was natural and well integrated. Nor did this outlook exclude less visible but important qualities. So intimately were the body and "person" connected for the Greeks that the cultivation of the former was vital to one's identity.[5] Thus the body, by incorporating balance, harmony, personality, and a "capacity for action," represented for the Greeks the reality of beauty and not just the appearance of it.

Figure 1.1. Eugen Sandow, founder of the sport of bodybuilding, posing as the Farnese Hercules. *Sandow's System of Physical Culture*, 54.

SANDOW THE MAGNIFICENT

Greek conceptions of arete had a compelling influence on the physical-culture movement. This lifestyle, which sought development through weight training, diet, aerobic activity, athletic competition, and mental discipline, was in vogue by the end of the nineteenth century. It was often dubbed "the strongman era," owing to the amazing feats of a Montreal behemoth named Louis Cyr and others. Their exploits were reported in the *National Police Gazette*, which, despite its title, was the foremost source of sporting news. The strength athlete who did most to focus popular attention on the body and cultivate interest in physical development was Eugen Sandow (Friedrich Wilhelm Muller). A native of Konigsberg and a protégé of the legendary Professor Attila (Louis Durlacher), Sandow attained worldwide fame in the 1890s after touring North America with Florenz Ziegfeld Jr.'s Trocadero Company.[6] In 1902, the noted physical educator Dudley Sargent of Harvard University examined Sandow and pronounced him "the most perfectly developed man the world has ever seen."[7] His resemblance to the statues of ancient Greece provoked much admiration and comment. But Sandow's genius was his ability to give concrete expression to a number of social trends. Most notable were the influence of the German physical-culture (*Turnen*) movement, the popularity of bodily displays on the vaudeville stage, and the importance of photography (superseding painting and sculpture) as an aesthetic medium.[8] Sandow, one of the most photographed stage performers of his era, virtually founded the sport of bodybuilding.

Sandow's "Great Competition," staged in London's Royal Albert Hall in September 1901, was the first noteworthy physique contest of the modern era. About 60 finalists, drawn from over 1,000 entrants in county contests, competed in a packed arena of 15,000 spectators for recognition as the most perfectly developed man in Great Britain and Ireland.[9] Prizes for the top three contestants included gold, silver, and bronze statuettes of Sandow, valued at £580. In the publicity generated for the contest, it was apparent that classical proportions, rather than showy muscles, would figure most prominently in the judges' criteria. "It should be clearly understood," stated Sandow, "that prizes will *not* be awarded to the men with the *biggest* muscles, but to those whose development is most symmetrical and even. Consequently a man who only weighs eight stone will have just as good a chance of success as his Herculean brother who brings down the scale to twice as much."[10]

The judges were prominent artistic and literary figures who had been chosen to lend credibility to the proceedings—Charles Lowes, a noted sculptor and amateur athlete, and Arthur Conan Doyle, an Edinburgh-trained physician and creator of Sherlock Holmes. Sandow would serve as referee if the judges could not agree. All three men possessed an intimate knowledge of the body balanced by a broader view of humanity. They selected William Murray of Nottingham as winner. Regarded by contemporaries as a great all-around athlete, Murray was adept at running, cycling, and football, but there is no evidence that lifting heavy weights played a significant part in his regimen. His superb physique was a natural by-product of regular physical training, and not something pursued for its own sake.[11] Sandow's great competition was a huge success. That "bodybuilding had come of age almost overnight," as his biographer concludes, might be an overstatement, but it was certainly introduced as a legitimate competitive endeavor for physical-culture enthusiasts.[12] Much as the Olympian gods served as ideal types for the ancient Greeks, Sandow would serve as an inspiration for generations of bodybuilders worldwide. Furthermore, as Michael Budd recognizes, the Sandow phenomenon was congruent with a broader societal "shift away from thinking of the body in terms of its 'being' to a conception of what it 'ought to be.'"[13]

BERNARR MACFADDEN

Closely watching Sandow's extraordinary success was the American entrepreneur Bernarr Macfadden. After emerging from the poverty-ridden Ozark Mountains of southwest Missouri, he spent his life overcoming physical challenges and fears of early death. Inspired by the exuberant personalities he encountered in the *Police Gazette*, Macfadden engaged in such hardy sports as boxing, wrestling, and gymnastics; to preserve his health, he abstained from alcohol, tobacco, drugs, and meat. Much like his celebrated contemporary Theodore Roosevelt, he believed in the strenuous life and thrived on hard work and outdoor living. Work, he once stated, was his swimming pool, and he loved to splash around in it. "Macfadden was unable to loaf," observes the biographer Robert Ernst. Once when urged to take a vacation from his work, he responded that he would take a long walk from New York to Chicago. He thrived on struggle and achievement, and idle conversation made him uncomfortable.[14]

The event that had the greatest impact on Macfadden's development as a physical culturist was the 1893 World's Fair in Chicago. There he was deeply moved by a replica of a Greek colonnade that supported an entablature with naked men and women in heroic poses. According to another Macfadden scholar, "The sight of the entablature was really all that he needed in the way of a classical education."

> It fixed forever his idealistic conception of classical times. The Greeks had reached a pinnacle of artistic, political, and intellectual development, and their celebration of the beauty of the human form, in stark contrast to American norms, was a revelation to Macfadden. He vowed to restore the idealism of the Greeks to his own society. These sentiments could only have been reinforced by his witnessing the exhibitions of Sandow at the Fair, for Sandow was the closest modern society could come to the realization of the Greek ideal.[15]

Figure 1.2. Bernarr Macfadden, "Father of Physical Culture." *Physical Culture*, August 1903, 105.

Whether he interacted with Sandow in Chicago is uncertain, but in 1897 Macfadden ventured to England, where he collaborated with the bicycle entrepreneur Hopton Hadley to market a wall developer (an exercise apparatus that could be attached to a wall for arm, leg, and torso development) he had invented. In the following year, Sandow and Macfadden founded the world's first muscle magazines, *Physical Culture* and *Physical Development*, respectively. After Sandow changed the name of his publication to *Sandow's Magazine of Physical Culture* in 1899, Macfadden appropriated *Physical Culture* as the title for his American magazine.[16]

Further evidence of Sandow's influence on Macfadden was the world physique competition that the latter began publicizing in the spring of 1903. It definitely had Sandow's imprimatur. Yet Macfadden's contest offered $1,000 prizes for "The Most Perfectly Developed Man" and for "The Most Perfectly Developed Woman." Winners from a dozen American and a dozen British contests would be brought to New York to take part in a "Mammoth Physical Culture Show" at Madison Square Garden. As with Sandow's promotion, pictures of prospective entrants were published regularly, but Macfadden, in order to lend a classical cast to his proceedings, offered *Physical Culture* readers a port-folio of such sculptures as Michelangelo's *David*, Giambologna's *Mercury*, and ancient works including the Venus de Milo, the Apollo Belvedere, and Diana. He was determined to provide competitors with "the best representations of perfect physical manhood and womanhood."[17]

In addition, Macfadden attempted to define the "ideal" figure: "We have always contended that where there was harmony of proportion, proper strength, and good health, the development was natural, i.e., what nature intended should be the proportions for a body."[18] Like the Greeks, Macfadden desired a balanced physique across the entire body. One con-tributor to the magazine, the strongman Gilman Low, was so obsessed with proportions that he attempted to quantify the ideal male figure.

> The figure[,] to be perfect, should be 7½ heads in height. From the roots of the hair to chin, first head; from chin to nipple, second head; from nipple to umbilicus, third head; from umbilicus to os pubes, fourth head; from os pubes to just above the knees, fifth head; from just above the knees to just below the knees, sixth head; from just below the knees to just above the ankles, seventh head; from just above the ankles to the heels, seventh and a half head.

Low believed that "no sculptor or artist of any note pays any atten-tion whatever to girth measurements; symmetry is his guiding star, and many of the gigantic, heavily-built, huge-muscled men of today are not in any sense pleasing to the truly artistic mind and temperament." But he conceded that there were a few modern athletes who would "almost rival the ideal Greek in form, weight and height."[19]

Low's idealized kind of development resulted not so much from lifting weights as from the sorts of competitions that Macfadden in-cluded in his show—wrestling, running, and fencing events, for both men and women. All-around development was Macfadden's ideal, and his imitation of the ancients was evident in an advertisement claiming that the interior of Madison Square Garden would be trans-formed into an idyllic classical setting: "The Days of Ancient Greece and Rome Revived."[20]

PERFECTLY DEVELOPED MAN AND WOMAN CONTESTS

Macfadden's great event took place from December 28, 1903, to Janu-ary 2, 1904. As with Sandow's contest, the goal was "not to decide who is the most wonderfully developed man" but "the most perfect

Figure 1.3. Contestants at Macfadden's "Perfect Man" Contest, regarded as virtually the first Mr. America Contest. *Physical Culture*, March 1904, 186. Far right: Al Trebar, the winner.

specimen of physical manhood." Although muscular development was important, the sculptors and physical culturists who served as judges looked for classical features—"uniform, healthy and wholesome development of each and every limb and muscle, and the relative proportions that they bear to each other."[21] The winner, Albert Toof Jennings, was a native of Michigan and 1898 physical education graduate from Harvard University. But his fame as a physical culturist was already well established. While at Harvard, his physique was deemed by Dr. Dudley Sargent to correspond exactly to the scientific standard for perfect proportions that he had been using for thirty years. Upon graduating, Jennings became a professional poser for artists and sculptors and embarked on a stage career, performing, as Al Treloar, strength stunts with a juggler. He was billed as the "Perfect Man."

However much Treloar's reputation might have influenced the judges, he deserved the title of "finest developed and best proportioned man living." To Macfadden, he was "a perfect Greek in proportions . . . a rare specimen among our modern athletes." Furthermore, Treloar was not just a well-built strongman. He was extremely agile, especially for his size (5'10", 185 pounds), and could perform a "round-off" (cartwheel-handspring) and reel off a row of "flip-flaps" (handsprings) with ease. He had useful muscles. Most important for his victory were Treloar's "lofty and ennobling" views. He believed self-improvement to be "a duty to the community as much as to the individual," one that would raise the moral tone of the nation. "The man or woman who brings his or her body to the highest possible state of perfection," he stated, acquires "a store of health and happiness for personal enrichment" and bequeaths to future generations "a legacy of strength, vigor and life, a freedom from evil tendencies, and a pleasure more valuable than palaces or titles."[22] Macfadden's winner exhibited what was healthiest and most wholesome in American manhood. The competition was, according to David Webster, "virtually the first Mr. America contest," and for Ernest Edwin Coffin, an authority on Sandow, Treloar was the very first Mr. America.[23]

The women's contest exhibited a similar idealism. As with the men, the females were judged by a panel of athletes, sculptors, physicians, and physical culturists who employed criteria of health, strength, and beauty. The winner, Emma Newkirk, of Santa Monica, was 5'4½", weighed 136 pounds, and had a 35" bust, 25" waist, 36" hips, and 23½" thighs. Declining offers from artists and theatrical revues seeking to capitalize on her fame, she returned to California to marry her hometown sweetheart. Whether this was the response of "a true woman," as Macfadden concluded, it was in keeping with the practice of many Miss Americas several decades later.[24]

So successful was Macfadden's enterprise that he began planning and advertising a more extravagant competition for October 1905, at which women would figure even more prominently. The men's competition was limited to amateurs (women were presumed to be amateurs). Contestants from both sexes were expected to display perfection of form, and in keeping with Macfadden's belief in all-around development, they had to demonstrate athleticism by engaging in a series of athletic events, seventeen for men and eight for women.[25]

PHYSICAL CULTURE OR PORNOGRAPHY?

Unfortunately, planning for the event was disrupted by a police raid on the *Physical Culture* offices led by the postal inspector Anthony Comstock, founder of the New York Society for the Suppression of Vice. The assault on "pornography" was motivated by two posters featuring winners from the previous year's contest. The first, as reported in the *New York Times* (October 6, 1905), showed "ten or twelve young women in white union suits with sashes around their waists," simulating nudity, and the other featured Al Treloar in a revealing pose, "wearing a pair of sandals and a leopard's skin breechcloth." Inside Macfadden's offices, Comstock uncovered more "obscene" material, including physique photographs and a painting of the Venus de Milo. In successive issues of *Physical Culture*, Macfadden railed against "the mental and moral perversion of Comstock," whom he called "King of the Prudes . . . the last dregs of human degeneracy." Far from corrupting the nation's youth, "the sex principle, properly controlled, leads us on to the highest and grandest characteristics of which human beings are capable."[26] Macfadden's focus on the Greek ideal became sidetracked into a crusade against prudery.

In 1907, Macfadden was indicted by a federal grand jury in New Jersey for publishing a story about the dire consequences that befell a sixteen-year-old youth whose parents never explained to him the facts of life. Ruling that it contained obscene, lewd, and lascivious material, the judge sentenced Macfadden to two years in prison and fined him $2,000. Although President Taft extended a pardon for his prison sentence, he did not remit the fine.[27] Fulton Oursler, a Macfadden aide, correctly attributes the failure of Macfadden's sanatoria projects in New Jersey and Michigan to his "fight against prudery and the conspiracy of silence regarding love and venereal disease."[28] A less obvious casualty was his physical-culture extravaganza, which was on the verge of becoming an annual affair.

Thereafter, Macfadden conducted photographic contests. The first such event, held in 1908, featured separate categories for the most perfect specimens of men, women, and children. Macfadden insisted that entrants' photographs should "show their proportions hampered as little as possible by clothing." It was evident from pictures published as examples that some contestants were photographed in the nude and then had garments painted over their private parts. All of Macfadden's displays of human form were ahead of social norms of the era, but one in particular, of ten-year-old Margaret Edwards, of Oakland, seemed in questionable taste. Her touched-up torso barely disguised her developing areolas and nipples—a depiction that verged on child pornography. Yet an accompanying letter from Margaret's proud mother, a high school teacher, reveals not a hint of prurient intent.

> Margaret eats but one meal a day, uses practically no meat and even a smaller amount of candy. Her strength and endurance are now simply wonderful. She has been reared out-of-doors and spends a good part of

her time riding horseback. . . . Three years ago she was pronounced to be one of the most perfectly developed children ever seen in this part of the country. She can tense or relax any muscle in her body at her will. . . . Margaret is Nature's own child, but lest you think that she is all muscle and no brain, I wish to state that she is in the high-fifth grade and quite a musician.[29]

Nor can the purity of Macfadden's motives be doubted. Implicit within the photograph and narrative are ideals—strength, endurance, beauty, athleticism, mental development, dietary discipline, and love of the outdoors—that had been popularized by the Greeks centuries earlier.[30] As pointed out in an article on games played by boys in the gymnasia of ancient Greece, "over one half of all education was devoted to the body." The Greeks believed that "if physical perfection were cultivated, moral and mental excellency would follow."[31] Macfadden's aim was to modernize and improve upon the Greeks by applying this standard to women and even children.

THE MODERN QUEST FOR ARETE

While there were virtually no physique contests in the United States for the next seven years while Macfadden reconstructed his finances, he and his staff continued to preach the gospel of all-around development, the virtues of the Greeks, and bodybuilding for all ages and both sexes. Ella Wheeler Wilcox advocated exercise for "every limb and muscle every day" and claimed that "moderation, regularity, and perseverance" should be the physical culturist's watchwords. But the key to success lay in balancing physical and mental exertion, body and mind.[32] Perhaps the most brilliant of Macfadden's authors, Carl Easton Williams, employed this theme of harmony in a 1914 article that compared the modern physique to the Greek ideal by juxtaposing photographs of figures from both eras. The Greeks, he contended, "could not conceive of excellence of mind without excellence of body," since "their whole scheme of life was to be found in the identification of the beautiful and the good." They were "inseparable, the one being the manifestation of the other." The major difference between moderns and ancients was that "we *have* athletes," but "they *were* athletes": "All of the citizens, philosophers and poets included, were models of physical development." Notwithstanding such modern specimens as Sandow, Thomas Inch, Al Treloar, Jeannette Baird, or Bernarr Macfadden, the true athlete was the exception rather than the rule. Unlike the Greeks, modern athletes were "in the game, not for self-improvement, but only to win." "We have a few examples of perfect development," Williams believed, "whereas the Greeks were at one time, nearly all examples of perfection."[33]

Although modern athletes usually fell short of their ancient counterparts, Macfadden featured illustrations of the best-developed youth as models for his readers. Two of them from nearby Brooklyn became the most important bodybuilding icons of the 1920s. Earle Liederman, first featured in a 1914 ad for weight-gain tablets, was a noted all-around athlete who built up his physique largely by swimming, acrobatics, boxing, and wrestling. He was strong, but he worked mainly for total conditioning, for example, by doing dips on the parallel bars and backflips.[34] Angelo Siciliano, later known as Charles Atlas, first appeared in a 1914 article by Macfadden as an exemplar of all-around development. Though less recognized as an athlete, Atlas exhibited supreme development. According to an October 1915 article on ideal body weight, he built his magnificent physique by practicing "hand-balancing" and "all around gymnastics." Significantly, though no mention is made of any technique resembling "dynamic tension," for which Atlas eventually became a household word, the article does confirm that his training incorporated "weight-lifting!"[35]

ALAN CALVERT AND "MANUFACTURED BUMPS"

Meanwhile, a rival entrepreneur was vying for the attention of physical culturists. Alan Calvert, scion of a Main Line Philadelphia family, had been inspired by reading William Blaikie's *How to Get Strong and How to Stay So* and by watching Sandow perform at the Chicago World's Fair.[36] Unable to procure weights like those Sandow was using, he founded the Milo Barbell Company in 1902, America's first manufacturer of weightlifting equipment. To instruct trainees on barbell use, Calvert published a pocket-sized guide and then, in 1914, founded *Strength* magazine, which publicized bodybuilding activities and showcased his products.[37] These initiatives, along with the presence of William Herrmann's gym and occasional strongman exhibitions staged by Calvert, led Philadelphia to become known as America's weightlifting and bodybuilding mecca.

Calvert's approach to physical culture was different from Macfadden's. Calvert emphasized training and scarcely mentioned any appreciation of Greek ideals. Instead of developing a magnificent physique naturally through a variety of sporting activities, Calvert advocated a shortcut that would allow youth to procure what were sometimes called "manufactured bumps." In 1916, Calvert boasted that since he had "introduced bar-bells and dumb-bells . . . magnificently built men have been appearing in all parts of the country, for nowadays practically anyone who can spare two or three hours a week for training purposes can . . . develop himself in his own bedroom." Calvert's only nod to the Greek ideal of general health was to stress the importance of "harmonious all-round development." He advised trainees not only to exercise "the whole body" but also to apply heavy weights to "the great muscle groups" in order to stimulate "the digestive and assimilative organs" and to improve blood circulation.[38] That the concept of whole-body health remained paramount to Calvert is apparent in an advertisement entitled "A 'Perfect Man'" published in a 1915 issue of *Physical Culture*. "This man is as healthy as he is strong, and as strong as he looks; we can say no more"—so read the caption of a picture showing a strong-man hoisting a heavy kettlebell over his pubic bone.[39]

MEASURING THE IDEAL PHYSIQUE

Increasingly, the emphasis of both barbell- and athletics-centered muscle camps was on the art of posing. Calvert's models exuded an aura of strength, while Macfadden's figures exhibited beauty suggestive of inner serenity. Strength lent itself to objective measurement through records and games, whereas the proponents of beauty seemed obsessed with proportions, seeking to derive body-size formulas from the physiques of Greek statues. In a 1915 article titled "Posing the Physique Beautiful," L. E. Eubanks advises anyone wishing to make such comparisons to obtain "a rule, a tape-line and calipers" in order to "go at the matter thoroughly." Then it was important to select an appropriate model: "If you are slender you would look ridiculous posed as the Farnese Hercules, and if your figure is heavy you would not make a good Apollo. A woman of eighteen with a girlish figure cannot consistently represent Juno; nor can a heavy woman in middle life succeed as Psyche." Upon selecting an appropriate model, the aspiring physical culturist should study his or her "pose thoroughly and aim at exact imitation."[40]

Milo Hastings, another *Physical Culture* writer, was less convinced that classical statues always furnished the best physique models. Examples of physical perfection might be more prevalent in the present than the past. "Why not let us sail under our own colors," he queried. "We have our own rivers to swim, muscles to measure, mirrors to reflect the result; and we have photography, half tones and kinematographs that can tell us American truths about one thousand seven hundred times faster than Greek sculptors could idealize.

Figure 1.4. Charles Atlas. *Physical Culture*, October 1921, 19.

As for the Greeks—they are dead."[41] Hastings chose Sandow and the swimmer–movie star Annette Kellerman as modern exemplars of excellence, but they were still measured by Grecian standards. In an elaborate diagram that allowed readers to "chart their own measurements with black or colored pencil," Hastings provided comparative data on Sandow and Kellerman compiled by Dr. Sargent at Harvard. By such means, modern bodybuilders could determine how closely their "proportions approach the Greek idea." Hastings concluded, however, that "the eye rather than the tape measure and calipers is the tribunal at which judgment on grace and symmetry must be sought."[42] This interest in measuring proportions was an outgrowth of the anthropometric craze that swept Europe and America in the late nineteenth century. It was based largely on the scientific works of Francis Galton and Karl Pearson and was later popularized in the iron game by David Willoughby.

Following conventional wisdom, Macfadden employed anthropometrics as a judging criterion at his Physique Beautiful Prize Competition in 1915. Male and female contestants were required to submit photographs of themselves, along with a detailed list of body measurements. But outward physical appearance alone was not the point of Macfadden's competition. "It is not essential that the measurements of contestants approach the ideal," he advised, "or the proportions of an Apollo or a Venus. The first purpose is to determine the results men and women have attained by physical culture." Edwin Crapo, of San Francisco, and Nana Sterling, of Houston, proved to be deserving winners of the Physique Beautiful contest. Sterling, according to Milo Hastings, not only possessed nearly ideal measurements, but also was as "strong as she is symmetrical," the result of "her work as hand balancer and acrobat."[43]

It was also evident that photography, unavailable to the ancients, was an excellent medium for depicting physiques. Gordon Reeves, in a 1917 article titled "Artistic Body Photography," extolled its virtues. "We cannot all be sculptors and transfer to bronze or marble a record of the human form. But by one of man's most ingenious inventions we can record such likeness for ourselves and friends." Unfortunately, it was "easy for the forces of prudery to decree that while nude painting and sculpture were 'art,' nude photography was an abomination" and that to be caught possessing such photographs was an "outward sign of inward disgrace."[44]

To combat prudery and to give the medium dignity, Macfadden

instituted the Physique Photography Contest, in which artistry rather than bodily development was stressed. The hundreds of photographs submitted were almost entirely from subjects with "ordinary physiques" rather than "big-muscled athletes." The winners, Arthur Gay, age twenty-one, of Rochester, New York; Mabel Lantz, aged twenty-six, of Tillamook, Oregon; and Elena D'Agosteno, age eight, of Meriden, Connecticut, struck poses that were natural and unaffected. All reflected serene composures and purity of spirit. Finally, Macfadden instituted a photographic contest to honor the woman who most fully preserved her youth and beauty into advanced age.[45] By such inclusiveness, he seemed determined to surpass the idealism of the Greeks, who placed so much emphasis on youth.

CHARLES ATLAS

The culmination of Macfadden's attempts to combine anthropometric and photographic methods came in the fall of 1921 with his contest to identify the most handsome man and most beautiful woman, based on facial appearance and bodily form. As in his earlier competitions, the male winner would be chosen for "symmetry and beauty" and not merely his "muscular development," a standard designed to ensure fairness: "This will not rule out the athlete or the gymnast but it will permit the man who is of slighter build to compete on equal terms with the more Herculean specimen of manhood."[46] Angelo Siciliano (aka Charles Atlas) triumphed over more than a thousand other entries. According to Atlas's biographers, Macfadden reviewed the photographs and summoned Atlas to his office in New York City: "Wearing his leotard skin under his trousers, Atlas hurried down to Macfadden, who gave him a glass of carrot juice, observed him in the flesh, immediately declared him the winner, and handed him a check for $1,000, calling Atlas 'the living realization of my lifelong battle for the body beautiful.'"[47] This romanticized account differs little from testimony that Atlas provided Paul Niemi in 1972. According to Niemi, the top three men were asked "to come to New York and be examined in person," the result being that Atlas won the $1,000 prize, with $700 and $300 going to the second- and third-place winners.[48]

What neither of these accounts recognizes is that Siciliano (as Atlas) was already well known to Macfadden and had appeared frequently in illustrations for articles and products in *Physical Culture* for nearly a decade. He was also a noted artist's model and stage performer. Like

Treloar two decades earlier, he was hardly unknown and clearly had an advantage over other entrants. Nevertheless, Macfadden's "discovery" of Atlas was trumpeted in a special pictorial feature of his magazine. "Mr. Siciliano has the face, physique, stature and carriage of an Apollo," according to one of the captions.[49] The 1921 contest no doubt stimulated a greater interest in physical culture, but it is likely that Atlas had been favored to win from the outset.

Subsequent issues of *Physical Culture* detailed the training protocol of Atlas. Readers learned that he used a weight-based regimen. In addition to a barbell consisting of a stick and two twenty-five-pound stones that he "faithfully" used at first, he "contrived a set of pulleys and weights . . . and used them regularly."[50] While this early evidence dispels the long-standing myth that Atlas developed his perfect body through dynamic tension and without weights, it should be noted that weightlifting was only one of a "great many" techniques he employed. As an adherent of Macfadden's principles, he sought "an all-around development rather than an abnormal one." His favorite exercises were walking, dipping (push-ups), chinning, and bending (including sit-ups). As for sports, he favored swimming or wrestling. Atlas supported his choices by referring to Greek mythology: "You have read the story of the wrestling match between Hercules and Antaeus. Every time Antaeus was thrown to the earth by Hercules, he grew stronger. Finally Hercules conquered him by squeezing him to death. . . . As the Greeks seemed to know more than any other people about developing the human body I have always looked on wrestling as the one best contest exercise." Atlas was interested in more than acquiring muscles. He knew he could get big muscles without gaining health, but acknowledged, "[I] could not very well acquire robust health without incidentally developing my muscles."[51] It is questionable whether these words were written by Atlas, whose immigrant English hardly matched his perfect body. But the sentiments reflect the spirit of Macfadden's contest. In subsequent issues of *Physical Culture*, Macfadden idealized Atlas as a "superman." To sculptors, he was known simply as "the Greek God."[52] He was a physical ideal, reflecting the sort of "dignity, sanctity and beauty" that all Americans could emulate.

The winner of the most beautiful woman prize was Gertrude Eggett, of Fresno. Macfadden recognized her endowments with a string of superlatives. She not only possessed "beauty of face and figure," but was also "a superb example of the modern athletic girl, a veritable Diana."

WINNING second place in the Perfect Woman Contest at the Physical Culture Exhibition, Miss Alaska Liederman is an example of extraordinary symmetry as well as a picture of vital and splendid womanhood. In an athletic sense she is a veritable Diana.

Figure 1.5. Helmar (Miss Alaska) Liederman, described by Macfadden as "a veritable Diana," who was barred from the 1922 Miss America Pageant for being married and being from New York, not Alaska. *Physical Culture*, January 1923, 37.

As "a consistent physical culturist," she wore neither corsets nor high heels, never used tea or coffee, ate only two meals a day (with little meat), and was "a beautiful dancer."[53] She seemed a fitting complement to Atlas.

THE FIRST MISS AMERICA PAGEANT

Meanwhile, another kind of beauty contest was being staged in the seaside resort of Atlantic City, where the emphasis was not so much on health, symmetry, and athleticism as on physical appearance. Conceived by hotel owners to prolong the summer tourist season, a "National Beauty Pageant," featuring eight contestants sponsored by major metropolitan newspapers, was held on September 7, 1921. Unlike Macfadden's shows, where contestants shamelessly flaunted their scantily covered bodies for the sake of physical culture, the pageant complied with an Atlantic City ordinance that forbade the display of nude limbs. This prohibition, long understood by striptease artists as a sure means of arousal, added a furtive, almost risqué element to the pageant. As Frank Deford notes, "Atlantic City constables just made sure that nobody was watching them as they watched whenever any of the more daring beauties rolled down their stockings on the beach to reveal dimpled knees to the sun."[54] The covering of young bodies under knee-length bathing ensembles, baggy wool tunics, and stockings succeeded only in tantalizing eager onlookers.

That this beauty pageant was set within a male cultural context with sexual overtones is evident not only from its inception as a businessmen's enterprise but also by the paternal dominance of King Neptune, to whom the "sea nymphs" (contestants) gathered to pay homage. "I have met here very pretty maids and matrons," pronounced Neptune, "all interesting to me, and I like the way they comport themselves. There is beauty of figure and of face, and beauty in grace and reserve, not to say modesty. All my sea nymphs are charming that I have met during my reign." Further illustrating how the contest was designed for male viewing pleasure, a local reporter noted that Neptune "unconsciously, as many thought, showed his personal absorption in the judging of the Inter-City Beauties on the Garden Pier stage": "He left his throne while the municipal selections for loveliness were pirouetting before the judges to secure a close-up view. The light that illuminated the stage seemed to shadow the visions of beauty."[55] The winner of the first Miss America Pageant was Margaret Gorman, a sprightly fifteen-year-old student from Washington, D.C. Reflecting the traditional values governing her selection was the response of Samuel Gompers, the president of the American Federation of Labor, who thought Gorman was "the type of woman America needs, strong, red-blooded, able to shoulder the responsibilities of homemaking and motherhood."[56] But her winsome smile and alluring figure were more likely foremost considerations for the judges.

AMERICA'S MOST PERFECTLY DEVELOPED MAN AND BEAUTIFUL WOMAN

Encouraged by the success of his 1921 photographic contest, Macfadden staged a live physical-culture extravaganza at Madison Square Garden. To no one's surprise, Atlas carried off the $1,000 prize by winning the title "America's Most Perfectly Developed Man." Again, health and overall development, not muscularity, were critical. Atlas recalled that a panel of sculptors, illustrators, and doctors examined each contestant "extremely carefully" for five nights in October: "Eyes, ears, nose, throat, heart, lungs, and blood were all checked. Measurements and weights were carefully recorded." Atlas also pointed out that "some of the 75 contestants had bigger arms or legs than he did, but none had his overall symmetry."[57]

The winner of the "Most Beautiful Woman Contest" was Dorothy Knapp, of New York City. Second place went to Miss Alaska, Helmar Liederman, "an example of extraordinary symmetry as well as a picture of vital and splendid womanhood." Significantly, she was the wife of Earle Liederman, who, in full-page advertisements for his courses, appropriated the moniker "Acme of Physical Perfection."[58] He hoped to use his wife's fame to enhance his commercial standing.

While Macfadden's extravaganza, unlike the first Miss America Pageant, might appear to have been innocent of arousing any sexual or prurient interest, there was "mud in the show," as Earle Liederman later revealed to Ottley Coulter. Liederman had the story from a colleague named Ken Terrell:

> [Terrell] confessed to me that during the judging of the ladies' section, all the gals had to strip to nothingness and parade forth and back before Macfadden and dozens of his friends and judges, etc. etc. and of course *all for art's sake ya know*—Nuts on that! Old Macfadden had arranged numerous *peep* holes in the rear drop on either side of the judges stand or rather seats, and Ken Terrell confessed to me that he was a privileged personage who peeped and saw the entire *naked girl show*. And to con-

firm this—my own wife confessed to me that night that everyone had to parade in the nude to be eligible to compete. I had it practically arranged for Miss Alaska to *win* this affair, as I needed such for a vast publicity campaign I had planned and so those last line words rather confirm my statements on the Macfadden hypocrisy.[59]

Physical-culture displays had the potential of degenerating into lewdness, immorality, and commercialism. Macfadden was not the only purveyor of prurience. Liederman insisted to Coulter that he could "reveal true tales" of many other promoters "that would make your hair stand up." For men as well as women, physical culture retained a seamy underside, real or imagined, that would long hamper bodybuilding from gaining respectability.

In 1922, Atlas could claim the coveted title Most Perfectly Developed Man, which was tantamount to recognition as Mr. America. Macfadden felt vindicated by having his editorial decision of the previous year confirmed by five professional authorities on the body. In fact, his Greek god was so perfect that Macfadden again ceased holding physical-culture competitions. "What is the use?" he allegedly said. "Atlas will win every time."[60]

What this off-the-cuff remark fails to take into account is that bodies as well as times change. Atlas soon embarked, as Liederman's commercial rival, on one of the most successful mail-order businesses in American history, but body ideals and preferences soon entered a new phase. Still, Sandow and Macfadden had established a solid basis for the physical-culture movement. The former invented bodybuilding through his matchless physique and showmanship, and the latter, more than any other person, conceptualized the sport for Americans by combining it with Greek ideals of physical development. Admittedly, as one of Macfadden's editors perceptively observed in 1915, "classical statuary was created by idealists who painted and chiseled what they had dreamed rather than what they had seen."[61] Macfadden was no less a visionary, yet he attempted to see his dreams realized in human flesh and thereby to surpass the Greeks. As the ancients sought to emulate the excellence of their gods and heroes, Macfadden sought to identify the finest specimens of live humanity—the likes of Treloar, Crapo, Gay, Liederman, and Atlas—in order to inspire a U.S. culture of physical excellence. An actual Mr. America contest was still nearly two decades away, but a solid conceptual basis for it was laid with the selection of Macfadden's "Greek god" as America's Most Perfectly Developed Man in 1922.

2

THE ATHLETIC BODY

FOR ALL THINGS THAT HAVE A FUNCTION OR ACTIVITY, THE GOOD AND THE "WELL" IS THOUGHT TO RESIDE IN THE FUNCTION.

ARISTOTLE, *NICOMACHEAN ETHICS*

AFTER WORLD WAR I THERE WAS A GROUNDSWELL OF INTEREST IN athletics, possibly as a reaction against the war, the ensuing flu epidemic, and the postwar economic depression. "Never before, nor since, has there been such a concentration of athletic genius" is the assessment of a popular history of sports. In 1950, when the Associated Press asked four hundred American sportswriters and broadcasters to name the greatest athletes of the first half of the century, 1920s champions finished first in six of the nine sports polled. Stars of this golden era swept the field in baseball (Babe Ruth), boxing (Jack Dempsey), golf (Bobby Jones), horse racing (Man o' War), swimming (Johnny Weissmuller), and tennis (Bill Tilden).[1] "Americans enjoyed a golden age of sport in the 1920s," writes the sports historian William Baker. By the 1930s, observes Donald J. Mrozek, "the rhetoric of a golden age . . . gave attention to excellence and the pursuit of the ideal in sports performance."[2] Baseball, football, and track enjoyed the greatest popularity, but it was also the era when, through formal regulations, records, judging, and a sanctioning authority (the AAU), weightlifting became a sport.[3] Although there were virtually no physique contests for nearly two decades between the world wars, bodybuilders sought an outlet by engaging in other physical-culture endeavors, especially weightlifting. In addition, they could apply their erstwhile all-around training approach (an updated version of arete) to a variety of sports, sometimes with remuneration. Greek ideals of beauty and grace remained, but bodies took on a more athletic look, and the "capacity for action" became the overriding principle in physical development. Function rather than form became the foremost concern of strength athletes in the interwar period.

THE OLYMPIC MODEL

Nowhere was this preoccupation with athleticism more evident than in the Olympic movement, itself a legacy of ancient Greece, dedicated to the tripartite ideal of "swifter, higher, stronger." In this era the games reached maturity.[4] From its inclusion in the first modern Olympic games in 1896, weightlifting had become a permanent fixture by the 1920s, when it was contested at Antwerp (1920), Paris (1924), and Amsterdam (1928). Critical to the permanent acceptance of weightlifting as an Olympic sport was the formation of a worldwide governing body by several European nations at Duisburg, Germany, in 1905, followed by its transformation into the Fédération Internationale Haltérophile (FIH) under Jules Rosset, president of the French federation, in 1920.[5] European and world championships in the 1920s coincided with the international competitive and patriotic fervor of the Olympics, and at the 1928 games the so-called Olympic lifts—press, snatch, and clean and jerk—were first contested.

This regularization of the sport was complemented by the growth of national organizations and competitions. When the strength enthusiast David Willoughby conducted the first American national championships at the Los Angeles Athletic Club in 1924, he followed FIH rules.[6] Similarly, the American Continental Weight-Lifters Association (ACWLA), founded by George Jowett and Ottley Coulter, and its successor, the American Bar Bell Men (ABBM), under Mark Berry, were strongly influenced by European models. When the latter joined the AAU, under Dietrich Wortmann, in 1929, American weightlifting rose to a new level of prestige by becoming an appendage of the International Olympic Committee (IOC). In 1932, Berry led an American weightlifting team (the first one to compete at the Olympics since 1904) to the Los Angeles games.[7]

MUSCLES FOR ACTION

Both Jowett and Berry served as editors of *Strength* in the 1920s, which allowed them to promote the new sport nationally. But earlier editors had been moving the magazine in that direction. Like *Physical Culture*, it was dedicated to muscular development, but the very title—*Strength*—and its emphasis on using barbells (not unrelated to the parent company's profits) suggested that muscles should be doing something. Results were measured in pounds lifted, records held, and competitions won, not in physical proportions. An emphasis on vigorous activity is evident throughout the January 1921 issue. An editorial informs readers that "the people who get ahead in this world are the people who do things." They were urged to join the weightlifting association that was being formed. "Are you Physically Fit?" is the title of an article advocating exercise for every body part: "Sitting in an armchair won't produce results." A pictorial section is devoted to such action heroes of the day as Ed (Strangler) Lewis, world-champion wrestler; Carl Appolo, a professional weightlifter and hand balancer; and Jack Dempsey, the heavyweight boxing champion. A seven-page section provides wrestling instruction. Included also, in a respectful nod to the classical origins of physical culture, is a photograph of a sculpture of Hercules, symbol of strength, in an action pose.[8] These articles conveyed the need for activity, the highest form of which was competitive sports.

This message was reflected on subsequent covers of *Strength*, which included action depictions of the oarsman Jack Kelly (the "Dempsey of the Sculls"), the Princeton football captain Stanley Keck, a female ice skater, a Detroit Tigers slugger, and a runner crossing the finish line. Even articles relating to physique, such as one titled "The Body Beautiful," stressed practicalities. As important as the methods that a bodybuilder used to obtain his physique was his reason for doing so: "What's he gonna do with it now that he has it?" No mention is made of the nature of his physique or of what constituted a "body beautiful," aside from what it could do. Another article, "The Boxer's Physique," similarly focused on action. After assessing how several boxers' physical attributes relate to their ring skills, it concluded that Jack Dempsey, was "the most perfectly-built man for boxing": "In ring togs, ready for action, Dempsey is a sight for sore eyes; believe me, he 'has everything'—the ranginess, the neat, compact look around the waist and hips, the muscular shoulders, good arms, and strong, lithe legs. Look at that wrist and forearm! In Jack's work they are worth far more than an 18 inch arm would be."[9] However well formed Dempsey may have been, particularly for boxing, few bodybuilding buffs of later generations would consider him Mr. America material.

Preoccupation with function was also evident in depictions of female figures. Dubbed the "American Venus," Gertrude Artelt of Philadelphia had "the most perfect figure" in a group of two thousand girls nationwide. But aside from accompanying pictures, *Strength* gave no indication of her physical attractiveness. At 5'10" and 165 pounds, she was hardly an all-American beauty. Rather, her appeal lay in her athletic achievements in gymnastics, basketball, track, and, especially, aquatics, in which she broke numerous records and won many gold medals, cups, and watches. She "won her honors by . . . seriousness of purpose, and not of mind or face."[10] The Roaring Twenties were full of this kind of pent-up energy, epitomized in action sports but evident also in perceptions of the body and its utilitarian purpose.

THE PROPORTIONAL MAN

A more traditional view, however, firmly rooted in Greek ideals of physical development, was still prevalent. In a 1922 article entitled "The Latest Addition to the 'Perfect Man,'" Alan Calvert praises the physique of Siegmund Klein, of Cleveland: "[His] physical proportions are just about as fine as anything I have ever seen. Note that I do not say 'muscular development'; although that is certainly extraordinary. It is his *proportions* that I admire." To Calvert and many physical culturists, "the ancient Greek statue" remained the ideal. Pictures of Klein revealed a "roundness of body" so admired by the Greeks: "There is the same depth of chest and abdomen, the same roundness without the least suggestion of fat; and above all the same appearance of being 'well-knit,' 'well-coupled' or 'finely put together.'"[11] To achieve such balance and integration, Klein used barbells to obtain muscular development, not to see how much he could lift.

Klein later refined this training approach into an adage: "Train for shape—strength will follow." Seemingly at odds with the existing emphasis on competition, a 1923 barbell advertisement in *Physical Culture* praises Klein for his dedication to higher ideals—symmetry, health, and organic power: "The average physical culturist thinks of a bar-bell user as a man who is always training to make or break records. When we questioned Mr. Klein we found that he had no idea of how much he could lift. He has used his bar-bell not as a lifting machine, but as a developing instrument which would furnish him with the graded resistance that is necessary to bring each part of the body to the peak of its power and the summit of its development." Still, one senses a nagging need, in tune with the times, to reassure readers of Klein's athletic prowess: "You can take our word for it that he is strong—for we tried him out against bigger and heavier athletes of the highest class. This man can run, jump, lift weights like Sandow, tumble like an acrobat and bend like a contortionist."[12]

Had a Mr. America contest existed in the mid-1920s, Klein would probably have won it. Instead, he won the "Beauté Plastique" title awarded by *La Culture Physique* in France in 1925 for the world's best-built athlete. It was Klein's only competition, and he entered it unintentionally by sending some photographs to the publisher Edmond Desbonnet.[13]

ATLAS AND LIEDERMAN

Only Charles Atlas held greater claim than Klein to having perfect (Greek-like) proportions, and he quickly sought to capitalize on his "Most Perfectly Developed Man" appellation. Guided by the English naturopath Frederick Tilney, he established (in the style of Macfadden) a Temple of Health at Woodcliff, New Jersey, and published a book, *Secrets of Muscular Power and Beauty*, that not only revealed Atlas's secrets of success but also promised to "make any man physically perfect, abnormally strong and beautifully proportioned." Interestingly, Atlas also recognized the need to explain what he could *do* with America's most perfect body, boasting he could easily tear a New York telephone book in half, break a tempered twelve-inch spike, and bend a three-quarter-inch iron rod with his teeth in seven seconds. He could also lie on a bed of 2,500 sharp nails while eight men jumped on a plank atop his nude body. Finally, perhaps in imitation of his mythological namesake, Atlas allegedly walked two city blocks with an 800-pound weight on his shoulders.[14] It is likely that Atlas, a modest man, was exploited by his zealous collaborator so that they could keep up with other mail-order muscle peddlers of the day.[15] Unwary scrawny young men, ignorant of the tricks of the trade and the commercial impetus behind them, trustfully parted with immense sums of money on courses, books, programs, pictures, and apparatuses promising to make them look like Greek gods and able to take on the neighborhood bully.[16]

By far the most successful muscle entrepreneur in the 1920s was Earle Liederman, whose enterprise once occupied an entire floor of a Manhattan office building and employed nearly a hundred people to handle his mail. In 1923, Liederman launched a correspondence physique contest to determine which of his pupils had shown the greatest improvement over nine months. The winner, Andrew Passannant, of New York City, received $1,000, and photos showing his deep chest, shapely biceps, muscular back, and all-around symmetry appeared prominently in Liederman's ads. But the promoter's pitch was more about health and strength than muscular development: "If you are weak, I guarantee to make you strong. If you are strong, I'll make you stronger. What I did for Andrew Passannant and thousands of others, I will also do for you."[17]

Liederman's contest inspired Atlas to offer $5,000, a princely sum in those days, to *his* most perfectly developed pupil. But the latter's pitch was directed more against his competitor's practices than toward the virtues of acquiring either form or function. So Atlas—or, more precisely, Tilney—denounced the reckless claims made by other physical directors and defied them "to produce a pupil so gracefully built, so perfectly proportioned, so radiantly healthy, so strong and powerful" as his own students. Atlas's winner, Anthony Sansone, of New York City, was magnificently endowed, acclaimed to be "physically perfect"—with "nothing overdeveloped" and "nothing underdeveloped."[18] He became one of the most admired physiques in the interwar era. To Vic Boff, even from a 1987 perspective, Sansone was an "Uncrowned Mr. America." He was "like a Greek god who had stepped out of the classic world of the ancients." A statue at the "Hall of Man" exhibit at Chicago's Field Museum of Natural History personified Sansone as the standard of physical perfection for the twentieth century. David Webster calls him "the most widely acclaimed 'poseur'[sic] of the age."[19]

The immediate result of Sansone's selection was that Liederman increased his prize for 1924 to $2,000 for distribution to the top fourteen contestants, along with fourteen-karat gold medals. The judges included two sportsmen, Budd Goodwin (swimming) and George Pritchard (football), along with the physical culturists Arthur Hyson, Macfadden, and Liederman—no more physicians or artists. In succeeding years, the Atlas competition faded away, but Liederman added a "Best Developed Man" contest (worth $1,000 and a free trip to New York) to find "the finest looking muscles." It was open to old and new pupils. And, Liederman added, "the colored boy has just as much chance as his white neighbor."[20] No blacks took top honors, but some did well, and it was obvious that Liederman's event was a melting pot for first- and second-generation Americans. Above all, with such winners as Wesley Barker, Gregory Paradise, and Kenneth Terrell, it provided a showcase for some of America's best physiques.

GEORGE JOWETT AND THE ACWLA

In the meantime, *Strength*, edited by Jowett from the mid-1920s, staged its own photographic physique contest. Called a "posing competition," it featured the unique practice of allowing readers to judge entrants from their pictures in the magazine. Selections were to be based on "all-round development" and "quality of the pose."[21] The 1925 winner was Lurten Cunningham, an Indiana native who, after attending a physical training school, became physical director of the Atlanta YMCA. His winning pose, selected over seventy-five other entries, was "an illustration of the body beautiful in its highest conception," according to *Strength*. At 5'7" and 175 pounds, Cunningham had a rugged, manly physique. Like Jowett and many others, he had started bodybuilding not so much to look good but to develop strength and use it. Sickly as a child and too weak at six to enter school, Cunningham recalled, "[I] soon acquired the name of 'sissy' because of my weakness." Recalling the severe drubbing he once received from an older boy, he vowed some day "to crush that boy," adding, "I have realized that ambition."[22] Cunningham later moved to the Athens YMCA, where he formed a lifting club and was indirectly responsible for introducing weight training to the University of Georgia. Except in New Orleans and a few isolated centers, barbell men and physical culture hardly existed in the South. The notoriety that Cunningham received from his award (including a loving cup, but no cash) enabled him to popularize weight training in the region.[23] But the 1926 posing competition, though vigorously publicized, was mysteriously phased out, with no winner declared.

That *Strength* should so quickly relinquish sponsoring physique competitions is hardly surprising given the bias of its editor. As a disciple of his fellow English strongman George Hackenschmidt, Jowett believed that "development and strength go hand in hand," since "a real orthodox strongman . . . must have the physique." But he made clear his choice "between the two": "[I] would choose strength . . . because I know with strength I would get development." Jowett's proclivity for useful muscles is evident in his editorials. "Physical strength is really the most important thing in life" was his view. He advocated "heavy, strenuous exercise" such as wrestling, weightlifting, tumbling, and gymnastics, "those forms of exercises which make you aware of the fact that you have done something after you have finished." Jowett advised readers, in the title of one article, to "*Play* to Keep Fit" and to engage in competitive sports. He complimented Germany, where weightlifting was "an integral part of existence" and thus the reason why that nation produced such "prodigies of physical might and bodily perfection."[24]

To instill this kind of competitive spirit in America, Jowett and others organized the ACWLA as a regulatory body for competitions and records, and he staged regular strength exhibitions at the Milo Barbell Company headquarters in Philadelphia. Most importantly, he started a monthly column in *Strength* that reported on lifting activities throughout the country. Unfortunately, Jowett's egotism and bombast led to a conflict with three close associates—D. G. Redmond, his publisher, over money; Charles MacMahon, a fellow writer, who espoused shape over strength; and Mark Berry, an ambitious understudy who was acting as a foil to Jowett on the ACWLA board of directors.[25] In early 1927, Jowett and his ACWLA were displaced by Berry and the ABBM.

SHAPE AS A MUSCULAR VIRTUE

It would be tempting to attribute Jowett's demise to his obsession with strength and his relative neglect of other aspects of physical development. Yet the magazine also published articles by MacMahon and Calvert that addressed symmetry, harmony, shape, and beauty. "The reason that the old Greek statues are so beautiful is because they show such wonderful symmetry," observed the former. Likewise, many modern strongmen exhibited perfect development. One article asked: "Now, did it ever strike you that these were 'strong men' because they were 'perfect men'? That they have great strength *by reason of* their perfectly symmetrical development." Ideally, size and strength should not be ends in themselves but desirable by-products of an all-around exercise program. What fascinated MacMahon was muscle shape and proportion, and both he and Calvert recommended the use of measurements to determine the relationship between muscles and overall development. They also recognized the importance of proper posing for representing the muscular ideal.[26]

Nonetheless, it was MacMahon who most fully captured the mood and frustrations of fledgling bodybuilders in the 1920s. Despite the existing emphasis on strength, movement, competition, and record making in the iron game, he perceived that "most of those who take up physical training do so for the main purpose of developing an admirable shape." This was a frank acknowledgment of human vanity as a motivation: "A lot of them may not care to admit it, but this does not alter the fact that most people want to have a body that will look well and be admired in a bathing suit, athletic costume, or in street clothes. Health and strength is desired, too, of course, but a clean-cut muscular figure is the most craved of all physical assets."[27] MacMahon could not have known that his emphasis on training for appearance, however out of fashion during the golden age of sports, was the wave of the future, an idea that Joe and Ben Weider would use to transform modern bodybuilding.[28]

Not only did Jowett provide opportunities for associates to promote their ideas about bodybuilding, he penned his own share of physique articles. Much of it was self-serving, as in a 1926 article titled "Muscular Proportions *You Can* Build," in which, with lavish illustrations, he likens his own physique, "representing the Herculean type of manhood," with that of Siegmund Klein, who, because of his "grace and physical beauty," resembled Apollo. Further to boost his credibility with bodybuilders, Jowett claimed that he won a "most perfect man" contest and that his newly published book, *Key to Might and Muscle*, was "the finest contribution to the cause of body-building." A quick glance at Jowett's poses indicates he had a heavy build that exuded strength rather than grace and beauty; even he admitted that his small knees, ankles, and feet were disproportionate to the large bones of his arms, torso, and hips. Jowett eschewed measurements as a way to identify the "perfect man." Yet he contended that "if you keep your mind fastened on '*shape*,' and not so much on '*size*,' you are less apt to get into the unbalanced state."[29] However imperfect his own shape, Jowett would hardly have encouraged the bodybuilders of later generations who were obsessed with size.

THE FEMININE PHYSIQUE

Despite Jowett's insistence that he found "more to admire in the form of a man than in that of a woman," as editor he lavished much attention on women's physical development. Most articles focused on beauty and the need for vigorous exercise to achieve it. "Beauty is based upon activity, for 'Strength is Beauty,'" wrote Florence Whitney in early 1925. She believed that women were becoming more attractive because they were stronger and living healthier lives, especially since millions were taking up swimming, tennis, and other outdoor sports. Women with strength also have "shapeliness": "You can prove this by endless examples of athletic girls, swimmers, dancers, runners and those who do more or less athletic performances in circus, vaudeville and musical comedy. They all have strength—from top to toe—and therefore have symmetry and shapeliness. If our flabby, non-athletic women had the strength with which to do things with their bodies, they, too, would have beauty."[30] Many other articles on female shapeliness appeared in *Strength*, as well as a monthly column entitled "Health—Strength—Beauty," edited by Marjorie Heathcote, which printed reader correspondence. Heathcote conducted a Well Formed Woman Contest that encouraged amateur physical culturists to display in photographs the effects of exercise. The winner, Rose Heather, of Catalina, California, was "the ideal type of the modern athletic girl." Her development was totally harmonious, and Heathcote held her up as an example: "Many girls would profit by leading an athletic life such as Miss Heather is leading."[31] Many articles featured professional models and budding starlets in nearly nude, touched-up, risqué, or highly suggestive poses. Whether these provocative pictures were designed to inspire male or female readers is uncertain, but the message was always the same. As for male bodybuilders, the way for women to achieve shapeliness and beauty was through exercise, the more the better.[32]

Such depictions of the body beautiful were standard fare in *Physical Culture*. In 1928, Macfadden revived his perfect woman contest, perhaps in response to *Strength*'s photo competitions, but more likely because the Miss America Pageant was struggling. While entrants to the annual seaside event were expected to be prim and proper, petty controversies—often fueled by feminists—over bobbed hair, long stockings, and the cut of swimsuits had a liberating effect, resulting in the display of more skin and a sexier appeal. Bishop William Hafey of Maryland decried the 1927 pageant as "an exploitation of feminine charm by money-mad men" and demanded an end to it.[33] Hotel owners who had promoted the event became increasingly embarrassed by scandals, charges of indecent exposure, and the presumed loose morals of the contestants. Negative publicity and lack of financial support led to a five-year abandonment of the pageant.

Into this void slipped the enterprising Macfadden, who launched a nationwide search for a modern physical-culture Venus. His contest was limited to "athletically inclined unmarried girls" between the ages of sixteen and twenty-five who possessed "the greatest gift of all that young womanhood can be endowed with—beauty of body." Macfadden was looking for more than just another pretty face and figure: "The winning girl will certainly have to be athletic in every sense of the word. She will have to be a representative of wholesome, robust young womanhood, symbolizing the future motherhood of America." The judges included himself as well as America's greatest showman, Florenz Ziegfeld Jr.; the radio personality Major Edward Bowes; and William LeBaron, vice president of FBO Pictures, who offered the winner a $1,500 Hollywood movie contract. Attempting to dissociate his competition from the scandal-ridden Miss America Pageant, Macfadden called on "America's fathers and mothers who have reared their daughters along health-building, clean-living, constructive ideas." Unlike other beauty pageants, Macfadden's would be a physical-culture event, stressing health, athleticism, and overall well-being. His wish for respectability was fulfilled with the selection of Marjorie Jane Douglas as the winner, "a New England society girl" who participated in outdoor sports, especially riding, and attended a private school in Boston.[34]

Macfadden's 1929 contest took on the format, though not the context, of the defunct Miss America Pageant: winners of sectional competitions would represent their cities or states at a Madison Square Garden finale just after Labor Day. The idealistic aim was to promote "clean living, right eating, right thinking and the cultivation of health and strength." So emphatic were organizers about wholesomeness that they offered a $1,000 prize to the winner's mother for "an exclusive story telling how she reared this beautiful specimen of girlhood."[35] From a field of six thousand contestants, thirty-two finalists emerged, mostly college and high school students. *Physical Culture* provided rail fare and lodging for each girl and her mother. The competitors represented "some of the finest types, possessed of the most symmetrical proportions," according to the contest's "editor."

More than ever before, the painfully thin, hipless, bustless girl stood in the background. The measurements of the entries proved conclusively that America's vast army of young girls are well developed . . . robust, vital, strong of shoulder, firm of chest, and solid of thigh. They did not represent the rapidly waning type that the anemic flapper characterizes physically. . . . There were no so-called exotic airs about them. The physical type of well-constructed girlhood . . . came and convinced everybody that she is of the wholesome type, who cares more for a jaunt in the outdoors, a round of golf, a tilt on the tennis courts, a swim, or a hike, than for all the bridge and cocktail parties in the world.

In addition to being repeatedly measured and examined for physical flaws, contestants had to pass a swimming test, and in anticipation of a Miss America innovation of the 1930s, they had to appear in evening gowns.[36]

The winner, Regina Mona, Miss Detroit, received a large bronze statue of Venus de Milo—an allusion to the classical roots of beauty— and an engraved Helbros watch with a large second hand, to time her athletic activities. At the crowning ceremonies, thousands cheered as America's Physical Culture Girl, escorted by Macfadden and another beauty dubbed Miss United States, descended a carpeted staircase in red velvet robes and filed past the other finalists to the tune of the "Stars and Stripes Forever."[37] Though influenced by the prevailing passion of the day for athletics, the affair featured some of the ideal qualities that stressed all-around development, which would characterize the Miss America and Mr. America contests by the 1950s.

However much Macfadden may have provided a template, neither female nor male Americana productions looked promising by the late 1920s. Macfadden failed to build on his stunning 1929 success with any further competitions that might establish the tradition of selecting a perfect woman. Instead, he undertook a less ambitious course in 1930, offering $1,000 in prizes for the best letter and accompanying photograph on the theme of "What I Have Learned and Done to Make My Body Beautiful." Unlike previous contests, he wanted stories of readers' accomplishments—and this one was open to men. It was not until the fall of 1932, however, that a winner was announced. Inga English, of Truro, Nova Scotia, once labeled the "sickest woman in the world," had weighed only seventy-seven pounds, could not walk or stand, and had a paralyzed and twisted face. Over five years, through exercise and right eating, she recovered her health and learned to lead a dynamic life. Success stories, though distorting the perfect-woman ideal, no doubt appealed to Depression-era readers. Hence, Macfadden's other

Figure 2.1. Siegmund Klein, the "Modern Physical Ideal," depicted in 1926 as a gentleman athlete. Author's possession.

contests during the decade, with such titles as "How Keeping Fit has Enabled Me to Make More Money" or the "Best Improvement Contest," stressed self-improvement rather than physical perfection.[38]

THE BERRY ERA

Briefly, it appeared as if *Strength* might resume its quest for America's best-developed male. After the departure of Jowett, Mark Berry became its editor and chief publicist for the iron game. After "an ardent exercise enthusiast" complained about the lack of articles on "shapeliness" in *Strength*, Berry replaced the ACWLA, which was primarily devoted to weightlifting, with his ABBM, which emphasized "the exercise side of barbell work." Thereafter, he published an abundance of physique-related articles, many written by him, and in 1928 revived the idea of a photographic posing competition. First prize, a loving cup, was awarded to Robert Ranous, of New York City, a pupil of Sig Klein, who showed exceptional abdominal and overall development. So popular was the contest that Berry decided to award gold and silver medals for the two best photos received each month. Significantly, the first gold medal winner, who had placed third in the earlier contest, was a black bodybuilder, Stanley Smith, from Bermuda, who displayed remarkable bicep-deltoid separation and a finely rippled back. Recognition of later winners assumed a familiar, almost matter-of-fact pattern: photographs, along with information on hometown, height and weight, and their poses. Eventually, the awards decreased in significance. *Strength* did stage a major Silver Cup Posing Contest, won by Walter Podolak, of Syracuse, but there was no accompanying fanfare regarding his formidable physique, and there were criticisms about the quality of judging.[39]

What seemed to interest Berry more than physique were strength and the feats that a well-developed body could perform. This preoccupation was evident in the issue that carried Podolak's prize-winning pose, in which Berry boasted that never before had so many weightlifting shows been held in such a short period time. No less than fifteen events were staged within several weeks, culminating in May 1929 in the National AAU Championships, "the greatest carnival of weight lifting in the history of the game, in America."[40] By then Berry, who had been conducting national championships since 1927, was combining his efforts with those of Dietrich Wortmann, head of the AAU. Each month the exploits of America's strength athletes were featured in lavish detail in *Strength*, along with updates on weightlifting records. Interestingly, the illustrations often featured weightlifters not in a lifting mode but in some sort of classical pose that showed off the fine physiques the athletes had developed. But form was never divorced from function in these displays.

Even in his depictions of the era's best bodybuilders, Berry emphasized their strength and what they could do with their muscles—indicating that they were not mirror athletes. Sig Klein epitomized the
physical-culture ideal. Berry explained that until the advent of Sandow,
the belief persisted that it was impossible for any "living person to rival
the classical 'gods' of sculpture in physical beauty and idealistic proportions." Since Sandow's retirement and death, "idealists" had been
"seeking one who could take his place in their fanciful adorations."
Berry believed that Klein was Sandow's successor, "the possessor of the
super-physique among all living men."[41] But it was Klein's strength
that provided credibility and respect for his physique.

Photographs in a 1928 article amply illustrate Klein's claim to be a
"modern physical ideal," but the text focuses on his physical prowess.
As a youth, Klein was inspired by his father, who, while serving in the
German army in the Franco-Prussian War, was "regarded as the strongest man in his regiment." Allegedly, he could take a 112-pound ring
weight and lift it to the top of a table with his little finger. Sig, following his father's example, displayed "unusual strength" in impromptu
hand-balancing exhibitions with friends. Later, to dispel rumors that his
magnificent physique lacked strength, Klein embarked on a campaign
of contests and record-breaking attempts. He not only defeated two of
America's best strongmen, Robert Snyder and Antone Matysek, but
also challenged any lifter to compete against him in the Olympic lifts,
offering $1,000 to anyone willing to vie for the title "Strongest Man in
America." His official lifts at a body weight of 148 pounds included a
270-pound clean and jerk, a 205-pound military press, and a 300-pound
squat for five repetitions. Further to illustrate the all-around qualities of
this "modern physical ideal," and prove that he was more than just a
beautiful body, Berry portrayed Klein as a "gentleman athlete," posing
him in top hat, tuxedo, and cane—a true man of the world.[42]

AMERICAN HUSKINESS

Especially apropos of Berry's conception of balanced development was
the American trait of huskiness, a blend of the Greek physical ideal
with a modern passion for sports and survival in a man's world. Berry
believed that "ultimate physical appearance" had the "greatest appeal"
to physical culturists who followed the teachings of *Strength*: "The
reader sees examples of perfect physical manhood, and the desire to
emulate a certain type or ideal begins to throb through his entire be-

ing. As his interest grows, his lifeblood seems to surge with the one idea; every fibre seems to be saturated with the desire for a physical appearance which will make it unnecessary for him to tell anyone that he possesses strength and super-abundant physical powers. There is one simple little word to describe the thing he most desires—husky."[43] Epitomizing huskiness was Lurten Cunningham, the winner of *Strength*'s 1925 posing competition, whose photos continued to be published for many years. "If there is one physique which suggests that quality of huskiness," it was Cunningham's, noted Berry. That he was also "quite classy as a sprinter and ball player" strengthened a statement that would otherwise be interpreted as referring to appearance only.[44]

Even women were expected to display athletic prowess, as was suggested by frequent representations of the movie star Clara Bow, the "It Girl" of the 1920s. Along with weights, bars, rings, "horses," and Indian clubs in her Beverly Hills gym were "several pairs of boxing gloves." *Strength* noted that Bow was "rather expert in their use." For men, the enduring public icon of muscles put to use was Charles Atlas. When introducing his dynamic tension system in 1930, Atlas drew on a pugilistic metaphor: "[I am] the Champion in my field just as the Heavyweight Champion of the World is in his!"[45] In succeeding generations, Atlas inspired millions of skinny youth to use their functional muscles to get even with beach bullies.

By the end of the 1920s, the Greek ideal was still intact. Although some doubted whether the Greeks in fact measured up to the standards of their statues or whether it was possible even to achieve such proportions, balance and the integration of physical and mental properties remained an inspiration for modern bodybuilders. David Willoughby concluded that the perfect man, according to benchmarks set by Greek sculptors, should be 5'10" and 180 pounds. But bodybuilding standards were becoming more fluid. They were animated by the great interest in sports that emerged in the 1920s. Even for Macfadden, the perfect physique was no static stereotype but rather one brought to life by function. In 1929, he employed a sporting metaphor to illustrate the actualization of perfection: "In the equine world, the perfect draft horse or the perfect race horse is determined largely by achievement, as in the case of Man o' War and his records, as well as by build and shapeliness. The same should be and is true of humans."[46] No one had heard of husky nineteen-year-old John Grimek when his nude photograph, taken in the sand pits near his home in New Jersey, appeared as one of the monthly silver-medal winners in a 1929 issue of

Strength.[47] But Grimek went on to become one of the greats of the iron game by combining the ancient Greek ideal of beauty with the new sporting craze.

THE DEPRESSION AND ADVENT OF YORK

The physical-culture movement underwent a metamorphosis in the early 1930s. Hard times, brought on by the Depression, had a devastating effect on the numerous muscles-by-mail vendors that had theretofore flourished. In April 1931, George Jowett estimated that the iron game was "ruined beyond measure." He told Ottley Coulter that Liederman, the most successful of the muscle peddlers, had suffered "a worse blow than anyone": "His agency is broke for over $100,000 in bad advertising for 1930." Liederman's wife, Helmar, a former Miss Alaska, had run away "with another fellow[,] taking Earle's imported Italian car and," since he had trustfully placed his securities in her name, "robbing Earle of every penny he possessed."[48] The Milo Barbell Company suffered too during these doleful times, and *Strength* and Berry's ABBM felt the pinch along with it. The magazine, to preserve its resources and broaden its appeal, took over *Correct Eating* in 1930 and the *Arena* in 1932. However much business sense these mergers made, they moved the scope of *Strength* further away from bodybuilding and made it unlikely that the national weightlifting championships would be complemented by a national physique contest.

The most significant iron game event of the early 1930s was the 1932 Olympics in Los Angeles. Berry served as coach of the U.S. weightlifting team, which was accompanied by an assistant trainer named Bob Hoffman, whose lifters from York, Pennsylvania, made up most of the team. Originally from Pittsburgh, Hoffman had become interested in weightlifting as a way to supplement his other athletic pursuits, chiefly aquatics. After serving in World War I, he and a partner started manufacturing automatic oil burners in York. He was "the world's greatest salesman and promoter" in the view of all who knew him. Profits increased steadily during the 1920s, and even through the early 1930s he was selling oil burners and making money at a prodigious rate.[49]

Once he became interested in weightlifting, he used his oil burner employees and facilities to manufacture weights and assemble a team, dubbed "the York gang." Hoffman was soon a major force in weightlifting. In Los Angeles, the U.S. team made a respectable showing, finishing third behind France and Germany, but Hoffman regarded it as a defeat. He realized that his men "had not advanced to the point of being a serious threat in international weightlifting" and that foreign lifters "looked upon the United States team as something of a joke."[50] He therefore used his financial resources to rejuvenate the sport and overturn the influence of his rivals—the Milo Barbell Company, *Strength*, and Mark Berry.[51] Thus Hoffman, who dominated the iron game for nearly a half century and was dubbed the "Father of American Weightlifting," based his claim to fame on weightlifting, not physique, competition.

A foremost factor in Hoffman's successful bid for power was *Strength & Health* magazine, founded in 1932 to inspire American weightlifters, advertise York products, and promote his philosophy of life. His inaugural editorial called for more physical activity. "The mass of people in the United States are not keeping up with the rest of the world physically," Hoffman warned. "Most of us ride everywhere, never walk or run, eat the wrong sorts of foods and don't exercise. The majority of us are only half alive."[52] Hoffman summoned Americans to engage in the active life. The November 1933 issue included articles on athletic training, feats of strength, muscle control, exercising the waistline, and hand balancing. Significantly, a monthly section entitled "Shows and Events" reported weightlifting results from the United States and abroad. The new magazine's emphasis on action reflected American tastes in the 1930s.

FORM OR FUNCTION?

Hoffman, however, did not ignore form, realizing (as did Berry) that most young trainees took up weightlifting to improve their appearance. Thus some early *Strength & Health* articles were entitled "The Sandow Biceps," "How You Can Change Your Physical Structure," and "The Beauty of the Male Physique." Jowett's ACWLA, with which Hoffman was affiliated, even staged a beauty contest, albeit for women, in conjunction with a 1933 lifting show in New York City. For several years, Hoffman emphasized physique development. "Shapeliness comes first with us," he asserted, "strength follows and increased bodyweight will result." The preoccupation with shapeliness stemmed from a twenty-week training program to which Hoffman subjected himself in 1933 in order to prove that he was the "world's foremost physical trainer." While gaining 23 pounds of "good solid muscle," Hoffman added 102 pounds to his weightlifting total, but he seemed most pleased with his new dimensions—17⅜" arm, 49" chest,

14" forearm, 29" thigh, 17¼" calf, and 34" waist at 243 pounds body weight. "A much greater shapeliness was attained by this training that was the marvel of all who saw it," he insisted.[53] To prove his point, he displayed before and after pictures of himself in 1934 issues of *Strength & Health*, along with a pitch for York barbells. The retouched after photograph shows not only a more youthful and shapely physique but also the addition of hair on Hoffman's formerly bald head!

Hoffman's flirtation with shapeliness was short-lived, and he soon returned to his first love, weightlifting. Although he remained interested in physique development as an appendage to lifting, he soon developed an alternative to Siegmund Klein's dictum of training for shape as a means to gain strength. Hoffman came to believe that "shapeliness alone is not enough; a chorus man may be shapely, but if he is not strong he loses any cause of admiration." Men like Hoffman's weightlifting champions, "who are beautifully proportioned, tremendously strong and the possessors of other desirable physical and mental characteristics," were his ideal, and remained his ideal for the rest of his life.[54]

THE BERLIN OLYMPICS

What caused Hoffman's change of heart was a series of events that shaped the course of bodybuilding for the next generation and culminated in an annual Mr. America Contest. First was the elimination, owing to the Depression, of Hoffman's major rivals. Upon the bankruptcy of the Milo Barbell Company and the termination of *Strength* in 1935, Hoffman acquired their assets and copyright entitlements for $4,000, making York virtually the only barbell manufacturer in the country.[55] Yet Mark Berry refused to recognize Hoffman's supremacy, and through his influence with Dietrich Wortmann and the AAU, he secured reappointment as Olympic coach for the 1936 games in Berlin. Chagrined, as he had been four years earlier at being excluded from leading a team that he had largely trained, and unwilling to remain sidelined, Hoffman resorted to desperate measures. While waiting in Le Havre, France, to return home on a ship, Hoffman, outweighing Berry by nearly a hundred pounds, assaulted his defiant rival.[56] A chastened Berry quickly fell into line, and Hoffman soon made his peace with Wortmann. Although Atlas remained a formidable rival in the marketplace, Hoffman, by dint of his financial resources, promotional skills, and size, became the dominant force in the iron game.

No less important to Hoffman's rededication to the sport were events that transpired at Hitler's games. Although disappointed that the U.S. team again placed third (behind Germany and Egypt), Hoffman was consoled that one of his boys, the featherweight Tony Terlazzo, became America's first Olympic weightlifting gold medalist since 1904. Further encouragement came from the results of the next two world championships, in which the U.S. team under Hoffman won two gold medals at Paris in 1937 and two gold, one silver, and a bronze at Vienna in 1938 in close pursuit of the Germans. The United States had "really arrived as a world lifting power," Hoffman boasted. These successes encouraged him to sell his interest in the oil-burner business and devote all his energy to making barbells and promoting weightlifting competitions. "I like weight lifting and weight lifters," he wrote in 1939, revealing his deep commitment to the sport.[57] Competitive bodybuilding was not yet part of his vision.

THE BLACK ATHLETE

Hoffman pondered the factors behind America's international success. That the iron game was more accepting of minorities than most sports, especially baseball, or U.S. society in general no doubt contributed to Hoffman's progressive attitudes about race. In his zeal to recruit the best weightlifters, color meant nothing to him. The ability to outlift the world's best athletes and bring glory to the United States—and himself—meant everything. It is not surprising that the 1936 Olympic team included a black featherweight named John Terry, who was trained by Charles Ramsey, of New York City, and promoted by Hoffman. Set up by Bob with his own business in York, Terry eventually won national championships from 1938 to 1941 and set an unofficial dead-lift record of 600 pounds. He was portrayed in *Strength & Health* as a muscular phenomenon; there were frequent photographs of his exceptional physique and references to his strength and wholesome character. Another African American, John Davis, whom Hoffman recruited from Brooklyn, quickly ascended the heights of weightlifting, winning the world light-heavyweight title at age seventeen in 1937 at Vienna, and setting two world records. After the war, he became the world's premier heavyweight, setting more records and winning seven Olympic and world titles. Hoffman even featured a nude picture of Davis's fine physique on the cover of *Strength & Health* in January 1941.[58]

Hoffman's pride in the accomplishments of black athletes and curiosity about their potential was unique. In his magazine's first year, he published an article titled "The Advent of the Colored Strength Athlete," extolling the achievements of Wesley Williams, who won distinction not only for his lifting ability and physique but also for becoming an officer in the New York Fire Department. Special attention in the 1930s was lavished on lifters from Panama, all of whom exhibited a mixed racial heritage, but there were also pictures of men of color from Barbados, Grenada, Jamaica, and Burma as well as the United States. Especially striking was the physique of a black bodybuilder showcased in November 1933 and identified simply as "Johnson" from New Jersey. Johnson exhibited large, well-defined arms, a deep chest, a narrow waist, and lumps of muscle all over his symmetrical back. The magazine noted: "There is muscular beauty in the contours of this bronze Hercules."[59] And probably few *Strength & Health* readers realized they were looking at a lighter-skinned black athlete when a physique photograph of Chester Fields, of Panama, appeared on the July 1934 cover, a first for a major muscle magazine.

So impressed was Hoffman with these success stories that he attributed superior athletic abilities to black athletes, especially in sprinting and jumping events. He noted as well that they quickly profited from weight training: "Many of the colored boys have bought York barbells. And in a surprisingly short period of time muscles appear all over them." Admittedly, the physical endowments of these black worthies were extraordinary, but unlike white bodybuilders such as Sandow, Macfadden, Jowett, and Berry, it was not possible to place them in the cultural tradition of the ancient Greeks. Rather, Hoffman looked to their African ancestry. It was survival of the fittest, not the quest for arete, that prevailed. After the 1936 Olympics, where African Americans won every track race up to 1500 meters, Hoffman elaborated on this theme, attributing their success to willpower rather than genetics: "Whether or not negroes are superior physically, it has been proven that the chief reason for their success is their mind."[60] Hoffman was perhaps trying to apply the Greek mind-body synthesis to African Americans, but his observations were some of the first on what would become a controversial issue by the end of the century.[61] Most importantly, he was always willing to give them a fair break, a rarity in the 1930s. Unlike most of his contemporaries, he believed they had the potential, if provided the opportunity, of moving the iron game to a higher level.

JOHN GRIMEK

Yet it was a white bodybuilder, John Grimek, who most invigorated the sport and epitomized physical perfection for the next generation. As a young weight trainee in Perth Amboy, New Jersey, he showed outstanding development, especially in the limbs, and was soon in demand by professional photographers in New York City. Later he found employment as an artist's model for studio classes at Princeton University, the University of Illinois, and the Art Institute of Chicago. He earned $80 weekly—excellent wages in the early years of the Depression—but he had to work 80–100 hours a week.[62] Meanwhile, Grimek's pictures were appearing regularly in *Strength*, described by superlatives such as "splendid," "marvelous," "incomparable," and "unexcelled." "This young man is beyond any doubt the outstanding example of muscular shapeliness in the world today," observed Berry in 1934. "Photographs simply give no true indication of his impressiveness." Unfortunately, since there were no physique contests to compete in, a 1935 caricature of his achievements extolled mainly his weightlifting feats.[63]

Grimek, in fact, had to make his mark first as a weightlifter, to show "capacity for action," in order to lend credibility to his physique. He displayed his awesome strength at the 1934 national championships in Brooklyn, where he pressed 242.5 pounds, the highest weight in the meet and 11 pounds over the American record. It caught Hoffman's attention, along "with the huskiest physique" he had seen, described as "broad, brown, shapely, terrific."[64] After placing second in 1935, and with the Berlin Olympics approaching, Grimek moved to York. The results were spectacular. At the ensuing senior nationals in Philadelphia, he pressed 258.5, snatched 220, and clean and jerked 308 pounds at 183.5 pounds body weight. Had he weighed 2 pounds less, he would have eclipsed the light-heavyweight world press record by 9 pounds.[65] Grimek registered the highest total of the meet, and with his national-record press, he was entitled to the designation of America's strongest man. In light of those accomplishments, Grimek's Olympic experience was anticlimactic. Although he pressed a creditable 253, he finished a distant ninth; Germany's Josef Manger, the winner, pressed 291.5 and made a three-lift total that was 121 pounds higher than Grimek's. Yet John lifted more than any American and displayed considerable nerve by competing against some of the physical giants of his sport.

In succeeding years, Grimek continued to show that pound for pound he was one of the strongest men in the world. In 1938, he pressed 261 pounds as a light heavyweight and became one of few lifters to defeat (by 15 pounds) the remarkable John Davis. "The man's just too strong for words," Hoffman once remarked. But Grimek never mastered his form in the quick lifts, and he was confronted with the question whether he was seriously committed to weightlifting. It was obvious that, as a lifter, he could never take full advantage of his great natural strength until he met or exceeded the body weight of his competitors. But to put on thirty or forty pounds, in an era when lifters ate regular food and did not take drugs, would mean losing much of the sharpness of his physique and likely developing a larger midriff. Whatever hopes he cherished as a bodybuilder would be jeopardized. Hoffman, who understood this conundrum, provided wise counsel.

> I frequently say that a man can't have everything. John Grimek has more than his share and has done more than his share for weightlifting. His physique is the finest, I believe, in the world at present and I doubt much if the greats of the past could match him. . . . He became a weightlifter to prove that there is power in a shapely physique. But there is one thing I can't believe. That a man can have a build like Grimek and be world's weightlifting champ. . . . I think his physique does weightlifting and the entire cause of weight training more good than would his winning of the world's championship.[66]

Had Grimek focused on weightlifting, the world would have been deprived of his classic physique at its height. Bodybuilding would never have been the same.

What deflected him from this course was Hoffman's zealous promotional bent. Grimek's physique proved irresistible to Hoffman, who sought to use it to advertise his products and publicize his philosophy of fitness. Grimek became something of a mascot of York Barbell. He was projected as "the present day perfect man," and his images became the most admired of any American bodybuilder. In May 1935, his picture appeared on the cover of *Strength & Health*, the first of twenty-seven times, more than any other person in the magazine's fifty-three-year history. In his 1936 assessment of the relative merits of the physiques of Klein, Grimek, and Sansone, the Canadian promoter Norman Miller concluded that Sansone "more closely resembles the ancient Greek sculpture that we are to this day prone to rely upon for a correct standard of the masculine physique."[67] Few, however, would gainsay Grimek's claim, in the action-obsessed 1930s, to be as strong as he looked. More than any other bodybuilder, Grimek opened the way for a separate sport to showcase the muscles that strength athletes developed for health, fitness, and weightlifting competition. In anticipation of such a phenomenon, Grimek epitomized the most perfectly developed American male.

MISS AMERICA—A HIGHER VISION OF BEAUTY

In 1935, the quest resumed in Atlantic City for America's most beautiful female. But unlike its male counterpart, the contest had no obvious connection with Greek physical culture or contemporary sporting enthusiasms. It was chiefly a body show in which glamour and glitz seemed to be the attractions. The Miss America Pageant was subsumed within a weeklong series of entertainments and sporting events billed as the Showmen's Variety Jubilee. The festival included vaudeville troupes, trapeze acts, clowns, comedians, high-diving horses, canine surfing, string bands, a fashion show, a hairdressers' contest, bicycle races, a yacht regatta, an aerial sham battle, and a six-mile ocean swim for a $1,000 prize.[68] It was a spectacle designed to lure tourists to Atlantic City for "A Thousand Thrills" and "A Wonder Week of Pleasure." Garish advertisements depicted drawings of scantily clad or unclad women frolicking freely and wantonly in "The Summer Amusement Capitol of America." One seductive flyer entitled "Girls! Girls! Girls!" displayed a topless bathing beauty with a ribbon that identified her as "Miss America 1935."[69]

Although the pageant never descended to an outright skin show, it was intended to satisfy the male desire to look at attractive women. The train that brought the forty-eight contestants from Philadelphia was called the "Beauty Special," and King Neptune presided over the festivities. Perhaps the remark that most revealed the emphasis on appearance was the caption accompanying a local newspaper picture of the girls in swimsuits: "There are Dangerous Curves Ahead for the Judges in the Jubilee Beauty Pageant."[70] As a fitting denouement to the tawdry spectacle, a nude statue of the 1935 Miss America, Henrietta Leaver, an "exotic" beauty from Pittsburgh, was unveiled after the competition. She unceremoniously left Atlantic City, protesting that she had innocently posed for the statue in a bathing suit.[71]

Soon steps were taken that permanently changed the pageant, drawing it closer to the nation's ideal of perfect womanhood. It remained part of the Showmen's Variety Jubilee until 1940, but in 1935 contest organizers had borrowed Lenora Slaughter from the St. Petersburg (Florida)

Chamber of Commerce to supervise the pageant. She stayed for thirty-two years, during which time she raised the moral tone of the contest. A sign of change was the inclusion of a talent competition, a rough equivalent to what athleticism would later be for Mr. America. It had little impact at first. The judges "*still* picked the pretty girls," Slaughter ruefully noted, but a decisive shift came in 1938, when a talent performance became mandatory and worth one-third of the balloting.[72]

Other changes followed. "I didn't like having nothing but swimsuits," Slaughter later stated. "I had to get Atlantic City to understand that it couldn't just be a beauty contest."[73] It should instead be a honorable undertaking. Atlantic City mayor C. D. White fully subscribed to Slaughter's standards, and as early as 1936 he stressed the event's "cultural" aspect in his welcoming address. "We are past the time when beauty parades are in the nature of floor shows," he said. "This is a cultural event seeking a high type of beauty."[74] What White meant by "cultural" soon became apparent. Henceforth the pageant, under Slaughter's steady hand, disallowed commercial sponsorship of contestants, limited entrants to girls between eighteen and twenty-eight, imposed a one a.m. curfew, prohibited smoking in public, and banned contestants from bars and nightclubs.[75] Also, no competitor could appear with a man, even her father, during pageant week. This "no males" regulation was enforced by a chaperone system put in place by Bette White, the mayor's wife.[76] Gone too by the end of the decade was King Neptune, a symbolic vestige of the contest's male-dominated past. No one would ever label Lenora Slaughter a feminist, but it would be difficult to find a more persistent advocate in the 1930s for the respect and advancement of women in such a visible feature of American life.

The Miss America Contest, by then an annual affair, suggested new possibilities for presentation of the male body. Hoffman was aware of this connection, as was obvious from his two-page spreads in *Strength & Health* of swimsuited Miss America contestants in 1936 and 1937 on Atlantic City's Steel Pier. Accompanying articles stressed a healthy and wholesome lifestyle. In "What Are Your Chances for Success and Happiness?," Hoffman argues that the development of muscles is a lifelong activity and that "physical training will lengthen life and improve one's feelings and appearance." In "A Woman's Life Is a Real Beauty Contest," he uses the byline of his wife, Rosetta, to criticize the deplorable physical condition of women. The Miss America Pageant was indicted for its superficiality, since it fostered a preoccupation with physical appearance derived from beauty aids rather than exercise: "The men have gotten a long way ahead of us in body culture, they have discovered how to mold a beautiful figure *and keep it*! It's about time they passed the 'secret' on to us."[77] Herein lay the irony between perceptions of male and female physiques when Slaughter was implementing her reforms: the ideal male, unlike his female counterpart, represented more than just physical appearance.

The inauguration of the Mr. America Contest must be seen against this background of rising attention being focused on women's bodies. That male bodies also deserved consideration became more evident not only in the revival of festivities in Atlantic City but also from momentum imparted in the 1920s and 1930s by such iron-game patriarchs as Calvert, Jowett, Berry, and Hoffman, who nurtured interest in muscular development within the context of sporting activities, chiefly weightlifting. Conceptually, this pent-up desire to recognize the perfect male body resulted from earlier seeds planted by Bernarr Macfadden in the fertile soil of neoclassical physical culture. It was hardly fortuitous, after a gestation period of four decades, that six physique competitions suddenly appeared at once.

The year 1936, highlighted by the Olympics, provided the most defining events in this progression. The attention of the weightlifting community was drawn to the awesome strength of America's pocket heavyweight, John Grimek, and his Herculean physique suggested that bodybuilding might be worth pursuing for its own sake. The Berlin Olympics were also important for awakening the world to the potential of America's black athletes, especially Jesse Owens, but also the weightlifter John Terry, whose well-developed physique attracted as much admiration as his strength did. "I have always believed," Hoffman later stated, "that there never was a better built man than John Terry."[78] No one as yet, except possibly Hoffman, had thought of exploiting such a magnificent resource as Terry strictly for display purposes. Another factor that encouraged the emerging Mr. America idea was the implementation of reforms in the Miss America Pageant by Lenora Slaughter, beginning in 1937. Previously, public displays of male and female bodies adhered to contrasting definitions of beauty. While the former, inspired by the Greeks and fostered by Macfadden, incorporated health and muscular function as important criteria, the latter adhered to a less noble perception of only skin-deep beauty. Slaughter not only brought the Miss America Pageant closer to the physical-culture ideal of a "high type of beauty," but also provided a template for the staging and publicity possibilities of a Mr. America counterpart. Both contests became embodiments of American ideals. Finally, it was in 1936 that Peary Rader, of Alliance, Nebraska, started publishing *Iron Man* magazine, and that Joe Weider, of Montreal, embarked, at age thirteen, on his long career as "Trainer of Champions." In succeeding decades, Rader and Weider had a major impact on the development of bodybuilding and the Mr. America Contest.

PART 2: THE GOLDEN AGE

3

THE FIRST MR. AMERICA CONTESTS

BODYBUILDING AS SUCH NEVER BECAME A SPECIAL ITEM UNTIL AFTER 1939 REALLY. BEFORE THAT ALL THE TOP MEN CAME FROM LIFTERS, STRONGMEN ETC. JOHN GRIMEK EVEN WAS A WEIGHT-LIFTER THOUGH THE FIRST TOTALLY DEDICATED BODYBUILDER. OTHERS LIKE TONY SANSONE WERE NOT REALLY TOP PHYSIQUE MEN JUST GREAT POSEURS.

OSCAR HEIDENSTAM TO JOHN TERPAK,
APRIL 7, 1972

IT WAS STRIKING THAT AFTER MANY YEARS OF NEGLECT AND SUBSERVIENCE to weightlifting, so many physique contests were held in 1938–1939. While ones in Schenectady, New York; New Haven, Connecticut; the Bronx, New York; and York, Pennsylvania, can be dismissed as having little more than local significance, those in Amsterdam (New York) and Chicago were nationally prominent and marked the beginning of a long tradition. Much debate has centered on which of these contests was the first true Mr. America competition. Most iron game aficionados conclude that both of them and their respective winners, Bert Goodrich and Roland Essmaker, deserve the appellation of Mr. America.[1] While the Amsterdam affair occurred earlier and first employed the title, the Chicago contest gained credibility from its association with the national weightlifting championships and its sponsorship by the AAU, the umbrella organization for future Mr. Americas. What these arguments fail to comprehend, however, is the all-important cultural component—a legacy from the Greeks— that had permeated bodybuilding over previous decades and would prove vital to Mr. America's ongoing existence. Under that criterion, the Amsterdam show clearly qualifies as the premier event.

JOHN HORDINES AND THE EARLY SHOWS

The tiny village of Pogar, buried deep in the Carpathian Mountains of Ukrainian Galicia and the site of heavy fighting in World War I, seems an unlikely source of inspiration for the first Mr. America Contest. That is where John Hordinetz (later Hordines), the fourteenth child of Russian Orthodox parents, was born on October 1, 1908. At age four, he immigrated to Centralia, Pennsylvania, where his father worked in the coal mines. Hordines escaped this harsh environment by winning a scholarship to Syracuse University, where he lettered in football (as varsity tackle) and three other sports. After graduating in 1934 with a degree in physical education, he occupied many niches in the burgeoning field of physical culture, first as physical director of the YMCA in Troy, New York, and then at Carroll "Pink" Gardner's Health Institute and Reducing Salon in Schenectady.[2] Gardner, according to the sportswriter Louis Cline, excelled as a wrestler and was "the most perfect specimen of physical man outside of Eugene [sic] Sandow I had ever seen."[3] It was Gardner's physique, athletic prowess, and clean living that inspired Hordines to stage the Eastern States Body Culture Contest on December 1, 1938, at Gardner's gym. An art director, a sports editor, and a former wrestling champion judged forty contestants. According to a local reporter, the event attracted "a large crowd cramming every nook and corner of the gym to get a glimpse of the fine physiques."[4] At the contest, observed Alton Eliason, a Connecticut gym owner, rules for judging included a point system and a three-pose protocol for athletes. There was no overall champion, only awards for height division winners, best body parts, and muscle control. Afterward, in deference to York's preeminence, the judges sent honorary awards to John Grimek and Gord Venables for their outstanding physiques.[5]

This politically savvy gesture proved invaluable in moving the Mr.

America concept forward. In the February 1939 issue of *Strength &
Health*, Hoffman carried a feature article entitled "America's Best Built
Men," which covered Hordines's contest. It opened auspiciously:

> Atlantic City has long been famed for the annual pageant in which they
> select Miss America, purported to be the most attractive American girl.
> Many cities select their best formed and most attractive model sending
> her to a district or state meet. The winners then contest in Atlantic City
> for the supreme honor, the title of Miss America. Miami, Florida and Hol-
> lywood, California have their pageants too, to glorify the American girl.
> The male physique, which shows to best advantage when developed to the
> limit, has in the past not had the opportunity to be shown under similar
> circumstances.

Hoffman then described the Schenectady contest and provided detailed
biographical sketches of the winners. He predicted that next year's
contest would be bigger, better advertised, and more representative of
the best-built men in the country. No less important was an article in
the following month's issue in which Hoffman expressed his determination "this year to select America's best developed man, a sort of Mr.
America." With a passing nod to similar contests in Britain and France,
he hoped someone would challenge Grimek, whose great strength and
magnificent physique seemed unbeatable. The national weightlifting
championships in Chicago or the New York World's Fair in 1939
seemed ideal locations. Hoffman intended it to be "the biggest event
of its kind in the entire world."[6]

Meanwhile a spin-off of Hordines's contest was held by Eliason
on April 4, 1939, in New Haven, Connecticut. "Looking like Greek
Gods," observed the *New Haven Register*, thirty of the state's finest
physiques "strutted their stuff . . . to the plaudits of nearly 400 enthusiastic spectators."[7] Each contestant in three height divisions performed three poses on a turntable. Isadore Urbanivicius, of Waterbury,
Connecticut, won the tall class, Eliason later recalled, but the winners
"were all outstanding both as lifters and in physical proportions." Hordines assisted with the judging, and the three winners won a free trip
to his next contest.[8] A Best Built Man Contest, staged at the Bronx
YMHA on April 23, attracted fifty-five entrants, Hoffman as master of
ceremonies, and Hordines as a judge. The contestants were evaluated
on muscular development as well as "excellence of proportion, poise,
health, condition of skin, hair, etc." Again there was no overall winner, but a Californian named Bert Goodrich "was outstanding as a sore

AMERICA'S FINEST PHYSIQUE CONTEST

At the JUNIOR HIGH SCHOOL AUDITORIUM
AMSTERDAM, N. Y.

SATURDAY, JUNE 10, 1939 *at 6 P. M.*

To select the Finest Physique in the United States as representing "Mr. America"

Under the direction of JOHNNIE HORDINES, Gardner's Gymnasium, Schenectady, N. Y.

Contest held in honor of Bernarr Macfadden's Fifty Years of Great Physical Culture Work

Proceeds of this contest will be given to the Knothole League, an organization doing fine work among under-priviledged boys, especially giving guidance and material help in baseball and athletics. Remember that "BUILDING BOYS IS BETTER THAN MENDING MEN."

DIVISION OF ALL CONTESTANTS

All models will be divided into three classes:

Class "A"—From 5 ft. to 5 ft., 8 in.
Class "B"—From 5 ft., 8 in., to 5 ft., 11 in.
Class "C"—From 5 ft., 11 in., to 6 ft., 4 in.

From the entire United States, twenty (20) contestants will be chosen for each of the three classes, making a total of sixty (60) in number.

ELIGIBILITY

Contest open to any male resident in the United States, regardless of race, creed or color. All entries will be given a square deal.

ENTRIES

Please send photographs showing different views of your body. More than one photo showing muscular development and body symmetry will greatly increase your chance of selection. Any photograph that has been "touched up" or improved beyond the original figure will cause disqualification from this and other future contests. All candidates sending photographs should inclose postage for return mailing.

Winners in the 1938-39 State Physique Contests automatically qualify but should send in their photographs early.

The selected candidates will pay an entry fee of two dollars ($2.00).

All entries close Saturday, June 3, 1939, with Johnnie Hordines of 918 State Street, Schenectady, New York.

POSING

Each candidate will receive three minutes posing time. In this period, a front pose, a back pose and a pose on a revolving pedestal will be taken. Each of these three poses will take one minute. A chime will signify changing time. All posing will be done to specially arrange violin and piano obligato rendered by Mrs. Mabel McLay and Mrs. Bertha Marquet.

WEARING APPAREL

In posing, tights or short trunks only will be permitted. Wearing apparel similar to that worn in the first Finest Physique Contest held at Gardner's Gymnasium, Schenectady, New York, December 1, 1939, is suitable. Those who have not seen the winners, please refer to the February issue of "Strength and Health" magazine.

Contestants are free to use oil on their bodies if they wish. Shaving off of superflous hair from the body is also permitted. (We believe that it is only fair to let all candidates display their bodies to the fullest advantage. Nature is not always kind in distributing hair over the male body.)

METHOD OF SELECTION

From each of the three height classes, three contestants will be chosen for Semi-final judging. Those chosen will be given three additional minutes of posing time. After these three have posed, a winner will be selected, representing Class "A." In the same manner, a winner from Classes "B" and "C" will be selected. From these three class winners, one will be selected as representing the Finest Physique in the United States or "Mr. America."

ADDITIONAL HONORS

Awards will be given for the Finest Chest and the Finest Abdomen. After "Mr. America" has been selected, each class of twenty models will pose on the stage in a group. From these three groups, three class winners will be selected for the Finest Chest and also three class winners for the Finest Abdomen. From each of these three winning classes, one will be selected as having the Finest Chest and one as having the Finest Abdomen in America.

AWARDS

To the winner of the Finest Physique in the United States as representing "Mr. America," a handsome plaque will be given.

To the winners of Class "A," "B" and "C," plaques will be given.

Similar awards will be made to the winners of the Finest Chest and Finest Abdomen.

The other contestants will each receive a Certificate emblematic of their honor as having been selected to compete in the contest.

The following are invited as judges:

1. CHARLES ATLAS—Renowned exponent of Body Building and Physical Culture.
2. PROF. WILLIAM J. DAVIDSON of Syracuse University—Greatly admired and learned Physical Education teacher.
3. MR. EATON G. DAVIS, Schenectady, N. Y., Noted Sculptor and Art Critic.
4. JOHN EVERS of Albany—Famous Big League Baseball star.
5. CARROLL "PINK" GARDNER of Schenectady, New York—Former World's Light Heavyweight Wrestling Champion.
6. BOB HOFFMAN of York, Pa. — World's leading authority on Body Culture and editor of "Strength and Health" magazine.
7. BERNARR MAC FADDEN—Eminent Physical Culturist and editor of "Physical Culture" magazine.
8. JACK MINNOCH—Prominent Sports Editor of the "Amsterdam Evening Recorder," of Amsterdam, New York.
9. WALTER REAGLES—Director of Art at the General Electric Company at Schenectady, New York. Judge at the annual Atlantic City Beauty Contest.

Master of Ceremonies—LEO BOLLEY, Tydol Sports Commentator and familiar voice on WGY and NBC networks.

Director of Art, Lighting and Decorating—LLOYD T. LAMBERT, Prominent Sportsman and Photographic expert.

OUR AMBITION IS—

A World's Finest Physique Contest at either the New York or San Francisco World's Fair in September, 1939.

Figure 3.1. Promotional poster for the first Mr. America Contest. Used by permission of the *Amsterdam (NY) Recorder.*

thumb and won the unanimous acclaim of the judges," noted Hoffman. The most interesting feature of his report, however, was his description of the winners' athletic achievements. Hoffman believed that muscles should be useful, and he was intent on showing "physiques the best athletes earn for themselves."[9]

THE FIRST MR. AMERICA CONTEST

Hoffman's approval of these early shows, which stressed athleticism along with health, symmetry, muscularity, and general appearance, set the stage for a national competition and encouraged Hordines to schedule his America's Finest Physique Contest on June 10, 1939. Promotional materials stated the winner would be designated "Mr. America."[10] Held in the early evening at the junior high school auditorium in Amsterdam, New York, it was preceded by weightlifting and bent press contests and a softball game, to set a proper athletic tone. Proceeds went to the Knot-Hole League, a local junior baseball circuit. The list of fifty-eight entrants from eleven states featured the

Figure 3.2. Bert Goodrich, the first Mr. America. *Strength & Health*, September 1939, 1.

iron-game notables David Asnis, of New York City; Gene Jantzen, of Los Angeles; and Walter Podolak, of Syracuse.[11] The judges were Hoffman, Adolf Rhein (New York gym operator), Joe Bonomo (Hollywood stuntman), Otto Arco (hand balancer), Easton Davis (sculptor), and William Davidson (Hordines's former mentor at Syracuse). Hordines recalled that in organizing the contest, he was "greatly influenced by the Miss America Contest": "I figured the women had their contest, so why not the men?" Furthermore, he was interested in more than "external beauty": "Not just muscle or weightlifting ability, but personality, character, and the way you lived. . . . All-around activities— that's what I stressed." Hordines especially wanted to have a sculptor as one of the judges "because he knew the shape of the body." Since Hordines "wanted to go back to the Greek ideal," "bulging muscles wasn't the most important thing—but how the muscles blend." In an effort to lend prestige and an air of tradition, he publicized his contest as being "held in honor of Bernarr Macfadden's Fifty Years of Great Physical Culture Work."[12]

Unlike preceding physique competitions, this Mr. America Contest selected just one winner. The posing protocol required each contestant to perform three poses (front, back, and optional) for a minute each on a platform that revolved on the third pose. A chime signified the time, and all posing was done to a violin and piano obbligato rendered by Mabel McLay and Bertha Marquet. On hand to administer special effects were Walter Reagles, the art director for the General Electric Company and a former Miss America Contest judge, and the noted physique photographer Al Urban, under whose auspices lighting equipment was installed "to best display the muscular effects of contestants' bodies." Muscularity, symmetry, and general appearance were the criteria. "I was simply overwhelmed by the many beautiful examples of male physique," commented Hoffman. "Practically every entry . . . had every requisite of the statues of Greek Gods which have been famous through the centuries."[13] Ultimately, Bert Goodrich, winner of the tall men's class, was designated Mr. America, followed by Elmer Farnham (short), of York, and Carl Hempe (medium), of Easton, Pennsylvania.

BUILDING ON THE PRECEDENT

More than any other factor, it was the follow-up publicity provided by Hoffman (in a feature article) on the "many supreme masculine beings" he had seen in Amsterdam that made this event significant. "This contest was more truly representative than any similar event ever held in America," he exclaimed.

> There are 450,000 words in our language . . . but words simply cannot describe the magnificent display we saw at Amsterdam. It is the forerunner of other similar contests and I hope that every reader in the future will either compete in such a contest or at least be present to witness the events. Physique contests have become tremendously popular. . . . Every district should stage such a contest to select the best built men in their section. Later send them to the larger contests so that they can win truly national honors.[14]

Joe Peters, of Schenectady, winner of the best chest award, concurs that Hordines's contest set a precedent. "In the thirties we practiced lifting as well as bodybuilding," he recalls. "No one thought of doing bodybuilding independently. Physique was an afterthought." What made this contest unique was its emphasis on physique—symmetry and muscular development.[15] For judges, accustomed to the objective standards of weightlifting meets, these subjective qualities, blending artistry, athleticism, and showmanship, made their task difficult.

Hoffman was confident that decisive steps had been taken toward a new tradition, and he looked forward to two future physique contests that might provide continuity, one for the weightlifters at the AAU championships in Chicago on July 4 and one at Hoffman's annual birthday show in York on November 18. He hoped that the latter would "be the biggest of the year" for entrants and spectators: "The other contests will be over . . . and a winner here will be a real Mr. America." The Chicago event, limited to selecting America's best-built weightlifter, was marred by controversy over the presence of female artists and art teachers as judges, and so received little publicity. Indeed, *Strength & Health*, which carried a full report of the weightlifting championships, made no mention of the physique contest! A passing reference was made to Roland Essmaker in a later issue, but without any recognition of his being Mr. America.[16] As Essmaker later noted, his name appeared nowhere on the program, even as a lifter: "I was a complete unknown and no one was more surprised than I was to be chosen the *1939 MR. AMERICA*."[17] Technical problems plagued Hoffman's York's Perfect Man Contest. Although won by Grimek and heavily promoted, it did not attract a national body of entrants and was something of an anticlimax to other 1939 contests.[18] Significantly Essmaker was not even a finalist in his height division at York.

Hoffman, though often vilified later as being opposed to body-building, was a key figure during the sport's emergence just before World War II. Through his promotion of all six 1939 contests and his nurturing of Grimek and other future physique stars, he did as much as anyone to identify and shape the course of the new competition. The other critical figure was John Hordines, who, by organizing two competitions, defining their format, and projecting a national image, crystallized the concept of Mr. America. Yet he had "no idea how important the contest would be" or that it would serve as a precedent. Hordines's lack of further association with his creation may be attributed partly to his being an iron-game upstart and partly to the influence of the powers that be, who would hardly have allowed such a promising enterprise to remain in an obscure place like Amsterdam, New York. It is also likely that Hoffman coveted control of the contest. "Hoffman was a big shot," Hordines ruefully recalls. "He knew it all." Given the effort required, it is hardly surprising that Hordines was willing to turn over the reins to a larger organization.[19] In any case, by assuming a teaching position at Coxsackie Reformatory, 135 miles north of New York City, Hordines abdicated all future rights to the Mr. America Contest. He would be no Lenora Slaughter.

THE GRIMEK ERA

Others quickly filled the void. Hoffman, after staging his Perfect Man Contest in York, displayed continued interest in physique by sponsoring two photographic contests in *Strength & Health* in early 1940. But the hand of New York promoters was most evident at the 1940 Mr. America Contest, held at Madison Square Garden. The blue-ribbon judging panel included Macfadden, Hoffman, Sig Klein, Charles Dieges (an AAU executive), John Kilpatrick (president of Madison Square Garden), H. J. Reilly (president of the Physio-Therapy Society), and Dan Parker (noted columnist for the *New York Daily Mirror*). All, except Hoffman, were from New York City. To no one's surprise, the winner was John Grimek. According to Klein, Grimek was there "in all his glory."

> I have seen Grimek poses in pictures, I have seen him perform at many, oh, so many exhibitions, but this evening he was at his best. He looked to me like the reincarnation of Hercules, with the grace of Apollo. When he struck his first pose, well, he did not strike it, he just glided into it,

he looked supreme. . . . Wave after wave of applause greeted him. Many judges who have never seen J. C. G. before rubbed their eyes, they never saw such grace, and development, such magnificent physical majesty.[20]

In addition to winning the overall title, Grimek won an award for best arms and the designation "Most Muscular Man in America." Unlike the other sixty contestants, he entered the lifting contest as a heavy-weight the same day, placing third to Steve Stanko and Louis Abele, both of whom greatly outweighed him. Klein noted at the time that Grimek "will be for some time to come the greatest boon to weight lifting and body building . . . since the days of Eugene [sic] Sandow."[21] There was no one else in his league.

Yet controversy plagued this second Mr. America Contest also. However obvious it might have been that Grimek was the winner, only 1.75 points (99.25 to 97.5) separated him from the runner-up, Frank Stepanek (Leight), a New York policeman. "Telling tales out of school," Klein explained that while five of the judges had decisively chosen Grimek, Reilly and Parker had placed Stepanek first, the impli-cation being they favored a local man.[22] But Parker went on the offen-

Figure 3.3. The inimitable John Grimek, Mr. America 1940. Author's possession.

sive in his newspaper column, suggesting that Hoffman had exercised undue influence and should not have been a judge when his "own man"—an employee, no less—was a contestant.[23] Hoffman retorted that it was impossible for his votes to outweigh others, since he was "outnumbered by six New York City judges." While the winner was from York, "the men who finished second, third, fourth, fifth and sixth were all New Yorkers."[24] Criticism of another kind, directed at the fledgling contest itself, came from a popular tabloid called *Pic*. "Bulging biceps, like dinosaurs, are in the parade of the past," it noted in a two-page pictorial spread: "Joe Louis, Johnny Weissmuller, Max Baer, Bobby Bruns or the thousand and one other logical contenders for the title of 'Mr. America' would not walk across the alley to compete in such a contest." To Jim Howlett, of Dorchester, Massachusetts, and other iron-game enthusiasts who complained to Hoffman, this article was full of "outrageous lies," but to a large majority of Americans, it no doubt reinforced deep-seated prejudices against musclemen.[25]

Bodybuilding was still outside the ken of mainstream sports and popular culture, but owing to the publicity surrounding Grimek and the Mr. America Contest, it was finally emerging from the shadows. A sure sign of progress was the appearance of Bosco, the legendary strongman creation of the cartoonist Harry Paschall, to wrest control of the contest just after the winners were selected. "'Hey, Joodge,' hollers Bosco, 'vot you mean—Meester America? You ain't seen nothing yet.'"[26] That Grimek and his title, like Miss America, might become household words seemed possible. "John Carol Grimek will have to get used to being Mr. America," predicted Sig Klein. "He should be proud of the title, and it will be a long time before he will be surpassed by any of the present crop of physical culturists."[27]

What seems remarkable in retrospect is that Grimek, the greatest bodybuilder of his era, considered himself chiefly a weightlifter. It was evident in his unwillingness, despite Hoffman's urging, to enter (or even attend) the first Mr. America Contest, in Amsterdam. Furthermore, his motivation for attending the second contest, according to Alton Eliason, was to enter the weightlifting competition. Eliason added that Grimek "hated John Davis" and chided Ray Van Cleef for writing an article on that "God-damned nigger" for *Strength & Health*. Grimek insisted that the only thing he wanted to do in New York was to "break the press record," which "Davis held . . . at 280": "Grimek wanted to do 284. He had a very flexible back and could get away with things. It was more important than winning the Mr. America Contest.

That was his prime interest that night." It should be remembered that Grimek's only bodybuilding competition thus far had been Hoffman's Perfect Man Contest in 1939, where he hardly had a choice. Decades later, Grimek pointed out to the author Fred Howell, "You know, I never planned to enter a physique contest. I was talked into it."[28] Had Hoffman not persuaded him to enter that lackluster affair in his own backyard, the bodybuilding world might have been denied one of its greatest stars. It served to prepare the reluctant Grimek to win the second Mr. America Contest.

By the 1941 contest, held at the Arena in Philadelphia, there was never any doubt that Grimek would win again. He looked "better than ever," according to Sig Klein. "His posing was magnificent, his muscularity unmatched, his proportions symmetrical, his appearance majestic." The point spread between Grimek's 146.5 and the 125.5 for the runner-up, Jules Bacon, of Philadelphia, seemed agreeable to everyone. Only Grimek's refusal to contest any of the subdivisions allowed others to win some honors. So sweeping was his victory that AAU officials ruled that no Mr. America could enter the contest again; otherwise, Grimek would have won indefinitely.[29]

ANCILLARY ISSUES

Such a standard also applied to the Miss America Contest, as did the practice of attracting contestants who had won previous contests throughout the country. Frank Leight (formerly Stepanek) was Mr. New York City; Jules Bacon, Mr. Philadelphia; and Tommy O'Hare, Mr. New Orleans. The latter and his coach, Cy Bermudez, had their expenses paid by the New Orleans Athletic Club.[30] Charges of favoritism were reduced by the decision to have ten judges: one from New York City, four from Philadelphia, and one each from Rochester, Cincinnati, Wilmington, New Orleans, and York. Although he did not vie for the overall title, John Davis, the heavyweight lifting champion, set a precedent by entering and winning the best back competition. The decision was hardly without controversy. Klein, for example, observed, "Johnny just stood with his arms at his sides and I was surprised that he won," but he concluded that the judges must have been influenced by photos they had seen, "for he was given the award almost with unanimous acclaim." In this instance, prejudice, racial or otherwise, seem to have worked in Davis's favor.[31]

Some months later, however, controversy emerged over a photographic contest organized by the *Police Gazette* editor Edyth Farrell that selected Walter Lasky, of Brooklyn, as Mr. Police Gazette of 1941. Gord Venables, in a scathing *Strength & Health* article, objected that Lasky's picture appeared in many newspapers as "Mr. America," "Best Built Man in America," or "America's Most Perfect Male." Also, the involvement of the burlesque queen Ann Corio and some leading boxing and wrestling figures led Venables to make some tongue-in-cheek statements that went beyond the bounds of propriety.

> The judges included Sig Klein, Arthur Donovan, the fight referee, Jack Pfeffer, wrestling promoter, Ann Corio and several "strip-tease" artists and a case of Scotch. The case of Scotch vied for interest with the physique photos from which the winner was to be selected and finally the Scotch won. I have it from a reliable souse that such men as Bert Goodrich, Jules Bacon, Ludwig Shusterich, Jack Long, and Frank Leight were not even in the judges' final tally! And those men are plenty fast company in any physique contest. Do you blame me for saying the contest smelled of smelt?[32]

Not surprisingly, Klein and the others singled out for abuse were incensed by Venables's intemperate remarks. Some threatened to sue.[33] Although Klein tried to serve as mediator, he had difficulty putting his personal feelings aside. "It was not very decent of Gord to write that material and his 'informer' was all wrong," he told John Terpak, Hoffman's general manager. The article, he said, "gives one the impression that the gym was turned into a bordello that evening," adding, "You know John, that it is a slur on my family as well as myself." But there is no indication that Venables or York ever provided an explanation, much less an apology for the "awful mess."[34] The fiasco illustrated the potential for misinformation to reach a public ill informed about the nature of bodybuilding. Beyond that, it was perhaps inevitable that the nascent Mr. America Contest should be confused with other physique shows and associated with other events where the body was displayed for artistic and entertainment purposes. And it was probably Venables's own "case of Scotch" rather than one at the *Police Gazette* contest that was the real culprit.

THE WAR YEARS

The increased popularity of the Mr. America concept was shown by the inauguration of a Junior Mr. America Contest in 1942. It was held at the high school auditorium in Bristol, Connecticut, on April 19 in conjunction with the junior national weightlifting championship, by then a permanent fixture, and the "Hale America" program, a fitness movement promoting the war effort.[35] The physique contest was won by Kimon Voyages, of the Bronx, but far more attention was drawn by a flamboyant eighteen-year-old named Dan Lurie, from Brooklyn, who lost by only a half point. Though superbly fit and possessing a magnificent physique, he no doubt offended the judges by his effrontery. Eliason, the meet director, recalls that when Lurie filled out a contestant card beforehand, listing his achievements, the list of titles was so long it would not fit on the card. When he got to "Mr. Swimming Pool of Brooklyn," Eliason walked away. Lurie was, in Eliason's view, "the most egotistical and arrogant individual I've ever met."[36] Venables, in his "Incredible But True" column, credits Lurie with performing 1,225 parallel-bar dips in one and a half hours, but like other elite bodybuilders during the war years (Stanko, Grimek, and Bacon), he was rejected for military service (the reasons were, respectively, phlebitis, high blood pressure, and a heart irregularity).[37] Still, Lurie added some color to an otherwise drab period.

At the 1942 Mr. America Contest, held in Cincinnati, Lurie again "was very much in evidence," according to Hoffman. Possessing a "remarkable development," Lurie won awards for best arms, best legs, and most muscular man on his way to taking third place, perhaps because he was "rather short for a Mr. America." Hoffman agreed that Leight was a deserving winner, but he disagreed with the selection process. Instead of scores being allotted for muscularity, symmetry, and general appearance, as in previous years, judges were instructed to distribute points for arms, chest, back, abdominals, and legs. Citing the grotesque appearance of the deformed black bodybuilder Kenneth Pendleton (whose physique was cramped and emaciated) and the midget weightlifter Joe De Pietro, both of whom had well-developed parts, Hoffman again drew on the contest's Atlantic City female counterpart, and the comparison was not flattering; there was, he said, "no consideration for symmetry, carriage, posing ability, general appearance, facial appearance or hair, all of which should be important . . . in selecting a 'Mr. or Miss America.' I wonder how the results of the judging of 'Miss America' would have been if they were judged by best legs, best abdominals, best chest, etc. They made their selection from general appearances, selecting the girl who was most beautiful in face and body, who was most graceful and presented the best general appearance." Also at variance with Miss America protocol was the procedure adopted by Cincinnati officials of disallowing leading competitors from posing side by side. Otherwise, Hoffman believed that John Davis would have won the best back award again. In fact, his entire physique was "more than extraordinary." In Hoffman's view, Davis had "as good a physique as any of the men who were present at Cincinnati and were it not for the handicap of color, he might have been 'Mr. America.'"[38]

A different view prevailed of the 1943 contest, held in Los Angeles, which was won by Jules Bacon, by then a York employee. It was a "glorious spectacle," according to Hoffman, "comparing favorably with the big 'Mr. America' contests of past years." Judging criteria returned to muscularity, symmetry, and general appearance, which Hoffman believed were "the same rules as were in effect in the 'Miss America' contest held each year in Atlantic City." Hoffman seemed pleased that he had influenced the meet director, David Matlin, to restore these traditional standards. While Lurie held an edge in muscularity and symmetry, Bacon won the title for his superior posture, posing, and hygiene. "It has always been my thought in selecting a 'Mr. America' that a man's hair, face, skin, teeth, etc. should count heavily," stated Hoffman. "That a man was hardly deserving of the 'Mr. America' title only on the strength of his physique."[39] However disappointed Lurie must have been, these standards of male beauty inherited from the Greeks, via the Macfadden era, fit prevailing ideals for a Mr. America.

These criteria also applied to the 1944 Junior Mr. America Contest, held in Pittsburgh, at which Steve Stanko, another York employee, was ranked "head and shoulders above the other competitors." Stanko had "everything desired of a 'Mr. America,'" observed Hoffman. In addition to an outstanding physique, "he has fine posture, an engaging smile, is handsome in a manly sort of way, with thick black hair and fine teeth, is modest to the extreme, one of our world famous weight lifters, a fitting example of America's best young manhood."[40]

Venables describes how Stanko also won the Mr. America title three weeks later, in Chattanooga, but under adverse conditions.

He had injured his left leg in weightlifting and had a severe case of thrombophlebitis. Dangerous blood clots had formed. I doubt that the judges knew this for Steve went through the contest with a superb posing routine and was unanimously voted the winner. A party was given after the meet at the German-American Club. It was about three blocks away so Steve and I started to walk it. . . . I know the pain must have been intense though he never complained; he just had to sit down on the curb and rest for twenty minutes. When he got back home he spent a week in bed with his leg propped up—the only Mr. America confined to bed after winning the title.[41]

Lurie, under the prevailing rules, was relegated to second place and most muscular man in both 1944 contests.[42] A developing pattern was evident also in Hoffman's yearly reports, in which he traced in loving detail each of the Mr. America contests since Amsterdam. Representatives of Hoffman's club had won the title in four of the last five years, and Lurie was "perennial runner up." Venables, always disinclined to conform, preferred that the title be called something other than Mr. America "which somehow smatters of a bevy of non-swimable bathing beauties at Atlantic City."[43] More typical was the perspective provided in *Your Physique* by George Weaver, who viewed the Mr. America Contest as "analogous" to the Miss America Contest. What was once the "Greek Ideal of Manly Beauty" was now the "AMERICAN Ideal."[44]

POSTWAR CHALLENGES

An aura of idealism of a different kind permeated the 1945 contest, won by Clarence Ross, of Oakland, a private first class in the U.S. Army Air Corps. "This story could easily be called, 'Unknown Makes Good,'" wrote Hoffman. "It would have made a good Horatio Alger story." While stationed at Las Vegas during the war, he sculpted a championship-caliber physique, and Hoffman saw "his winning the Mr. America title" as "just one more proof of how wonderful it is to live in America."[45] Hoffman again had reason to feel satisfied because of the role he played in reestablishing traditional selection procedures. American idealism, of a geographic and ethnic sort, was evident in the 1945 Junior Mr. America Contest, won by Joe Lauriano, of Honolulu, who embodied mixed ancestry. Conspicuous by his absence from both 1945 contests was Dan Lurie, who, either from frustration or a desire to convert his muscles into money, had turned professional. Advertisements for his photos and physical-culture studio in Brooklyn soon began appearing in Joe Weider's Canadian publication *Your Physique*.[46]

The most significant indication of Lurie's new direction was his decision to challenge Grimek in a special contest for the title "America's Most Muscular Man." Lurie, with Weider's magazines as his mouthpiece, contended (incorrectly) that although it was assumed that Grimek was America's most muscular man by virtue of his two Mr. America victories, he had never actually won the title—whereas Lurie had won it thrice. The current Mr. America, Clarence Ross, resented Lurie's effrontery. "It makes me hot to think that I have just won the title for 1945," he told John Terpak, "and then a guy like him goes around claiming he is the most muscular man." At first Grimek tried insulting Lurie, referring to his "supercilious actions" and "self-inflated ego," hoping he would go away. When Weider and Lurie persisted, Hoffman organized a most muscular man contest at Philadelphia in May 1946. Grimek easily triumphed over the likes of Stanko, Sam Loprinzi, and Kimon Voyages while Lurie watched from the audience. When taunted by Hoffman to compete in an impromptu contest with other professionals, Lurie lost to Sig Klein, who was past his prime. According to Lurie, "A riot began at the back of the auditorium. People began throwing chairs and loud booing rang throughout the building."[47] Lurie later insisted that the challenge was Weider's idea, but it was not difficult for Grimek to identify the "opportunists" who "thought they could snag some cheap publicity by playing another man for a sucker" because "they themselves lack the necessary qualification."[48]

Yet controversy has continued to swirl over the circumstances surrounding the inception of this encounter and its intent. Weider denied that it was his idea, saying that the title of most muscular man "went to Lurie's head."

> This could have been a bad joke, but Lurie did it in my magazine. Some have said that I engineered everything to stir up controversy with York. Grimek, after all, was Bob Hoffman's superstar. Give me a break! Never, ever, would I do such a thing; Grimek was my idol. . . . The way it really happened, Lurie put his challenge into an issue just closing while I was out of town. I came home, saw the challenge, and had a fit, but it was too late to pull the thing out of the magazine.[49]

What Weider minded most was that Grimek had allegedly "wanted to come work with me," and talks had started "about him making the switch . . . but then that stupid challenge spoiled everything," since Grimek would never join Weider as long as Lurie was with him. Further, Weider was in a bind: "Insults started flying in Hoffman's *Strength and Health*, and I felt I had to back up Lurie because he appeared in my magazine." Weider regretted taking "the wrong side out of loyalty": "Think of the opportunity missed—Joe Weider and John Grimek as a team!"[50]

Randy Roach, in *Muscle, Smoke, and Mirrors*, rightly reckons it was unlikely that Grimek considered leaving York and Hoffman, "who was basically 'King Kong' of the industry[,] for a 24 year old Joe Weider who was at that time inexperienced and infantile in comparison." Although Lurie was unaware of any Grimek-Weider talks, Grimek verified that Weider was offering to pay him "$20,000 a year and set him up in Paris." It was a preposterous offer, and Grimek never trusted Weider, having observed how he would "build a guy up and then discard him."[51] Besides, though Hoffman never paid well, Grimek and his family were comfortably situated in York, where he was attached to a publicity medium that acclaimed him the world's greatest bodybuilder. What Weider's magnanimous offer signified was the importance of not only Grimek but also the Mr. America title, on which his fame chiefly rested.

The Lurie-Weider challenge helped define the changing course of bodybuilding and how it should be conducted. Weider was able to capitalize on the contest's lack of showmanship.

> Why can't strong man shows be put on with some semblance of professional theatre? We, the audience, are accustomed to showmanship. We have it in radio, the movies, the dramatic and musical comedy stage, and when we pay more than a buck for a seat we resent being steeped in corn. Why can't there be a Master of Ceremonies with a smooth line of talk and a brisk but easy manner to keep the show moving? Why can't there be good music to put a little spirit into the evening? When Turners tin can piano began to beat out the Star Spangled Banner we all knew what we were in for. When that ordeal was over Mr. Hoffman assured us the man at the piano was a very fine musician, but that he hadn't heard him since he played at his mother's funeral!

Readers of *Your Physique* no doubt found that comment amusing. But the comedy highlight of the evening occurred after a strongman act in which

> Sig Klein had juggled a huge barbell with super-human strength and really superb showmanship. When he had finished he put the bell down with a terrific thud that might have torn a hole through the floor of the stage. He took his bows amid thunderous applause and ran off. Just then the huge bell began to *roll*. Right toward the audience it came! We sat with bated breath as it crashed into the footlight trough, breaking some bulbs. Then, trying to be helpful, some little guy in a business suit ran on stage, grabbed up the bell in one small hand and ran off with it![52]

Most importantly, as a muscularity contest, the challenge signified a

Figure 3.4. Alan Stephan, Mr. America 1946. Courtesy of Stark Center.

growing difference in the way the ideal male physique was perceived. While Hoffman and the AAU, as inheritors of the Greek tradition, viewed musculature as an outward manifestation of other desirable qualities, including health, character, beauty, and athleticism, the Weider camp placed more emphasis on muscles or appearance for its own sake.

To Frank Leight (Mr. America 1942) and most bodybuilders after World War II, the choice seemed clear: that the only valid bodybuilding competition was one where "muscularity, general appearance, symmetry, proportions, cleanliness, character and general health are taken into consideration." The winner was supposed to be an exemplar of more than just muscle mass: "Call the contest what you will, 'Mr. America,' or 'Mr. Nobody.' It isn't the name that counts but what such a contest would symbolize. Namely the selection of a man who would become for the future generations of Body Builders, Weight Lifters, Physical Culturists etc. a pattern to look up."[53] Lurie's challenge, stressing muscular development alone, ran counter to Leight's holistic views and helped establish the philosophical bases for the Hoffman-Weider schism, which lasted for decades.

Meanwhile, World War II and its aftermath brought changes in the Miss America Pageant that made it, like its male counterpart, more representative of the feminine ideal and less like just a body show. During the 1940s, Lenora Slaughter worked incessantly to enhance the pageant's image by securing state, rather than city, representation and by enlisting the Junior Chamber of Commerce to stage grassroots competitions.[54] The most significant figure, aside from Slaughter, in upgrading the Miss America format was the 1943 winner, Jean Bartel, of California, the first college graduate to be crowned. After her selection, she refused to pose in a swimsuit. "I wanted to focus on a singing/acting career," she recalled. "It wasn't the image I was trying to present." While Bartel and Slaughter were visiting the University of Minnesota during her reign, a female student suggested offering scholarships to Miss Americas. This idea coincided with Slaughter's vision. "I don't want my Miss Americas to have to take Hollywood careers," she stated. "I want them to *become* something." She subsequently built a scholarship fund of $5,000, which was awarded to Bess Myerson, Miss America of 1945, to attend graduate school at Columbia University.[55] Quickly the fund grew, and by 1948, including local and state scholarships, $50,000 in awards was being distributed annually.[56] Such innovations resulted in another criterion for selecting America's symbol of femininity—intelligence. Since 1936, personal interviews had become an important part of the judging. In 1945, Slaughter told judges to deemphasize physical measurements and to consider facial beauty, voice and articulateness, wholesomeness, poise, special abilities, health, hygiene, and dress.[57] Intelligence, talent (including athletic ability), and presentability seemed appropriate criteria for Miss Americas.

ALAN STEPHAN

These traditional values were no less evident at the 1946 Mr. America Contest, held in Detroit. Five judges, all from America's heartland (Cincinnati, Columbus, Rochester, Indianapolis, and Lafayette, Indiana) chose Alan Stephan of Cicero, Illinois. It was a popular, all-American choice. Besides serving in the Seebees during the war, he became a model for recruiting and war bond posters because of his handsome face and impressive build.[58] Like Leight (Stepanek) and Bacon (Baconskas), this Mr. America exhibited the anglicizing effect by shortening his name from Steponaitis to the more English-sounding Stephan. To Peary Rader, the editor of *Iron Man*, he epitomized "the finest manhood" in America.

> If you are interested in Shape he has it. If it is separation, we doubt if any of them [earlier Mr. Americas] have had more. If it is measurements that interest you, you will find his are probably larger than any winner thus far. If it is strength that interests you, this young fellow ranks at the top with John Grimek. Here is a handsome young fellow with a personality, grace and posture that seem natural to him. Here is a man with everything you could ask for. He has the height that so many people demand in a "Mr. America."[59]

Stephan was also a true amateur. The 1946 competition was his first physique contest, and he had trained for only six weeks for it. Most impressive was his strength. He pressed 260, snatched 240, clean-and-jerked 325, and did curl repetitions with 205 pounds at a body weight of 205. As an indication of the quality of Stephan's competition, the 1946 Junior Mr. America, Everett Sinderoff, placed only ninth. All agreed that it was the best Mr. America Contest ever and that Stephan was a deserving winner. "Nothing has thrilled the athletic world like these Mr. Americas," observed Earle Liederman. "They are the final achievements in presentations of muscular masterpieces."[60]

In an article titled "The Modern Apollo," Ray Van Cleef linked the Mr. America Contest with earlier traditions—the Greeks, Macfadden's perfect-man contests, and the Miss America Pageant. Since "the very first one in Atlantic City skyrocketed into the spotlight of public attention," he noted, "the title 'Miss America' has almost magical appeal and 'clicked' with the general public." Although Van Cleef realized the women's pageant "greatly overshadowed" its male counterpart, he praised John Hordines "for attaching the title 'Mr. America' to what has proved to be the most outstanding and successful of all the annual physique contests." The "ideal title" played "a role of immeasurable importance, like the 'Miss America' title," enabling the competition to "secure extensive publicity through newspapers, magazines and news-reels." Alan Stephan, who was photographed more than any previous Mr. America, personified "all of the attributes that this title is symbolic of"; his physique was "a combination of an Apollo and a Hercules; an ideal type." Most impressive about Stephan, however, was his respect for the Greek ideal of a sound mind in a sound body. Though likened to manly images projected by Robert Taylor, Frank Sinatra, and Charles Boyer; viewed as a prospective Tarzan or Superman; and "swamped with attractive movie offers and stage contracts," Stephan intended to further his education. On the day after becoming Mr. America, he traveled to the University of Michigan to enroll for the fall semester. He planned to pursue a physical education degree, compete in wres-tling, gymnastics, or track, and enter the next Olympics.[61] Stephan's youthful aspirations and exemplary traits of well-rounded manhood compared favorably with the feminine ideals of Miss America winners.

Despite the aura of idealism surrounding Stephan's victory, Lurie's earlier muscularity challenge had left its mark on the criteria that se-lected him. Instead of the traditional balance between three categories, muscularity was worth seven points, symmetry five, and general ap-pearance three. That muscularity, aside from other desirable traits, was gaining favor was evident in the tendency of some bodybuilders to train only for the most muscular award. Such was the case with Sam Loprinzi, of Portland, Oregon, who had been inspired by winning his height division at Hoffman's muscularity contest. He then remained in York to train for the title of most muscular man at the Mr. America Contest a few weeks later. He ignored the Mr. America competition itself, feeling that his diminutive stature would be a disadvantage.[62] Lo-prinzi placed second to Stephan overall but edged him out on muscu-larity. Much the same thinking was revealed by Karo Whitfield, an At-lanta promoter who was a York ally and frequent Mr. America judge. He informed Terpak about "a 165 pounder" named Harry Smith who had just returned from the service. Whitfield was preparing him to contend for the title of most muscular man at the 1947 Mr. America contest, noting, "He's the nearest to looking like Grimek at 21 years of age that I've seen." Although Smith was "only 5'6" in height which would hurt him in the Mr. America contest," Whitfield was convinced he would "give someone a run for the Muscular Man title."[63]

"THE PERFECT MR. AMERICA"

Though Smith became Mr. Georgia in 1947 and Junior Mr. America in 1948, he did not attend the 1947 Mr. America Contest, held in Chicago. It was won by Steve Reeves over the largest field yet to compete in a physique contest (36) with 3,000 spectators. "He is the most perfect personification of what weight training can do," exclaimed Gene Jantzen, another competitor. "His face is about as perfect as they come, with regular strong features that fit his physical development to the letter. He has all of the physical assets that go to make up a truly phenomenal muscle man. He has a lot of native intelligence and plenty of ambition."[64] Steve's 1948 successor, George Eiferman, remembers him as "the perfect Mr. America." He was 6'1", 215 pounds, and had a twenty-nine-inch waist. Eiferman asked him whether "he had intestines," since there seemed to be "no room" for them. Eiferman noted Reeves's lack of flamboyance: "People misunderstood Steve because he was quiet—kind of like Gary Cooper in the movies. He was a cowboy and was more reserved by nature."[65] Peary Rader was impressed by Reeves's muscularity, balance, and definition as well as his overall masculinity. He had a complete package of male attributes: "Here was a man who combined the massive muscular development that appeals so much to barbell men with the broad shoulders and slender hips that the average man prefers."[66] It was the physique photographer Lon Hanagan, however, who established a Greek connection and its relevance to American social norms.

> I am sure if one of these Ancient Greeks came to life today and saw our new MR. AMERICA, Steve Reeves—he would find it hard to believe that Steve was not a re-incarnation of the body of one of those superior beings from Mount Olympus. Yes, Mr. and Mrs. American public, we have a great winner this year in Steve Reeves. There are great things ahead for this boy, and I can see him following the star-dust trail to Mount Olympus![67]

Such superlatives obscure the fact that he was not an obvious choice. He and the muscular marvel Eric Pedersen, Mr. California, were deadlocked in the balloting with 72 points each. An additional vote by the nine judges declared Reeves the winner and awarded Pedersen most muscular honors. Pedersen is little known outside the iron game, while Reeves went on to higher levels of competition and eventually international stardom through his movie career. Similarly, few observers at the contest could have imagined that Reeves's popularity could exceed that of Stephan, the most publicized Mr. America to date. Yet Stephan (appearing as a guest with his wife, Grace ("Miss Legionnaire"), never fulfilled his early promise. Instead of pursuing his university studies or becoming a box-office attraction, Stephan opened a gym in Minneapolis and later lapsed into obscurity.[68]

REFINING THE MR. AMERICA IDEAL

Aside from its glitz and glitter, the chief interest in the 1947 contest lay in the application of new rules allowing contestants just three poses of fifteen seconds each, which expedited the show and enhanced audience appeal. In Rader's estimation, "The entire show was smooth compared to other years."[69] Ray Van Cleef applauded action taken on a more troubling issue: "Unquestionably the greatest menace . . . is the invasion of this competition, which should personify masculinity, with practices provoking a suspicion or assumption of homosexuality." He found it "disgusting" to observe bodybuilders "employing facial and body makeup," and was pleased that the AAU forbade the use of cosmetics, oils, and artificial coloring. Van Cleef also saw the need to ban the use of "chorus-girlish" attire with sequins and of "trunks so abbreviated as to resemble a burlesque girl's 'G-string.'"[70] Whatever desirable similarities there might be to the Miss America Pageant, the showcasing of effeminate qualities in men was taboo.

A different view came from Lon Hanagan, who was gay. In his report of the Chicago contest for *Your Physique*, he adopted the same mocking tone that Joe Weider had employed for Hoffman's "most muscular" show a year earlier.

> Why cannot a Mr. America show be a REAL show. A little theatrical atmosphere would not hurt a bit. . . . There were too many conflicting people walking around the wings and poking their faces out. No theatre performance would allow this. Let's get away from the ordinary, this Mr. America show should be planned and produced with much more "finesse." I also noticed that oil on the bodies was forbidden. This left the bodies "flat" in appearance unless the contestant was lucky enough to possess an oily skin. . . . At a Miss America contest I'm sure that if no makeup were allowed we could see a drab procession of females. . . . Who started this oil-on-body business anyhow? Our history tells us of the Greek athletes who always rubbed olive oil on the body to give it a healthy glow.[71]

In a less inhibited era, Hanagan might have added that homosexuality, anathema to Van Cleef and Rader, was an important aspect of ancient Greek culture. But the point could also be made that oil and theatrics, by placing undue emphasis on musculature, detracted from other important attributes.

Another issue raised by Hanagan was the disappointing ninth-place finish of Keevil Daly, of New York City. Originally from British Guiana, a region noted for producing outstanding physiques, Daly exhibited great promise, winning the Mr. Metropolitan and Mr. New York City titles in 1947. Even Gord Venables was impressed. "I never saw better muscular separation in the shoulders," he wrote. And "Keevil may well lay claim to being the strongest man in the Mr. America contest for in the weightlifting he snatched 245 at a bodyweight of 170."[72] If, as was widely assumed, height discrimination was part of the idealistic conception of American manhood, was it not as likely that there was also racial discrimination?

MR. AMERICA AND MR. UNIVERSE

The greatest problem for Mr. Americas themselves, however, was the lack of a higher title to which they could aspire. To fill this void, Walt Baptiste, a San Francisco gym owner, devised a Professional Mr. America Contest in 1946. A poorly run affair, it hardly justified its title. Nearly all the judges and entrants were Californians, there were no scorecards, and each contestant was limited to four poses of three seconds each. No one disputed the choice of Clarence Ross as winner, but a faux pas occurred after the other awards were announced. According to Alyce Stagg, a strongwoman and the wife of the gym owner Ed Yarick, Baptiste returned to the stage to announce that Leo Stern, of San Diego, Mr. California 1946 and third-place finisher in the Mr. America Contest, was not runner-up in this contest, but fourth. Above him were Norman Marks and Phil Courtois, gym owners in the Bay Area. Later, when Stagg asked the contestants to stay for pictures, "they were pretty disgusted," and she added, "I can't blame them." The idea of a contest for professionals went back to the Lurie challenge, and even after the San Francisco fiasco, Earle Liederman clung to the hope that there would be more professional events. But the concept of a Professional Mr. America in 1946, unlike its amateur counterpart in 1939, lacked adequate precedents.[73]

Another possible direction for physique contests was to make them international in scope. Theretofore, the only international event was a French contest held since the 1930s to identify the "best built man in Europe." But the world weightlifting championships that Hoffman would be hosting in Philadelphia in September 1947 would provide an opportunity to stage a worldwide event and title. Grimek predicted that the competition would be "as big or bigger than our Mr. America contest and should inspire other nations to conduct similar affairs." Furthermore, by stressing "muscular development," it would be liberated from some of the cultural constraints of competitions likened to Miss America contests and would address a growing demand for more muscle display. It was initially called the "Mr. World Contest," but Hoffman's public relations agent, Erwin Rosee, told him the title would not rhyme. So it was changed to Mr. Universe. "It's okay by me if they want to call it Mr. Universe," quipped Venables. "I doubt very much any Martians or Venusians will compete."[74]

In fact, as in the world weightlifting championships, international participation was low. The contest was won by Steve Stanko, followed by the Americans John Farbotnik and Eric Pedersen. The only foreign competitors were René Leger, Mr. Canada 1947, and Juhani Vellamo, of Finland. Far more attention was lavished on the weightlifting events, and the Mr. Universe Contest seemed an afterthought. "Time was limited this particular night," remarked Grimek, "so the usual point system was eliminated and each judge was compelled to make his own selection by writing his choice on a ballot."[75] Despite the growing popularity of physique contests, the Mr. Universe Contest, as a sort of AAU foster child, had an inauspicious birth.

By this time, the Mr. America Contest had become the most popular and prestigious bodybuilding competition in the world. It was especially evident at a physical-culture extravaganza staged by Vic Tanny in Los Angeles in December 1946, when five Mr. Americas (Goodrich, Grimek, Stanko, Ross, and Stephan) took the stage together. "It was a sight that many of us will not forget," observed Tanny, seeing "the world's greatest physiques . . . all on stage together in tableau."[76] It was an exhilarating experience, even for cosmopolitan Californians. What distinguished these early Mr. Americas was their spontaneity—none of them were quite sure what they were doing or where it would lead. They were "a new breed," according to Marla Matzer Rose, the author of *Muscle Beach*. Goodrich "really didn't train per se for the Mr. America contest: he just walked in, showed off his body, and won."[77] Virtually all his development had come from training for track, gymnastics, and acrobatics. Likewise, Grimek, though the idol of all aspiring bodybuilders, never relinquished his love for heavy athletics. "John is still terrific as ever," Tanny told Terpak after seeing Grimek pose at a sellout show in Los Angeles. "He's got the muscles to lift anything."[78] Even Clarence Ross had an unprepossessing attitude toward his physique. "I am just an ordinary chap and I live a normal life," he insisted. He had been exercising with weights for several years and learned about the Mr. America Contest only three months earlier. "I entertained no illusions about my chances of winning."[79] All the Mr. Americas thus far considered themselves amateurs and athletes rather than showmen or career bodybuilders. All seemed to have well-balanced lives in which their celebrity status was kept in proper perspective.

In this springtime of the Mr. America Contest there remained a firm link with its classical origins, fostered by judging standards that still emphasized health, general appearance, symmetry, and athleticism as well as muscularity. These standards were enforced by the AAU establishment and bolstered by Hoffman, Van Cleef, Matlin, and Rader. The Lurie-Weider challenge, with its emphasis on muscle for muscle's sake, marked the beginning of a departure from that tradition. Indeed, a 1946 editorial by Joe Weider seemed to belittle the ancients: "I suspect that most of their muscle marvels would have seemed rather small as compared to our first-class heavyweight strong men." Yet he shared with the Greeks several basic principles of bodybuilding—good health, progressive training, regularity, and patience. His brother, Ben, subscribed to similarly sensible principles in describing the newly crowned Mr. America 1946: "Stephan's strength is in proportion to his development and he excels in all physical pastimes from barbells to swimming and gymnastics, thus making him an all-round athlete."[80] No doubt the Weiders were still searching for their own distinctive niche in the iron game, but their remarks seem sincere. In immediate postwar America, where homogeneity remained strong, there was considerable consensus on what constituted perfect manhood. Tall, blond Alan Stephen epitomized this ideal. To the film star Mae West, who encountered him backstage at the Selwyn Theater in Chicago in 1947, Stephan was more than Mr. America—he was "Mr. Absolutely Everything!"[81]

4

THE GLORY YEARS

**HE REPRESENTS THE TOWER OF STRENGTH
AND STRONGMEN OF THE PAST,
AS THE IDEAL MR. AMERICA,
HIS GOAL ACHIEVED AT LAST!**

**TO ONE AND ALL A BIG SALUTE
TO YOUR UNDYING FAME.
MAY ALL THE WORLD REMEMBER YOU
WITH REVERENCE FOR YOUR NAME.**

VIRGINIA CAGLIETTA

AFTER WORLD WAR II, IT APPEARED AS THOUGH THE GOLDEN AGE OF AMERICAN weightlifting, spurred by the victories of Bob Hoffman's teams in world competitions, would be complemented by a golden age of bodybuilding likewise under his aegis. Through his control of muscle publications and his influence in the AAU, Hoffman had fostered the early development and character of muscularity as a desirable derivative of the athletic body. He helped popularize the Mr. America Contest as an ideal of American manhood, drawing inspiration from the annual Miss America Contest, which was fast becoming an enduring component of national iconography. Hoffman virtually dominated bodybuilding competitions, as he did those for weightlifting, from the early 1940s to the mid-1960s. As the iron-game scholar Terry Todd later observed, "It's hard for people around now to imagine what a potent place York was at that time."[1] American prosperity, accompanied by an increased interest in health, sports, and physical appearance, had an important bearing on bodybuilding. But physique competitions were susceptible to other cultural forces—professionalism, commercialization, internationalization, and a demographic shift westward. The Weider organization, which emphasized muscle size, definition, and flare, pushed the sport in these new directions. But it served initially to enhance rather than diminish the prestige of the Mr. America concept and left amateurism and Greek ideals of beauty and balance intact.

THE GOLDEN WEST

The movement of large numbers of Americans to the West Coast after 1945 had a great impact on the development of bodybuilding. "People seem to be pouring into Calif. and at present, the state is in throes of a tremendous upswing," wrote Vic Tanny, who was the most enterprising gym owner in the West after World War II. Bodybuilders and lifters regarded Southern California as a "hotbed" and "Santa Monica as the focal point of activity."[2] Muscle Beach played no small part in this attraction. Popularized in the 1930s by gymnasts and acrobats, it was attracting weightlifters and bodybuilders by the late 1940s. The beach culture furnished opportunities for displaying muscles—biceps, latissimi dorsi (lats), trapezoids (traps), and quadriceps (quads)—in a natural setting. In 1948, Earle Liederman noted, "The West has finally surpassed the East in turning out the best men in the country. Ross, Reeves, Pedersen, Page . . . are the outstanding Western bodybuilders." After predicting that Reeves would become the 1947 Mr. America, Liederman believed that the next one would also be "a Western boy."[3] Although the 1948 winner, George Eiferman, hailed from Philadelphia, he had won the Mr. California title and spent the rest of his life in the West. From 1945 to 1955, seven Mr. Americas came from the West, and four times the contest was staged in Los Angeles.

This development was encouraged by a proliferation of physique contests in the region, such as Mr. Muscle Beach, Mr. Los Angeles, and Mr. California, often accompanied by beauty contests for women. Most spectacular was the Mr. USA Contest, sponsored by Bert Goodrich and Vic

Tanny at the Los Angeles Shrine Auditorium in March 1948. Though inspired by the Mr. America Contest, it offered a $1,000 prize (and a colossal trophy) to the winner and featured a Mr. Western America Contest for amateurs. Clarence Ross defeated a strong field that included two other Mr. Americas (Stephan and Reeves), Eric Pedersen, and Floyd Page, and the future Mr. America Jack Delinger took top amateur honors. Les Stockton (a Muscle Beach performer whose wife, "Pudgy," was the first female bodybuilder) told Sig Klein that Ross "received the longest and biggest ovation" that he had ever seen, adding that he "seems to have the same age-old appeal of Grimek."[4] Befitting the physical tone of this affair were the whistles that filled the auditorium for the Miss USA Contest, counterpart to the men's competition. One observer thought the event, won by the "curvaceous Val Njord," gave "Atlantic City's 'Miss America' affair plenty of competition in attracting beautiful belles." Among the 5,000 spectators was Al Treloar, winner of America's first physique contest. He rated the Goodrich-Tanny show "tops." So respected had the Mr. USA Contest become by 1949 that it attracted Grimek out of retirement; he defeated Ross and Reeves, thereby ensuring his legendary status. Although the Professional Mr. America Contest in San Francisco continued to be marred by organizational snafus, both it and the Mr. USA Contest were credible, though short-lived attempts to elevate bodybuilding to a higher level.[5]

THE IFBB

Drawing on the energy of the West and the popularity of the Mr. America Contest were Joe and Ben Weider in distant Montreal, the legendary "cradle of strongmen." In launching the International Federation of Bodybuilders (IFBB), they sought to professionalize and internationalize bodybuilding, thereby liberating it from control of the American weightlifting establishment.[6] It was the lackluster Mr. Universe Contest in 1947 that had prompted the Weiders to act. An ensuing article by Gene Jantzen in *Your Physique*, took the organizers to task for not selecting "the most perfectly built man in the world." The contest lacked international entrants, and was overshadowed by the weightlifting competition, and the greatest asset of the winner, Steve Stanko, was that he worked for Bob Hoffman, who sponsored the affair. "Prominent bodybuilders in the audience," according to Jantzen, commented that other contestants, including George Eiferman, John Farbotnik, and Eric Pedersen, "looked better than Steve." Jantzen added a touch of Olympian disdain: "Even the Grecian Gods of masculine beauty must have laughed at what took place." The Mr. America Contest, though merely national, was a classier affair.

> It is to prevent such a farce like this from sweeping the bodybuilding game that the International Federation of Body Builders is being organized. Every decent intelligent bodybuilder in the world will be invited to join. The I.F.O.B.B. will sanction and sponsor bodybuilding contests in the various cities and districts of every country interested. Proceeds of these small meets will go towards sending the local winners to the provincial or state meets. The winners of these contests will then meet in a national contest. . . . When the National Champions . . . are named in each of the countries . . . then the International Federation of Body Builders will hold an honest to goodness Mr. Universe Contest.[7]

Jantzen, however, later contended that the report published under his name did not represent what he had witnessed in Philadelphia: "Weider didn't like what I wrote, so he changed the whole article. Practically everything I wrote was opposite from what he published. . . . And he never did pay me for it!"[8] A half century later Jantzen remained furious over his article that launched the IFBB.

Whatever the flaws of the Mr. Universe Contest, trashing it in print was merely a pretext for "a revolutionary venture" that the Weiders had been planning for many months. The conception of the IFBB owes much to Emmanuel Orlick, a Weider editor who wrote to George Jowett in March 1948 about the origins of the group:

> [I] suggested such an organization to Joe some two or three years ago when he first began to have trouble with the A.A.U. of C[anada]. I pointed out to him the possibility of creating his organization and successfully competing against this body. . . . Eventually Joe came back to me with HIS sensational idea of the International Body Builders Club or some such thing. . . . I backed him up the idea—gave him the name International Federation of Body Builders and spent quite a few hours outlining the scheme. . . . Then I wrote the first blast which appeared under his name, about the organization, this brought him a lot of letters.[9]

This evidence, brought to light by Randy Roach, contradicts Dan Lurie's claim that he "established the IFBB name" by having it "registered" in 1947 for the first IFBB event, the Mr. New York State Contest that he held on January 15, 1948. As Roach notes, Lurie has "no legal documents or proof to support his assertions."[10] Although the Weiders admitted that the IFBB name "was linked to this show," they heaped contumely on Lurie for charging "high prices" for tickets, which resulted in low attendance—not the image they wished to convey: "It is unfortunate indeed that such a fiasco should even be mentioned in the same breath as a worthy organization with lofty principles." Based on the chronology of contests and magazines in which their reports appeared, it is virtually certain that the Most Perfect Physique and Most Muscular Man Contest in October 1947 (reported in the February 1948 issue of *Your Physique*) was the first IFBB event.[11]

Questions also surround the Weiders' story that the IFBB resulted from a letter (sent by Dietrich Wortmann) withdrawing their sanction for the Mr. Montreal Contest in October 1946. "To Hell with the AAU and Bob Hoffman," they allegedly responded. "As of this moment we have our own governing body," they told contestants. "We're calling it the International Federation of Bodybuilders, and it's going to make bodybuilding bigger and better than ever."[12] Curiously, neither the contest nor the contretemps was covered by Weider publications of the time.[13] A full report on the contest by a Canadian official named Lionel St. Jean, however, appears in *Strength & Health* with no mention of irregularities or evidence of the brothers' involvement. The only Weider reference appears in an unrelated insert congratulating Joe on his recent marriage to Diane Ross in Manhattan. While Charles Smith, who attended the 1946 Montreal contest as a spectator, confirms that the Weiders announced an intention to form "their own bodybuilding society" on that occasion, he calls Ben's alleged sanctioning difficulties "bunk," since Wortmann had no jurisdiction over Canadian lifters or bodybuilders.[14] A more likely scenario is that generating a fake controversy about the Montreal contest, along with the seed planted by Orlick, enabled Ben, much in the manner that Joe had claimed to be a "Trainer of Champions" since 1936, to establish historical credibility for the IFBB.

Indeed, as the IFBB concept pullulated in Ben's mind, it helped spur his purported recruitment visits to "22 countries" in the spring of 1947 and the creation of "offices" in France and South Africa. The launching of the IFBB really took place, as Jantzen's article suggests, when the Weiders staged their first contest in October 1947, two weeks after the Philadelphia affair and fully a year after the alleged Montreal incident. They declared instant success in their rebellion against "pseudo amateurism." The "rush for membership" was "reaching the proportions of a torrential flood," and supposedly the IFBB would soon be staging contests worldwide.[15] To support such rhetoric, the Weiders adopted the Goodrich-Tanny idea of handing out cash awards and big trophies in order to attract participants.

AAU authorities took a dim view of these developments. Even before Jantzen's landmark article, Hoffman had published a lengthy rebuttal to charges that the Mr. Universe Contest was fixed or improperly conducted, including an explanation of how the judges had been selected and how they had voted. One of them, Larry Barnholdt, attested to the propriety of the affair: "Nobody offered me any bribes or promised me anything if I voted for a certain entrant." Hoffman claimed that he "took practically no part in the Mr. Universe Contest" and that 90 percent of the spectators agreed with the judges that "Stanko was the best man." Hoffman also denounced Lurie's show in January 1948, calling the IFBB an "outlaw" organization and any bodybuilder participating in its contests would lose AAU eligibility.[16]

The Weiders, of course, were not the only sponsors of professional shows. Walt Baptiste had been doing it in San Francisco for two years, and even Peary Rader lent his support to the Professional Strongman Association. This organization held a "Mr. 1949 Contest" in Los Angeles, which was won by Armand Tanny, but the field consisted mainly of lesser lights. As Rader and others (mostly Californians) became interested in promoting physical culture more generally, the organization became the American Physical Improvement Association and held no more physique contests.[17]

TWO MR. AMERICAS

In a bold move to exploit and perhaps even appropriate the image of the nation's leading bodybuilding event, the Weiders launched their own Mr. America Contest under the IFBB. "Cash for Mr. America, Money! Money! Money!" was the title of a *Muscle Power* article criticizing the AAU for its old-fogey ways and challenging it "to come out of its shell and be modern": "If the A.A.U. would give a thousand simoleons, the Mr. America who got it could start something." And abolishing the rule prohibiting winners from entering later contests would provide more incentives for bodybuilders.[18] Coincident with this initiative, virtually every issue of *Your Physique* and *Muscle Power* was filled with references, pictures, stories, and training routines of AAU Mr. Americas (usually Stephan, Ross, and Reeves). One report of an IFBB-sponsored Mr. Calcutta Contest in India noted it was "run on the lines of a 'Mr. America' Contest." Plans were also in the works for an

IFBB Junior Mr. America Contest (for teens ages thirteen to seventeen), featuring winners of state competitions.[19] By organizing a professional Mr. America contest, the Weiders appeared to be blurring age-old distinctions between amateur and professional while capitalizing on the title and those who had earned it under AAU auspices.

On November 6, 1948, at the Roosevelt Auditorium in New York, Alan Stephan, AAU Mr. America 1946, won another Mr. America title, a forty-inch trophy, $250 in cash, and a free trip to Miami. According to the IFBB reporter Leo Gaudreau, Stephan's muscular exhibition was greeted with "a continuous round of applause and cheering from an enthusiastic house that was packed to the walls." The second- and third-place finishers were French Canadians, Joffre L'Heureux and Leo Robert, as was the winner of the short-men's class, Ed Thierault. Johnny Icino, of New York City, won the Junior Mr. America Contest. Clarence Ross, the so-called King of Bodybuilders, did not compete, but his guest-posing routine highlighted the show. "Ancient Greece had nothing like this," exclaimed Gaudreau. Although the fledgling IFBB failed to follow up its Mr. America Contest with a Mr. Universe event, it conducted a Mr. North America Contest in New York in April 1949.

BEHIND THE SCENES

HARRY PASCHALL

Figure 4.1, "Bosco," Harry Paschall's iconic portrayal of strength and integrity. *Strength & Health*, July 1947, 21.

Ross claimed a $1,000 prize for defeating some of the best men on the continent. The Weider editor Barton Horvath called it the "GREAT-EST EVENT OF THEM ALL!"[20]

In the meantime, some changes, no doubt inspired by the IFFB competition, were occurring in the AAU Mr. America Contest. In striking contrast to his predecessor, the taciturn Steve Reeves, George Eiferman, was outgoing and full of fun. Commenting on his premature birth in 1925, he quipped, "I was in a hurry so I could start training for the Mr. America title." But Eiferman's most notable feature was his size. "He is one of the shortest men to win the title," noted Peary Rader. "What enabled him to overcome this natural disadvantage was his thick musculature, especially in the upper body." No less impressive was the runner-up, Jack Delinger, of Oakland, who succeeded Eiferman in 1949. He too was "a real stocky guy," recalls the former *Strength & Health* editor Jim Murray—very short but thickly muscled and proportional.[21] Ray Van Cleef, in his contest report, used the adjective "Herculean" repeatedly in describing Delinger's physique. And Delinger, like Eiferman, easily won the best chest award. "He has a deep and high arched chest," remarked Rader, "with fine pectorals." Well-developed pecs, traps, lats, and quads were identified with the Weider organization in Harry Paschall's caricatures in *Strength & Health* of the narcissistic Weedy Man (whose humiliating encounters with Bosco, a tower of strength and integrity, became legendary) and Paschall's demeaning references to the IFBB.[22] But Weedy Man's traits could just as easily be applied to an increasing number of Mr. America contestants. Indeed one of them, Steve Reeves, was often characterized, in snide and indirect references, as a mirror athlete whose muscles lacked real strength or the capacity for athletic achievement.[23] During the next decade, as the European physique remained lithe and symmetrical, big, thick, brawny muscles became the hallmark of the American bodybuilder.

BIGNESS—QUESTIONING THE GREEK IDEAL

This evolution invoked a lively discussion among muscle pundits about what constituted the ideal physique. No longer did the Greeks provide the gold standard. "It may be true that they worshipped a fine and beautiful physique," commented Rader. "But it is also true that their standards and ideas of what a perfect physique is did not compare with those of our modern bodybuilders."[24] At the current rate of progress, Paschall predicted that there would soon be "an avalanche of 20-inch arms and 55-inch chests" among aspiring Mr. Americas. His idea of perfection, however, related less to size than to "pleasing proportions and well rounded muscles." Paschall extolled standards established by Alan Calvert in a bygone era, when Sandow was everyone's image of the perfect man. Perfection for Calvert meant more than 16" biceps and a 44" chest: "His ideal man must not only look strong, but he must be strong. He must be an athlete plus."[25] Paschall believed that there would be "even better Mr. Americas if they would also be reasonably good weightlifters." Such a qualification would be "similar to that employed in the Miss America contest where talent counts."[26] A pioneer bodybuilder himself, Paschall represented a strong independent link with the past and the sport's amateur tradition.

Especially given Paschall's attacks, it is surprising that a Weider author should sympathize with his bodybuilding philosophy. Yet George Weaver expressed many of the same concerns over the muscular hypertrophy afflicting current bodybuilders and signaling a departure from classical standards. Weaver concurred that the physiques of the Mr. Americas since the war, when seen as a proportion between muscular bulk and height, "were of the order of Superman rather than Ideal standards," leading to confusion among bodybuilders.[27]

> It appears that the Mr. America contests cannot rightly be considered a quest for the athlete who most nearly approaches the *ideal* physique. . . . We might as well face the fact that physique contests of this nature are a form of harmless and pleasant childishness, exactly like reading fairytales or listening to **SUPERMAN** on the radio. The boy who worships the Lone Ranger and the older boy who worships Mr. America are both indulging the human passion for the *heroic*. There can be no objection to this as long as the heroic Superman physique, or the still more massive Herculean physique, or the absolute ultimate or Maximum physique, are not confused with the Ideal Physique.[28]

It was this confusion that led to Peary Rader's belief that the ancients were not "nearly as well built as modern barbell athletes."[29] He thereby abetted the growing importance of bigness over beauty as the modern standard.

Nor did Rader endorse Weaver's dismissive views on extremism in bodybuilding. He defended it on grounds that "appearance means a lot to a young fellow" whose "huge arms, pectorals or whatever it is he excels at, holds the spot light at that time in his life." What concerned Rader far more was a public perception that the morality of bodybuilders was "the lowest and worst of any group of humanity" and that the sport tolerated "abnormal relations whose adherents are generally referred to as 'queers.'" A "major and immediate" goal of his new American Physical Improvement Association was to clean up such depravity. To ensure that unsuspecting youth were not led astray into appreciating the male physique in the wrong way, Rader adopted a policy requiring all physique ads in his magazine to "include a by-line that all photos advertised are of models wearing trunks" and that all "nude photos of genuine strength athletes" appearing with articles "have trunks painted on them."[30] Whatever apprehensions Rader may have had about bodybuilding, he remained steadfast in support of the AAU, weightlifting, and weightlifting's importance in building an ideal physique.

THE FORGOTTEN MR. AMERICA

Ironically, the 1950 IFBB Mr. America embodied many traditional values and could hardly have been less like Paschall's Weedy Man. Jimmy Payne was born in 1926 to a Jewish father and an Italian Catholic mother in Oakland, a hotbed of physical culture. He became a bodybuilder after joining Carl Cathy's gym and later Jack LaLanne's studio, where he, along with Steve Reeves, received personal instruction from Clem Poechman, a Bay Area physical culturist. At nearby Neptune Beach, a resort featuring a dance hall, picnic grounds, and swimming pools, he did hand-balancing acts with LaLanne and the Oakland gym owner Ed Yarick. After joining the navy in 1943, he met Sam Loprinzi, who was a barbell instructor at Treasure Island, a major embarkation point for men being shipped out. Owing to his background in wrestling and boxing from school and association with Loprinzi, with whom he did balancing and barbell work, Payne was assigned to be a physical trainer in the service. After his discharge, he opened a health studio with the bodybuilder Norman Marks and started entering lifting meets and performing stunts. According to Alyce Stagg, Jimmy and LaLanne "worked up a sensational act" and were featured at many Bay Area shows.[31]

Occasionally, he and LaLanne would drive the nearly four hundred miles to Muscle Beach. Payne later recalled: "We would perform on the beach all day and go to the Brown Derby and other clubs in Hollywood at night to drink. Jack put away quite a few." Later, he performed a nightclub act in San Francisco. Equally adept at hand balancing and muscle control, he was a much sought-after emcee, comedian, and tap dancer. Payne recalled what conditions were like in those days: "[I] worked in some pretty tough places that were both topless and bottomless. I worked on Broadway in San Francisco when it was amateur night for strippers. I worked with Tempest Storm, Lily St. Cyr, Candy Cane, Sugar, Tassle-twirling Tammy from Big T Texas, and Satin Doll. I never worked with Gypsy Rose Lee. Good strippers didn't show everything. There was no vulgarity."[32] In the tradition of vaudeville physical culturists, Payne was versatile, "unlike the current physique guys who can do nothing more than show muscles," he says. His muscles were functional. Weighing only 145 pounds, he could press 245, snatch 210, and clean-and-jerk 280, enough to have earned him third place as a lightweight at the 1951 world championships in Milan. He could also squat 325 and deadlift 500 pounds, and on his fifty-second birthday he performed fifty-one handstand dips, surpassing Jack LaLanne's mark of thirty-five.[33] Payne started to enter physique contests in 1945. In 1947 he beat the future Mr. America Jack Delinger to win the Mr. Northern California Contest, and placed third in Baptiste's professional contests in 1948 and 1949.[34]

Although Ben Weider was overseas promoting the IFBB, anticipation for his organization's 1950 Mr. America Contest was great. According to Liederman, it was "going to be an extremely important event and **ALL** the best men are invited." He hoped that owing to AAU rules on professionalism, many bodybuilders, including previous Mr. Americas, would enter the contest.[35] None showed up. Details are sketchy, but the contest was directed by the West Coast photographer Russ Warner for the Weiders on February 17 at Oakland Auditorium; Ed Theriault appeared as guest poser. Payne, the winner, recalled a packed house with perhaps as many as a thousand fans and a dozen contestants, virtually all Californians. But the quality of physiques was high: Phil Courtois placed second, Norman Marks third, Vince Gironda fourth, and Bob McCune fifth. Despite winning a professional contest, Payne had trouble collecting his prize:

> I won $180 and didn't get the publicity I should have got. But I got the money, and that mattered more to me at the time. I had to ask Warner for the money. Warner said, "Fuck you," so I went for him. One of Joe's men held me back, and Joe gave me a check. I don't think Joe wanted me to win. He probably wanted Marks or Gironda, but the audience had a great impact and really favored me. I was proud that I won because I was small and it showed that I could accomplish something.[36]

Remarkably that Mr. America Contest and its winner received almost no

Figure 4.2. Jimmy Payne, the 1950 IFBB Mr. America, with "Miss Americalf." Author's possession.

recognition in Weider magazines. A picture of Payne with his trophy is tucked into an article entitled "I Gained 100 Pounds of Bodyweight" in the July 1950 issue of *Muscle Power*, but it is accompanied by no text. A much larger photo of Phil Courtois and article appear elsewhere in the magazine as "a tribute to a great bodybuilder who achieves his greatest triumph after 20 years of weight training"—for finishing second![37] Far more coverage was provided of the 1949 Mr. Armed Forces Contest in Honolulu and the AAU's Mr. Los Angeles Contest in 1950.[38] When asked why so much more attention was devoted to AAU than IFBB physique contests of that period, Ben Weider responded with an air of glib insouciance: "There was no particular reason. It is just the way the journalist wrote it up and the information and photos that he supplied."[39]

Yet Payne did more to promote the Mr. America image beyond the contest, and in a more traditional sense, than most other Mr. Americas. "I believe that it is the quality of the muscle that counts and not size," he argued. A big bicep "sure looks good, but what can you do with it?" He hoped that his son and daughter, ages two years and three weeks in 1948, would become Mr. America and Miss America in 1968![40]

In the early 1960s, after Jack LaLanne launched his highly successful television fitness series for women, Payne and his wife, Jane, started a weekly family program called *Mr. and Mrs. America*. It was featured in a belated *Muscle Builder* article that calls him "America's most versatile athlete," whose talents surpassed those of Jim Thorpe.

> On the rings Jimmy works out like an Olympic star. He is a consummate artist on the high horizontal bar . . . the parallel bars . . . the trapeze. He is a champion weightlifter . . . an expert tumbler . . . a trampolinist of the first order . . . and he excels in diving, judo, wrestling, muscle control and all the track events at which Jim Thorpe was noted for!
>
> He can perform a One-Finger Chin with each of his index fingers *four* times. He does a complete routine while suspended 400 to 500 feet above a crowd while fastened to a Helicopter.[41]

But the author, Clem Poechman, makes no mention of his having won the Mr. America title.

Payne obtained recognition elsewhere, being introduced as Mr. America when he appeared on the television shows *You Asked for It* and the *Wide World of Sports* and when he emceed the World Wristwrestling Championships in Petaluma, California. And his own televised program was recast as the *Junior Mr. & Miss America Club*, sponsored by "Super-Strength Alcoa Wrap." On it, he led children in such exercises as elephant squats, zebra steps, rhino raises, and duck dips. Jimmy also lifted a calf named Miss Americalf onto his shoulders (Milo of Crotona style).[42] Yet virtually no listing of Mr. America titleholders recognizes Payne's 1950 victory. Even an official one furnished by Tony Blinn of the IFBB, compiled at the behest of Ben Weider, does not include him.[43]

A WEIDER REVERSAL

A likely reason for this omission and lack of coverage of its own contests is that the Weider organization, though attracting leading bodybuilders—such as Page, Eder, Tanny, Robert, Stephan, Goldberg, and Ross—and such notables as Sig Klein, George Yacos, Tony Lanza, and Lon Hanagan as judges, was having second thoughts about divorcing itself from the American weightlifting establishment. Increasingly favorable references to the AAU in Weider publications indicated that an accord might be in the offing. One article even created a hypothetical scenario of the AAU and IFBB "blending in serene harmony."[44] Negotiations ensued with Wortmann, followed by a surprise announcement in the January 1950 issue of *Your Physique* that the two bodies had "ironed out their difficulties" and would thenceforth "cooperate fully with each other." The Weiders admitted that they had been at fault for failing to recognize the distinction between amateur and professional, thereby jeopardizing the eligibility of American athletes in international competition. Though still based in Canada, they claimed to have "feelings of patriotism as much as the next guy": "We desire . . . to see the USA remain **TOP DOG** in the world of weights. So many thousands of young men were entering on physique competitions that we saw we were endangering the supply of future championship material. That we should have foreseen this eventuality, is a reproach which *could* be flung at us, but we HONESTLY believed that so long as a man did not ACCEPT a money prize, then he retained his amateur status."[45] Even more surprising was the Weiders' willingness to reach an accord with Hoffman, whose "unostentatious generosity has provided the financial sinews of the American weightlifting teams"; they acknowledged that it was "time someone else helped." Thus they intended "to publish a third magazine devoted entirely to COMPETITIVE LIFTING."[46] In light of later perceptions of Joe Weider as the bodybuilder's best friend, it seems remarkable that he and his brother seemed eager to redirect their energies to support weightlifting, the AAU, and Hoffman just when bodybuilding was starting to blossom.

To prove their sincerity in launching this initiative, the Weiders' publications featured an instructional article entitled "Your First Weightlifting Contest," which supported AAU efforts to recruit lifters and offered short tributes to Grimek and Stanko, no doubt intended to placate York.[47] Likewise, Liederman lauded the AAU Mr. Los Angeles Contest for 1950 as "a truly splendid show." Although a separate publication devoted to competitive weightlifting never materialized, a monthly weightlifting news section, edited by Charles Smith, a member of the New York (Metropolitan) AAU, soon appeared in *Muscle Power*, which was dubbed "two magazines in one."[48] Noticeably understated were articles or announcements about Weider shows (chiefly Mr. Montreal and Mr. Canada), and the IFBB logo appeared only on pictures of winners mounted on leftover pedestals. Most striking, in light of the absence of coverage of the 1950 IFBB Mr. America Contest, was the attention lavished by Weider magazines on the AAU Mr. America Contest and its 1950 winner, John Farbotnik. Liederman described Farbotnik as an "anatomical sensation" and "the most sensational poseur these old optics have ever seen." Smith, despite his partiality toward the black bodybuilder Melvin Wells, recognized that Farbotnik was "as good a man to ever wear the crown."[49] Further evidence of the power of the AAU Mr. America title and its influence on the Weiders was their frequent use of it to increase their magazines' appeal and the sales of their products. The April 1950 cover of *Your Physique* featured four AAU Mr. Americas, and the inside back cover displayed one of them (Ross) making a pitch for "Y-O-U-R MR. AMERICA DE LUXE SPECIAL" barbell set. For all intents and purposes, the IFBB had disappeared.

Most importantly, the Weiders' conversion to the AAU and the promotion of weightlifting was accompanied by a philosophical pronouncement that aligned them with the best traditions of physical culture. In response to a reader's query about the validity of bodybuilding for its own sake, Joe explained, "The ancient Greeks trained the mind and body as one inseparable unity. This was part of their very civilization. . . . The Ancient Greeks were interested in all-around development and keenly interested in the beauty of the male body. They developed their bodies and minds first and then went in for specialized training for competitive events."[50] Weider's ideas about maintaining a sense of balance coincided with those of other authors. Liederman warned against fanatic bodybuilders obsessed with "big lumps": "The shape of a muscle is of far greater consequence than size." These sentiments were echoed by Rader: "We have many young fellows who are being encouraged to concentrate ENTIRELY ON BIG MUSCLES. In this zeal for huge measurements they forget that there is such a thing as HEALTH, Mental Development, and Spiritual Growth." Hoffman, from a weightlifting perspective, subscribed to the notion of all-around development: "Our champion weight lifters who regularly train for a symmetrical body and great strength bear the closest resemblance of any modern athletes to the ancient Greek and Roman statues."[51]

THE ONGOING FEUD

In light of what appeared to be a meeting of minds and the contrite spirit displayed by the Weiders, it might seem surprising that dissension soon set in. Beyond the fact that Hoffman still harbored a deep distrust of his commercial rivals and never subscribed to the IFBB-AAU accord, it was the ceaseless and snide attacks of Harry Paschall on bodybuilders (and by implication on the Weiders) in his *Strength & Health* column that aroused their ire. In the August 1949 issue, for instance, he pointed out that Weider-trained men were just mirror athletes, while at least four of the six top men in that year's Mr. America Contest were "real strength athletes." Joe Weider responded to these jibes in a strongly worded article, "Getting It Off My Chest," in which he defended bodybuilding, launched a personal attack on Paschall, and urged readers not to buy York magazines.[52] Harry's counterblast was classic Paschall:

> Politics makes strange bedfellows. A year ago Weedy was hollering that the A.A.U. was unfair to bodybuilders, who should be highly paid for their efforts in achieving biceps with a larger circumference than their heads. Now we find him all snuggled up to the A.A.U., using the well known Red tactics of infiltration. . . . The plain facts are that the IFBB (Informal Brotherhood of Boobs) did not work out quite as well as Weedy expected, and now he is prospecting for gold on the other side of the street in the field of weightlifting.[53]

Obviously, money was a factor in the Weiders' sudden change of heart. Equally revealing is the extent to which they realized that their bid for a share of power in the iron game was premature. Not so obvious is how much the Weiders' moneymaking prowess underscored the motives of their York adversaries. From E. M. Orlick's perspective, "Hoffman got angry because he knew Weider was making money. There were things that Joe did that I didn't approve of, but he had as much right to make money as Hoffman."[54]

Neither side gave any quarter as the feud was waged through months of mud-slinging articles, but the Weider camp, perhaps as underdog, adopted a more philosophical approach and even expressed interest in a settlement. After tracing the roots of their conflict back to Joe's setting up his headquarters in Jersey City, the founding of his second magazine (*Muscle Power*), and the Weider-Lurie challenge—all in 1946—Joe offered in the summer of 1950 to "bury the hatchet" and "work hand in hand" with his York rivals: "Thousands will benefit if we swallow our pride and extend the hand of friendship and forgiveness to each other." Indeed, as Orlick remembered it: "Joe never talked ill of Hoffman. I always thought it was Bob who had the ill feelings."[55] But this gesture of peace was not reciprocated, and the level of rancorous rhetoric only escalated.

Few could have predicted that the quarrel would persist for decades. Throughout this long power struggle, the AAU Mr. America Contest and its winners were shamelessly exploited by both sides for commercial and political advantage. One of the winners (George Eiferman), in addition to endorsing York products, admitted to Hoffman that he was training to beat Clancy Ross in the 1948 Mr. USA Contest: "He is representing Weider and if I can beat him it will help a lot I guess—wont it."[56] Though stating in a *Your Physique* article that he was "NOBODY'S PUPIL," Alan Stephan declared: "The Weider system incorporated all the exercise principles that I personally used to develop my own body, and which I teach to my pupils."[57] But Hoffman claimed credit for all Mr. Americas through 1949, insisting that they had "trained with York equipment and training methods." In a way, Hoffman claimed that York was essentially responsible for the men's success: "Three highly publicized Mr. Americas, Clarence Ross, Alan Stephan and Steve Reeves were York barbell men and not publicized by and claimed as pupils by another barbell company, UNTIL THEY HAD WON THE MR. AMERICA CROWNS."[58] It is safe to say that both sides exaggerated greatly in their efforts to wring maximum publicity from bodybuilding's most valuable commodity.

THE FARBOTNIK CONTROVERSY

Any possibility of consensus broke down when John Farbotnik was featured in a *Muscle Power* article that he neither approved nor was compensated for. The story claimed that the workouts leading to his victory in the 1950 AAU Mr. America Contest were "almost identical to the Weider System."[59] In a *Strength & Health* rebuttal, Farbotnik took offense at the use of his name and photographs: "I have neither seen nor

Figure 4.3. Melvin Wells, named most muscular man and Mr. America runner-up for 1950 and 1951. *Strength & Health,* January 1949, cover.

used a Weider barbell or Weider course. My first training equipment consisted of York super cables and cable courses written by Bob Hoffman. At Fritsche's Gym we used nothing but Milo weights which Bob Hoffman had bought out some time earlier. If my course is so similar to that of Weider's then Weider is using York training methods."[60] Further confirmation of the Weiders' villainy, according to Hoffman, was evident in the fracas surrounding Farbotnik's victory at the amateur Mr. World Contest held in Paris with the world weightlifting championships in October 1950. When Reg Park, Mr. Britain, was disqualified because he had competed in a professional (Weider) show a month earlier in New York, he protested by claiming (with evidence obtained from Weider) that Farbotnik too had violated amateur rules. Turbulent scenes involving Park's parents and the French police followed, and Park's disqualification was sustained. But without him, Farbotnik had virtually no competition. As Hoffman put it, "The entries were not as extraordinary as those in the major American A.A.U. physique contests."[61] Mr. World meant far less in real terms than Mr. America. It was an empty title.

Not surprisingly, Weider refused to accept his adversary's version of events. Park had been disqualified, he insisted, because Farbotnik was being groomed "as York's new wonder man." For this reason, he had been allowed to enter the Mr. World and the Mr. America contests, although he had received compensation on numerous occasions. Park, on the other hand, though awarded $500 at Weider's contest, "did not accept this award for himself" and in fact used it to advance the cause of another sport: "He was so appreciative of the swell reception he had been given by the American public in general that he donated this prize to the American AAU Weightlifting Fund, giving it back to me to hold for Mr. Wortmann when he returned from the World Championships." Weider also contended that given the low quality of the other Mr. World contestants, Hoffman had no fear of anyone except Reg Park beating Farbotnik, asking plaintively, "Now do you get the full import of what took place in Paris?"[62] Hoffman shot back against all of Weider's claims: "Reg Park did not donate, as claimed . . . in Weider's slanderous article, the $500 to the American Weightlifting Fund. . . . The truth of the matter is that the only money obtained by the A.A.U. from Weider's show, aside from the sanction fee, was the required 10% of the gross receipts. This sum of less than $200 was turned over after a long delay when official pressure was exerted." It was Hoffman who had borne the expense of sending the American weightlifting team and Farbotnik to Paris.[63]

In succeeding months, the feud became even more vicious and personal, leading Weider to mock Hoffman's athletic credentials and to challenge him to a lifting and physique contest. "I have been insulted and my reputation has been unfairly and maliciously blackened," claimed Hoffman. "I want and demand satisfaction." He therefore accepted Weider's challenge but also proposed a boxing match, which would allow him to take advantage of his superior size, to precede the other events.[64] Needless to say, this physical showdown never took place.

Meanwhile, recognizing Mr. America iconography as the hottest commodity in the iron game, the Weiders continued to use both it and AAU winners through the 1950s, even launching and relaunching a magazine called *Mr. America* in 1952 and 1958.[65] What seems remarkable is that they made no attempt to rejuvenate the IFBB or their own Mr. America Contest during these years. Even in reports of the Mr. Montreal and Mr. Canada contests that they administered in 1950s, there is no mention of IFBB sponsorship.[66] Notwithstanding his inability to break the York hold on the AAU, Joe Weider remained true to his agreement with Wortmann, announcing in the April 1952 issue of *Your Physique* that during the previous year he had donated $2,000 in physique contest profits to the Olympic Weightlifting Team Fund. The motive behind this seemingly irrational display of generosity was not so much to support American weightlifting as to undermine its dependency on Hoffman. In a veiled reference to York, he argued that his bodybuilding shows could liberate AAU athletes from "certain controls" wielded by "powerful influences in National weightlifting circles."

> Only by making our weightlifters and our weightlifting teams completely financially independent can these controlling bonds be shattered. It is not fair to them, or to the people of America that certain dictatorial policies, nourished and condoned solely because of need of private support of our teams, should delegate these sterling athletes to a serf basis. . . . Therefore, next month I am writing an article which sets down a plan which . . . will make our weightlifting teams 100% self sufficient, self respecting and free to act . . . to select their coach, trainers and deserving team members, without regard to anyone except those who believe in them the most . . . the American Public.[67]

This editorial shows that Weider, in Harry Paschall's words, was still "prospecting for gold on the other side of the street" and that the financial infrastructure of weightlifting was still the mainspring of power in the sport.

But no plan that would enable Joe Weider to stake a claim on weightlifting through his bodybuilding enterprises ever materialized. He simply lacked the resources from his magazines and his Mr. America Barbell Company to mount an assault on fortress York, whose corporate assets had been growing since the 1930s. Thus, in a 1954 editorial in *Muscle Builder*, Ben Weider displayed all the signs of a true believer by encouraging athletes to join the AAU and enter its contests.[68]

THE ADVENT OF AFRICAN AMERICANS

An important subsidiary issue emerged from these antics. In the course of criticizing Hoffman's heavy-handed influence over the AAU, Joe Weider questioned the judges' decision at the 1950 Mr. America Contest to give the best back award and overall title to Farbotnik over Melvin Wells, a black bodybuilder from Buffalo known for his arm and upper-back development. "It's not always what you have, but sometimes WHO you know" was Weider's view of this outcome. Wells was reported to have said, "Gosh! I wonder what I have to do to win this title." Most accounts of the contest, however, attribute Wells's second-place finish to his weaker lower-body development (especially in his calves) and lack of symmetry. From the audience, Joe Peters, a contestant in the first Mr. America Contest, thought it was a fair decision: "Wells had tremendous arms and deltoids but not a balanced physique and not comparable to Farbotnik's."[69] Even reports in Weider's magazines acknowledged Wells's less than perfect chest, abdominals, and legs and expressed no criticisms over the AAU selection process.[70] Further to counter Weider's insinuations, Hoffman published a letter in which Wells denied any resentment regarding his placement: "I truly appreciate everything that has been done for me. . . . Never did I dream that I would be elevated so high in the physique world." He attributed the outcome to "people who have the backbone to stand up and face an issue regardless of race, creed or color."[71] Like Lurie during the war era, Wells had to be content as runner-up and most muscular man in successive years, and Weider, however broad his suggestion that the Mr. America Contest was fixed, never overtly raised the specter of racial discrimination.

Soon a new black muscular sensation, the Cuban-born George Paine, appeared on the horizon. After winning the Mr. New York State title in 1950, he became the first of his race to win the Junior Mr. America crown, edging out the magnificent Marvin Eder by a half point in 1951. Charles Smith in *Your Physique* praised him lavishly: "Paine looked wonderful. His separation of muscle is something to see and he easily ties the great Melvin Wells at his best." Lon Hanagan concurred that Paine "has EVERYTHING! Large muscles, sensational definition, perfect proportions and rugged power." His appearance, along with those of other black stars—Rocky Kent, John Rogers, Leroy Colbert, and Robert Shealy—prompted an article by Earle Liederman entitled "Are Colored Athletes Physically Superior to Whites?"[72] At the 1951 Mr. America Contest, Paine displayed, according to Liederman, "the greatest back development . . . seen in many, many years." The writer then reached into his bag of superlatives: "To term it *Great* is a weak word. *Incredible* perhaps describes it better." Peary Rader was also impressed, calling Paine "the sensation of the show," but his superlatives lapsed into a racial attribute, perhaps to justify why Paine placed only third overall: "Like most all of his race his calves are his weak spot."[73]

RESTORING THE ALL-AROUND IDEAL

Yet no one seemed displeased with the choice of Roy Hilligenn as the new Mr. America. Though a native of South Africa, he had won the Mr. Pacific Coast and Mr. Northern California titles. *Iron Man* heralded him as "just about perfect in every way, plenty of definition, exceptional bulk, excellent proportion and symmetry, beautiful skin texture and coloration and an ability at posing and display that is seldom equaled." Hilligenn was the first non-American to win the title. He also displayed real athletic ability by placing second to the great Norbert Schemansky in the weightlifting championships. *Strength & Health* made much of the fact that the contest was held at the Greek Theatre in Los Angeles: "The body worshippers of ancient Greece must have smiled down approvingly from the heavens as Roy Stanley Hilligenn, a sun-tanned young modern god whose body typifies in every way the models of those ancient Greeks, smilingly stepped forward to accept his trophy. . . . Aphrodite herself probably sighed with regret that she had lived her time B.A. (before the advent of Mr. Americas). No previous Mr. America title was ever won in more fitting surroundings."[74] In keeping with this Hellenic theme, *Muscle Power* stressed Hilligenn's well roundedness, which included his popularity, especially with women, and his ballroom dancing. He bowled 281 and played "the banjo, violin, piano as well as the harmonica," in addition to being "a tumbler, hand balancer and all round athlete." Finally, Hilligenn was the fourth Mr. America (the others being Ross, Reeves, and Delinger) from Yarick's gym in Oakland.[75] Notwithstanding his foreign origins, Hilligenn seemed to be an all-American who typified the physical-culture ideal.

Opinion varied greatly about what constituted the ideal physique, but most modern authorities would have sympathized with R. G. Kocsis's 1951 assessment that there was "nothing to substantiate any theory . . . that the ancients possessed muscular development superior to ours."[76] No longer was it possible, as in the days of Sandow's and Macfadden's contests, to use just the Greeks as a universal standard. "Modern civilization seems to have no ideal," wrote Eric Askew, "unlike the Greeks who had two well-known characters, Apollo and Farnese Hercules."[77] Such was the extent of modern progress in bodybuilding, even since the first Mr. America Contest in 1939. Much though Askew admired the Greeks, he believed that modern physique contests needed a more relevant model.

> Perhaps it is possible to learn from the Miss and Mrs. Contests a few pointers that could, with a few years' judicious application, raise the level of the standard of our contests, until they hold a place in the news world comparable to the Miss America contest. The Miss America contest . . . is also much more profitable to the contestants with its $25,000 in prizes and scholarships. . . . Singing and dancing may have their place in girls' contests, but we could surely use other mental tests to show that weight-trained men can and do have intellect as well as brawn. This would not be done with the object of lowering the standards of physical perfection. Rather with a few such alterations the general standing of the Iron Game would be measurably improved, for it has been recognized that the aspirant to the title of Miss America should have some intellectual capabilities, is it not just as true that her male counterpart should be equally endowed.[78]

What Askew desired was a few points allotted to mental capabilities: "I.Q. tests such as psychologists use would fit the bill perfectly." Similarly, he sought some test of physical prowess to provide further credibility for Mr. America. The dead lift and mile run, as tests of strength and stamina, would force contestants to use their weight-trained muscles, "proving to the public that this is not for show only."[79] As if to assure readers that such all-around standards were not the peculiar province of York athletes, Joe Weider boasted in 1950 that he could military-press 235, bench-press 330, and curl 180 pounds. But his difficulty in negotiating a 200-pound press with a "big backbend" on the fourth try at the 1951 Mr. Universe contest in London showed how distant such claims were from reality.[80]

For Miss America contestants, however, subjected to the draconian measures of Lenora Slaughter, all-around development was more than a distant ideal. In 1951, Yolande Betbeze (of Alabama) dealt the body-show aspect of the contest a severe blow when she refused, after her coronation, to embark on the traditional swimsuit fashion tour of the United States. Understandably dismayed, Catalina Swim Wear, a pageant sponsor, insisted that Betbeze be disqualified. When pageant officials refused, Catalina withdrew its support and helped found the Miss Universe Contest in 1952. This establishment of an alternative venue for external beauty enabled Slaughter to pursue more freely her anti-sexist agenda. It did nothing to diminish the popularity of the Atlantic City contest. The 1954 winner, Evelyn Ay, of Pennsylvania, became one of the most celebrated Miss Americas, chiefly for her all-around feminine virtues. A press report noted the twenty-year-old combined "a level head and stage poise with her ravishing figure and charm, for in the crucial question-and-answer period, she came through with colors flying so high that there were expressions of amazement up and down press row." It seemed almost incidental that Ay won the swimsuit competition too.[81] With television coverage introduced in 1954, the recruitment of Bert Parks as emcee in 1955, and his introduction the next year of "There She Is," which became the show's theme song, the pageant entered its golden age. Perfectly packaged, it became a beacon of dignity and middle-class respectability for a generation.

THE PARK CONTROVERSY

The Mr. America Contest was less self-consciously moving toward a similar set of ideals, perhaps because there was greater agreement about what it meant to be an American in the 1950s. Reports in *Iron Man* indicated that the 1952 show, conducted by John Terlazzo in New York City, was the best ever, and the winner, Jim Park, of Chicago, was "one of the finest built men of our time." Not unlike the Miss Americas of his time, Park was thrilled with his celebrity status, and friends began calling his wife, Ethel, "Mrs. America." "In fact it's the greatest thing that could happen to one guy," he remarked. "All of a sudden everyone knows who I am."[82] Not everyone, however, was pleased with the outcome. Weider publications, increasingly critical of AAU events, called it the "most unpopular and incompetent decision ever rendered" in a Mr. America Contest, expressing outrage that George Paine was not selected most muscular man and that Malcolm Brenner, of Los Angeles, did not win the overall title. When Park was announced the winner, "about 2,000 bodybuilding fans and weight training authorities booed the decision for a solid 10 minutes, with such genuine annoyance at the

Figure 4.4. Five-time Mr. Universe Bill Pearl at the time he won the 1953 Mr. America Contest. Courtesy of George and Tuesday Coates and Richard Thornley Jr.

'raw' decision, that for a while it appeared as though a riot would break out." To emphasize their displeasure, "a group lifted Malcolm Brenner onto their shoulders and walked him off the platform to his dressing room in a victory march."[83] Barton Horvath, calling the contest a "fiasco," insisted that in his twenty-five years in bodybuilding, he had

117

"never seen such a violent demonstration."[84] Jim Murray, reporting for *Strength & Health*, completely disagreed. Calling Horvath's charges "an extravagant exaggeration," he reported that "an extremely noisy group in the 'peanut gallery' had shown up simply to discredit Park in the minds of judges" and then "boorishly protested the final decision." But this group was a clear minority: "Far more members of the audience were crowding around Jim Park for his autograph."[85] Further to defend the process, Murray named the judges and listed the criteria used since the war—six points each for muscularity and symmetry and a point each for general appearance, face and skin, and posing. In fact, Brenner had recently won the Junior Mr. America title in Oakland with exactly the same number of points (70) awarded by "a different set of qualified A.A.U. judges."[86] Later, Brenner settled the controversy on a CBS radio interview, stating, "I think the better man won!" Murray recalled, from the perspective of a half century, "Park was better than you think."[87]

Weider was unwilling to let the matter drop, particularly when Park became a York employee. No mention was made of race in relation to the Brenner controversy, but in Weider's *American Manhood* (a spin-off of *Mr. America*) it was raised by a reader, "a colored bodybuilder," who stated that Wells and Paine "appeared to receive anything but fair judging" at the Mr. America Contest.[88] And *Muscle Power* featured a fictional dialogue between bodybuilding buffs. "I saw the whole thing with me eyes," stated the protagonist.

> There was a lotta them boys who had lumps bigger than the winner but they were colored fellers and didn't have a ghost of a chance there. There wuz a guy named Melvin Wells who has the greatest arms in the land—did he get a tumble? . . . Naw, he got disgusted, that's all he got and I don't blame him for walking out of the show as he did. Then how about this other colored feller, George Paine, who is all muscle from his dome to his dogs. If any guy deserved to become the most muscular man, it was this guy Paine. And y' can scratch him off too. *Why?* Betcha *can't* answer that one.[89]

When Park won a Mr. World Contest staged by Hoffman in Philadelphia in October 1952 over Hilligenn, Delinger, and Paine, there was less sniping from the Weider camp. But questions emerged about the outcome, Park's amateur status, and a lack of international entries. A contestant named Tom Manfre attributed both Park's victory over Paine and his own placement below Yaz Kuzuhara (a York entry) in the short class to Hoffman's control of the AAU and contest: "Everybody who was a judge worked for him. It stunk like dead fish."[90] Charles Smith chose to play up Norbert Schemansky's world-record clean and jerk (408 pounds), which was performed as a sidelight. Only by his victory in the 1954 Mr. Universe Contest, in London, did Park attain full credibility in the iron game.[91]

FUNCTION OVER FORM—SYMMETRY OVER SIZE

Part of the reason for this dissension, aside from politics, was that the AAU, true to its amateur code, was moving toward the all-around standard used in the popular Miss America Contest, while the Weiders' promotional pitch increasingly emphasized muscle size, especially in the arms and chest. Articles entitled "Could Your Arms Become Too Large?," "Gain 15 Inches on Your Chest," "Skinny, You Can Gain Weight," and "Get Massive Biceps Size" in successive issues of *Muscle Power* fed the desires of skinny youth to get big.[92] The 19" bicep became an ideal for top-flight bodybuilders. The Weider cover man Clancy Ross reportedly became "raging mad" over an article crediting him with only an 18" upper arm and a 50" chest: "I resent being slimmed down by a typewriter! . . . My arm now hits a hot 19" and my chest is 51½".[93] For much of the American public, however, this passion for bigness seemed grotesque. An article entitled "Mr. America Isn't All He Looks to Be" in a Los Angeles magazine illustrated the point: "One of the phoniest aberrations of these times is the Mr. America cult, composed of the Big Bicep Boys and their worshippers. They seem to think that the top-heavy human pouter-pigeons who compete for the Mr. America title are stronger, healthier and more beautiful than a football tackling dummy. . . . There are dozens of magazines devoted to picturing near-nude photographs of the Big Bicep Boys, strutting and smirking and displaying the rippling bands and cords of imitation muscles that have gruesomely been built into their body by weightlifting exercises."[94] To counteract this impression of inflated muscles and unnatural lifestyles, the AAU establishment, guided by York, tried to emphasize function over form—muscles as strong as they looked. Indeed, the 1952 Mr. World Contest, while using the same all-around judging criteria as the Mr. America Contest, added a category for athletic ability.[95]

Such was Hoffman's interest in weightlifting and his influence in the AAU that it seemed likely athleticism would loom larger in future physique contests, leading Ray Van Cleef to speculate that Park's successor would also compete in the national weightlifting championships.[96] Len Bosland, a contestant in the recent Mr. World Contest, interpreted athletic points as a means for Hoffman "to get bodybuilders to take up weightlifting" and "stay in weightlifting."[97] At the moment, however, Hoffman's vision was more in line with the kind of balance sought by the ancient Greeks: "We are not trying to pick America's most handsome man when we select 'Mr. America,' but neither are we trying to select an abysmal brute with much more of his share of muscles. We want to select as physique contest winners the man with the best development, the most symmetrical proportions, who is a good poser, an athletic type, a man who is good-looking in a manly sort of way, a man who is the superior physical specimen."[98] But his instructions to judges in 1953 drew on criteria similar to those used in choosing Miss Americas: "The winner should have good character, reasonable intelligence, athletic ability and personality, as well as muscles and pleasing appearance." These mostly intangible qualities fit the judges' choice, Bill Pearl, of San Diego, leading Paschall, in a rare display of optimism, to remark: "These muscle contests are now on a

Figure 4.5. Judges (Bob Hoffman, Alvin Roy, Peary Rader, Karo Whitfield, Ray Van Cleef [hidden], Harry Paschall, and John Terpak) interviewing Steve Klisanin at the 1955 Mr. America Contest. Author's collection.

sounder footing than they have been for years. Bill is exactly the type of young American who will do the game a lot of good. He is strictly NOT a musclehead."[99] Tellingly, however, Pearl did not compete in the weightlifting championships.

Others in the iron game shared Paschall's gratification. While Rader admired Pearl's size and symmetry, "a picture of perfection," he seemed more impressed by his intangibles, especially his retiring and modest manner: "He is one of the finest fellows ever to win such a title and will surely bring it nothing but honor and respect." Most importantly, Pearl was a "sincere Christian and a member of the Baptist church" and appeared to satisfy the "demands in character and clean living" embodied in the Mr. America title.[100] There was a striking similarity between the all-around masculinity of Pearl and the feminine virtues exhibited by 1954 Miss America, Evelyn Ay. Both contests aspired to respectability according to the white, suburban, middle-class values that became a set feature of the 1950s.

Even Weider editors expressed satisfaction with the outcome. Charles Smith observed there was "something sleek, not slick mark you, but sleek about Bill's development." And his posing was "beyond any doubt, the best since John Grimek, the Master." In fact, Pearl had spent the previous week in York picking up pointers from Grimek. Jim Murray recalled the impression that Pearl made: "Pearl was just a kid when he came to York and just in awe of Grimek. There was a skylight in the dressing room of the old gym on Broad Street and we had him stand under it. Grimek and I looked at each other and said almost in unison, 'Well, there's your winner!'"[101]

The close resemblance between Pearl's posing style and Grimek's further signified the classic look of Mr. Americas in the 1950s. Equally revealing was Liederman's staunch defense of AAU judges. "There is more to winning a title than large muscles," he explained. "The largest arms do not necessarily make a Mr. America. . . . Muscle shape, proportions, contours, posture, skin condition, features and general personality all contribute to judging."[102] It is not surprising that these perceptions of the Mr. America ideal, as espoused by a Weider writer, closely coincided with those of Hoffman and Rader, since AAU Mr. Americas had become permanent fixtures in promoting Weider magazines and products. More remarkable was the lack of Weider contests, the proceeds of which, as stipulated in the Wortmann accord, went to the Metropolitan AAU. In contrast to the coverage of Mr. America contests, the Weiders' 1953 Mr. Eastern America competition, won by

121

Leroy Colbert against a lackluster field, was buried in the back pages of *Muscle Power*.[103] Despite their ongoing feud, Hoffman and Weider displayed remarkable respect for the Mr. America Contest and the ideals it represented.

MR. AMERICA GOES HOLLYWOOD

Richard Dubois, the 1954 Mr. America, won paeans of praise. Like Pearl, he seemed ideal for symbolizing the nation's manhood. Hoffman described Dubois as "superbly developed, handsome, smiling, likeable, popular."[104] Despite being only twenty, the youngest winner yet, he looked and acted the part. "He was all that a person would visualize a Mr. America to be," remarked the California gym owner George Bruce. "If only more young Americans would follow his example, we could wipe out sickness, ill health and lack of bodily vigor."[105] Especially appealing was the rags-to-riches story of how Dubois had risen from poverty in the South Bronx. When his father died, he was sent to a Catholic orphanage, where he excelled in swimming, diving, and boxing. But Dubois also displayed an artistic bent, and while shining shoes and selling newspapers in Manhattan's theater district, he became acquainted with actors, who secured minor stage roles for him. After starting serious bodybuilding, he was drawn to Los Angeles, where he could maximize his talents in Hollywood and on Muscle Beach.

The publicity from his Mr. America victory helped Dubois land a role in the MGM film *Athena*, starring Debbie Reynolds, Jane Powell, and Vic Damone. "A typical American Horatio Alger story" was the description that appeared in the publicity release introducing Dubois (who performed under the name "Richard Sabre"), "a 21 year old, athletically built, clean-cut young man, with natural acting ability and a willingness to work hard for a career." He combined the best of Victor Mature, Clark Gable, Douglas Fairbanks Jr., and Charles Boyer, having "all the romantic aspects of Mature with the masculinity of Gable's virility, blended with the dash of Fairbanks and the woman appeal of Boyer." Liederman predicted that Dubois's cinema career—there was a long-term contract at Universal Studios in the offing—would "rise with meteoric speed" and that he would become "the most commercial Mr. America of them all."[106]

It would be easy to assume that Dubois was simply following the lead of Steve Reeves, but his illustrious film career was only beginning, and it seems just as likely that Dubois helped Reeves achieve success. In

Athena, the two Mr. Americas competed against each other in a mock Mr. Universe Contest in which, after a tie, Reeves defeated Dubois by lifting more weight overhead. Most importantly, the technical director on the film was Bert Goodrich, who used the occasion to employ numerous local bodybuilders, including Jerry Ross, Ed Holovchik, Irwin Koszewski, Joe Gold, and Malcolm Brenner, as extras, thereby reinforcing the Hollywood–Muscle Beach connection. Liederman predicted that *Athena* would "do more for the bodybuilding game than anything that has happened during the past few years."[107] Several years later, Reeves became a box-office star by playing Hercules in a series of films. Dubois at first fancied himself "a Shakespearean actor," predicting, "Within five years I will be the greatest actor that Hollywood has ever known!" But he turned his muscles into quick cash by joining Eiferman, Koszewski, Gold, Armand Tanny, and others in Mae West's road show, and he was soon playing Las Vegas for $1,000 a week.[108] Eventually, Dubois became a born-again Christian and disappeared from the muscle and movie scenes.

Although critics of the Mr. America Contest were distracted by the youthful exuberance of Dubois, there remained a reservoir of discontent, especially in the Weider camp, and a general feeling that the competition could be better run. While Liederman called the 1954 contest "the finest presentation that the Amateur Athletic Union has ever accomplished," he chided local organizers for contests (preceded by weightlifting) that lasted over six hours, for failing to relay judges' scores to the audience and contestants, and for adhering so closely to amateur standards that bodybuilders could not earn a living by displaying their muscles in movies. And never far from the surface was the race issue. "Will George Paine ever win the Mr. America contest," queried Liederman, "or for that matter will any colored bodybuilder? Calves seem to let these boys down." Finally, owing to the subjectivity of physique judging, there were always contestants disgruntled over not winning or placing higher. Such was the case with Lud Schusterich, who, after a long layoff, trained his body to its best shape ever at Leo Stern's gym in San Diego, only to finish fifth. Hoffman tried to convince him that Mr. America contests were judged fairly, a "thankless task" by which "friends are lost." Stern too was disappointed with the 1954 contest, so much so that he decided to discontinue sponsoring physique contests. Henceforth "a man should also be judged on character and intelligence—either that, or call him America's Best Built Man—not 'Mr. America.'"[109]

THE QUEST FOR THE PERFECT MAN

Judging from the increasing popularity of the Mr. America contests, the system was working reasonably well, but there were continual calls from iron-game leaders for reforms. Interestingly, none of them aimed to satisfy popular demands for increased muscularity; instead, all addressed the need to fulfill the highest ideals of American manhood, stressing character, education, personality, health, and "muscular efficiency," a euphemism for athletic ability. Rader, who was uncompromising on these points, assumed a strong moralistic stance: "WE ARE ALL AGREED THAT WE MUST EITHER HAVE A MR. AMERICA WHO WILL BE AN IDEAL AMERICAN IN EVERY WAY or change the name to something like 'Best Built Man' or some other less inclusive title."[110] Hoffman, a longtime supporter of all-around development and useful muscles, strongly supported Rader's proposals. Sensing how closely they coincided with the criteria of the Miss America Pageant, which stressed personality, intellect, and talent as well as physical endowments, Bob Hise, of Los Angeles, even suggested that "the Mr. America should be held with the Miss America contest." This idea met with little favor, but support for Rader's proposals was strong among AAU bigwigs. Pending full implementation, the national committee, before the 1955 contest, held in Cleveland, decided to "gradually adopt" such criteria as character, education, career aspirations, and athletic ability in a "rather informal way" through an interview process. And judges would be insulated from crowd influences by a prejudging procedure, another Rader idea.[111]

The impact of these changes on the 1955 Mr. America Contest was dramatic. Virtually all reports on the victory of Steve Klisanin, the 1953 Junior Mr. America, emphasized his all-around assets, almost to the exclusion of muscular development. "The youthful Marine makes an ideal Mr. America winner," reckoned Van Cleef, "with his fine musculature, a pleasing personality, outstanding athletic ability and good intelligence."[112] A former football star and lifting champion, Klisanin planned to return to college after leaving the service. "It was just another contest," he later recalled. "I was interested in weightlifting mainly and did bodybuilding exercises."[113] Writing for *Iron Man*, Mabel Rader admitted there were other physiques as good as Klisanin's, but "the scales were tipped in Steve's favor" by the new standards of officiating: "No longer does the title 'Mr. America" designate the one quality, 'Superior Physique.' It also includes character, insofar as it can be determined, education, personality, and past and present athletic ability. While this method of judging and selecting a winner is quite new and still rather crude in use, the leaders in our game feel it is a move in the right direction. . . . Those responsible for these changes feel that a man bearing the title of 'Mr. America' should be fully representative of the finest in American manhood in every way." That Klisanin was a Marine and "would much rather be a World Champion lifter" than Mr. America no doubt further endeared him to the judges.[114]

Weider editors concurred with the spirit of the new rulings. When zealous AAU officials in Los Angeles started requiring physique contestants to register totals three times their body weight in the Olympic lifts, Liederman approved: "The more you think about it the more logical it seems, for if muscles are not strong or useful, what good are they?" No less committed to all-around development was Joe Weider, who offered particular advice to young men: "[Do] not neglect the training of your mind or the development of masculine culture while building your body. A real Mr. America should be the ideal male—muscularly perfect, well schooled, cultured, and the possessor of a magnetic personality."[115] Poise and personality, already key standards for Miss Americas, became foremost criteria for those choosing a Mr. America.

The desire for all-around manly development was hardly new. It harked back to the early contests staged by Macfadden and to Johnny Hordines's stress on "personality, character, and the way you live."[116] Ideals of symmetry and athletic ability were likewise inherited from earlier eras. John Grimek, still bodybuilding's leading icon, observed that the winner of a current physique contest was rarely the biggest man with the largest measurements. Typically, he would exhibit a classic appeal "without any one outstanding feature," but his "whole physique" would have "that 'something' which is becoming and pleasing to the eye." He added that symmetry was the "factor that separates the winners from the also-rans." This was in keeping with classical standards of beauty: "For ages now ancient Grecian statues have been upheld as a criterion for masculine perfection, although some are modeled along comparatively slender lines. All these ancient masterpieces, however, have balanced proportions."[117]

The growing emphasis on big muscles and ongoing nagging criticisms of AAU policies, so evident in Weider publications just after the war, seemed not to disturb this equilibrium or to detract from the Mr. America ideal. In fact, it could be argued that the Weiders only increased its appeal by showcasing the male physique and popularizing bodybuilding. "In America," wrote Joe Weider in 1955, "where bodybuilding activity is presently at a fever pitch, millions of men and boys train regularly with weights, with one major goal in mind; the plucking of the Mr. America plum." A reader even credited Weider's publication with inaugurating the interviews at the 1955 contest, in which contestants "were questioned about their hobbies, athletic background, what work they did and other details designed to determine good character."[118] That the promotion of these traits, so reminiscent of the Greek ideal of a sound mind in a sound body, was shared by the triumvirate of bodybuilding in the mid-1950s—Hoffman, Rader, and Weider—accounts in large part for the popularity of the Mr. America Contest as it entered upon the heart of its golden age.

5

MULTIPLE MR. AMERICAS

IT WAS SUPPOSED TO REPRESENT AN AMERICAN IDEAL. THAT WAS THE GRANDEUR OF IT. ORIGINALLY I THINK IT WAS THE EPITOME OF THE ALL-AMERICAN MALE, AND THEY WANTED FUNCTIONALITY WITH THAT. . . . THEY WERE LOOKING FOR A MUSCULAR BOY SCOUT.

JAN DELLINGER, INTERVIEW BY THE AUTHOR, MAY 22, 2008

MUCH OF MODERN SCHOLARSHIP HAS PORTRAYED AMERICAN SOCIETY FROM the mid-1950s through the early 1960s as staid, complacent, and boring. To Todd Gitlin, the "dead, dreary Fifties" was a time when "consensus intellectuals," to accommodate the nation's newfound affluence, "were busy settling their accounts with the postwar order." They "presumed that America was melting down to a single sea of national satisfaction."[1] But the apparent stasis of this era concealed a restless energy that would eventually bring momentous changes to American society and physical culture. While the Mr. America Contest (like its Miss America counterpart) remained unaltered until the late 1960s, internal pressures were mounting that would change the face of American bodybuilding. The concept of emulating the Greek ideal by training for functional muscles and all-around development became institutionalized during this period, but it awakened the antithetical notion of muscularity for its own sake. The Weiders, effectively excluded from the established order by Bob Hoffman and the AAU, provided both a focal point for dissident elements and the necessary energy to provoke change.

MUSCLES AND MORALITY

For a while, in the aftermath of the 1955 Mr. America Contest, consensus seemed to prevail. More than ever, amateurism (a derivative of the Greek ideal) was universally respected, especially with the demise of Walt Baptiste's Professional Mr. America and the inauguration of a "Teen Age Mr. America Contest" in April 1956 at the Duncan YMCA in Chicago. Peary Rader observed that as the judges were tallying the scores, "all the boys came out and gave some strength demonstrations, such as dead lifts, squats, bench presses, curls, etc., and they all showed unusual strength and ability, which is very desirable in physique contestants."[2] Coinciding with this outlook, AAU officials meeting in Los Angeles in 1956 adopted sweeping rules changes that Rader himself had had a major hand in formulating. Henceforth, "athletic ability" would account for 25 percent of the judging criteria, 50 percent was allotted to symmetry and general appearance (including education, personality, and character), and only 25 percent was awarded for muscular development. This emphasis on intangibles and athletic ability was something that Rader "had long wanted" in judging: "It is desirable that anyone bearing the title of 'Mr. America' should represent the Ideal of American Manhood in every phase of his being."[3] But underlying his crusade for integrity and all-American values was a strong sense of Christian morality. Haunted by the possibility that bodybuilding might attract the wrong element, he allowed *Iron Man* to become a forum for homophobia. In a guest editorial, Leo Stern enlisted tradition and religion in the cause: "For centuries there has been a distinct difference between the two sexes. Let's keep it that way. I am sure God so intended it to be." Ironically, the same issue featured a full-page picture of an epic struggle between two nude men (Hercules throwing Lichas into the sea), reminding readers that physical culture had long been perceived as the pursuit of either perfection or perversion.[4]

On the cusp of this cultural divide were Weider publications, which not only featured ads for photographs of nearly naked young men but also included titles appealing explicitly to homosexuals, such as *Body Beautiful* and *Adonis*.[5] Rader, though moralistic, never rebuked the Weiders for these associations. But York, with serious commercial considerations at stake, was unrestrained. Harry Paschall, the managing editor of *Strength & Health* from 1955 till his death in 1957, addressed it in an article entitled "Let Me Tell You a Fairy Tale":

> In the past several years a flood of undersized booklets featuring the male physique in all stages of nudity have appeared. . . . Under the guise of wholesome physical culture, these dirty little books are aimed directly at a profitable market, the homosexual or 'fairy' trade. They are on the stands for one reason only—*to make a profit*. Circulation figures show they do just that, because they outsell the regular physical culture journals, and are so cheap to print, that the profit is obvious.

It was obvious to Paschall that for puzzled bodybuilders searching for truth, "even Diogenes with his lantern could never find it in a Weedy publication." While Rader and Hoffman had taken measures against smut, Weider magazines were full of "ads of fairy photos who sell nude and suggestive pictures directed at the Swish Trade."[6]

York's defense of morality seemed justified by a reader's report that a police censor had confiscated copies of *Body Beautiful*, *Adonis*, and other sexually oriented and girlie magazines from newsstands in Detroit. Local physical culturists prevented the removal of *Strength & Health* and other mainstream muscle magazines, but their cause was hardly helped by revelations in Weider's *Mr. America* about Hoffman's sex habits.[7] While Weider may have been vulnerable for skirting the limits of morality and legality, Hoffman was no paragon of virtue.

The morality issue, however, was merely an extension of a larger debate over muscular development, and Paschall brought it into sharp focus. In keeping with the Greek tradition, he stressed "sensible physical training," heaping scorn on "boobybuilders," particularly followers of Weider principles who valued muscles for their own sake: "These fellows are no longer training to become strong, to be more athletic, to enter into wholesome competition with others. They no longer go through a sensible system of basic exercises. They are devotees of a strange cult of 'lumps at any price.'" Paschall's point about useful muscles was made even clearer in his cartoon character Bosco, whose strength and integrity stood in striking contrast to the effeminacy and narcissism of Weedy (i.e., Weider) Man, who seemed concerned only with appearance. "Muscles are made to use, to lift, to pull, to carry, to run, and jump," contended Hoffman, who seemed pleased that athletic ability at last figured in the scoring of most physique contests.[8]

These nonmuscular criteria initially received tacit acceptance from the Weider camp, which expressed no displeasure over the Mr. America winners in the mid-1950s. After all, Joe Weider had started as a weight-lifter and devoted a considerable portion of his magazines to the sport. But Charles Smith was unconvinced that a bodybuilder had to prove his strength: "No man who has developed big muscles, definition and proportion IS weak." He believed such rules would in fact jeopardize lifting meets, which were always paired with physique contests: "Run an Olympic Lifting Meet on its own and there's more than a good chance you'll lose money."[9] Smith's point about the popularity and financial importance of physique contests was well taken, and the ongoing role of bodybuilding as a handmaiden to weightlifting would become a source of discontent to readers of Weider magazines. They were also beginning to question the outcome of AAU-sanctioned contests. "How is it that Mickey Hargitay who placed only 5th in the last [1955] Mr. America Contest," queried John Allerdice, of Chicago, "was able to go on to London and win the greatest bodybuilding title of all—Mr. Universe?" To lessen this possibility, Weider editors recommended that judges' scorecards be made public and that bodybuilders report any irregularities to local AAU officials.[10] Notwithstanding the obvious benefits that such innovations would confer, they would not address the growing disparity between the new AAU rules and the perceptions of an increasing number of bodybuilders championed by the Weiders.

THE VIRGINIA BEACH FIASCO

These differences surfaced soon after the 1956 Mr. America Contest, which was won by Ray Schaefer of Michigan City, Indiana. At 210 body weight, Schaefer could press 250, squat 450, bench press 380, and curl 160 pounds and seemed to have all the requisite personal and muscular assets. Controversy surfaced a week later, however, when Schaefer pitted his muscles against those of 1955 winner, Steve Klisanin, a longtime Hoffman favorite, at an impromptu Mr. Universe Contest staged by the Virginia Beach Junior Chamber of Commerce and a local promoter named Buck Cowling. The three-day event (June 8–10) included a Mr. Universe Ball, with a floor show and dancing; a Mr. Universe Parade featuring the contestants, along with thirty-two groups of marchers; and many acrobatic, balance, lifting, and clown acts interspersed with the physique competition. Although Rader called it "one of the finest physique and variety shows we have ever seen," none of the judges knew "what [they] were judging" on the first evening of contest, when Schaefer placed first with 70.5 points, followed by Robert Hinds (68), Gene Bohanty (68), and Klisanin (66.5). The judges were Rader, Barton Horvath, Doug Biller, Dr. Howard James, George Greenfield, Bill Colonna, and Bob Hoffman.[11]

By the second night, Hoffman, acting as vice president of the AAU Weightlifting Committee and head judge, replaced Horvath, a Weider editor, and James with Paul Anderson and Ottley Coulter and also ruled there should be no height divisions. Both decisions, which were opposed by contest organizers, "created a terrific disturbance back stage among both the officials and the contestants," leading to the exchange of "many hard words" and putting "all relations" under "considerable strain." Bill Colonna later recalled that Cowling got up on the bleachers and scolded Hoffman for what he had done: "You big son of a bitch, you rigged my contest, and I'm going to fix your ass." Nevertheless, Hoffman had his way. Klisanin won with 69.5 points, Schaefer took second with 68, and Bohanty and Harry Johnson tied for third with 65 each.[12] (Only the second-night scores determined the final places.) Perhaps to cover up what appeared to be a flagrant manipulation of the results, Hoffman agreed to pay Schaefer's way to the far more prestigious Mr. Universe Contest, which was being staged by Oscar Heidenstam's National Amateur Bodybuilders' Association (NABBA) in London the following weekend. Hoffman probably reasoned that it would be pointless to send Klisanin, since he was already a Mr. Universe.[13] There, the 1949 Mr. America, Jack Delinger, won the professional division, and Schaefer won the amateur title over a distinguished field that included such stars as John Lees, of England, and Paul Winter, of Antigua.

Hoffman's gesture, however, was insufficient to appease the Weider organization, which seized on the contretemps at Virginia Beach to launch an assault on Hoffman, the AAU, and the weightlifting clique. A blast from Hoffman's old bête noire, Dan Parker of the *New York Daily Mirror*, was followed by a full exposé by Horvath in the October issue of *Muscle Builder*. "For far too long," he claimed, "Hoffman had bellowed his way into the limelight of AAU bodybuilding contests, usurping powers never officially delegated to him in a series of ludicrous attempts to establish himself as the czar of the muscle world." He noted the contest director refused to accept the judges' decision and was instituting legal proceedings against Hoffman as a "liar," a "fraud," and an "incompetent official." As further proof that Hoffman had "rigged" the outcome, Horvath provided pictures comparing the physiques of Klisanin and Schaefer with those of other entrants, along with copies of the score sheets (furnished by contest promoters), which showed how closely the marks awarded by Coulter and Hoffman (seated side by side) coincided, and how Doug Biller was allegedly pressured to rate Schaefer lower and Klisanin higher on the second night. Most damning, however, were Hoffman's remarks to the local *Virginian-Pilot* about why he had removed Horvath, a physical culturist for twenty-five years: "I don't consider him a qualified AAU official. . . . I only put Horvath in there the first night to try to educate him around the right line." Hoffman also expressed disdain for bodybuilding: "I'm interested in getting rid of these physique contests anyway. They are sissified things."[14] The Virginia Beach encounter between two Mr. Americas brought to a head the growing rift between weightlifters and bodybuilders, and between their leaders.

ETHICAL REVERBERATIONS

Not surprisingly, Hoffman's seemingly outrageous actions and remarks triggered a firestorm of controversy within the bodybuilding world. They are comprehensible only within the context of the prevailing AAU rules structure and climate of opinion. Harry Paschall, in his in-imitable style, was "moved to wonder why a number of very preju-diced magazine writers have been blowing their stacks about unfair competition," characterizing "critics of the athletic-type physique of Klisanin" as "a very thin fringe of lump-happy characters whose profes-sional business is the creation of monsters." Further to cast aspersions on critics of AAU standards, Paschall pointed out that Klisanin was a recent graduate of the University of New Mexico who had a "B.S. degree in the highly technical subject of geology."

> Most of his detractors have great difficulty in spelling "cat." Klisanin is an all-round athlete of exceptional merit, and much prefers the sport of weight-lifting to posing on a platform with a rose between his lips. . . . We are proud of Steve Klisanin as one of our most representative Mr. Americas, as a man who can lift 350 pounds overhead while standing on his own two feet instead of reclining on a bench, and who can appear before the non-muscle-conscious public as a credit to weight training and clean-living American manhood.[15]

Hoffman was no less defensive of AAU standards, especially athletics points, and wanted to see an all-around contest between Klisanin and Schaefer that would feature running, jumping, swimming, wrestling, lifting, and other events. He reckoned that Klisanin could "give Schaefer a ten yard start in a hundred and beat him to the tape." Sportsmanship and morality were other grounds for criticizing Schaefer. Not only did he refuse to accept his second-place trophy at Virginia Beach, but he also accepted $700 from Hoffman for his flight to London "with the verbal agreement that he would repay" Hoffman's organization "with pictures and articles." But "without a thought of his obligation," Schaefer "signed up with Weider." Hoffman saw this lapse as an indictment of all bodybuilders: "Do you wonder why we prefer weight-lifting to the physique contests?"[16]

Schaefer's pictures, articles, and testimonials were soon appearing in Weider magazines. "During my entire training career I have used Weider methods entirely," he is quoted as saying. "My victories in the 'Mr. Junior America'—'Mr. Universe' and 'America's Most Muscular Man' contests prove how effective they are." Letters from Weider magazine readers indicated that Schaefer's treatment at Virginia Beach was becoming a cause célèbre and that many bodybuilders theretofore supportive of York were being swayed by Horvath's exposé. "Each day," observed Joe, "we receive letters, telephone calls and bits of information from many sources which point to a Hoffman dynasty and a dictatorial rule."[17] Weider kept the pot boiling over the next year by publishing more scorecards and sending letters (via Horvath) to Clarence Johnson (AAU weightlifting chairman) and AAU president Carl Hansen, requesting an investigation of Hoffman's conduct. "One rumor has it Mr. Johnson, that you are merely a puppet official and that Hoffman pulls the strings while you dance to his tune," wrote Horvath.[18] For those who witnessed Hoffman's behavior firsthand, the effect was devastating. The local iron-game patriarch George Greenfield, formerly a York supporter, "lost a lot of respect for Hoffman and stopped going to York picnics," according to Bob Crist. Stunned by the revelations, Bill Colonna gained the impression that Hoffman often predetermined the winners of physique contests, especially Mr. America: "Why Bob did it I'll never know. He didn't have to do it, but it did permanent damage to his reputation."[19]

Meanwhile further evidence of Hoffman's bias, this time with a racial edge, was served up to bodybuilders when he headed a panel that selected the weightlifter Thomas Ewing over a superbly built African

American bodybuilder, Robert Walker, at the Mr. Apollo Contest in Los Angeles. "Walker has committed the unforgivable sin of being born a Negro," observed one reader.[20] In a feature article, *Muscle Builder* editors speculated on Walker's chances of winning the coveted Mr. America title.

> He learned the hard way in the 1956 Mr. Apollo event.
> "Robbed of the title," is what they say.
> Why?
> Bob refuses to comment. His faith remains unshaken in his fellowmen. But he's aware of the rumors. They persist—
> "A negro will never wear the Mr. America crown!"
> Facts have also reached his ears.
> "Art Harris was forced by officials to stand out in the rain during a Florida contest. He lost by ¼ point after a huddle and an official recap.
> "Melvin Wells lost the 'best arms' trophy to a man with much smaller, less impressive arms in a Mr. America contest.
> "Leroy Colbert—George Paine, how far did they get?"
> Bob is determined to see for himself.[21]

But Walker never entered the 1957 Mr. America Contest, which was held at Daytona Beach and won by Ronald (Speck) Lacy, a recent graduate of the University of Kentucky, where he was a football star. It was the first time that athletic points were officially implemented. Although separate judges were used for the Most Muscular Man selection and no York men sat on the Mr. America panel, the Weiders aired criticisms from a Miami Beach reader who claimed that too many points (13.5) separated Lacy from the field for the results to be believable. Lacy was also more committed to weightlifting than bodybuilding, had spent time in York before the show, had traveled to Florida by car with Hoffman, and received a big buildup when Bob addressed the audience before the show. The reader commented: "Then it was evident who the winner would be. Another frame-up? Another kick in the teeth to bodybuilders? The scoring speaks for itself."[22]

Denigration of Hoffman then led to another controversy, this time at the 1957 Junior Mr. America Contest, proving to the Weiders that physique competitions had sunk to a "new low." The title was won by Jim Dugger, a comparative unknown from Georgia, but many higher-profile men—Irwin Koszewski, Doug Strohl, Robert Hinds, Art Harris, Lynn Lyman—though eligible, had not entered, allegedly because of the rigged judging at Virginia Beach. "Prejudices, partiality and a one man rule have so undermined the precepts of fair play that those that know the score refuse to enter the big events," claimed the Weiders. With fan support, they vowed to "fight harder than ever to clean up the sport."[23]

However true to ancient traditions and the highest ideals of manhood the new AAU rules may have been, Hoffman had made a strategic error by forcing the issue, thereby jeopardizing fairness and impartial judgment, especially at Virginia Beach. It not only damaged his reputation, but also was a missed opportunity for a man who had otherwise been an iron-game visionary. Had he acted wisely, Hoffman could have appropriated the nascent Mr. Universe title in 1947, much as he did the Mr. America Contest in 1940, turned it into a higher echelon of competition for Mr. America winners, superseded Heidenstam's event in England, and staved off future challenges from the Weiders.[24] In retrospect, the fiasco at Virginia Beach gave a big boost to the Weiders, prompting them in 1958 to break their 1950 accord with the AAU, revive the IFBB as a sanctioning body, reinstitute their own Mr. America Contest, and renew their ultimately successful thrust for dominance in the bodybuilding world.

HOFFMAN VERSUS WEIDER

Instead of stressing the positive aspects of his philosophy, Hoffman turned negative, employing the brilliant but poisonous pen of Harry Paschall to pillory and caricature his enemies. Harry had contempt for the "strange cult . . . fostered by the Weedy type muscle magazines that will do anything for a buck" and only made weight training look "ridiculous in the eyes of the general public." His description of "booby builders" should sound familiar to observers of a later generation of hyperdeveloped physiques: "We will admit they have developed a strange type of super-lumped physique. All you have to do is drop in at one of the boobybuilding gyms or beaches where this type prevails and you can readily see for yourself. The bodies they are turning out could come out of a mold—they are alike as two peas from the same pod. . . . Their physiques lack cohesion. They are not together. They have no resemblance to real athletes."[25] To Paschall, these bodybuilders were effeminate creatures, not deserving the respect of real men, and victims of the homosexual market. When a grand jury in Union County, New Jersey, indicted Weider's body-beautiful publications for conspiring to sell indecent literature, York was gleeful: "Anyone who takes one look at their current publications, such as *Jem*, and their small, dirty homo books *Body Beautiful* and *Adonis*, cannot fail to see the category into which such literature falls. Indecency is a mild word for it. Pornography is better." Peary Rader too, fearing a general "mental and moral degeneration," was harshly critical of magazines that catered to "sexual deviates," but he was careful never to associate them with the Weiders.[26]

For Hoffman and Weider, their ongoing feud was fueled more by ego, power, and commercial superiority than by morality. In a 1957 article in *Muscle Builder*, "People Who Live in Glass Houses," the Weiders delivered a stinging rebuttal to York's charges, claiming that Hoffman's "disregard for the truth has been as notorious as his arrogant interference in physique competition." To Hoffman's charge that their magazines "suborn homosexuality," the Weiders countered by saying, "*He's done it in spades!*" Regarding nudity: "What is done in *Adonis* and *Body Beautiful* has been done for years in Hoffman's magazine." Since the founding of *Strength & Health* in 1932, its readers "have been beguiled by a veritable daisy-chain of gentlemen with bulging biceps, bare behinds and bugle-beaded jock straps." Heading the list were photos of Hoffman, but his publications carried revealing pictures of such iron-game celebrities as Sandow, Klein, Van Cleef, Grimek, Paschall, Park, and countless lesser lights. Furthermore, Grimek, "Mr. Everything[,] . . . probably posed in states of nudity more frequently than any other physique star," having made a living during the 1930s by modeling for art classes at prestigious educational institutions.

But the most flagrant example of Hoffman's "hypocrisy," argued the Weiders, was the Strength & Health League, founded by Hoffman and Jowett in the 1930s. "This column was the meeting place of more homosexuals than Kraft-Ebing [*sic*] or Kinsey ever dreamed of! Ostensibly a 'pen pals' club, it became notorious with the passing years and was finally discontinued by 'request,' rumor hath it, of higher authorities." It was "the *first time in history the faggots have ever been organized*."[27] While admitting some past errors of judgment, Hoffman boasted that *Strength & Health* had not been "banned by any organization for publishing indecent pictures or articles or carrying questionable advertisements, a claim that our illustrious friend from Union City can't make."[28] With supremacy of the iron game seemingly at stake, neither side would give quarter.

The feud deepened in early 1958 when the Weiders followed their exposé with three articles revealing Hoffman's attempts to defraud the government, his unsavory personal life, and his prejudice against bodybuilders.[29] By this reckoning, fixing physique contests appeared to be the least of his sins. Hoffman's rebuttal was equally vicious. In an editorial entitled "Birds of a Feather," he pelted Joe Weider with names such as "rat," "skunk," "jackal," and "hyena," and accused him of making a "laughing stock" of the AAU abroad and "causing our beloved nation incalculable harm and loss of prestige."[30] In the latest instance of villainy, Weider had allegedly tried, at the 1957 Mr. Universe Contest, to seduce Lacy into switching his allegiance from York to Union City, much as he had done with Ray Schaefer.

> But Lacy is a man, a real man. He told Weider and he told the world that he is a York man, that he owes his success largely to York barbells, *Strength & Health*, and Bob Hoffman. . . . Schaefer is not our kind of bird. Lacy is. Klisanin, Farbotnik, Hilligen, Pearl, Frank Leight, Grimek, Stanko, and Bacon, all Mr. America winners, are our kinds of birds. They stick with York because they are honest, because they cannot be bought. Others who began as York men and who reached the top as York men sold their souls for a few pieces of silver, sold their honesty and integrity for a mess of potage [sic]. . . . The opposition has a number of magazines, we have only one—and so he has much more room to tell of the exploits of his stooges and promulgate his lies.[31]

It was likely for these reasons, as well as differences in training philosophy (form over function), that other Mr. Americas—Ross, Eiferman, and Delinger—had defected to Weider and that increasing numbers of bodybuilders, especially on the West Coast, were identifying with Weider and viewing the AAU and Hoffman as contrary to their interests. Nowhere was this development more evident than at Muscle Beach, where a group of bodybuilders chanted, "Down with Bob Hoffman" as they hoisted him in effigy.[32]

In *Brothers of Iron*, Joe Weider explains that his association with sexually oriented magazines was inadvertent. His two "girlie" magazines, *Jem* and *Monsieur*, had allegedly been started only to please his distributor, American News. He likens them to Hugh Hefner's *Playboy*, which combined "high-tone writing, racy humor, and shots of nude women showing their breasts." Though he claims that his heart was never in them, they "took off like rockets anyway." Likewise, his "picture magazines with artistic physique shots of men" had been undertaken only to please one of his editors, a gay man who lacked the resources to produce them himself. Since Weider had "no hang-ups in that direction," he went through with the project: "[I] published another couple magazines I never would have put out on my own." Especially after his homosexual magazines (though profitable) proved an embarrassment in

his feud with Hoffman, it is hardly surprising that Weider, hoping to enhance his historical image, later claimed that they "were other peoples'
ideas": "I had almost nothing to do with them."[33]

The verdict of modern scholarship, however, is that Weider and other
physique magazine publishers in the 1950s were pioneers in establishing an identity for the gay liberation movement, which blossomed a
decade later. David Johnson argues that "such consumer items validated
gay men's erotic attraction to other men, contributed to their sense of
participating in a larger community, and provided particular class, race
and gender-based models for what it meant to be gay." Furthermore,
Maria Wyke contends that "beefcake" photographers and publishers, in
order to avoid prosecution, often used the "rhetoric of classicism" to
"safeguard mass-produced but privately consumed visualizations of gay
desire."[34] Neither this circumvention nor any commercial motivation is
mentioned in Weider's account.[35]

E. M. Orlick, however, contends that "Joe did his gay and female
magazines for the money in it."[36] Also, writing to Rader shortly after a
1964 White House scandal jeopardized Lyndon Johnson's election for
president—a top presidential aide was arrested for "disorderly conduct" with another man in a YMCA restroom—Orlick argued Joe
would be a "prime target with his outright homo magazines and may
even get hurt with his other magazines, on which a number of homos
are working."

> Of course this has always disturbed me and the few other so-called nor-
> mal people left. Lud Shusterich [sic], a very fine religious man, (Euro-
> pean Representative) has been violently opposed and vowed he would
> remove all of them from the organization before he was finished. He told
> [the York defector] Gord Venables and I more than once that he felt that
> the homos would eventually destroy Weider and his organization and
> thus all with him.
>
> When Venables went back to Hoffman he was replaced by a homo.
> Gradually they are taking over and you can see their influence in the
> mags. The other homos see their influence in the mags even though the
> average reader may not be aware of it . . . certain expressions, words with
> double meanings, camera angles of physique shots, blurbs, costumes etc.
> etc. Most of them used a number of different aliases.
>
> To add to the confusion Weider may interpret my stand against the
> homos as a stand against him, whereas I would actually be saving him
> from extinction. The *best* thing for him and all of his magazines and for
> his business as a whole would be to get rid of all his homo magazines and
> all of his homo editors, artists, writers etc. With nice, clean acceptable

magazines he could go right into the high schools, colleges, etc. reaching a potential readership into the many millions.[37]

At best, Weider's denial of an active role in producing his gay magazines is self-deception or delusion. At worst it is humbug, which fooled no one in the business.

MR. AMERICA DERIVATIVES

In Weider's and Hoffman's quest for superiority and control of body-builders, iconography continued to play an important role in their promotional strategies. While lip service was still given to "Herculean," "sound mind in a healthy body," "Graecian Torso," "*Discobolus*," and other references to the sport's ancient origins, the most popular symbol of strength, physical development, and manliness in the mid to late 1950s was the Mr. America title.[38] An added attraction in 1956 was the Teenage Mr. America Contest, won by John Podrebarac, of Kansas City, after less than two years of training. At the 1957 version in Berkeley, California, the competition had become keener and was accompanied by a national teen lifting meet. The winner, Mike Ferraro, of Buffalo, eventually became a leading contender for Junior and Senior Mr. America titles.[39] The Weider organization, more than York, appropriated Mr. America associations in its articles, advertisements, and symbolism, featuring stories and pictures of winners, a "Mr. America Improvement Contest," and even an article entitled "What It Takes to Be a Mr. America." One reader was struck by how often the phrase "getting a Mr. America physique" appeared in Weider publications: "You apply this to everybody, it appears."[40] So struck were the Weiders by the Mr. America moniker that they launched *Jr. Mr. America*, a magazine for teenage bodybuilders, in 1956 and relaunched their *Mr. America*, dubbed "The magazine of the Champions," in 1958.

In March 1957 they employed a derivative title, "Mr. America's," for a Pan-American contest in Mexico City featuring contestants from eleven nations. Unlike the Mr. America title, which could be conferred only on U.S. athletes, the Mr. America's award was open to bodybuilders in North, Central, and South America. Despite his criticisms of the AAU, the judging criteria imposed by Ben Weider resembled the new Mr. America rules, including an athletic ability test, posing and stage presence, and an emphasis on the total physique. In a report on the contest, *Muscle Builder* noted: "Physical proportion, muscle tone

Figure 5.1. Harry Johnson, who, in 1959 at age thirty-five, became the oldest bodybuilder to win the Mr. America Contest. Courtesy of Harry Johnson.

and general physical condition were rated above huge muscle girths. A 'balanced' physique earned a top mark." Already, Ben boasted, the Mr. America's title "ranks with the Mr. Universe and Mr. World crowns in bodybuilding importance."[41] Exhibiting more vision than the AAU, whose Mr. America Contest was merely national, the Weiders were moving to a grander, international level.

Only in retrospect can it be seen that the Weiders, by their constant use of Mr. America associations and with their worsening relations with Hoffman and the AAU were inching toward a break from the 1950 accord and another attempt at establishing bodybuilding hegemony. A hint of such ambitions was evident in the resurrection of the IFBB, under Ben's tutelage, as the sponsor of the Mr. America's Contest. But the event that precipitated a crisis was again, as in Philadelphia in 1947 and Virginia Beach in 1956, a Mr. Universe Contest. When Doug Strohl, Joe's entrant at the 1957 event in London, placed well below the leaders, an article questioning the fairness of NABBA judging appeared in *Muscle Builder*. Six months later came an announcement that the IFBB would stage four major physique contests in early 1959 for the titles Mr. Canada, Mr. America, Mr. Universe, and World's Most Muscular Man, however odd it might seem that a second Mr. America Contest should be held—in Canada! Nevertheless, the Weiders likened participation in any of these events to "playing in the World Series or driving at Indianapolis," calling it "the top attainment for the bodybuilder." Unlike what contestants allegedly experienced at AAU and NABBA productions, the Weiders guaranteed them "fair and impartial treatment throughout." Judging would be based on "muscularity, shape, and symmetry—and on nothing else!"[42] Coverage of these events in Weider publications, however, was amazingly slight, although the winners, Chuck Sipes (Mr. America), Germain Godbout (Mr. Canada), Eddie Sylvestre (Mr. Universe), and Tom Sansone (World's Most Muscular Man), had outstanding physiques. Much greater attention was devoted to Sansone as the 1958 AAU Mr. America. According to the Weider author Leroy Colbert, his physique was the product of the "Weider training principles" followed by "every modern bodybuilder." Hoffman and Rader simply viewed Sansone a deserving winner.[43] The Weiders' hyperbole showed a lack of confidence in their own contests and winners; to sustain credibility, they drew on as many associations as possible with the more prestigious AAU event.

ATHLETICS POINTS HULLABALOO

Still, the Weiders' strategy, no doubt relating to their Canadian origins, of raising bodybuilding to an international level of recognition was sound. To stave off this threat, Hoffman continued to send Mr. America winners to the NABBA Mr. Universe Contest for increased exposure. The Weiders' Mr. America Contest and harsh criticism of the AAU version presented a greater problem for Hoffman, especially since Peary Rader, the man most responsible for the current rules structure, seemed to be backtracking. As a result of "some agitation," he believed too large a portion of scoring for most physique contests (50 percent) was devoted to athletic ability and general appearance, since a contestant who was only "average in muscular development and symmetry" might win the title. Other aspects of the classical ideal were questioned: "Education is important, of course, but most certainly it should not be so predominant in a physique contest as to throw it out of balance." Using the Miss America Contest as a guide, Rader believed that the current judging criteria might be limited to just the Mr. America Contest, where "certain qualities" that went "above and beyond" physical development had to be considered, "for the title denotes the ideal of 'American Manhood.'"

Figure 5.2. Milton R. Smith, "Winners of a Recent National Physique Contest": (*left to right*) "Best Chest, Best Abdominals, Mr. America, Biggest Arms, and *Miss America*." Author's possession.

Eventually, the AAU's weightlifting committee, at a 1958 meeting in Chicago, retained the current standards for all "Mr." contests, which were meant to symbolize "the ideal American man or youth," while other physique contests could dispense with athletic and general appearance points.[44] Indeed, athletics points and a winning personality helped the less bulky Harry Johnson edge out Ray Routledge to become (at thirty-five) the oldest Mr. America ever in 1959, and "athletic ability" enabled Elmo Santiago to become Junior Mr. America over a strong field.[45] Still Rader had to explain that "the public too often misunderstands" why athletes with superior physiques, such as the African Americans George Orlando and Art Harris, might place only fourth or eighth at the Mr. America Contest.[46] Even contestants seemed confused about scoring procedures. Johnson, though ecstatic about becoming Mr. America after five attempts, later admitted, "Art had a better physique than mine and should have won the contest."[47]

The issue of athletics points and other nonmuscular criteria was highlighted in a sharply worded exchange between Ed Jubinville, a prominent Massachusetts physical culturist, and Hoffman. Jubinville complained that the 1958 Junior Mr. New England Contest, which usually attracted over twenty-five contestants, had only eight. He checked into the matter for himself: "I've asked quite a few fellows why they didn't enter, the answer is one and the same: 'We don't believe in the Athletic Ability part.'" Bodybuilders believed that the object of that rule was "to eliminate 'Queers' in the game," but Jubinville asserted the needlessness of such a provision: "Out here in New England we know of none, have yet to see any of them use so-called cosmetics or bleach their hair. There is one simple A.A.U. rule that covers this, any entrant may be rejected by SPONSORS OF THE CONTEST." In response, Hoffman revealed both his contempt for bodybuilders whose physiques were not a natural outgrowth of athletic activity and the rationale for current AAU policy.

> [It was] the opinion of the Body Building Committee that when the contest is called Mr. Universe, Mr. America, Mr. New England, or Mr. Holyoke, that our game would be subject to much censor, much ridicule and even hilarity if we were presumptuous enough to pick some of the muscle specimens who have been picked for the Mr. titles. . . . Most body builders are body builders because they can't do anything else. It reached the point at the preliminaries of the Mr. America contest when the members of the committee would say, "What can't you do, snatch, or can't you hold your jerks." Most men who want to enter Mr. contests do

> not have athletic ability, cannot use their muscles. It is the opinion of the national bodybuilding committee . . . that muscles are made to use, and a man should be able to use them.

Hoffman believed if promoters "don't want to follow the Mr. America rules, which include athletic ability, why don't they hold contests just to select the Most Muscular man."[48] For Hoffman, unlike Rader, it was not so much morality but American middle-class ideals, derived from the Greeks, that should dictate criteria at "Mr." contests.

To settle the matter and avoid future misunderstandings, Van Cleef conducted a poll of *Strength & Health* readers. About two-thirds voted that "Mr." events should continue to be held alongside weightlifting contests and that the judges' scores be made public. Nearly three-quarters supported the new scoring system and its emphasis on "athletic skills." One respondent wanted to go "further by introducing some endurance test and other objective physical fitness tests, plus a check on the moral and mental qualifications of the candidates." Even more pleasing to Van Cleef was the 71 percent approval that readers gave to the proposal that Mr. America finalists should display a physical talent, such as tumbling, hand balancing, strength, or flexibility feats. "Not only would it add far greater entertainment variety," he argued, but it would make the public "aware that a superman development and exceptional physical skills go hand in hand." This consideration was a practical matter as much as a nod to classical ideals, as "proved by the national prestige significance the Miss America pageant has gained since making [talent] a factor in the selection of the winners." Most likely a poll of Weider magazine readers, with a greater proportion of bodybuilders, would have yielded contrary results. In fact, Van Cleef was certain that all the "hullabaloo" was being contrived to exploit bodybuilders for personal gain, by one culprit in particular: "The prime offender in this is so well known by his finagling antics that there's no need to identify him."[49]

THE MISS AMERICA TEMPLATE

Ironically, the Miss America Pageant that Van Cleef and others wished to emulate was grappling with similar questions of how properly to project the body to an admiring public. Despite its popularity, the pageant was becoming perceived as staid and boring by the late 1950s and early 1960s—the "status quo sixties," according to one author. Even the choreography added in 1960 to provide life and movement for television viewers "was simple in its complexity and sterile in its sensuality." As the dances became more "torrid" over the ensuing decade, pageant organizers left "no stone unturned in creating a pristine Miss America environment," leaving "the erotically clad Miss America dancers [to] bump and grind with a ferocity incongruent with the rest of the setting." While a modicum of eroticism was necessary to satisfy the growing television audience, it could not infringe on the dignity and middle-class values embodied in the Miss America image. Before the 1959 event, the *Atlantic City Press* illustrated how far the pageant had progressed since its turbulent beginnings in the 1920s: "The winner of the nation's most important beauty title is not merely the most beautiful girl, nor the most talented girl, nor the most intelligent girl. She must be a combination of all these, since the typical American young woman is neither beautiful to the exclusion of all other characteristics, talented beyond measure, nor an 'egghead.'" Similarly vapid sentiments and an air of self-satisfaction permeated articles on Lenora Slaughter and her vision of the ideal Miss America. She was, according to Slaughter, "a girl who possesses the loveliest qualities of womanhood—grace, charm and spiritual beauty." The combination was necessary because "outward beauty alone is not enough."[50]

What lay behind this façade of decency, however, was increasingly the lure of money, quite a lot of it. Although the Miss America organization operated as a nonprofit, it had a budget of $500,000 in 1960, and its sponsors, including General Motors, Pepsi-Cola, and Toni, spent as much as $1 million, mainly on television rights. Indicative of the title's commercialization: the 1953 Miss America, Neva Fickling, estimated that she earned over $100,000 in the year of her reign. By the end of the decade, a Miss America could expect to earn $1 million. Even state winners were earning $20,000. That there was "profit in pulchritude" was unquestionable.[51] Money, almost as much as beauty and wholesomeness, had become embedded in the Miss America Pageant by the early 1960s.

The AAU Mr. America Contest was not nearly as lucrative, and loyalists viewed the Weider Mr. America Contest as little more than an attempt to commercially exploit the title. Bill Wheless, of Austin, Texas, wanted to know who was the real Mr. America for 1959, Harry Johnson or Chuck Sipes. Wheless predicted greater confusion ahead: "It won't be long till there are three or four Miss Americas, Mr. Americas, along with as many Mr. Universes claiming the title each year." The *Strength & Health* editor Bob Hasse dismissed Sipes as a misguided young man who, after tying for ninth place in the 1958 Mr. America Contest, forfeited his chance to become a real Mr. America by "succumbing to the lure of publicity in Weider's string of publications." There was "only one true Mr. America," Hasse stated, "and that is Harry Johnson."[52] But the Weiders were straining to lend credibility to their own Mr. America, even cropping calf, quadriceps, biceps, and latissimus dorsi muscles from a before photograph of Sipes to show how much he had improved by following Weider principles.[53] Plus, they scoffed at AAU claims to exclusive use of the Mr. America title: "Do they possess the title by divine decree? Is it *sacred* . . . and are *they*? No . . . the A.A.U. has no more legal sanction or right to the title than the I.F.B.B. It is NOT a copyrighted title!"[54]

Another mocking jab at the AAU rules seemed irresistible. To be an IFBB Mr. America, unlike the AAU version,

> you *don't* have to prove your athleticism by running the mile—playing a game of tennis—swimming the backstroke. You are not required to throw the javelin—wrestle—you don't have to lift a ton of weights to prove that you're a worthy candidate for championship.
>
> No one will examine your educational background to see if you had a 98.6 average in high school—you'll not be asked to recite a literary selection to prove that you can speak intelligently—no one will examine your mouth to see if you have all 32 teeth![55]

Yet another source of vulnerability was the AAU's decision to hold regional Junior Mr. America contests in 1960 without picking an overall winner. "There are *four* of 'em," mocked *Muscle Builder*, "take your pick! There's a *Junior Mr. A. Eastern Section* . . . a *Junior Mr. A. West Coast Section* . . . a *JMA Southwest Section* and a *JMA Southern Section!* Isn't that the silliest thing you've ever heard? . . . Here's the question, Doc: Is you *is* or is you *ain't* a *Junior-Mr.-America-Eastern-Western-Northern-Southern Section?*" Hardly did the Weiders realize that in their zeal to capitalize on the title, they committed the same impropriety by recognizing the winner of each height division at their 1960 contest in Montreal as a Mr. America.[56] So along with the 1960 AAU winner, Lloyd "Red" Lerille, there were four Mr. Americas and four Junior Mr. Americas, and the title, which both organizations viewed as special, was at risk of losing its uniqueness.[57]

THE IFBB MR. AMERICA

That the title did not lose its luster owes much to its continued recognition as a national symbol, not unlike Miss America, during the Cold War era. The 1960 AAU contest, according to Peary Rader, "was probably the best event ever" for the quality of the physiques on display and the closeness of the competition. Bob Hasse estimated that Lerille, who also took home the prize for most muscular man, impressed the judges not so much by his "symmetry and general excellence" as by his "mass and muscularity," a reversal of previous AAU criteria.[58] Curiously, the Weiders seemed to take an opposite tack, one more in line with classical traditions. A 1960 *Mr. America* article advocated imitation of the "ALL-AROUND PERFECTION of the Greeks who combined the CREATIVE MIND with the MAGNIFICENT BODY." Mental development, effective speech, confidence, a dynamic personality, and personal appearance were all deemed necessary complements to a well-developed physique. In *Muscle Builder*, Joe Weider took aim at the "Giantism Complex," arguing that training just for bulk would ultimately "ruin" a competitor's "Mr. America physique." Bodybuilders, he argued, "should train for *proportion* first" and "then work for muscle size."[59] But the pragmatic Weiders always seemed able to adapt ideals from the past to some current promotional purpose.

Taking a cue from the Miss America Pageant, the IFBB made plans to send its Mr. America and Mr. Universe winners out to make public appearances and offer muscle-building demonstrations throughout the country. To indicate the likely popularity of such an initiative, the Weiders claimed that "long lines of people" had waited outside Montreal's Eaton's department store during the three days of the 1960 competition while "inside, many of the stars who took part in the contest gave stunning demonstrations of the efficacy of weight-training, and boys and men of all ages—not to mention interested mothers and sisters—simply ate it up!"[60] Overlooking the more diminutive IFBB Mr. Americas, Larry Cianchetta and Germain Godbout, the Weider publicity machine featured the winner of the tall man's class, Gene Shuey, of Dallas, Texas, as *the* Mr. America. Heretofore, according to the Weider pitch, Shuey had been merely a draftsman-architect who took acting lessons at night and performed in little theater productions: "Now his muscles by Weider and his thesping by [Konstantin] Stanislavsky have combined to make him a winner! No sooner had talent scouts spotted him in his dynamic posing routine than they rushed to sign him up for several TV appearances in New York. . . .

Yes, your Weider-built muscles can carry you to fame and fortune just as they have done for STEVE REEVES, ED FURY, DICK HARRISON, GORDON SCOTT, LOU DEGNI . . . and now GENE SHUEY!"[61]

Much the same kind of hyperbole was applied to Chuck Sipes, the previous year's winner: "Before his *Mr. America* victory Chuck operated a small Modesto gym which was doing rather well, although not sensationally." But after he won the title, it "flowered into a gigantic Sacramento Health Studio" that was "thriving beyond Chuck's wildest expectations." Furthermore, Sipes had "dozens" of offers for television appearances, Walt Disney productions, and "lucrative posing exhibitions all over California." Supposedly, none of this notoriety would have been possible without his Mr. America victory and the publicity generated by *Muscle Builder* and *Mr. America*, "now read by talent scouts everywhere!"[62] Few readers probably remembered, however, that the 1959 IFBB Mr. America Contest was a small event tucked away in Canada and that the magazines provided almost no coverage of the event. Gene Shuey never became a box-office idol.

Even more dissembling were the remarks of Gord Venables, a defector from the York-AAU ranks, about the 1960 Weider contest. Attempting to draw on the Mr. America–Miss America connection in order to gain credibility for his employers, he noted that "bodybuilding has come a long way" since Johnny Hordines had staged the first Mr. America Contest two decades earlier. Hordines had hoped that "Amsterdam would be to 'Mr. America' what Atlantic City is to 'Miss America.'"

> It didn't work out that way but he started the ball rolling. The ball rolled along until it was picked up and carried by the *International Federation of Body Builders* under the capable direction of Ben Weider. It was carried to a touchdown for the IFBB has made the "Mr. America" title the goal of all bodybuilders in the United States and Canada. I have seen a lot of "Mr. America" shows but none the equal of the Montreal show.[63]

To Venables, it was "The Greatest Show on Earth."

Equally misleading was his take on the Mr. Universe Contest, which had been conducted annually in England since 1948. Venables explained that the object of that event was "to find the best built man in the world!" Doing so was an arduous, expensive task: "That job is difficult; it requires a large organization, a world-wide contact with all bodybuilders and—money. The IFBB took on the staging of the 'Mr. Universe' contest" and "will stage the 1961 show in New York."[64] By sleight of hand, Venables shifted the site of the show, making no mention of Heidenstam's far more prestigious contest in London and giving readers the impression that it had been replaced by the IFBB production.

RAY ROUTLEDGE

Despite all the ballyhoo, there was no IFBB show in 1961. There was only one Mr. America for that year, Ray Routledge, who had been narrowly edged out for the title in 1959 and 1960. Rader was especially pleased, noting, "It would be hard to find a man more representative of ideal American manhood." Routledge not only was serving his country with the air force in Germany, but also was married (with five children), had a good education, and was active in church and civic affairs—"a leader and an example to all the youth of our nation, not just physically, but mentally and spiritually." Lest readers and even some competitors not understand fully the criteria for choosing a Mr. America, Rader pointed out that much more was at stake under the scrutiny of experienced judges than meets the eye, including posture, personality, and character, and flaws in general appearance and muscularity not readily apparent under the glare of bright lights. Rader pointed out that "quite frequently the best built men do not place as high in a contest" as others who "possess some of these other less apparent qualities to a high degree." A Mr. America must "represent the 'Ideal of American Manhood,' not just a physique. He must be a real credit to the title he holds."[65] Van Cleef concurred, noting that the "biggest liability" to the title's acceptance was "the distorted notion that the Mr. America is strictly a physique event." Overall excellence was needed: "A Mr. America must be a first rate athlete and have a quality of character and intelligence of a desirable order, plus having a superman physique." Related to this vision, and closely resembling a practice at the Miss America Pageant, was his idea that the current winner should attend the selection of (though not to crown!) his successor.[66] The only departures from tradition at the 1961 contest were a prejudging session, at which the judges did all the scoring, and the presence of three minorities in the top ten—two blacks (second and fourth) and one Hispanic (seventh)—a harbinger of things to come.

Quite a different view of the AAU affair was offered by Eugene Hanson in *Mr. America*. Though not finding fault with the contestants, Hanson was harshly critical of the organizers, whose chief failing seemed to be that they did not bring the Mr. America Contest up to Miss America standards.

Figure 5.3. Larry Scott, the 1962 IFBB Mr. America and in 1965 the first Mr. Olympia. *Iron Man*, December 1964, 1. Used by permission.

Why was it not nationally televised?

Why Was the auditorium only half filled with spectators? Why was it run off with less drama than a community dog show?

Obviously, the sponsors who have taken over the once glamorous *Mr. America* contest—the tired old men who are the petty tyrants of the AAU—must be blamed.

The Amateur Athletic Union was at its worst in this presentation.[67]

Nevertheless, with no Mr. America of their own in 1961, the Weiders laid claim to the winner of this supposedly flawed production. In "the story of our newest Mr. America," Ben explained how Routledge had been "a total misfit in the athletic department of his school" as a teenager. Then a kind of miracle happened. Routledge, according to Ben, came across an issue of *Muscle Builder* and was impressed by the physiques of such Mr. Americas as Delinger, Ross, and Reeves. So "just a few days later Ray sent for a set of weights and the famous Weider courses and was officially enrolled as a Weider pupil." Then "he began at once to gain in muscle size, in bodyweight, in measurements . . . and—to his surprise—the inch of height that made him a full six feet tall!"[68] An increase in height strains belief, but it was part of an all-out effort by the Weiders, now boasting modern corporate offices in Montreal and Union City, and branches worldwide, to establish credibility among bodybuilders and create a larger-than-life scenario.

Not surprisingly, the York organization, then in litigation with the Weiders over claims of slander, scoffed at its archrival's claims and vehemently objected to criticisms branding the AAU as "obsolete and incompetent." Van Cleef retorted, "Anyone intimately acquainted with the situation is aware that the greater part of this criticism is grossly distorted." As for the Weiders' claim on the 1961 Mr. America, York rebutted with a testimonial from Routledge, who repudiated Ben Weider's article on him: "[It was] published without my knowledge or consent." Routledge went on to disavow completely any connection with the Weiders: "I have *never* met Mr. Weider, spoken with him in person, or over the telephone at any time whatsoever. I have *never* exchanged correspondence or had any monetary dealings with him at any time. This man has exploited me. . . . He has claimed I am one of his star pupils, which is absurd and openly ridiculous." York ads pictured Routledge holding a York barbell, above a caption stating that he had "used York Deluxe Barbells throughout his bodybuilding career."[69]

Refusing to admit defeat, the Weiders argued that their claim on

Routledge as a pupil stemmed from an article entitled "What Weight-Training Has Done for Ray Routledge, Jr.," which was written by Liederman under the pseudonym Jack Black in the July 1958 issue of *Mr. America*: "So if Ray Routledge was a Weider-built champion by his own admission to Earle Liederman, obviously he is still a Weider-built champion." Notwithstanding Liederman's allegations that his articles had been "plagiarized" and published "without permission" after he left the Weiders' organization in 1958, the Weiders insisted that they had "paid for every scrap of information Liederman had to offer," which granted them rights to it.[70] Such questions of publishing rights and fair compensation remained an issue, especially since Liederman was now employed by Hoffman and had become part of the ongoing, litigious feud between York and the Weiders. He certainly never became rich during the fourteen years he worked for the Weiders.

THE 1962 MR. AMERICAS

No such controversies surrounded the 1962 Mr. America, Joe Abbenda, of Long Island City. Even Gord Venables, writing for *Mr. America*, had to admit that the event "went off well." The highlight came when Abbenda displayed his manliness while being awarded the large Mr. America trophy by Miss Highland Park. The audience wanted more: "From the crowd came a dozen shouts of 'Kiss her, Joe, kiss her.' The young lady giggled and Joe blushed. But Joe is a man, and a man that couldn't resist a beauty like the trophy donor." Abbenda was more than just a muscle man to Venables. He was "a swell guy": "He speaks effectively and has a million dollar smile. I doubt they could have picked a better man to wear the mythical Mr. America crown." Peary Rader assumed a loftier air, calling the contestants "the finest in any branch of athletics." They were "interested in self-improvement, not just their physiques, but their minds and morals as well." In fact, they were "fine, clean living young fellows with high ideals and ambitions and most of them are college graduates."[71] It seemed a triumph not only for Abbenda, but also for the AAU Mr. America Contest and everything good about America.

While Abbenda was one of the most popular Mr. Americas, there were strong countercurrents at work. Exactly when anabolic steroids became part of bodybuilding is open to conjecture. Although documentary evidence confirms that Dr. John Ziegler, the "Father of Dianabol," was administering them to York weightlifters as early as 1959, there is some indication that bodybuilders in Chicago and California had had access to a related drug, Nilevar, by 1958. Bill Pearl states that he took "dosages of 30 mg a day for 3 months" five years after he won the Mr. America contest and thereby made rapid gains in body weight and strength, but there is no evidence that other winners of his era took steroids.[72] Abbenda admitted to being the first Mr. America to take them, but only after he won the title and before he became Mr. Universe in London later in 1962. Unaware of the circumstances surrounding Pearl's and Abbenda's use, the 1963 winner, Vern Weaver, stated that he was "the second Mr. America to take steroids."[73] Drugs, and their amazing transformative effects, would accelerate the emphasis on appearance as the sole criterion for judging physique contests.

It was also at the 1962 contest that race became a more serious consideration. Harold Poole, an African American, finished just two points behind Abbenda. In his autobiography, Larry Scott, who did not compete, recalls sitting

> in the nosebleed section of the Santa Monica Civic auditorium watching Joe Abenda [sic] fight it out for the Mr. America title. The show was won by Joe, but frankly from my position and most everyone else in the audience, it looked like it should have gone to a young 19 year old bodybuilder by the name of Harold Poole. There had never been a black Mr. America and everyone suggested there wasn't going to be one this year either. . . . I felt sorry for Harold, but most of my sympathies were for Joe Abenda—the booing was so bad. It made for a hollow victory.[74]

Abbenda, however, vehemently denies Scott's story, saying he was "wrong about the booing" and "did not even attend the contest." There is no evidence of disenchantment with the decision in *Iron Man*, and according to *Strength & Health*, there was "not a single boo or other mark of disapproval."[75] Both magazines displayed pictures of a smiling Poole congratulating the winner. Furthermore, Poole was from Indianapolis, not New York, as Scott claims, and the contest was held in Detroit, not in Santa Monica. What Scott's flawed account does indicate, however, is a retrospective view from the 1990s, conditioned by years of rivalry between the AAU and the IFBB, including disputes over racial matters, for control of muscledom.

It appeared for a while too that the Mr. America contest won by Abbenda might be the only one held that year, since the Weiders were struggling to find a venue. At first Chicoutimi, a remote town 300 miles northeast of Montreal, was chosen, chiefly for its large auditorium. Then the location was switched to the Hotel New Yorker in Manhattan. Finally, along with the IFBB Mr. Universe show, it was moved to the Brooklyn Academy of Music and scheduled for September 15. In the hype that preceded the contests, Joe Weider described in detail the dimensions of the trophies and promised winners movie and television screen tests, stage auditions, a wardrobe of fall fashions by a "world-renown" designer, and "3 fun-packed days in fabulous New York City—AT OUR EXPENSE!" All contestants would receive a solid bronze medallion bearing the inscription "1962 IFFB Mr. Universe–Mr. America Contest" and an etching of "Joe Weider's famous crossed-arms-on-chest pose," by then a standard icon (accompanied by the slogan "Trainer of Champions") in Weider magazines.[76]

Hyperbole reached even greater heights in Weider descriptions of the show itself. "From out of the West they jetted," according to the staff writer Hal Warner, "four young bodybuilders—Californians all— to win, place and show in the *biggest* (it was merely *colossal*!) . . . *bestest* (there has never been another like it!) . . . *fastest* (it lasted five hours but seemed like five minutes!) . . . and *smoothest* (it ticked right along like the 'syncopated clock') *Mr. America–Mr. Universe* show on record!" Winning the Mr. America Contest was Larry Scott, originally from Pocatello, Idaho, who "burst on stage like a bomb shell while the other contestants took to the hills!" He was "the most impressive *Mr. America* of the last decade," exclaimed Warner. The huge muscular dimensions were matched by huge trophies, some larger than the contestants.[77]

Scott, who gained a reputation for his supersized arms ("loaded guns") and "all American boy image," was Weider's first superstar of the 1960s. He had aspired to win the AAU Mr. America title, but after being snubbed by Hoffman, allegedly in Santa Monica, he defected to the Weiders; they assured him that he would be judged "only on [his] physique" and not subjected to AAU politics and "all that other nonsense." The Weiders' decision, however tentative, to stage their contests in New York was a stroke of genius. The spectators were, Scott recalls, highly motivated: "There was no money for the winners, but the outpouring of approval made all the years of work, worthwhile." Yet he still felt an inexplicable void after realizing his most cherished dream.

> I had returned to my room alone about 2 AM with the Mr. America trophy. With oil still seeping from my deeply tanned skin, I caught my reflection in the mirror as I set the trophy on the chest of drawers. . . . I asked myself, "this is it? After all these years and all this hard work, this is all there is to it? Where is the glowing sense of satisfaction and accomplishment?" . . . Yes, I was bigger outside but inside I didn't feel

any more secure or confident than I ever did. . . . I had finally won Mr. America. Here beside me was the trophy to prove it, yet it felt like a hollow victory.[78]

Had Scott entered the AAU version, involving tests of physical, mental, and spiritual qualities, he might have felt more fulfilled. But appearance became the sole criterion for Scott's victory, which catapulted him to stardom, bestowed credibility on the IFBB Mr. America Contest, and enhanced the Weiders' reputation as physique promoters of the first order.

LAST-DITCH REFORMS

Much of the spiritual fulfillment that Scott hankered for was embedded in Rader's aspirations for American manhood. Yet Rader believed that the AAU system was far from perfect and suggested even more reforms, ones that, if accepted, would bring the entrants under scrutiny rivaling that paid to Miss America contestants. Rader believed that an entire day should be devoted to the judging process. The contestants, during the interview phase, would strip "so the judges can observe them for an hour or so while they are relaxed and walking around." Then they would pose under spotlights and under normal lighting. In the interests of fairness and verifiability, athletic points would be determined by whether the contestants could total three and a half times their body weight in the Olympic lifts. Finally, he suggested that the Mr. America show be held in the evening, with no lifting preceding it, and that clinics be held for judges. Van Cleef pointed out that "quite a number of physique contests" were not following AAU protocol in selecting the winners, but that lapse did not seem to deter Rader or AAU leaders from pressing their agenda for a contest to recognize total manhood.[79]

The Weider organization, though pursuing an alternate course, seemed no less intent on seeking the imprimatur of tradition. Capitalizing perhaps on the success of their recent contests in New York, the Weiders again sought respectability by tapping into the AAU power structure. In the December 1962 issue of *Muscle Builder*, Ben Weider expressed a desire to "participate in publicizing and sponsoring AAU-sanctioned weightlifting and physique events." He envisioned an IFBB-AAU accord that would lead to a unified national weightlifting championships and a Mr. America Contest, culminating in an annual Mr. World Contest. The liaison for such a move was the former Mr. America contender Lud Schusterich, who headed the Weiders' European operations.[80] The key to opening any AAU door was Hoffman, and Schusterich had an opportunity when the two shared a room at an international coaches conference in Paris in February 1964. Joe Weider quickly followed up this encounter with a personal bid for cooperation: "Please write Bob that if he desires a get together I will be glad to telephone him, meeting him in Philadelphia or some such place, and spend all the time necessary to work out a good arrangement where one could act as intelligent adults and co-operate for each other's good." When Hoffman did not respond, Schusterich sent a follow-up letter to him and to Rudy Sablo, chairman of the weightlifting committee. But his remark to Bob that "the only barriers to a peaceful get together between rival bodybuilding groups is personality and ego clashes," however true, was probably counterproductive. It is hardly surprising that neither Hoffman nor Sablo responded to Schusterich's appeal.[81] Neither Hoffman nor Joe probably realized at this point the vulnerability of the AAU's position or the potential strength of the IFBB. Societal forces beyond the control of either of these tycoons of sport were about to make an irrevocable impact on the world of Mr. America.

6

THE REAL DIVIDING LINE IN RECENT AMERICAN HISTORY IS THE LINE BETWEEN THOSE WHO LIVED THROUGH THE 1960S AND THOSE WHO DIDN'T. ALL OF US WHO EXPERIENCED THE 60S, THAT PROFOUND UPHEAVAL AFTER WHICH NOTHING WAS EVER THE SAME AGAIN, WERE UNAVOIDABLY MARKED FOR LIFE.

CHRISTOPHER LASCH, "THE BABY BOOMERS"

IN FEBRUARY 1960, THE BRITISH PRIME MINISTER, HAROLD MACMILLAN, famously stated in a visit to Cape Town, South Africa: "The wind of change is blowing through this continent."[1] Macmillan's remarks were seen as a harbinger of colonial liberation, and few could have predicted their relevance in future decades to many areas of social and political life, including the obscure sport of bodybuilding half a world away.

For example, by 1963 numerous blacks had entered the AAU Mr. America Contest, but none had won the top prize. Despite protestations to the contrary by AAU officials, detractors increasingly suspected that the judging process was racially biased. "Our enemies are always trying to show that we are anti-negro, anti-semitic, anti-body-builder or something," noted Bob Hoffman, even though, in his opinion, the AAU was committed to neutrality and objective standards: "We try to pick the best man regardless of club, color, race, creed."[2] Indeed, nothing in Hoffman's past suggested that he held ethnic, religious, or racial biases. However disinclined he was to support bodybuilding for its own sake, his support for minorities was solid. But by the mid-1960s, a new cultural dynamic was sweeping the nation, one that sought a higher standard of fairness and greater empowerment for those not in America's mainstream. That no man of color had ever been crowned Mr. America suggested a flaw in the system. Concurrently, there appeared a black bodybuilder who challenged the AAU's classically based judging tradition.

HAROLD POOLE

No previous black contestant had shown quite so much promise as Harold Poole, a bodybuilder from Indianapolis who entered the Mr. America Contest in 1960 at age sixteen and placed eighteenth, then rose to fourth the following year. Rader observed that he had "the most outstanding physique there from the standpoint of shape, development, definition, and general overall proportions," adding, "Here is a colored boy who has good calves." He had "the foundation for becoming the greatest physique his race has ever produced." Poole, who planned to enter Purdue University, seemed to have it all, and no one was surprised when he was runner-up to Joe Abbenda and winner of the most muscular title in 1962.[3] Nothing seemed to stand in his way of becoming the first black Mr. America. It was obvious, from smiles all round on the winners' dais, that Poole was fully expected to win the top spot the next year.

Unfortunately, those expectations were not realized. At the 1963 contest, held in Harrisburg, Pennsylvania, Poole was again awarded the trophy for most muscular man but was outscored by the York native Vern Weaver, whom he had easily bested in earlier outings. Bob Hasse reported that Poole's muscular development had improved even further and that he "accepted the huge Most Muscular trophy with obvious satisfaction."

> But his reaction to the announcement that he was placed second in Mr. America scoring gave proof positive that he is not yet ready for that honor. Confused and perhaps abetted by hooting and booing from a loud-mouthed minority in the audience, the Indiana teenager foundered on stage, seemingly unable to make up his mind whether he should accept the runner-up trophy or not; when he did, amidst the uproar he continued to move about the stage. Not knowing what to expect next, the emcee . . . had the curtain drawn shut. Some minutes later the curtains

Figure 6.1. The 1963 Mr. America Contest: (*left to right*) Bill Seno (Chicago, fifth place), Vern Weaver (York, winner), Harold Poole (Indianapolis, runner-up and most muscular), Craig Whitehead (New Orleans, third place), and John Gourgott (New Orleans, fourth place). Courtesy of Stark Center.

parted again, and Weaver was announced as the winner. With apparent reluctance, Poole shook the victor's hand. A short time later the five top men were asked to pose as a group on the elevated posing platform. Poole, in tears, hesitated momentarily behind the other four, then walked off stage.[4]

Two weeks later, at the Teenage Mr. America Contest, when Poole was again relegated to second by the surprise winner Jerry Daniels, of Georgia, he repeated his disappearing act, then smashed his trophy offstage.

A flurry of letters to editors ensued from stunned bodybuilding fans, some expressing outrage at Poole's unsportsmanlike conduct and others expressing displeasure with the scoring system that allegedly caused it. "All I can say is that sportsmanship is all very well when you are treated fairly and squarely," sneered a reader from England. An Indianapolis letter to Rader described the audience attending the teenage event as "fighting mad": "As soon as Poole was announced as 2nd place someone from the crowd shouted 'What kind of a fuck goes on here tonight?"'[5] Only one reader raised the subject of race, insisting that Poole had "won the title two years in a row, but because he is a Negro, he is relegated to the 2nd spot."[6] Poole's own story eventually appeared in a 2008 interview.

> There was a general understanding at the time that a black man could not win the AAU Mr. America contest because of some racist attitudes. Before the judging of the 1963 contest I was pumping up backstage with some of the other competitors. A curtain had been put up to give the competitors privacy. York Barbell founder Bob Hoffman came into the area and was talking with York official John Terpak. I guess they didn't know I was on the other side of the curtain. I heard Hoffman tell Terpak, "As long as I run the AAU Mr. America, I have the last word, and no Jew black or Puerto Rican is ever going to win this contest."

Still, Poole decided to compete, "to prove them wrong." When Weaver was named winner and Poole smashed his trophy "against the wall, Hoffman came running over and yelled, 'You will never compete for the AAU Mr. America again!' I shot back, 'Get away from me, you prejudiced son of a bitch, or I will put you in the hospital!'"[7]

Questions, however, surround Poole's account. Why did it take forty-five years for Poole to tell his story, which, in condemning Hoffman, sounds almost staged for posterity as a way to rationalize his loss? Also, unlike the Virginia Beach debacle, there is no corroborating evidence for his version of events, which differs somewhat from other accounts. Poole, according to *Iron Man*, crashed his trophy "to the floor in little pieces" rather than "against the wall," and this might be a trivial discrepancy, but the expression of outrage occurred at the Teenage Mr. America Contest, not the Mr. America Contest, which casts doubt on his description of Hoffman's reaction. Poole also makes no mention of his having shown up for the teenage event six hours late on the first night of judging; though disqualified from the most muscular man event, he was allowed to enter the Teenage Mr. America Contest on the second night. A racially prejudiced panel would hardly have made such a concession. In a broader view of this incident, it is obvious from his depiction of Weaver as "smooth as glass" that Poole's view of judging criteria, though shared by the majority of fans, differed from the AAU Mr. America rules and tradition, and the incongruence could easily be misinterpreted as "a general understanding" that blacks could not win the contest because of "racist attitudes." Yet the incident enabled Rick Wayne to say that Poole was "to black bodybuilding . . . what Joe Louis and Muhammad Ali had each in turn been to race and boxing."[8] Certainly, no one at the time realized that they were witnessing the dawn of the civil rights movement in bodybuilding.

AAU officials, oblivious of these developments, continued responding to criticisms by citing the facts of the selection process. Hoffman explained that six of the seven judges rated Weaver ahead of Poole, mainly because of symmetry and general appearance. Poole had the edge in muscularity, for which he was recognized as most muscular man. Both contestants received maximum athletic points. To refute any charge of racism, Hoffman noted that the only black judge, Rudy Sablo, rated Weaver a half point higher than Poole in total scoring. Sablo's placement, like those of the white judges, reflected the idealism of the times. He recalled later, "Mr. America was to be a complete physique, and Poole didn't have that."[9] Poole's most serious handicap, according to another AAU official, Ralph Countryman, was a severe speech defect, which supposedly cost him victory in 1962. Seeking a remedy, Poole enrolled in an institute for stammerers, but the impediment persisted, and was likely a factor in his 1963 setbacks. Bob Crist, a future national AAU chairman, recalled that Poole "looked great" at Harrisburg, but "people talked about his having a speech impediment." Bob Bendel, a veteran judge of about twenty-five national physique panels, thought that Poole "should have won," but he was disappointed in his behavior. Val Vasilieff, who placed ninth, believed that "Weaver should have won over Poole. . . . When he did a back shot the place went wild."[10] However justified Weaver's selection might have been, nothing could console Poole, and it was no surprise that he soon found employment with Weider Enterprises in Union City.

Peary Rader, seemingly stunned by the fallout from the 1963 contests, called for "some outside group" to take them over to prevent further tarnishing of the Mr. America image: "Too many incidents such as we saw at the Mr. America and the Teen Age Mr. America, are causing the contests to deteriorate in the eyes of the public." Instead of defending the criteria that he had been so instrumental in implementing over the previous decade, he beat a quick retreat in an effort to disengage himself from responsibility for unpopular decisions. The judges, he noted, had a difficult decision and "did what they believed was right whether or not anyone agreed with them."[11] Playing the role of Pontius Pilate, Rader remained aloof as letters poured into his office questioning Poole's runner-up placement. He explained that judges and AAU officials worked with a broad set of standards.

A Mr. America is different from any other physique title holder and must be able not only to display a first class physique but also to be able to appear in public and give lectures and represent the ideal of American manhood in other ways than physique. I have felt, many times in the past, that men with inferior physiques (not the best, I mean), have been selected as Mr. America because of these other rather intangible qualities. This (of course) makes for disapproval with the audience and public because they see only the physique. It is somewhat similar to the Miss America, where I feel they pick one of the less beautiful girls because of other qualities the judges think are required. There is no question but that Harold had the finest physique by far at the Teen Age nationals, according to men who were there . . . but here again other factors were involved in the placing.[12]

Vern Weaver found the discussions in *Iron Man* disturbing and accused Rader of stirring up enmity against him. "I, as 'Mr. America' 1963 would prefer to live out this year with the least amount of contempt as possible. I find it very difficult to elevate the meaning of the 'Mr. America' title as long as contemptuous premises continue to be injected into the contest itself."[13]

Decades later, Weaver remained bitter. He felt that Poole had a good physique but that his own symmetry was better: "Poole had teeth missing. He was the typical muscle-head with few social graces." It is impossible to know how much any lingering resentment contributed to Weaver's eventual suicide, but he always felt that the controversy engendered by Poole "threw a cloud" over his title. The York aide Dick Smith, for whom Weaver was "like a kid brother," viewed him as a magnificently endowed person who always had deep-seated problems. "I said, 'Vern, suicide is a permanent solution to a temporary problem.' But he said, 'My problems are not temporary.'" Smith was "close to a lot of the Mr. Americas, but after Vern took his life, I didn't have the same feeling for bodybuilding."[14]

A FLESHY ALTERNATIVE

Benefiting most from the controversy was the Weider organization. AAU troubles as well as the success of the IFBB's previous year's event energized the Weiders for their 1963 contests, to be held in Brooklyn. To their Mr. America title, won by Reg Lewis, they added a Miss Americana event, a play on the Miss America title, which was won by Lewis's wife, Sheri. But it was obvious that the criteria used for the female contest were nothing like those Lenora Slaughter had implemented for

Miss America. It was a beauty show, a fitting complement to the IFBB Mr. America, at which physical appearance was the only factor. "As each gal stepped into the spot to parade before the fans," reported *Muscle Builder*, "cheers and applause drowned out the band's music—and encouraged each contestant to give her very best." What "give her very best" meant was not explained, but it was a sexist display, reminiscent of King Neptune gazing at the entrants in Miss America shows of the 1920s. Hoping to satisfy a largely male audience, the Weiders, according to the journalist Gene Mozee, "got their first Miss Americana contestants mainly out of local strip clubs."[15] But the Americana contest was too obscure to spawn protests from the feminist movement, still in its infancy.

Above all, the 1963 contests were designed to show how many AAU bodybuilders had come "over the fence" to join the IFBB. Fourteen were identified, including such champions as Arthur Harris, Hugo Labra, Carlos Rodriguez, and Freddy Ortiz. During intermission fans gathered in the lobby to discuss the "great beauties and muscular giants" they had just seen. "Many notables in the AAU" were congratulating their friends and admiring the six-foot trophies. "Among them," noted *Muscle Builder*, "was Joe Abbenda, who especially wanted to see his ex-rivals." Climaxing the festivities was the Mr. Universe Contest, won by Harold Poole. Racial discrimination was never cited in the IFBB official report, but lest anyone miss the point, readers were assured that Poole, "one of the greatest bodybuilders in the world," had "for some unknown reason—failed to make the mark with the AAU." He was the Weiders' "star attraction."[16]

Unlike some of the Weiders' previous reports, descriptions of their 1963 contests were no idle boasts. Nearly ninety men competed, noted Ben, compared with just fifty-six in 1962. A live band, as well as performers doing hand balancing, strength feats, and karate, entertained spectators between competitions. Afterward, Bud Parker, who orchestrated the affair, held a victory party at his home for about 150 bodybuilders and guests, "making it the largest gathering of muscle stars ever." "It was a great party," according to *Muscle Builder*, "good company and good food." Parties were "becoming a traditional part of Weider/Parker IFBB shows," serving as a "perfect 'nightcap' to a great competition." Significantly, the Weider show drew attendees from all over the country, along with nineteen foreign contestants, chiefly from Canada and the Caribbean.[17] Owing to Ben Weider's efforts, the IFBB was becoming an international entity.

What enabled the Weiders to achieve such success at their 1963 show, according to Joe, was the absence of a point system or any other sort of objective measure to quantify subjective impressions. "Muscular development should be the determining factor in any physique contest," he explained. "If you start with experts who have been in the field for years . . . who are well aware of what constitutes a good physique according to the times, then these men will determine the winners regardless of points." Ultimate justification for such a system, Weider believed, was "the mass audience—whose roars of approval clearly indicated that the judges' decisions were also the popular—or, choice of all."[18] Implicit in these statements was the notion that little counted in IFBB judging aside from muscularity, and decisions were rooted more in the proletarian standard of pleasing the crowd and less in any idealistic standards of manhood or respect for bodybuilding traditions.

It was a new era of physical culture, and the Weider organization appeared to be in the vanguard. Bodybuilders, utilizing such novel principles as "cheating" and "triple range training," were encouraged by the "trainer of champions" to "bomb" and "blitz" their muscles to unprecedented heights.[19] Physiques were bigger and more muscular, owing in part to the impact of anabolic steroids. Since their introduction by John Ziegler to York weightlifters, the drugs had spread to other sports, but they were having the most striking impact on bodybuilders. *Muscle Builder* reported that "the phenomenal muscular growth of Joe Abbenda and Bill Pearl . . . may be due, in part, to *Dianabol*," and another former AAU Mr. America, Tom Sansone, was rumored to be taking either Dianabol or Nilevar.[20] The Weiders and other promoters warned against the dangers of tissue-building drugs, but featured prominently in their magazines were musclemen who benefited from steroids.

Whether Weider publications did it more flagrantly than others is debatable, but it is indisputable that the Weiders were the foremost at using sex to publicize their products and programs, especially through visual images. In a 1964 article in *Mr. America*, Betty Weider, Joe's wife and "winner of innumerable beauty contests," is pictured with the former Mr. America Larry Scott. She queries young men: "Are you the epitome of manliness? Or do you look like something the cat dragged in? Are your shoulders capped with masses of muscle, or are they bony protrusions? Are your arms skinny pipe-stems, do your ribs look like Venetian blinds, do your legs look like skinny twigs? . . . Make no mistake . . . a beautiful girl wants a real he-man, a *Mr. America* type for her companion." The best way, of course, to a real he-man physique that would satisfy "Miss America" was through Weider methods—utilizing weight sets, courses, and "the latest Weider product, *Crash Weight-Gaining Formula #7:*" "With it you can gain up to 15 pounds of solid, he-man muscle; add an inch or more to your arms; about 2 inches to your chest in just the next two weeks!"[21] Much the same pitch was evident in an article entitled "Why You Can't Find a Girl," which appeared in Weider's new publication, *Young Mr. America*; Betty was featured with the 1963 Mr. America, Reg Lewis. In the same issue, Russell Fornwalt assured young readers that a surefire way to develop sex appeal is to build one's muscles "fully and symmetrically" by using Weider food supplements.[22] Glitz and glamour, and an emphasis on physical appearance, characterized the Weider style.

RETHINKING MR. AMERICA

Occasionally, Weider publications recognized the Greek origins of body-building, with such articles as "That Classical Look for Physical Perfection" or "The Quest for Beauty is Eternal," but any connection between ancient ideals and the aspirations of scrawny youth for big muscles was hardly obvious.[23] Admiration for the ancients was more evident in rival magazines. "The Greeks considered a strong and beautiful human frame as important as a good mind," wrote A. J. Papalas in a 1964 article titled "Dietary Habits of the Ancient Greek Athlete" in *Strength & Health*. In the same magazine two years later, the champion weightlifter Bill March observed, "It seems very silly . . . to have a body that looks like a Greek god and not have the strength to go along with the image." In 1968 in *Muscular Development*, David Willoughby traced the history of the Hercules legend through a set of illustrations, including the oil painting of the twelve labors of Hercules displayed in the foyer of the York Barbell headquarters. Pictures of Greek sculpture accompanied Otto Wolfgang's 1968 article "How to Become a Male Artist's Model" in *Muscle Training Illustrated*, which advised prospects to study Greek and Roman statuary along with modern muscle magazines featuring graceful poses by some of the world's best-built men.[24] But it was the support for all-around development in the Mr. America Contest that did more than journalistic wisdom to keep the idea alive. This spirit was best embodied in a trophy inspired by the Farnese Hercules. Donated by Karo Whitfield of Atlanta and awarded to the "Best Built Weightlifter" at the 1963 Senior Nationals, it was won by John Gourgott, of New Orleans, who placed fifth in the mid-heavyweight class and fourth in the Mr. America Contest. Quite unknowingly, he epitomized amateur athleticism.[25]

In the wake of the controversies surrounding Poole in 1963, attention was focused on the need for further revision of rules and the relevance of athletics points. Again Rader took the lead, arguing that at one time weightlifting and bodybuilding were "almost synonymous" and that it seemed "natural that lifting and physique contests should be held together." But times had changed: "Today there is very little in common between bodybuilders and weightlifters. . . . I know of few, if any, bodybuilders who approve the athletic points used in selecting a Mr. America." Though less willing to compromise on education and character issues, Rader could see that his moral crusade for a Mr. America who was "truly representative of ideal American manhood in every respect" was being questioned: "I still feel this way, but apparently Mr. Public does not agree with me, for he voices vociferous objection to the selection of anything but a physical specimen." Richard Cavaler, who joined the Michigan AAU in 1965, reflected a growing sentiment. He was disgusted by the "mumbo-jumbo" part of the Mr. America Contest, which resembled "the Miss America Contest where Bert Parks asked them questions." The athletes hated it because it "had nothing to do with bodybuilding." They felt like "trained animals" from having to "look perfect and act goody-goody." As Randy Roach notes, "The voice of the times was demanding victory for the most muscular physique regardless of whether it could lift, run, jump, walk, or talk."

To accommodate these competing visions, Rader brought two resolutions to the 1963 national AAU convention. First, the AAU should drop the Mr. America Contest and let an outside group handle it "somewhat in the manner of the Miss America contest." Failing that, he would request a separate AAU committee to administer it. Owing to "red tape," neither plan succeeded.[26] Hence the Mr. America Contest, along with many lesser titles under AAU sanction, remained shackled to weightlifting and forced to perpetuate the notion that physique shows were athletic contests and somehow related to the Miss America Pageant.

For the Weider brothers, the picture was clearer. Having been excluded from weightlifting over the previous decade, they were actively promoting bodybuilding as an alternative.[27] Emboldened by their successful shows in 1963 and 1964, Joe announced his organization's divorce from weightlifting, athleticism, and any traditional distinctions between amateurs and professionals.

> The IFBB recognizes the fact that bodybuilders train for one sport and one sport only. Bodybuilding is that sport—the building of as perfect a

body as possible. . . . Therefore, the IFBB recognizes that bodybuilders are not interested in participating in amateur events, and that being an amateur is of no value in a bodybuilder. He will never enter swimming events, athletic events or weightlifting events. The bodybuilder knows he can never win them or rise to top honors and be great in bodybuilding. He has one purpose—to be a champion in muscle building and win "Mr. Perfect" titles.[28]

Contrary to AAU contests, at which winners were often booed because of a selection system that awarded points for "sports ability, diction, clothed appearance, I.Q., and the like," IFBB winners were picked "solely on muscular development," and decisions were always in "full accord with the critical fans," Weider contended.[29]

Ironically, while Joe was trying to please the bodybuilding masses by disallowing athletic tests at Weider competitions, he was pursuing closer connections with the highest level of weightlifting officialdom, seeking to trump AAU influence and give the IFBB international credibility. Since the early 1950s, Hoffman had been sending winners of the Mr. America Contest to London to compete in the NABBA Mr. Universe Contest. Meanwhile, the Weiders had developed a close association with Oscar State, secretary of the International Weightlifting Federation (IWF) and an adversary of Oscar Heidenstam and NABBA.[30] The IWF had been conducting a Mr. Universe Contest off and on since 1954. Through connections with State, Weider hoped to revitalize this event and use it both to provide a higher level of competition and to exercise influence over the parent body of AAU weightlifting, heretofore controlled by Hoffman. Joe intended to send winners of his Mr. America and Mr. Universe contests to the IWF affair annually. State admitted to Rader that Joe paid him "very handsomely" for his "contributions" (articles and reports for Weider publications, as well as political leverage), and Bob Hasse observed that State was "making no bones about giving the F.I.H.C. [IWF] to Weider." He predicted that "some real fire will come of this."[31]

Ben Weider had an even more grandiose idea: getting the sport into the Olympics. He later recalled, "The Olympic quest [became] the focus of my professional life."[32] Had bodybuilding become an Olympic sport, it would have been the ultimate reconciliation of an activity epitomizing form, as defined by Joe in the 1960s, with an event symbolizing the highest level of functionality.

THE CARIBBEAN CONNECTION

Ben's internationalization ideas, however, served a more immediate function of providing a means to break down racial barriers, potentially a key factor in hitting the AAU where it was most vulnerable. Repeatedly, as if to imply strongly that the AAU Mr. America Contest discriminated against blacks and Hispanics, the Weiders insisted that "every bodybuilder regardless of race, color, creed or birthplace has an equal chance to win an IFBB title!" But however much any individual judge may have had a racial agenda, the AAU Mr. America and its weight-lifting counterpart were as open to minorities as ever. It was just that the Weiders, either for prestige or commercial purposes, were eagerly recruiting newfound talent, especially from the Caribbean, which had the effect of giving the AAU an archaic appearance. At the Weiders' 1960 show in Montreal, Chuck Sipes became Mr. Universe, but the hit of the evening was the "phenomenal" Serge Nubret, Mr. Guadeloupe, who won the most muscular man award and, according to Gord Venables, "all but 'stole the show.'"[33] Also receiving lavish praise was Michel Hercules, twice Mr. Trinidad and runner-up to Sipes. So great were the superlatives used to describe these two dark-skinned athletes in Weider magazines that one wonders how they could possibly have not won. Ben vividly describes the impact of Nubret.

> Bodybuilder after champion bodybuilder, star after noted star had filed across the great stage of Montreal's Monument Nationale to the enthusiastic applause of the huge audience. Then it happened! . . . What an awe-inspiring sight it was when Serge Nubret strode majestically across the stage and confidently mounted the podium. With all the ease of a professional he went through pose after pose. . . . At each new revelation the audience cheered Serge to the echo and when he departed from the stage they stood up as one man and yelled themselves hoarse!

Equally overwhelming was the "terrific muscularity" of Hercules, whom Weider called the "Titan of the Tropics": "I had never seen anyone like him! . . . My poor old typewriter can't begin to tell you about Michel Hercules—you just have to see him in person . . . what a man!"[34]

Of the West Indian stars lured to the IFBB, none had greater impact than Rick Wayne (born Learie Carasco), from the tiny island of St. Lucia. After immigrating to Britain at the dawn of the swinging sixties, he soon gained notoriety as an entertainer and bodybuilder. Wayne became, declared Ben Weider, "England's golden-throated 'Music Man' with Muscle": "The lights dim in a fashionable London nite club. Action ceases on the dance floor as the girls hold their collective breath. The spotlight falls on a young, lithe, and good-looking West Indian boy. Walking amidst the enthralled audience he glides over to the mike . . . then . . . Wham! As he opens his mouth to sing the girls in his audience open theirs to scream and swoon. Ricky Wayne has enchanted another packed house." When Wayne, sporting twenty-inch arms, won the Mr. Britain Contest in 1963, Weider likened it to "Frank Sinatra winning the *Mr. America* title!"[35] In 1965 he made his American debut, placing second to the Barbadian Earl Maynard in the IFBB Mr. Universe Contest amidst an audience that was predominantly black and Puerto Rican. Eventually, Wayne won the IFBB Mr. World (1967) and the WBBG Mr. America (1970) titles.

In the Weiders' competitions, then, seemingly unlike the AAU Mr. America Contest, was a climate of congeniality and welcome for black bodybuilders, especially for those from French islands in the Caribbean.

Figure 6.2. The "Blond Bomber," Dave Draper, winning the 1965 IFBB Mr. America Contest. Author's possession.

Nor were there any athletic points or other criteria to complicate the judging—just muscularity. The Weider brothers' Jewishness may have led them to take this inclusive approach, but an unmistakable bond was evident. It was reinforced by the presence of IFBB representatives, contests, and products in the Caribbean, first in Trinidad and Jamaica, then in Martinique and Guadeloupe. The West Indies was a "bee-hive of athletic activities," observed Bud Parker in *Muscle Builder* in 1963, and bodybuilding was "playing a vital role in creating and maintaining this interest." Bodybuilders and their admirers were alike caught up in the fervor: "Contests attract as many as fifty contestants and one-thousand spectators"[36] Nubret and Hercules were simply the most notable of many Caribbean bodybuilders showing up at the Weiders' contests and appearing in their magazines. That they were so prevalent in a Mr. Universe Contest held in Canada, never a natural site for a Mr. America Contest, further boosted the IFBB's international appeal.

No less impressive was "fabulous" Freddy Ortiz, a Puerto Rican who moved to Brooklyn in 1958. After being discovered by Bud Parker's brother at a concession stand on Coney Island in 1962, he was encouraged to enter the upcoming IFBB Mr. Universe Contest. Despite having never competed, Ortiz won first place and the award for most muscular in the short-man's class. The reporter Hal Warner observed that "he gave a display of muscular perfection that was as poised and well-presented as that by any veteran muscle man. . . . He's real Mr. America Material!"[37] Soon Freddy, as "America's Newest Muscular Sensation," was appearing in virtually every issue of the Weider magazines—as cover model, purveyor of products (often with an attractive female on his shoulders), and author of articles on building a prize-winning physique. Most striking were Ortiz's arms, alleged to be 19", even though he was barely 5'6". In 1963, he was runner-up at the IFBB Mr. America Contest, where he was joined by many other entrants from the islands, most notably Mike Torres and Carlos Rodriguez from his homeland. Rodriguez, an ex-marine who had placed twenty-sixth in the recent AAU Mr. America Contest, was especially impressive.[38] Clearly, the Weider welcome mat was out for Caribbean bodybuilders, many of whom had defected from the AAU in order to win titles and fame (but little money!) with the IFBB.[39]

Bodybuilders of color were much in evidence at major Weider shows in 1964 and 1965 at the Brooklyn Academy of Music. *Iron Man* reported that the 1964 extravaganza was "a really sensational show, the best seen by many in years." Harold Poole became the IFBB Mr. America, and

Christopher Forde, of Trinidad, won the tall class and most muscular man award in the Mr. Universe Contest. Ortiz was "simply sensational" in the Mr. America event, as well as the show's best poser. According to the magazine: "He can control a crowd with master precision."[40] Only Poole's more muscular legs enabled him to edge out Ortiz.

Likewise in the Miss Americana Contest the emphasis was on the body. "Unlike the men, the girls don't use a posing dais," reported Bud Parker: "They walk onto the stage into the center area and go through a very pretty routine. One follows the other—and after each gal, the statistics on the next one are given. Each contestant poses and then steps into the stage wings. Later, after the individual posing—all the contestants come back so that the judges and fans see them together." Unlike the men, the Miss Americana contestants lacked luster, somewhat reminiscent of Miss America shows of the 1920s. Although "the fans cheered and whistled approval," according to Parker, the greatest crowd-pleaser was Larry Scott, who copped the 1964 Mr. Universe title. Parker raved: "In all my years in the Iron Game I have never witnessed anything like it. . . . Scott is a master of the platform. . . . Not since the days of Reeves has any one bodybuilder received such an ovation."[41]

The 1965 Weider extravaganza was an even bigger affair, not least because of Dave Draper, a native of New Jersey who later gained fame as the "Blond Bomber." Although he easily bested Chester Yorton, another white contestant, in the Mr. America Contest, the Mr. Universe title again featured a heavy Caribbean presence; six men of color represented Trinidad and Tobago alone. The winner was Earl Maynard, who had also won the 1964 NABBA Mr. Universe Contest. The new Mr. Olympia Contest, though won by the inimitable Larry Scott, was a showdown with Maynard and Harold Poole. Audience approval, so important in Weider competitions, was much in evidence, observed a *Mr. America* report. For Scott, "the crowd cheered louder than anyone . . . in any contest before," and Draper and Maynard "received the greatest ovation of all contestants" in their respective events. What made the contest special, according to Draper, was its "spontaneity" and "energy" and the magnificent field it attracted, including the future great Frank Zane. Even Draper's father, who was in the audience, was besieged by autograph seekers. "Muscle up," was the message conveyed in *Mr. America*, "you're in the Weider generation of champions."[42]

THE WEIGHT OF TRADITION

From the Weiders' perspective, AAU physique shows were languishing under the weight of tradition. Draper noted that the AAU was still powerful, but it was "losing ground" in a world that was "paying attention to the IFBB Mr. America," which was unencumbered by athletic points. In an editorial, "How the IFBB Is Saving Bodybuilding," Joe Weider described this changing state of affairs while recounting the 1965 Mr. North America Contest, held in Montreal by the AAU after the weightlifting championships. In contrast to IFBB shows, it attracted only five contestants.

> [It] was held as an "afterthought"—at 2 in the morning, before an audience of approximately 150. It was boring . . . it was tiring . . . it came and went as if it had never happened.
>   Who knew about the contest? Almost no one! Who covered the event? Almost no one! Who came to see the event? Almost no one!
>   Such are the affairs of the AAU . . . so low are its standards. If the IFBB weren't on the scene to rescue bodybuilding from the stranglehold of the AAU, our sport would die a quick death.

Weider rightly recognized that American weightlifting, controlled by the same clique, was also declining. "We cannot help weightlifting, but we can boost bodybuilding because our hands are not tied here—and because the IFBB is the leading bodybuilding organization throughout the world."[43]

The Weiders focused their attention on Rader, who, as an unaligned supporter of the AAU, must have seemed vulnerable to co-optation. One of their writers, Jon Twichell, insisted to Rader in 1964 that the AAU could hardly match the current list of IFBB champions, who were "judged solely on physique." Ben Weider, boasting that his organization had affiliates in forty-four countries, invited Rader to join the IFBB board of directors. And John Valentine, who distributed American magazines in Britain, reported to Rader that *Strength & Health* and *Iron Man* were being edged out: "The Cockney boys are all flocking to the Weider banner."[44] But only in retrospect can it be seen that the AAU hold on bodybuilding was slipping.

Most AAU traditionalists were prepared to make no such admission. The selection of Val Vasilieff, of Sicklerville, New Jersey, as the 1964 Mr. America was, according to Rader, "a fairly popular one," as was the selection of Chicago's Bill Seno as most muscular man. To Hoffman,

Vasilieff was an ideal choice: "He is handsome, he is symmetrical and best of all he is strong." At a *Strength & Health* picnic, he "deadlifted 600 pounds without a warmup" at 198 body weight. But his most impressive feat was a one-arm curl of 135 pounds, which was "the talk of the contest!"[45] As always for Hoffman, functional muscles led to pleasing form. Rader was most impressed with third-place finisher Randy Watson, who had "a terrific posing routine" and near faultless physique: "He is very handsome, with a dynamic, sparkling personality, is well educated and has fine character." As a Church of Christ minister in Manchester, Tennessee, he trained parishioners in his church basement gym. Most extraordinary was the eighth-place finish of John DeCola, of Framingham, Massachusetts, who had recently beaten Vasilieff for the Junior Mr. America title. "What happened????" was the reaction of the *Iron Man* columnist Bob Hise. What happened was that DeCola earned only three athletic points, although he had received a full five at the Juniors. Although a bad back prevented him from doing the Olympic lifts, Rader could see "no weak points" on his "marvelous physique," leading him further to question AAU scoring procedures. When DeCola approached Hoffman about the anomaly, hoping for some understanding, "Bob remained silent."[46]

SERGIO OLIVA

The most spectacular bodybuilder to emerge from the 1964 contest, however, was Sergio Oliva, a dark-skinned Cuban weightlifter who had defected from his team at the Central American Games in Jamaica in 1962 and moved to Chicago, leaving behind a family of eleven brothers and nine sisters. Although Oliva placed only seventh, he was "one of the most muscular men we have ever seen," remarked Rader. "His shoulders are very, very broad and tremendously muscled, and he tapers down to an unbelievably small waist." To the Chicagoan John Balik, "It was Bosco come to life!"[47]

In 1965, Oliva rose to second place and was named most muscular man, but the AAU scoring system denied him the top title. It went to the massive and symmetrical Jerry Daniels, who, according to Gene Mozee, represented "the best all-round ideal specimen of American manhood both physically and mentally."[48] As Rader explained to Jon Twichell:

> There is no question but that Olivia [*sic*] has the best physique by far, he was very outstanding. However considering the method by which the

> Mr. America contest is judged, it was not unusual that he did not win. Due to the fact that he is not a citizen and also it is very difficult for him to speak the English language, even though he had the outstanding physique of the show, he, in the eyes of the judges probably would not have made a representative Mr. America in other respects.[49]

Ironically, Rader had just used his influence on AAU ruling councils to place more emphasis on physique in the Mr. America Contest by separating it from the lifting competition, discarding the point system, and lessening the criterion of athletic ability.

Although Daniels had already bested Oliva for the 1965 Junior Mr. America title, the result at the senior contest surprised fans at the Embassy Auditorium in Los Angeles *Strength & Health* reported: "Oliva was definitely the favorite of the audience and competitors alike and received by far the greatest ovation of any of the contestants." Daniels also expressed surprise: "When they called out my name as the winner, it felt like my blood just stopped running through my veins."[50] According to the second runner-up, Bob Gajda, Daniels was in a state of "disbelief," saying, "'I don't believe it, I don't believe it.' And I don't either," Gajda said. Oliva was "very upset."[51]

In 1966, after Oliva won the Junior Mr. America title over Gajda, his training partner, expectations were high that he would become the first black Mr. America. But again he was denied the grand prize, chiefly because of his broken English and some physical flaws, and had to settle for most muscular man. Oliva accepted his placement with both a sense of humor and a racial barb: "The AAU guys who don't know the Civil War is over say Gajda is the winner when everyone in the house knew it was me." From that point on, said Oliva, "[It was] goodbye AAU for me and hello IFBB and super-bodybuilding status."[52]

After defecting to Weider, Oliva won the Mr. World title. A year later he beat such greats as Poole, Draper, and Sipes to become Mr. Olympia. "Sock it to me, baby!" he screamed as he rammed a fist full of hundred-dollar bills and an engraved silver platter overhead. Oliva likened his departure from the AAU ("Antique Archaic Underdogs") to his 1962 escape from "Castroland."[53] Years later, Rick Wayne put a racial spin on this event. "He had the best possible revenge for the AAU's injustices to his race; he'd landed bodybuilding with a new king—who was black!"[54] In retrospect, however, Oliva regarded the Weiders not as racist, but as little better than the old AAU establishment: "Joe Weider was a businessman that I didn't trust. In my opinion, and the opinion of many, he was only after one thing—money and he didn't give a damn about whom he screwed along the way. . . . I admit that Joe Weider made bodybuilding what it is today. . . . But it's also true that he pulled all kinds of tricks, changed judges, changed votes in competitions and did as he pleased."[55] According to his fellow islander Ken Rosa, Oliva "doesn't call himself black, but calls himself Cuban."[56] Like many others from the Caribbean, Oliva seemed oblivious of the color line and viewed bodybuilding as a highway to success. But he learned that he did not fit the cultural expectations of the Mr. America Contest.

The Weiders were much more attuned to cultural change, and their exploitation of the rich bodybuilding potential of the Caribbean was in full swing. "If you were to visit the Weider sales office in Union City any day," remarked Ortiz, "you would find it necessary to understand Spanish. Spanish-speaking bodybuilders from all over the globe are always here on their visits to New York." Reports, promotions, and contests steadily drifted in from such IFBB hotbeds as Venezuela, the Bahamas, and Trinidad and Tobago.[57] So great was the influx of international bodybuilders that the IFBB instigated a new Mr. World title, the first five winners of which—Jose Casteneda Lence (Mexico), Jorge Brisco (Argentina), Kingsley Poitier (Bahamas), Sergio Oliva (Cuba), and Rick Wayne (St. Lucia)—hailed from south of the border. Wayne recalled that leading musclemen from the Caribbean, "mainly Puerto Rico and blacks from the Bahamas, Jamaica, and Trinidad—were making hot names for themselves via Weider's *Muscle Builder* magazine" and were "at the front lines in the wars against York."[58] The Weiders were not only tapping some of the best-built men in the hemisphere, but also creating a host of international titles that challenged the Mr. America title for prestige in the eyes of bodybuilding enthusiasts.

THE WORLD BODYBUILDING GUILD

Another outlet for these energies appeared in 1965 with the creation of the World Bodybuilding Guild (WBBG) by the veteran promoter Dan Lurie, who misleadingly claimed to be "Winner of More 'Mr. America' Titles than Any Athlete Living." Lurie's organ, *Muscle Training Illustrated*, drew heavily on New York's immigrant community and was made possible, as Randy Roach points out, by Lurie's television earnings as Sealtest Dan the Muscleman on Sealtest Dairy's popular *Big Top* circus show over the previous decade.[59] In blatant imitation of the AAU and IFBB Mr. America contests, Lurie launched a "Mr. Americas" Contest in 1967 at Roosevelt Auditorium, offering $1,000 in prize money. He declared a "new bodybuilding era" in which everyone could compete, "regardless of whose products he plugged, whose system he claimed he followed, what food supplements he ate, or anything else."[60] Although Harold Poole won the title, entrants from the islands were much in evidence; George Paine (Cuba) placed third, Elliot Gilchrist (Grenada) fourth, and Warren Frederick (Antigua) fifth—all men of color. Lurie also tapped Bob Russell, who had hosted the Miss America Contest for twelve years and written the show's theme song, to emcee his event. At the 1968 contest (dubbed the WBBG Pro Mr. America) Poole was again the winner. It was ironic, in light of the 1963 AAU fiasco, that Poole became the only bodybuilder to win three Mr. America titles—1964 (IFBB), 1967 (WBBG), and 1968 (WBBG). That Lurie's production had at least local credibility was evident from the one thousand fans who showed up at the Brooklyn Academy of Music, and from a judges panel with such iron-game notables as Dave Asnis, Vic Boff, Walter Podolak, and Val Pasqua.[61]

It became Lurie's aspiration, as it was for the Weiders, to seek a higher level of recognition for his champions and greater influence for himself. Hence, he announced that the 1968 runner-up, Freddy Ortiz, would be seeking the Mr. Universe title in London and that the WBBG hoped to "create close ties with NABBA in the near future." By this time too, Lurie was prepared to declare the nonexistence of racism in bodybuilding: "Happily, there is no racial prejudice; it does not matter what color a man's skin is in our sport. A man's greatness (or lack of it) in bodybuilding is directly and solely related to his physical development, be he white, black, brown, yellow, or red. Bodybuilders, in fact, are so totally unconscious of racial origin that it is impossible for most to conceive."[62] Pictures of dark-skinned bodybuilders (largely from the islands) in every issue of Lurie's magazine gave meaning to these fine words. Most telling was a photograph of Poole, Ortiz, and Frederick on the winners dais of the 1968 contest and a feature article on the guest appearance of Oliva, entitled "Sensational Sergio Oliva Brings the House Down."[63] The WBBG, with its base in Brooklyn, was ideally positioned, even more than the IFBB, to take advantage of New York's multiracial mix.

In 1969, Lurie sought greater fame in the bodybuilding world by staging more events that, unlike Weider productions, complemented rather than detracted from his Mr. America Contest. That competition included a testimonial dinner at the Granada Hotel emceed by a local television personality named Alan Burke. There were speeches by local dignitaries and the presentation of an award for "outstanding contribution to bodybuilding" to the 1967 AAU Mr. America, Dennis Tinerino, an Italian American from Brooklyn who had recently won the NABBA Amateur Mr. Universe. The Puerto Rican immigrant Johnny Maldonado won Lurie's Pro Mr. America title, and Arthur Harris received a trophy honoring him as the "Unclaimed Mr. America," an obvious slap at the AAU.[64]

The 1970 event featured a public round of preliminary judging in Brooklyn's Union Square, along with a Teenage Mr. America Contest, which was won by Carl Greenridge. Rick Wayne won the Pro Mr. America title, although he worked for the Weiders and was not an American. Controversy emerged when Poole, after learning that he was only third after early judging, failed to appear for the evening show at the Irving Auditorium. Even worse sportsmanship, reported George Larsen, was displayed by Tinerino, who "stormed off the platform" when Wayne was declared winner. This was done "in 'full view of the audience, a shocked audience.'"[65] Such antics indicated perhaps that Lurie was now a major player whose titles were eagerly sought.

ASSESSING THE IFBB MR. AMERICA

Notwithstanding Lurie's access to metropolitan New York minorities, the Weider organization, with its higher profile in the sport, was in a better position to exploit national and international talent. While its Mr. America Contest attracted fewer minorities because it was limited to Americans—interestingly, the AAU did not bar noncitizens from its Mr. America Contest—the Mr. World event served foreign bodybuilders almost exclusively. After Poole's 1964 victory, the IFBB Mr. America was won by white contestants over the next decade, almost as if it was sustaining the traditional image projected by the AAU Mr. America and the Miss America competitions. Maynard, Nubret, Oliva, and Wayne loomed large among the West Indian stars lured to the IFBB, but its Mr. America Contest, seemingly a feeder for the more grandiose Mr. Olympia and Mr. Universe events, remained largely white.

In 1966 it was won by Chester Yorton, and in 1967 the title went to Don Howorth, both Southern Californians. The latter show was preceded by an IFBB Junior Mr. America Contest, won by Howorth, and another copycat competition, this one called the Miss American Beauty Contest. For Yorton and Howorth the Mr. America Contest was overshadowed by other events in their lives. Yorton was nearly killed in an auto accident several years later. After his miraculous recovery, he conducted a publicity campaign for drug-free bodybuilding and won the NABBA Professional Mr. Universe Contest in 1972. In the same year he became Mr. America, Howorth survived a triple set of tragedies. Driving in the hills above Malibu, he failed to negotiate a turn, and his car, according to the gossip editor Dick Tyler, "flipped fifty feet in the air and landed upside down." Although Don acquired just a few scratches, he "came close to competing for the Mr. Heaven title." Then his apartment above Vince Gironda's gym caught fire, turning his trophies into "a shapeless wad." Finally, the sports car of his friend Bill McArdle, not properly secured, careered down a hill and crashed through the wall of Howorth's new apartment. Each of these near tragedies could have jeopardized his Mr. America career.[66]

Howorth's most telling experiences, however, were otherworldly. His titles came on the heels of an LSD trip nine months earlier in which he envisioned winning the Mr. America Contest. "I saw a person on the stage in a body without a face, then I finally saw the face," he recalls. "It was a premonition." In addition to steroids, Howorth had been taking recreational drugs, in a search for spiritual meaning, and he was stoned on the night of the Mr. America Contest. As he put it, "In those hippy days nothing was weighed or measured. Everything depended on the right vibes." Later he was sentenced to five years in the state penitentiary for transporting drugs. In contrast with the decorous public engagements of Miss America winners, it was in the unlikely environment of Vacaville that he had some of his most fulfilling experiences as Mr. America.

> I was like a god in prison. What else could you ask for than a Mr. America? I got more appreciation from the guys than I ever did outside. Everyone wanted to know my training secrets. I was in euphoria. Outside I was looked on as a faggot. It saved my life. I helped one guy gain 60 pounds and another 80. There was a free doctor running the medical area, and he had fifteen containers of steroids. I distributed them, and that's how the guys got big. "If you ever have any trouble, let us know," they told me. I saw Charles Manson at Vacaville. Timothy Leary was there too. It resembled "One Flew over the Cuckoo's Nest."

Otherwise Howorth received little satisfaction from winning the Mr. America title: "There was never any future in it. I could never make any money out of it, and dealing with Weider was a pain in the ass. The title never really meant anything."[67]

As for pride in bodybuilding's ancient origins, Howorth regarded the Greeks as "really weird" people who "did a lot of crazy things" and mistreated women. Nor did he respect the AAU standards inspired by the Greeks. It seemed "ridiculous" for "AAU officials [to] expect a guy to hold down a job, go to college, and in some cases support a family, and still have time to develop a great body and be an outstanding tennis player, swimmer, football star or weightlifter *all at the same time.*"[68] Howorth subscribed to the modern line that "the guy with the best body deserves the title, *not* the best athlete with the best body" and regarded Weider's version to be the "REAL *Mr. America Contest.*"[69]

Like several of its predecessors, the Weiders' 1968 Mr. America Contest was held at the Brooklyn Academy of Music, but the Miss Americana Contest was conducted a week later, with the Mr. Universe Contest, in Miami. Frank Zane, recently wed to Christine Harris, the 1967 Miss Americana, was the new IFBB Mr. America and Mr. Universe. In contrast to the increasingly massive, steroid-induced physiques of the late 1960s, Zane's body revealed an Apollo-like suppleness and balance. Ironically, far more coverage in *Muscle Builder/Power*, yet another Weider magazine, was given to the twenty-inch arms of Boyer Coe, the Louisianian who had just been named most muscular man at the AAU Mr. America Contest. "It's the man of massively-muscular size," wrote Joe Weider, "who's winning the big titles today. . . . Naturally he is totally familiar with Weider bomb/blitz techniques."[70] It is uncertain whether he was trying to induce Coe to defect to the IFBB or was simply trading on the credibility of AAU physique stars, as he had often done, but it is telling that he virtually ignored the less muscular Zane. Yet Zane's proportional look resulted in three Mr. Universe titles and three successive Mr. Olympia wins in the 1970s. The Grecian look, despite powerful countervailing cultural and commercial forces, remained alive.

That the IFBB still paid lip service to it was evident in a 1966 *Muscle Builder* article on Chuck Collras, a rising Greek American bodybuilder dubbed the "Golden Greek." He allegedly fulfilled "ancient Greek ideals both physically and mentally." At a body weight of 155 pounds, Collras could bench press 360, did not drink or smoke, followed a healthy diet, and had a perfect tan. He also rejected anabolic drugs. In faux–Damon Runyon style, the article gave the reasons: "Others were taking the critters—why shouldn't he? The 'Big D'—they shyly call it—was making them big, making them strong. So damn the consequences, anyway, he went for the ride. For four months everything went swell. He got big, he got strong. His progress was hot, but he began to notice his dinners at home getting cold. Family life and Dianabol make a bad mixture. . . . So he stopped taking Dianabol. Besides, possible prostate cancer casts a cool shadow across any hot progress from these muscle building critters."[71] Unlike Zane, Collras never reached bodybuilding's top echelons with his golden Greek image, and Weider editorials hammered away at the sham amateurism of AAU policies. "This 'amateur' kick has gotten out of all proportion," wrote Dick Tyler in 1967. "The whole setup is filled with deceit and double standards."[72]

More successful in infusing erstwhile amateur ideals into the Weider approach was John DeCola, who, after his disappointing experience with the AAU in 1964, retired for a few years, then came back to win the IFBB Mr. America crown in 1969. He cited Richard Nixon, who had become president after "many heart-breaks and defeats," as his inspiration. DeCola initially had difficulty severing his loyalty to the AAU, and even after winning the IFBB title, he still adhered to the AAU ideal of all-around development. "I've always thought of the 'Mr. America' title as something more than a physique crown," he explained in a 1970 interview: "I believe it should also be emblematic of those qualities we would like to see represented as an ideal person both physically and spiritually. . . . As Mr. America I have a unique opportunity to influence today's young Americans by setting some kind of example. If I can steer just one so-called 'turned on' kid away from smoking, drinking and drugs then the title has served its purpose. I'm proud I'm an American so you can imagine how proud I am to be called 'Mr. America.'"[73]

It did not seem to matter to DeCola that it was not the traditional version of the contest he had won. Indeed, after attending Weider shows at the Brooklyn Academy for several years, he convinced himself that the "IFBB Mr. America meant as much as the AAU Mr. America would have." But he realized that graduating to the next level of physique competition would necessitate taking steroids. After the veteran bodybuilder Kimon Voyages assured him that they would only damage his health, DeCola decided he "didn't want to do that" and, like Jerry Daniels, who had reached the same conclusion several years earlier, quit competitive bodybuilding.[74]

MIKE KATZ

In 1970, the IFBB Mr. America title was won by Mike Katz, a former professional football star who displayed magnificent chest development. Bud Parker, who organized the affair, along with the Miss Americana, Mr. World, and Mr. Olympia contests, called it a "great" show featuring "the greatest bodybuilders in the world today." Not surprisingly, the Mr.

America Contest was overshadowed by the World and Olympia events, won respectively by Dave Draper and Arnold Schwarzenegger. But Parker's report focused mainly on warnings about drugs. On arriving for the preliminary judging, he could "hardly recognize a few old friends."

> Their faces were beet-red. What looked like inverted bags under the eyes gave their faces a skull-like appearance. When standing relaxed their muscles seemed puffy. . . . Are we witnessing the making and breaking of champions? Can the sacrifice be worth it—jeopardizing one's health for a handful of shiny metal and a title which is rendered meaningless because its winner is not worthy of it? Have some of us forgotten the purpose of bodybuilding—not only a means of attaining visual perfection but also inner perfection?[75]

Although Parker focused on health risks to individual steroid users, the implication of his message was collective—that the single-minded pursuit of appearance (muscles for muscles' sake), which was largely fueling the success of the Weiders, was making physique titles meaningless and destroying the sport. Although what he saw was "not peculiar to IFBB contestants," it was clear that if drugs were "responsible for so many 'monsters' who are taking home awards left and right these days," then the world's three top bodybuilders—Katz, Draper, and Schwarzenegger—must rank high on that list.[76]

For Katz, the prestige of his Mr. America title was compromised not only by a public increasingly wary of how athletes acquired their magnificent bodies but also by a political wrangle resulting in the awarding of a second IFBB Mr. America title, this one to Sergio Oliva, already the winner of three Mr. Olympia titles. Perhaps feeling slighted from never having been a Mr. America or peeved by his loss to Schwarzenegger in a Mr. World Contest two weeks earlier in Ohio, Oliva threatened to enter the contest. But if he did, it would result in a boycott by other contestants, since he would be such a prohibitive favorite to win. The prospect horrified contest organizers, as Joe Weider explained:

> If Sergio entered it wouldn't be a contest. He'd win hands down and deny the title to some deserving guy on his way up. Bud Parker, the promoter, finally satisfied Sergio by agreeing to name him honorary Mr. America and giving him a duplicate trophy. He also got honorary wins and trophies for his bodyweight class and all the body parts awards like best arms, best back, and so on. This nonsense took some of the excitement out of the Mr. America contest, but at least we could get going with the events that built up to Mr. Olympia.[77]

Rick Wayne added, "One is left to wonder how meaningful to Katz the title has been considering the circumstances surrounding its acquisition." As for Oliva, the importance of his Mr. America title paled in comparison to his unsuccessful bid for a fourth Mr. Olympia title a few hours later, resulting in a rage that still boiled over in his life story decades later: "So Joe Weider got his man Arnold, a white man, for his magazine covers." How little being Mr. America meant to Oliva at that point is evident not only from its omission from the text, but even from the list of his titles at the back of his book![78]

It could have meant a lot more to Katz, but its importance became embroiled in a legal altercation with the York organization. When the editor John Grimek refused to retract the statement that Katz had "never won the Mr. America title," made in the April 1971 issue of *Muscular Development*, Katz, claiming injury to his reputation, sued for punitive damages in Connecticut Superior Court. He insisted that "the pot of gold at the end of the rainbow, after winning the Mr. America Contest" had been denied to him because of Grimek's statement in what was "the bible of the sport." Katz was prevented not only from turning professional but also from cashing in on "posing exhibitions, seminars, training camps, and endorsements." The most damaging evidence against York was a letter from Richard Pruger, a former York employee, to Katz, which showed possible malice. It stemmed from Pruger having to withdraw an invitation (and a fee of $500 to $1,000) to Katz to pose for a show he was staging in Pittsburgh: "I had a letter of agreement all typed up when I spoke with my boss concerning the meet. It seems that you and York have some sort of legal disagreement, all of which is tied into the authenticity of the I.F.B.B." Although the defense tried to downplay the bad feelings between Hoffman and Weider, the plaintiff's attorney was able to show that Katz had been victimized. The court awarded him $75,000, which was reduced to $17,500 on appeal.[79]

The verdict signified the growing strength of the Weiders. Their version of Mr. America had come a long way since Gene Shuey's win a decade earlier. That it was dominated by Caucasian bodybuilders was hardly noticed, chiefly because men of color were so prevalent and successful in the other, more prestigious contests they staged. Whatever message it conveyed about ideal American manhood was overlooked.

HOLDING THE CULTURE LINE

Thus the last bastion of whiteness appeared to be the AAU and its centerpiece, the Mr. America Contest, still regarded by many as the world's most prestigious physique competition. To a great extent, its stance on issues of bodily display and racial diversity tapped the same body of conservative social sentiment that guided the Miss America Pageant. Both mixed uneasily with the liberation movements emerging in the late 1960s. A premonition of change for the women's contest came with Lenora Slaughter's retirement in 1967. In parting comments, she recognized that there would always be a swimsuit competition and that two-piece models would eventually be acceptable: "But there will be nothing vulgar. Fashion will prevail."[80] Still, for all of Slaughter's efforts over the years to lessen the judges' focus on the body, increase the age of contestants, and preserve the event's nonprofit character, about two hundred feminist protestors descended on Atlantic City the next year. Insisting that pageant misplaced priorities were "on body rather than brains, on youth rather than maturity and on commercialism rather than humanity," the protestors, calling themselves the Women's Liberation Front, "marched on the Boardwalk . . . chanted anti–Pageant slogans, and tossed bras, girdles, makeup, and hair curlers into a 'freedom trash can.'"[81] A few ardent spirits eluded security personnel and managed to toss a stink bomb on the Convention Hall runway during the television broadcast. They returned in 1969, still unaware that the Miss Universe Contest was a worse example of female exploitation and commercialism.[82] The protestors focused on the Miss America event probably because of its popularity, as the most widely watched of the pageants, and its representation of American bourgeois values. In essence, what the feminists found objectionable was Slaughter's worldview. Although she may have sought advancement for women, she did so within a set of traditional assumptions about women and their place in society. Feminists sought to empower and liberate women from the social, economic, and cultural constraints of the past.

The AAU Mr. America Contest, drawing on the same set of middle-class values (cast in classical conceptions of the body and manhood) was also subjected to countercultural stirrings in the late 1960s. By this time, AAU officials had become adept at staging well-organized competitions. Of the many contests Peary Rader had seen, he had never witnessed "one that was better organized, had more excellent acts or was better presented" than the first Over 40 Mr. America Contest in

1966, conducted by Lyell Ryden in Denver. It was won by Harry Johnson who, at forty-two, "looked better than he did when he won his Mr. America title in 1959." In 1967 in Columbus, Ohio, Jim Lorimer and Frasher Ferguson held one of the most successful Mr. America contests ever. "I can't say enough fine things about the show," exclaimed Bob Hoffman.[83] Yet *Muscle Training Illustrated* speculated that it could go down in history as "the start of the decline of the AAU bodybuilding empire," since it attracted only fourteen contestants. Still, argued Ralph Countryman in *Iron Man*, "the quality of the top men was high as ever, possibly even better. . . . And it's still the Mr. America show that draws the crowd."[84]

Indeed, the selection of Dennis Tinerino as winner was well received. In *Strength & Health*, Bill Starr recognized him as "a deserving young man" who started Olympic lifting in order to gain his athletic points and became an accomplished weightlifter: "The Mr. America Crown is in good hands."[85] For Tinerino, it was "a dream come true," evoking "tears of joy." It was a culmination of his efforts over six years, and he attached a meaning to it that fit traditional expectations. Charles Atlas, a "good friend of the family," had once told Tinerino that he was "a natural." "The 'Mr. America' title stands for more than an ideal muscular physique," he reflected. "It stands for the things which are a great part of our American heritage, namely sound character, athletic ability and a sound and spiritually alert mind."[86]

These were fine words, conveyed in the euphoria of his victory. But fulfilling the Mr. America ideal proved more difficult. Tinerino later signed a contract with Joe Weider and fulfilled another "lifelong dream" by moving to California, where he admittedly made some "poor choices."

> I got to liking the high life. I was famous. I was on the "A" party list. I got caught up in the pride of life, got in with the wrong people. Some friends and I organized an "escort" service, which is just a fancy name for a prostitution ring. . . . I did not know it at the time, but the police had been following my activities closely. Eventually I was arrested and sentenced to a year in jail under the organized crime statute. I was married and had two small children. So you could say I hit the skids.

It was a sobering experience, and Tinerino was able to turn his life around and continue his involvement in the sport. But bodybuilding had been more fulfilling before he won his Mr. America title: "There was no money. We did it for the sheer love of it. . . . There was a real camaraderie then."[87] Not unlike the 1967 IFBB Mr. America, who also

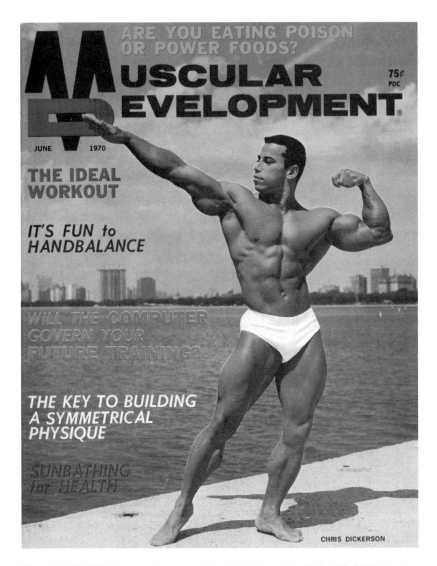

Figure 6.3. Chris Dickerson as he appeared just before becoming the first black Mr. America, in 1970. *Muscular Development*, June 1970, 1.

turned to criminal activity, Tinerino's victory left a spiritual void. He ultimately found solace with his conversion to Christianity in 1979.

From 1968 to 1970, AAU Mr. America winners, with almost mechanical regularity, were drawn from the previous year's runner-ups, and the 1968 contest even featured the same winner sequence as the Junior Mr. America event a month earlier. It also attracted a surfeit of spectators (hundreds had to be turned away) to York, where Jim Haislop, of Tampa, described in *Muscular Development* as a "handsome, blond Adonis with a wider V-shape than any Mr. America," triumphed over a field of twenty-seven. But Ralph Countryman reported in *Iron Man* that Haislop's selection was "hotly disputed by the muscle-conscious audience," which favored Boyer Coe.[88] Coe went on to win in 1969 at Chicago, but the contest was marred by booing, according to Countryman. *Iron Man* commended the winner anyway: "Unfortunately this is usually interpreted as dissatisfaction with the winner himself, and it takes a pretty gutsy man to face the catcalls he doesn't deserve when the decision is unpopular." Otherwise there were highlights, including "the largest assortment of big trophies . . . outside of the office bowling tournament." Most striking, aside from the high quality of contestants, was the masterly emceeing of Len Bosland, of Glen Rock, New Jersey: "He made the introductions with style and effect. He doesn't oversell the man, and he maintains the pace of the contest. He uses mike silence more effectively than some use words."[89] Like the title itself, Bosland was becoming an icon—the Bert Parks of the Mr. America Contest.[90]

When Coe won the title, he was a senior at the University of Southwestern Louisiana, and by coincidence, Judy Ford, who won the Miss America title in 1969, was attending the same institution.[91] There was "lots of publicity over a Miss America and Mr. America being from the same school," but according to Coe, "If the national media noticed, I missed it."

> Judy got lots of attention in her own right as Miss America, of course, and in addition to her various prizes, she was sent around the country on tour. Although she dropped out of school to take advantage of her contest rewards, I caught her when she was back in Lafayette several months later to visit and we discussed the things she had won as Miss America. These included a $10,000 scholarship, a $10,000 wardrobe, $80,000 in endorsements and a year of public relations travel as Miss America. So at 19 years old she was virtually set for life, if she played her cards right.

By contrast, Coe got a trophy, and Red Lerille had to pay his way to the contest. For him, it was a goal accomplished. When asked later how it felt to be Mr. America, he recalled: "Honestly I never gave it a second thought; my mind was already on to the next goal."[92]

Coe's next goal was the NABBA Mr. Universe title, which he won. Much the same attitude was expressed by Frank Zane, the 1968 IFBB Mr. America, for whom the title, though "a long-term goal," did nothing for him in an "immediate sense": "It was my first big title, and it all counts. I would have moved up anyway." Indeed, it preceded a "high point" in his career, beating Arnlold Schwarzenegger at the IFBB Mr. Universe Contest in Miami three weeks later. In other words, being Mr. America, unlike being Miss America, was meaningful not as an end in itself but only as a step leading to some higher goal. Its mystique, the embodiment of a holistic ideal of American manhood, was quickly giving way to an emphasis wholly on muscular development. Coe doubted whether there was anything left of the Greek ideal of a mind-body balance: "If there was ever such a thing as the 'Greek ideal,' it must have gone out of vogue at the time of Sandow."[93]

Doubts about the ideal's viability also concerned AAU officials. In response to widespread appeals, Peary Rader had been suggesting the elimination of athletic ability points and substitution of a place system (which had been adopted by NABBA in the 1950s and the IFBB in the 1960s) for points in judging. Given physique politics, nothing could be done about duplicate Mr. Americas, Rader argued, but it "does nothing to improve the public image of the title." At the 1968 AAU Convention in Las Vegas, the national committee approved (just barely) a proposal by Don Haley, of California, to eliminate athletic points.[94]

Joe Weider was jubilant over this landmark decision. Henceforth,

> Mr. America contestants . . . will be judged solely on physique alone, and not on ability to excel at sports. This is how it should be. . . . For more than 13 years the AAU doggedly held onto rules which were recognized immediately as being absurd. Its practice of judging physique contestants on things other than muscular development, such as athletic performance in an unrelated activity, or a bodybuilder's ability to perform Olympic lifts which were not normally practiced, caused more than one top champion to lose a title to a lesser man, physically, who excelled at athletic performance, or someone who had straighter teeth and a flawless complexion.

Significantly, Weider took credit for the change, viewing it not so much as an advance for the AAU as a victory for his organization, "which again proves that the IFBB is close to the hearts and interests of bodybuilders." He expressed pride in the part the Weiders had played in the whole affair: "We were at long last able to reverse the AAU ruling and wipe out that dirty deal." Furthermore, in light of the IWF's recent elimination of its Mr. Universe Contest, Weider gave credence to rumors suggesting that the AAU might "give up all control of bodybuilding, enabling the organization to concern itself solely with weightlifting and powerlifting."[95]

That did not appear to be a realistic notion, but its discussion in 1964 in Houston at the annual AAU meeting had implied that it was not out of the question. Rudy Sablo, chair of the national committee, admitted, "The only reason . . . we have for keeping the Mr. America contest under A.A.U. jurisdiction is for the financial support it provides for the weightlifting game."[96] A less cynical view was held by Bob Crist, who took a hand in reforming the Mr. America Contest. In 1968, he discussed upgrading "the show along the lines of the Miss America pageant": devoting an entire day to it (separate from the lifting), choosing representatives by state, and interviewing the ten finalists "on stage like the Miss America" so that "the public could see and hear their favorites." Further to enliven the affair, he proposed a variety show with "a full evening program," similar to the format of the NABBA Mr. Universe Contest.[97] Crist gave every indication that whatever changes were made, the AAU would maintain the elevated tone of the Mr. America Contest and never allow it to become just a muscle show.

CROSSING THE COLOR LINE

Throughout the late 1960s, whites dominated the AAU Mr. America lists of entrants and winners. Aside from such notables as Chris Dickerson, Bill Grant, and Ken Covington, there were few blacks. And with the exception of the Puerto Rican Anibal Lopez, who placed sixth in 1970, there were virtually no Hispanics, and none of the rich confluence of race and culture that enlivened the Weider, Lurie, and Heidenstam contests. Whiteness was also reflected in the articles, ads, and photographs in York magazines, and in such reader-participation sections as the self-improvement and man-of-the-month contests.[98] Clearly, the cultural dynamic operating within the AAU contrasted with the one at work in the other bodybuilding organizations, but pressures for greater diversity within the organization had been mounting since the Poole and Oliva incidents, and also within American society, fully in the grips of the civil rights struggle.

Within the larger context of the times, however, the Mr. America Contest was far less vulnerable to accusations of racism than its female counterpart. Despite increasing strides made by the civil rights movement, Miss America officials seemed oblivious of the need to include blacks in the contestant pool. Progress occurred at a snail's pace, beginning with an "all-Negro float" in the 1966 Miss America Pageant parade, which placed second in competition with eighty other floats. The 1967 version featured Miss Sepia Pennsylvania, Patricia Freeman, and "eight other talented beauty queens" who had competed for a $10,000 scholarship to the University of Pennsylvania. Then in 1968 a black contestant was runner-up for the Miss California title, and another was a semifinalist in the Miss Indiana Contest. In 1969, Dr. Zelma George, a sociologist, educator, and actress, became the first black to serve on the Miss America judging panel.[99]

In 1968, a black profit-making organization, Fashionable Publications, headed by Morris Anderson, had staged the first Miss Black America Pageant at the Ritz-Carlton Convention Hall on the same evening as the Miss America finals. Though poorly organized and attended, it included swimsuit, talent, and intelligence categories. One contestant, too embarrassed to sing her song, "threw her hands up to her face and ran off." Another, after the wrong song was played repeatedly for her choreographed dance, finally "walked offstage and set the record herself." The *Philadelphia Bulletin* greeted such spontaneous goofs with delight, since they "gave the show a refreshingly innocent touch," "a quality that had long since disappeared from the highly polished Miss America Contest."[100]

The 1969 pageant went more smoothly. The winner, Saundra Williams, of Philadelphia, was outspoken on the shortcomings of the *other* contest regarding race: "Miss America does not represent us because there has never been a black girl in the pageant. With my title I can show black women that they too are beautiful, even though they do have large noses and thick lips. There is a need to keep saying this over and over because for so long none of us believed it. But now we're finally coming around."[101]

Black women were liberating themselves from traditional (white) ideals of beauty, but they were creating a separate sphere in the process. Although Cheryl Browne, Miss Iowa 1970, became the first black contestant in the Miss America Pageant, much of the pressure in the ensuing decade for racial equality was removed by the coexistence of the Miss Black America Pageant.

That no Mr. Black America Contest emerged may be attributed to the multiplicity of bodybuilding organizations in which black men had already made significant inroads. When Chris Dickerson became the first black AAU Mr. America in 1970, his racial profile was distinctive. Unlike many who competed in the IFBB, WBBG, and NABBA contests, Dickerson was light skinned, but he had Caribbean connections, being of mixed French and African descent on his father's side. His birth certificate reads "Henri Christophe," in honor of a liberator who led a black army that drove the French out of Haiti in 1803.[102] Though he spent most of his adult life in New York and Los Angeles, both national melting pots, Dickerson was born in Alabama, the self-proclaimed "Heart of Dixie." In that sense, he was homegrown. But unlike such black power activists as Harold Poole, Sergio Oliva, and Rick Wayne, Dickerson was at peace with the predominantly white AAU establishment. "I wanted very much to be Mr. America," he stated. "I wanted to prove that a black man could win the title. I figured that if it meant not being able to wear an Afro hairstyle, well, that was a small price." By 1970, Dickerson sensed that the AAU was changing and "anxious to have a black Mr. America": "I felt that they were in my corner, and I really felt that my race . . . would be in my favor because of times being what they were."[103]

Dickerson met all the expectations of the AAU with his exceptional muscularity, symmetry, character, education, poise, and other qualities that made the Mr. America competition more than a muscle show. Dickerson evinced a willingness to play the game by the white man's rules. Hence, he was critical of those who refused to wear a suit, speak politely, remove facial hair, show up on time, or who engaged in other subtle forms of dissent. "There is politics in everything and no one is above it," he advised. "There must be rapport, an identification on both sides of the judging table. In order to build that communication, you must dress and conduct yourself accordingly."[104]

What set Dickerson apart from previous black physique stars was his ability to assimilate, a strategy acquired from Bill Pearl, who groomed the first three black Mr. Americas. Pearl was aware of the cultural prejudices against blacks and the AAU's adherence to Miss America standards of comportment.

> I made sure their fingernails were manicured. I made sure the kid's shoes were shined and they walked up there in a suit and a tie and looked as professional as they possibly could be. . . . Even backstage, if there were black kids in the contest, my black kids did not associate with them because if one of those black kids had said something wrong while he was there, he's automatically pegged. . . . I had specific criteria I talked to those kids about, constantly. Even going on stage, never looking down, making eye contact with everybody and smiling. Even the way they talked. How they answered something. And there were certainly phrases I didn't want them to use. And they were kind enough to listen to me.

Essentially, Pearl was training his charges to be black white people. Bill called it "all-American" as that term was understood at the time.[105]

Dickerson's ability to transcend the bounds of black culture attracted the attention of a nationally syndicated newspaper columnist, who compared the Mr. and Miss America contests. Aside from the difference in monetary rewards and the hard physical training required of Mr. Americas, the two titles seemed strikingly similar as representative American icons.[106] By assimilating, Dickerson, in the words of Rick Wayne, "had blasted through the color barrier."[107] But Dickerson's assimilative powers extended beyond color to challenge another iron-game taboo. The Greek gods must have been laughing as AAU officials inadvertently selected their first gay Mr. America.

PART 3: DECLINE AND FALL

7

THE ARNOLD ERA

ARNOLD BROUGHT BODYBUILDING OUT OF THE CLOSET AND MADE IT FASHIONABLE TO BE FIT. HOWEVER, I RESPECT HIM MORE TODAY FOR HIS MIND THAN HIS BODY. FROM A BUSINESS STANDPOINT ARNOLD IS A GENIUS. BEYOND THAT, HE EPITOMIZES THE AMERICAN DREAM.

JESSE VENTURA, *MUSCULAR DEVELOPMENT,*
FEBRUARY 1988

ARNOLD SCHWARZENEGGER NEVER HELD A MR. AMERICA TITLE FOR ANY of the physique federations, but by the end of the twentieth century, he had become an icon of what it meant to be an American. Indeed, his accomplishments represented more than repeatedly winning major competitions in what had always been a minor and ill-defined sport. By dint of his remarkable physique, business acumen, and winning personality, Arnold not only raised the status of bodybuilding but also stimulated a worldwide fitness craze and helped redefine the male body image. To such an extent did he become an international reflection of American values that, despite his foreign birth and pronounced accent, he in essence became a Mr. America, more so than any bodybuilder of his era who bore the title, and as familiar a symbol of America as McDonald's. At his naturalization ceremony in 1983, wearing a red, white, and blue suit, Arnold publicly embodied the fulfillment of the American dream. After singing the national anthem, he told reporters: "This is the realization of the dream I have had ever since my childhood, to come to America and become an American. I really am convinced . . . this country is the No. 1 in the world."[1] The impact of Arnold cannot be overestimated. To such an extent did Schwarzenegger represent America and where it was going, in bodybuilding and society, in the 1970s that he overshadowed the significance of the Mr. America title.

THE NEW *MR. AMERICA*

A critical factor in Schwarzenegger's rise to fame was his ability to relate to changing social values in the late 1960s. He did so by associating with Joe Weider, who brought the young Austrian to America after he won the amateur (1967) and professional (1968) Mr. Universe titles in London. They became an effective team, complementing each other as promoter and star even more effectively than had Hoffman and Grimek in an earlier era.[2] Recognizing the need to get in step with America's youth culture, Weider decided to make Arnold the centerpiece of his new *Mr. America* magazine in 1969, which was intended to introduce "a revolution in Muscle Publishing." In an editorial, "Growing Up with Our Readers," Joe promised that the old *Mr. America* would soon be "as extinct as the dodo bird and as obsolete as the Ford Tri-Motor." He insisted that unlike bodybuilders of the past, who were just musclemen interested in adding weight and dimensions to their physiques, those of the present were educated and worldly: "The contemporary weight trainer is interested in improving his physical appearance by packing on well-proportioned muscle, but he also is interested in general health, proper nutrition, and all-around fitness. He wants to know what current fashions appropriately set off a muscular physique, what hair style will enable him to look his best, how to plan for the future, and—last but not least—how to come on strong with the groovy gals." Weider intended "to publish what the readers want . . . and what they need."[3] In so doing, he planned to make money by catering to popular tastes, but on a more symbolic level Weider was turning a corner in his exploitation of the Mr. America label, replacing its staid AAU association with a hip, revolutionary image of the 1970s and a foreign-born hero.

Successive issues of *Mr. America*, subtitled "The Virile Fitness Magazine for Today's Man," featured such articles as "A Celebration of the Flesh," "The Big O[rgasm]: How Important Is It for the Woman?," "Four Aphrodisiac Drinks for Sexual Vigor," "Is 'Big' Best? . . . The

Truth about Genital Size," "Beer: The Bodybuilder's Beverage of Nutrition," "The ABC's of Drugs," and "Secrets of Hatha Yoga for Increased Sexual Power and Drive."[4] The most prevalent topic was sex, and many articles included the kind of testimony and advice found in psychology or sex therapy columns. "I want my husband to treat me like a common whore," admitted Mrs. Geraldine M., twenty-four, in an article entitled "Women's Shocking Sexual Desires." She elaborated: "If I refuse him anything he should belt me in the mouth." The article is illustrated by pictures of nine women, including a bevy of beautiful females surrounding the 1968 Mr. America, Frank Zane, none of whom appear to be clothed. "What women have to realize is that nothing that pleases both partners is abnormal," explained M. Brothman, M.D., the author of the piece. "Where sex is concerned the modern day thinking is 'Anything goes.'" Another article, "Mr. America Swings at These Zingy Spots," encouraged readers to enjoy a modern lifestyle by visiting "exotic/erotic ports of call" such as London, Trinidad, Montreal, and Amsterdam. Rick Wayne had suggestions for those vacationing Amsterdam: "After you've done the usual touristy thing, "you'll want to groove in on two of the wildest clubs . . . the *Fantasia* and the *Paradiso*. Anything goes! Marijuana is smoked openly here, but since you're not on 'pot' you can turn on with beer, dancing, stripping, making love . . . you name it and it's there!"[5] This was not the sort of fare that had appeared in past muscle magazines.

Sexual themes were evident in all aspects of *Mr. America*. A "Weider Wildcat" ad for chewable vitamin E tablets featured a shot of a scantily clad bodybuilder and a woman meeting on the beach, captioned by, "You've got a lot of living, loving and fun-ing to do and you need a lot of endurance/stamina-building Vitamin E to do it," suggesting the product could improve one's sex life.[6] But it was the covers, often shots of models on the beach in revealing attire, that were most striking. The one for the April 1970 issue featured the 1965 Mr. America, Dave Draper, with two young girls pawing at his legs, one peering through his crotch from the beach front, and Betty Weider on his shoulders, straddling his neck. Though middle-aged, Betty was fit and fetching, no less sexy than her younger counterparts. Her image appeared twenty times in that issue alone (as often as Arnold's), and she graced the covers and ads of Weider magazines more than any other female over the years. She and Draper, the Blond Bomber, struck a perfect chord for the California muscle-beach-culture image that Joe was trying to present.

Ironically, observed Draper, the image did not coincide with reality:

"I seldom made it to the beach and was never on a surf board. It was usually too cold to get in the water. Most muscle guys were working 25 weeks a year and collecting unemployment. Some were sleeping in cars. I didn't have time for the beach."[7] Also, after winning the 1970 Mr. World title in New York, Draper retired to a more sedate existence infused with alcohol and drugs. As "the sport took off like a rocket," he recalled, his own life went "out to pasture." His existence in Venice became almost completely self-contained: "Someone could say the '70s never happened and I'd believe 'em."[8]

A NEW "AMERICAN" ICON

The bodybuilder who capitalized most on Draper's retirement was Schwarzenegger. The Blond Bomber was soon replaced as a popular icon by the Austrian Oak. Furthermore, after a losing to Frank Zane in the 1968 Mr. Universe Contest, Schwarzenegger bounded to the top of the physique firmament by winning the competition in 1969 and 1970. He defeated Sergio Oliva at a Mr. World Contest in Columbus, Ohio, and at the Mr. Olympia Contest in New York, both in 1970. His upward trajectory was explained by Chuck Sipes in an article entitled "They Call Him 'Sexy' Schwarzenegger Now!" Joe Weider not only provided Schwarzenegger with training advice, but also "transformed his image *socially*, for now he is no longer the naïve young man from the 'olde worlde' but a swinger who really makes the scene!" The metamorphosis began with Arnold's hairstyle.

> Joe suggested that he put himself in the hands of a Hollywood hair-stylist like Sebring who works on movie stars like George Hamilton . . . physique stars like Dave Draper, Don Peters and John Tristram . . . and on famous models like Mark Nixon. This is what *Mr. America* has been urging: that you build not only a muscular, slim-line physique, but "showcase" it with an *individualized* hairstyle, and with *personalized* designs in clothes. . . . Next Joe urged Arnold (who is very fair-skinned) to get a *slow* tan, the California way . . . a *measured* tan that "lives" all year 'round. This kind of tan gives that tawny, turned-on-from-within glow that girls find so devastating! He further suggested that Arnold develop a personal *mystere*, and that to do this he must first begin to take things easy. And so instead of his customary Great Dane *bound*, Arnold began to develop a more casual, sexier walk. . . . Instead of breathlessly telling his life story in ten seconds he began to cultivate a slower, sexier, more intimate way of speaking.[9]

Figure 7.1. Sexy Schwarzenegger "muscling up" with a "007" Twister and draped by three bikini-clad beach bunnies, including Betty Weider, who "just can't leave him alone," according to the caption. *Mr. America*, August 1969, 1. © Weider Health and Fitness/Zeller.

The transformation resulted in a five-part series in *Muscle Builder/ Power* in 1971 on Arnold's adventurous lifestyle. There were many revealing photos of him; on the cover of the July 1971 issue of *Mr. America*, he holds a naked female while kissing her torso. An ad in *Muscle Builder/Power* for a new "Sexi-Waist Plan" shows a nude female (her buttocks revealed) with her face on Arnold's abdomen as if preparing to fellate him, and another displays a shadowy naked Arnold suggestively hovering over a shadowy naked female. The caption reads: "Find out what it's like to be more of a man. Ignite your world and hers with the MARK OF THE BEAST . . . I. BRUTE . . . 100% Oriental Ginseng Herb Tablets."[10]

It is hardly surprising that both magazines had had "skyrocketing" sales since the launching of the "new *Mr. America*." That publication could show a young man "how to develop not only his body, but the attitudes and his life style of the coming New Man," vouched Schwarzenegger, under the pseudonym "Arnold Strong." So frequently did Schwarzenegger 's image and articles appear in Weider magazines that one reader asked, "Don't you think you are overdoing it"? Joe's response pointed out that "Arnold gave our sport a terrific shot in the arm" and that Schwarzenegger was carrying on a tradition: "Steve Reeves gave bodybuilding a fantastic boost by helping to raise it to greater . . . heights during [the] 1950's, and now we have Arnold doing the same thing."[11]

Weider can justly claim credit for shaping Arnold's commercial image. "Of all the fantastic achievements of Joe Weider with his pupils," observed Rick Wayne, "surely his work with Arnold Schwarzenegger must go down in bodybuilding history as the most astounding."[12] But his Americanization, in a more human sense, stemmed largely from his relationship with Barbara Outland, a California student-waitress with whom he lived for six years in the early 1970s. She not only helped him with his English skills and his finances but also gave him love and a stable social environment, which were critical to his success. Outland identified her role as part of his transplanted family: "Joe, the successful father through whom he could become a respected man; Franco [Columbu], the malleable brother he could both control and adore; and Barbara, the ideal mother he could love, respect, and guide." But she was the only real American. As one of Arnold's early coauthors later told Outland, "Arnold wanted me to meet you because he respected you for having opened up a classy place for him. He looked at you as a really nice person, a true American."[13] Unlike most other accounts of Schwarzenegger, Outland's provides insights on his Americanization.

THE SEXUALIZATION OF BODYBUILDING

Not surprisingly, the Weiders' emphasis on sex was reflected in competition reports. A premonition was provided in the 1969 Miss Americana Contest. After a juggling act, according to Dick Tyler,

> it was time for the studs in the audience to watch their blood pressure rise as the girls in the Miss Americana began to strut their stuff. I do mean strut. This isn't like the Miss America where the girls sedately march down the promenade and do a few turns. The girls in the Miss Americana are far more "athletic" as some of them go into all types of contortions before the yelling throng. It's pretty great . . . when the girls get before the audience—the only holds that are barred are those the men in the audience would like to get on the contestants. One of the girls even did a strip on the stage which came as a surprise (a pleasant one to all).[14]

Further to imbue his organization with this liberated spirit, Joe moved his headquarters to Woodland Hills, California: "That's where it's at, where everything happens." He argued that New York was two years behind Los Angeles in muscle culture, which seemed to thrive in an environment of sun, beaches, palm trees, and leisure.[15]

It was fitting, therefore, that the 1971 IFBB Mr. America Contest was moved from the Brooklyn Academy to a Hollywood nightclub, where "garish gold statues" of nude women graced the lobby and a West Coast version of the sexually liberated musical *Hair* had recently been performed. Skin, both male and female, was much in evidence in a photograph of Chuck Collras, runner-up in his class, embracing a Miss Americana contestant: "You might say that Chuck's all set to muscle up and make out." Again the females received special attention from Tyler. "The Miss Americana . . . girls present a display that must be seen. I mean—how can you describe a bouncing 40" of you know what with mere words. 'Ah, yes. What pretty little fillies,' as W. C. Fields would say.'" But the Mr. America winner, Ken Waller, received scant recognition. Even the puritanical *Iron Man* devoted undue attention to the IFBB Americana, noting that 4'11" Liz Daniels won the title "'Most Voluptuous' a sort of best chest award for females."[16]

It was inevitable that so much emphasis on sex should stir up controversy. While one reader approved of "spicing up MR. AMERICA with photos and subjects of interest to *real men*," another felt he had lost a "close friend" and wondered whether it was still a physique magazine.

Weider replied that "far from being merely a sex magazine," it was "for the bodybuilder who wants to find out what really makes him tick!"[17] The most vociferous criticism, however, emerged from the York media. Loyd Poplin, of Arkansas, believed that Weider magazines gave the impression that "all weightlifters were perverted or gay" and that Joe, by employing the "most distasteful tactics," was "exploiting the entire sport to make a few bucks." James Carlson, of Oregon, admitted that there were "nice-looking girls" in *Mr. America*, but he "didn't want a stag magazine." He noted that one article, "Skiing and Sheing," featured "a man skiing off a woman's bare bosom": "All it mentioned was where to go to pick up girls in tight ski slacks; and drinks; and hamburgers . . . ridiculous." William Ely, from Maryland, believed that the IFBB's only purpose was to produce winners for Weider ads and that the "muscle up and make out" mentality detracted from sportsmanship and bodybuilding's healthful benefits.[18]

To distinguish the AAU's approach to projecting the body from Weider's, Chris Dickerson, pictured under an unadorned statue of King Neptune in Florence, Italy, penned an article titled "The Nude Syndrome" for the Mr. A Series in *Strength & Health*. It was natural to admire nude male and female physiques, as did "the Greeks and the Romans."

> [But] many people fail to appreciate the nude physique man simply because they fear the stigma that may go along with such appreciation. . . . We seem to have developed . . . a standard that dictates to us that the physique must be covered from the oblique muscles down to three inches below the pelvis. . . . Think to yourself of the great men of today, or of your favorite bodybuilder. Wouldn't you be inspired by a first rate, well thought-out nude or semi-nude photo, created with dramatic lighting, and artistic insight of this man?[19]

It became evident that such liberal views were linked with Dickerson's sexual orientation. A Venice firm released a series of 8 mm films entitled *Nude Physique Studies*, which featured Dickerson, the "most popular Mr. America of the decade," posing with "classical muscular elegance, tasteful, 'class' . . . at the peak of his bodybuilding perfection." Provocative films of the IFBB stars Rick Wayne and Bill Grant (WBBG Mr. America 1972) were also available. There was no doubt, despite the films' artistry and good taste, who were the intended patrons. George Parker, of Ringoes, New Jersey, expressed dismay to Rader that Dickerson, whom he had "long admired" as "holder of our highest and reputedly most respectable title[,] would stoop to this."[20] Although these productions confronted Parker with what he did not want to believe about bodybuilders, they revealed the fine line that has always existed between artistic and prurient exposure of the body, a distinction that seemed especially pertinent to the culture of the early 1970s.

CLIMACTIC AAU CONTESTANTS

Increasingly, the IFBB Mr. America title, won by a series of outstanding bodybuilders—Ed Corney, Lou Ferrigno, Bob Birdsong, Robby Robinson, Mike Mentzer, and Dan Padilla—was playing second fiddle, until its demise in 1977, to a variety of Mr. Universe, Mr. World, and Mr. Olympia contests sponsored by several federations. But the AAU version seemed poised to continue indefinitely its proud tradition of symbolizing American manhood, despite its rivals and even the dominating presence of Schwarzenegger.

Casey Viator, from New Iberia, Louisiana, after placing third in the 1970 Mr. America Contest, "came on the scene like gang busters and destroyed the competition" at the Teenage Mr. America Contest in York, according to Bob Crist. Winning the award for most muscular award, and the prizes for all the subdivisions except best abdominals, Viator represented "the fine young talent" showing up in the sport. The "clean cut" contestants were "quick to answer the panel's questions and show good judgment in their responses," offering "a good solid projection of the 'whole person' concept." No less glowing in his praise was Peary Rader, who noted that Viator had created the most comment because of his rapid improvement and his arms, which "were among the largest in the world." When Viator captured the 1971 Junior Mr. America title, Mabel Rader commented: "If anyone deserves the title of Hercules, certainly Casey Viator is the man, as we have never seen a man of his height with such huge, yet shapely, proportions." Additionally, she proclaimed him to be "a very fine young man of high character and ideals, who will do justice to any title that he wins."[21] Much speculation centered on how he would fare in the upcoming Mr. America Contest, where he would confront some of the world's best physiques.

One of them, a Kentuckian named Ken Waller, was expelled early for violating amateur rules by posing for a *Life* magazine ad. Viator easily demolished the remaining field, which included such notables as Pete Grymkowski, Ed Corney, Mike Mentzer, Bill Grant, Kent Kuehn, Bob Birdsong, and Don Ross, all of whom would eventually gain distinction in the IFBB. "Too often in the past spectators did not agree with the selection of the judges," noted *Muscular Development*, "but this time there was complete harmony." And there were many others to wow the audience, leading Peary Rader to state that "the top ten men were as good as you will find anywhere at any time in any contest."[22] The AAU amateurs were holding up well against the IFBB professionals. As the three-time Mr. Universe Reg Park observed, "The public identifies more readily with a Mr. America title than a Mr. Universe. Whenever you say to someone outside of bodybuilding that so-and-so was a former Mr. America, they're always more impressed than if I said the same guy was a Mr. Universe."[23]

Yet resentment persisted that the Mr. America title meant much less than its female counterpart. One bodybuilding enthusiast noted, after Dickerson's win, that "this year's Miss America measures 34-21-34 and for this she gets a $10,000 scholarship, new wardrobe, a year's travel and instant fame," whereas "this year's Mr. America measures 49-30-34 and for it gets not much," little more than a few weightlifting meet exhibitions and the title itself.[24] Nevertheless Hoffman's vision of Mr. America remained tied to the Miss America tradition. "Our contests," he reiterated, had always been conducted "somewhat like the Miss America contests": "Just as a woman with the biggest bust measurement, with a slender waist and voluptuous hips, does not win. Personality, education, talent, poise and beauty, are all considered in selecting Miss America, consideration was always given in the Mr. America contests to what a man could do with his muscles. This came under the heading of athletic ability."[25] The AAU title, like the Miss America crown, still signified a gender ideal and embodied many desirable traits, but muscle mass, always a hallmark of masculinity, was becoming increasingly important, owing largely to the influence of Schwarzenegger and anabolic steroids.

STEVE MICHALIK

Muscle mass was evident in the 1972 Junior Mr. America, Pete Grymkowski, a twenty-six-year-old from Rochester who was an "easy winner" over a more symmetrical Steve Michalik, of Valley Stream, New York. "He has tremendous bulk and excellent shape and the largest deltoids we have ever seen on a bodybuilder anywhere," reported *Iron Man*.[26] Expectations were high that he would be the next Mr. America. But Michalik won it by a large margin, though he won none of the subdivisions and Grymkowski was named most muscular man. Michalik attributed his victory to a downsizing that revealed a classic V shape between his 27-inch waist and 54-inch chest. According to Michalik, "People hadn't seen that kind of physique since Steve Reeves." He also reduced his arms from 22 to 19 inches to match his calves and neck. He noted that these efforts were part of a deliberate strategy: "Symmetry was beauty and was going to win me that title."[27] But it was the prestige of the Mr. America title that motivated Michalik. The contest still had meaning.

From the vantage point of thirty years, Michalik detailed the intensity of his commitment to training:

> If you're not one of these genetically gifted guys or girls whose ancestors worked in caves, you've got to be willing to train hard and have the desire to go beyond anything there is. The New York *Times* once quoted me as saying I would drink crankcase oil to win. That was an understatement of what I would have done! When I was 8 years old I wanted to be Mr. America. . . . My goal was to do it or die trying. To me death would have been a release. By accepting the possibility of death, I was ready to do anything in the gym to achieve that goal.[28]

Michalik was one of the first Mr. Americas to train on Arthur Jones's revolutionary Nautilus machines and to adopt his high-intensity training program. Unlike the long hours he had formerly spent at the gym, Michalik now trained only twice a week for thirty-eight minutes each. So pleased was Peary Rader after this well-groomed and well-spoken champion appeared on the Dick Cavett show that he pronounced him an ideal Mr. America who would do nothing to tarnish the image of manhood that the title represented.[29]

Yet suspicions were growing that the massive physiques becoming the norm in bodybuilding were chemically enhanced. In an article entitled "The Mr. America Syndrome," Joseph Gallucci argued that young trainees, aspiring "to win the big one" and ignoring "all warnings about steroids," would "venture to the quack's office in order to attain more 'get-big-quick' pills." The magic era of Grimek and Stanko, when a man was as strong as he looked, no longer existed. Now ends alone justified the means, according to Gallucci.[30] Michalik, however, vehemently denied using steroids in 1972, even publishing a notarized statement that read: "I have never taken drugs in any form as an aid to my bodybuilding career." What enabled him to win the Mr. America Contest, he insisted, was mental discipline and mind-over-matter techniques that he learned from Buddhist monks during his military service in Vietnam.[31]

But he confessed to taking them before winning the 1972 NABBA Mr. Universe Contest.

> It was obvious that the competitors at that level were bigger and harder than me, so I agreed to take steroids. I started out cautiously, taking one pill a day. When I started seeing the results, I began getting bolder and figured, if one pill works, two will work even better. Before you know it, you're taking a handful of anabolic steroids a day and injecting half a dozen shots a week. . . . Slowly, I learned the harsh realities. At first, it was my mental state. I was more aggressive, meaner. You could say I was outright nasty. Then the headaches came. Headaches? They were more like jackhammers pounding at my brain. Oh, and yes, there were the nosebleeds. That was fun. All the while, I was getting bigger and bigger as my blood pressure rose higher and higher. Sure, I won the heavyweight division of the Mr. Universe competition all right, but at what price? To begin with, there was depression, impotency, and infertility. I was quite the man all right, a real Mr. Universe. I looked great, but the machinery didn't work. . . . It was my body telling me, "Listen jerk, you're going to die if you don't quit this stuff." It turned out I had these tumorlike cysts the size of golf balls on my liver.[32]

Yet he turned to steroids again to help him recover from a car accident in 1975 that immobilized his lower body. Not only was he able to walk after three years, but his addiction also enabled him to train hard enough to enter IFBB Grand Prix events. Only when bodybuilders started taking insulin in the 1980s did he quit taking steroids.[33]

Regardless of his personal failings, Michalik's perspective on Mr. America was no less steeped in tradition than Hoffman's. The AAU had a system of ethics and morals.

> They wanted you to be a Mr. America. When you won, they wanted you to go out there and represent America as a clean cut American, the old fashioned '30s, '40s viewpoint—"Over there, over there, over there." These were all the old guys that were running it in the '60s and '70s. They remember the old era of red, white, and blue, and leaving your doors open, and farmlands, and people working hard, and everybody helping everybody. And that's the work ethic they instilled in Mr. America. When they faded out, and died and lost control and the new era came in, there was no control.[34]

Likewise for Bill Pearl, Mr. America once represented pride in being an American. The titleholder was envisioned as having "the look of some guy on a *Life* magazine cover during World War II"; Mr. America was "like an American soldier, keeping us safe from our enemies." "There's a time, I think they tried to do that," he said, adding, "I think that's when the Mr. America Contest was the most popular."[35]

To reassert control over that image, argued Michalik, the AAU needed a renewed commitment to its ideals and a leader.

Arnold had a chance to be that guy, but he became the other guy. Pot smoking, promiscuous, fun loving, and wearing rags and stuff. And so everybody followed. They all became sheeple. You know when one sheep falls off the cliff, they all follow him off the cliff. They all became sheeple. There was no firm leader to rein it in and say, "Wait a minute. You guys can't be in this contest. You got eight hundred tattoos." They got guys now where their whole faces are tattooed and scars and swastikas. Forget about it! If you had a pimple you lost the Mr. America. When Eric Pedersen competed against Steve Reeves they were tied for an hour. They found a pimple on Eric Pedersen's leg, and Steve Reeves became Mr. America. Yeah, that's how critical it was back then. So that's what happened. . . . The leadership changed.[36]

"It's Arnold's America now," as Kim Wood bluntly put it, "and the bad guys have won."[37] Arnold's impact on the course of bodybuilding in the 1970s may have been at least as great as Hoffman's in the 1940s, but between them lay a seismic change in social values and culture that obviated any meaningful return to the past.

THE WILLIAMSBURG BROUHAHA

A quite different scenario engulfed the 1973 AAU Mr. America Contest, held at the College of William and Mary. In the wake of the racial precedent set by the 1970 event, there appeared on the horizon a black bodybuilder who seemed a darker version of the relatively light-skinned Dickerson. James Morris, a native of New York City, had been training for eighteen years and had won many major physique contests. He retired after placing seventh in the 1969 Mr. America Contest, but was coaxed back to serious training by Bill Pearl at his Pasadena gym. Morris improved greatly, winning the Mr. USA Contest and placing third at the 1972 Mr. America competition. Peary Rader noted he had such a "fabulous physique" that it would not have been a surprise "had he come out in first place."[38]

The main obstacle to fulfilling this ambition in 1973 was massive Pete Grymkowski, runner-up for the previous two years. But with continued improvement and exposure in leading muscle magazines, Morris took the 1973 crown, and Grymkowski again came in second. What shocked everyone was the thirty-point spread between them, while less than twenty points separated the next six contestants. "How was this possible?" asked John Grimek, since "it's virtually impossible for any man to be that far ahead of others in today's competition." Consequently, the announcement of scores was greeted by prolonged booing from the assembled throng in the huge auditorium at Williamsburg.[39] A flurry of letters to editors ensued, none attacking the concept of a black Mr. America or denying that Morris had an outstanding physique and would represent the title well, but virtually everyone wondered how Morris deserved thirty points more than the man many thought should have won.

Only *Iron Man* carried an analysis of the results, observing that Morris, with the possible exception of his calves, had excellent "balance and proportions" along with "amazing cuts and definition, probably the best of anyone in the contest." Furthermore, he had "a personality that matches his spectacular physique; he is a man that we and all Americans can be proud of." As one of the seven judges, I recall that our selection of Morris was unanimous and strong, based largely on his combination of muscularity and symmetry. But he also came across as well educated, mannerly, articulate, and poised in the interview process. His muscles were not larger than those of other contestants, but they were nicely defined, shaped, and integrated. I was especially impressed with the definition of Morris's thigh biceps (hamstring) muscles, the best I had ever seen—and a rarity in those days. We might have been distracted from any deficiencies in his calf development by those of another leading black contestant, Willie Johnson, of Akron, whose slender calves starkly contrasted with his awesome back. Grymkowski's size (especially of his deltoids) was impressive, but his physique needed more definition, and his posing was not as effective as that of Morris and some others.[40]

In the interview process, Grymkowski came off as almost too eager (even as obsequious) to please the judges—a sign of insincerity. These impressions were confirmed years later when he revealed that he was "a little sick of the old style of judging where every guy had to be Mr. Prim 'n' Proper. And you all had to talk nice to the judges. At the time I thought that half of the judges were homosexuals anyway."[41] Morris, on the other hand, was natural all the way. However unobvious it may have been to onlookers, it was clear to me and other judges that Morris was the winner, even by a substantial margin. Whether racial considerations played any part in our decisions is less certain. I do not think any of us had a racial agenda, even though the contest was held in the South, and three of us represented southern states. But I recall that all of us were pleased that a second black man (and a homosexual, as we later learned) had so admirably fulfilled the AAU's stringent requirements for ideal American manhood.[42]

An unfortunate aspect of the 1973 contest was the jettisoning of the set of Mr. America rules crafted by a committee that had "worked long and hard" under Bob Crist to "do the athletes justice." The judging criteria set a traditional standard of twenty-five points each for muscularity, symmetry, and presentation, and five points for the "vital area" of the interview, which was retained because "the man chosen must be in the public eye and project the best image of [the] sport." The Raders had argued for years that the subjective nature of physique judging lent itself more readily to the placement system than point-based scores, and disenchantment over the 1973 result seemed to justify rethinking the point system.[43] Calling it "That Mr. America Problem," Peary Rader advocated its abandonment on grounds that it was "complicated and difficult to work with" and that the Mr. America and other AAU contests were the only ones still using it.[44]

Responding to the overwhelming weight of bodybuilding opinion and following the precedent set by the Weiders, the AAU national committee quietly substituted placements for points. What Rader did not understand was that his revered standard of the whole physique and man, initially jeopardized by the removal of athletic points in the 1960s, was now probably doomed. Although traditional judging criteria and the ideal of picking the best overall specimen of American manhood theoretically still applied, the absence of mandatory points in critical categories rendered these time-honored standards meaningless. The AAU Mr. America Contest was no longer unique.

THE "WASH YEARS" OF MISS AMERICA

The Greek ideal of balance in body and life was almost never mentioned in an era increasingly dominated by the image of "sexy Schwarzenegger."[45] Still, the ideal of perfect manhood, as a counterpart to the highly popular Miss America icon, remained. Peary Rader, commenting on the recent brouhaha at Williamsburg, noted, "I almost never agree with the judges of the Miss America contest, but I don't immediately say that the judges are crooked or incompetent." His wife, Mabel, believed that judging at Mr. America contests would be more effective if it took place over at least two days, which would bring it "more in line with the present arrangement of the Miss America contest."[46] A *Strength & Health* reader, after viewing the 1971 Miss America Pageant on television, suggested that it should serve as a model for Mr. America contests: "Miss America had 50 contestants from every corner of the country and only one contestant from each state. Three States however supplied 17 contestants in the Mr. A competition with five states providing 2 each and the remaining 6 states one each. The question arrives: Why should some states enter 6 or seven aspirants and 31 remaining states have no entries? . . . Don't *Mr. State* titles mean anything?"[47] The obvious answers to these queries are that the Mr. America Contest, aside from promotional articles in muscle magazines, lacked a grassroots qualifying system and naturally favored populous states.

At least Mr. America organizers, despite their envy of the Miss America Pageant and their feelings of inferiority, could take pride in being more advanced and more in tune with the times than their female counterpart in regard to race. The latter, even with the retirement of Lenora Slaughter, seemed impervious to substantive change as it entered the 1970s. Addressing the predicament faced by organizers, pageant chairman Albert Marks ruefully observed that their charter stated the contest was open to women of all races and creeds. Much though they might want to see black contestants in Atlantic City, they could not just "conjure up" such women.[48] Zelma George echoed this frustration before Cheryl Browne's arrival in 1970: "Look I would love to have a colored girl here to take the heat off this thing, but we won't fix anything, so we just have to wait."[49]

Affirmative action was not yet part of national consciousness, but in 1978 Frank Deford observed that in the post-Brown years, "the black state queens chosen have usually come from states with small black populations: Wyoming, Delaware, Nebraska." There had been one exception—"Miss Indiana in 1971 was a Black from an urban state"— and, unsurprisingly, "no black queens have yet come from the South." While the Miss Black America pageants in the 1970s no doubt drained the pool of black Miss America aspirants, they reinforced the concept of all-around feminine attributes. As Deford noted, "The new wave of segregated black pageants has been produced strictly out of protest against *Miss America*. The sardonic turnabout, though, is that they imitate, exactly as they oppose."[50] Nevertheless, the Miss America Pageant remained virtually lily white throughout the 1970s. Unlike the Mr. America Contest, it had no tradition of racial integration and harbored no internal rebels, female equivalents of Poole and Oliva, to arouse moral indignation.

Protests regarding women's rights and dignity, which had seemingly been addressed by Slaughter's reforms, were more vocal and emotionally charged. In 1968, Pepsi-Cola withdrew its sponsorship because the pageant no longer represented "the changing values of our society," and the feminist movement contended it was "a degrading image of woman as a brainless, smiling sex object, a piece of meat."[51] In 1970 pageant officials thwarted an assault by militant feminists by conspiring with a regional bus company—protestors were told that all their chartered buses had broken down at the same time!—and obtaining an injunction against the burning of bras in protest, on grounds that it would be a fire hazard on the boardwalk. The *New York Sunday News* (September 6, 1970) found it difficult to understand "why the Girl Scout atmosphere of the Miss America Pageant should so enrage [the protestors] when most of the imitators—Miss Universe, Miss World, Mrs. America and Miss Nude Universe—all dwell almost exclusively on the image of women as sex objects." The Miss America Contest "has distributed more than $6 million in scholarship grants to more than 1,000 girls" who could "liberate themselves." Deford concurred, noting "the Liberationists have laid so many evils at the Pageant's door, that it becomes perfectly obvious that they are only flailing, hoping to land a lucky punch."[52] Their inability to articulate the point of their protest also impressed Chairman Marks: "So far as I can see, the feminists are saying that we are exploiting female flesh. They never say that we are exploiting it *vis-à-vis* anything—just that we are exploiting it."[53] The National Organization for Women (NOW), borrowing a strategy from Miss Black America organizers, staged a convention in Atlantic City during pageant week in 1974, in a desperate attempt to upstage the "sex objects" in Convention Hall. Most authorities agree that the feminists received so much attention because the pageant had been made bland by television in the 1970s, its content designed to appeal to the Geritol set. And the spectacle of watching women walking around in bathing suits (even two-piecers) lost its ability to titillate in an age of R- and X-rated movies, *Playboy*, *Penthouse*, and other aspects of the sexual revolution. They were "the wash years of the Pageant," commented Michele Passarelli, Miss Rhode Island of 1972. "It seemed to me that the times were very anti-Pageant. *Exceptionally* so!"[54] The decade ended with a whimper.

Figure 7.2. Drawing by Peter Viachursako, of Athens, Greece, illustrating the choice physique contestants faced in the early 1970s over which federation to follow. *Iron Man*, May 1972, 37.

THE MR. WORLD CONTEST

More than ever, the Miss America Pageant was problematic as a template for how to increase public awareness of the Mr. America Contest. What was needed was a higher-echelon competition to which Mr. America winners could aspire. Coming forward to put this nascent sentiment into action was Jim Lorimer, who had become aware of the importance of weight training as a high school football player in Pennsylvania. On moving to Columbus, Ohio, in 1959 as a Nationwide Insurance executive, he became a successful coach and administrator for women's track and field. Lorimer's organizing ability led AAU officials to solicit him to direct the 1967 national weightlifting championships and Mr. America Contest.[55] Impressed by his conduct of the meet, one of the best ever, the AAU and the IWF asked Lorimer to host the 1970 world weightlifting championships in Columbus. Concerned about funding, he added a Mr. World Contest as a way to arouse popular interest and asked ABC's *Wide World of Sports* to cover it—an iron-game precedent. Most importantly, he called Schwarzenegger at Gold's Gym in California and sold him on the idea of entering the contest.

Excitement reached a high pitch because of the television coverage, the disqualification of nine lifters for drugs, and the world's first 500-pound clean and jerk, which was accomplished by the Soviet heavyweight Vasily Alexeev. Arnold, who had just beaten the bodybuilding legends Reg Park and Dave Draper for his fourth Mr. Universe title, arrived just in time. Ken Waller, later an IFBB Mr. America, won the amateur event against lackluster competition. Arnold, on the other hand, electrified the crowd by defeating Sergio Oliva in the first-ever posedown before a record audience of 5,000.[56] "The crowd went absolutely wild," Lorimer recalled. In *Muscular Development,* John Grimek commended the winners, the organizers, and the spirited crowd: "Everything was just perfect." Most pleased of all was Schwarzenegger, who told Lorimer that it was the best contest he had ever been in. "When I am done competing in the sport of bodybuilding, I want to go into the promotion of the sport. I want to raise the cash prizes up to $100,000, I want to professionalize the sport. . . . And I'm going to come back to Columbus, Ohio, and ask you to become my partner."[57] It was a premonition of the future Terminator's now-famous line: "I'll be back!"

In retrospect, the Columbus show provided a golden opportunity for the AAU to capitalize on publicity generated by Schwarzenegger, bodybuilding's hottest commodity, and to offer Mr. America winners a higher level of competition. Such a possibility had been realized by the Weider brothers with their creation of the Mr. Olympia Contest in 1965, but it had thus far not generated much interest or participation. What made a difference was their recruitment of Arnold. Just after winning his second NABBA title, in 1968, he agreed to come to America to work for Weider and compete in IFBB contests. "Business fascinates me," wrote Arnold. "I get caught up in the whole idea that it's a game to make money and to make money make more money. Joe Weider is a wizard at it, and I liked being able to watch him operate."[58] Once ensconced with Weider, Arnold won two IFBB Mr. Universe titles and reeled off six Mr. Olympia victories, 1970–1975. Henceforth, as Alan Radley and David Gentle observed, "a new type of physique took centre stage" as "massive muscles became the norm, and proportion seemed to have been thrown out as in baby and bathwater." But it was Arnold, contended Joe Gold, "by his appearances and talk shows around the country," who made bodybuilding acceptable. He had "the charisma that people sensed," could "speak well in public," and could "take the negativity of an interviewer and turn it around and show him just how stupid HE was!"[59] Schwarzenegger's achievements and imagery became a critical factor in the rise of the Weiders and the Mr. Olympia Contest to dominance in the physique world, and served as a springboard for his own movie career.[60]

The AAU had always regarded the NABBA Mr. Universe Contest in

London as an outlet for its Mr. America winners, but unlike the IFBB's version, the show was sponsored by another national organization, under Oscar Heidenstam. Many regarded it as inferior to the Mr. America Contest. Acting on the Columbus precedent and attempting to raise the stakes, York planned a second Mr. World Contest along with the first World's Powerlifting Championship. It would be, promised Gord Venables, "the start of the biggest physique contest of them all." But the fact that it was held on the nearest Saturday in 1971 to Hoffman's birthday "to honor Bob," who "has done so much for physique contests," lent a parochial air to the event. Although *Muscular Development* called it "highly successful," *Iron Man* labeled it "the most disappointing" of the year's major contests, since it did not represent the world. The only non-Americans were the NABBA representatives Al Beckles and Paul Grant, who won first and second.[61]

Ben Weider chided Terpak on this issue and tried to use it as leverage to obtain AAU affiliation for the IFBB: "When I went to school, I was told that there were approximately 130 nations in the world. Correct me if I am wrong, but I understand that in your Mr. World A.A.U. amateur contest, you had exactly one nation participating, other than America, and that was England. . . . This is all the more reason why the A.A.U. must reach a conciliation with us."[62] Notably absent too were any former Mr. Americas, for whom the contest could have been a capstone. Nor were any present for the 1972 version, which featured only four foreign entrants, noted Herb Glossbrenner, a "mild turnout internationally for a Mr. World." *Muscular Development* expressed disappointment that only twenty-one of the thirty men who sent entries showed up, none of them "big names." A well-built Ron Thompson, of Flint, Michigan, won, but his ninth-place finish in the 1973 Junior Mr. America Contest indicated that the Mr. World title was far lower on the pecking order than Mr. America. Dickerson and Coe dropped their amateur standing and took home multiple NABBA Mr. Universe and WBBG Mr. America and Mr. World titles from 1970 to 1975.[63]

The 1973, 1974, and 1976 AAU Mr. World contests, won by Roy Duval (England), Ian Lawrence (Scotland), and Bertil Fox (England), were equally anticlimatic. The emcee Len Bosland rationalized his disappointment at the 1973 turnout: "It takes a great deal of time to build the prestige of a contest." Most likely, in light of the monetary pulling power that Arnold was bringing to the sport, another amateur contest of dubious distinction had little attraction for ambitious bodybuilders. Although the IFBB Mr. Olympia award was still only $1,000, Dan Lurie boasted of awarding over $4,000 in cash prizes, trips, and trophies for winners of his 1973 contests.[64] While the AAU Mr. World was languishing, the IFBB Mr. World and Mr. Olympia and the WBBG Mr. World and Mr. Olympus contests were capturing the best physique stars of the day, including Franco Columbu, Frank Zane, Robby Robinson, Serge Nubret, and Schwarzenegger. Despite considerable effort and expense, York partisans, confronted with the sport's growing professionalization, abandoned support for a higher form of amateurism after 1976. AAU Mr. America winners would be forced to leave the fold for greener pastures.

INTERNATIONAL POLITICAL LEVERAGE

What motivated York's efforts on behalf of its ill-fated Mr. World Contest was the growing international presence of the IFBB by the early 1970s. For the previous two decades, it had consisted of a loose-knit confederation overseen by Ben Weider from his headquarters in Montreal. Hoffman's organization had a firm link with Heidenstam's London contest and longtime influence in the IWF through Hoffman's confidant Clarence Johnson, who was either vice president or president of the group from 1953 to 1972. The Weiders had a close association with Heidenstam's archrival, Oscar State, who was the IWF general secretary from 1960 to 1976 and a contributor to Weider magazines since the early 1950s. In 1972, Johnson lost the IWF presidency to Gottfried Schodl, of Austria, an event that coincided with the IFBB's admission in 1971 to the General Assembly of International Sports Federations (GAISF), a Switzerland-based body with seventy-three national affiliates and jurisdiction over numerous Olympic events.[65] The IFBB seemed poised for IOC recognition, which could elevate bodybuilding to an Olympic sport.[66]

Heidenstam was furious, attributing this Weider triumph to the intrigues of State, who was soon elected general secretary of GAISF and awarded an OBE by the queen of England.[67] He urged John Terpak, Hoffman's chief aide, to "use your powers and contacts against this wretched man," who was a "fly in the ointment and doing all in his power to get Weider any recognition possible." Oscar hardly underestimated his adversaries: "I imagine that State and the Weider brothers are of the same political and [Jewish] racial fraternity. I am surprised that you in USA tolerate this in State. . . . Weider really wants to isolate us in Europe and is telling everyone this. Ourselves and the French are the only bodybuilding bastion in Europe and a stumbling block to Weider taking over." Heidenstam was especially frustrated that the GAISF seemed unconcerned that the IFBB was a commercial enterprise. Often expressing despair to his York friends, he could not comprehend how State had gained such an advantage, even to the extent that "no one else can get in." Heidenstam believed that York had the clout to stop the Weiders, and when he heard that Ben Weider was seeking AAU affiliation for the IFBB in 1972, he expressed the "hope that you will hit him hard and take him down many pegs."[68]

All was not well at York, however. Hoffman was aging and ill, his weightlifting empire was crumbling, and his company was losing its share of the barbell and food supplement market. In a satirical article, "The One Nation 'Mr. World' Contest," Ben Weider displayed his organization's muscle, claiming that the 1971 AAU Mr. World had so few international entries because he had notified the IFBB's thirty national affiliates that they would be violating the federation's constitution if they sent participants. The winners, Albert Beckles and Paul Grant, although allegedly professionals, were able to compete because Heidenstam had secured amateur cards for them from Wally Holland of the British Amateur Weight-Lifters' Association (BAWLA).[69] Further evidence of increased Weider leverage, according to a surprised Rader, came from an admission by John Terpak, the outgoing chair of the AAU weightlifting committee, who observed that GAISF recognition of the IFBB automatically permitted its athletes to enter AAU-sanctioned contests.[70] It was a virtual validation of the IFBB's dominance.

GAISF membership enabled the Weiders to gain the ear of the new AAU president, Jack Kelly Jr. Responding to a letter from Ben Weider, he indicated his familiarity with the Mr. America Contest; desiring to see "a more harmonious relationship" between the AAU and the IFBB, he hosted a meeting between the two sides at his Philadelphia apartment in November 1971.[71] Terpak was accompanied by Dave Mayor, Pete Miller, and Rudy Sablo, while Ben Weider was joined by Ralph Johnson, Bob Hise, and Jack King. Little common ground was found, since the York side shunned Weider's conciliatory gestures. The IWF had no authority to meddle in the affairs of another GAISF affiliate, he admitted, but there was no reason why the IFBB could not affiliate with the AAU and enter its athletes in the Mr. America Contest. Obviously, York would never allow such an intrusion. It is hardly surprising, given York's distrust of Weider, that the discussion centered on personalities and ethics. To York's objection that the IFBB (with its lifetime president) was not democratic, Weider offered to resign, but added, "I will be re-elected anyway." To discredit the opposition, Sablo reviewed IFBB activities since 1947. Weider, "noticeably annoyed, asked that . . . bygones be bygones," and stated "that he was not interested in history," being interested only in helping bodybuilders. He believed that each organization should recognize the other's athletes and "work towards a grand climax—one Mr. America contest."[72] He even offered to change the name of the IFBB Mr. America Contest to the American Bodybuilding Championships, and to alter the IFBB constitution to differentiate between amateur and professional competitions.[73] It was evident that the IFBB side had made a favorable impression on Kelly and that the Weider brothers had the energy and determination to dominate bodybuilding in the United States even as they were increasing their global presence.[74]

THE AMERICAN AMATEUR BODYBUILDING ASSOCIATION

In ensuing months the Weiders moved aggressively on several fronts, buoyed by the popularity of Schwarzenegger and the participation of increasing numbers of AAU elite bodybuilders in IFBB contests, most recently Ken Waller and Boyer Coe. In 1972, they announced an upgrade in their nutritional products and equipment, a new publication called *The Bodybuilder*, and the movement of Joe's headquarters to California, the center of physique culture. Most importantly, at an organizational meeting in Philadelphia, Ben Weider awarded Kelly an IFBB Certificate of Merit for his "contributions to sports and physical fitness." There Kelly witnessed the creation of the American Amateur Bodybuilding Association (AABBA); Ralph Johnson was elected president, and there were six regional affiliates. These efforts had their intended effect of drawing Kelly to the Weider side: Ben was awarded a life membership in the AAU.[75] Later Weider attended the annual GAISF congress in Lausanne, Switzerland, where he reveled in his "efforts to get bodybuilding recognized as a true amateur sport," on the same level as "hockey, skiing, weightlifting, swimming, track and field," and other high-visibility sports. In addition to schmoozing with the GAISF president, Thomas Keller, and the IOC notables Avery Brundage and Lord Killanin, Weider attended an IOC executive committee meeting. Thus "sports history of a sort was created," and it was obvious that Weider was dreaming of Olympic participation as his next step. He was greatly satisfied, stating, "My cup runneth over." He soon applied for IOC affiliation, expecting "a favorable answer . . . in the near future."[76]

In addition to the interpersonal skills that Weider brought to bear in raising the status of the IFBB was an ample amount of bluff and bluster. While his argument that only ten sports in the GAISF had more national affiliates than the IFBB was in some measure true, his boast in 1973 that "the vast majority of American bodybuilders are members of the A.A.B.A. and not the A.A.U." was wholly untrue. Although there were hastily created AABA committees for medicine, arm wrestling, and public relations, there was little evidence of local, state, or regional competitions. The great advantage the IFBB had over its adversaries was logic. Ben could rightly argue that it alone was the international amateur organization that determined which national federation should represent a particular country. He pointed out, by contrast, the limitation of the AAU: "Since the A.A.U. is a national organization that controls specific sports only in America it has no power outside the U.S.A." Only by affiliating with the IFBB/AABA could it send competitors to international events. It was this logic, even though the IFBB was largely professional and the AABA little more than a paper organization designed to further Weider's Olympic ambitions, that appealed to Jack Kelly. "It is my hope that the A.A.U. might become the American member of the I.F.B.B.," he wrote Weider eight months after their meeting, "and organize all amateur bodybuilding in the U.S.A., thereby having our Mr. America qualify for your Mr. Universe Contest."[77] While Olympic recognition for the IFBB was not developing as quickly as Weider hoped, political leverage was emerging from another quarter.

In 1973, Senator John Tunney of California spearheaded a congressional effort to create a national sports board that would both coordinate all amateur sports and separate bodybuilding and powerlifting from the AAU national weightlifting committee. Furthermore, the international federation for each sport would recognize only one affiliate in each country. But the measure failed to pass. How much impact the lobbying of Ben Weider, a Canadian residing in Montreal, had on these initiatives is uncertain, but at one point he enlisted the aid of Schwarzenegger, an Austrian citizen, now known as the "King of the Bodybuilders" after four Mr. Olympia victories. In a guest editorial, no doubt ghosted by Weider editors, Arnold and his bodybuilding friends, virtually all of whom were professionals, were supposedly "burned up" and "fighting mad" about amateur bodybuilders being forced to enter only AAU events. "I strongly urge them *all* to join the *American Amateur Bodybuilding Association* (A.A.B.A.), which is the *only* amateur federation in America permitted to control amateur bodybuilding abroad and for the Olympics."[78]

THE WBBG

This incessant political infighting did not appear to be harming body-building contests. As Len Bosland noted in 1974, "the physique contest is emerging to a place of respect which has been unprecedented," and the AAU Mr. America and Mr. World contests were no longer relegated to the end of lifting sessions. The next year, James Morris validated the perception that the sport had grown in prestige: "The general image of the sport has improved tremendously over the last five years. Public acceptance of the sport has gone up, like 10,000 percent. I mean, it's now on TV. I won the Mr. America about a year and a half ago and at last count I've done about thirty TV shows."[79] The continued favorable name recognition of the Mr. America Contest, the popularity of Schwarzeneg-ger, and the showcasing of elite bodybuilders as inspirations for American youth no doubt contributed to this higher level of acceptance.

Another way in which the sport was brought to the public, albe-it with a sweet-sour flavor, was through Dan Lurie's version of Mr. America. By parading his bodybuilders through the streets of Manhat-tan on the day of the 1970 contest, he sought to generate the "kind of publicity that helps educate the public and wins followers." His 1971 show, however, nearly ended in disaster when Ken Waller, told he could not enter the Pro Mr. America because he had just won the IFBB Mr. America Contest, "caused a terrible fuss." No doubt Waller's loss to Boyer Coe in the Mr. World Contest, which he *was* allowed to enter, had not improved his demeanor. A misunderstanding over photograph-ic and financial arrangements then led, in Lurie's words, to "arguments and unfair accusations on Waller's part, as well as a scuffle, in full view of hundreds present": "It was a black eye for bodybuilding." The new Pro Mr. America, Peter Caputo, was hardly mentioned in Lurie's report, indicating that the winner and his title were relatively meaningless.[80]

The 1972 contest, on the other hand, was "a test of real men and gut-wrenching sportsmanship" between the local favorite, Lou Ferrigno, winner of the 1971 WBBG Teenage Mr. America; the veteran Warren Frederick; and Bill Grant. When the thirteen judges chose Grant, he broke down in tears.[81] It was his "best win," he recalled. "After all those years of trying for the AAU Mr. America, it was the best moment of my career." Grant credited Lurie with "getting guys before Joe had them."[82] But Ferrigno, the faster-rising star, soon defected to the IFBB. He won its 1973 Mr. America Contest and successfully sued Lurie for $100,000 for using his image to promote his Jet Weight-Gain Formula

707 supplement. According to Lurie, "[These events] broke my heart," but he moved on: "I forgive Lou and wish him well."[83]

In 1973, Chris Dickerson won Lurie's Mr. America title, but his victory, almost a foregone conclusion, was overshadowed by a welter of other contests that attracted three thousand fans to the Hunter College auditorium in New York and featured a hundred contestants. Highlights included posing routines by former IFBB Mr. Americas Frank Zane, Dave Draper, and Sergio Oliva, but the major attraction was the appearance of the immortal Steve Reeves, who had not been seen in bodybuilding circles in decades. Earlier in the day, Reeves had appeared in several televised interviews, including one by Howard Cosell, and New York honored him by giving him a key to the city and designating September 8 as Physical Culture Day. Nat Haber reported that Lurie's contests attracted an "appreciative, overcrowded, standing-room-only audience," but everyone was there to see one guy: "Two Hercules film-clips were shown. Our guest of honor stepped out on the stage and at that moment no one in the crowded auditorium could hold back his enthusiasm for this moment of actually seeing in person the fabulous Steve Reeves."[84] Probably no one made the connection between Reeves's box-office triumphs and bodybuilding's Greek traditions, least of all through the WBBG Mr. America Contest.

LURIE VERSUS WEIDER

In 1974, Warren Frederick edged out Mr. California, Ralph Kroger, and Mr. Michigan, Don Ross, after having competed for the Mr. America title in all three federations. Frederick later explained: "I felt I should have been winning before, but it was the color barrier that kept me back. When you're black you got to do better." He felt there was discrimination in the IFBB, but "in the AAU it was even more." His take on the latter: "I won the AAU Mr. America Contest in 1969 and didn't." Lurie helped him by paying him to appear in promotional ads, but Frederick still felt shortchanged overall: "I was never making money like I should."[85]

What was new was a Pro Mr. America Over-40 Contest, which the former Mr. Universe Elmo Santiago won over George Paine and Kenny Hall. "While everyone seems concerned with the bodybuilder until he hits the age of 30," noted Rick Wayne, "it is good to note the WBBG plans events to keep the older bodybuilder interested in staying in shape." A former Miss Nude America, Kellie Everts, "dominated the scene" in the Miss Body Beautiful U.S.A. Contest over twenty other girls. Unfortunately, the proceedings were marred by the guest-posing appearance of Sergio Oliva, whose routine was interrupted by fans "shouting for Arnold" in response to Lurie's promotion of a showdown between Oliva and Schwarzenegger for the "World's Best-Built Man" title. Although Oliva's posing went well, "his remarks over the microphone were in the worst taste," Wayne declared. "Sergio's private war with Weider should be kept between them. Fans should not be forced to be a part of this kind of ugliness."[86]

Although a Schwarzenegger-Oliva showdown never materialized, months later, Arnold successfully sued Lurie for $100,000 for using his name in promoting the WBBG's inaugural Mr. Hollywood Contest, insisting that the publicity was what made the contest profitable.[87] In retrospect, the incident was the latest chapter in a feud going back to the 1940s and was reminiscent of the Lurie-Grimek challenge. With York's influence on the wane, there was an all-out fight for hegemony in the physique world, and the Weiders used the power of the courts— seen in the litigation brought by Ferrigno and Schwarzenegger—to restrain Lurie, an upstart competitor. With Oliva in his camp, Lurie hoped to attract Arnold through the one-on-one challenge, and further hoped that Ferrigno might even return. Lurie, who was playing for high stakes, recognized, as did Weider, that California was the hot spot for bodybuilding. "The WBBG Smashes into California" was the heading for Lurie's Mr. Hollywood Contest. He crowed in the pages of *Muscle Training Illustrated*: "Recently the World Body Building Guild walked into bombing, blitzing, zonking, honking, whacking, and thwacking land—California—and ran its first sanctioned show in the Big Bear State. We all know who has his headquarters in that state over in Woodlawn Hills; yes, the great dictator of the sport J. W. To you, J. W., I say 'The WBBG is here to stay and give bodybuilders an even break, and "you ain't seen nothing yet"!'"[88] "Weider wanted to destroy me" is how Lurie viewed the lawsuits brought against him by the two giants of the sport. But according to Joe Weider, "Lurie tried to stir up trouble with me just to try to get a little attention.... That guy was like gum on my shoe."[89] However easy it might be to think of the Weiders as having a great advantage over Lurie, they still lacked the political and financial control they would have a decade later. The full impact of the Schwarzenegger phenomenon was yet to be felt, and they could hardly allow Lurie to gain any advantage.

Lurie had attracted considerable talent: Boyer Coe won his Mr. World Contest for five straight years, and Oliva won his new Mr. Olympus

Contest, a challenge to the Weiders' Olympia, in 1975 and 1976. Former Mr. Californias Ralph Kroger and Scott Wilson won Lurie's next two Pro Mr. America contests, indicating his growing West Coast presence, but the title seemed devoid of any meaning other than to support the sponsor's ego and commercial enterprises. When asked how it felt to be Mr. America, Wilson seemed confused: "It's just another contest. I don't know, maybe tomorrow it'll hit me. I guess it's great. Yes, it is great!" Lurie's greatest contribution to the iron game was perhaps his hosting the first annual WBBG Hall of Fame Testimonial Dinner in May 1975, at the New York Sheraton. The honorees were Dickerson, Draper, Joe Bonomo, and ninety-four-year-old Joe Greenstein, the "Mighty Atom," who was the main attraction.[90] The award dinner evolved into the Olde Time Strong Man Association and annual dinners organized by Vic Boff and Artie Drechsler in succeeding decades.

MUSCLEMAG INTERNATIONAL

Robert Kennedy, an English bodybuilder with an artistic background, wrote articles for physical-culture publications. In the fall of 1974, a magazine that he launched from his Ontario base showed promise of bringing sanity to the sport.[91] Kennedy declared allegiance to the sensible traditions of bodybuilding in the inaugural issue of *MuscleMag International*: "I do not believe in the building of enormous muscle size—nor do I believe in the dangerous practice of drug taking that 99% of these out-size fellows ingest to build such awesome muscle." Reinforcement for Kennedy's view came from David Webster's article "The Ideal Physique," which drew inspiration from the ancients by advocating a "finely built but moderately proportioned manhood." Another article, "Turn Your Back on Steroids," and a full-page drawing of Hercules set the tone for Kennedy's magazine. Aware that he might offend fans of such "huge muscled fellows" as Oliva, Schwarzenegger, Katz, and Ferrigno, he was careful in his second issue not to condemn them, only the judges: "These gargantuans train like men possessed, and, who's going to condemn them for it? . . . We know that 'the Oak' realized his dream." That issue featured full-page photos of the more proportional physiques of Reeves, Tinerino, and Zane. The fourth issue included an article by the 1975 AAU Mr. America, Dale Adrian, titled "Mr. America's Secrets of Proportions." Dick Falcon contributed a piece on Richard Baldwin, Mr. Sunshine State, who was inspired to take up bodybuilding by studying ancient Greek civilization: "Its history, its literature, the great men the country had spawned like Homer, Plato, Socrates, Aristotle, Hippocrates and Alexander the Great, fascinated him. He marveled at the pictures of the ancient Greek statues depicting the human form in all its beauty."[92]

Kennedy's appreciation of the body extended to the female form and eroticism. Many magazine issues featured pert young females in revealing outfits, such as the one facing Kennedy's editorial in the summer issue of 1975: "We thought you would like to see this photo of Anulka" the caption innocently reads. The same issue carries a full-page set of ads, of the sort usually found in pulp men's magazines, for books entitled "How to Pick Up Girls!" and "How to Make Love to a Single Girl!," with a picture of an enticing bare-breasted young woman. In addition, perhaps to the delight or dismay of readers, *MuscleMag* featured occasional full-frontal pictures of male nudes. The magazine defended these photos: "If you are offended by nudity and want only to see pictures of bodybuilders and lifters decently clad, then buy IRON MAN. It is a great magazine and will offend no one. . . . If you want to see every wrinkle in a man's penis then 'In Touch' would be your journal. It caters for 'gay' fellows, or you can visit your friendly supermarket and flick through 'Playgirl' or 'Viva.'" He would continue to display "well-built fellows both nude and in swim wear," knowing that many top physique models, Grimek, Ross, Reeves, Sansone, Dickerson, Grant, Morris, Lurie, and Atlas, had posed nude: "If the male sex organs happen to be showing on a photograph we choose then, so be it, they will remain." In contrast to Weider's commercially driven depictions, Kennedy's nudes were more artistic and, like those made in ancient Greece, depicted the body within the context of the whole man. Finally, Kennedy formed the World Bodybuilding Association, offering products to address readers' training needs; but without a contest agenda to build a fan base, it seemed uncertain whether his enterprise could survive the rough-and-tumble world of bodybuilding journalism.[93]

THE AAU IN EQUILIBRIUM

Philosophically, Kennedy was more in synch with the AAU, whose Mr. Americas seemed less driven by drugs and size. There were no giants among the thirty five contestants at the 1974 contest at York. Gone was Pete Grymkowski to the friendlier confines of the IFBB, and present was the diminutive Danny Padillo, later called "giant killer." Ron Thompson, who took no subdivisions and had placed thirtieth three years earlier, was the surprise winner. Yet he was a true amateur who had overcome all odds. As manager of a building-supply company, he trained during off-hours in his basement gym on homemade equipment. His height was a disadvantage, and unlike Weider and Lurie stars, he had very white skin that did not tan well. Also distinctive was Thompson's claim that he did not "use growth drugs," since as many as 90 percent of his rivals were using them. He expounded on the topic: "How extensive is the use of growth drugs in our sport? The following illustration was very depressing to me. At some of the big contests, on a number of occasions, a top bodybuilder would come over to talk to me and . . . he would ask what I was on, referring to growth drugs. Not IF I was but WHAT was I on! The assumption was that everyone was!" What enabled him to win was his symmetry, an attribute increasingly valued by AAU officials, who were starting to denigrate the Weider giants as "monsters" and "freaks." The 1974 AAU contest, having recovered from the 1973 fiasco, was the first to use the placement system, but according to Clarence Bass, it took seven judges seven hours to reach a decision; only one point separated Thompson from Paul Hill, and Doug Beaver was only a point behind Hill. Yet Bass pronounced the contest "a spellbinding success."[94]

"The ANNUAL AAU Mr. America contest is the thing that bodybuilding dreams are made of," wrote Bill Reynolds of the 1975 event, staged at the Culver City Veterans Auditorium, "across from MGM's movie studios." What enabled Dale Adrian, of Canoga Park, California, to win over thirty-two others was his "symmetrical and shapely physique," declared Reynolds. Along with sufficient size and cuts, he presented "a harmonious whole body." The crowd favorite, however, was Robert (Robbie) Robinson, who was named most muscular man but placed fifth overall. Though rated high for his chest, arms, and back, he lacked thigh cuts and calf size.[95] Adrian later added that Robinson was "not a good poser," since "he posed way too fast." In addition, he had a distracting skin growth dangling from his underarms. Race, Adrian believes, was not a factor. What enabled Adrian to beat others who were bigger and more gifted genetically was his symmetry; and he was in the best shape of his life. As he put it: "I was peaked." Adrian admitted to taking steroids, but "the amounts were small," and he "was under a doctor's supervision." Others were taking much more. In fact, "everybody was on steroids in the 1975 Mr. A Contest," he claimed. In retrospect, the title neither hindered nor helped him. Three decades later, he had to hold down three jobs in order to make ends meet. Adrian considered the Mr. America Contest "prestigious because of who had won it before," and it still had that prestige in 1975. It was "perhaps the best in recent memory," reported Franklin Page for *Iron Man.* "Every physique in it was of exceptional quality."[96]

The U.S. bicentennial edition of the AAU Mr. America Contest, staged by York Barbell in Philadelphia, was disappointing. Reynolds reported that only twenty-four contestants showed up, and "overall depth was a bit shallow." But the biggest problem was the absence of physique lights at the public show, which forced the men to pose under house lighting. According to Reynolds, "the organizing committee blew a fuse on this one!" Bob Kennedy was even more critical: "The AAU runs the worst bodybuilding contests of any organization in the U.S.A. Philadelphia was a classic example. No spotlight. No stage decoration. No music. And the AAU has been running bodybuilding contests longer than any other group in this country."[97]

The winner, however, was outstanding. For Kalman Szkalak, the son of refugees from the 1956 Hungarian uprising, it was only his third contest, the second being his Mr. California victory a month earlier. Reynolds made a prediction: "Kal's going to be one of the real greats *very* soon. His shape is outstanding and his symmetry almost flawless." He also had size, so much so that many compared him to another central European émigré. This was the view of the physique pundit John Mese: "Szkalak reminds me a little of Arnold Schwarzenegger, particularly his arms." Reynolds observed that "the resemblance between Kal and Arnold when the former strikes his side chest pose is uncanny." According to Ken Sprague, the proprietor of the Gold's Gym where Szkalak trained, "Arnold is the only other bodybuilder who trains with the tenacity and determination displayed by Kal. His mind is locked on physique perfection."[98]

But the superlatives lavished on Szkalak merely made more obvious the manifold pressures brought to bear on the AAU by Schwarzenegger's growing fame in the mid-1970s. Peary Rader was frustrated by the organization's inability to detach Mr. America from the national weightlifting championships, where it was always considered an afterthought: "Something must be done, and quickly. . . . The Mr. America can be made one of the most spectacular shows in this country, but it will take work, planning and innovation."[99] But its secondary status behind the lifting competition was only one of the problems confronting organizers. Unlike other bodybuilding federations but like the Miss America Pageant, a Mr. America could win the title only once and could not afterward readily advance to a higher title or receive cash awards. And despite energetic leadership from Bob Crist, he and virtu-ally all AAU leaders were unpaid volunteers whose interests, efforts, and funds were spread among weightlifting, bodybuilding, and powerlifting.

AN IFBB AFTERTHOUGHT

For the Weiders, their Mr. America Contest was becoming merely one component of a growing bodybuilding empire. To Rick Wayne, by 1973 the Mr. Olympia Contest had transcended all other bodybuilding shows: "It was simply the greatest. All you had to show, to be allowed in, was a pack of incredible muscle." In that year Lou Ferrigno, at 6'5" and 260 pounds, became the tallest and heaviest Mr. America ever, and Joe Weider considered him "the only man *naturally* big enough to knock-off Arnold." But Ferrigno regarded the title as merely "the first of his goals," and it was soon overshadowed by his winning the 1973 Mr. Uni-verse title in Switzerland. To Bob Birdsong, of Kentucky, winning the 1974 IFBB Mr. America was the realization of a dream. He recalled that at fourteen, "I told myself that one day I would become Mr. America." But it was likely the AAU Mr. America title, in its prime in 1962, when Birdsong was that age, and not the IFBB version, then in its infancy, that he coveted. It was the AAU version that he first entered, placing tenth in 1972. Also, it appeared that he entered the IFBB Mr. America to recover from the "bitter defeat" of losing the Mr. Universe Contest in Italy nine days earlier—making what he called a dream more a con-solation prize of sorts. He expressed gratitude to Joe Weider for "train-ing advice and money," indicating that this holder of the IFBB's leading amateur title was actually a professional.[100]

It was also soon obvious to Birdsong that being Mr. America hardly fulfilled his expectations. As so many aspiring bodybuilders discovered in pursuit of this dream, it was impossible to support their lifestyle—long training hours, lodging, supplements, and drugs—without com-promising their moral standards. Birdsong later admitted to becoming a "typical Hollywood hustler," adding, "It was so cool depending on the Hollywood big shots for money. . . . [I] did whatever they wanted me to." In addition to his title, Birdsong had all the trappings of American success, including a sports car and lots of women. Later, to the delight of Peary Rader, he became a Christian after encountering two elderly women at a Santa Monica restaurant, and then retired.[101] Far from being an exemplar of American manhood, Birdsong discovered that his lifelong goal and the culture associated with it were devoid of meaning or moral content.

Even the title of Birdsong's dream was changed to "Mr. Americas" in order to avoid legal action by the AAU, which had seized ownership of the Mr. America copyright.[102] The Weiders brought back their Miss Americana, "the cutesy girlie show" and introduced a Mr. USA (another AAU duplication), which was won by Danny Padilla in 1975. The AAU's proprietary claim on the "Mr. America" name was no doubt a factor in the demise of the IFBB title in 1977. The last three winners were all defectors from AAU ranks. Robby Robinson, the 1975 Mr. Americas, believed that the AAU was more interested in showcasing track athletes than in promoting musclemen. He noted that for bodybuilders, the organization had little beyond the one contest: "There is not much they can offer besides the AAU Mr. America, and after the luster of that wears thin, you might as well hang up the posing briefs. I was being stifled." The IFBB was far more accepting of Robinson. Soon he was Mr. World 1975. In a full-body picture of him in *Muscle Builder*, the caption notes that he "needed only four blockbuster poses" to win the armful of trophies he is carrying—a striking contrast to AAU criticisms of him for inadequate posing.[103] It was obvious that the IFBB Mr. America (Americas) title had outlived its usefulness. It survived another two years, but it was merely a stepping-stone for Mike Mentzer in 1976 and Danny Padilla in 1977 on their way to higher titles that rewarded greater muscle mass.

IFBB SUPERSTARS

What was drawing the life out of all the Mr. America versions was not only the Mr. Olympia title but also its larger-than-life titleholder from 1970 to 1975. An important aspect of Schwarzenegger's master plan was to become a film star, much in the manner of the legendary Steve Reeves.[104] But his first film, *Hercules in New York* (1970), where he openly exploited his muscles, was a bomb. "Often cited as one of the worst films of all time," his biographers note, "it nevertheless opened doors in Hollywood" and exposed him to a larger audience. Then in *Stay Hungry* (1976), starring Jeff Bridges and Sally Field, he won a Golden Globe Award for best actor in a film debut. It was based on a novel by Charles Gaines, who also wrote (with George Butler) *Pumping Iron*, a nonfictional overview of the IFBB bodybuilding subculture. Schwarzenegger was only one character in the book—which went into twenty-five printings, as Laurence Leamer notes—but he dominated it "as the highest exemplar of this hidden world." According to Leamer, the book had a large impact on Schwarzenegger's life: "Gaines and Butler helped elevate Arnold to a unique place, not only in bodybuilding but in American popular culture."[105]

They later adapted the book into a movie focusing on the 1975 Mr. Olympia Contest in South Africa, featuring a confrontation between Schwarzenegger and Ferrigno. The latter, according to Louise Krasniewicz and Michael Blitz, "was taller and bigger than Arnold, but he lacked the one quality that had made Arnold so successful in bodybuilding: confidence." The film brought bodybuilding to a public that had only hazy or incorrect ideas about the sport:

> The movie also focused on Arnold's masculinity, showing him being the center of attention of women at the beach, in a photo studio, and at the gym. This effort to take bodybuilding out of a gay subculture and bring it into the mainstream is considered to be one of *Pumping Iron's* greatest successes and is thought by many historians of American society to be a major turning point on the development of America's fitness culture.[106]

Ferrigno's Olympia loss, however, did not diminish his popularity. In 1976, he competed successfully against forty-six elite athletes in a variety of events on ABC-TV's "Superstars" program in Sarasota, Florida. "I wanted to erase the muscle-bound image that a lot of people have of us," he explained, "the idea that bodybuilders are unable to do well in other sports." To the reporter Jack Gurney, "the results were stunning." Ferrigno did well in rowing, weightlifting, bowling, the half-mile run, bicycling, and baseball hitting, and collected $18,000.[107] His appearance was also a step to his becoming the star of the popular television series *The Incredible Hulk*.

Pumping Iron became an iron-game classic, attracting worldwide attention and helping legitimize bodybuilding as a sport. Whether it contributed to the demise of the Mr. America Contest is debatable, but Wayne DeMilia attributes much of his own success as a promoter and that of the Weiders to its appearance: "If they had done the film on the AAU Mr. America or on the NABBA Mr. Universe, they would have become bigger." Butler and Gaines had met Arnold, "this charismatic guy hidden away in this nothing sport," while doing a bodybuilding story for *Sports Illustrated* in 1972. The article, which centered on Arnold and led to the book and movie, allowed the IFBB to share a leading role. According to DeMilia, "that's what buried the AAU."[108]

Another unexpected offshoot of *Pumping Iron* was a program called *Articulate Muscle: The Male Body in Art*, sponsored by the Whitney

Museum of American Art in February 1976. It featured a photo exhibit; a panel discussion featuring art, literature, and medical professors from Columbia, Rutgers, and New York University; and posing displays by Ed Corney, Frank Zane, and Schwarzenegger. It was a momentous occasion, and potentially a boost for bodybuilding. Although the overflow audience consisted largely of modern physique aficionados, the discussion centered mostly on the ideal of beauty as conceived by the ancient Greeks. According to Colin Eisler of NYU's Institute of Fine Arts, figural representation, which was divinely sanctioned, provided "a field day for the Greeks": "They were free to render forceful forms in art commemorating victories in the Olympic Games, honoring the gods, the highest personification of human and divine endeavor in thousands of marble statues." Mason Cooley, a professor at Columbia, checked his university library's card catalogue for entries on bodybuilding, but there was "nothing there." But he found plenty on other body-related subjects: "I turned to the next card which had to do with 'Body and Mind,' 'Body and Spirit,' and there was card file after card file after card file on such entries. I think this might tell us something about the curious illness of the relations of mind and body that has overtaken us in the last century and a half." Cooley hoped that the "socially significant" event at the Whitney was a symptom that "this long, long, sick and destructive dichotomy of man and body" was coming to an end.[109]

The posing routines of the three bodybuilders, however, gave no indication of any healing. While Corney and Zane were well received by the audience, the applause for Schwarzenegger was "deafening," reported Al Antuck. Unbefitting the distinguished surroundings and academic discussion, "there were loud shouts for Arnold! Arnold! Arnold! Arnold!" Then Eisler put a damper on the celebratory mood when he dismissed the notion put forward by Charles Gaines and Schwarzenegger that a bodybuilder was a sculptor: "There is a saying that a man who is self-educated has had the disadvantage of having a very ignorant teacher. I must admit if you are a work of art, you have had the disadvantage of having a bad art teacher because to me, your poses are the personification of 19th century camp. I do not find it beautiful. (Boos and catcalls from the audience)."[110] The Whitney gathering was a defining moment in how far representations of an ideal physique had departed from the Greek ideal or any modern conception of beauty.[111]

What was left was muscle mass, a concept that had been growing in popularity for decades but had been accelerated by the spread of steroids in the 1960s and the Schwarzenegger phenomenon of the 1970s.

Having transcended the "Sexy Schwarzenegger" image created for him by Joe Weider, Schwarzenegger was busily creating his next persona. Unlike other bodybuilders, he was unwilling to be exploited. "Not once did Joe take advantage of Arnold," recollected Dave Draper, "and Joe loved it."[112] But it was Schwarzenegger who most inspired the latest Weider emphasis on large muscles, and it was his image that appeared most prominently in *Muscle Builder*. The April 1976 issue included articles entitled "Building Muscular Mass—That Stays," "Building Mass without Fat," and "Mass, I Am Joe's Muscle Power," as well as ads featuring Arnold's "Mindblowing Biceps" and his "Super Arm Blaster."[113] On the other hand, Robert Kennedy opposed the "Giantism Complex" that was sweeping bodybuilding. Schwarzenegger, he argued, was a "natural" who had twenty-inch arms at age eighteen, and should not necessarily be seen as someone to emulate: "If you can't quite match him in size then be content to build a body which suits *your* frame and *your* inherited qualities." Inspired by the ancient Greeks, Kennedy was trying to project "the bodybuilding image of the future." His watchwords were "proportion, goodly size and fine definition."[114] Yet *MuscleMag International*, with no contests of its own and few "natural" stars from which to choose, and trying desperately to retain readers, continued using photographs of those bodybuilders who contributed most to the giantism complex. Schwarzenegger eventually appeared sixteen times on the cover of Kennedy's magazine.

The competition that stood the greatest chance of recapturing the essence of the Greek ideal was the AAU Mr. America Contest, but with its abandonment of athletic ability and the point system, its increased emphasis on muscularity, and the removal of such intangibles as character, education, and general appearance, it relinquished many of the qualities that made it special and emblematic of American manhood. This collapse coincided with demands for racial equality, the Weiders' commercial aspirations, professionalization of the sport, and an ego-driven desire of bodybuilders to get big and win at any price. Randy Roach captures its essence: "By surrendering their traditional, idealistic judging standards in order to fall in line with the new growing orthodoxy of competitive professional bodybuilding, the AAU was basically signaling an acknowledgment of the end of their dominant reign. Changing rules now had them playing catch-up to the competition and it was their stringent rules that helped protect bodybuilding from Hoffman and Rader's greatest fears. The Mr. America would become simply just another pure physique show, unbridled, ripe, and open to the growing chemical invasion already on the horizon."[115]

Replacing it was the Mr. Olympia Contest and its heroic six-time champion. So great was the star power of Arnold Schwarzenegger by the mid-1970s that a *Muscle Builder* reader who heard that he had lost a leg in an accident in South Africa, could not "see anyone beating" even a one-legged Schwarzenegger "for a long time." Rumors were also circulating that Arnold, now fluent in English, working on a college degree, and becoming wealthy, was buying *Iron Man*, where he could further project his own version of manliness. Joe Weider, who had risen with the tide of Arnold's success, could claim that the sport had a "new image" and that "bodybuilding has come of age."[116] That image had been focused largely on the AAU Mr. America Contest for decades, but Schwarzenegger introduced a new version of the American dream. When he retired from competition in 1975, it remained to be seen whether the energy and image that he had brought to bodybuilding and physical culture could be sustained and what form it would take.

8

THE SPRAGUE REVOLUTION

**KEN HAD A BIG INFLUENCE IN THOSE DAYS ON EVERY-
THING. HE HAD HIS FINGERS IN EVERYTHING. AND IT WAS
RIPE TO BE PICKED IN THOSE DAYS BECAUSE THERE WAS
NOTHING. NO FRANCHISES. AMERICA WAS READY.**

STEVE MICHALIK,
PERSONAL COMMUNICATION WITH THE AUTHOR

KEN SPRAGUE, LIKE ARNOLD, WAS NEVER A MR. AMERICA, BUT UNLIKE Arnold, he is unknown to most people other than iron-game insiders. Yet he had a remarkable impact on bodybuilding—forging a link with the homosexual community, transforming Gold's Gym into an internationally recognized symbol of physical culture, breathing new life into the AAU Mr. America Contest, and leading a movement that ended nearly a half century of York-AAU domination. Through these initiatives, Sprague set in motion a series of events that changed the course of amateur bodybuilding. He quite likely contributed as much, in his own idiosyncratic way, to the fitness revolution of the late 1970s as Jane Fonda, Jack LaLanne, Kenneth Cooper, and other popular icons, including Schwarzenegger.

"DAKOTA"

Sprague was born on July 14, 1945, and grew up in Cincinnati's Over-the-Rhine neighborhood, a traditionally German area where lifting weights and drinking beer were part of the culture. Naturally robust, Sprague was easily able to build his body. He played football, ran track, and boxed. And although he ate what he pleased, "it all just seemed to go to muscle," he recalled. Energetic and self-confident, Sprague always had "too many irons in the fire." While studying chemistry at the University of Cincinnati on a track scholarship, he was married with two children and working at a machine-tool company at night: "I'd often work twelve hours a night, seven nights a week, when they were busy." He also worked out at the YMCA, and his physique was good enough that he became Mr. Cincinnati in 1967. With an imposing physical presence and personality, "Sprague was the bull of the woods in Cincinnati," observed Kim Wood.[1]

Then a friend encouraged Ken to apply for a modeling job with Colt Studios in New York. It would entail posing in the nude, but that "was the furthest thing from my mind," he claimed. When the photographer asked him to disrobe, Sprague "didn't think twice about it": "I just naturally don't seem to have any inhibitions."[2] An old-timer at Sprague's home gym recalls that he even showed nude photos of himself to others during workouts. According to Marvin Jones's 1974 interview with Sprague: "Colt Studios sent [pictures of] their new model, christened 'Dakota,' out to their customers. The response was enthusiastic, and further pictures seemed in order." When Colt offered him the opportunity to model in California, Ken concluded that being photographed in the nude was an easier way to make a living than working long hours at a Cincinnati tool company. He had just arrived in March 1970 to complete "his second session of straightforward nudes for Colt when he was approached by a private collector to appear in a hard-core sex film."

> "I had about $10 to my name," he explains, "when this fellow said. 'Hey, you can make $200, if you'll just be in his film.' So I said, 'Great!' Back in Ohio, I'd work my butt off for a week and a half for $200!" . . .
> His costar in that first hardcore film was another handsome young bodybuilder named Jim Cassidy. The two have since become the Nelson Eddy and Jeanette MacDonald of the gay films, appearing in several highly successful movies together. In fact, Cassidy has costarred in all but one of Dakota's handful of hardcore movies.[3]

Eventually, as a gym entrepreneur, Sprague enlisted various bodybuilders to "star" in his gay pornography productions, most notably Bob Birdsong, the 1974 IFBB Mr. America.

Sprague also capitalized on the "wide range of people" he met through his modeling, who enabled him to "piece things together and package business deals." He observed of the modeling and bodybuilding world: "Hundreds of so-called models come and go, but there are few that ever make use of all the contacts that they make while they're at it. . . . It's the packaging that I supply, and the initiative and the time." He regarded what he was doing as "a legitimate business arrangement" and had no moral qualms about it "as long as everything is all out front." To Sprague, his enterprise was no less legitimate than running a grocery store or a service station. Wood called him "the connector between bodybuilding and homosexuality."[4]

Much of what Sprague revealed in his interview served as a template for a novel, *The Iron Game*, by David Carter (the pen name of David Beckman), which used fictitious names thinly disguising real ones. The narrator described the character based on Sprague as never feeling "any guilt," someone who "would take whatever position was necessary to insure that he would end up in good shape financially." According to the story, Keith Spaulding (Sprague) and James Cass (Cassidy), as a result of their films, each earned at least an additional $100,000 a year by turning "tricks," and the former was worth about $4 million.[5]

Sprague admits that he made a great deal of money, but not in the way that Carter portrays it. He first attempted to become a "major, legitimate influence in the field of pornography" by setting up a production facility and doing business openly from a street address. But "the legal climate just wasn't right for that sort of thing," so he decided that "all the sleepless nights just weren't worth it." On discovering that profits were just as good in the "legitimate field," he opened his studio "as an independent rental sound stage." According to Sprague, business was good in 1974: "Over a quarter of all the television commercials made in Hollywood are shot on my stage, as well as a lot of your independent television productions. The volume of work done at the studio is really heavy." Jones pointed up a made-for-Hollywood irony: "Among the studio's major clients are the street-corner evangelists Tony and Susan Alamo, who tape their weekly religious telecasts on the same sound stage that a couple of years ago produced the gay hardcore epic, *Loadstar*."[6] Sprague contended that his "colorful entertainments" became "less and less" a part of his business. As for turning "tricks" or making arrangements for bodybuilders to hook up with gay clients, "people jump to conclusions."[7] He was neither a prostitute nor a pimp, but he was definitely a catalyst for the burgeoning gay pornography industry.

Another occurrence relating to Sprague's colorful career, conveyed in Carter's novel, involved Arnold Schwarzenegger, whose posing footage was included in a porno production called *Going Down*.[8] When Arnold heard that it was playing to packed houses, he was livid. As his girlfriend Barbara Outland (Baker) relates in her memoir: "When I arrived home one winter afternoon, I heard Arnold screaming into the phone, 'You fucking prick! How dare you screw me like dis! I'll have your ass, you *Gott*-damn cock-sucker. Jayzeus Kreest, you fucked me over, and now you are fucked, believe me!' . . . He slammed down the phone, screaming, 'Dat fucking asshole put my posing routine in his supposed documentary—a movie where faggots are jacking off while watching me pose. Dat bastard!'" Upon visiting the theater in North Hollywood where the supposed bodybuilding documentary was being shown, Outland expressed concern about what that kind of exposure would do to Arnold's budding film career. What she saw on the screen was "rows of actors, seated in a movie theater setting . . . groaning in self-joy over my lover."

> The scene flashed to Arnold in a double biceps pose, then to the audience of men holding gay men's *Schlongs*. The camera took me back to Arnold doing a full back pose, his Olympian muscles bulging and taut, and then it slipped back to rows of rapid hand and mouth movement. Then the camera flipped back to Arnold performing a side-view of glistening muscularity, and then shrunk back to ejaculating penises, shriveled in compliance under their own muscular feats.
>
> I knew some of these scumbags. They were the Bills and Dennys of our distant social life on that silver screen, sucking their way to financial gain.[9]

Sprague insists that "it was nothing like she describes." It was a film featuring some gym members with footage inserts from a show. "Arnold and Franco were irate," but Joe Weider told Schwarzenegger to "just go over and settle it with" Sprague, who explained why: "Joe didn't want to ruffle me because I owned Gold's. So Arnold came up and said ah, we've got to settle this, so I said I'll give you $50 each. Okay."[10] So even when Schwarzenegger was Mr. Olympia, $50 was enough to buy him off.

According to Carter's account, the underlying cause of this gay porno trade was the inability of bodybuilders to earn a living through their sport: "Every top bodybuilder must find something that will free his time so that he can train. I was finding out more evidence now that the super straight image given in Wilson's [Weider's] publications was becoming more and more of a cover-up. Actually, the gay community either directly or indirectly, almost completely supported the existence of high-level bodybuilding."[11] Sprague confirmed that his actors were well compensated and "made more money than they did for Weider."[12] Another aspect of the gay porno scene was hustling, which the sociologist Alan Klein describes as "an economic survival strategy in a subculture where competitors are hard-pressed to find the time and money to train." He concurs with several of Carter's conclusions: "The buying and selling of favors and goods in a barely concealed black market is in striking contrast to the clean-cut image publicly presented. Many aspiring bodybuilders fall into this network out of need." The importance of performing sex services as a way to pay for long hours of training, food supplements, drugs, and basic needs of life shows up in the testimony of a bodybuilder who told Klein, "I trained for the [Mr.] America contest eight hours a day . . . I couldn't do that working twelve hours a day in some shipyard."[13] Carter also claimed that "many Mr. Americas" were capitalizing on the gay porn bonanza. From 1950 to 1965, "at least half of them were gay," and the rest "at least turned a few tricks." More believable is his contention that Sprague and Cassidy "made the gay movie industry grow by leaps and bounds," and by instituting telephone contacts with clients, "brought modeling off of the street."[14] At least some bodybuilders were high-ticket call boys.

Doubts about Carter's book are justified. It is full of errors and exaggerations, as befitting a novel, and its facts are acceptable only with far more than a pinch of salt. Yet Mike Graham, who trained at Gold's at that time and read the book, insisted, "Most of the stories really happened. There was an awful lot of hustling going on at all levels."[15] Sprague offers a unique perspective on Carter.

> He trained at the gym, and I hired him also at the studio to guard it. And he lived in a little camper. We called him the Missing Link because he was an unusual lifter and an unusual character. . . . He used to send pictures of himself to the magazines, and we used to sit around and laugh about how he would take a black marker and draw in definitions on his body. He was one of those freaks that gathers at gyms. He was bright, really bright and a fun guy, a fun guy. He was just out to make money.[16]

Yet, like any novel, *The Iron Game* offers a virtual representation of truth, most evident in Carter's concluding statement about the gays he encountered in Hollywood and Beverly Hills: "[They] could realize, to some degree, the spirit of the bodybuilder while the straight world could not. Many of the houses seemed to be designed along the lines of the Greek and Roman houses of the past. These cultures were represented throughout by the décor. Both of these cultures used to be heavy into bodybuilding as a natural endeavor."[17]

What Sprague had identified and Carter publicized was a connection between bodybuilding and its ancient cultural roots that had been lost or shunned by other promoters.

GOLD'S GYM

In 1971, Sprague was not yet rich, yet through contacts, foresight, and self-confidence, he managed to foster one of the most important phenomena in bodybuilding by parlaying his meager resources into the purchase of Gold's Gym in Venice. Gold's had only sixty members, according to Sprague, and was "never mentioned in *Muscle and Fitness*." Adjacent to it was a drug haven occupied by a motorcycle gang. Gironda's gym in North Hollywood and Pearl's in Pasadena were far better known. Joe Gold "no longer wanted anything to do with the gym business," so Sprague stepped in: "I bought Gold's as a hobby. I never really wanted to run a business, just a place to work out." Sprague put up $15,000 of the $77,000 sales price, half of which he borrowed.[18] Marvin Jones noted that it was "with the cooperation of wealthy friends and acquaintances" that Sprague was able to purchase Gold's, two Venice apartment complexes, and his massive Hollywood studio. Like Arnold, much of Sprague's financial success stemmed from his real estate holdings. He is straightforward about this: "I invested very early in Venice, and everything skyrocketed. Some went up twenty times. I paid $2,000 for a house along a canal that went up twenty or thirty times in a matter of three or four years. That's where I made the money. A lot of it." But as Jones noted, his links with the gay community through pornography were "the key to a wealth of business opportunities," including an institution critical to establishing bodybuilding culture.[19]

That Joe Weider, still on the East Coast, was involved in Sprague's purchase of Gold's seems doubtful, but he did help promote it. Dan Howard, a former Mr. Oklahoma who managed Gold's while Sprague was tending to other enterprises, noticed Joe "taking pictures in the gym of everybody." He told Weider, "'Hey, you ain't going to take no more pictures in here unless a guy has a Gold's tank top on or Gold's shorts.' Within a year we were making more money off mail orders than members." Sprague attributed much of his success to an arrangement with movie studios: the gym was free for their use as long as actors wore Gold's Gym shirts.[20] This cinematic exposure led to the sale of tens of thousands of T-shirts. Gold's became an icon for a generation of physical culturists.

Soon the chain was attracting an elite bodybuilding clientele nationwide. But on his 1976 West Coast trip, Bob Kennedy found Gold's "cold and soulless": "At Gold's everybody is working for himself. Sergio Oliva, who was visiting a short time ago commented to Arnold, 'This place is unfriendly. No one talks.' 'They don't give a damn,' said

Figure 8.1. Ken Sprague with Manuel Perry, the 1976 Mr. USA, at the front desk of Gold's Gym before the 1977 Mr. America Contest, in which Perry placed second. Courtesy of Stark Center.

Arnold. And he meant it in a non-critical way. At Gold's people train for the ultimate. They have no time for talk and lengthy salutations."[21] In 1978, Ed Giuliani, a perennial Mr. America aspirant, described the "spirit" of Gold's more positively: "When you train at Gold's you automatically fall into a pattern of training with champions. A lot of it rubs off. There's motivation and spirit in the gym. . . . You're with the best and you know it, so you start to concentrate a little more. When you're in Gold's Gym you have all these men around you who have won Americas, Universes and Olympias, and you get a fever to train."[22] For

Rick Wayne, "Gold's is the Ultimate Bodybuilding Experience.... Hey, the intellectual stimulation is admittedly nil. But who ever heard of a gym that specialized in intellect development?"[23] Wayne, like virtually all modern bodybuilders, did not realize that the Greek concept of the gymnasia combined physical exercise and mental stimulation and did not concern muscle building.

But Gold's sense of serious purpose made it special. Much of *Pumping Iron* was shot on the premises, and Weider's photographer, Artie Zeller, shot most IFBB photos at Gold's rather than at the Mid-City Gym in Manhattan. According to Sprague, he "had something Weider wanted," and Weider's relations with Tom Minichiello "worsened as [Sprague] got closer to Weider"; Sprague added, "Weider was the key." Another advantage of Gold's was that the beach—a location for stunning photos—was just a block away. Sprague was well aware of the power of photography: "Pictures helped to make Gold's. Bodybuilders were misfits in every other part of the country, but in Venice everyone was a misfit, and the bodybuilders fit right in." So many major bodybuilders were gravitating to Gold's that Sprague claims there were years when "every bodybuilder winning an elite contest" came from his gym.[24] In contrast to the first year, when the gym earned only about $25,000, Sprague noted there were "select days" in the mid-1970s when "receipts from contest spectators and product sales exceeded $250,000." In addition to appearing in the *Wall Street Journal* and CBS's *60 Minutes*, Gold's was featured in thousands of media spots. In 1977, when the University of Nebraska strength coach Boyd Epley was putting together the National Strength and Conditioning Association, he toured Gold's. By the end of 1978, Sprague was planning to open a second Gold's in the San Fernando Valley, near the Weiders' headquarters, three times larger than the old one.[25] Sprague never lacked audacity.

Gold's proximity to Hollywood also fostered film opportunities outside the porn industry. For instance, Sprague took credit for securing the Hulk role for Lou Ferrigno.[26] But hustling and making porn were always options for aspiring bodybuilders, much like "modeling" for would-be female starlets. Indeed it was "widely rumored," according to Jones, that Sprague was "a favorite companion of famed film director George Cukor."[27] Connections with the gay community were maintained, Bill Pearl notes, by a separate phone in Gold's.[28] Sprague, however, insisted that there was "never more than one line into Gold's gym," adding incredulously, "Where do they get this stuff?" Dan Howard could not support Bill's story but explained there were several doc-

tors, including Mike Walczak, who "used the boys" by supplying nutritional products, advice, and drugs in return for sexual favors.[29] But the
homosexual bodybuilding culture was not limited to Gold's, leading
Carter to speculate that "most of the entertainment industry was gay,"
that at least a million gays lived in greater Los Angeles, that a main motivation of bodybuilders was not to impress women but men, and that "all
weightlifters were latent homosexuals."[30] Although Pearl was not aware
of it at first, at least one-third of the members in his gym were gay.[31]

It was Sprague's achievement to turn success rooted in California's
gay culture into a greater business venture, transforming a relatively
obscure sweat gym into the mecca of bodybuilding. The outside appearance remained austere, almost fort-like, but he created a palatial
environment inside, along with adjacent living space for himself and
his wife, Maryon. It was, in Jones's estimation, the "Place To Train for all
serious Mr. America and Mr. Universe contenders." But knowing how
it came about, and given Sprague's desire to gain greater respectability,
it was only natural for Jones to ask him: "Do you ever regret your past?
Would you rather forget that Dakota ever existed?"

> "Sometimes," he admits reluctantly, "in the middle of the night, I do. I
> lie there and think, 'Oh, God, what is this going to do to my future?'
> Back in Ohio I always thought that I would like to go into politics, and I
> think that that is pretty well out of reach now. You can talk around a lot
> of things, but I don't know how you could parlay my past into a political
> career. But whenever I start thinking about the future, I realize that if it
> weren't for all that, I wouldn't have a future to think about. I'd still be
> back in Ohio running a machine . . . for a living."[32]

Therefore, Sprague sought opportunities for advancement within the
sport that would allow him to use the prestige, power, and money gained
from Gold's to greatest advantage and possibly influence the course of
physique politics.

TO AFFILIATE OR NOT?

Securing a stake in amateur bodybuilding, especially the Mr. America
Contest, had been a major goal for the Weiders for several decades.
Part of the impetus, according to Joe, was to separate amateurs from
professionals—"in one direction the bodybuilder would be recognized
as a competitive athlete, and in the other he becomes a figure in a
theatrical staging of muscles." Enshrining this distinction in a series of

contests would give the Weiders access to the two glittering prizes that had thus far eluded them—the Mr. America Contest and admission to the Olympics. Their dogged persistence against York, their gaining the IFBB's admission to the GAISF, their promotional success with Arnold Schwarzenegger, and the increased appeal of their contests, products, and magazines enhanced this possibility, but it was Sprague who in the late 1970s engineered the merger.

The course of events began in December 1975 when the national committee, chaired by Bob Crist, approved a restructuring plan to stave off a government-mandated breakup.[33] Henceforth, weightlifting, powerlifting, and physique would each be governed by its own subcommittee, all overseen by a national executive. Each subcommittee could affiliate with an international body.[34] Crist predicted a "period of uneasiness" but believed that the sports were "more alive and growing than ever." Some assurance that physique was moving ahead came from the Southern Pacific Association's chairman, John Askem, who proudly noted that Gold's Gym, "the West Coast mecca of top bodybuilders," had become an AAU member club.[35]

Ralph Countryman, a retired naval officer and district attorney from Oakland, chaired the new National Physique Committee (NPC); the Florida bodybuilder Richard Baldwin acted as secretary. Heading their agenda was an organizational plan submitted at the 1976 Mr. America Contest. A significant feature was the number of voting members on the committee, which was large, including the physique chairmen of all AAU associations and all former Mr. Americas, and could be made larger by a provision that the chairman could appoint yearly members at large. Countryman had been pondering the possibility of the AAU affiliating with the IFBB and forming an alliance with the AABA (now AFAB, the American Federation of Amateur Bodybuilders); he intended to visit Montreal to discuss these matters. Most striking, however, was Sprague's offer of $1,000 to the National AAU, $2,500 to the Southern Pacific Association (plus profits), $10,000 to the Physique Athletes Travel Fund, and travel reimbursement to the winner for the right to host the 1977 Mr. America Contest. Although it was an amazing offer and the only bid submitted, the committee accepted it only tentatively because Sprague was suing another member of his association.[36]

At the July meeting of the NPC in Tallahassee, no action was taken on the IFBB's request for affiliation, but rules were adopted. At the first national meets staged with no accompanying lifting competition, the Teenage Mr. America was won by Mike Torchia, and the Past 40

Mr. America was won by Vic Seipke. Sprague not only served as a judge but also received his national judging card, and Countryman appointed him to the committee as a member at large and to three subcommittees. In November, he was appointed secretary after Richard Baldwin resigned. "Within a year I had control over the NPC" is how Sprague described his meteoric rise.[37] Significantly, AAU ruling #76-182 specified that IFBB and AFAB athletes were eligible to compete in AAU contests, and all physique contests had to be sanctioned separately from any lifting event. "Association Chairmen should guard this badge of independence zealously," Countryman advised. But independence was hardly the scenario envisioned by the Weider brothers. They showed up at the Mr. Los Angeles Contest in January 1977, with Sprague and the maverick Bob Hise, to stake a claim in the new order. Confident that AAU bodybuilding would become a national affiliate of the IFBB and the GAISF in coming months, Ben was already counting his chickens, "anticipating news from the international Olympic Committee for recognition soon."[38]

THE SPRAGUE COUP

These events set the stage for Sprague's coup d'état. On April 9, 1977, the Physique Committee held a special session in Cincinnati. By then, Sprague was not only its secretary but also chairman of both Region XIII and the Southern Pacific Association of the AAU, as well as the director of a Mr. Midwest Contest in Cincinnati's symphony hall. It was an impressive show that served as a dress rehearsal for his Mr. America Contest held several months later in Santa Monica. Although the intent of the NPC meeting was to discuss the impact of AAU #76-182, a lengthy discussion ensued over whether to affiliate with the IFBB and on what terms. There were concerns over the AAU's loss of control to the AFAB, international interference in AAU internal matters, possible replacement of AAU physique officials, and "one-man control" by Ben Weider. *Muscle Digest* observed that the IFBB had close ties with commercial interests, which could impinge on the responsibility of an international federation to govern democratically. But as the magazine noted: "The obvious lack of organization and direction in the AAU presents no better alternative." The committee voted 11–5 to place affiliation on the Santa Monica agenda.[39]

On that occasion, Ben Weider was on hand to answer questions, some of which were hostile. It was a historic occasion at which all bodybuilding factions were present, noted Peary Rader. The major point of contention: "Mr. Weider feels he has a completely democratic organization while some in the audience felt that it was not democratic and said so in pointed terms." At one point, Countryman lost his temper. "I didn't mind the pot shots from Committee members," he later told Weider, "but I did not appreciate the loud and irrelevant remarks of Dan Lurie. . . . Even York seemed subdued and friendly by comparison." Although the pro-merger West Coast was heavily represented, the motion to affiliate failed, 16–13, to gain the necessary two-thirds vote. Still the committee approved continued AFAB-AAU cooperation, and Countryman was satisfied that "the door has been opened" and would "remain open" for his successor.[40]

Clarence Bass, a committee member from New Mexico, was even more upbeat about the outcome in a letter to Countryman:

> The handwriting is on the wall and it is only a matter of time before the U.S.A. will begin to have some say in bodybuilding on the international level. . . . From my personal standpoint I suppose I am on York's blacklist now and forever more. Just think of it, casting a vote in favor of Weider right there in front of Terpak, Grimek, God and everybody. . . . I do not think we are going to be able to find anybody to adequately fill your shoes. I am, however, going to recommend to Ken Sprague that he proceed ahead to seek the chairmanship. I do not think he can handle the job with the even handed dignity that you have, but I do think he is the best man around with the interest, the intelligence, not to mention the money, to move physique forward in the next few years. Ken I believe made a start on defusing the issue of his past, and "the picture" and that fact when taken with his very successful and competent handling of the Mr. America just might make him electable.[41]

The problem of Sprague's "past" referred to a compromising picture from his porn-star days that circulated in the bodybuilding community. Ira Hurley, of Chicago, wrote Jerome Weis, chairman of the NPC rules committee, that it represented such "a *major set-back* and *discredit* to the Sport of Physique" that Sprague had to go: "Should the picture be true in fact, I as an AAU member would insist upon your action to remove him from his positions of responsibility." Weis responded: "Mr. Sprague deeply regrets certain incidents in his past as do we all. If he is to be purged from the Committee there might be a few other members who will have to follow him because of similar incidents." On a technical note, Weis pointed out, according to the AAU Code (454.10.b.3), such action could be taken only by the subject's association (which Sprague chaired) and for activities that took place during competition.[42] On the other hand, as the puritanical Oscar State pointed out in an article on the projected AAU-IFBB merger, "we cannot apply our amnesty to those who have abased our sport through their known association with pornographic or homosexual activities."[43] A broad application of this penalty would have automatically jeopardized many NPC leaders, including the outgoing chairman.

Sprague remained secretary, and when he "got Jim Manion elected chairman of the NPC" at the 1977 AAU convention, in Columbus, Ohio, they presented a united front for affiliation. "Without Ben and Joe bodybuilding would not be where it is today," stated Manion. "I am very much in favor of the move," concurred Sprague. Additionally, a plan was adopted to make each sport committee independent, with "no control from the AAU." Henceforth, it would serve as just a coordinating body. Finally, to attract television revenue, the Mr. America Contest, the centerpiece of the NPC, was moved from June to September (in proximity to the Miss America Contest), and Cincinnati became the venue. The hand of Sprague was evident in these transactions.[44] Finally, at an NPC meeting on January 29, 1978, in Santa Monica, with two city policemen on guard, a motion to affiliate carried by a 23–5–1 vote.[45] Credit for this coup was attributed to Sprague, who, was described this way by *Muscle Training Illustrated*: "[He] crashed upon the bodybuilding scene like a comet, a veritable meteorite slashing and burning through the physique world atmosphere. Aside from being known for his merchandising of a small 'pumping iron' palace called 'Gold's Gym' . . . into a giant, internationally-known fitness household word, Sprague in a period of roughly two years consolidated a political punch that slipped the AAU 'Old Guard' a severe crack which changed the face of bodybuilding in America for all time." Jan Dellinger called it an "ambush of the old AAU crowd."[46] Another vote eliminated the formal interview at the 1978 Mr. America Contest, restricting it to "the normal course of conversation during the check-in of contestants," thus removing any nonmuscle criteria from judging. Subsequently, the NPC decided that any bodybuilder placing in the top three in any Mr. America or Mr. USA Contest would be eligible to represent the United States at the IFBB Mr. Universe Contest in Acapulco, Mexico, just one step from the coveted Mr. Olympia title.[47]

THE 1977 EXTRAVAGANZA

Meanwhile, Sprague had already assumed the role of promoter in the straitlaced AAU amateur circuit. Success came quickly when he won the bid to stage the 1976 Mr. California Contest, a Mr. America feeder event. Previous Mr. Californias who became Mr. Americas included Bill Pearl, Chris Dickerson, Jim Morris, and Dale Adrian. In front of a packed audience of 3,000 at the Santa Monica Civic Auditorium, Kal Szkalak upset "highly favored" Dave Johns in 1976. Both had recently migrated to Gold's from other gyms and aspired to become Mr. Americas. Sprague organized an equally successful Gold's Classic, featuring the likes of Oliva, Ferrigno, Padilla, Grant, Robinson, and Szkalak. More a muscle show than a contest, not all the men were in top shape, but *MuscleMag* observed that Oliva "looked good enough to bring the house down with every pose."[48] Sprague's triumphs contrasted sharply with that year's Mr. America show, which was poorly conducted and attracted barely 500 spectators.

That bitter memory, Sprague's organizational talents, and his $16,000 donation to the AAU enabled him to hold the 1977 version in Santa Monica. It cost him about $100,000, including $46,000 for programs and $10,000 for posters that were mailed all over the country. "We've hired a publicity firm," he explained before the contest, "that handles such shows as 'Network' and stars like the former Peter Finch."

> They will saturate the Mr. America pageant with celebrities. *Cosmopolitan* magazine will do a story on the show from a woman's angle. *People* magazine, *Time* and *Newsweek* will cover it. C.B.S.'s *60 Minutes* has done sixty minutes of filming in the gym which will be shown to sixty million people. This is going to be the biggest event in physique contest history. . . . We want to put bodybuilding before the eyes of the public which takes costly publicity. It will help every gym operator, bodybuilding magazine publisher and bodybuilding marketeer in the United States. We want to create a new bodybuilding awareness.[49]

Responding to the observation that Arnold represented the advent of a new bodybuilding era, Sprague boasted, "We are going beyond Arnold. Bodybuilding itself is the star." He wanted to humanize the sport in a way that neither the Mr. Olympia Contest nor *Pumping Iron* had been able to achieve, by professional planning and follow-up. The key was to coax magazine writers into portraying competitors as real people to whom readers could relate: "What's the bodybuilder thinking about on Saturday night when he's alone? What does his family think?" Even nonwinners could be identified from precontest stories. On all fronts, "interest and excitement can be built."[50] In an effort to make body-building mainstream, Sprague tapped media techniques that would soon become commonplace.

There were many naysayers, especially given Sprague's tainted back-ground, who doubted his ability to pull off such a coup. Rick Wayne expected "chaos" and predicted that the highly publicized parade down Ocean Avenue to inaugurate "Mr. America Day" would be a "fine ex-ample of a well-intentioned dream gone haywire." Even "hotshots" at Gold's and local gyms were disturbed by the prospect of greased bodybuilders on elephants and camels and gaudily decorated vintage cars and ostentatious politicians in bizarre costumes and baton-twirling maidens and clowns marching to the thumps of a big bass drum.

> Hey, it sounded too much like some Mardi Gras carnival! . . . "The whole thing will set bodybuilding back fifty years," said one aging Mr. America aspirant with a huge axe to grind. "It's gonna be a big show for the limp-wrists and the Venice Beach weirdos. . . . Ken Sprague is selling us all down the drain. It'll take fifty years to set us back on course again after this one. Mark my words."

Another former bodybuilder believed that Sprague was "making a mockery of bodybuilding." As for Wayne, he envisioned an expensive, tawdry spectacle gone awry.

> But we were all wrong as it turned out. Sprague scored a tremendous hit with his mid-morning parade and the hordes who lined up to watch the spectacle let the promoter know how they felt about his show in no uncertain way. They applauded, cheered, whistled enthusiastically, swung cameras from every conceivable angle, some even attempting to partici-pate in the parade. Yes, the fears earlier expressed by some of bodybuild-ing's better known purists turned out to be completely unfounded.[51]

Led by Bert Goodrich, the first Mr. America, the parade featured a cavalcade of musclemen on elephants and a hundred units, including seven marching bands. A float with a banner heralding Gold's Gym was lined with musclemen and shapely females. Over a hundred thousand spectators witnessed the two-hour extravaganza.[52]

In the evening, in front of 3,500 spectators, Sprague conducted one of the most spectacular physique contests ever held. In a country still reeling from the Vietnam War, a huge American flag served as a backdrop onstage, with "Gold's Mr. America" superimposed on it in bold letters. The Mr. America symbol had been reawakened, this being the first time since its inception that it was held as a single event.[53] Sprague had infused the title with a new sense of pride in what it meant to be an American. The atmosphere was further enhanced by a twenty-piece orchestra, an original Mr. America overture, a hand-balancing act, and guest posing by Robby Robinson and Bill Grant. The new Mr. America, Dave Johns, was "in true battle form," observed Wayne: "Veins as big as telegraph cables zig-zagged his pectorals, biceps and deltoids." Johns was presented a six-foot trophy by the silver-screen star Mae West, who sighed, "Oh, what perfect parts." For Johns, his "dream finally came true." Wayne exclaimed, "Ken Sprague deserves full praise for a job well done." Joe Weider called it the "best-staged AAU bodybuilding show ever."[54]

Sprague looked back on the event with pride. His object was to give Mr. America "some promotional pop" and to transform it into "a performing art, but more than that, a spectacle."[55] The staid and drab AAU Mr. America Contest had been recast as an exciting mixture of sport and entertainment. The Mr. America dream was still alive, but what did it mean?

THE BARNUM OF BODYBUILDING

As remarkable as the Mr. America Contest was, in 1978 Sprague staged four other major physique contests and a powerlifting meet. Plenty of hype preceded the Gold's Classic held on July 29, an event dubbed by Armand Tanny "the Greatest Bodybuilding Show in History." Sprague, the so-called Barnum of Bodybuilding, was set to "come up with a four-ring circus . . . that promises to tout muscle with unprecedented pomp, puff, bombast and hoopla." It would feature a professional World Cup with cash prizes of at least $20,000 and a Cadillac for the winner, a USA versus World Amateur Challenge Match, the AAU Teenage Mr. America, and the AAU Past 40 Mr. America. The show, in the newly renovated Shrine Auditorium, where Steve Reeves had become Mr. America thirty-one years earlier, would feature oversized video projections of the contestants, enabling patrons in the back rows to see them easily. As with the recent Muhammad Ali–George Foreman fight, distant patrons could view Sprague's production in gyms and theaters by closed-circuit television. Celebrities from movies, television, and sports were expected to be "much in evidence[,] since bodybuilding contests had become 'in' things to attend." An orchestra would play an original score predicted to have an impact similar to Igor Stravinsky's *Firebird*, which had jolted the ballet world earlier in the century. Afterward there would be a victory party with music and dancing and large ice cream and cake sculptures of bodybuilders. Sprague predicted that his event would be "the biggest AAU bodybuilding promotion ever," bigger than the 1977 Mr. America and "bigger than the Mr. Olympia." Lest the Weiders feel threatened by Sprague's wizardry, he credited Ben with the idea of the World Cup and recognized his outstanding work "as contagious," adding, "Now I've got the fever."[56]

Sprague did not disappoint. What impressed Denis (Denie) Walter was Sprague's "four ring" judging process, with the teens on the left of the stage, over-forties on the right, World Cup contestants in the center, and the USA versus World event downstairs, each with its own panel of judges.

> It would naturally happen at a Gold's Gym–promoted event since, of course, it has the creative mind of Ken Sprague behind the action. Sprague's 1977 AAU Mr. America contest . . . still remains a dynamic landmark in the sport. . . . It's far too exciting for the audience's eyes, and much more efficient, to boot. A new phrase might better describe the concept and production values of this, or any Gold's promoted event. Anything Sprague does in this line is sure to be innovative. He's got a particular class all his own. So you might refer to his events in Hollywood terms. You might call it "Spragavision."[57]

Even the saturnine Wayne grudgingly agreed that it was "The Greatest Bodybuilding Show on earth." The *Rocky* star Sylvester Stallone awarded the Teenage Mr. America trophy to Rudy Hermosillo, his bodyguard, and Earl Maynard won the Past 40 Mr. America title. Both trained at Gold's. In the USA versus World challenge match, the USA team of Mike Mentzer, Ron Teufel, and Danny Padilla easily won. The show featured virtually a who's who of physique, leading Sprague to boast that the competitive level was "unparalleled," bigger than the Mr. Olympia: "You know, it's a far cry from when you won the Mr. America trophy and that was that. It's becoming a real money sport to people; these guys could literally be rich, and that's great!"[58]

At the rate Sprague was moving, it appeared he could soon outdistance bodybuilding's big three promoters—Weider, Hoffman, and Lurie—and exceed even Arnold in media exposure. Initially, the 1978 Mr. America Contest was scheduled for Lafayette, Louisiana, but given the brilliance of the 1977 event, the national committee moved it to Sprague's hometown. Again it was preceded by a parade, this time led by Cincinnati's mayor, Jerry Springer, who took off his shirt and did double bicep poses for the crowd. Bill Pearl began the festivities with a dazzling posing display to commemorate the twenty-fifth anniversary of his winning the title. The winner was Tony Pearson, another product of Gold's. But his defeat of the favorite, Ron Teufel, the recent winner of Mr. USA and Mr. California titles, disappointed many fans. "Teufel was stunned, nearly uncontrollably on the stage," reported Roger Schwab for *Iron Man*. Rick Wayne reported that he was inundated with letters and calls declaring Pearson not good enough to place even fourth. According to Wayne, Pearson "had achieved his big dream but not for one moment had he anticipated the North Pole winds that greeted him in Santa Monica," where he was virtually ostracized. Yet it was an extraordinary field, especially given the uncertain state of AAU bodybuilding. Kent Kuehn, one of the judges, was in awe, noting that at one time the first half dozen "would [have been] the top competitors." Such was the quality that "the guys are like twenty-five deep." Richard Baldwin, who placed third in his height class, concurred: "I think this is the best Mr. America contest yet. Anybody who even places can be happy."[59] Some of this improvement can be attributed to steroids, but it was also the first Mr. America Contest since the AAU-IFBB merger.

GODFATHER OF BODYBUILDING?

Sprague's coup was virtually complete, but to some bodybuilders and officials he was an antihero, not so much because of his past associations with pornography as for his influence and conflicts of interest. Sprague had risen quickly to prominence through his skills as a businessman and promoter and his willingness to take risks at long odds. Especially after Tony Pearson became "the most controversial Mr. America to date," Bill Reynolds identified a body of opinion that considered Sprague "the Godfather of AAU Bodybuilding," meaning that "*his* judges confer the title—like Santa giving a present—on whomever will do Sprague the most good economically." Sprague called it "bull guano." Rick Wayne observed, "Sprague promotes some of the biggest shows, gives the largest prizes, owns the world's most famous bodybuilding gym, and is a power in AAU bodybuilding. Should he be penalized for his success, or congratulated for it?" Many bodybuilders suspected a Sprague-Weider plot to monopolize the sport. One experienced bodybuilder spelled out the possible consequences of such collusion:

> In the old days when Robby and Mentzer and other champs were dissatisfied with the way the AAU ran things they simply quit and joined the IFBB. But now you have to sit still and swallow your vomit. For when the AAU drops you, or when you fall out with Sprague and his friends on the AAU committee, there is every chance the IFBB will also place a ban on you. That way, Sprague and Weider can control bodybuilding to their own advantage. After all, Sprague is in business at Gold's and Weider has his own various enterprises.

Joe Weider called these insinuations "sheer nonsense": "Sprague was elected to his position in the AAU. Neither my brother nor I could have had anything to do with that." He denied that Gold's trainees got special consideration in judging, that it was possible for Sprague to fix a contest or judges panel, or that his magazines favored Gold's. "Thanks to people like Ken Sprague," he concluded, "bodybuilding is being seen in the very best light on television . . . radio and the print media." Sprague's view was pragmatic: "When you have power you have to exercise it. Sometimes that's not very popular."[60]

Concerns that Sprague was gaining too much power had dissipated by the fall of 1978, when his promotional genius was no longer so evident. Sprague conducted the Senior National Power Championships in Los Angeles in August 1978, and Terry Todd described it as "the best of meets . . . the worst of meets." Although the lifting caliber was outstanding, there was no program or scoreboard, the audience had difficulty seeing the action, and the organization was inadequate. Sprague was to blame; his wife Maryon's illness caused him often to be out of touch. Sprague recovered his promotional zeal enough to stage his Mr. America Contest in Cincinnati in September, but Maryon's cancer worsened, and he felt compelled to resign as NPC secretary. "In one full swoop the roof caved in on the man in his personal life," explained Walter.[61] Sprague later pointed out that promoting Gold's "7 days a week, 14 hours a day for 7 years" had taken its toll, but it was "a combination of things" that knocked him "out of the picture."

> I was pretty well used to taking a lot of flak, grievances, and a lot of criticism. Because any time you try to accomplish something, I do believe

that happens. It's par for the course when the "new order" is on a collision vector with the "old order" of things. The situation was one where I just couldn't admit to myself she was going to die. . . . I couldn't make any arrangements to transfer my responsibilities or hers slowly; I just kept trying to make everything go on as it was. Now, of course, I was being attacked as an administrator. I didn't leave because of that, I was used to it. But losing Maryon took out a part of me, and I went off to be by myself and regroup and see which direction I wanted to take my life.[62]

By the summer of 1979 he had sold Gold's to Pete Grymkowski and his partners Ed Conners and Denny Doyle, moved to Orcas Island in Puget Sound, and remarried.

NATURE ABHORS A VACUUM

But he did not totally relinquish his interests or responsibilities. Still regarded as "gym mogul and contest promoter supreme," he accepted election as one of four vice chairmen at the NPC meeting in San Antonio in November 1978, but the sudden absence of his controlling hand was evident in the "not so harmonious" election for chairman, in which Mike Katz challenged Manion. Katz, according to Walter, made no secret of his displeasure with how the committee was functioning. He was quoted in *Muscle Digest* as saying that "if he lost the election the only alternative . . . was to 'write the AAU off' and start a new association."[63] But Sprague manipulated the voting by flying in thirty delegates approved by Manion, as allowed in the constitution, and secured the removal of five others. Still it appeared as if Katz would win; his supporters had counted the votes in the room. Mabel Rader, Mike Walczak, and Sprague were selected to count the votes. As Sprague later explained, the ballots were "little pieces of paper on which they could write Manion or Katz." Before the vote count began, he "took about a dozen of them and wrote Manion and took about a dozen random ones out."[64] This tale of skullduggery is corroborated by evidence from Wayne DeMilia and Randy Roach, but the national secretary, Mike Graham, insisted that it did not happen: "It's old men giving themselves more credit than they deserve."[65] After losing 27–19, Katz refused a vice chairmanship, left with his followers, and in a separate meeting formed the United States Federation of Bodybuilders, with himself as president. It was obvious to Walter that the NPC without Sprague "burned out of control," for he, Manion, and Maryon "had formed an administrative force which had now been broken," and "the oncoming AAU-IFBB affiliation went wild" without its internal power base. Sprague continued to attend meetings, vote, and serve on committees, but he was no longer a dominant force.[66]

Katz was not the only obstacle to the NPC and IFBB's continued affiliation and hegemony. As Joe Weider realized, it was still necessary to secure absorption of the AFAB into the AAU superstructure: "The rub lies in satisfying AFAB officials, who have worked the past three years in building what was once a rival to the AAU . . . when affiliation seemed to be a very remote prospect." For this reason, Weider shifted the focus of his Mr. America Contest from a recognized brand name to a less desirable, nondescript entity. This ploy was only partially successful. Mike Mentzer took the title in October 1976 at Madison Square Garden, stating afterward that "winning the Mr. America has been a lifetime goal." But it was called the American Bodybuilding Championships, devoid of a "Mr." prefix. In a posedown, Mentzer, Danny Padilla, and Robby Robinson (who did not compete) qualified to represent the United States in the IFBB Mr. Universe Contest. Scant attention was paid to the Miss Americana winner, Marilyn Person.

The 1977 "America" contest, staged in June by Franco Columbu in Los Angeles, was attended by the comedian Dom DeLuise and the actors Sally Field and Burt Reynolds, thanks to Arnold's Hollywood connections. The lightweight Padilla earned the sobriquet "giant killer" by upsetting Pete Grymkowski (dubbed the "uncrowned Mr. America") and Roger Callard.[67] When asked whether he felt cheated because he got to hold the title just seven months, Mentzer replied, "It didn't matter to me at all since the prestige of the title and the springboarding action to world fame were the more important aspects of winning the title. The fact that I had a 'reign' as Mr. America never really occurred to me; once you win Mr. America, so I thought, you are always Mr. America. . . . As Mr. America a bodybuilder is insured an inviolable niche in the sport's history." Mentzer seemed unaware that his hard-won title was no longer "Mr. America" and was being phased out, but for Ed Guiliani, age forty-two, who finished second among the lightweights, it meant the denial of a lifelong ambition. As Wayne noted, "A Mr. America contest without Eddie Giuliani is analogous to spaghetti Bolognese with the spaghetti left out." The 1977 American team for the IFBB World (aka Universe) Championships in Nimes, France, was selected at the Mr. USA Contest, and there was no Miss Americana.[68]

THE DEMISE OF THE WBBG MR. AMERICA

In light of the excitement generated by NPC contests, much less attention was focused on the WBBG Pro Mr. Americas. Although Scott Wilson, Don Ross, Anibal Lopez, and Tommy Aybar were worthy winners in the late 1970s, the contest itself seemed submerged, not only by the hustle, bustle, and hassle of New York City but also amidst all the other titles Lurie offered—Pro Teenage America, Pro Mr. America Over 40, Pro Mr. America Over 50, Miss Body Beautiful USA, Pro Mr. World, and Mr. Olympus. Many contestants had been contenders for the AAU Mr. America crown. One of them, Don Ross, the 1977 winner, attempted to extract some meaning from his title, noting that it had more value since the renaming of the IFBB version. Now there were only two Mr. Americas! As for monetary rewards, he claimed that his victory resulted in more members for his Detroit gym, higher purses for his professional wrestling bouts, and cash for promoting Lurie products. Lurie sent Ross to the NABBA Mr. Universe Contest in London, where he ranked a disappointing fifth out of six, hardly a credit to his Mr. America title. Nor did Lopez (1978), third out of six, or Aybar (1979), eighth out of ten, fare better in their classes. In addition to credibility issues, Lurie's 1979 contest was plagued by disputes over judging and special guests. "After the show ended, Dan headed for the aspirin," commented Walter. It was the last WBBG Mr. America show.[69]

An unexpected highlight, however, was provided by the Miss Body Beautiful USA Contest conducted by the newly formed the Superior Physique Association (SPA). According to Walter, Doris Barrilleaux, as head judge, coached the girls in "posing displays devoid of the gross 'bimboism' that usually brings out the worst, foul and undignified response from the audience." Instead, the contestants "were received as ladies and athletes who train for shapeliness and can be proud to take it into competition . . . called Women's Bodybuilding." Walter added: "Let's hope the idea which is ripping popularly across the country keeps right on. Somehow an 'iron maiden' has more dignity as a 'body-buildress' than a raunchy 'cheesecake' audience 'mooner.'" The winner, Georgia Miller (Fudge), of St. Petersburg, Florida, and others, by doing "standard muscle poses modified slightly to fit their feminine curves," were transforming women's contests from crass spectacles, so characteristic of the Miss Americana and early Lurie shows, into dignified displays of the female physique.[70] Men's shows, on the other hand, were gravitating toward massive displays of muscle.

WEIDER AFFILIATES

Although the Weiders had amply laid the groundwork, the AAU board of governors, contrary to expectations, tabled the question of affiliation at its San Antonio meeting, which allowed the opposition nearly a year to make itself heard. It had already crystallized under the rubric of the AFAB, led by Jubinville, Schusterich, and Minichiello, which formally separated from the IFBB and refused to be absorbed by the AAU.[71]

On another front, Serge Nubret, once an IFBB vice president, formed the World Amateur Bodybuilders Association (WABBA) in 1976 for the purpose, as Oscar Heidenstam explained to John Terpak, of "driving Weider from Europe." WABBA, NABBA, and York could mount a challenge to the Weiders' international ambitions. In November 1977, Nubret conducted a Mr. Universe Contest in Paris, won by Ahmet Enunlu, of Turkey, and the AAU Mr. America Dave Johns was named most muscular man. The presence of Sergio Oliva, who won the professional title, and Steve Reeves, who was given a Greek statue and a Sandow statuette, lent credibility to the event. Also on hand was Heidenstam, the titular head of WABBA, and Jubinville, doing his muscle control act, to provide an anti-Weider tone. According to Bill Reynolds, "[It was] one of the best shows I've seen, and for a maiden effort it was particularly remarkable." By 1982, WABBA was claiming to have affiliates in fifty nations, and its U.S. branch, the United States Bodybuilding Federation (USBF), had allegedly staged fourteen contests the previous year, including a WABBA Mr. America.[72] Whether the USBF-WABBA could break the NPC-IFBB power structure forged by Sprague would depend on the ability of all anti-Weider elements to unite.

With power slipping away after years of preparation to claim bodybuilding's greatest prize, and with Sprague no longer their champion, the Weiders acted quickly. Despite a pronouncement from Jim Fox, the AAU Physique Committee liaison, that there was as yet "no affiliation between the IFBB and the AAU," Ben Weider suspended the 1978 Mr. America, Tony Pearson, for violating IFBB rules. Weider then claimed that *Muscle & Fitness* was the official magazine of the NPC. Manion's committee informed Weider that his charge against Pearson was invalid, and Sprague secured passage of a motion instructing Weider to contact the NPC concerning any problems with AAU athletes and to cease circulating letters from his office to committee members.[73] It was evident to Sprague that the Physique Committee was becoming a "parrot" of the IFBB.

Figure 8.2. "Where Is Women's Bodybuilding Going?" This depiction by Robert A. Moody illustrates the dilemma facing women's bodybuilding at the time Laura Combes became the first Ms. America in 1980. *SPA News*, November 1980, 1.

I was probably the prime mover to get the AAU to affiliate with the IFBB, and "conceptually" I still feel it's a good idea. But the closer I became involved with the AAU-IFBB affiliation, I see that Weider—if the AAU is not kept very, very strong—will take advantage of his power position. . . . Ben is not using the IFBB political position for the honesty of bodybuilding. He's using it to enhance the Weider position commercially. Yes, there's no doubt in my mind about that . . . absolutely no doubt.[74]

But Sprague was unable to stop the movement he had initiated. At the 1979 AAU Convention, in Las Vegas, the Physique Committee approved IFBB affiliation. "The world changed and moved on that November day in Las Vegas, where two Caesars met at 'Caesar's Palace,'" quipped *Muscle Training Illustrated*. "Not a word passed between them. Bob Hoffman, 'The Father' of American weightlifting watches his stepchild grow up and away from him. . . . Joe Weider looks on as a concerned rich uncle." Sprague, pronounced "a 'winner' in more ways than one," was credited with having packed the committee with California votes, a consequence of his earlier actions as power broker. Yet "he never said a word." His machinations were also evident in the yearly-contest bids, which mostly went to the West Coast. Ed Jubinville, of New England, "found this very frustrating" and Pete Miller, of Washington, D.C., "found his bids steadily rejected." Nor was it any surprise, owing to a "massive California pressure group vote," that Lisa Lyon, of Santa Monica, was elected chair of the new women's physique organization.[75]

AAU RETALIATION

While it was natural for the NPC, as sole representative of amateur bodybuilding in the United States and purveyor of the Mr. America title, to expect that its bid for U.S. Olympic Committee (USOC) membership would be successful, it was rejected in June 1980 on grounds that the sport would not likely be become a part of either the Olympics or the Pan-American Games. To facilitate future negotiations with the USOC, the NPC intended to drop "AAU" from its title, which would "demonstrate to the few die-hard invincibly ignorant . . . that the AAU, national or local, has no jurisdiction over our sport." That approach, however, played into the hands of NPC detractors. "The [AAU] Weightlifting committee, or at least a few die-hards among the old crowd there," argued Jerome Weis, "have resented the divorce of our sport from theirs and would like to see it returned to the status of a demonstration sport to help increase the gate at their events." NPC leaders perceived their opponents as reactionaries who wanted to "turn the clock back." They suspected that the old York crowd would stage a counterrevolution to overturn the recent Weider infiltration.[76]

Those fears soon materialized when AAU president Joe Henson made a bold attempt to gain the upper hand in amateur bodybuilding. According to his son Josh, Henson's initiative was prompted by the NPC's decision to sever its AAU ties and by his visit to the 1980 Mr. America Contest: "There was no AAU banner, no reference to the

AAU. There was all sorts of squawking about drugs and so forth, and my father came back and made a report and said Mr. America means something. . . . You could still see Steve Reeves movies, and he represented something. These guys are into rumors, there's backroom politics, there's drugs. I'm not sure they're doing the Mr. America name justice."[77] Concurrently, Henson was approached by a group of dissidents who agreed the contest was not receiving the respect it deserved and that the AAU owned the title. On Henson's request, they drew up a petition stating that NPC leaders were "abusing the sport" and allowing drug use. Henson thereupon appointed a Mr. America Committee (MAC) of AAU-York loyalists dedicated to amateurism, and installed Bob Crist as chairman.[78]

It met in February 1981 in Indianapolis. After AAU vice president Richard Harkins explained the AAU's ownership rights to "Mr. America" service marks, the committee agreed to a number of resolutions: the NPC could not issue AAU cards, AAU athletes could compete in NPC contests, bids awarded to the NPC for 1981 America titles would be honored, judges for these contests must have AAU approval, and the MAC must oversee all events titled "America." Henson conveyed these decisions to Manion, further stating that no sanctions should be taken against athletes who competed in non-NPC meets and that Crist would attend all 1981 contests using the term "Mr. America."[79] To Clarence Bass, the requirements were unacceptable on grounds that the committee was "heavily weighted" towards powerlifting and weightlifting, and that the AAU was trying to impose itself on the NPC by holding the Mr. America title over its head: "Obviously we cannot allow them to interfere to this extent."[80] The NPC and its mother organization (now a nuisance) were drifting apart. But no mention appears in the records of either body of the real reason for their separation, the disenchantment of AAU-York traditionalists with the Weiders' affiliation with, and apparent takeover of, the NPC.

At the AAU annual meeting in St. Louis in November, Bass observed that Henson had "no quarrel" with the NPC and regarded it as "the national governing body for physique." Henson had established the MAC for "the sole purpose of protecting AAU ownership of the 'Mr. America' servicemark." The AAU, according to its lawyer, owned an "incontestable copyright." The NPC had merely leased the title for several years. Bass believed that the NPC must either rename its contest the "American Bodybuilding Championship" or pursue legal action. He suspected that the real reason for Henson's intervention was that "the

AAU is in serious financial difficulty" and was using the Mr. America Contest to bolster its sagging finances: "The AAU is a sinking ship trying to find a reason why it shouldn't go down for the last time. Unfortunately they still have enough steam left to cause the NPC trouble."[81]

NPC MR. AMERICA TRIUMPHS

Meanwhile the NPC, following precedents set by Sprague, conducted three highly successful Mr. America contests. Ken "Doc" Neely staged the 1979 version at the recently renovated Fox Theatre in Atlanta, where *Gone with the Wind* had premiered in 1938, and secured the nearby Hilton as headquarters, thus providing athletes and officials with a touch of class. *Muscular Development* conceded that while York was known as "'Muscletown,' Atlanta seemed to be the 'new muscle capital,'" where more muscles were on display than in any other city in the world. Serving as a backdrop for the fifty-two contestants were massive Styrofoam letters that spelled A-M-E-R-I-C-A, flanked by statues of Moses and Hercules. All seemed pleased with how the contest was organized. *Iron Man* called it the "greatest Mr. America Contest" in its thirty-one-year history, attributing its success to the recent AAU-IFBB affiliation: "Every qualified amateur contender in the U.S. now had one specific quest, The A.A.U. Mr. America Contest." Amid so many accolades for the event and the reorganization wrought by Sprague, the physical attributes of the winner, Ray Mentzer, were nearly overlooked.[82]

The 1980 contest reached another milestone by attracting eighty-nine contestants, so many that there were four judging panels. Still running under steam generated by Sprague's earlier triumphs, the event was sponsored by Gold's Gym and its new owner, Pete Grymkowski, in the Santa Monica Civic Auditorium, filled to capacity with many waiting outside. But Sprague directed the show behind the scenes. In *Iron Man*, Dave Sauer pronounced it "the most awesome display of muscularity ever seen in over forty years of Mr. America contests." The official view was similar: "Rod Miller, one of the judges, said it all. . . . 'In the past, the best way for me to pick the places was to look for outstanding body parts. Now it seems that I have to hunt for the weak points and it's very difficult to find weakness in many of these physiques.'"[83] A vastly improved Gary Leonard, of Fresno, took the main title.

A major innovation was the inclusion of a Ms. America Contest preceding the main event. "The same appreciative chorus of mass oohs and aahs that greeted the posing endeavors of the Mr. America contestants echoed resoundingly through the halls of the Civic Auditorium as nearly 40 of this country's top female iron pumpers took to the stage," reported Kristy Stover. The first Ms. America, Laura Combes, was crowned by Lou "Hulk" Ferrigno. Similarities with the Miss America Contest were obvious, especially the short runway that jutted into the orchestra pit, much as in the Atlantic City event, where the "muscle girls" could strut and pose. But already the Ms. America Contest was moving away from the Miss America model, and judges favored the more muscular contestants. To Bill Dobbins, Combes was "overwhelming—powerful delts, well-developed arms, full, sweeping lats and cut-up thighs." He asked a question more than one spectator was probably asking: "Is this what a *woman* bodybuilder should look like?" "Where is women's bodybuilding going?" asked Jan Caswell. "Will there be a place for the slimmer, more symmetrical, less muscular girl who combines femininity and grace with a firm, well-toned physique?"[84] The Mr. America Contest, with help from steroids and the lack of any non-muscular criteria, had resolved the question a decade earlier.

Nevertheless comparisons with the Miss America Contest were irresistible, even for the men. "It could have been Bert Parks singing 'Here she comes, Miss America,'" noted Caswell, "as the contestants introduced themselves and the state they represented." Although Gary Leonard appeared to be an "all-American boy," few of the many new faces showed charisma, and the impact of drugs on the massive male physiques was evident. There was also a mixed-couples competition, won by Shelley Gruwell and John Brown, and weight classes replaced height classes. The men's show appeared on cable television, the major press services were present, and the famed gossip columnist Rona Barrett covered it, leading Clarence Bass to "realize from experiences that go back to 1977 that the Gold's Gym people are very good promoters . . . particularly Ken Sprague." Though ostensibly retired from promoting, he was still laying golden eggs.[85]

The 1981 contest, in Las Vegas, featured the elimination of the most muscular man award, implying what everyone had known for a decade, namely, that the Mr. America title itself was just that. Indeed, the winner, Tim Belknap, of Rockford, Illinois, epitomized muscularity.[86] "It is hard to conceive of anyone who stands less than 5'5" weighing in excess of 225 pounds," observed John Grimek, adding that Belknap "not only has size, but his muscularity is sharp and his proportions blend." To Franklin Page, he was "muscular mass personified." Belknap's legs were "so large that squats are counterproductive": "At one point he was squatting with over 700 pounds and had a 30 inch thigh." Also remarkable was the arm development of the runner-up, Lance Dreher. "The forearms, biceps and triceps muscles on this man have to be seen to be believed," commented Chris Lund.[87] Tickets were sold out months in advance, and closed-circuit television handled the overflow from Caesar's Palace. There were one hundred competitors.

No less spectacular, with fifty-seven entrants, was the women's contest. Carla Dunlap, an African American who had been training less than two years, won a first-place trophy taller than she was. And the future physique stars Jeff Everson and Cory Kneuer (Everson) won the 1981 mixed-pairs competition. "Both are blond and have the healthy look of the All-American athlete," noted Sheila Herman. "As bodybuilders, they're beautifully matched." The physique judge Charles Simkovich was impressed by "the amazing growth that the Mr. America spectacular has experienced in recent years," and was certain that there would be "more progress in the future!" The contest was filmed by HBO for an even larger audience, creating the hope that it could eventually rival its popular Miss America counterpart.[88]

DRUGS: THE SCOURGE OF BODYBUILDING

What was most striking about the male physiques on display was their increasing size and muscularity, a result of two decades of steroid use.[89] Virtually all the muscle magazines condemned them. In an article entitled "Drugs: The Scourge of Bodybuilding," Ed Giuliani noted that "today's bodybuilders are more cut, are bigger, and produce a better show," but "nobody talks about health anymore." He pointed out the problem with this inattention to the drugs' possible side effects: "Is the Mr. America or Mr. Olympia really worth the risk of kidney troubles?" Joe Weider agreed that something had to be done. Bodybuilders had fallen prey to the "fatal psychology" that "if two Dianabol pills are good, then 10 pills are five times as good." But Pete Grymkowski used Weider's magazine to justify his own use of drugs (under medical supervision) and to attest to their efficacy. He concluded, "People who are more open-minded can excel with steroids." Schwarzenegger, on the other hand, decried the use of steroids and even suggested that their effect could be "imaginary." He wanted to see competition without drugs. And he admitted his own past use: "Too many magazines have been pretending the top bodybuilders don't use steroids. Hell, they all do. And I realize it's stupid. Perhaps one of the best things about my retirement from competition is that I don't have to take steroids as I used to. I think we should come right out in the open and warn bodybuilders of the risks involved."[90]

Robert Kennedy, a lifelong opponent of steroids, took much the same position.

I don't blame the bodybuilders who take the stuff—they can't help it. They know that to win, they *have* to go the steroid route; and their competitive nature can not be dampened—winning is everything and I understand that. . . . Now, with Pro bodybuilding contests offering bigger and bigger money, and the same judging standards giving the awards to the biggest and most vascular physiques, things are going to get worse. There will be more diseased organs, internal bleeding, wrecked and destroyed young bodybuilders than ever.[91]

As proprietor of Gold's Gym, Ken Sprague had a unique view of the steroid epidemic.

I have seen people take 100 times the recommended dosage of the common steroids used. And they are not just taking one steroid but 100 times the recommended dosage of several different steroids at the same time (synergistic effects). I have known people to go into shock and have to be rushed to the emergency room. One fellow dropped dead at home.

One time in the gym, a guy's heart stopped . . . and he was only 30. He went into shock after taking an injectable steroid. I saw another guy take 100 Dianabol tablets after breakfast (500 milligrams) and 50 Anavar tablets. He does this every day when he is training for a contest. Plus he takes injectables every day . . . also thyroid in heavy dosages. . . . Sometimes these guys go on zero carbohydrates for two months before a contest, combined with the many drugs and thyroid extracts, and poor, unhealthy diets. I can't see that not killing somebody.[92]

Although drug use was most visible among professional bodybuilders, it thoroughly permeated the amateur ranks too. After Dr. Walczak attended the Mr. USA and Junior Mr. America contests on the East Coast in 1981, he realized that "abuse was ballooning": "Testosterone, H.C.G., and you stack this, and you stack that. They're all taking ten times what they need. I heard one fellow was taking 8,000 mg. of Testosterone."[93]

Most distressing was the possibility that this addiction might spread to the nascent sport of women's bodybuilding. At the highly successful U.S. Women's Bodybuilding Championships, emceed by Sprague in April 1980 in Atlantic City, hopes were high when the ultrafeminine Rachel McLish, of Texas, won. "I think these women are tremendous as athletes," stated Denie Walter. "And frankly, since this is the home . . . of the Miss America Pageant, I'll take any of these women, anytime. I think they're more beautiful, because they take what they have to begin with and build on it." Yet Walter, along with Dr. Bob Goldman, realized that steroids were already infesting the new sport. "By God, does that have to go the way of Men's Bodybuilding?" they asked. If so, they predicted a worst-case scenario of women turning into men, asking sarcastically, "What guy could keep his hands off a muscular, hairy, puss-filled [sic], well-pimpled, balding woman with a deep sexy voice."[94] Peary Rader believed that drug use by women was "more insidious" than for men and feared it would destroy the sport. And he had seen its adverse effects for himself: "I have often been shocked to come into a room and hear a woman I have known for a long time as a woman talking with a deep voice."[95] Oddly, these observations did not coincide with the views of the scientific community, at least those put forward by Ann Grandjean of the American Societies for Pharmacology and Experimental Therapeutics. She concluded from twenty-five clinical studies that "research does not show evidence that steroids increase dry weight muscle mass or strength."[96] Those inside the sport, however, knew the connection was real.

NATURAL MR. AMERICA

It was only fitting, in light of the hypermuscularity of so many bodybuilders and rampant steroid abuse, that a drug-free movement should emerge. Chester Yorton, the 1966 IFBB Mr. America and NABBA Mr. Universe, seized the initiative by forming a Natural Bodybuilders Association (NBA) and staging a Natural Mr. America Contest in March 1978 in Las Vegas. Contestants were required to pass blood tests. It was, according to the runner-up, Bob Gallucci, "muscle against muscle rather than needle against naturals."[97] The event gained credibility by enlisting such iron-game notables as Bill Pearl, Joe Nista, Mike Dayton, Leo Stern, and Earl Maynard as judges, giving out expensive trophies, and awarding cash prizes totaling $7,000. Dan Lurie devoted nearly an entire issue of his magazine to the contest, noting that "macho man" Yorton ran it "with a feeling of vendetta toward *artificial* modern bodybuilding standards": "He seemed to have blood in his eye."[98] Although he strongly supported Yorton's initiatives, Peary Rader noted that drug tests were not always accurate and expressed concern that enforcement could lead to legal problems. In 1979, Yorton added Teenage and Over 40 Natural Mr. America titles, which were won by Doug Brignole and Jerry

Engelbert, and awarded $10,000 to professional winners and $2,000 in silver cups to the amateurs. There was an increase in the number of contestants (44) and audience members (1,000), and plans were put in place for regional championships. Three competitors tested positive, including Rufus Howard, who would have won the amateur division.[99]

Such was the popularity of drug-free bodybuilding that the Natural Bodybuilders of America (NBBA) appeared in 1981, under the leadership of Tom Ciola. It used a polygraph to catch contestants who might beat the blood test by staying off drugs for several months after having used them extensively. Also featured was a Natural Miss America Contest. From all over the nation, 110 contestants came to Utica, New York, seeking what the male winner, Bob Gallucci, called "the most sought after physique title in the country." He was especially impressed by the women, who "presented an outstanding, toned and aesthetic physique." The winner, Darci Dmitrenko, "performed a graceful, flowing routine with gymnastic stunts which brought the 1600 spectators to a roar." He considered her "a symbol of what bodybuilding could be like: healthful, competitive and with great participation."[100]

The 1981 NBA version also featured a Natural Ms. America, won by Heidi Miller; the men's title went to Eddie Love. Curiously, the audience was treated to a posing exhibition by the WBBG Pro-Mr. America Don Ross, a known drug abuser, who also served as a judge. The NBA magazine *Natural Bodybuilding*, which published the results, carried an article by Ross on muscle density and mass and an ad for his course titled "Size, Power and Muscularity." The greatest curiosity, however, was that while the IFBB and WBBG Mr. Americas were dissolving, two new versions of the title were arising, each purporting to be the true representative of American bodybuilding. Plans were even in the works for the NBBA, in imitation of the NPC-IFBB, to stage a Mr. Universe Contest and to ally with the nascent AAU MAC, headed by Bob Crist.[101]

RESURRECTING THE GREEK IDEAL

Such a move might resolve the problem of multiple Mr. Americas, but could the resulting contest be reattached to its ancient roots? Rarely did references appear in magazines to the Greeks, and then only with a vague notion of their relevance. A 1980 *Muscle & Fitness* editorial, "Heirs of Hercules," compared ancient heroes with "the Frank Zanes, the Arnold Schwarzeneggers, the Larry Scotts, and the Robby Robinsons of the world." Modern bodybuilders were "lucky to have the blood of the ancient heroes in their veins." Likewise, Joe Weider could sound a traditionalist note: "The Greeks believed in all-round development. In the ancient Olympic Games men were glorified for the attainment of physical perfection, an achievement labeled *arête*—total perfection of mind and body. The ideal of excellence also encompassed the intellect, for it was believed that a well-developed and finely tuned body had to be accompanied by an alert mind and a pure conscience." Whether these were truly Weider's sentiments is uncertain, since his editorials were largely penned by Armand Tanny, whose views were also rooted in a bygone era. Joe's attachment to the ancient Greeks likely reflected a more utilitarian bent, in that he shared his brother's ambition for bodybuilding to take its "rightful place as an Olympic sport."[102] Otherwise, he seemed oblivious of the erosion of traditional values that had accompanied his rise to eminence.

Bob Kennedy, on the other hand, a longtime admirer of the Greek ideal and one of its most celebrated sculptors, Lysippus, believed that modern physiques were "at the pre-Lysippus era of their art." Symmetry and proportion were at best secondary considerations: "Aesthetics seem to be thrown out the window. The more advanced a bodybuilder becomes the more imbalanced becomes his physique." To Kennedy, Steve Reeves was the "perfect specimen," and bodybuilding had regressed since his day. In the late 1940s, "the aim of bodybuilding was to build proportionate muscles that respected the frame" and "had to look 'right' on a person." Although Reeves would hardly qualify for a Mr. America Contest of the 1980s, Kennedy hoped for a return to sanity. He believed that "the Reeves physique is not dead . . . just resting, waiting for the resurrection!"[103]

Whether the bodybuilding clock could be turned back several decades before the transformations wrought by Schwarzenegger and Sprague through the Weiders seemed doubtful, but that was the intention behind Joe Henson's initiative to reassume AAU control over the Mr. America Contest. According to his son:

> Mr. America was supposed to be the embodiment of the American male and that has been distorted in recent generations to mean big. Everything is big in America—big cars, big houses. Ever since *Playboy* we all know what the most perfect woman looks like. But there's nothing to tell us what the ideal male looks like. I would suggest we look back to the Greeks. The Greeks believed in moderation. Steroids and freaks go against everything the Greeks stood for. That's where the concept started, and we've lost it.[104]

Whether the Greek ideal could be restored seemed to depend on whether the AAU, which at one time stressed all-around development and a balance between mind and body, and the natural associations could take the sport in a different direction, away from the obsession with steroid-induced mass and toward an integration of musculature and the total man. But first the AAU would need to regain control of its Mr. America rights and the bodybuilding infrastructure that supported it, which had both been so easily relinquished over the previous three years. As Sprague later recognized, it was the greatest advantage accrued by the NPC and its IFBB affiliate: "Weider and the IFBB stole the grass-roots organization that the AAU had once controlled."[105] Even if the AAU could take back the head of amateur bodybuilding, the IFBB would retain the body.

9

PROFESSIONALIZING AMATEURISM

A MAN'S AESTHETIC APPEAL DISAPPEARS WHEN HE CEASES TO LOOK NATURALLY MUSCULAR RATHER THAN A TRIUMPH OF THE PHARMACIST'S ART.

= DAVID L. CHAPMAN, IN CHAPMAN AND GRUBISIC, =
AMERICAN HUNKS

WHILE THE MR. AMERICA CONTEST AND OTHER PHYSIQUE SHOWS continued into 1981, the National Physique Committee and the Mr. America Committee prepared for a showdown over rights to the coveted Mr. America title. What ensued over the next two years was a series of court encounters designed to settle entitlement issues and ultimately determine the course of amateur bodybuilding. In addressing the NPC's possible violation of federal antitrust laws as well as its claim to prestigious trademarks, the courts would decide whether the MAC could exist, and on what level. Neither side was willing to accept control over just local or national competitions. Each wanted all the pie. Beyond matters of jurisdiction, however, the critical question over the next decade was the extent to which either organization could control the hearts and minds of bodybuilders. Much would depend on the construction of a network of professional images and icons that would transcend amateur traditions.

A LEGAL SHOWDOWN

On May 18, 1982, the U.S. District Court for the Eastern District of Tennessee, responding to a suit filed by the local MAC secretary, Ken Alexander, charging harassment by the NPC, issued an injunction preventing the NPC from punishing any athlete who entered an AAU contest. Although the judge stated that his ruling was equally applicable to the AAU, MAC officials proclaimed "a victory for the individual athlete's rights." Jim Manion argued that the lawsuit was merely a "pointless" harassment tactic by the AAU because NPC policy had never excluded anyone from its competitions. Manion later qualified those remarks, however, by stating that eligibility for the NPC Mr. America depended on an athlete's performance in previous NPC competitions—for example, "Winning the AAU California does not qualify you." Also the IFBB, as an international organization, "is not subject to the same legal restrictions that govern the NPC and the AAU." Thus, it could penalize athletes from rival organizations, and "while the IFBB is not in the business of making life difficult for bodybuilders," Manion made it clear that MAC crossovers would receive no special favors, since "the AAU seems bent on virtually destroying the NPC through a variety of subtle and not-so-subtle methods."[1]

This dispute was merely a prelude to the more serious question of who could claim the Mr. America title and other "Mr." contests for which there were duplications. The intention of the MAC to hold a Mr. America Contest in Worcester, Massachusetts, in 1982 prompted the NPC to file a retaliatory suit contending the title had been transferred to the NPC when it was created in 1978 and that its forthcoming Mr. America Contest in New York was the only valid one. "Suddenly we have two Mr. America contests," Manion argued.

> And the situation tends to diminish the prestige of the title itself. Some athletes are happy about this because the level of competition in the AAU event is not as difficult. . . . If the competition between the NPC and the AAU were based on the ability of each organization to present significant and exciting contests, the NPC would win hands down. So the AAU is trying to avoid this kind of showdown, preferring instead to take its fight to the courts, hoping the legal system can accomplish what its own promoters cannot.

For this reason, Manion appealed to bodybuilders, promoters, gym owners, and fans for donations to assist the NPC with its legal expenses, claiming that the NPC, "unlike the AAU, . . . is not as huge and doesn't have as many resources and means of raising money." His arguments, however, were flawed. While the NPC originated in 1978, the AAU could claim precedence from 1940, and it had never relinquished its control of the Mr. America title. With regard to loss of prestige from title duplications, the same could be said of the Weiders' initiation of Mr. America contests in 1949 and 1958. It could hardly be determined whether the quality of NPC contests was better, since the MAC was not yet operational. Finally, whether the NPC was in greater financial need than the MAC was questionable, since the latter was an amateur organization run by volunteers answerable to the nonprofit AAU, while the former was linked to the commercially based Weider magazine and fitness-product empire, which had seemingly unlimited resources.[2]

The NPC lost its suit to stop the Mr. America Contest in Worcester, at which point the AAU sued the NPC to prevent it from using the Mr. America title in its forthcoming New York contest. When the judge granted a temporary injunction to that effect, Ben Weider intervened by approaching Joe Henson at a GAISF meeting in Monaco. This led to an out-of-court settlement whereby the NPC gave up its claim to the Mr. America title and agreed to call its contest the American Bodybuilding Championships.[3] Later rulings in Tennessee and Florida prohibited the NPC from not allowing AAU athletes to participate in its contests, and prohibited non-AAU promoters from using the "Mr." prefix in their titles.[4]

Manion claimed the settlement actually worked to the NPC's advantage, since it coincided with IFBB policy regarding contest names. He noted that "the IFBB has realized for some time that the 'Mr.' titles have an old-fashioned, beauty contest connotation," while championship titles were more appropriate designations for an international sport. It was as if the NPC, which had desperately sought voluntary support for its case months earlier, never really wanted to win! Once the dust had settled in the courts, the AAU–NPC rivalry could focus on the contests. The athletes would decide which organization "does the better job." It was also obvious to Manion, as it likely was to his adversaries, that their contests were merely stepping-stones to international competitions, where success would ultimately validate their national counterparts.[5]

WAYNE DEMILIA

What neither side could have foreseen was the impact of a young body-building enthusiast whose messiah-like appearance in the late 1970s changed the face of bodybuilding over the next several decades. Wayne DeMilia, the Italian American son of a New York policeman, was raised in Brooklyn and earned an engineering degree from Queen's College. As an AT&T employee, he became aware of the impoverished state of bodybuilders when he attended the 1973 Mr. Olympia Contest at the Brooklyn Academy and saw Arnold take the microphone after his victory. "He walked around the stage and looking at the check. He goes, 'I trained all year. Last year they paid me a $1,000, and this year they paid me $750.' He throws the mike down and walks off. Wow, what a crazy sport this is, I thought. The place was half empty. Reports were that people were breaking down the doors, but it was half empty."[6]

Obviously there was little money to be made, but he accepted an offer from Tom Minichiello, owner of the Mid-City Gym, where he worked out, to run the 1975 Mr. Eastern America Contest. By enlisting local sponsors and promoting the event among fellow trainees, DeMilia made $2,000. Confident that he could make physique shows profitable, he visited Weider headquarters in California.

> I walk in, and here's Joe Weider behind this big desk. I see somebody's making money from bodybuilding. I'm looking at the building too. The building is impressive. And he goes, "What do you want?" That goofy voice he has. I said, "I want to run pro shows. You don't need amateur shows. Bodybuilding should be like golf and tennis, with a grand prix circuit. You get points, and that's how you get into the Olympia." "Ah, nobody's gonna do that. You can only support one pro show. There can't be more than the Olympia. Anyway, you're talking to the wrong guy." "So what do you mean?" "Talk to my brother." "Who's your brother?" "Ben Weider." "You mean there's two of you?" . . . Three months later I read Joe Weider's editorial. "I've come up with a great idea. I'm gonna turn bodybuilding into golf and tennis. I'm gonna have a grand prix circuit, and people are gonna get points to go into the Olympia, and run shows all over the place." . . . He stole it all from me.[7]

Meanwhile DeMilia not only aired his ideas to Ben but also managed, through a chance elevator encounter with Schwarzenegger, to get appointed to the newly formed IFBB pro committee, which Schwarzenegger chaired.

Though the committee included such notables as John Balik, Jim

Lorimer, and Paul Graham, it was DeMilia, assisted by Charlie Blake, the vice president of a New York marketing firm, who in 1978 launched the first non-Olympia pro show. Taking a cue from the boxing promoter Don King, he named it "Night of Champions." It was successful, a "sellout, standing room only," DeMilia recalled. "Robbie [Robinson] won, and there were all these stories about how I promoted it." Susan Fox, the only female judge, reported in *Iron Man* that she had witnessed "a new standard . . . for physique productions" and that DeMilia "delivered all he had promised."[8]

His 1979 Night of Champions was equally successful. The most critical step in securing the trust of the Weiders was to win the favor of Oscar State, whom they placed in charge of the Mr. Olympia Contest, along with DeMilia, in the early 1980s.

> Oscar in the beginning didn't like me. Who's this young wise guy from New York coming in here? I'm from the Olympics and weightlifting and this and that. And he's some kind of a phone man or something, but when we got to know each other, we were on the same page. Oscar liked me because "the rules are the rules, Oscar. Let's follow them." I remember he looked at me shocked. "You're correct, you know."[9]

Eventually, after leaving AT&T, DeMilia became head of the IFBB professional division and successfully promoted a plethora of shows in stylish venues with generous prizes. They included various Grand Prix competitions and twelve Mr. Olympia contests from 1984 to 2003. Gene Mozee called DeMilia "a real hustler" who "made the Olympia the way it is."[10] According to DeMilia, he also seized the reins from Manion by representing the NPC in the 1981 court hearings with the AAU, executed the surrender of the NPC Mr. America title (even taking down and reprinting posters), and promoted the new American Bodybuilding Championships, which were won by Lee Haney in 1982.[11]

In contrast with the Mr. America show in Worcester, DeMilia boasted that his contest attracted twice as many contestants and 3,000 spectators. He also claimed that the Mr. America title was not worth fighting for. The NPC national championships were "really a Mr. America Contest under another name that then became a feeder for the pros and that's what everybody wanted to do was get into the pros and make a fortune."[12] Most critically, he was able to sell his strategy to Weider and Manion. He told Weider the reason that so many contestants had turned out for his recent show: "They wanted into my pro shows. Because you win the AAU Mr. America over there, you go to the NABBA

Figure 9.1. Wayne DeMilia (seated), as impresario of the IFBB, played a critical role in professionalizing amateur bodybuilding in the 1980s and 1990s. He is shown with the Australian photographer Wayne Gallasch in Amsterdam in 2002. Courtesy of Wayne Gallasch.

Universe, even the NABBA Pro Universe, you don't get money, and where do you go? And they're seeing all these shows I'm running."

As for the Mr. America name? "Just give it up," he told Weider. Manion concurred.

> I said, I'm gonna call Carl Morrelli. He's our attorney here in New York, and I'm gonna tell him. . . . Ben goes, "Are you sure you're right?" I say, "Ben, you gave Jimmy $25,000 for legal bills. The legal bills in three states are now up over a quarter of a million dollars. Where is this money going to come from? You ain't gonna give us any more money. What are we going to do, run contests to pay legal bills? For what? A title doesn't mean anything. Everybody wants to go into pro shows. They want to be in Night of Champions, and they want to be in Mr. Olympia. Nobody cares about going to the NABBA Universe any more. They don't give any money. They're coming for money." He says, "Sounds good to me." . . . I called the lawyer and said drop it.[13]

It was a risky strategy, especially since the Weiders had spent over three decades trying to secure a hold on the world's most prestigious physique contest, only to see it slip from their grasp. But it enabled DeMilia, as impresario of the IFBB, to develop a highly profitable amateur and professional hierarchy of events on behalf of the Weiders. That success relegated the AAU to exercising exclusive control over the means by which they would ultimately, à la Hamlet, be "hoist with [their] own petard."[14]

REBIRTH OF THE AAU

For the moment, it was possible for AAU organizers to celebrate their legal victories. They began publishing *AAU Physique News*, which dubbed itself the "Official Journal of the AAU Mr. America Committee." The editor, Ken Alexander, thanked "the several hundred athletes, promoters, officials and publishers for braving both abuse and threats" and counted on their continued support. The biggest challenge would be to restore a grassroots organization. Alexander boasted that by the spring of 1982 the AAU had over five thousand registered athletes in fifty states, and that physique committees were operating in twenty-seven states and serving over 70 percent of the population. Efforts were afoot to establish medical and women's subcommittees, prepare a new rulebook, attract commercial sponsors, and offer fitness products. No less important were MAC initiatives to affiliate with WABBA in order to provide a higher non–IFBB echelon of competition. Oscar Heidenstam was invited to the forthcoming Mr. America Contest in Worcester to seal the deal. Additionally, the MAC wanted to design a Mr. America award that would mimic the Motion Picture Association of America's Oscar and Mr. Olympia's Sandow. Alexander was even looking into gaining IOC membership for the AAU physique organization. But as Jan Dellinger explained, the AAU had "lost the title for a few years": The barn door was open and the horse was gone." The AAU had to rebuild its structure.[15]

Meanwhile, the MAC was sanctioning contests. One of the first, a Mr. Los Angeles held in February 1982 in Long Beach, was overseen by Jack O'Bleness, who inherited Sprague's mantle as Southern Pacific AAU chairman. Jay Carroll reported that the show opened with some "straight facts" regarding the AAU's plans. Then the show began: "As flashing and twirling lights played around the stage, the National AAU emblem was spotlighted . . . and a gilded figure stood flexed upon a podium. It was Dave Dupree who looked more like a statue than does a statue." After that dramatic introduction, competition ensued for Mr. Los Angeles and teenage, over-40, novice, and women's versions of the title. It was "one of the finest Mr. Los Angeles events ever staged." But it was national contests that most defined the AAU's new image and intent, beginning in April with the Mr. Collegiate America, won by the massive Jeff King, followed in June by the Junior Mr. America Contest, sponsored by York Barbell. To establish credibility, contestants could request the removal of any judge believed to be biased. The competition ran smoothly, a sporting atmosphere prevailed, and Mike Antorino appeared to be a deserving winner. Still, observed Al Antuck, "The road back to bodybuilding for the AAU is not without its curves, bumps and pot holes."[16]

THE 1982 MR. AMERICA CONTEST

The real test for the fledgling organization came in August with the Mr. America Contest, which was staged by Cliff Sawyer in Worcester. According to Antuck, it marked the return of an event "as American as apple pie and hot dogs" and reflected the "open friendliness and genuine wholesomeness of a medium sized New England city." A celebratory mood prevailed. Joe Henson made statements about bringing physique back to "respectability," past Mr. Americas were recognized, and service awards were presented to John Grimek, Peary Rader, and Mabel Rader. The contest was "no longer under the domination of a couple of foreigners," noted Antuck, but now enjoyed "democratic representation" from all parts of the country. All officials were "citizens of the USA."[17] The winner, out of forty-nine contestants, was Rufus Howard, a butcher from Encino, California, who cried openly when his name was announced. Howard was the fifth African American to win the title, and Sawyer confirmed that even with white judges, it was a unanimous decision: "The numbers and caliber of contestants was outstanding."[18] The veteran competitor Tom Willert noticed "many former NPC competitors switching to the AAU." He rejected Manion's view that the AAU Mr. America was less prestigious. Its lineup even included two national NPC titleholders. Was the AAU reviving its grassroots? Listings by the nonaligned *Muscle Digest* show thirteen AAU shows and thirty-four by the NPC from February to October 1982, a good start but still a steep climb ahead.[19]

Less enamored with these developments were the editors of *Muscle Training Illustrated*, now in league with the Weiders, who believed amateur bodybuilding had prospered under the NPC and that the AAU's return ("Monsters from the 'ID'") was motivated by money.

> Remember the old AAU days? Physique contests at two in the morning after a 15 hour brutal Weightlifting event? Bodybuilding athletes were always treated as suspect second class citizens in those days. They were the tolerated necessary "trash," "faggots" or worse. They were exhibitionistic "sockos" because they posed instead of intelligently ripping their guts out with silly barbell snatches and clean jerks [sic] that popped your joints and crushed spinal columns to "shit." Well bodybuilders who are none of those "bad things" kept posing and . . . departed for parts in the non-exploiting wild blue yonder . . . and made it! No thanks to the AAU—but thanks to the NPC-IFBB.[20]

No less incensed was Doris Barrilleaux, chair of the American Federation of Women Bodybuilders, an IFBB affiliate, who feared that duplicate contests planned by the AAU would be a setback to the great strides made in women's and mixed-couples competitions in recent years.

But the NPC seemed prepared to face the AAU challenge. Apparently confused at first, it staged Teenage and Past 40 Mr. America contests in San Jose in August 1982, but later, to abide by court rulings, relabeled its Mr. America Contest, held in October, as the American Bodybuilding Championships.[21] It was held in a "shabby, run-down theatre" in the Times Square area of New York City, reported Dave Sauer, where "officials and spectators had to walk carefully to avoid stepping on inebriated winos that littered the sidewalk." Inside, despite poor lighting and music, the audience was treated to "one of the most exciting amateur bodybuilding competitions of all time." Leading the parade was Lee Haney, whose American championship triumph was complemented by that of American women's champion Carla Dunlap, and a mixed-pairs victory by Rick and Cathy Basacker. Al Antuck acknowledged that the NPC championships were a "great" show, but the Mr. America Contest remained "the most prestigious of all bodybuilding contests in the USA." There was "magic in the Mr. America name, and everyone craves either to win or control the title."[22]

INTERNATIONAL HEGEMONY

The real issue, however, was whether the NPC, despite losing this coveted title, would be able to control amateur bodybuilding. It held several advantages, the greatest being its affiliation with the IFBB, which brought with it publicity through the Weiders' magazines and their international network. Attempting to put the best face on his organization's recent court losses, Manion pointed out that Rufus Howard merely "holds the AAU title," but the winners of the NPC championships went immediately to Bruges, Belgium, where three of the four-member U.S. contingent won their weight categories against thirty-eight other teams, making them eligible for the Mr. Olympia Contest. In Bill Reynolds's assessment, the lightweight James Gaubert was "a clear winner from square one," the middleweight Dale Ruplinger "was the most convincing winner of any class," and the physique of the heavyweight Lee Haney had "no weak points." He called it "the best amateur show" he had ever seen and noted how the world championships, previously held in Nimes (1977), Acapulco (1978), Columbus (1979), Manila (1980), and Cairo (1981), kept getting better. For Manion, the implication for the NPC was obvious: "You don't make a contest a real national championship by simply giving it the name. A real national championship exists only when the best competitors in the country contend for it. When the NPC champions are able then to compete against the best international amateurs the IFBB can muster and completely blow them away, it offers as much proof of their superior quality as any rational person could require."[23] He neglected to mention that Rufus Howard, at York Barbell's expense, had competed in the NABBA Mr. Universe Contest in London. That he could fare no better than second in his class gave credence to Manion's argument.

Aside from the practical and prestige value of a higher level of competition, the driving force behind the world championships was Ben
Weider's desire to make physique an Olympic sport. Although that motive could be read into the Mr. Olympia Contest, which the Weiders
established in 1965, that was a professional event. But IFBB recognition by the GAISF, which had an indirect association with the IOC,
gave them grounds for hope. Hence, in 1977 they established an amateur world championship with weight divisions, much like wrestling,
weightlifting, and other Olympic sports. According to Bob Kennedy,
"Oscar State taught Ben how to organize federations. The compulsory
poses and the pose down was set up by State to make it more like an
Olympic sport." Weider also pursued Juan Antonio Samaranch, president of the IOC, relentlessly, but, according to Kennedy, "Samaranch
said he couldn't accept all of the gifts Ben was sending." Kennedy added
that although bodybuilding "was finally accepted as a demonstration
sport . . . others on the committee laughed at it."[24] Although the
AAU's recapture of the Mr. America Contest was a temporary set-
back, Ben remained confident that the AAU's plans for Olympic
recognition were pointless: "Why would an amateur bodybuilder
waste his or her time competing in AAU-sanctioned events if it
were understood that winning such contests would lead absolutely
nowhere?" He dismissed NABBA and WABBA as lacking the legitimacy and international stature of the IFBB, and also as unlikely to
achieve Olympic recognition. Yet despite decades of lobbying the
IOC, inclusion of bodybuilding in the Olympics would also prove
to be beyond Weider's "impossible dreams."[25]

JEFF KING

In 1983 the Mr. America Committee continued to expand its reach,
sponsoring thirty-two contests between July and December, licensing
a Mr. America Fitness Center in Gaithersburg, Maryland, and establishing an American Bodybuilding Hall of Fame at York Barbell. The new
MAC chairman, Cliff Sawyer, boasted a registration of 2,000 athletes,
while the NPC's enrollment had allegedly decreased by 500, indicating
that "the prestigious AAU America titles unquestionably take precedence." With links to NABBA and WABBA, according to Sawyer, "the
AAU has certainly shown its athletes that there is 'life' beyond the 'Mr.
America.'" He claimed that such greats as Oliva, Pearl, Mentzer, and
Coe were pledging assistance to AAU bodybuilding, and that Lance

Dreher, winner of the 1981 Mr. Universe title, was denouncing the NPC and supporting the AAU.[26]

On another front, a federal court ruling in Florida disallowed use of the prefix "Mr." on any non–AAU local or regional events. By then, Joe Weider, making a virtue out of necessity, had concluded that "the Mr. title hurts bodybuilding."

> In the minds of the press and public alike it creates the image of a beauty pageant such as the Miss America event. That is the very image we have strived to overcome for so many years.
>
> In all areas of the sport . . . we have made great strides forward. Yet all of our progress is diminished by the Mr. America, the Mr. California, even the Mr. Red River Valley titles. They do not suggest sport, they suggest pinup contests. They are throwbacks to the Dark Ages from whence we came.[27]

The irony, bordering on hypocrisy, of Weider's remarks was not lost on a perceptive *Muscular Development* reader, who pointed out that "not too many years ago, the Weider-formed IFBB *copied* the Mr. America title" and that the only "Mr." title that Weider wished to retain was the Mr. Olympia, which he, of course, invented.[28]

Coincidentally, the Mr. America Committee changed its name to the AAU America Committee, not out of deference to Weider, but because of the rapid growth in the number of women bodybuilders. Hence, the Ms. America title received equal billing with the 1983 Mr. America Contest, held at the University of South Florida. There were fifty-five male and twenty-seven female contestants. Kerrie Keenan, a South Florida student and local favorite, easily won the women's title. Among the men, noted Al Antuck, were a "high number of cross-overs from the NPC to the AAU," a sign of democratization. A recent graduate of Springfield College, Jeff King, dominated the proceedings.

> Jeff King was awesome. . . . He was huge when he won the '82 AAU Collegiate Mr. America title. Now he was even more huge, but with greater definition. His upper body was as massive as his lower body. His thighs and calves have been compared with those of Tom Platz. . . . Jeff King will make a fine Mr. America. He has the physique, personality, intelligence and charm to be an exemplary bearer of this title—the best known and most recognized bodybuilding title in the world.[29]

He was "the king of muscledom": "Long live the king!" To Jan Dellinger, the editor of *Muscular Development*, King not only had a fabulous physique but also epitomized the Mr. America ideal. He was lev-elheaded, personable, and aspired to be "a professional person and not a muscle head," he told Dellinger. When asked what it was like to win the Mr. America Contest, King's response resembled that of Larry Scott years earlier: "It's funny. Think of it like Christmas. When you were a kid waiting for Christmas. You could hardly stand it. As soon as Christ-

Figure 9.2. The rippled back of Joone Hopfenspirger, the 1985 Ms. America. Courtesy of Stark Center.

mas day came and you opened all your gifts, it was a letdown. I felt like I had worked my ass off for nothing."[30]

Part of King's frustration lay in the fact that winning the Mr. America Contest was no longer the ultimate goal in bodybuilding, but merely a stepping-stone to other, more grandiose titles. Next on the agenda was the NABBA Mr. Universe, to which the AAU, mimicking Weider but using York funding, was sending an American team of four height-class winners. King was the standout, the first American to capture the amateur crown since Coe won in 1969. "After I won that, it became a job," he recalled. But he was not able to win the NABBA professional contest or the WABBA Mr. World event the following year. Nor was he able to translate his Mr. America victory into greater glory in the Weider hierarchy. However much AAU officials sought to deny it, professionalism had been the order of the day since the advent of Schwarzenegger and DeMilia, and Mr. Olympia was the most coveted title in bodybuilding. Joe Weider courted King and even flew him to California for a photograph session and possible articles. That their relationship went no further, says King, may be attributed to "politics": "If Weider put me on the cover of his magazine and I wasn't an NPC man, then he would be recognizing an unaffiliated bodybuilder. It would not be promoting their business." It came down to "dollars and cents."[31] The AAU administrator Fred Yale concurred that politics got in Jeff's way: "When things were changing he got caught in the pinch." While *Muscular Development* provided ample coverage of AAU contests and revived its once-popular Mr. America series, *Strength & Health* was virtually defunct, and York Barbell was swiftly declining as a force in bodybuilding. Still, King made his mark. Denie Walter predicted that he would "pull the AAU out of oblivion with the finest physique . . . in the history of the title."[32]

APOLLONIAN VERSUS HERCULEAN ARCHETYPES

Weider's magazine empire, on the other hand, was growing. *Muscle & Fitness* was entering its heyday, and *Flex*, inaugurated in 1983, was catering to bodybuilding's hard-core base. Both were promoting the leading icons of the 1980s and creating the impression that NPC-dominated physique contests at home, and IFBB ones abroad, led to fame and fortune.[33] One such icon was Bob Paris, an Indiana native who "took America by storm," reported Rick Wayne, at Weider's Mr. America equivalent, the NPC National Championships, held in San Jose: "Bob

Paris is what Steve Reeves might have been had he been born 40 years after his actual birthday. . . . If ever a man deserved to be called Mr. America or Mr. Universe, that man is Bob Paris." Though never a Mr. America, Paris was being elevated to the stature of what that title once stood for, and both he and those whom he defeated, especially Mike Christian and Rich Gaspari, became part of the Weider-constructed imagery of bodybuilding. Jeff King, who held the title of Mr. America, soon lapsed into obscurity as a physical therapist.[34]

Unlike Paris, however, King's physique helped inaugurate a new era of bodybuilding, one in which mass would predominate. "How To Get Really, Really Big and Massive" was the title of a 1982 article by Schwarzenegger, who still exemplified a fixation on size. What *Muscular Development* called "the herculean superstructure" of Joe Meeko, of Catasauqua, Pennsylvania, dominated the seventy 1984 Mr. America contestants (from twenty-five states) who competed in Pasadena. His victory over the less massive Rick Poston reminded Al Antuck of the historical distinction between body types. The 1947 contest had featured the "Herculean physique" of blond-haired Eric Pedersen against the "V-shaped physique" of dark-haired Steve Reeves, who ultimately won the contest. But "in 1984 it was Pedersen's physique in the form, shape and possession of Joe Meeko that won the Mr. America title." The women too were getting bigger. Ms. America Jill O'Connor, borrowing the heroic victory pose popularized by Sergio Oliva, displayed her muscularity to the fullest, especially her arm development. "When I first started training, my arms were about 11," she stated. "They now measure 15" pumped." They became her "showpiece." Muscle size was also important for the 1985 Mr. America, Mike Antorino, of Tuckerton, New Jersey, who had earlier captured collegiate and junior America titles, but his shape and muscularity were critical, according to Bob Gruskin: "Mike's abs were thick as bricks, traps to his ears, legs cross striated and deeply etched." Likewise the female champion, Joone Hopfenspirger, of Golden Valley, Minnesota, was "ripped beyond belief!"[35]

Nowhere was the Apollonian-Herculean cleavage in bodybuilding more clearly delineated than in *Pumping Iron II*, a 1983 female version of the highly popular *Pumping Iron*. In the book that inspired the film, Charles Gaines and George Butler described two camps of women bodybuilders. There were women whose bodies were "only slightly more muscular than female gymnasts' and dancers' and whose key aesthetic concerns were femininity and symmetry."

And then there were the others, the "freaks" as some people called them.
. . . These women wanted nothing to do with beauty-contest aesthetics. They wanted *muscles*, and they were interested not only in taking women's bodybuilding further . . . but, in the words of a popular song . . . "Take It to the Limit"—to the max.[36]

In the film, this latter image was conveyed at a Caesar's Palace contest in Las Vegas. Beverley Francis, an Australian bodybuilder, challenged the traditional conceptions of the female physique displayed by Rachel McLish, Carla Dunlap, and Lori Bowen. Francis's physique was "qualitatively different and—because there is no frame of reference for it—existentially unsettling." She was "the unprecedented woman." Yet the powers that be seemed unwilling to accept the hypermuscularity normally associated with the male physique in a female body. "What we're looking for," asserted Ben Weider, "is something that's right down the middle. A woman who has a certain amount of aesthetic femininity but . . . has the muscle tone to show that she is an athlete. Women are women, and men are men."[37] McLish tried to dispel women's potential doubts about bodybuilding: "Many women fear that they'll look too muscular. But you won't look like a man." A difference in hormones and skeletal frame would prevent it, she believed.[38]

However true this rationale may have been in an earlier era, dramatic changes in training protocol were narrowing the gender gap. "I guess no formerly masculine domain is free from female intrusion," a perceptive reader of *Muscular Development* concluded, "even muscle building." As a result, "many of these women look disturbingly masculine—the result of steroids, no doubt!" Herein lay the crux of the controversy over how far women bodybuilders should follow the course of their male counterparts. "Women were already mimicking the men in that they are using drugs," observed Pam Shotzberger, a finalist in the 1983 Ms. America Contest. "Is drugs what bodybuilding is really all about?" she asked. A 1985 reader of *Flex*, contending there were "fundamental biochemical differences between the sexes," argued that the "only way a woman can become as beefed as Bev [Francis] is, is to either ingest or genetically possess an overabundance of male hormones."[39]

In a 1985 issue of *Muscle & Fitness*, two sports medicine specialists agreed that steroid usage among female athletes had been increasing for ten years, owing to the prospect of financial rewards. Steroid abuse was evident, for example, in female athletes from Soviet bloc countries at the 1976 (and later) Olympics. According to Dr. William Taylor, "bodybuilders are the greatest users of anabolic hormones," including human growth hormone. Dr. Robert Kerr concurred, noting that nearly 80 percent of female bodybuilders took performance-enhancing drugs. He stated, "Drug usage among female athletes is definitely on the rise, and until anything comes along that's better, they are going to take these drugs."[40] Bob Goldman's *Death in the Locker Room*, the harshest condemnation of steroid use in sports, includes testimony from Doris Barrilleaux, who insisted that steroid use is "not a laughing matter": "[It is] sad enough that women will resort to its use to try to improve their physical performance. But why on God's earth will they resort to it to change their physical appearance?"[41]

Ironically, where women were concerned, beauty of face and figure remained the most prominent image projected by the muscle media. A 1984 issue of *Muscle & Fitness* featured the newcomer Kris Alexander, who combined "beautiful musculature" with an attractive face, along with sexy photos of Rachel McLish, Shelley Gruwell, and Candy Csencsits in articles titled "The New Femininity" and "Beautiful Breasts." There was no mention of the growing drug menace. For McLish, whose "flex appeal" was often regarded one of bodybuilding's most valuable commodities, the solution was obvious: "If steroid use isn't checked, people will keep asking 'Is this a man or a woman?' . . . Drug testing will legitimize our sport."[42]

LEGITIMIZING THE SPORT

Despite recent court rulings forbidding use of the "Mr. America" title outside the AAU, two drug-free events held in October 1982 sported its name. The chief interest surrounding the Natural American Bodybuilding Championships in Pittsburgh was the attendance of the iron-game notables Bill Pearl, Clancy Ross, and Anibal Lopez. According to Jan Dellinger, when Greg Tefft, winner of the Natural Mr. America title, walked out on the stage, "the female half of the audience came alive," "instantly branding the blond-haired, blue-eyed Adonis as 'hunk' material." The Natural Ms. America winner, Terri Rouviere, gained an edge in posing from her gymnastic background. Meanwhile, over a hundred contestants entered a NBBA drug-free contest in Utica, New York, that featured Natural Mr., Miss, Teenage, and Over-40 categories. Only one failed the polygraph test. Mike Ashley, a future IFBB champion, won the Natural Mr. America title, and a former IFBB Mr. America, Reg Lewis, won the Over-40 title. Most notable to Bob Gallucci were the poise and attractive physiques displayed by females and the "lack of boisterousness or braggadocio which is exhibited by bodybuilders at other contests." Although the NBBA, loathing the "bad name" given to bodybuilding by the "drug gang," claimed that it was growing "by leaps and bounds," it was unable to merge with the AAU, or to tap the prestige of the Mr. America title any longer. Henceforth, its winners would carry such lackluster titles as Mr. and Miss United States Natural.[43]

In addition to initiating testing at women's contests, Joe Weider seized on bodybuilding's Greek heritage to restore respectability to the sport. Coinciding with the 1984 Olympics in Los Angeles and in support of his brother's lifelong attempts to include physique in the games, he penned an editorial entitled "Bodybuilding: It's Greek to Me." While repeating the usual platitudes about the Hellenic ideal, it emphasized how the Weider lifestyle and organization had refined the Greek tradition: "The ancient Greeks might experience cultural shock were they to see what we have done with the human body today. We have created phenomenal specimens of muscular development that would boggle the minds of those early idealists." Joe reminded readers that in 1965 he had created the Mr. Olympia Contest as a way to "enter the hallowed ground of the ancient Greek gods with incarnate image." Ensuing articles—"The Classical Look: Returning to the Ideal," "Flexibility," and "The Classical Mind"—followed the same theme. That more than respect for Greek ideals was motivating this sudden surge of interest in the "classical look" was evident in an ongoing feature titled "Physical Perfection: The Eternal Quest," which assured readers that the Trainer of Champions since 1936, with 7.5 million successful students, was dedicated to physical perfection through the application of science: "The Weider Research Clinic scientists, together with the greatest bodybuilders of our day, are on the cutting edge of the incredible new technology that allows them to develop phenomenal perfect physiques. You see, the Weider Research Clinic realizes, as did the ancient Greek athletes, that physical perfection is the birth-right of every man and woman." It was through "Joe's nutritional products" that aspiring bodybuilders would achieve the Greek ideal and gain "the winning edge."[44] No mention is made of bodybuilders' athleticism or the place of steroids in their lives.

LEGITIMIZING MISS AMERICA

How far bodybuilding had become unbalanced and unmoored from any Greek or American ideal was made obvious by comparisons with the Miss America Pageant, which was coping with feminism and modernization. To glorify the 1984 AAU Ms. America, the reporter Reg Bradford mimicked words popularized by Bert Parks when he introduced Miss America winners: "'There she is . . .' and there she was—Ms. America, Jill O'Connor."[45] But Parks had been sacked in 1979 by the pageant chairman, Albert Marks, and in 1982, owing to a contract dispute with the composer Bernie Wayne, "There She Is" was discontinued as the show's theme song. Now Miss Americas were serenaded with "Look at Her" and "Miss America, You're Beautiful."

But the most significant change was the obliteration of the race barrier. In 1980, two African American contestants broke into the top ten—Miss Washington, Doris Hayes, and Miss Arkansas, Lencola Sullivan. The latter reached the top five. Three years later, two more black women, Vanessa Williams, of New York, and Suzette Charles, of New Jersey, were named Miss America and runner-up. "I must have taken my vitamins today," was Marks's reaction. This precedent became poignant when a scandal erupted toward the end of Williams's reign over nude photos of her (taken years earlier) that appeared in *Penthouse*. Fortunately, Williams bowed out gracefully by resigning and even appearing contrite. Fortuitously—and fortunately for the image that the pageant was trying to project—Suzette Charles, who served as Miss America for the rest of Williams's term, was also black. Still there were naysayers. The Congress of Racial Equality insisted the relatively light-skinned Williams and the mixed-race Charles were not black enough. It was not until the fourth black Miss America (1991), Marjorie Vincent, of Illinois, the daughter of Haitian immigrants, that "a woman with dark skin and classically Negro features" triumphed. As one journalist observed, "Vincent with her luscious lips, broad nose and full cheeks, didn't fit what had fit the conventional mold."[46] It had taken two decades for the Miss America Contest to reach the same level of racial parity as the AAU Mr. America Contest had attained with James Morris in 1973.

What enabled Atlantic City officials to keep up with the times and transcend challenges of the 1980s was a new sense of professional commitment exhibited by contestants. It can be traced to the 1974 Miss America, Becky King, who, unlike many of her predecessors, was unwilling to settle for just marriage and a career as a homemaker, or the unlikely possibility of a break in show business. "Although Miss America contestants had a long history of fostering college education," she recalls, "I was the first who said I wanted to go to law school, and that I was in it for the money. Al Marks was appalled, but I told him being

Miss America was a job." Much though Marks may have dreaded the increased professionalism of aspiring Miss Americas, which was easily interpreted as commercialism, it strongly reinforced the intelligence and education criteria already in place and further detracted from the beauty show concept. In a prepageant profile in 1981, an Atlantic City journalist concluded, as a safe assumption, that "Miss America 1982 will be intelligent," since "there are several high school valedictorians, at least three Phi Beta Kappas, and a score of high honor students among the candidates." Ann-Marie Bivans notes how the program by 1990 was attracting "increasingly accomplished women who view their participation as a means to furthering lofty academic and career goals." She then lists numerous examples of contestants who attained degrees and honors at the nation's most prestigious universities.[47] Thus, the Miss America Pageant cleared the gender and racial hurdles that had appeared so formidable only a decade earlier, thereby achieving a bona fide legitimacy.

AAU VERSUS NPC

The Miss America Pageant marked a clear departure from the Mr. America Contest in its emphasis on intellect and function and by rejecting the notion that women were just physical objects to be gazed upon. Yet both the AAU and the NPC persisted through the mid-1980s with parallel Mr. America–style men's, women's, teenage, over-40, and couples titles. It was obvious that physiques in both organizations were becoming bigger and more defined. "Muscularity has gradually become a more and more significant factor in competitive bodybuilding," noted Jerry Brainum in 1983. "Bodybuilders learned early on that steroids allowed them to overtrain, get ripped and still stay big." After winning the 1984 NPC men's version, Mike Christian discussed the symbolic importance of the Mr. America title in an article entitled "Bigger *Is* Best": "Ever since I was a kid . . . I've wanted to be Mr. America. When they changed the title it made no difference." For his AAU rival Joe Meeko, "Winning the Mr. America title had been a dream of mine ever since I was a teenager as I always believed that it was the most prestigious title available. . . . Talk to youngsters starting out in body-building and they will tell you they 'want to look like Mr America.'" The critical question was whether adoring muscle fans would accept the NPC's synthetic version.[48]

A test of sorts occurred when Bob Gruskin attended the AAU and

NPC teenage and masters contests only three weeks apart in 1983. Both attracted an equal number of entrants; the former had superb organization, and the latter elicited greater crowd response. Gruskin regretted that the AAU-NPC split was resulting in "too many contests." But both organizations appeared to be robust.[49] The NPC, of course, had the powerful backing of the Weiders and their publicity network, which had grown fortyfold in seven years and was grossing an estimated $200 million a year by 1985.[50] The AAU, under chairman Cliff Sawyer, allegedly added over 2,000 members in 1985, established strongholds in previously weak areas of the country, and boasted the support of York Barbell, which housed a Bodybuilding Hall of Fame and *Muscular Development*, an AAU organ.[51]

A factor giving the NPC a significant edge, despite its having relinquished the Mr. America title, was its connection with the international network that Ben Weider had assembled. It was the channel by which its national champions, dubbed the "Best in America" for 1983, became eligible for the world championships, held in Singapore. According to Fred Hatfield, nearly 4,000 people showed up "to cheer the 137 bodybuilders from 46 countries who competed for the world's most prestigious amateur bodybuilding title."[52] Led by the national overall winner Bob Paris, the Americans took three of five weight divisions and won the team title. Paris explains how he adjusted to the confusing nomenclature of his titles.

> Even though the NPC didn't call it that anymore, I was the new Mr. America. . . . The IFBB was now trying to call what had always been the Mr. Universe the World Bodybuilding Championships; that was its official name. They thought that the title *world champion* was more in line with the ambitious plans to eventually have bodybuilding in the Olympic Games; it gave the champion more of an international sporting flair, something like world gymnastics champion, perhaps. The title Mr. Universe smacked of being attached to a beauty contest, they felt, and it betrayed the athleticism of the competition. We didn't wear evening gowns or have a Mr. Congeniality winner, after all.[53]

An equivalent women's amateur world championship took place in London, drawing 37 entrants from 22 countries. The Americans, known for femininity and lean lines, placed second, and were somewhat taken aback by the international stress on muscularity. "Bodybuilding means muscle," the 1981 Ms. America, Laura Combes, later observed, "and lots of it!"[54]

Much the same scenario played out for the men in 1984, when

the American amateur champions, led by heavyweight Mike Christian, won the world title in Las Vegas. The American women's champion, Cory Everson, became that year's Ms. Olympia, the first of six, and Lee Haney, after working his way up from the AAU Teenage Mr. America to the NPC national title, won his first of eight Mr. Olympia titles. Both became bodybuilding superstars and boosted the NPC-IFBB's stock immensely. Though none of the NPC champions could claim to be a Mr. America or Mr. Universe, that was exactly what their victories against tough competition entitled them to be.

SEEKING A PROFESSIONAL PARTNER

The AAU, on the other hand, was struggling to establish an international connection as a way to position its top-ranked amateurs for the commercial benefits of professional status. For many years, Mr. America winners had sought a higher level of competition through the NABBA Mr. Universe Contest in London. Despite its prestige and list of eminent winners, NABBA, strictly a national organization, offered virtually no opportunities for advancement.[55] To remedy this shortcoming, Oscar Heidenstam had linked NABBA with Serge Nubret's WABBA. Although Oscar became president, Nubret exercised controlling influence. Hence, the 1979 Mr. Universe Contest followed WABBA rules, used fewer British judges, and allowed Nubret to play a leading role.[56] Though Heidenstam found the arrangement distasteful, he tolerated it for several years, hoping to present a united front against the Weiders. But his resentments boiled over at the 1983 WABBA world championships, held in Switzerland. It was a "scandal," Heidenstam wrote to Grimek, how the proceedings were dominated by Nubret and his wife. "No wonder people write me and ask me about 'Nubret's Association.'" Using "the worst tricks of Weider," Nubret had manipulated victory for himself in the professional class. Likewise, the meeting of national delegates was a "farce," spent mostly in haggling over money. Therefore, Oscar withdrew NABBA from WABBA, hoping that other federations would follow and join a new entity called NABBA International.[57]

Key to Heidenstam's departure was Cliff Sawyer and the AAU America Committee. Heidenstam assumed that AAU America and other WABBA affiliates would follow NABBA's lead. As Heidenstam wrote to Grimek: "[Sawyer] told me quite emphatically that he would be guided by us." But Sawyer had second thoughts. By February 1984, seventeen WABBA countries were following the United States rath-

er than the United Kingdom. The ostensible reason for Sawyer's retreat was the need for unity against Weider. But the real explanation,
Heidenstam insisted, was money, a subject he held in contempt. Indeed,
the recent NABBA–WABBA rift "revolved round *money for professionals*." It was "all Nubret ever thinks of," he told Grimek, mainly how to
"wangle" a "cut" from contestant earnings. Talks had broken down in
Switzerland over Nubret's opposition to a Yugoslavian bid to hold the
1984 Mr. World Contest in Belgrade, "because they could not guarantee the amount for pros!" It seemed clear that prospects for personal
gain had influenced Sawyer's decision to stay with WABBA; a com-
muniqué from the association stated that he would receive a "$1,070
reimbursement" for his airfare to Switzerland. It appeared to be a corrupt bargain in which Sawyer's support was tied to personal financial
considerations.[58] Although Heidenstam still had support from NABBA
mainstays in Britain, he had alienated the new AAU leadership and split
non-IFBB bodybuilding worldwide. In 1984, two Mr. World and Mr.
Europe contests were held as each amateur federation tried to upstage
the other.

THE 1985 WABBA PRO-AM WORLD CONTEST

Much of the problem stemmed from Heidenstam's traditional, amateur mind-set, which prevented him from seeing how important a professional connection was to any anti-Weider initiative. Owing to his
organization's financial straits, Heidenstam could offer no more than
£5,000 to professional Mr. Universe winners, far less than the IFBB
awarded. Yet attempts to heal the rift proved fruitless. In 1985, Sawyer
made a polite inquiry about the status of NABBA, hinting that his
WABBA plans had not worked out as well as expected. Despite men-
tioning the $50,000 in cash he would be offering professional win-
ners at the forthcoming WABBA World Contest in Worcester, his letter
was clearly an olive branch. Heidenstam responded to Sawyer's contrite
gesture with a stream of invective that was condescending and cruel.
In a seven-page single-spaced screed, Heidenstam detailed the sins of
Sawyer and WABBA over the past six years, his core complaint being
their obsession with money. "More than once I have said 'is it not called
"World *Amateur* Bodybuilders Association,"'" why do we always have to
pin everything on a handful of professionals, when there are about 50
amateurs competing!" As for his not supporting the Mr. World Contest,
he blamed Sawyer: "It's not a question of NOT supporting you but a

question of our not belonging to WABBA any more. Had you come with us, as we hoped, then we would have been there." Beyond his grudge over Sawyer's alleged betrayal, Heidenstam was distressed by the emphasis on professionalism.[59] It was a result, owing to the Weiders, of the biggest and best athletes being drawn to contests offering the most money, but a professional component was necessary to attract aspiring bodybuilders for whom being Mr. America was no longer enough.

Sawyer's Mr. World Contest held in November 1985 tested whether the AAU could reach the lofty heights achieved by the IFBB with its Mr. Olympia Contest and other events promoted by DeMilia. Greg Zulak called it "Mayhem in Worcester" in *MuscleMag International*, having witnessed some unusual and "downright amusing" practices. The women's competition resembled a "beauty contest" featuring women with "lean lithe muscles," along the lines preferred by Nubret, who abhorred "large muscular women." The top amateurs would have placed no higher than sixth in the NPC nationals. The women's pro winner, Maria Concetta Serio, "very pretty" and an easy winner, "lacked the hardness, density, size and muscularity" displayed by "top physique women lately." For the men's amateur contest there seemed to be "no rules" and "nobody to keep the judges in line."

> For example, in the IFBB, the judges are not allowed to speak to other judges, are not allowed to shout out instructions to competitors onstage, and are not allowed to have cameras and take pictures while judging. In WABBA . . . almost every judge had a camera and the head judge from France who sat one row in front of me even had a video camera! He spent most of the contest filming and spent very little time judging, from what I could see. . . . At the same time, I heard various judges shouting up at the stage to give instructions, especially the same head judge and Serge Nubret who sat right beside him.

But real fireworks occurred in the men's professional division, which attracted some top stars, including Jeff King, Warren Frederick, Lance Dreher, three-time WABBA Mr. World Ed Kawak, and 1983 Mr. Olympia Samir Bannout, an IFBB defector. There was chaos, marked by a prolonged "pushing and shoving" match, at the preliminary-judging posedown. Then Kawak, miffed at his third placement, grabbed the microphone from the emcee and shouted "WABBA is bad, WABBA want me down. . . . Everyone know that I'm best." Bannout was pleased with his first place and $22,000 prize, but when handed a check for only $15,000 and told that the remainder would be a tanning bed worth

$7,000, he replied, "I don't need a fucking sun bed, I live in California. I want my money." For several hours he wrangled with WABBA officials. At 3 a.m. he showed up at Sawyer's house and pounded on the door. Sawyer refused to see him and called the police. Still, Zulak conceded that "WABBA is a young organization and you have to give them E for Effort."[60]

In *Muscular Development*, Jan Dellinger provided some damage control for WABBA and the AAU. Kawak, he admitted, had been "visibly irked" and had offered some "parting comments, but "despite what you may read in other bodybuilding magazines with a differing political persuasion," Kawak "did not verbally attack WABBA or state that he was fleeing to the IFBB." Nor was Bannout quite so visibly upset, especially after Sawyer offered to buy the tanning bed, and Jeff King, contrary to rumors, was not unhappy with his second-place winnings. Dellinger also contended that "no WABBA judge was taking pictures of contestants" during the judging. Far from being a "debacle," the men's events were stellar attractions that breathed life into the sport, and the women's events, which offered $10,000 in prizes, were also successful.[61]

Roughly on the same side of the political fence, Denie Walter in *Muscle Training Illustrated* congratulated WABBA and the AAU for attempting "to counter the general IFBB dictatorial and arrogant 'Napoleonic Code' which now pervades the World Bodybuilding sport scene." He observed that Kawak brought more discredit on himself than WABBA by his tasteless remarks and that Bannout stated he was "very glad" to be part of the contest and would continue to support WABBA and the AAU. Bannout wanted to encourage "the people that support Bodybuilding and live Bodybuilding, not that other California 'bullshit.'" What Sawyer and his comrades had in mind was a democratic alternative. "The professional access circuit we're developing," Sawyer asserted, would "make a quantum leap for the amateur who wants to turn pro when the am-titles run out." His goal, like the Weiders', was Olympic participation, and Sawyer in fact claimed that his committee already had USOC support.[62]

Such intentions caused concern for Ben Weider, whose reaction took the form of a condescending letter to Dellinger (printed in *MMI*) specifying the controversies at the WABBA world meet and challenging him to prove his "honesty, sincerity, and integrity . . . by reporting the facts of this event as they were." He also wanted Dellinger to know that while only about 550 people were in the audience at the Worcester contest, attendance figures at the recent Mr. Olympia Contest in

Brussels and the IFBB world championships in Gothenburg, Sweden, were 7,000 and 10,000. No doubt Weider was disappointed by Dellinger's rebuttal and his estimate of attendance having been "close to 1,000." The WABBA world meet had attracted eighty-three entrants from twenty countries, the United States won the team title, and the total money package of $50,000 exceeded the $35,000 offered at the recent Mr. Olympia Contest. Furthermore, the appearance of so many iron-game notables, a mixture of IFBB defectors and curiosity seekers, included not only Bannout, Dreher, Nubret, King, and Kawak but also Tim Belknap, George Snyder, Artie Zeller, Dave Draper, John Grimek,

Figure 9.3. Bob Gruskin congratulating the 1986 Junior Mr. America, Rich Barretta, who became Mr. America the following year. Courtesy of Wayne Gallasch.

George Paine, Tom Minichiello, Ed Jubinville, Denie Walter, and Dan Lurie, indicating that WABBA and its AAU affiliate might be able to stake a claim to the future of professional bodybuilding.[63]

SEEKING A HIGHER PROFILE

All depended on whether the AAU could both sustain a high profile by sealing a connection between its Mr. America Contest and the WABBA and establish a reputation for credibility and profitability. It did not help that Jeff King placed only second at WABBA's world meet and that Joe Meeko and Mike Antorino did not compete. Additionally, relations between the AAU chiefs and Nubret, always shaky, soon broke down, and their separation became permanent. To Dellinger, it seemed imperative that the AAU establish a professional division in order to bolster its stock. As he put the matter in a letter to Jon Rieger.

> The top people have to have a place to go . . . or go to Weider. I can guarantee that Cathey Palyo (won medium class at the '85 Ms. A) will not be at the Ms. A this year because she's won the NPC California, her class at the NPC USA, won the Denver Gold's Classic and, frankly, won't want to screw up her political standing with the NPC-IFBB by going into the AAU Ms. America. Even winning the title isn't worth risking for fear of the possible repercussions. . . . The AAU Mr./Ms. America titles have been seriously devalued.

But the lack of a professional or international outlet was only part of the systemic problems plaguing the AAU. As Dellinger told Rieger, he was troubled by its lack of organizational efforts and miffed at its failure to use *Muscular Development* fully as a publicity medium.

> Yes, the NPC benefits enormously from its alliance with Weider—primarily from an image and reputation standpoint. And this is precisely where the AAU is losing the battle. However, less from not being associated with Weider than it tends to "shoot itself in the foot!" . . . The NPC promoters are much better on the notification issue—and I don't print half their announcements. . . . NPC promoters, of big shows anyway, are just so much more professional. And, frankly, this appearance of mediocrity by AAU promoters contributes greatly to the AAU's "minor league" moniker in the sport.

He summed up his frustration: "I never cease to be amazed at the ineptitude of the AAU."[64] A sampling of local competitors' feelings by Rosemary Hallum, of Alameda, California, confirmed Dellinger's views. In a letter to Rieger, she concluded that the NPC was more professional, that NPC-related magazines were top of the line and were supported by more money and power, that some AAU shows were tacky and poorly organized, and that local AAU promoters "go around in circles . . . like a cat chasing its own tail."[65]

Still, opportunities for the AAU to raise its competitive level abounded. In March 1985, Joe Tete conducted an AAU international championship in Atlantic City, but it attracted only one entrant from outside the United States. Likewise, an international natural-bodybuilding event in Cherry Hill, New Jersey, got little notice. A more noteworthy attempt to fill the void left by the divorce from WABBA was the first AAU Mr. World–Ms. World competition, which was staged by Lance Dreher and Tom Tabback in April 1986 in Phoenix. It was sponsored in part by Tabback's company, Sportstar Nutritional Supplements. Though only ten men and three women competed, the quality was high, featuring two future Mr. Americas, Glenn Knerr and Bill Norberg. The enthusiastic crowd of 2,300 was treated to an exhibition by the powerlifter Ed Coan, who deadlifted 800 pounds thrice. Then there was an inaugural AAU Mr.–Ms. Universe held in Tucson, which was broadcast on ESPN. The winner, Marlon Darton, exhibited cuts and size on a massive, 6'5", 250-pound frame. The presence of the physique legends Reg Park and Bill Pearl provided a note of distinction. Finally, NABBA hoped to enhance its stature when it staged a world championship in Las Vegas in 1986; Canada's André Maille took the overall title. It was followed by a NABBA Grand National event in 1987, which had numerous Mr. and Ms. Americas as entrants.[66]

Despite this profusion of higher-level competitions, the notion persisted that "Mr. America" was "the most prestigious amateur bodybuilding title in the land." To Bob Gruskin, it was "the dream of every aspiring physique devotee." For Dan Lurie, "the Mr. America title itself is really the only important one in the Bodybuilding world," symbolizing "for men and women every where the earth's mightiest and most technologically superior country." So attractive had the Mr. America title become that officials imposed eligibility requirements for the 1986 event, held in St. Louis. It was becoming too difficult, noted Ira Hurley, "to handle the big numbers we're getting," especially since there was superb quality "across the board." Still, observed Jon Rieger, "nearly 70 competitors showed up to fight for the right to call themselves Mr. or Ms. America." Curiously, the 1986 Mr. America, Glenn Knerr, had already won Mr. World for that year, yet placed only third in the AAU Mr. Universe Contest. Terri Nordaby, who won the 1986 AAU Ms. Universe title, became Ms. America in 1987.[67]

A "PROFESSIONAL" PLANNING CONFERENCE

Efforts needed to be made to dispel the confusion due to the proliferation of titles brought on by promoters and athletes seeking a higher form of recognition. To that end, Ken Alexander hosted an AAU America Corporate Planning Conference in January 1987 in Knoxville, Tennessee. First and foremost, the fifteen leaders sought to establish a professional-bodybuilding component, possibly through NABBA. Dellinger, the first speaker to "sound off" on the subject, later told Rieger, "We probably got hung up on the pro issue too long, particularly since the AAU is only geared for amateur events"; but, he added, overall "the dialogue was terrific."[68] Other agenda items included a possible drug-testing program, the creation of media outlets to improve the visibility of champions, fund-raising, and the resolution of conflicts with the NPC. In addition, AAU leaders planned to provide a channel for Olympic recognition by organizing a Pan American Physique Federation (PAPF) under Pete Miller and Carlos Rodriguez. It conducted a championship in San Juan, Puerto Rico, in 1987; Joe Meeko won the men's division, Candelaria De Eraza won the women's title, and Marlon Darton, the "Jolly Black Giant," was guest poser.[69]

The subject of drug testing, which included input from Dr. Don Hatcher, the president of ABM Laboratories, provoked extensive discussion, but it was only later that Cliff Sawyer received a request from AAU president Richard Harkins for the America Committee to institute testing.[70] Sawyer reminded Harkins of the exorbitant costs ($175 per athlete); the remote testing sites; the time required to administer the tests, transmit the samples, and perform laboratory work; and possible legal implications. But the committee agreed to comply with Harkins's request if the AAU would "raise the money for all aspects and expenses" related to testing, assume all legal expenses and liability, and require other senior sports to institute similar programs. On his own, Sawyer started soliciting local promoters to look for sponsors who would assume the prohibitive costs ($5,000–$10,000 for each competition).[71] "Drug-testing is coming," he warned. By July, the America Committee had issued a list of testing procedures, along with a new physique manual prepared by Jon Rieger, which seemed to set the stage to move forward on this critical matter.[72] Despite Harkins's statement at the annual convention in Indianapolis in September 1988 that the AAU had no money for testing and was concerned about litigation, the committee adopted a resolution to begin drug testing in 1989.[73]

Regarding AAU-NPC relations, *Muscle Training Illustrated* reported that after the meeting a call was made to Jim Manion to establish "a continual dialogue" for settling territorial disputes: "Each felt the current sniping situation between the organizations on regional, state and local level is silly and bad for the sport overall—and that they as leaders could talk and achieve a finer control over the issues involved. . . . To date both groups have lost up to approximately $120,000 each on the national level in the courts of the land. That comes from the athletes who support these systems, which is everyone's loss."[74] In effect, the AAU had sought a truce, signifying its weakened position.[75] The accord was complemented by the decision of Jan Dellinger, following Grimek's retirement, Hoffman's death, and the demise of *Strength & Health*, to start carrying NPC features and views in *Muscular Development*.[76]

THE ROAD TO FAME AND FORTUNE

Reciprocity was another matter, however, and there seemed to be no reason for the Weiders to relinquish their publicity edge by carrying AAU features. Therefore, the AAU, until it could find a higher tier of bodybuilding titles outside IFBB jurisdiction, had to devise a source of financial gain for its athletes. The Mr. America title could be a means to this end, and the New York promoter Bob Gruskin, who had prepped seven winners, helped create an awareness of how to exploit it. "He knew how to train people with very intensive workouts," according to Bob Bonham, owner of the Strong and Shapely Gym in East Rutherford, New Jersey. "And he taught them life's lessons. He made them have jobs, keep their jobs, not become bodybuilding bums." Gruskin liked "a certain type of guy": "Square jawed, blond hair, very Aryan." And they usually had potential before they met him.[77]

Gruskin set up a whirlwind tour of Germany that called for the 1985 titlist Mike Antorino to give twenty seminars in nineteen days. "I didn't realize that everyone knew that I was Mr. America," Antorino reflected, "but they did." And he recognized its worth, both for himself and for the public:

Winning the Mr. America title was a dream come true. It's the most prestigious amateur title in existence and a greater segment of people can relate to it as the average Joe on the street has heard of Mr. America. . . . Even when training for the Mr. America I didn't foresee myself raking in tons of money if I won. Well, I did win, and it hasn't been tons, but I can surely say "pounds!" . . . Winning the Mr. America title is nothing like winning the Miss America title (beauty pageant). When you win the title, that's about all you get . . . if that's all you want!

On the other hand, if you are willing to work hard there are numerous doors open to you.[78]

Glenn Knerr and Teri Nordaby sought to capitalize on their titles by endorsing Sportstar products. "Take Sportstar every day," advised Knerr in an ad entitled "Mr. America" that ran in leading muscle magazines. "I've tried them all and Sportstar is the best!" Joe Meeko, soon after becoming Mr. America, started his own company, Power Grips, to help bodybuilders train efficiently. But by 1988 the demands of his business were taking a toll on his ability to advance in the physique world. Bill Norberg, after winning the 1988 title, faced a similar quandary. He was a full-time accountant. Could he parlay his Mr. America fame into gym ownership and rise to a higher level of competition?[79]

For NPC athletes, such questions did not loom so large, since their fame was promoted by Weider publications and their prospects of fortune were seemingly ensured if they could graduate through the amateur system and secure a "pro card." By the mid-1980s, that grass was looking greener for most Mr. Americas. In 1987, Knerr realized that the NPC-IFBB network was his best option. "Glenn claims he's just not making the money he thought he would with his 'A' title," reported *Muscle Training Illustrated*.[80] But in the 1988 NPC Nationals, he only placed fifth. Likewise, Cathey Palyo switched to the NPC in order to compete against "higher quality women": "There are too few high-level AAU shows, while there are scores of IFBB amateur and pro events." Palyo became the 1986 NPC champion. "Movin' On to Better Things" was the title of the article in *MuscleMag International* that described the move of the AAU champions Rick and Debbie Poston to the NPC.[81] After winning virtually everything that the AAU and NABBA had to offer, Joe Meeko decided, "It was time for me to do something I should have done a while ago."[82] He entered the 1987 NPC Nationals, in Atlantic City, but failed to place in the top five. In 1988, the veteran AAU champion Marty Vranicar finally defected. He was clear about why he did it: "My main reason for switching was publicity. I have put a lot of time and effort into the sport and have done well, but even with all the titles I have won in the AAU, I was an unknown. The IFBB and the NPC promise me not only the opportunity to compete against the best known figures in the sport, but also to reap some of the benefits. Eventually I want to go professional, and the only way to do that is through the IFBB."[83] When asked why he switched organizations, the aspiring professional Vince Taylor replied that he "looked at the AAU as kindergarten in comparison to the NPC."[84] Taylor quickly ascended the heights by placing third in the 1989 Mr. Olympia Contest.

Meanwhile new opportunities were opening for NPC competitors every year. In 1985, Ben Weider included the "World Games" in the IFBB's repertoire. Held in London and won by the up-and-comer Berry DeMey, the event was not unlike the NPC World Championships; the winners of each weight class became eligible to turn professional and enter Mr. and Ms. Olympia contests. Weider argued it was special because it was held only once every four years—"Another Triumph for the IFBB." Jim Manion argued that "the NPC/IFBB graduation system . . . offers the competitor the logical progression of his or her bodybuilding career," from NPC national championships to IFBB amateur universe to IFBB pro status. He noted, "Within this system lies the highest quality of competition in the USA today."[85] "Bodybuilding has made it" was the IFBB line. With the sport's growing popularity, enterprising champions could promote "profitable, high-gloss productions."[86]

In 1988, the Men's National Championships was hosted at the Atlanta Civic Center by "TotaLee Awesome Lee Haney." "Big-Time Productions Are Big Business," exclaimed an article title in *Flex*. According to NPC national coordinator Dan Forbes, the list of former NPC athletes "now striking it rich as IFBB professionals reads like a 'who's who' of bodybuilding: Lee Haney, Cory Everson, Phil Hill, Mike Quinn, Cathey Palyo, Mike Christian, Rich Gaspari," all of whom "qualified for professional status by progressing through the NPC system." Exemplifying the IFBB's professional lure was Edward Kawak. "All I want to do . . . is earn a decent living," he stated. "Sure, I've won many WABBA titles, but to me a Mr. Olympia title means ultimate success in the sport."[87] By 1989, according to Lou Parees, "making gains" was "the NPC Story." Under Manion, it had grown to 1,500 contests and 20,000 athletes from just 200 and 2,000 in 1977, and the *NPC Newsletter* had doubled its page count, supplementing information in *Muscle & Fitness* and *Flex*.[88] Meanwhile, York sold *Muscular Development* in 1989, and like *Iron Man* and *MuscleMag*, it was providing more NPC-IFBB than AAU coverage.

The demise of loyalist AAU publications and Manion's management skills contributed significantly to the increasing popularity of NPC contests in the 1980s. But the most potent factor in their success was the magnetic force of the professional network put in place by Wayne DeMilia, whose efforts had accelerated IFBB growth over the previous decade and ultimately led to the professionalization of amateur bodybuilding. In retrospect, it can seen that DeMilia completed a transformation set in motion by Schwarzenegger and Sprague. Amateur bodybuilding became an indispensible link with professionalism in much the same way that college football is for the NFL, and farm clubs are for Major League Baseball. "Yeah, everything was my ideas," he says, "but they [the Weiders] took credit for them." Furthermore, DeMilia never received a salary. "The Weiders didn't pay me a dime." His only income came from shows he promoted, but the Weiders demanded a heavy cut. "At the Olympia they were taking two-thirds and leaving me one-third," yet he was doing most of the work and wielding much of the power on their behalf.[89] To say that DeMilia was largely responsible for the growth of professional bodybuilding and contributed greatly to the influence and fortune amassed by the Weiders would be an understatement, yet nowhere in their memoir *Brothers of Iron* does his name appear.[90]

BODYBUILDING'S ACHILLES' HEEL

By the end of the 1980s, the popularity of the Mr. America Contest (if not the image) had been superseded by that of its virtual rival, and the IFBB and its NPC affiliate seemed poised to lead bodybuilding into the Olympics. What stood in the way of widespread public acceptance was the same problem plaguing all strength-related sports.[91] As Greg Zulak observed in 1988, elite athletes, who are supposed to represent the "best that bodybuilding can offer (and to whom we all want to emulate) have all kinds of problems."

> Invariably, they have huge, thick bloated waists. Oh sure, when they suck their waists in, the abs look good and the waist looks tight but if you watch closely, as they pose they often forget to hold their waists in and as they start to "belly-breathe," the gut hangs out like the abdomen of a pregnant woman. You see, steroids make even the intestines grow so they push the waist out. And when the waist thickens and pushes out, it not

Figure 9.4. Matt DuFresne "put the 'mass' in Massachusetts" as Mr. America 1989. Courtesy of Bob Gruskin.

only lessens the V-taper but visually appears to make the shoulders look narrower and ruins the body's symmetry.

Then of course gynecomastia is as common as dirt these days. And steroid acne is too. All from too much steroids. Another commonplace thing is to see top stars with bodies totally out of proportion. Many of them look like they were put together by a demented Dr. Frankenstein. . . . This comes from a fetishism that most bodybuilders have for freaky bodyparts.[92]

Joe Weider admitted, "You can't scare a lot of athletes by listing the dangers of using steroids," noting that over a hundred Olympic athletes stated they would take a pill, knowing it would kill them a year later, if it would guarantee a gold medal. Ben Weider nevertheless, knowing that bodybuilders were among the worst drug abusers, was determined to gain Olympic recognition. Hence, the IFBB instituted drug testing at the Ms. Olympia Contest in 1985 and at the men's world championships in 1986. "Bodybuilding will comply with the IOC's wishes," Ben announced, by using IOC-approved laboratories.[93]

Further to bolster credibility, Weider enlisted as his drug czar Dr. Bob Goldman, who declared that the IFBB would test for the full IOC list of 3,100 banned substances. Testing not only would remove an obstacle to seeing the sport join the Olympics, but also could shame rival organizations. "Only the IFBB (with the NPC starting this year) is fighting the steroids problem," observed Jeff Everson. "If we seriously want to get rid of these drugs, many more organizations need to follow suit—the AAU, WABBA and NABBA must unite with the IFBB in this effort." Anxious to show the efficacy of their procedures, IFBB officials announced that all contestants at the 1987 Madrid World Championships passed their drug tests, and only two women were disqualified of the twenty-seven tested at the 1988 Pro World Championship.[94] Then after all twenty-eight competitors tested negative at the 1989 women's Pro World, Gayle Hall proudly announced, "It's *finally happened!* Drugs have been successfully eliminated from the sport of women's pro bodybuilding!"[95]

Naysayers, however, were not convinced that the IFBB was winning its antidrug initiative. In an "open letter" to *MuscleMag*, Daniel Burke, of Daytona, Florida, queried:

Ben Weider are you out there? So, your life long dream is to put bodybuilding into the Olympics? I can tell you how—start steroid testing in NPC-IFBB contests at all levels. . . . No one is fooled by these token Ms. Olympia tests. Those women are most definitely on steroids. And frankly, to be competitive in today's contests they have to take them. Otherwise

they'll get up there and look like—gosh—women. And they will lose.
. . . Let's face the facts. In order to be competitive in bodybuilding or
powerlifting you simply *must* take drugs—or you're going to be blown
off the stage.[96]

Although Terry Todd applauded the Weiders for instituting testing, he
warned that the judgment of history would depend on their ability to
"to implement a rigorous, year-round program that tests the top pros at
the Mr. Olympia for steroids." Joe's response, however, dodged the issue.
Though "aware that many of the top champions *do* use steroids, I'm still
proud of them because steroids didn't build their bodies." Steroids he
regarded as "secondary," and as no substitute for hard work, dedication,
and nutrition. According to Boyer Coe, the Mr. Olympia Contest was
tested just once: "Everybody looked terrible. Then Joe came to realize
. . . if the guys looked as bad the next year as they did this year people
were not coming back to see them. So that was the end of it."[97]

No less damaging to the IFBB's testing efforts was the belief that
bodybuilders could dodge detection, the subject of a 1988 *MuscleMag*
article, "Catch Me If You Can! How the Pros Beat the Drug Test," by
Dr. Winston Smith.[98] Peter McGough grappled with the issue in a 1989
article, "Debating the Drug Tests," that questioned whether "cleaning
up the sport will lead to Olympic recognition, mass acceptance, and
bigger sponsorship deals." Mike Quinn, a world champion, challenged
the basis of the whole exercise in drug testing and claimed that it was
in fact pointless.

I don't see how testing at the pro level helps to achieve that goal, as the
Olympics are for amateurs. Personally I just can't see bodybuilding *ever*
getting into the Olympics.
As for going mainstream, I'm a pretty positive guy, but I can't see that
happening either. If the general public were interested attitudes would
be changing now, and they're *not!* Being in the public eye, being instantly recognizable as a bodybuilder, I come face to face with a lot of
stereotypical pre-judgments of bodybuilding. The public's view is that a
bodybuilder is not a total person, and I don't anticipate any shift from
that position because of drug testing.[99]

Further doubts about testing were reinforced by the extreme devel-
opment of the men at the NPC Junior National Championships in
Memphis, and by the muscularity of future eight-time Ms. Olympia
Lenda Murray.[100]

The AAU began testing its Junior Mr. and Junior Ms. USA, and

Mr. and Ms. Teenage USA, events only in 1989. "Both were success-ful," reported AAU chairman Crist, who planned three more for 1990. Furthermore, potential sponsors were impressed, and there had not yet been any "legal problems." In Crist's opinion: "Pure and simple, it worked."[101] No Mr. America, however, the inspiration for thousands of young men, had yet been tested.

THE HERCULEAN LOOK

Indeed, Mr. America contestants in the 1980s, though less in the public eye than their NPC brethren, were showing just as much evidence of steroid use. Lest any doubts lingered about their impact, the steroid guru Dan Duchaine was emphatic about it: "Without steroids it would be impossible to achieve the size and hardness that is regularly achieved by many top bodybuilders. This is not to say that there wouldn't still be tremendous physiques. The physiques would just not be as freaky."[102] Duchaine thus heralded the age of freaks, but the person most respon-sible for the emphasis on mass and muscularity, with a legacy going back to the 1950s, was Joe Weider. In 1987 he proudly broadcast the "Herculean look" as the most desirable goal for bodybuilders.

> What is the quintessential factor that sets bodybuilders apart from other athletes? Of course, it's hard, deep chiseled *mass*. The name of the game in bodybuilding is as it's always been—get big and cut. You must take your muscles to a level of physical development that transcends the bounds of mere locomotion. If you fail in this singular mission, then you are not a super-bodybuilder.
>
> Over the years that I have coached and learned from the great body-builders, I have always insisted that mass should take precedence over all else in their quest for Mr. or Ms. Olympia stature.[103]

Weider's emphasis on size, of course, was related to the promotion of his products, such as Joe Weider's Sugar-Free BIG Weight Gain Powder, and the sale of his magazines. The September 1989 issue of *Flex* was full of such articles as "Mr. Size" (about Gary Strydom), "Big, Bulging Biceps" (John Hnatyschak), "Super Legs" (Juliette Bergmann), "They Don't Come Any Bigger Than Eddie Robinson," "Big Man, Big Shake" (Lou Ferrigno), "How I Built 21 Inch Guns" (Johnny Morant), "Bertil's Beefy Chest" (Bertil Fox), and an ad entitled "Reach Higher Peaks," which was for Joe Weider's Super Arm Blaster.[104]

Other vendors followed suit, doing their part to create the freak phenomenon. Most striking was "The Brutally Huge System," peddled by Bill Davis, of Tucson, in a 1989 issue of *MuscleMag*. Rather than urging bodybuilders to resort to steroids or spend thirty hours a week in the gym, he wanted them to buy his fourteen-videocassette course, which included such titles as "When Huge is Not Enough," "Yard Wide Shoulders and 22" Arms," "Brutally Ripped," "Somewhere on the Other Side of Huge," and "30" Thighs and 21" Cows." It promised to make skinny trainees "brutally huge."[105]

Though fostered mainly by the Weiders and popularized by Schwarzenegger, the size complex was no less evident in Mr. America contestants. After witnessing Rich Barretta win in 1987 at Atlantic City, Jan Dellinger observed: "[His] most muscular shots were exceptional. Of course, this is a trademark with any bodybuilder prepped by Bob Gruskin; they look like they were poured into a form of a most muscular pose. Watch King, Meeko, Antorino, Terra, etc.! Ask them for their favorite pose and you'll get a most muscular of some type on reflex."[106] The appeal to bigness was implicit too in the plans of the promoter Wally Boyko, who launched the Pro Bodybuilding Association, modeled after Vincent McMahon's World Wrestling Federation. It would offer $120,000 in prize money, and there would be no preliminary judging, no compulsory poses or comparisons, and no judging panel. According to Boyko, the outcome would be decided "by the audience," whose response would be detected by a computer that measured decibel level and sound duration. Boyko admitted the obvious: "Someone said to me that through this system, the best physique may not win, and that may be so. But the audience knows what constitutes a good physique." But bodybuilding fans, more than judging panels, would invariably prefer massive, drug-induced physiques.[107]

Contestants who refused to conform to this image, like Bob Paris, were forced to leave the sport. For Jeff Everson,

> Too much emphasis was being placed on steroid-induced hardness and outright mass. Excluded were programs for proportion, symmetry, shape. The day when the Steve Reeves physique made a woman melt and a man burn with envy were gone. Physiques now turned the stomach of the average woman and made most men snicker at the oddness of it all. Bob Paris had had enough of the illusion. . . . It got to the point where Bob flat out quit using steroids.[108]

Although Frank Zane had managed to pitch his more slender physique in such a way as to win three Olympias in the late 1970s, there was no longer a place for classical lines. The age of freaks had arrived.

BODYBUILDING: *QUO VADIS?*

While the Weiders were the chief enablers of freakish bodybuilding culture, their careers harked back to an era when the Greek ideal predominated. Hence, it is hardly surprising that Joe responded favorably to a suggestion by Nellis Eddington, of Cambridge, Massachusetts, that the classical form of Rachel McLish be captured in photographs taken among statues in Greece: "We're one step ahead of you, Nellis. We are just now setting up the logistics of an ambitious photo shoot of Bob Paris with the ancient Greek ruins—the Acropolis, the Parthenon and the like—as a backdrop. We've chosen Bob because he is one of the most classically built of all current bodybuilders, and also because he is of Greek extraction himself."[109] Such an event never materialized, and both Paris and McLish quickly receded from the bodybuilding scene. But with the 1988 Seoul Olympics approaching, Weider magazines featured a series of Greek tableaus, including statues (human and stone), columns, and a tasteful emphasis on male and female nudity. Armand Tanny reminded readers that "bodybuilding as art is based on nudity."[110]

Attaining the classical ideal, however, would be difficult, especially given the woeful state of bodybuilding. In an insightful letter in 1989 to *Iron Man*, Grover Porter, an Alabama professor, pointed out a recent Gallup poll showing that "the general public looks with favor on 'moderately well-muscled bodies' but that it looks with disdain on the 'steroid monsters' that dominate bodybuilding today."[111] In a follow-up letter in *Muscle & Fitness* entitled "Bodybuilding: Quo Vadis?" Porter cites the iron-game pioneer George Jowett's three categories of male physique derived from the Greeks: Apollo Belvedere, Theseus Olympus, and Farnese Hercules. The Theseus type was the most popular, Jowett noted, and the one best suited to be the symbolic Mr. America. Thus, Porter reasoned, "the one-of-a-kind physique of Steve Reeves is the epitome of the Mr. America type body." But steroids had induced near-total acceptance of the Herculean look by modern bodybuilders. It was time to ask, "Where are we going? And if we seriously want it to become an Olympic sport and the world's number one fitness activity, we must get to work on bodybuilding now." And one thing was necessary above all others: "We must get drugs out of the sport!"[112]

More emphatic against the cult of bigness, stemming from his artistic training, was Bob Kennedy: "They have no idea what they are doing or what they're training to achieve. The body is a work of art. No work of art is judged on sheer size alone. Big turnip-shaped thighs, bloated, thick waists, droopy pecs and lats and a bunched up physique are disgusting." In his 1988 article "Bodybuilding—Where Did We Go Wrong?," Greg Zulak reminds *MuscleMag* readers that forty years earlier bodybuilders followed "the Greek ideal of a healthy body and a healthy mind. The emphasis was on symmetry and proportion and athleticism." Zulak attributes much of the later departure from ancient ideals to the decision of the IFBB, when it became the world's most powerful bodybuilding organization, to subsume the "most muscular" and body-part awards into its overall titles.[113]

Yet it was the Weiders, whose glorifying of steroid-induced massive physiques set the pace for the sport in the 1980s, who most strongly focused on Greek ideals throughout that decade. It was a conundrum. Although espousing health, fitness, and athleticism, by showcasing unhealthy freaks they sent the wrong message to the public and hampered bodybuilding's general acceptance. As Zulak pointed out, "Some bodybuilders can barely walk properly, and have no interest in health." The IFBB champion Mike Mentzer once said, "'Why talk to me about health? I'm not a health nut. I'm a bodybuilder.' In most modern competitors' minds, there is no relationship between bodybuilding and health and fitness." For the general public, there was a disconnection between what bodybuilding presumed to be and what it actually was. Mike Quinn said it best—in the public eye "a bodybuilder is not a total person."[114] Bodybuilders had been corrupting the Greek ideal since the 1960s, and the more the Weiders stressed massive physiques, though the result was lucrative and gave physique fans what they wanted, the less chance there was for the sport to gain Olympic recognition. They failed to understand that while the Greeks revered humanity, the IFBB was displaying only a virtual humanity.

For those who sought refuge in the pre-Weider world, it was the Mr. America contests of the 1950s, held under the auspices of the AAU and promoted by Bob Hoffman and Peary Rader, that most epitomized the Greek ideal. Yet the amateur tradition was corrupted and swept away in the 1980s by a culture of professionalism created by DeMilia under the IFBB banner. When asked why the Mr. America declined in the 1980s, Boyer Coe, whose bodybuilding career spanned three decades, answered simply, "Money." He explained that in the beginning, "the top title . . . was the Mr. America Contest; that was the big goal." But then things changed: "As soon as professional bodybuilding emerged, each guy wanted to get good enough to turn pro. You earn your pro card, and if you are really outstanding you are able to make money, and the title of Mr. America is no longer important." Were it not for DeMilia, "there would have never been professional bodybuilding." As Jan Dellinger explained, "The IFBB made the NPC into an effective feeder system." So compelling was DeMilia's formula that the AAU started imitating NPC-IFBB judging criteria. It was muscularity that triumphed at the 1989 Mr. America Contest, held in Worcester. The report in *Iron Man* was entitled "Matt DuFresne and Mary Adams Put the 'Mass' in Massachusetts."[115]

Notwithstanding the earnest efforts of those acting in behalf of the AAU to reclaim the Mr. America title at the beginning of the decade, the contest itself became Weiderized. Like the competitors in the NPC's contests, those who aspired to become Mr. America, though amateur in name, were actually budding professionals. The real had become virtual. The Weiders, in their enthusiasm for hegemony and profit, had allowed bodybuilding to become more a spectacle than a sport, and despite all their efforts to make things appear otherwise, it was a perversion of the Greek ideal.

10

ECLIPSE OF AN ICON

COMPETITIVE BODYBUILDING IS INHERENTLY AN EVEN MORE PROBLEMATIC INSTITUTION THAN THE MODERN OLYMPIC GAMES FOR WHICH TO SEEK SOURCES IN THE ANCIENT WORLD. CONCERNED WITH THE DISPLAY OF STATIC MOMENTS OF EXTREME PHYSICAL TENSION, MALE BODYBUILDING INVOLVES THE PLEASURES OF LOOKING AT A MUSCULAR BODY THAT PERFORMS NO OTHER FUNCTION THAN THE DISPLAY OF ITSELF.

MARIA WYKE, "HERCULEAN MUSCLE!"

HOWEVER MUCH PRIDE WINNERS EXPRESSED IN THE MR. AMERICA TITLE, it was becoming an anachronism, overshadowed by its NPC rival and offering little prospect of future rewards. Matt DuFresne went on to win the Amateur Mr. Universe Contest in London, but admitted to feeling "shock" on achieving the goal he had desired for nine years, admitting, "It's hard to know what to do next." Likewise the 1988 Mr. America, Bill Norberg, having reached the AAU heights, lowered his sights and entered the 1990 NPC Junior Nationals in New Orleans.[1] Nor did there seem much virtue attached to being Mr. America. Despite reminders by such pundits as Bob Gruskin that it was "the most coveted title in amateur bodybuilding" and followed in the tradition of Grimek, Reeves, and Pearl, negative publicity tarnished its image at the outset of the 1990s. *MuscleMag* reported that DuFresne, a year after his victories, got busted for possession of 35,000 bottles of "something that sure wasn't amino acids"; Bill Grant, the 1972 WBBG Mr. America, was convicted for trafficking cocaine and would be "spending time in the big house." Readers were also reminded that the 1974 IFBB Mr. America, Bob Birdsong, whose career spanned three decades, had formerly not only taken angel dust, smoked pot, and dropped acid, but had been a sex hustler for older men and an actor in gay porn videos.[2] What contributed to this errant behavior was a departure from the sport's early traditions. The journalist Steve Neece mocked the naïveté that prevailed when bodybuilding was dominated by Hoffman.

> Bob disapproved of the west coast lifestyle and the events had a category called "athletic points" which were part of the scoring. If you were an Olympic style weightlifter or perhaps another form of athlete, you got 'em, if you weren't, tough luck. The AAU also had a category called "personal appearance" which supposedly covered such things as clear skin, teeth, grooming and general facial features. That took care of anybody who made it past the athletic part but wasn't desirable in AAU, (Bob's) eyes. Just a little history lesson, kiddies, to show ya how far we've come.[3]

There was no going back to the innocent days when character, education, and athleticism were integral to winning the Mr. America crown, but where was there to go now?

THE CONTEST TO WHICH NOBODY CAME

The 1990 Mr. America Contest, held in Chicago, was ideal in many ways. It was supported by American Airlines, Budget Rent-a-Car, Twinlab, and several muscle magazines, and the meet director, Nick Ganakes, left no stone unturned to try to guarantee a flawless contest. There were nearly a hundred contestants vying for Mr., Ms., Teen, Masters, and Mixed Pairs America titles, all of whom received first-class treatment. The quality of competition was excellent, there were plenty of amenities, and all events started on time. Alan Paul reported it was "one of the best organized and most tightly-run competitions" of the year, one in which people were "treated like neighbors rather than numbers." Yet the contest was disappointing, mainly because of a lack of spectators. "What if they held a contest and nobody came?" queried Paul. "It's somewhat difficult to understand why the Mr. America—the title that has the most recognition value beyond the outer fringes of the body-building community—failed to draw in Chicago." In contrast to the Mr. Olympia Contest, which had been a sellout there a fortnight earlier, only a few hundred occupied the Sheraton ballroom. The promoter likely "took a very un-neighborly kick in the wallet," Paul concluded.[4]

The new Mr. America, Pete Miller, of Evanston, Illinois, was not displeased. Like so many recent winners, he had "fantasized" about the title: "I remember seeing pictures of Joe Meeko and Jeff King and guys like that, and remember thinking that I could never look like that. But there's something about the title that always sounded so good—Mr. America." The title meant so much that Miller professed not to "care if I get anything out of it financially." In succeeding months, as reality set in, he found that any advance beyond his current job as a personal trainer would require a great deal of effort: "Nothing just comes to you on a platter."[5] Though big money eluded AAU winners, Bob Gruskin observed that Miller's physique, "thick, round, and ripped," was "equal to that if not better than most professionals." Another reporter noted that the size of Teenage Mr. America, Paul Grafas, with twenty-inch arms, rivaled that of the youthful Schwarzenegger. Such superlatives, however, were wasted on an anonymous former Mr. America who confided to Bob Kennedy that however good bodybuilders might look at showtime, they resembled overweight wrestlers the rest of the year: "These guys can hardly walk."[6]

PROFESSIONAL AMBITIONS

Countless pundits weighed in on how such a state of affairs had emerged and what could be done to restore the Mr. America title to its former glory. Don Ross observed that "the AAU and NABBA were the first bodybuilding organizations" and that their "historical significance alone should warrant more attention." He hoped that such talent scouts as Ed Connors on the West Coast and Bob Gruskin in the East could breathe new life into the faltering contest, which still had a glittering image. Joe DeAngelis seemed to be the future phenomenon that Ross was looking for. An admirer of Jeff King, DeAngelis wanted to win the same titles as his role model had. "Though the NPC champs get more publicity, calling yourself 'the champion of this' or 'the champion of that' just isn't as impressive as *Mister* America and *Mister* Universe."[7]

It was also the intent of Joe Tete, who staged the 1991 contest at the Showboat Hotel and Casino in Atlantic City, to draw on its storied past.

"There is no bigger honor than having the AAU America. It's the oldest, most famous amateur contest in the world," he exclaimed. It could be "the most lucrative ever."[8] Tete took advantage of the Miss America locale to put on a show steeped in symbolism. The host asking the question "May I have the envelope please?" followed by a dramatic pause and the announcement of the new Mr. America was reminiscent of Bert Parks.[9] For Tete: "Miss America was such a big kind of name and people looked forward to watching it every year. It was in Atlantic City and so forth, and then you had Mr. America, and well, that's the male version. The main similarity I think of is the name because mainstream knows Miss America, and guess what? They know Mr. America as well. Oh, he's Mr. America! They don't know the Nationals or the NPC. They know Mr. America. That's what made the contest so prestigious." Miss America nostalgia no doubt helped Tete attract 2,000 spectators: "It was packed." Contest reports placed as much emphasis on tradition as on the physique of DeAngelis, who was invited to take his place among the sport's legendary figures. Grimek was on hand to receive a special award for his contributions to the sport.[10]

In a resurrection of the monthly "Mr. America Series" in *Muscular Development*, DeAngelis claimed that he built his body with the basic movements used by "the great AAU Mr. Americas," from Grimek to "the modern day giants."[11] He became the NABBA Mr. Universe the next year, but with nowhere else to go, DeAngelis petitioned the IFBB for pro status. Surprisingly, it was granted. But his inaugural trip to the 1993 NPC Nationals, in Fort Lauderdale, was sobering. "When he realized at the judging that he had no chance of landing in the top five," observed Lonnie Teper, "he was disappointed. When he realized there'd be no chance of making the top 10, he was crushed. By the time he was officially placed 15th, he was numb."[12] Nor did he make the cut the following year or place in the 1995 North American Championships. With his Mr. America title slighted, DeAngelis took up powerlifting, did bit parts in movies, and worked as a personal trainer.

Tete conducted the 1992 Mr. America, held in Cherry Hill, New Jersey. The winner, Mike Scarcella, though claiming the title was a "dream" that he had cherished since his youth, was an NPC castoff. After entering one of Wally Boyko's professional shows in Los Angeles, Scarcella trained to enter the 1989 NPC Junior Nationals. He had been dieting for two months when Jim Manion called him a week before the contest. According to Scarcella: "He told me I was disqualified from the NPC because I had competed in the PBA and was now considered a professional. I explained that I had refused the money, but he wouldn't listen. . . . After a week or so of being totally depressed and eating about a dozen pizzas and ten gallons of ice cream I phone up the promoter of the AAU Junior Mr. America contest, which was to be held in three weeks, to ask him if I could compete in it. He accepted me totally."[13] Unlike most Mr. Americas of the time, who sought greater glory or financial gain, Scarcella wanted to support the kind of charitable cause normally undertaken by Miss Americas. He wanted to do something for the nation's youth because "so many are so mixed up, not knowing where they are heading . . . and into drugs." As Mr. America, Scarcella could be a role model for kids, showing them the benefits of staying in school, working toward a career, and being drug-free. Scarcella's noble aim was reminiscent of Paul Anderson's creation of a youth home once he had reached the pinnacle of the strength world.[14]

Unfortunately, Scarcella had to deal with demons brought on by the bodybuilding lifestyle and by expectations that had little to do with charitable endeavors. What ultimately drove Scarcella was not so much a desire to help people as personal ambition. He realized he had gone as far as he could with the AAU, observed Greg Zulak, and "would love to compete as a pro in the IFBB to test his physique against the likes of Lee Labrada, Vince Taylor, Shawn Ray and Kevin Levrone."[15] That kind of commitment required drugs. As Mark Donald explained: "Scarcella had dedicated his life to health and fitness—dieting, weight and cardio training, posing—measuring every aspect of his existence like some sort of body chemist. But somewhere along the way, from West Virginia farm boy to admired Mr. America to high-priced personal trainer, he lost the discipline that made his life make sense. Whether that was caused by GHB, steroids or a fundamental insecurity that made him overcompensate on the outside for what was missing on the inside, his story was far too common in the world of bodybuilding."[16] Scarcella never made it to the professional ranks, but his desire to secure a pro card, which fueled his addiction to GHB and steroids, led to his death in 2003.

THE WBF

A new opportunity for aspiring professionals emerged with Vince McMahon's announcement that his Titan Sports organization would sponsor a World Bodybuilding Federation (WBF) to complement his popular World Wrestling Federation. The first competition would be

held at Donald Trump's Taj Mahal in Atlantic City in June 1991.[17] Tom
Platz, the WBF's director of talent development, believed that the Weiders lacked the skills to "take bodybuilding into the real world mar-
ketplace." He intended to transform the sport from a subculture to a
mass-entertainment spectacle by recruiting thirteen top IFBB pros and
offering them lucrative salaries and national media exposure. Joe Weider responded by offering his remaining stars better financial packages,
leading Don Ross to observe that "because of the new organization and
the threat of competition to the Weider organizations, *everybody's* getting better deals." WBF marketing manager Jonathan Flora announced
there would be drug testing, but there were no immediate plans for it.[18]
Jan Paul reported that a near-capacity crowd witnessed the WBF World
Championship on Father's Day weekend. Hosted by Regis Philbin, it
was "the most lavishly appointed and professionally produced bodybuilding show ever seen, complete with dancing girls, flashing lights, costumes,
pulsating theme music, special effects and Las Vegas-style glitz aplenty."

> It was as memorable a bodybuilding show as this reporter has ever seen
> . . . though not for all the right reasons. . . . Relatively poor in quality
> and content, it was clear that whoever was behind its production knew
> little about the wants and needs of the typical bodybuilding fan. . . . The
> thirteen WBF Superstars were, with a couple exceptions, far from their
> best condition. . . . There was absolutely no sense that these thirteen
> men were athletes in *competition* with each other for the honor of being
> named WBF World Champion. This was a bodybuilding *show*—and a
> very good one, to be sure—not, in reality, a competitive event.[19]

Perhaps the evening's most telling image was that of WWF personalities
Randy Savage and Miss Elizabeth receiving greater ovations than Gary
Strydom, the winner, or any of the WBF contestants. The Weiders could
breathe a sigh of relief.[20]

In the meantime, however, McMahon was pursuing a higher form
of recognition in the bodybuilding world by attempting to secure the
Mr. America title. Infringement of the AAU trademark had become a
problem in the late 1980s, when promoters tried to lend prestige to
their events by using "America" or "Mr." in their publicity. To clamp
down on these violations, the AAU engaged two law firms to protect
the "America" title from promoters in Pennsylvania, New Jersey, and
Minnesota who were calling their contests "Mr. Natural America" and
"Natural America." Unfortunately, the initial expense was over $5,000,
which the cash-starved committee could ill afford.[21] For this reason,

and to provide a higher level of competition, McMahon's proposal to buy, lease, or underwrite the Mr. America Contest seemed attractive. In November 1991, four America Committee members met with Linda McMahon, Vince's wife, at WBF headquarters in Stamford, Connecticut. "At first," Crist reported, "the AAU team felt the WBF wanted an amateur group to feed their professional ranks and contests. We asked the WBF to use our credentials and officials rule book. . . . The second day of the meeting showed the bottom line to be their insistence on *complete control* of the sport, and re-write the rule book, and the use of the America Trademark for an indefinite period. . . . Our team projected a 'Corporate Sponsor Approach' where they would fund the national series and other regional events." In subsequent meetings, it was obvious to Crist that the WBF would "do an end run" around his committee by proposing to buy the trademark from the AAU. According to AAU president Stan Hooley, such overtures had already been made. *"This is our primary grievance and concern,"* stated Crist. A telephone survey of committee members confirmed these fears. Crist adamantly opposed any sale: "The America Trademark is our corner stone, our identity symbol and life blood. *The sale of the Trademark would be the end of AAU Bodybuilding."*[22]

In a bid for greater credibility, McMahon recruited Lou Ferrigno by offering him the most lucrative contract ever given a bodybuilder. But there were no follow-up contests to sustain momentum, and highly paid WBF athletes lacked incentive to stay in shape. Then televised news stories began to appear on such programs as *20/20, Donahue,* and *Larry King Live* about drug abuse and sexual misconduct among McMahon's WWF heroes. One of the alleged steroid abusers was Hulk Hogan. McMahon denied the charges, but "his WBF athletes" were not "thrilled with the type of hype their boss has been receiving," observed Lonnie Teper. "They're afraid of the guilt-by-association tag." WBF bodybuilders were even more upset when McMahon, owing to media pressure, instituted the strictest drug-testing policy of any sport.[23] Then Ferrigno suddenly resigned and rejoined the IFBB. "You'd have to ask Louie," Boyer Coe stated, "but I would assume it was because of the steroid issue."[24] While Flora diplomatically called it "contractual differences," the WBF athlete David Dearth was more candid about Ferrigno's response to his fellow athletes: "He came out of nearly 20 years of retirement to show the world the best bodybuilder ever, and he was told he was going to be drug tested. He said, 'If any of you show positive on a drug test, big deal. But if *I* show positive on a test, every tabloid in the country will be screaming about the Incredible Hulk being found guilty of taking steroids. I have so many kids looking up to me, and so much to lose.'"[25] With his biggest star gone, McMahon started downsizing, suspending publication of *Bodybuilding Lifestyles* magazine, which was losing as much as $200,000 a month, and moving his championship from the Long Beach Arena to a smaller venue.[26]

The contest was another dazzling display, but one more suited to a wrestling audience. Ross reported that it took place "amidst the roar of fireworks and the most spectacular stage setting in the history of body-building." Strydom was the easy winner, but drastic physical changes were evident among the other contestants, especially Mike Quinn, who "was the talk of the contest":"The audience was shocked at the amount of bodyfat he carried." It was the "first time they had ever seen a top pro competing with his belly hanging over his trunks." No less pathetic was Mike Christian, who "seemed drained and listless." Bill Phillips concurred that Christian's physique looked "tired and weathered . . . down some 30 pounds from his peak Olympia form." He not only appeared to be "in pain while on stage" but also "came close to fainting once backstage."[27]

All the finalists passed the drug test, but the days of the WBF were numbered. "McMahon knew how to promote wrestling, but nothing else" is the view of Jan Dellinger.[28] Boyer Coe attributes McMahon's fiasco to his failure to provide television coverage, his pouring money into a pointless magazine, his ignorance of bodybuilding, and, most critically, the steroid charges that emerged from his wrestling sector: "It suddenly appeared out of nowhere and cut him off at the knees. How did that happen? Who headed that up? If I remember correctly it was [Senator] Orrin Hatch out of Utah . . . that took the wind out of Vince's sails. They had to do steroid testing. So he was forced to do that in bodybuilding too. It just so happened who was one of the biggest, if not the biggest, employer in the state of Utah? Weider Foods. Can't prove anything, but it makes you wonder."[29] McMahon's final misstep was his choice of Mauro Di Pasquale, a no-nonsense drug scientist, to do the testing. "If you want effective drug testing, let me handle it" was his motto. "You know what happened to the WBF when I did the drug testing? They had to depend more on the suits, their persona, because they'd gone down in size and were holding more bodyfat." Their "ridiculous shapes" contrasted sharply with the physiques previously induced by their unfettered drug use.[30] Bob Phillips noted that "not even 'a McMahon' could compete with Weider," which sent "a strong message to anyone else who might think about trying to topple 'the King.'" The result? "Weider and the IFBB" were "stronger than ever." McMahon's physique stars were clamoring for reinstatement.[31]

DRUG-TESTING TRIBULATIONS

By 1993 the IFBB and the NPC, driven by Ben Weider's quest for Olympic status, were instituting drug testing for men and women, overseen by Bob Goldman, at some of its biggest contests. In 1989, Tonya Knight received a two-year suspension and was forced to give up her Ms. International title for sending a surrogate to take her test. The bodybuilding world was even more shocked when four men at the 1990 Arnold Classic, Shawn Ray, Samir Bannout, Nimrod King, and Rolf Moeller, tested positive for banned substances. Ray, the overall winner, had to relinquish $60,000 and his title to second-place Mike Ashley, who always claimed to be drug-free. According to Jim Manion, the most talked-about topics at the 1990 Olympia contest was drug testing, its effect on appearance, and who would fail. Of the twenty competitors, five—Mohammed Benaziza, Vince Comerford, Berry De-Mey, J. J. Marsh, and Van Walcott Smith—failed.[32]

These incidents coincided with a national crackdown on steroids, driven partly by football superstar Lyle Alzado's attributing his inoperable brain cancer to the massive intake of steroids and human growth hormone.[33] "Around Gold's nobody is selling to strangers," reported *Muscle Training Illustrated*, "which frustrates a lot of people that come from all over the globe to partake of what they believe to be state-of-the-art 'roids."[34] As athletes learned to cope with more rigorous tests, the IFBB instituted a random year-round program in 1992 in which 6–10 IFBB professionals were chosen monthly by a computer for IOC testing by Goldman. Penalties included a year's suspension for the first positive test, two years for the second, and life for a third. Steve Neece was "not impressed." It meant if 10 athletes were tested monthly, 60 of the 180 pros would be untested each year.[35]

Even less impressed was Di Pasquale, who regarded the IFBB-NPC drug testing over the years as "a joke." In many cases, bodybuilders passed what he calls "the sink test," in which samples were poured down the drain. Nor did he trust natural bodybuilders, who were obviously "hyped to the hilt with drugs": "When there's money involved and when there's recognition, power, influence, etc., it's very difficult to stop people from using the stuff." Ben Weider approached Di Pasquale, who

Figure 10.1. Ted Karnezis chaired the AAU America Committee during its demise in the 1990s. Courtesy of Max Furek.

told him, "The only way I would do the drug testing was if I had total control and there wasn't any bullshit." There would have to be mandatory suspensions. But the Weiders did not impress Di Pasquale: "They weren't serious enough. Had they been serious I would have taken it over."[36]

Di Pasquale admitted, however, that even his rigorous procedures are not foolproof. If a particular steroid is not in the mass spectrometer database, it cannot be detected without spending a lot of time and money to analyze the whole spectrum of what is in a sample and possibly identify it as a new designer drug. Testosterone gels and oral testosterone, which are eliminated from one's system in twenty-four hours, are another way to escape detection. He pointed out what testers are up against: "Unless you have very, very, very strict out-of-contest, instantaneous, unannounced blood testing and you do it frequently, you're not going to catch these people." Even more elusive is human growth hormone, which is used ubiquitously but for which there have been few positive tests. For Di Pasquale, "it's all about appearance" for athletes and promoters. They try to project what they "want people to believe, and they'll do what they have to do to make people believe that their drug-testing is effective." Beyond that, drugs are deeply embedded in American culture: "We pop pills for any reason. We use alcohol. We use nicotine. We use over-the-counter medications. We use prescription medications. It's a drug-using world."[37]

Reverberations from drug-testing protocols initiated by the IFBB, NPC, and WBF, as well as ongoing respect for natural contests, inspired the AAU to initiate similar procedures. Crist seemed determined to move forward despite getting little more than lip service from the AAU and virtually no alternative sponsorship or funding. While there were no complaints or legal problems, Ira Hurley, a member of the AAU America Committee, took Crist to task for "ethical failure, abuse of office, and financial mismanagement" for his conduct of the 1992 Mr. and Ms. USA Contest in Hampton, Virginia. At issue was Crist's unauthorized payment of $3,450 to the Nichols Laboratory in San Diego to defray personal expenses for the drug testers. Crist vigorously defended his conduct to AAU president Bobby Dodd, calling Hurley's accusations "without foundation," but it was obvious to Hurley that Crist's conduct did not follow the guidelines in the physique handbook.[38] An investigation by an internal board of review determined that there was "great ambiguity regarding responsibility for payment of drug testing," and Crist had "acted in good faith" despite lack of authorization. To resolve the issue, Crist agreed to reimburse the physique fund $1,232 for the urine testing, although he had already lost $4,778.80 from the contest. Not surprisingly, Crist, daunted by the whole affair, resigned, still maintaining his innocence. "It was always my contention," he explained to AAU physique coordinator Ray Mozingo, "that when the National Office became involved with choice of a lab to do the testing, they would assume this cost. This was my error to *assume* something not in writing."[39]

But he remained committed to testing and was vindicated in principle by the committee's resolve to begin testing Mr. and Ms. America contestants in 1995.[40] Ted Karnezis, the new AAU America chairman, credited Crist with boldly tackling an issue previously unaddressed: "Bob took a chance in 1992 to get a flavor to see what would happen, and he got spanked for it." Karnezis wanted to render AAU physique "drug-free" but realized the demoralization caused by this issue and the financial cost to promoters for implementing testing. He wanted to make the Mr. America title "the golden egg again and get the winner back on the Tonight Show." But "no one wanted to accept someone on drugs," and the AAU was as deeply steeped in the drug culture as the other federations.[41]

Steroid use was most evident in the protégés of Bob Gruskin, who, as noted in a 1991 *Muscular Development* article by China Blue, "rarely turns out anything but winners." Blue attributed Gruskin's success in producing Mr. Americas year after year to his nutritional aids: "Bob feeds all of these big thugs, who systematically and calculatingly, eat him out of house and home." Karnezis told a different story. Gruskin, who "always had someone in his stable ready for a major contest," was "well known to be involved in steroids": "His boys were stoked to the gills." Karnezis thought Gruskin was "making money directly and indirectly" from drugs and had a friend named Pierce who was "more openly involved in the drug culture." Karnezis elaborated: "Can I say that all of Gruskin's boys were involved in drugs and were provided medical assistance from him? No, but I can say that Gruskin was the most successful trainer ever. I don't have any facts. No syringes, rubber gloves, bottles, etc. No, nothing but his presence."[42]

To Bob Bonham, Gruskin's "knowledge" as a biochemistry professor was critical to his connection with steroids. He does not believe that Gruskin administered or sold them to his charges, but counseling was another matter: "Bob's thing was if one of his boys wasn't growing, 'double the dosage.' That's a joke we make. But he's the man with the knowledge, and where else are you going to get that knowledge unless the coach gives it?" Wayne DeMilia recalled going to Gruskin's house in the mid-1980s: "The refrigerator in the basement was loaded with steroids because he could get them, and he was doing experiments on rats. . . . I saw some of the rats one time. They were gigantic because they were loaded up with stuff. And Bob would set up the guys' drug cycles." Gruskin also understood genetics and could predict the muscle thickness of his charges—"He liked big thick good-looking white guys." Ending the culture of drug use would be difficult, but Karnezis insisted, "[It was] where my heart was." He tried to get cooperation from other drug-testing federations, but "egos and personalities got in the way," and no AAU testing took place until 1995.[43]

SIGNS OF TERMINAL ILLNESS

In the meantime the AAU America Committee accepted a bid for the 1993 contest from Jack Copeland and C. T. Minich of Fort Myers,

Florida, a recent hotbed of bodybuilding activity. Although the promoters had never conducted a major contest, Karnezis recalled their pitch: "This guy came to the committee representing town commissioners and said he was going to have great publicity." Committee members were swept away by the presentation and hoped that publicity generated by cosponsor *Muscular Development* would breathe life into the contest. Owned by Twinlab and the Bleckman family, the magazine wanted to revive the spirit of Hoffman and Grimek. Don Ross reminded readers that Mr. America was "the Granddaddy of all major physique events" and that "copy cat" organizations had to change their "Mr." and "Ms." titles to "national championships." The original title continued "to carry weight," since winners of those contests "often refer to themselves as 'Mr. America.'" The exclusiveness of the title remained important: "Today, the AAU still holds the only real Mr. America contest and only the winner of that show has legitimate claim to the 'Mr.' title."[44]

According to Harley Schwarz's *MuscleMag* report, the contest took place "before a crowd of screaming bodybuilding enthusiasts," indicating that the Mr. America title was alive and well. The promoters provided "excellent facilities . . . in their first attempt at holding such a high-profile national event." AAU administrators, however, were not impressed. According to Karnezis, it was one of the worst physique contests ever.

> What they said at the bids never lived up to what actually occurred. It was all hype. . . . When I got to Florida and went into the auditorium . . . the trophy table was draped in black cloth. I picked up the cloth and nearly threw up when I saw what was there: nothing more than plastic cups that a little league baseball coach would give to his kids. Labels were taped on. The guy said they took away his budget, and he had to cut corners. . . . The hardest moment was having to break the news to the athletes. What we're going to do is go through the awards, act like sportsmen, and I will make it up to you. I went back home, took $3,000 out of the physique committee treasury, contacted a local trophy shop, and worked out a plan with color-engraved silver plaques on wood. The Mr. and Ms. America winners received special sculptured awards made on pedestals. I also had Mr. America watches made with dials displaying bodybuilders and a John Grimek pose. The athletes took it extremely well.[45]

The Connecticut AAU official Fred Yale agreed that the promoter was "terrible" and "didn't know what was going on." Controversy also surrounded the women's event. What constituted the ideal women's physique, which had confronted the IFBB in the mid-1980s, was now an

AAU issue. Schwarz described Ms. America Karla Nelson, of Minnesota, as a "well-defined, extraordinarily muscled young lady who is in every way delightful and feminine," but she had taken "the female physique to a point that many people feel is *too far.*" Karnezis called Nelson "a bruiser" who "has her own website where she wrestles other women."[46]

The 1993 Mr. America was Billy Nothaft, another Gruskin boy, who had won the 1992 Junior Mr. America. Nothaft was pleased at winning bodybuilding's most prestigious prize, but he immediately expressed his intention to secure an IFBB pro card. Fred Yale thought he had "a pleasant physique but nothing overwhelming"; he was someone who would not be seen as special if he was "just standing there, but he was really good at posing." Then he disappeared: "He just vanished. But that's the way they all did at this point. If you get here, it's over." This invisibility "contributed to the diminution of the Mr. America Contest." Yale's point was underscored by the editors of *MuscleMag*, who had recalled a similar case back in 1990: "There was this real badass Mr. America winner, Pete Miller. The guy was in the AAU as opposed to the NPC so he didn't get much publicity, but he looked damned awesome. . . . Miller appeared as though he'd try to make the transition to the IFBB . . . but he just sort of disappeared."[47]

The failure of Miller and other Mr. Americas to achieve fortune and fame after turning professional stemmed largely from the IFBB's unwillingness to allow AAU athletes equal footing in the NPC, along with the AAU's inability to generate its own publicity medium. "Let's not pull any punches," advised Don Ross, "AAU bodybuilding is in serious trouble." Getting the Mr. America Contest "back on track" would require "funding." AAU officials were workingmen and workingwomen, and bodybuilding was not their job. It was "true amateurism." But they could at least pursue sponsors. Then publicity, including colorful circulars, advertisements, and television coverage, would be necessary, as would greater attention to presentation. According to Ross:

> You can no longer run a top contest on a stage with no interesting backdrop or set. Nor with trophies that come with a magnifying glass so you can see them. Huge trophies aren't necessary nor practical to take back home on a plane, but classy statues, carvings, or even very nice plaques are far better than those cheap, plastic figurines on a small plastic stand that look like they should say *"World's Best Dad."* Hey, guys . . . this is the *Mr. and Ms. America!*

Ross's final idea for restoring luster to the Mr. America crown addressed the perennial problem of "no place to go" after winning it. He advised reaffiliating with the NABBA Mr. Universe Contest, which, since its inception in 1948, had boasted a family tree of all-time greats. The trip to London could even be part of the prize.[48]

The 1994 Mr. America Contest was held at the University of Pennsylvania and hosted by Mike Charnik, who had conducted a Mr. and Ms. USA Contest four years earlier. "Many people have all but given up on the AAU as a competitive organization," observed Harley Schwarz. "Well, all those doubting Thomases had better think twice before signing a death certificate." But the event was marred again by a dispute over women's judging. Betsy Briggs, runner-up the previous year to Karla Nelson, again placed second, this time to the more muscular Midge Shull. Feeling she had been robbed, Briggs and a companion verbally attacked the judges. The men's winner was Andy Sivert, who, according to Schwarz, "put together a complete package of size, definition and symmetrical proportion" and was an easy winner. Fred Yale, however, could not remember Sivert. Yale would officiate a show, but next day he could not remember who won. There did not seem to be any point in making the effort: "Things in the AAU were going crazy. There were lawsuits. Half are worried, half are pulling out, some don't care, and the AAU is going down. I would go and judge and go home, knowing that the end is near."[49]

A NEW BEGINNING

For Schwarz, however, the Philadelphia contest marked the end of an era and the beginning of a brighter future. The Physique Drug Testing Committee, chaired by Pete Miller, adopted the USOC drug protocol.[50] Schwarz had faith in Karnezis's dedication to the amateur ideal and his ability to resurrect AAU bodybuilding. Unlike the commercially driven NPC-IFBB network, "the AAU clings tightly to its roots, subscribing to the purity of the sport itself with no desire for financial gain." Ross, in an article entitled "AAU Bodybuilding Is Planning a Big Comeback," expressed confidence in Karnezis as someone "very serious about reviving his organization." Critical to this outcome would be a consolidation of its frayed network under one Mr. America promoter. Karnezis chose Fairfax Hackley, a northern Virginia gym operator and former IFBB official. Karnezis explained to the committee members that he had been searching for a promoter who could "make a difference in our program." He added, "I actually prayed for the answer." His prayers were answered by someone "well connected and knowledgeable in the sport." The exuberant Hackley, proud to be the first African American director, had no lack of confidence: "As you are aware, the *America* was once the most prestigious amateur bodybuilding title, but owing to politics, poor planning and leadership, has fallen by the wayside in recent years. I will attempt to resurrect this title because it has a rich and storied history." Hackley intended to switch from height to weight classes and to institute random drug testing. There would be an award for the most muscular and a Steve Reeves classic physique award.[51] A movement was also afoot to allow Mr. and Ms. America winners, in the Mr. Olympia mode, to claim the title multiple times, creating possible AAU superstars. Ross was convinced that "the long-floundering AAU couldn't have found a better person" to get the physique committee "back on its feet."[52]

In a further step to resuscitate his organization, Karnezis attempted to tap the preeminence of the Weider organization, much as the Weiders had drawn sustenance from the AAU in the 1950s. On hearing of bodybuilding's acceptance in the Pan American Games as a demonstration sport, Karnezis congratulated Ben Weider and offered his support and cooperation. As a "relative newcomer" who was "not hindered by negative relationships" from the past, he broached the idea of a general association with the IFBB, much as Ben had attempted in the 1970s with the AAU: "I wonder if there is a possibility that in the future AAU athletes might be accepted into the pro ranks of the IFBB via qualification through the AAU USA and America championships. Would a tie with an organization that is already a USOC member strengthen your position in this Olympic effort? I personally think that the participation of amateur athletes from a member organization would be very appealing. Could an affiliation be arranged under your direction?" Weider was polite but firm in his response, sensing the AAU was a wounded warrior seeking a lifeline from its erstwhile adversary. Weider reminded Karnezis that the IFBB, representing 157 countries, was the only officially recognized governing body for bodybuilding by the GAISF, and that the NPC under Jim Manion was the recognized affiliate in the United States. What Weider offered was for Karnezis to "release bodybuilding from the control of the AAU" and become a member of the NPC executive council. The NPC could register all AAU athletes, and with "just one strong unified federation in the USA," the "duplication of various competitions would be eliminated."[53] Left unsaid was that the Weiders could thereby regain the Mr. America plum and monopo-

lize amateur bodybuilding. After a similar rebuff from Manion, Karnezis, with plans underway to revive the contest under Hackley and no
wish to sell his soul to the devil, pursued this strategy no further.[54]

As reality set in that the Mr. America Contest was only six months
away, many of the dissensions that had plagued the America Committee
reemerged, plus the new one of working with a promoter styled as the
"director" and endowed with unprecedented authority. Hackley took
a firm hand: "We will be doing things somewhat different than in the
past." He intended to pursue "sound business practices" but was finding
a lot of backbiting and finger-pointing, which he was determined to
stop. "There were people influencing Ted," he recalled, who "had their
own agenda." Whether Hackley was getting paid and possibly deviating
from the rulebook were among issues raised by the former chairman
Crist. He assured Karnezis: "I will not be silent on these issues, and will
use my skill and vigor to see our rules are not violated. Harry Silas, and
I worked for over 6 weeks to develop an entry blank and provide a
protocol for testing for the 1995 Jr. America and Masters America. We
expect the same follow through to . . . the rules and protocol for the
1995 America Contest." In a handwritten note to Rieger, Crist revealed
the real source of his displeasure: "This guy Hackley is an *IFBB* re-tread
judge & now is the *Savior* of America. Hackley has yet to put his address
on anything!"[55] These issues were at least partially resolved by a postal
poll approving (retroactively) Hackley's appointment (16–5–4), Karnezis's performance (21–3–1), and the use of physique funds to cover drug
testing (18–7). Crist then tendered his resignation as chair of the drug-
testing subcommittee.[56]

TRIAL BY ERROR

Despite high hopes for maximum exposure, media coverage of AAU
events and Mr. America contests was thinning out. The 1995 contest
was relegated to the "News Bytes" section of *Muscular Development*
long after it was news.[57] The 1996 show, according to John Romano,
fared no better: "[It] was poorly attended and its content ripped to
shreds on the Internet: the Steve Reeves tribute was hokey; the strength
exhibition was lame; the Macarena was stupid, blah blah blah blah blah."
Some of the best information on the two years that Hackley ran the
contest comes from David Chapman, who was a "fly on the wall" as
chairman of the advisory board that Hackley set up as window dressing.
It meant that Chapman was a "head nodder" with no responsibilities.

Hackley wanted to lend more prestige to the contest by putting "a little glamour and glitz into the show" and inviting iron-game celebrities to lend credibility.[58] In 1995, they included "Golden Eagle" Tom Platz, who received an honorary Mr. America title, and Bill Pearl, and in 1996 the legendary Steve Reeves.[59] The events were staged at Georgetown University in 1995 and at Fairfax High School in 1996. Such was the nondescript nature of the contest by then that Chapman could not remember the winners' names, but he recalled that "the guys competing in it, and the girls, . . . were pretty buffed and steroidal in appearance, so though it was nominally an amateur competition, I think it was going to be used as a stepping-stone to greater, i.e., professional places in the sport." Perhaps Chapman's most vivid memory was the lavish spending on celebrity guests, committee and advisory board members, and fancy hotels.

> I think by the time Fairfax's second year rolled around the AAU was getting a little nervous because he was spending tons of money. . . . I mean he spent a ton of money just renting the auditorium. And he had huge trophies that looked like brass wedding cakes with all sorts of ornamentation on them, and he had lots of those. . . . There were quite a few of us, and Fairfax rented this obscenely huge stretch limo that we all piled into to go off on various jaunts. We went to the White House and got a special tour. . . . I was having a great time. I got to go to Washington, D.C., and stay at fancy hotels, and I got to meet Steve Reeves and all of these other people. I was having a wonderful time. When it came to the power end of it, I couldn't have cared less about that stuff.[60]

Hackley told Chapman that the America Committee understood that some money would need to be spent. "I have their complete backing," he said. Unfortunately, the turnout for both years was "depressingly small," made more evident by "a whole lot of empty seats" in a large auditorium. Though a national contest, virtually all the contestants, fewer than fifty each year, were from the eastern seaboard, and none were from California.[61]

The 1995 and 1996 Mr. Americas were Terry Hairston and Doug Reiser. The contests, according to Chapman, "ran very smoothly" with "all the bells and whistles and these huge trophies." And the dimensions of the physiques matched the trophies. They were just "slabs of beef," which Chapman found very unappealing: "I don't think it's the historic or the moral goal of bodybuilding or physical culture. I think it goes against all of that. To me it's kind of a freak show. . . . To me it's lost all of its meaning . . . all of the symmetry and beauty as the human body is capable of. It's certainly not being exemplified in these bodies. . . . In my estimation they have nothing to do with beauty. They're ugly, they're grotesque, and they're unhealthy."[62] The "drug look" was evident to Russell Parker, second runner-up in the heavyweight class in 1996: "In the steroid world, a guy can weigh 290 and be totally ripped." It was also obvious to a local reporter that "the hyperdeveloped muscles of the drug look are still setting the contestants' aesthetic standards."[63] "I think Fairfax knew what he was doing as far as running a show was concerned," observed Chapman. He attributed this efficiency to Hackley's authoritarian manner and the fact that his lawyer had secured for him an "iron-clad contract" to do as he pleased.

> He could be a rather abrasive person. He always showed me the utmost respect and friendship. But I mentioned his name to Joe Weider once, and I got another one of the eye-rolls. "You don't want to have anything to do with that guy. He is difficult." So I didn't go into it. But I know that he had very clear ideas about how things should be run and how things should be, and I'm sure that if he didn't get things exactly the way he wanted them, he could be really unpleasant. I don't think he was a real team player.[64]

Bill Pearl confirmed that Hackley had "his own way of doing everything": "He probably set his own rules." Karnezis and the America Committee seemed content to allow Hackley as much latitude as needed to run the contests. Chapman observed that "whenever Fairfax and Ted got into their huddles, Ted would defer to Fairfax whenever he had to."[65] In both years this congenial relationship was put to the test.

DOUBLE DRUG DEBACLES

Part of the controversy surrounding the 1995 contest pertained to insufficient clarity in the rulebook. Hackley wanted a separate statement on drug policy issued by national headquarters, and members of the committee simply wanted some alterations in the rulebook; the discrepancy fueled dissension.[66] A more serious split developed in the contest itself over protocol when two of the five randomly chosen contestants tested positive. One was the winner of the contest. Hackley vehemently protested that proper procedures had not been followed when Karnezis, in lieu of hiring a trained technician, conducted the urine tests himself. Furthermore, the five chosen for testing just happened to be the top five. "If you have random testing and you only have twenty competitors, and you've picked out all five winners, that's not random," argued Hackley. When it appeared that Hairston, with Hackley's support, might sue, committee members, realizing that there were problems with the protocol and lacking the wherewithal to support seemingly flawed tests in court, backed down. Hairston contended he never saw the test results, never had his lawyer talk to anyone, and knew nothing about testing procedures. "I followed the rules for the contest & was drug free for over 12 months," he insisted. "Bottom Line is I'm the 1995 Mr. America and no one can ever take that away from me." Hackley's position followed suit: "Terry Hairston won the day of the show . . . irrespective of protocols. If you have as much doubt as I had and if you do not have a process in place, then the point is Terry Hairston was judged on that day to be Mr. America, period." Still Hairston fondly remembered his victory: "I think the AAU was a good organization . . . The Mr. America was put on well. Hackley did a great job." For Hairston, his title was not only a marketable draw for his successful California gym but also a continuing source of pride: "You say Mr. America and everyone can relate to red, white, and blue."[67]

Controversy over procedures in the 1995 contest continued into 1996, and was exacerbated by new sources of contention within the committee. Rieger had already receded from active participation, owing in part to infighting among his colleagues. In April, Fred Yale resigned as chair of the Doping Policy Committee because he disagreed with how Karnezis, in his own words, "handled the two individuals who tested positive at the 95 America." Then, acting on complaints from the law and legislation subcommittee, Karnezis removed Pete Miller, one of the longest-serving and hardest-working members, as chair of the credentials committee. Realizing that he had acted hastily, Karnezis apologized profusely, and the issue was quickly resolved, but it provoked anger, hurt feelings, and disharmony.[68] Yale, expressing surprise and dismay, sought to smooth ruffled feathers. "What's going on here?" he asked Karnezis. "Can't any of us work together anymore? . . . We're all friends here. Just sit down and work things out!" But too many seeds of discord had already been sown, not least between the director and certain committee members. Crist informed Karnezis that Hackley had called on July 3 "to chew [him] out on various subjects," including Miller's removal, drug testing, and physique committee rules. When informed that he had acted improperly by not submitting the 1996 America entry form for Crist's approval, Hackley "became very angry and used profanity." Next, according to Crist, Hackley lost control: "*He then told me, I will not be invited to the 1996 America Contest, in any capacity.* He was shouting over the phone. . . . I told him I would hang up, if he continued. He did continue, and I hung up. *Is this the type of person, who should be in charge of Mr. America?*"⁶⁹

Karnezis, ignoring this unpleasant exchange, expressed gratitude for Hackley's achievements in 1995 and anticipated "greater success with this year's show under his direction." To acquire a "higher profile," Hackley persuaded Karnezis to rent a booth at the Arnold Classic in March. "I got the first year under my belt now I'm really going to start to do some damage," he wrote to Chapman. In the meantime the medical subcommittee, after discussing the previous year's drug debacle, was prepared to deal with a possible dispute over testing, and Karnezis was satisfied that it had in place "the legal requirements of proper notification."⁷⁰

The winner was the middleweight Charles Durr, but he failed the drug test, so the title passed to the heavyweight Doug Reiser. According to a local reporter, five of the nineteen Mr. America contestants had tested positive for steroids. Karnezis was "'really pissed off' about it," adding, "The violators are 'basically thumb[ing] their noses at the process.'" As an unidentified newspaper clipping put it: "The No. 1 thumb to the nose would be from the Mr. America title-winner himself, Charles Durr of Chicago. His piss-cup test showed baldenone, nandrolone, and stenozolol (all anabolic steroids) in his system, according to Karnezis, as well as a testosterone level at least 32 times that of a normal man, according to Buddy DuVall, a spokesperson for Corning Clinical Laboratories, in San Diego, which conducted the tests. . . . So much for pure Mr. America ideals."⁷¹ But again there was a breakdown in protocol. "It's not a case of positive versus negative in the drug test," claimed Hackley in support of Durr. "Just like a court of law, there exists rules of evidence to protect people's rights." Hackley was at odds with Karnezis not only because of flawed testing procedures but also because of alleged manipulation of the rules.

> You cannot change the rules and regulations. You have to go back into the committee if you want to do that, because this is what happens as a result. Ted was trying to change the rules. . . . In 1996 there's no way in hell Ted Karnezis should have conducted that drug test. . . . Apparently, the person who was supposed to show up from the AAU to conduct the protocol and collect the samples did not. Ted collected the samples. The samples were collected unsupervised. And this is something we agreed upon. No one on the committee, no one directly involved with bodybuilding, could be involved in the collection and testing of the samples after the faux pas in 1995.

Every protocol was broken. As a matter of fact, the samples sat in the trunk of his car in ninety-degree weather for three days before they were forwarded to the lab. Now, I don't know if you remember your chemistry lesson, but let me tell you, there is no way that you could do a proper testing with those samples. It's as simple as that.[72]

When the final results came back two weeks later, Karnezis declared Reiser the winner. At that point, lawyers entered the picture and the matter was taken to court.

"Hold your hand while we wait for the judges' decision?
Dude - this ain't the Ms. America Pageant!"

Figure 10.2. *Musclehedz* cartoon featured in the September 2008 issue of *MuscleMag International*. Courtesy of John Gleneicki.

The controversy centered on the insufficiency of Durr's urine sample, and owing to his use of diuretics, he was unable to provide a full sample until after the contest, when he was able hydrate. Thus, he was tested out of sequence. And although Durr signed a form verifying his sample, he allegedly did so *before* it was collected. That Durr had had two previous tangles with dubious test results and that the testing lab in San Diego found no reason to question the samples may have influenced the results. Thus, Durr's attorney was unable in court to lift the AAU's ban on his client's use of the Mr. America title. Clearly, the AAU had the upper hand, but the case was costly and, for Crist, served as a premonition of future vulnerability. "The drug testing issue is square upon us," he warned Karnezis, "with added costs and legal challenges."

> *We have yet to do what is proper (in my opinion) with the Nichols Lab, in charge of all collections and testing.* Any time, our AAU staff, collect these samples, and handles the chain of custody, we're only asking for a legal challenge. We have yet to charge the $60.00 needed to do the test, and make this program pay its own way. *Yes, the athlete needs to pay it.* We have no money to pay these bills. . . . You have stood up on the Drug Issue, but have done little to protect yourself, or this committee.[73]

A year later, the case was finally resolved in favor of the AAU. Karnezis recalled meeting Reiser on a highway near Hagerstown, Maryland, to present him his award—hardly a dignified ending.[74]

AN HONORABLE TITLE?

Doug Reiser thus entered the lengthening list of unknown Mr. Americas of the 1980s and 1990s. Charles Durr died in 2005 of an alleged "enlarged heart," thereby arousing more speculation about steroids in bodybuilding in the blogosphere. Still, the title itself seemed unblemished, and there was no lack of AAU sympathizers who regretted the kinds of contests and bodybuilders it had come to represent. As Greg Zulak reminisced, "30 years ago the NABBA Mr. Universe and the AAU Mr. America contest were considered the two top physique shows on the planet, bar none. . . . The Olympia really didn't become the premier contest in bodybuilding until the early '70s. Before that the AAU Mr. America title was Mr. Big." Zulak further observed: "Many people today see the AAU Mr. America title as a secondary title, not as important as the NPC championships. But it shouldn't be seen that way." It was nice to be known as an NPC national champion, "but there will always be something very special about being called Mr. America."[75] John Romano traced the contest's decline since the 1940s: "The lure of money, prestige, and magazine exposure attracted many top guys to the other side and the Weiders won out. What Weider couldn't get was the rights to the all-time greatest bodybuilding title." Nor were the Weiders able to enshrine any of their titles in the American cultural mainstream. Romano challenged readers to test the prestige of Mr. America: "Ask the average Joe what bodybuilding title Arnold holds, or to name the pre-eminent bodybuilding title and you know what he'll say? I know because I tried it down at the market the other day—although a scant few people I asked said the Mr. Universe, most guessed it's the Mr. America title. They don't seem to know Mr. Olympia from Mr. Rogers."[76] A perfect example of mistaken attribution occurred after Lee Apperson won his class at the 1994 and 1995 Mr. America contests. Under the assumption that he had won the overall title, noted Charles Anderson, he returned to his hometown of Daytona Beach a local hero. His "Mr. America trophy" was displayed at his gym, and his achievements were celebrated "at a reception where the mayor presented him with the key to the city and named a day in his honor."[77] It is doubtful whether any Mr. Olympia ever returned home to a ticker-tape parade or received any local honor.

That the Miss America Pageant was able to retain its dignity to the end of the century and beyond may be attributed to its adaptability to changing ideals of modern womanhood. During decades of reforms, the greatest challenge it had to overcome was its traditional image as a beauty contest. As a *New York Times* writer observed in 1965, "The Miss America pageant, unlike most of its numerous imitators, is no longer merely a beauty contest and not at all the bathing-beauty contest it used to be, although girlie-show associations still persist in the public mind."[78] One such representative of the "public mind" was Frank Deford, who insisted in 1971 that "the basic, and base, pageant appeal is, and always has been, girl-watching—and the fewer clothes the better." That sentiment was expressed in 1981 by Frank Sinatra: "Hey, I'm a red-blooded American guy. If someone puts 50 beautiful girls on TV, you can bet I'm going to watch."[79]

Most unwilling to accept the sweeping changes made in the Miss America Contest since 1965 were radical feminists, whose perspective was rooted in the notion that the swimsuit competition was simply "where women parade in front of a panel of judges in a swimsuit." To Sarah Banet-Weiser in 1999, it remained "an event that both encourages and legitimates sexual objectification."[80] Such observations fail to comprehend that the nature of the swimsuit competition (worth only 15 percent of the overall score) has changed. Contestants are both beautiful and buff, inducing not so much sexual arousal but respect for the human form, thus approaching the ancient Greek ideal of "a sound mind within a sound body."

Critical to this transformation was the onset of the physical fitness movement in the late 1970s, inspired by such cultural icons as Arnold Schwarzenegger, Jane Fonda, and Gold's Gym. Being fit and flaunting it in revealing attire became de rigueur among ambitious young women—a symbol of their liberation and a fitting complement to talent, intelligence, and career. "By the 1980s," noted Ann-Marie Bivans, contestants had expanded their training to include "sprinting, fast walking, hydro-aerobic training, high-intensity aerobic classes, and computerized cardiovascular and weight-training programs." No longer was weight-lifting taboo for aspiring Miss Americas. It helped "hone their bodies into the healthiest condition of their lives." At first, Kay Lani Rafko, Miss America 1988, had difficulty understanding how a swimsuit competition fit into a scholarship pageant. But she eventually realized that emphasizing the body, outside any sexual connotations, was motivation "to keep physically healthy and to eat the right foods." And doing that brought its own rewards: "And I can tell you it feels good when you're healthy and physically fit. And *that's* really what the swimsuit competition is about."[81] It is hardly surprising that the swimsuit competition has evolved into what is a fitness event, although it is outweighed by talent, a functional component, which counts for 35 percent of a contestant's overall score.

Most physical culturists would not see any relevance of the Miss America Pageant to bodybuilding. The hard-core iron-game journalist Steve Neece, however, had a revelation on viewing the 1993 contest. Although he considered such activities "bourgeois" and "exploitative," he could not help but be impressed visually and personally by the contestants.

Brief "up close and personal" segments were done with many of the contestants, and several were shown practicing weight-resistance training as part of their daily activities. I assume this was their chosen way to maintain and/or enhance their appearance. Among those doing this was the eventual winner, Kimberly Clarice Aiken of South Carolina. Yes, she's a real beauty and seems sincere in her desire to help the homeless. Another contestant, also seen weight training, was shown working with AIDS victims and devoting time to dispersing information on this scourge. Truly the Miss America pageant has come a long way![82]

It was a harder sell for feminists, but Marianne Thesander, in the *Feminine Ideal*, could rationalize in 1997 that "women of today expect to be able to show off their female forms without being regarded purely as sex objects; but they realize that this requires them to be more than physical beings." The conclusion that Penny Pearlman reached after studying twenty-two former Miss Americas was that "the door closes with a bang if there is no substance behind the beauty." Tara Holland (1997) was "passionate about the program because it promotes the complete package of what it takes to live a successful life."[83] The Miss America Pageant, with contestants who not only had beautiful, functional bodies but also were talented and intelligent, presented a striking contrast to its male counterpart, which had only huge, drug-ridden bodies to offer.

A FITNESS ALTERNATIVE

Within the physical-culture community, however, a movement to restore some degree of function to hypermuscular bodies began to emerge. Not surprisingly, it appeared in the women's sector, where the masculinizing impact of drugs was most evident. "Last year at the Olympia I was backstage and I saw ugly sights, really ugly sights," observed Neece in 1993, "tortoise-shell skin, hairy faces, deep voices, and what looked like male genitals sticking out of their suits!" Although male muscularity was most evident among females at NPC-IFFB contests, it was also prevalent in the AAU. As Don Ross noted, the 1993 Ms. America, Karla Nelson, at 5'10" and 200 pounds, "created quite a stir when she strode up on stage flexing those monstrous, ripped thighs and huge arms that looked around 18 inches!" So prevalent was "the disheartening little rumble" among fans that one pundit asked whether the sport of women's bodybuilding was dying.[84]

In addition to the natural bodybuilding federations that emerged in the late 1970s, Wally Boyko initiated a women's movement in 1984, which featured a combination of bodybuilding and beauty pageantry, including interviews. As a physical-culture show, it attracted a different kind of entrant and audience from the Miss America Pageant. Laura Dayton reported that "one blonde, starry-eyed beauty" at a 1990 show, when asked what was her "biggest pet peeve," seemed "slightly confused" and cautiously answered, "My horse?"[85] After attending her first fitness show in 1992, Carol Ann Weber wrote up her impressions in a report entitled "Fitness Pageants or T & A on Parade."

> For a minute I thought I was caught in a time warp and had accidently been thrust into a wet-T-shirt contest at a local bar. Even though most of the contestants were . . . fit and toned, and some actually displayed a hint of muscle, I could hear the men in the audience shouting, "Show us your tits!" and "What a great ass!"—which is exactly the kind of attitude that makes my stomach churn. Then to top it all off, the women had to give a little speech to make sure they were literate enough to speak in complete sentences. So after parading around in high heels and near-thong bikinis proudly displaying what great plastic surgeons they've been able to afford, the contestants in these shows must don evening gowns and prove to the world that not only have they molded their bodies to exactly the form most men want to see in a Coors commercial, but they can talk too![86]

Nevertheless fitness competitions quickly gained popularity in the early 1990s, one of the most ambitious being the Fitness Festival Summer Tour, conducted by Lew Zwick and the American Sports Network in five cities. It included talent, swimwear, eveningwear, and interview rounds, and top finishers competed in a televised national championship in California. Zulak called it "one of ESPN's highest-rated shows of its kind." By 1992, Boyko was sponsoring twenty professional fitness shows a year, including two major titles, Ms. National Fitness and Ms. Fitness USA, and offering over $100,000 in cash and prizes.[87] As Bill Pearl observed, Boyko understood that women are more likely to draw a crowd than men: "He was the start of something."[88]

Increasing public acceptance of fitness shows attracted some former bodybuilding promoters hoping to capitalize on the desire for beautiful and fit women. One of them was George Snyder, who had inaugurated the Ms. Olympia title. "He wanted to create role models who would be accepted by the general public and encourage women to participate in fitness," observed Don Ross. Originally, the Ms. Olympia was supposed to be "a high-class event with hearty cash prizes that would give birth to these role models." Snyder never intended for judging criteria to be "identical with the male contests." He emphasized feminine shape, athletic aesthetics, and beauty, knowing that the greatest fear for women working out was the prospect of "ending up looking like a man." Rachel McLish, according to Snyder, was "the ideal role model": "She was pretty, had a good physique—not too muscular—could speak well and represent the sport in a positive manner. Women admired her." But after the fourth Ms. Olympia, in 1983, Snyder signed over the contest to the IFBB and, according to Ross, "women's bodybuilding went in the wrong direction." What Snyder attempted to do in 1993, by creating a Miss Galaxy Fitness Contest, was to restore the McLish look. "There's a reason that fitness competitions are outdrawing bodybuilding competitions," observed McLish. "Men and women can relate to a muscular woman and appreciate her athleticism and aesthetics. But, they can't applaud a manly or overly masculine woman." As female bodybuilders were becoming increasingly muscular by the early 1990s, it was McLish and others with her look who were increasingly appearing in muscle magazines. "T & A appears to be here to stay as far as the covers of bodybuilding magazines are concerned," noted Steve Neece. After three good years in Florida, Snyder moved his fitness show to "Mecca," the boardwalk and lawn of Venice Beach, where it "attracted throngs of happy, excited onlookers," according to Redd Hall, for an entire week. Entrants were scored 50 percent on beauty and 50 percent on athletic ability, which was determined by times run on a military-style obstacle course; ties were broken by scores on a written health and fitness exam.[89]

New Jersey-based Kenny Kassel and Bob Bonham produced another successful show, the Women's Pro Fitness, in connection with a women's strength show in 1993 at Kissimmee, Florida. "Some people are suggesting that women's fitness shows may be the beginning-of-the-end of women's bodybuilding," reported Reg Bradford. "We don't know about that, but it's clear that well-run fitness shows like this one are here to stay." Soon, the former WBF executive Jonathan Flora got in on the act by promoting a Fitness America Pageant, which by 1994 was being broadcast regularly on ESPN. In 1995, it attracted 115 contestants, and the 1996 winner, Amy Fadhli, a stunning and fit Iranian-born beauty, became the Rachel McLish of Bob Kennedy's media productions.[90]

On the other hand, as John Balik, the editor of *Iron Man*, noted in 1999, attendance at the Ms. Olympia Contest had been declining since Cory Everson's 1985 win: "The effect of the drug package on women's physiques is destroying the sport. I know they train brutally hard, but I also know that the bodies we see on stage would be totally different if the vast chemical shotgun were not being used."[91] John Romano, in a 2000 *Muscular Development* editorial, "They Shoot Horses, Don't They?" was blunt.

> Little Ms. Fitness is kickin' Ms. Olympia's ass. While the women bodybuilders were striving to look more like men, out of nowhere women's

fitness showed up and stole the show. Within just a couple of years it was T&A over pecs and glutes everywhere. Soon the fitness girls were competing for more prize money and signing more lucrative endorsement contracts than their distant cousins. Fitness shows were taped for TV to sellout crowds, while bodybuilding promoters couldn't give away tickets to the women's events. . . . This year, as Ms. Olympia entrants prepared for their show, poor ticket sales took their toll and it looked like the ladies were going to be all juiced up with nowhere to go. . . . Somebody shoot it.[92]

The Weiders even started their own fitness competition in 1996, and there were rumors that they were thinking of pulling the plug on women's bodybuilding, since no one was making money from it. Nor was it helping bring the sport into the mainstream.[93]

THE AGE OF FREAKS

Much of the message of the declining state of women's bodybuilding, however, was lost on the men, for whom there was no fitness alternative and whose physiques kept getting larger. "Size, Size and More Size" headed a letter from an *Iron Man* reader named John Canning, who blamed bodybuilding's woeful state on the economic system: "Americans have no sense of proportion, no concept of 'enough.'" When Dorian Yates, who carried size to a monstrous level, succeeded Lee Haney as Mr. Olympia in 1993, the legendary strongman Bill Kazmaier responded, "Dorian Yates? I wouldn't want to hand him a trophy for anything less than first place for fear of being killed or crushed!" Jon Hotten, in his book on "a sport with no boundaries," calls Haney "the last of the regulation freaks, the last man that a normal man might feel existed as a part of the same species." Yates was the first of the "really freaky freaks."[94] Lori Grannis likened the IFBB professional Lee Priest (whom Hotten calls the "smallest freak") to "a carnival caricature of the human form." Not surprisingly, his favorite physique type was his own, "the bigger, freakier and uglier . . . the better." Clearly, the trend among IFBB pros and aspiring NPC and AAU amateurs was to reach maximum size and definition with little regard for symmetry or overall appearance. The titles of articles and ads conveyed this image: "Big Beyond Belief," "If You Got Any Bigger You'd Need Your Own Zip Code," "Get the Biggest Freakiest Arms Ever!," and "Highway to Giant Quads."[95] In a letter to *MuscleMag International*, Robert Harrison, of Mississippi, protested.

> We need to clean up this sport. Everybody knows it. It can be done, but it won't be done because of the almighty dollar. I have been a fan and competitor for over 30 years and have always enjoyed reading the body-building magazines. But now I feel very depressed to say that I am part of this great big lie. Bodybuilding used to be about the ultimate in health and fitness. If you can tell me that these 275 to 330-pound monsters are the ultimate role models of health and fitness, without fearing your immortal soul will burn in hell for lying, I will admit that I'm wrong.[96]

Much though Harrison's views were out of step with the forces governing bodybuilding, they coincided with public perceptions of the sport.

Most greats of the game from previous eras, though big in their own time, expressed views coinciding with Harrison's. To the former Olympia competitor Lee Labrada, watching a bodybuilding show was "like going to the circus."

> You'll see men looking like obese caricatures who have somehow managed to push the bloat from their waist onto their limbs, parading around in the pajamas (two sizes too big, of course) or tight lycra tights, depending on which self-image disorder they're suffering from. Then there are the androgynous women with the facial characteristics and vocal pitch of men, strutting around in tiny strap dresses which look like they were borrowed from a local hooker. Competitive bodybuilding is turning into "the sport of more"; the stomping ground of reverse anorexics. And I'm sick of it![97]

Reg Park, on returning from the 1998 Arnold Classic, could not quite comprehend the physiques he had just witnessed.

> I didn't understand why they were in the contest. If I had been the promoter, I'd have said, "Look, you're not a good example of what we're trying to sell." But then, I guess I don't know what they're trying to sell any more. Apparently they only want to sell shocking, gargantuan size at all costs. There's no consideration of aestheticism these days. Look back at Reeves. He was a good-looking kid. He had a package. It's just not there any more.[98]

Reeves was equally outraged by what he was seeing.

> For over 30 years I've remained silent and just watched the transition that bodybuilding has made. And in my opinion, and in the opinions of many who have talked to me, bodybuilding, as it's practiced and promoted today, is dying—and dying fast.
>
> Well, it's a good thing! Never in my life would I have imagined that such a terrific sport would be filled with so-called "champions" who are held up as

heroes and adulated for physiques that are built with drugs. What kind of "real" bodybuilding champion is that?[99]

Admittedly, observed Frank Zane, one could still enter competitions without taking steroids, but without much hope of winning: "Nobody talks about physique quality any more. People just talk about size. They've lost track of what bodybuilding is all about." Zane cited an *Iron Man* poll that asked readers whom they would like to look like.

> I got 26%, Reeves 25%, Arnold 22%, Coleman 8%. Magazines publish how to look like a freak. A handful of people will pay big bucks to go to these shows, and they want to see freaky muscle. So every magazine builds that up. But nobody wants to look like that, so bodybuilding has taken a tremendous hit. Hardcore bodybuilding hasn't grown much since the '70s. There are more competitors, but there isn't more audience. . . . Everyone is in such a hurry to get muscle that they've become walking pharmaceutical companies. . . . The popular magazines with large circulations are into promoting monsters and selling products, mainly supplements. They wonder why bodybuilding isn't going anywhere. It's thanks to them it's not going anywhere. Wise up.[100]

Bob Paris, a Weider champion in the 1980s whose physique was often likened to Zane's, became aware of a generation gap when he attempted a comeback in the 1990s.

> A lot of guys I know in the sport want to be freaky; that is their driving principle—to be the biggest physical freak possible, crushing the competition through sheer brute size. It doesn't matter to them if the whole physical package looks exaggerated beyond recognition; in fact that's part of the point. The guy who works toward being a freak doesn't care that such an extreme distortion of the human form repels far more people than it attracts. . . . And especially during the last ten years, bodybuilding has continued to push even further toward freakiness as a guiding principle. . . . With each passing year more of the judges, fans, and athletes . . . seem blinded to the fact that they are preventing the sport from achieving more respect and in turn attracting more money and prestige.[101]

Paris applied the term "gorilla suit" to his own moderately exaggerated form, and it seemed applicable to the entire sport of bodybuilding. "How do you market a physique that just screams out, 'Drugs, drugs, drugs,'" exclaimed DeMilia.[102]

THE STEROID CONUNDRUM

Despite the prevalence of natural contests, repeated efforts to institute more rigorous testing, and vigorous denials that a problem existed, the bodybuilding community was confronted with increasing drug use by the mid-1990s, which resulted in more freaks and wannabe freaks at the highest level. Athletes and promoters responded in various ways. Ronnie Coleman, who succeeded Yates as the freakiest bodybuilder of all time, claimed in 1992 that he was drug-free and that he believed all competitors should take urine and blood tests. It was "nearly unbeliev-able" to Brian Dobson that Coleman's physique was drug-free. He must be "truly a marvel of genetic engineering." In a *MuscleMag* editorial, Steve Clark pointed out the humbug surrounding steroids, citing Den-nis Tinerino, who, after denying on a national broadcast that he had ever used them, admitted that they made him miserable. Then there was Shawn Ray and Rich Gaspari. The former claimed he was natural until he failed the drug test at the 1990 Arnold Classic, and the latter got busted in New Jersey after denying on a talk show that he was using steroids. Only after having to testify under oath at a trial in Uniondale, New York, did Hulk Hogan admit to using steroids. Previously project-ed by the WWF as a role model, he had always urged youthful fans to take vitamins and say their prayers. "Steroids are such a touchy subject," observed the IFBB pro Dennis Newman. "That's why so many body-builders deny ever touching them. Meanwhile, the guy's 260 pounds at 2 percent bodyfat. I mean, c'mon!"[103] Frank Zane, nicknamed "the chemist," skirted the subject, saying that he "always sought innovative alternatives to steroids" by using food and supplements "to produce druglike anabolic effects." Zabo Kozewski, however, recalled that Zane "walked around with a bag of drugs all the time." In an atmosphere of smoke and mirrors, any admission of drug use was rare, and avoidance of the subject commonplace. "When we drug-test," observed Wayne DeMilia, "they try every which way to circumvent the test."[104]

Magazine publishers and promoters faced an even greater conun-drum in how to present a sport founded on principles of health and fitness but whose champions were neither healthy nor fit. An *Iron Man* reader in 1993 complained that bodybuilding was "the only sport in which the fundamental competitive principle consists of mutual cheat-ing through illegal activity." Larry Scott perceived it as a "Catch-22 situation" for promoters, who "need to have the guys big in order to have successful shows," yet feel "it's not good to promote the use of drugs."[105] John Balik applauded efforts by drug-testing promoters and federations and recruited Mauro Di Pasquale as a columnist. But he also prominently featured freaks in every issue of his magazine. "It seems somewhat hypocritical," Balik admitted, "to talk about staying drug-free while admiring—and giving press to—those who choose the drug route. Many of the letters we receive address this, and . . . most readers applaud us for presenting bodybuilding as it is." Balik later rationalized his actions by noting that his predecessor, Peary Rader, "never made a judgment call as to who used and who didn't."[106]

Bob Kennedy, no less a believer in natural bodybuilding, echoed Balik's rationale of honesty and openness as a defense for at least indirectly promoting steroid use. *MuscleMag* flaunted freaks in every issue and carried ads on how to get big fast. One in March 1994 carried the enticing pitch "The Best-Kept Secret in BodyBuilding" and featured two handbooks, *How to Manufacture Testosterone!* and *How to Buy Deca-Durabolin, Equipose, and Winstrol V Legally*, available for $24.95 each from Anabolic Outlaw Publishing in Colorado. Next month, another ad offered free copies of Dan Duchaine's *Underground Steroid Handbook*, plus $3.00 for postage and handling. It was, after all, a free-enterprise economy and an enterprising free press! Only Steve Blechman, the publisher of *Muscular Development*, adopted an all-natural policy in 1997, excluding all nontested contests and bodybuilders from his magazine.[107]

In the wake of the deaths of Mohammed Benaziza and Andreas Munzer, Balik, Kennedy, and Blechman met to form a united media front against drugs. In a passionate plea to Joe Weider to join them, Balik minced no words.

> I am bewildered by your lack of leadership about IFBB pro bodybuilding and competitive bodybuilding in general. I'm finding it impossible to tolerate . . . your abdication of leadership in the crucial aspect of the health of our competitors. . . . Joe, you are the only one on the planet who can make a difference. I can write letters and talk to people, but without your direct support, it will take many more tragedies to get the attention of the athletes.
>
> I had suggested a meeting in Columbus, Ohio, at the Arnold Classic so that you and Ben and the other people who care about the future of our sport could all meet and discuss the future of bodybuilding. You chose to ignore my suggestion.
>
> What will be your legacy? Will it be similar to Bob Hoffman's? He built up Olympic weightlifting in this country and then watched it become a shadow of itself because of his timid leadership. Your legacy can

SPONSORED BY
Si-Flex Productions
1999
Mr./Ms. AMERICA
AAU NATIONAL ULTIMATE BODY BUILDING CHAMPIONSHIP
SI-FLEX MASTERS
UNLIMITED UNIVERSE
WORLD BODY BUILDING CHAMPIONSHIP

MOST PRESTIGIOUS CONTEST IN THE WORLD
DON'T MISS THIS SPECTACLE

Saturday, December 11, 1999
Lee Playhouse, Fort Lee, Virginia
BLDG. 4300, MAHONE AVENUE, FT. LEE, VA 23801

Tickets:	Registration:
Pre-Judging 12 Noon: $ 15.00 Gen. Adm.	COMFORT INN - Friday, December, 10, 1999
(Children Under 10 - $5.00 Military - $10.00)	5380 Oaklawn Boulevard (3:00 - 10:00 pm)
Finals 7 PM: $ 20.00 Gen. Adm.	Prince George, Va. 23875 Phone: (804) 452-0022
(Children Under 10 - $10.00 Military - $15.00)	I-295 - Exit 9B, Rt. 36 West, 1 mile on left
Combination Ticket: $ 30.00 Gen. Adm.	**Call: Harry E. Silas**
(Children Under 10 - $20.00 Military - $25.00)	**1-804-862-2391**

"Supplements of Substance & Affordable Quality"
TEAM BODYBUILDING
PROUD SPONSOR
1999 MR/MS AMERICA - SI-FLEX MASTERS UNIVERSE
(757) 421-4704
P.O. BOX 1412, CHESAPEAKE, VA 23328
1986-1999

Figure 10.3. Promotional poster for the last AAU Mr. America Contest. Author's possession.

be not only the progenitor of modern bodybuilding but also a shining example of a man who had the guts to bring it back from the brink of destruction. The future of IFBB pro bodybuilding is in your hands. Will it be a battlefield littered with athletes dying in an arena tilted toward deadly chemicals or will it tilt in the other direction toward the Greek ideal of a strong body and a strong mind. I believe bodybuilding should be a part of life, not a precursor to death.[108]

Weider's attitude, however, reflected both cynicism and the control he exercised over the sport. "We started drug-testing some time ago, but most of the athletes would always beat the tests," he admitted in 1997. "The only way to stop drug use for sure would be to test everyone constantly and that would cost too much." Still, he strongly favored testing, planned to implement it soon at his contests, and hoped to eliminate drugs from professional bodybuilding within three years. He hoped public acceptance would follow from that: "Right now we are perceived as an esoteric sport. That's one of the reasons why Ben and I have worked so hard at getting IOC recognition. It would greatly transform the image of bodybuilding for the better."[109] Perhaps Joe should have reasoned conversely that only by improving the image of the sport would IOC recognition be achieved.

Testing, of course, was the key, but few regarded it as foolproof. The most effective way to avoid detection, observed Michael Colgan, was to use one of the 150 new steroids or steroid-like drugs reported each year: "The drug test programs are always behind the times. It costs an arm-and-a-leg to set up a definitive test for any new chemical, so it's always a money problem. No one wants the expense of setting up testing for *ineffective* new drugs. So they have to wait for research studies showing how effective the drugs are. By then athletes have been using them for at least a couple of years." Furthermore, as Shawn Assael points out in *Steroid Nation*, a gas chromatograph or a mass spectrometer is "only as smart as the people operating it" and only finds compounds that it is programmed to detect. Nor could any test detect human growth hormone, and polygraph tests were inadmissible in court. "The IFBB loved to let people think that the professional division was drug tested," observed Bob Paris, and "drug free. There is not one person that I know of in the sport who truly believes in that. We all know it's a crock, a manipulation of perception surrounding a complicated issue that won't go away." It posed a moral dilemma for Paris, who knew that he could not be competitive unless he subscribed to the hypocrisy of bodybuilding's drug culture.[110]

Much of the motive force behind the problem was money. As Wayne DeMilia recognized, Olympia prize money had increased greatly over the decades from Scott ('66) to Columbu ('76) to Haney ('86) to Yates ('96). And linked with money were drugs. At the time of his death in 1996, Andreas Munzer was spending 10,000 deutsche marks a month on the two dozen chemicals he was consuming.[111] Competitive bodybuilding in the 1990s, according to an anonymous Olympia contender, was "all chemistry"—in fact, he called it "chemical warfare." He spent about $60,000 a year on drugs, $30,000 of which was for human growth hormone. His compensation, on the other hand, was "disgraceful," a situation he attributed to the promoters.

> They don't talk about how much drug [abuse] there is. And it's not just the steroids. We've got to use speed and stuff like that. We have to use a lot of diuretics, things that aren't too healthy, and they don't feel good. Lots of guys are using cocaine—not just because they like it, but it helps you get cut up, it helps you not eat.
> With drugs there's use and abuse. But at our level I feel we're getting exploited, you know? They pump us full of drugs . . . or we pump ourselves full of drugs to make ourselves look like freaks, and we get on stage and that's our job. But we don't get paid hardly anything. The guy who uses our pictures, the supplement companies, make all the money, and they don't give us nothing. If it wasn't for our pictures, they wouldn't have nothing to promote.

To earn an extra $10,000 a month, some bodybuilders resorted to hustling. "It's all a sacrifice," according to this competitor, mainly "your integrity, your pride. . . . The drugs, the prostitution. This whole sport is about being a bitch. You gotta be a bitch to pay your bills. You gotta be a bitch to win. That's what it's all about. Total exploitation."[112] To end this destructive cycle, it would be necessary to alter the dynamics of bodybuilding consumerism. But there was a serious problem: "Once you've seen extreme physique development, how are you going to train the eye of the audience to accept something less?" Ron Harris, an *Iron Man* reader, did not believe it was possible: "Being drug-free myself, I'd love to see the drugs magically disappear, but it's never going to happen. Once you have people with 23-inch arms, cross-striations on the butts, quads and triceps and the proportions of the old Marvel Comics superheroes, there's no turning back."[113] A culture of drift had settled into bodybuilding that no one seemed capable of reversing.

THE TRAGIC DEATH OF MR. AMERICA

Despite testing, the physiques of AAU competitors, largely through steroids for size and diuretics for definition, rivaled those of their NPC counterparts. But the control of the IFBB and NPC over contests, media, and money had relegated other federations to the fringes of the physique world. Likewise, those who took testing too far, like those labeled "natural," were stigmatized as losers. A statement appearing in the IFBB official journal defined natural bodybuilders as not having "the God-given muscle-building genetics backed up by a superhuman drive to go the whole nine yards."[114] They were bodybuilders "who know they can't hack it at the top level of the NPC and the IFBB and are content to be bigger fish in smaller ponds." The advent of the freaks served notice that a natural bodybuilder could never become a Mr. Olympia or win the Arnold Classic or the NPC Nationals, the most desirable titles in the sport. "One of the biggest misconceptions is that you can build a pro-quality physique without steroids," wrote Bob Kennedy in 1995. His magazine polled a sampling of stars in 1998.

• Jay Cutler: "I don't think a natural bodybuilder could ever compete on a large scale."
• Paul DeMayo: "The natural athlete is never going to reach the level of the bodybuilder who uses steroids."
• J. J. Marsh: "To make astounding gains one has to do drugs, period."

When the three-time Arnold winner Kenny "Flex" Wheeler, after wrestling with his conscience and with health issues, entered the 2002 Olympia natural, "the judges didn't know what to do with a leaner and cleaner Flex." After he finished seventh, a "famous competitor" offered condolences: "Doing it natural is your death sentence in this sport."[115]

It was obvious that the drug culture led to the creation of "monsters and freaks," and that a "new aesthetic" would be possible only by going "natural." Yet as a 1997 *MuscleMag* editorial pointed out, any "old-fashioned idealism" was going to "attract more anger and laughter than big bucks—as long as people want to pay for freak shows."[116] Nevertheless, the AAU, which joined forces with the Disney Corporation in 1994, and the Mr. America Contest, the nation's oldest physique competition, continued to draw purist elements of the iron game.[117] John Romano, in the "all-natural" *Muscular Development*, viewed the Disney association as a "perfect opportunity for those seeking an alternative to the current game of drug saturated events": "The Mouse isn't going to tolerate drug use."[118]

Although its 1995 and 1996 contests were fiascos, the America Committee persisted with testing. The 1997 event was held in a world-class facility with "state-of-the-art staging, lights and sound" and was directed by two experienced promoters, Tom Palermo and Rob Anderson.[119] Unfortunately, it lost all its media coverage, even *Muscular Development*. Even those running the contest could barely remember the winners' names. "No one cared who was in the contest because they had never seen the guys in the magazines," observed Bill Pearl. There was "no publicity whatsoever." With no publicity attached to their title, Jan Dellinger concluded, Mr. Americas would "drop out and become no names." Bill Davey and Harvey Campbell, the 1997 and 1998 winners, soon lapsed into obscurity. Drug testing, though it lent an air of credibility, proved to be a liability. As Fred Yale noted, the NPC was not testing and yet was getting all the attention. Freakishness was still a draw: "Natural bodybuilders don't sell products. Freaky sells tickets and products. Natural sells nothing." It was obvious to David Chapman after 1996 that Mr. America had "ceased to be a national contest . . . and had clearly lost relevance in the bodybuilding world." But the show did not disappear completely: "It was still those words that kept people coming back." He had witnessed the death throes of a proud tradition.[120]

Much of the blame for this downward spiral has been placed on the shortcomings of Ted Karnezis. In contrast to Cliff Sawyer, who was "solution-oriented" and "a consensus builder," says Jon Rieger, "Karnezis enraged people. He was arbitrary sometimes, not transparent, and not consistent. His style sometimes made people angry as hell." Despite Karnezis's desire to involve non-Weider media, Bob Kennedy recalled that he "did not run a good contest": "It was so disorganized. The worst lighting in the world, judges dressed in anything, starting three hours late, judges taking pictures. A bunch of misfits." Dellinger attributes this disorganization to AAU administrators' unbusinesslike attitude: "It was an avocation. They didn't even have a letterhead. Now that's pretty darn basic. They would never approach corporate sponsors. . . . There's your amateur politics." Additionally, the America Committee became increasingly out of sympathy with the AAU after the 1996 lawsuit. "It was supposedly a democratic organization," according to Pete Miller, but AAU president Bobby Dodd made his living from it and sidestepped the board of directors. Miller added, "There should have been a system of checks and balances." Bob Crist noted that under Dodd "the whole face of the AAU switched over to an emphasis on the Junior Olympics," adding that the organization seemed "no longer interested in adult sports." Indicative of Dodd's lack of interest in physique was his decision to rescind the disqualification of the 1996 light heavyweight Jamie Rodriguez, based on new evidence showing that he had not violated the AAU's doping code. It was Karnezis who had to cope with the fallout. "The national officers dumped on him after the lawsuit," recalled Crist. To Rieger, the demise of the Mr. America Contest can be attributed largely to the "unsophistication" of Karnezis in dealing with the testing issue. But all members of the America Committee supported it in principle, yet lacked practical expertise—they were all responsible: "All of us were amateurs."[121]

The immediate crux of the matter was not so much testing, the new direction of the AAU, the leadership of Karnezis, or even the lack of media coverage as it was the seemingly innocuous matter of insurance. As Yale explained, "Bodybuilding was a relatively small sport with a large liability." Although the AAU continued to insure Mr. America contests for the next two years, the 1996 debacle had left its mark on an organization struggling for bare existence. Meet promoters were required to pay $750 for insurance. In 1998, Reg Faust, of Annapolis, Maryland, protested to Dodd that after paying $800 for a venue, $500 for drug testing, and $750 for insurance, not to mention the cost of trophies, his contest expenses were well over $2,000.[122] Karnezis recalled that the 1999 Mr. America Contest "almost never took place." The AAU told him "in so many words" that if he could not raise additional money for insurance, the contest would not be held. The promoter, Harry Silas, of Petersburg, Virginia, had already made numerous plans and had spent a great deal of money, so Karnezis feared that Silas might sue him if the show fell through. So he went to the Potomac Valley Association, which contributed $5,000 in return for a like donation from Karnezis's father in California, who used it as a tax break. With another $5,000 from his sport fund, Karnezis was able to satisfy the insurance company. He noted, "We ran it like any other America."[123]

Tracy Dorsey, a Baltimore native who had been bodybuilding for only a year, became the 1999 Mr. America. Fred Yale recalled the December competition as "nondescript."

> Nobody knew anybody or much cared. It was not drug-tested, but most of the contestants appeared to be drug-free. No monsters. But everyone knew it was the last year. . . . There were many regrets and nostalgia at the last show. We finally got down to a group of people who were on the same page. No one was there for self-interest or to promote anything. It

was a sad time. We were finally getting the sport to where we wanted it for a long time. There was not a dry eye in the place.[124]

Karnezis, however, did not think it would be the last America. He thought they could work their way through the insurance problem and carefully involve AAU heads in the process.[125]

Karnezis seemed unaware of the mounting political pressures. Physique, with its dwindling popularity, financial burdens, and image problem was out of synch with the AAU's youth orientation.[126] It is not surprising that bodybuilding incurred the displeasure of the powers that be, but discontent was trickling down also to the rank and file who would attend the AAU's annual meeting in Puerto Rico in September 1999 to decide the fate of the sport. A more politically savvy Bob Crist, who had heard rumors of AAU plans to drop physique, took steps to line up votes to save it. Opposition came not so much from those against drug testing as from those who thought the organization was "not doing enough of it or not doing it right." But his efforts were to no avail. Karnezis was understandably bitter about what happened in Puerto Rico: "The committee was stacked with AAU officers who had never been involved with physique or my committee, and I was not allowed to testify. Our sport was not able to support itself, so they would have to abolish it. What they didn't say was that they had mandated drug-testing and provided no funding, assistance, or direction in handling the situation. Yet they told the convention that they had provided adequate support." Karnezis believed that the insurance company was "in cahoots with the AAU" and that the AAU was underinsured, leaving it with few funds for a vulnerable sport that was bringing no favorable recognition to the parent body. There were larger lawsuits and concerns in sports such as wrestling and gymnastics. Karnezis summed up his feelings in a letter: "I don't wish the organization ill, it's just got some people in it who need to be excised. The AAU was founded on legitimacy, but it has grown to be corrupt."[127] No amount of sour grapes, however, could restore the Mr. America Contest.

Beyond the obvious lesson to never underestimate the power of insurance, it was obvious that the contest was a casualty of the sport and the inability of promoters to control it. Few would disagree with Rieger's assessment that drugs were the problem: "Steroids ruined the sport because they led it into a place where a public which was already skeptical now had tangible reasons to look askance at what bodybuilders were doing. Steroids made it possible to develop such freaky looks and size that most people could not relate to." As Josh Henson pointed out, "The general public didn't care about big muscles. But those inside the culture did, and they made money from it." The IFBB and NPC and those who promoted their champions benefited most from the steroid–big muscle cult. The America Committee tried to have it both ways by encouraging athletes to mimic the physiques of their NPC-IFBB rivals, yet trying to go mainstream through the AAU. In the end both approaches failed. Gone too was the idealism that had given birth to the sport and provided its sustenance in the early days. As Fred Yale observed, "Greek ideals went by the wayside sometime in the 1960s; by the 1970s it was almost gone, and by the 1980s it was totally gone." Any mention of the Greeks by the 1990s only provoked ironic comparisons. As an example of how distorted the sport's reasoning had become, a 1998 *MuscleMag* reader likened modern bodybuilding to "a rebirth of the classical Greek pursuit of physical perfection." Current physiques were "even closer to perfection than those conceived of by the ancient Greek sculptors." Such musings show little understanding of the concepts of arete, sophrosyne, and *kalokagathia*, which made up the Greek spirit exemplified by early bodybuilders. It required not only an appreciation of balance, moderation, and beauty but also an embrace of man's mental and spiritual capacities. By the time of its finale in 1999, the Mr. America Contest had declined into a mere body show, a victim of the drug-crazed culture into which bodybuilding had descended.[128]

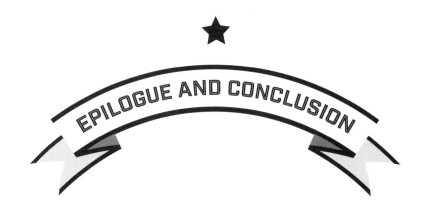

EPILOGUE AND CONCLUSION

IT IS STILL THE MOST IMPORTANT TITLE. IT USED TO BE A
MAGIC TITLE. IT IS A VERY CLEAN TITLE. MR. UNIVERSE IS A
BIT OUTRAGEOUS. MR. AMERICA IS DOWN TO EARTH AND IT
STANDS FOR THE RICHEST AND MOST POWERFUL COUNTRY
IN THE WORLD.

BOB KENNEDY, PERSONAL COMMUNICATION
WITH THE AUTHOR

THE FINAL SEQUENCE OF THE MR. AMERICA STORY HAS YET TO BE TOLD.
In the weeks and months after the decision in Puerto Rico there was
much discussion about a revival. But the AAU was unlikely to sanction a contest without drug testing, and as Fred Yale observed, holding the event without testing would mar the organization's "standards,
principles and reputation." Since an AAU-sponsored event was off the
table, Yale, Tom Minichiello, and Mike Bondurant considered purchas-
ing the title. With their many friends, they could possibly conduct a Mr.
America Contest in Florida, a leading bodybuilding state. AAU leaders
initially asked for $10,000, then $50,000, then decided not to sell it.
Some America Committee members, such as Yale, were relieved it was
over; they could finally take yearly vacations again. Others stayed active.
Karnezis joined the NPC, though he never conducted any contests.

Crist continued to run contests for the North American Sports Federation, which administered polygraph tests. Pete Miller got involved in USA Masters Weightlifting. Tracy Dorsey was able to overcome the stigma of his AAU title to win a major NPC title in 2001.[1]

MR. AMERICA REBORN

The Puerto Rico shutdown resulted in the Mr. America Contest going on a four-year hiatus during which there were no Mr. Americas. But the AAU had to continue using its service mark or else relinquish it to public domain. The Sacramento promoter Kelvin Fountano secured a lease for a Mr. and Ms. America Contest in 2003. The winners, Dan Elam and Trish Hamishin, as well as the figure titlist, Voncille Williams, were residents of California. Despite the organizers' best efforts, the contest lost money. Publicity for the 2004 event, like so many previous promotions, appealed to nostalgia. Fountano noted how "many bodybuilding buffs can rattle off the names and years of their favorite Mr. Americas as if they were World Series or Superbowl victories." There was still "a magic ring to the name Mr. America." The contest remained largely a local affair. Joe Rapisura and Joan Lopez joined the growing list of largely unknown winners since the 1970s. In the absence of drug testing, insurance was not a problem. What Fountano did not expect was the negativity of Jim Manion and the "backlash" from the NPC, whose "California rep was instructing athletes not to enter our contest." Despite hopes that a fresh bodybuilding public would be drawn to the name and that his Mr. America Contest, not unlike the Miss America Pageant, would be a culminating event for regional qualifiers, Fountano sponsored no further competitions.[2]

Meanwhile, Vince McMahon had applied the Mr. America moniker in 2003 to a masked character portrayed by Hulk Hogan, but it was unconnected with bodybuilding. By 2009, the copyright for the title had fallen into abeyance. It was secured by Bob Bonham, who, like many previous promoters, was attracted by its historic significance but wanted it strictly for its marketing value: "Business had been sucking. I was looking for another alternative to make money, so I wanted to make Mr. America more of a cottage industry. We would have a show, a magazine, cologne, whatever, you know. The Mr. America magazine wasn't going to be a bodybuilding magazine. It was going to be one on lifestyle. A web magazine. All I wanted to do was lease out the name and get paid the royalties. I didn't want to run the stuff."[3]

To administer his Mr. America contest, Bonham secured Wayne De-Milia, "the best promoter *ever* in bodybuilding." Despite, in his own words, having "made the IFBB what it is," DeMilia ended his involvement with the federation in 2004 after the Weiders sold their interest to David Pecker's American Media, Inc. So DeMilia pinned his hopes on a title that had a storied tradition and magical name recognition. He envisioned a classy, high-profile event that would draw 500 contestants, 2,500 spectators, national publicity, and cameo appearances by previous Mr. Americas. Such an approach would not only revive Bonham's business, but also recharge DeMilia's career and restore the Mr. America title to its former glory. When Bonham was unwilling to gamble for such high stakes, DeMilia bowed out, saying, "If I can't do it on a grand scale, I'm not going to do it at all."[4] Bonham then enlisted his family members, who worked gratis, and International Bodybuilding and Fitness, led by Charlie Carolla, a "cookie-cutter" organization known for its strict testing, which arranged rentals, judges, awards, backstage personnel, and lighting, all for under $10,000.[5]

The Mr. America Contest was reborn again on May 21, 2011, at Martin Luther King Jr. High School in Manhattan at an event staged by Bonham. Thirteen contestants competed in five open men's categories, and another seventeen in thirteen non-America events. When asked how many were in the audience, Bonham responded, "Not enough—too embarrassing to say." Short preparation time, a lack of publicity, and competition from three drug-tested contests elsewhere on the same day hampered his efforts. Most critically, he explained, "Manion called up all the editors and told them the Mr. America is not to be mentioned in any of the magazines." Even his friend Gregg Valentino, a columnist for *Muscular Development*, felt threatened. Thus, it was a lackluster affair.[6]

Two months later, Bonham could not remember who had won his Mr. America Contest and could not find a list of entrants or results. He could recall only that the overall title was won by "a skinny black guy who didn't deserve the name of Mr. America." The results and the winner, Rawle Green, showed up on a female bodybuilding website, but without any story. Still, Bonham seemed undaunted, conducting 2012 and 2013 contests in Secaucus, New Jersey. He deplores the state of modern bodybuilding, but sees the Mr. America title, by contrast, as a source of inspiration: "I want to go back to a more pure America. If I can influence people to a better lifestyle by running this show, I've achieved what I want."[7] Such aspirations are not inconsistent with the

Greek ideal. But the future of the contest and the glittering image and tradition it represents seems uncertain. That it even exists after decades of decline is remarkable. It is sustained only by its image.

THE MALE PREDICAMENT

The inability of bodybuilders by the end of the twentieth century to fulfill the expectations of such an eminent title cannot be understood unless viewed within the broader context of American society. Scholars have increasingly identified the bizarre culture that nurtured its demise as being symptomatic of the ills plaguing modern manhood. According to Alan Klein, the most striking feature of bodybuilding since the 1970s is irony, conveyed in his 1986 article, "Pumping Irony," a pun on the title of the 1977 film that raised public awareness of the sport. In *Little Big Men*, Klein reveals the dark underside of bodybuilding: men who appear healthy, fit, and confident but are actually unwell, unfit, and insecure. It is a world of glossy appearances that relies on "visual sleight of hand . . . to convince us that virile looks are synonymous with youth and health."[8] In her study of male body image, Lynne Luciano concurs that "it isn't body*building* but body *image* that really matters: this is less a sport than a physical display." Most professional athletes, she argues, "must be able to do something, not just look as if they can do it." Since the onset of the "fitness revolution," in the 1970s, "health objectives have tended to become secondary to remaking bodies for purely aesthetic ends."[9] Harrison Pope, Katharine Phillips, and Roberto Olivardia call this obsession with appearance the Adonis complex. They note that the circulation of *Men's Health* increased sixfold from 1990 to 1997, and other physical culture magazines posted similar gains. Though emphasizing health and fitness, "they are often heavily focused on male body appearance."[10] By this standard, the obsession of bodybuilders with appearance merely reflects the priority that society places on looks over substance.

Most scholars also attribute the prevalence of men's obsession with body image to the confusion of gender roles in postindustrial society and a consequent crisis of male identity. Traditional perceptions of gender, according to Harvey Mansfield, clearly differentiated between the sexes. By the 1970s, however, the cultural revolution carried on by baby boomers was causing major changes in gender relations. Men, according to Pope, Phillips, and Olivardia, experienced "threatened masculinity," an emotional problem unique to modern society. For most cultures throughout history, traditional male behaviors and pursuits "have received approval and respect." But in a postindustrial world, "what are these male behaviors and pursuits?" Superior physical strength, some men believe, always distinguishes them from women, but "muscles are a tenuous foundation on which to base all of one's sense of masculinity and self-esteem."[11]

If education is a reliable indicator of social advancement, then men are falling behind. Despite denials by the American Association of University Women of a "boy problem," data indicate that by 2005 women were earning the majority of bachelor's and master's degrees, and in thirty years of federal testing, girls increased their superiority on verbal exams while boys' lead in math narrowed. Girls earned better grades, received more academic honors, and had higher high school graduation rates. It was obvious to Tom Mortenson, a scholar at the Pell Institute, that "adult men are having a great deal of difficulty," presumably as a result of their upbringing: "We seem to know how to . . . prepare young women, but there's really no conversation going on about what we ought to be doing to prepare our boys."[12] With women excelling in so many areas and nearing parity with men, Pope, Phillips, and Olivardia conclude they are "leaving men with primarily their bodies as a defining source of masculinity."[13]

The male predicament is likewise acknowledged by the feminist viewpoint, poignantly expressed in *Stiffed*, by Susan Faludi, who argues that women are "asking men to share the public reins and men can't bear it." Men have lost their traditional dominance in so many areas critical for defining masculinity—politics, religion, the military, the community, and the home. Societal changes affecting both sexes since the 1960s led to what Faludi calls an "ornamental culture" constructed around celebrity and image. It is "the ultimate expression of the American Century," replacing "institutions in which men felt some sense of belonging" with visual spectacles "that benefit global commercial forces they cannot fathom." To Faludi, the Vietnam War was a "defining event of American masculinity, the bridge that collapsed just as the nation's sons thought they were crossing to manhood." Unlike their fathers, men today are deemed marginally useful, and personal worth is judged in ornamental terms. And a familiar icon symbolized all that: "If there was an enemy behind this cultural sea change, it seemed to most men to have a feminine face. . . . Men felt trapped in Miss America's boudoir. She was now their rival, not to be won over by a show of masculine strength, care, or protection, but only to be bested in a competition where the odds did not seem to be on the men's side."[14] Bereft of their traditional identities, men were seeking new roles. Carol Lee calls it "the male curse," in which young men view masculinity as "a version of *Jaws*": "Retreat is impossible and advance perilous." For George Mosse there was no longer a "simple test of manhood" or any "concrete signposts on the road to masculinity." But unsure whether the old measures of manhood are gone, he seeks a new masculinity.[15]

A COMIC-BOOK MASCULINITY

Mosse seems less sure about what form this new masculinity will take, but he puts little faith in bodybuilding, which, unlike the gymnastics movement a century earlier, no longer provides men a means of passing "the test of manhood through acquiring a properly structured body." Klein, who is even less sanguine about the future of American manhood, subscribes to Faludi's concept of ornamentalism, using the rubric "comic-book masculinity." Typically, it takes the form of a separation of the body from the mind or inner self that allows "the body [to] be *consciously* constructed." The "appearance of hegemonic masculinity" is used to "compensate for a vulnerable, weak sense of a man's self." Thus, bodybuilding is not an appropriate choice for men seeking "a more secure sense of masculinity." The sport is "about accruing size," and "to lose size is tantamount to becoming less of a man in every way." Bodybuilders cultivate the look of power and confidence because image is everything.[16] With the concentration on appearance to the exclusion of all else, laments a 1999 *MuscleMag* editorial, came the loss of romantic idealism to a mentality in which bigger is always better. Bodybuilders, having lost all sense of proportion, concern for aesthetics, and respect for human dignity, display physiques "contaminated with foreign objects, polluted by synthetic chemicals, deformed via injected oils, and degraded by the demand for and acceptance of hideous wobbling pot-bellied caricatures of well-muscled men." The writer goes on to ask angrily, "How the hell did calf implants, pec-padding, Synthol-filled biceps and triceps, roid guts and GH-distended organs ever win acceptance from judges and paying public alike?"[17] While promoters must share responsibility for this unhealthy state of affairs, societal factors—commercial, American, and modern—were facilitating these changes.

The authors of *The Adonis Complex* attribute this fixation on size to muscle dysmorphia, a condition fostered by a belief that one's bodily appearance is inadequate. Bodybuilders call it "bigorexia," a condition in which men feel that they are never big enough—a sort of reverse anorexia nervosa not unrelated to obsessive-compulsive disorders. The authors' studies revealed that college students desired at least twenty-eight more pounds of muscle and that even oversized weightlifters wanted another fifteen pounds. Steroids would enable them to increase muscle mass and thereby exhibit masculinity. Indeed "the male body simply cannot exceed a certain level of muscularity without the help of steroids or other chemicals." Pope, Phillips, and Olivardia also reckoned in 2000 that "a typical high school boy in the United States would think nothing of taking anywhere between 300 and 1,000 milligrams of steroids per week," and that a competitive weightlifter "might take up to several thousand milligrams per week." These estimates are in line with data from the Department of Health and Human Services cited by Klein, namely, that by 1991 "as many as 250,000 high school senior

Name	Year of title	Year of death	Age at death
Bert Goodrich	1939	1991	84
Roland Essmaker	1939	2002	86
John Grimek	1940/41	1998	88
Frank Leight	1942	1990	78
Jules Bacon	1943	2007	89
Steve Stanko	1944	1978	61
Clarence Ross	1945	2008	84
Alan Stephan	1946	2005	81
Steve Reeves	1947	2000	74
George Eiferman	1948	2002	76
Jack Delinger	1949	1992	66
John Farbotnik	1950	1998	72
Roy Hilligenn	1951	2008	85
Jim Park	1952	2007	79
Dick DuBois	1954	2007	74
Steve Klisanin	1955	2005	75
Ron Lacy	1957	2005	75
Tom Sansone	1958	1974	38
Ray Routledge	1961	2008	77
Vern Weaver	1963	1993	56
Dennis Tinerino	1967	2010	64
Casey Viator	1971	2012	61
Steve Michalik	1972	2102	63
Ron Thompson	1974	2003	59
Dave Johns	1977	1986	40
Ray Mentzer	1979	2001	47
Joe Meeko	1984	2009	48
Mike Scarcella	1992	2003	39

Table 1. Age at Death of Mr. America Winners, 1939–1992

males were using steroids."[18] In contrast with the ancient Greek notion of nothing in excess, bigorexia and anorexia, according to the feminist scholar Susan Bordo, "like so many contemporary disorders, are diseases of a culture that doesn't know when to stop."[19]

Since the 1970s, according to Mauro Di Pasquale, drug use by elite and professional bodybuilders has been "out of control": "It's not unusual for these athletes to use monthly amounts equal to what a normal male would produce in a lifetime." One top bodybuilder told him that in the four weeks before a contest he took ten kinds of steroids, 10,000 milligrams daily, in addition to "absurd amounts of other drugs and hormones." According to Pope, Phillips, and Olivardia, this fixation on size and body image rather than substance, so evident in bodybuilding, is symptomatic of a larger crisis afflicting modern males. They cite two sociocultural factors that distinguish the present generation from previous generations, "the availability of anabolic steroids and the increasing parity of women." It is hardly fortuitous that this crisis has coincided with the precipitous decline of the Mr. America Contest since the 1960s and the traditional values it represented.[20]

The obsession with size has also had a far-reaching impact on the health and well-being of bodybuilders. According to Di Pasquale, this unfettered drug use is reflected in early deaths, cardiovascular problems, and other ailments that afflict elite bodybuilders more than the general population. The scientific studies he cites strongly support this argument.[21] No less telling of the destructive impact of the bodybuilding lifestyle in general and of drugs in particular is the necrological profile of the sixty-two AAU Mr. Americas from 1939 to 1999, twenty-eight of whom have passed away (see table 1). What these data show is the extraordinary contrast in longevity of Mr. Americas before and after 1962, roughly marking the onset of the steroid era. While the overall age for those who have passed away is 68.53 years, it is 75.89 for pre-steroid-era winners and only 53.00 for steroid-era titlists, a difference of 22.89 years. If Tom Sansone, who is widely believed to have died from steroid intake, is included in the latter category, the age differential, 26.50 years (78.00 to 51.50), is even greater.[22] Admittedly, these figures do not tell the whole story, but they tell enough of it to suggest that drug use has had a serious impact on the well-being of the most recent generation of AAU Mr. Americas.

Among Mr. Americas from other federations, major health disorders seem more prevalent than deaths. Fewer winners, twenty for the IFBB and twelve for the WBBG, than in the AAU, along with a lack of data for the pre-steroid era, make it difficult to compare across governing bodies. But with the decline of the AAU Mr. America Contest, attention became focused on drug use by IFBB professionals, which reached a crescendo with the deaths of Mohammed Benaziza and Andreas Munzer.[23] As one competitor admitted to Alan Klein, "When we're up there (on the posing platform), we're closer to death than we are to life."[24] The athletes who run the greatest risks are most likely those who compete on the highest level. Bill Pearl recalled meeting the eight-time Mr. Olympia Ronnie Coleman at a Virginia airport around 2001 to help him open a health club. Walking "to the car from the plane probably took forty-five minutes to an hour." In 2010, the three-time Olympia winner Jay Cutler defended his title, but he had cut his water intake so drastically that his body nearly shut down. As Peter McGough reported, "For 45 minutes after the prejudging, Jay lay prone backstage; he didn't even have the strength to stand."[25] Chemical use by bodybuilders has gone far beyond the relatively minor Dianabol intake of the early 1960s and now includes scores of other drugs along with human growth hormone, diuretics, and insulin, all with multiple body-altering and mind-altering effects. Because of drug use, dietary regimens, brutal training routines, and an obsession with size, modern bodybuilders are neither healthy nor fit.

THE END OF IDEALISM

This tragic state of affairs stands in stark contrast with the early history of bodybuilding, which emphasized the integration of mind, body, and spirit and a blending of form with athletic function. Such was the intent of promoters and entrepreneurs from the 1890s to the 1960s, including Eugen Sandow, Bernarr Macfadden, and Bob Hoffman. Then, bodybuilding was not treated as a separate practice, but was chiefly the result of pursuing a fit and healthy lifestyle, or was seen as an extension of the sport of weightlifting. As the iconoclast Greg Zulak reflected in 1995:

> In the old days bodybuilding was called "physical culture," a term which comprised health, fitness (both physical and mental), strength and muscular development—in other words, a healthy mind in a healthy body. Training solely for muscular development with no regard to health would have been incomprehensible 60 years ago. Equally puzzling would have been the practice of training solely for muscular development with no regard to strength. In the first 50 years of the century you had to be as strong as you looked. Muscles were mostly a byproduct of training to lift heavy weights. . . . The other great change resulted from the introduction of anabolic ste-

roids to strength athletes in the late 1950s and early 1960s. Up until then the use of chemical enhancement such as steroids was a foreign concept. Taking drugs to win a physique or strength contest was tantamount to cheating. There was more sense of decency and honor back then.[26]

After gaining recognition as a competitive event in 1939, bodybuilding increased in popularity over the next several decades, but it retained a sense of equilibrium, to such an extent that criteria for Mr. America resembled those for selecting Miss America. In both contests, the body was embedded within the context of the whole person, which included character, intelligence, talent, athleticism, personality, and overall appearance.

The 1960s, however, witnessed a decline of idealism and a retreat to the body alone as the defining feature of masculinity. A newspaper report on the IFBB Mr. America in 1973, won by Bob Birdsong, provides a gender comparative: "Unlike the Miss America pageant, which tries hard to disguise its basic physical appeal beneath a lot of evening gowns, talent shows and scholarship talk, the Mr. America contest is a body show, pure and simple."[27] The contrast between these American icons was palpable. As Josh Henson pointed out, it was *Playboy* and Miss America that sustained an "idealized version of a woman." But nothing any longer epitomized manhood: "Young teenage boys have no such ideal. There might have been a time when Mr. America was it, but it's not anymore." Henson recommended that bodybuilders "look back to the Greeks," who "believed in moderation." The implication is clear: "Steroids and freaks go against everything the Greeks stood for." Yet the notion of Mr. America remains in the popular imagination, contended Steve Michalik, nourished by its association with Miss America imagery: "When you go anywhere and say you're Mr. America, people go, 'Wow!' because they equate it with Miss America. You're the NPC champion? Nobody cares. Nobody even cares about Mr. Olympia."[28] Though divorced from its male counterpart since the 1960s, Miss America continues to nurture an ideal.

This metamorphosis coincided with the displacement of Hoffman and the AAU by the Weiders and the IFBB. Joe Weider's rationale for challenging the status quo was that "all the top guys" in the AAU "looked upon bodybuilders as homosexual, little muscle guys with absolutely no power or strength."

They were perceived as mere showoffs. The AAU used it as a way to attract audiences. People would sit through the long, boring weightlifting meet—sometimes until 1:30 in the morning—just to see the bodybuilding contest at the end. The AAU would give the bodybuilders a little room inside the auditorium where the weightlifting meet was held, and a couple of bodybuilders would stand on a table and pose. That was the contest! They just made a mockery of bodybuilding.[29]

A less altruistic rationale for the Weiders' focus on bodybuilding was that it was far more profitable than weightlifting, and ripe for the picking. An emphasis on muscle display rather than lifting prowess was evident from the inception of Joe's magazines and Ben's contests. It was a selling point not lost on other promoters who, once the steroid era was in full swing, abandoned athleticism and the classical look for the sake of survival. Increasingly, young fans with appetites for big muscles settled for nothing less. As Tommy Suggs once observed, "Hoffman was for competence. Weider was for freaks." Editors, as Joe Roark explained in 1988, regardless of personal convictions, were "not willing to risk decreased sales by showing builders on the covers who could not place in a major contest."[30] It was all a matter of cash flow and keeping up with the Weiders.

THE WEIDER MACHINE

But sole responsibility for this transformation can hardly be placed on the Weiders. Their organization merely served as a vehicle for other iron-game agents of change whose outcomes were far less hegemonic or profitable. While Ben's initiatives on the international scene date from the late 1940s, it was the confidence, connections, and mentoring of Oscar State over the next several decades that invigorated the IFBB and laid the basis for the Weiders' international sovereignty over bodybuilding. As David Webster observed, "Oscar State set the thing up in such a way that it became a properly run organization. He gave the Weiders credibility."[31] It was State who created the IFBB's constitution and provided political leverage for its admission to the GAISF, which hastened the decline of the NABBA Mr. Universe and the AAU Mr. America contests.[32] On becoming secretary of the GAISF, Oscar helped establish links with the IOC for the Weiders, nurturing Ben's dream of making physique an Olympic event. "Oscar was a rather cool, reserved individual," recalled Ben, "and our relationship took a long time to ripen. After we met I had no idea that Oscar would be the best friend I ever had, outside my family." It was no exaggeration for Ben to say that "without him there would be less of a story to tell."[33]

Likewise the supercharged physique and star power of Arnold Schwarzenegger not only contributed to the visibility and cash flow of the Weiders but also raised the Mr. Olympia Contest above its Mr. America rival while paradoxically fostering public perceptions that Arnold was a Mr. America. As the York defector Bill Starr recognized, Hoffman "still had control of bodybuilding" in the early 1970s, and then "Arnold made the difference." It was Arnold, observed Dale Adrian, who created a public awareness of bodybuilding and "broke things wide open." But "if Arnold had just the body and not the personality he would have gone nowhere." He was, a 1978 study concluded, "the personification of modern bodybuilding." According to Fred Yale, "his iconography replaced that of Mr. America as a household word." To Jon Rieger, "Arnold was the Isaac Newton of bodybuilding."[34] Alan Radley and David Gentle recognize Arnold's emergence as "the beginning of a new physique standard, identified by mountains of flesh." The result was predictable: "Steroid abuse followed and development left the rules of classical proportion far behind." That Arnold was only dimly aware of this watershed is indicated by his response to a 1973 query from Charles Gaines: "Has it ever occurred to you that your body is like a classical piece of sculpture?" "What a brilliant idea," Arnold replied, "I have never thought of that."[35] As the cultural context of bodybuilding changed after the 1960s, Arnold became the greatest symbol of that shift. He was "the first fully self-constructed superstar," argues Clive James in *Fame in the Twentieth Century*.[36]

The third agent of change was Ken Sprague, who not only served as a catalyst for the male pornography industry and nurtured Gold's Gym to prominence but also engineered the transfer of amateur physique (under the rubric of the NPC) from the AAU to the Weiders. His association with the IFBB, however, was fortuitous. "Had I any association with Hoffman," he recollects, "I'm sure I could have taken the physique committee with York. But they didn't have the sense to try to work something out." Sprague's reputation as a wheeler-dealer no doubt contributed to another lost opportunity for the AAU in the late 1970s when he offered it a $250,000 option for yearly rights to televise the Mr. America Contest (à la Miss America) on a Saturday night with all proceeds going to the physique committee. The publicity and profits could have been enormous and might even have staved off a Weider takeover, but traditional thinking prevailed. Sprague became, as Randy Roach points out, "the biggest impact player in 1970s bodybuilding politics."[37] As they did with Arnold, the Weiders took advantage of opportunities provided them by Sprague for greater fame and fortune.

Whether they had the same aspirations for their bodybuilders, however, was not so evident. It was Wayne DeMilia who, by creating the professional division of the IFBB, demonstrated that the two could be mutually beneficial. "Everybody wants to make money," DeMilia believed. But his graduated system for professionalizing amateur bodybuilders, contributed not only to a departure from the gentlemanly Victorian notion of "playing the game" but also to the demise of the Greek ideals of sophrosyne and *paideia*. "Professionals and amateurs are different," Paul Weiss observed. "The one works for money, the other plays as part of an adventure at self-discovery and growth. . . . The task of the professional is to please, usually by means of a victory; the task of the amateur is to function excellently in the game. The objective of the one is economic security . . . but the objective of the other is to become more of a man." Contrary to common belief, the Mr. Olympia was the Weiders' only professional contest until DeMilia held his Night of Champions in 1978. Theretofore, the Weiders had been only marginally successful and were still struggling to outdistance rivals. As DeMilia observed, the Weiders were not that strong in the early 1970s, but "had all the right people to ride on their backs." In his view, their empire was largely built by others: "We were the guys behind the scenes doing everything, and the Weiders were taking the credit."[38] DeMilia led them to the pot of gold.

WHO KILLED MR. AMERICA?

Was it the "Master Blaster" and his brother from Canada, the English "Educator," the Austrian "Terminator," the Cincinnati "Golden Boy," or the Brooklyn "Whiz Kid"? All these outliers contributed to the death of Mr. America, but the greatest burden of responsibility must fall on the Weiders. The logic for this conclusion is well established in the groundbreaking insights of Randy Roach and Gordon LaVelle. In essence, the brothers' culpability for the catastrophe is rooted in their hubris. "While successfully marketing muscles," writes Roach, "the Weiders propagated the image of their own role and organization beyond that of reality and into the realm of historical deception." For LaVelle, Joe Weider let success go to his head: "He promoted his brand, and himself, like no other man in history. . . . Articles heaping praise on him would regularly run in his magazines, and these quite often tested the limits of vanity and pretentiousness." Furthermore, such was their control over "the relatively small and insular world of bodybuilding" that no events or circumstances escaped their scrutiny. "It all happened on their watch." Where the Weiders were most culpable, argued LaVelle, was in using their contests and magazines to glorify chemically enhanced bodybuilders and rejecting serious drug screening, largely for the sake of money.

> [Joe] Weider did not invent bodybuilding, nor did he invent bodybuilding drugs. He certainly did not give a small percentage of mankind the at-all-costs determination to attain incredible levels of size and muscularity. Rather, he was presented with, and capitalized on, the opportunity to exploit a combination of these things. In doing so, he built a large fortune. He also fostered the development of an activity with a strong correlation between fanatical participation, health problems, and early deaths. . . . For all his self-propping as the man responsible for bringing health and fitness to the masses through bodybuilding, if he were to be honest, he would also have to admit accountability for all other things that have come from his creation.[39]

Evidence that has been presented in this study reinforces LaVelle's perception of the Weider phenomenon. Admittedly, Macfadden, Liederman, Atlas, Hoffman, and even the Raders exhibited an entrepreneurial spirit, but the Weiders pursued it furthest. In this respect, their greatest success constituted their greatest failure.

The Weiders' rise was accompanied by an attitudinal transformation in American society. According to Godfrey Hodgson, between the assassination of John F. Kennedy and the resignation of Richard M. Nixon, the country saw the collapse of its liberal ideology, which "tore consensus to shreds." Hadley Cantril concluded from a 1959 public opinion survey that Americans, after a generation of unparalleled prosperity, were the most confident and satisfied people in the world. After multiple crises in the late 1960s, however, Americans were brought face-to-face with "moral ambiguity." Lack of clarity over right and wrong inaugurated a "prevailing mood of impotence and loss." Americans' "pilgrimage never reached the city the Puritan sought."[40]

This attitudinal change coincided with a generational divide in physical culture. Just as Hoffman's vision concerning the efficacy of weight training and nutritional aids contributed to his early dominance, the Weiders' focus on bodybuilding, professionalism, and the international scene, in synch with the cultural revolution of the 1960s, catapulted them to the forefront. A critical factor in this rise was their willingness to explore fields on the fringes of American morality and to question the sport's rigid amateur code. Their publications, especially *Adonis* and *Body Beautiful*, had a strong appeal for the homosexual community. "If it hadn't been for the gay community there wouldn't be bodybuilding," observed Mike Graham. "They supported the magazines, they supported the contests, they supported the boys."[41] Likewise, *Jem* and *Monsieur* were attractive to heterosexual American men. The soft-core pornography that they published in the 1950s anticipated the sexual revolution of the 1960s, and there was a lot of money to be made in it. Their *Mr. America* muscle magazine of the 1970s, featuring "Sexy Schwarzenegger," fully fit the times. In an earlier era, Hoffman's scandalous personal life had been carefully hidden, and Peary Rader became the moral spokesman for the AAU and the Mr. America Contest. However much the Weiders coveted the Mr. America prize, even to the extent of formulating ersatz versions of the contest, it never fit their cultural milieu.

THE RACIAL EDGE

Another cultural component of the transformation of bodybuilding was the entry of blacks into the sport. While there was never any official color bar in the AAU, the criteria for selecting Mr. Americas strongly favored the traditional values of a society whose discriminatory practices tended to exclude the culturally and economically disadvantaged U.S. underclass. The postmodern historian Joan Scott identifies this incongruence with the inability of a culture dominated by white males to accept women: "Women were culturally incompatible and simply could not just be added on without a fundamental recasting of the terms, standards and assumptions of what has passed for objective, neutral and universal history in the past because that view of history included in its very definition of itself the exclusion of women." For the world of bodybuilding, replace the word "women" in this passage with "blacks." As George Mosse recognizes, the male ideal derived from the Greeks was appropriated to justify racism, for example, serving as a model for German fascism, and that racist stereotype of masculinity was "not far removed from the image of the "clean-cut Englishman." Indeed, Plato's ideal of perfection is echoed in the classic modern work on Aryan supremacy. "What makes the Greek ideal of beauty immortal," wrote Adolf Hitler, "is the wonderful combination of the most glorious physical beauty with a brilliant mind and the noblest soul."[42] Thus, the Greek ideal, from a black perspective, was loaded with racial overtones. An emphasis on musculature enabled blacks to redefine bodybuilding and the Mr. America Contest to their own satisfaction. As it was bodybuilding for the Weiders, it was muscularity for blacks.

By the time of the Mr. America Contest in 1999, the AAU was no longer as susceptible to charges of racial discrimination, but the event had ceased to carry the status it held in former decades. That change might be attributed in part to a redirection of priorities in American society—from homogeneity to heterogeneity—in the 1960s. The civil rights movement accentuated that trend, as did the influx of elite athletes of color from the Caribbean. What was viewed as racial discrimination, owing to the failure of blacks to take the top prize before 1970, could just as easily be interpreted as the AAU's adherence to traditional values from an era when the United States had more definite ideas of what constituted perfect manhood. Looking back, Bob Bendel thinks that prejudice existed, but it was minor. Although hard pressed to name five prejudiced Mr. America judges, he believes that "with the judges of today, Melvin Wells would have won." Len Bosland thinks similarly: "There was racial prejudice on the Mr. America judges' panel, but I can't prove it." Especially suspect was Dale Adrian's victory over Robbie Robinson in 1975. Possibly judges after 1970, in tune with the times, were more predisposed to choose black winners, but there is no evidence of periodic reforms being introduced specifically to favor blacks. According to Bob Crist, there was "a lot of pressure to keep up with Weider," which led to the elimination of traditional judging procedures.[43]

During the civil rights era, blacks figured prominently in all Mr. America contests, with nine winners, including the final two, after 1969. It was not so much that earlier AAU officials were racists as it was that the cultural tradition stemming from the Greeks defined the contest according to traditional white American standards of what the ideal male should be. However appealing Martin Bernal's *Black Athena* might be as an explanation for the origins of Western civilization, modern black bodybuilders displayed little consonance between the Afrocentric model and the Greek logos. Rather, they aspired to a separate cultural identity. Black liberation had nothing to do with the Greeks.[44] Though the urge to do so must have been irresistible at times, there was never a need for the Weiders to play the race card. But their Jewish heritage and reputation as outsiders ideally positioned them to take advantage of this cultural disjuncture. Racial resentments that fueled the resistance of young black bodybuilders to Mr. America standards coincided with their acceptance of the Weider line of muscle for muscle's sake. But Robbie Robinson, perhaps the most militant of AAU defectors, lamented the IFBB judging standards in 2003, which ensured that "the biggest guy wins." Greater emphasis needed to be placed on "symmetry, definition and a good aesthetic look, minus things like bloated guts." The abandonment of such criteria was devastating: "We've lost our core audience." Likewise in retrospect Bill Grant, a WBBG Mr. America, could "see how personality and education are important": "You are, after all, representing America."[45] Robinson and Grant accurately identified the unfortunate trade-off that modern bodybuilders had made—by satisfying the tastes of the hard-core cult of muscle buffs, they had lost the respect of the mainstream American public.

RESTORING FUNCTION

That any restoration of balance might be possible seems unlikely now, especially given the prevalence of drugs in modern bodybuilding.[46] Furthermore, few would view a champion bodybuilder as representing an ideal American male, or would support Ben Weider's chimerical scheme to make bodybuilding an Olympic sport. How could an activity that epitomizes form fit into a venue where function determines results? The classicist Maria Wyke attributes this conundrum to a fundamental misunderstanding and misapplication of Greek history to the sport: "It is precisely the purely visual element in bodybuilding competitions that has constituted its greatest problem in gaining accreditation as a sport suitable for entry in the modern Olympic games and has set it at such a distance from the athletic practices of antiquity. Yet the constant reference back to classical *art* rather than classical athletic practice in Weider's comments and those of the popular historians neatly elides the entire problem."[47] Clearly, a cultural correction seems in order, but it is unlikely to happen by restoring the AAU formula from the pre-drug era. The world is vastly different in the twenty-first century, but as Laurence Goldstein recognizes, "the body needs to be rescued from its captivity by an unwholesome form of culture."[48] There are some cultural constants that can be tapped for inspiration that are no less true for humanity at present than they were for bodybuilding's founders twenty-five centuries ago. The Greeks were, above all, humanists who greatly valued the quality of life. Health and fitness are timeless values that are vital to survival and well-being, and Greek ideals of harmony and balance, cultivation of the whole person, moderation, and physical and moral excellence favor no one gender, race, religion, nationality, or class of people. That arete and *kalokagathia* were appropriated by what Michel Foucault categorizes as Western idealisms and power blocs in Germany, England, and the United States should not detract from their intrinsic value for constructing a civil society and a sporting climate. Nor should they be regarded as a panacea for resolving current ills. Daniel Dombrowski's comparative study cautions against using ancient Greece as "a primal paradise of ideas with which to examine athletics." Its ideals can provide, however, an "interesting standard" for judging current ideals and practices.[49] Yet almost no post-1960s bodybuilder or promoter interviewed for this study could think of any connection with the Greeks. Nor could they imagine any cultural similarity between Mr. America and Miss America.

Any reeducation would need to start with an understanding that form necessarily follows function. Such an approach would provide an antidote to the prevailing, degenerate subculture of size, which is virtually devoid of substance. "Display calls heavily on grandiosity as the hallmark of a champion bodybuilder," notes Klein. "One doesn't so much admire bodybuilders for what they can do as far as what they *look* like they can do." This shallow perspective on the body accounts for much of the popularity of bodybuilding vis-à-vis other strength sports. "In our world of advertising," observes Samuel Fussell, "it's no wonder why bodybuilding succeeded where powerlifting and Olympic lifting didn't." In the former, "the appearance of strength is more important than the application of strength. . . . How perfectly postmodern, where surface is substance and larger-than-life is life."[50] Bodybuilding is a form of virtual reality that has degenerated into a cult.

The current obsession with drugs, size, and commercialism would be impervious to any direct assault. It might be possible, however, to stage a flank offensive that would restore bodybuilding's integrity as a sport and its credibility with mainstream America. A possible template could be the first AAU Mr. America Contest, which chose a winner from weightlifting contestants, thus imparting a degree of athleticism to the title. That this concept was disgraced and eventually abolished should not detract from its intrinsic value. But weightlifting has been a dying sport in the United States for decades, and any attempt to add a physique component would need to be preceded by its own revival.[51]

A new option for bodybuilders wishing to develop physiques that reveal clean lines, symmetry, and tone is provided by the World Beauty

Fitness and Fashion (WBFF), founded in 2007 by the former IFBB pro Paul Dillett. At first, Frank Budelewski explains, companies refused to sponsor Dillett's shows, on the grounds that they did not "endorse freak shows." So Dillett changed up things: "Paul introduced divisions that had never been in bodybuilding competitions before. Fitness model, swimsuit, men's fitness model, and a brand new division muscle model. He also made his competitions more like a show, with fancy lighting, pumping music, and performances in between divisions by recording artists. He took amateur competitions out of the high school auditoriums and into top level venues." Muscle modeling best describes this new approach, in which most competitors are women. "The WBFF looks at everything," explained Dillett. "We look at your physique, your face, your hair, the way you put on your makeup—every single thing. We ask, 'Could this girl be on the cover? Could she be in an ad campaign for Nike or Reebok?' We judge the complete package."[52] Popular response to this saner depiction of the body, fueled by WBFF's free online magazine, *Fit and Firm*, has been exceptional.

"It's where it's at today," according to Wayne DeMilia, who estimated the magazine has 80,000 subscribers and a total circulation, through social media, of over a half million. Judging criteria for the WBFF's glamorous shows stress marketability (40 percent), physique (40 percent), and stage presence. Dillett's organization "judges the face where the IFBB doesn't," DeMilia observed. "Our society rewards pretty people, and their girls are pretty." The WBFF utilizes much the same strategy as Ken Sprague did, DeMilia admitted, stressing the entertainment and glamour aspect of physique shows. To convert this mainstream appeal into possible gainful careers for Dillett's contestants, DeMilia plans to offer screen tests through his entertainment company, make low-budget films through an independent studio, and use his Hollywood connections "to make some of these people stars." Why? "They all want to get into entertainment but don't know how. We can create the bridge."[53] But the WBFF's focus is almost totally on appearance rather than function, so entertainers rather than athletes are displayed. Thus raising the question—are these bodies really healthy and fit or do they just look like it?

A better template, one that incorporates athleticism into the conception of an ideal physique, would be a total-body sport testing all aspects of a competitor's makeup. Joe Tete recommends mixed martial arts. These guys are "built like hell because they train six hours a day"; although not bodybuilders, "some are built like bodybuilders." And their drug tests "are for real."[54]

CrossFit might be a better model. It is a strength and conditioning sport combining weightlifting, sprinting, gymnastics, plyometrics, rowing, and other movements. It is the "sport of fitness," according to the instructor manual, involving "constantly varied, high-intensity, functional movement." It is designed to test athletic proficiency in ten areas—endurance, stamina, strength, flexibility, power, speed, coordination, agility, balance, and accuracy.[55] But what is there to ensure Cross-Fitters are drug-free? Although organizers adhere to a zero-tolerance policy and higher-level competitors are subject to testing by labs approved by the World Anti-Doping Agency, there is nothing to prevent the intrusion of drugs into the sport other than the attitude of the athletes. But in the spirit of Greek idealism, CrossFitters seem dedicated to health and fitness. "The point of CF is to get better at life," remarked one devotee.[56]

Any consciousness of muscularity is an afterthought. CrossFit epitomizes natural physique development: form follows function. "I think appearance is the least you have to worry about" is the assessment of a former bodybuilder. "If you train and eat right the physique will follow." In an article entitled "Form Follows Function," Russell Berger observes that all CrossFit athletes "are motivated by the powerful force of physical accomplishment," not an obsession with body image: "It is not our primary goal to improve physiques, but we would be fooling ourselves if we didn't acknowledge the beauty of these CrossFit bodies at work."[57] David Nall, a natural-physique promoter in Austin, Texas, recognizes that CrossFitters are in "amazing physical shape."

> A lot of people who do it look like they could step on stage and do some drug-free competing. They have great physiques for it because of the compound movements and the Olympic lifting and all the stuff they do. You have to be a very well rounded athlete. . . . They look like a figure competitor or a drug-free bodybuilder looks like. A lot of those guys are in really good shape. You can't do all that stuff and have too much density. I would love some of the people to cross over and do some of our physique competitions.[58]

Though hardly a fan of CrossFit, Mike Graham of nearby Lockhart admits "that would be kind of fun."[59] Thus would it not be fitting for CrossFit champions to complement their athleticism with a physique competition to demonstrate that form truly follows function?

A GREEK TRAGEDY?

Such a natural format bears a likeness to the conception of the founder of the first Mr. America Contest, for whom the human body was like a flower—a natural wonder and an object of beauty and admiration. Yet this ideal floral form would not exist without the functional component of a healthy and fit whole plant, properly nourished with water, sunlight, and fertile soil. Beauty was not so much the direct object of development as a desirable outcome that both enriched the plant's quality of life and had a functional (reproductive) component. John Hordines, an avid gardener, started a National Flower Contest in his later years. Designed to "recognize beauty and honor people," it was a postal competition for the best floral pictures. Only his death at age ninety-five prevented him from establishing a National Flower Hall of Fame at his remote village in upstate New York. "Flowers and good bodies" complemented each other, and his flower contest can be viewed conceptually as a continuation of his landmark physique contest a half century earlier. As he put it, "I saw the need for it very badly." It is doubtful that Hordines was well versed in Greek aesthetics or had ever heard of Johann Winckelmann, but he had a taste for beauty. He viewed Mr. America as "just like the flower." Both typified "beauty." For Hordines, these ideals were linked with his love of America: "This country gave me a lot, and I want to pay something back. . . . We have a great country."[60] It was Hordines who, by channeling the inchoate notions of earlier promoters into a national ideal, transformed a Greek concept into an American icon.

Although he was soon marginalized and Mr. America contests and titlists ceased to be amateur, athletic, or drug-free, those unfortunate developments should not detract from the impact of ideals prevalent for more than six decades. Even in the twenty-first century, those ideals persist with the indelible image of Steve Reeves. To Steve Michalik, he was "absolute perfection": "Handsome, tremendous posture, well spoken, well groomed, a very beautiful, balanced physique that could appeal both to men and women. This was Mr. America. It wasn't about having big muscles. It was about having beauty and symmetry like any flower, or bird, or animal on earth that when you look at it and you see a panther run you say, my God, look at the symmetry in that. Well, Steve Reeves was like that."[61] Thus, the title still has strength in its virtual nonexistence! Failing Bob Bonham's efforts to revive the contest, a complete makeover of the NPC Nationals, the addition of a functional aspect to muscle modeling, or the incorporation of a physique component into CrossFit, there seems little hope of resurrecting either the title or the ideals it stood for.[62] At one time it embodied the intrinsic ethos of a burgeoning America, but in the 1960s it took on much of society's rejection of traditional values. Bodybuilding, as a subculture, is hardly vital to the nation's economy or status in the world, but its tragic history reflects an erosion of American idealism. How much it matters, given the failure of the sport to enter the mainstream of American life, is a matter of conjecture. But insofar as people as well as athletes are motivated by symbols, it does matter. If that perspective is to prevail, perhaps it is better to think of what has happened to the Mr. America icon as not so much a Greek tragedy as a Greek comedy.

.

AAU MR. AMERICA

1939	Bert Goodrich★
1939	Roland Essmaker
1940	John Grimek
1941	John Grimek
1942	Frank Leight
1943	Jules Bacon
1944	Steve Stanko
1945	Clarence Ross
1946	Alan Stephan
1947	Steve Reeves
1948	George Eiferman
1949	Jack Delinger
1950	John Farbotnik
1951	Roy Hilligenn
1952	Jim Park
1953	Bill Pearl
1954	Dick DuBois
1955	Steve Klisanin
1956	Ray Schaefer
1957	Ron Lacy
1958	Tom Sansone
1959	Harry Johnson
1960	Lloyd Lerille
1961	Ray Routledge
1962	Joe Abbenda
1963	Vern Weaver
1964	Val Vasilieff
1965	Jerry Daniels
1966	Bob Gajda
1967	Dennis Tinerino
1968	James Haislop
1969	Boyer Coe
1970	Chris Dickerson
1971	Casey Viator
1972	Steve Michalik
1973	James Morris
1974	Ron Thompson
1975	Dale Adrian
1976	Kal Szkalak
1977	Dave Johns
1978	Tony Pearson
1979	Ray Mentzer★★
1980	Gary Leonard★★
1981	Tim Belknap★★

1982	Rufus Howard
1983	Jeff King
1984	Joe Meeko
1985	Michael Antorino
1986	Glenn Knerr
1987	Richard Barretta
1988	Bill Norberg
1989	Matt DuFresne
1990	Pete Miller
1991	Joe DeAngelis
1992	Mike Scarcella
1993	Billy Nothaft
1994	Andrew Sivert
1995	Terry Hairston
1996	Doug Reiser
1997	Bill Davey
1998	Harvey Campbell
1999	Tracy Dorsey

*First Mr. America, but not AAU sanctioned
**AAU/NPC Mr. America

AAU/WBFA MR. AMERICA

2003	Dan Elam
2004	Joe Rapisura

INBF MR. AMERICA

2011	Rawle Green
2012	Dan White
2013	John Heart

AAU JUNIOR MR. AMERICA

1942	Kimon Voyages
1944	Steve Stanko
1945	Joe Lauriano
1946	Everett Sinderoff
1947	Edward J. Simons
1948	Harry Smith
1949	Val Pasqua
1950	John Farbotnik
1951	George Paine
1952	Malcolm Brenner
1953	Steve Klisanin

1954	Harry Johnson (East)
	Gene Bohanty (West)
1955	Vic Seipke
1956	Ray Schaefer
1957	Jim Dugger
1958	Tom Sansone (East)
1958	Ray Routledge (West)
1959	Elmo Santiago
1960	Frank Allen Quinn (South)
	Joseph Lazzaro (East)
	Hugo Labra (West)
	Gail Crick (Southwest)
1961	Joe Simon (East)
	Ronnie Russell(Southeast)
	John Gourgott (South)
	Lou Walter (Midwest)
	Harold Poole (Central)
	Franklin Jones (West)
1962	Joe Abbenda (East)
	Tony Munday (Midwest)
	Billy Lemacks (South)
1963	Randy Watson
1964	John DeCola
1965	Jerry Daniels
1966	Sergio Oliva
1967	Dennis Tinerino
1968	Jim Haislop
1969	Boyer Coe
1970	Chris Dickerson
1971	Casey Viator
1972	Pete Grymkowski
1973	Paul Hill
1974	Ron Thompson
1975	Willie Johnson
1976	Dave Johns
1977	Mario Nieves
1978	Tony Pearson
1979	Robert Jodkiewicz*
1980	Ernie Santiago*
1981	Marty Vranicar*
1982	Mike Antorino
1983	Michael McKinley
1984	Abe Cuesta
1985	Victor Terra
1986	Richard Barretta
1987	Brian Silk
1988	Jim Katsikis

1989	Mike Rollins
1990	Robert Harrop
1991	Mike Scarcella
1992	Bill Nothaft
1995	Chet Innamorati
1996	Bernardo Winston
1997	A. K. Leinbach
1998	Dietrich Horsey
1999	Jerome Brooks

★AAU/NPC Junior Mr. America

AAU TEENAGE MR. AMERICA

1956	John Podrebarac
1957	Mike Ferraro
1958	John Gourgott
1959	Joe Abbenda
1960	Jerry Doettrell (East)
	Gil Dimeglio (Midwest)
	John Corvallo (West)
1961	Steve Boyer (East)
	John Piscareta (Midwest)
1962	Michael Liscio (East)
	Mickey Majoris (Midwest)
1963	Jerry Daniels
1964	Bud Schosek
1965	Dennis Tinerino
1966	Boyer Coe
1967	Michael Dayton
1968	Ken Covington
1969	Bob Gallucci
1970	Casey Viator
1971	Scott Pace
1972	Sammie Willis
1973	Joe Ugolik
1974	Dan Tobol
1975	Ron Teufel
1976	Mike Torchia
1977	Jim Yasenchock
1978	Rudy Hermosillo
1979	Lee Haney★
1980	Danny Berumen★
1981	Mike Quinn★
1982	Anthony Watkins
1983	Victor Terra
1984	Ted Lopes
1985	Matt DuFresne

1986	Derrick Whittsett
1987	Frank Vassil
1988	John Vano
1989	Mike Goll
1990	Paul Grafas
1992	Branch Warren
1993	Jeremy Parmley
1994	Rodney Bizzell
1995	Jay Jaillett
1996	Jay Jaillett (18–19)
	Benjamin Lash (13–17)
1997	Justin Leonard (18–19)
	Benjamin Lash (13–17)
1998	Jarrod (Rudolf) Tucker (18–19)
	Shaun Critzer (16–17)
	Scott Proscia (13–15)
1999	Roger Morello (18–19)
	William McDermott (16–17)
	Scott Proscia (13–15)

★AAU/NPC Teenage Mr. America

AAU COLLEGIATE MR. AMERICA

1970	Carl Smith
1972	Ellington Darden
1973	Ken Holbert
1974	Bob Gallucci
1975	Clinton Beyerle
1976	Lance Dreher
1978	Ron Blackmon
1981	Michael Antorino
1982	Jeffrey King
1983	Al Bedrosian
1984	Peter Moen/Robert Gosch
1985	Scott Colangelo
1986	William Norberg Jr.
1989	Steve Kidwell

AAU (MASTERS) MR. AMERICA OVER 40

1966	Harry Johnson
1967	Frank Szymanski
1976	Vic Seipke
1977	Kent Kuehn
1978	Earl Maynard

1979   Phil Outlaw★
1980   Paul Love★
1981   O. J. Smith★
1982   Alex McNeil
1983   Walt Tyndall
1984   John DeCola
1985   Larry Robinson
1986   Butch Fairchild
1987   Max Reppel
1988   Carl Smith
1989   Brad Leavitt
1990   Walter Korzeniowski
1991   Frank Capullupo
1992   Tony Giello
1993   Robert Irby
1994   Dean Miller
1995   Chavers Todd
1996   Karl Herkert
1997   Eugene Hawkins
1998   Charlie Moss
1999   Robert Irby
★AAU/NPC Mr. America Over 40

AAU JUNIOR MASTERS
MR. AMERICA

1990   James E. McClain Jr.

AAU GRANDMASTERS
MR. AMERICA (OVER 50)

1991   Wiley Owen
1992   Jim Batick
1994   Harry Scott
1995   Doc Junkins
1996   Maitland Nance
1997   Gregg Amore
1998   Jerry Lindsey
1999   John McPeek

AAU GRANDMASTERS
MR. AMERICA (OVER 60)

1995   John Mangini
1996   John Mangini
1997   Jack King

1998   Dominick Duche
1999   Maitland Nance

AAU GRANDMASTERS
MR. AMERICA (OVER 70)

1999   Reggie Faust

AAU/WBFA MASTERS
MR. AMERICA

2004   Ben Wellen

INBF MASTERS
MR. AMERICA OVER 50

2011   Butch Paradis

AAU MS. AMERICA

1980   Carla Dunlap
1981   Laura Combes
1982   Tina Plakinger
1983   Kerrie Keenan
1984   Jill O'Connor
1985   Joone Hopfenspirger
1986   Connie McCloskey
1987   Teri Nordaby
1988   Cathy Butler
1989   Mary Adams
1990   Linda Slayton
1991   Teri Locicero
1992   Kathi Costello
1993   Karla Nelson
1994   Midge Shull
1995   Betsy Briggs
1996   Cynthia Barker
1997   Denise Richardson
1998   Denise Richardson
1999   Cathy Boulé

AAU/WBFA MS. AMERICA

2003   Trish Hamishin
2004   Joan Lopez

AAU/WBFA MS. AMERICA FITNESS

2004   Voncille Williams

AAU JUNIOR MS. AMERICA

1985   Karin Mitchell
1986   Teresa Nordaby
1987   Linda Bevelander
1988   Terri LoCicero
1989   Angela Terry
1990   Gina McPherson
1992   Linda Mignosa
1995   Johnna Carter
1996   Sonya Bond
1997   Cheryl Dater-Katz
1998   Sonyo Tillet-Bond

AAU TEENAGE MS. AMERICA

1996   Delores Serbin (18-19)
1997   Candace Samuel (18-19)
1998   Rachael Leo (18-19)
       Eveann Frazer Baptise (13-15)

AAU COLLEGIATE MS. AMERICA

1982   Melissa Orth
1983   Leslie Stamatis
1984   Jewel Campbell
1985   Jill Howe
1986   Beth Machael
1989   Casey Hensley

AAU MASTERS MS. AMERICA (40 AND OVER)

1990   Sophie Taggart
1991   Kathy Barette
1992   Pamela Costilow-Sebok
1993   Betsy Bates
1994   Gayle Schroeder
1995   Donna Karr
1996   Cathy Boulé
1997   Cathy Boulé

1998   Muriel Brewer
1999   Nancy Jason

AAU/WBFA MASTERS MS. AMERICA

2004   Lanna King

AAU JUNIOR MASTERS MS. AMERICA

1990   Charlotte Dimirack

AAU COUPLES AMERICA

1982   Tina Plakinger/Phil Dempskey
1983   Carrie Zupancic/Michael McKinley
1984   Katherine Thomason/
       Anthony Cusack
1985   Pamela Forte/Bruce Quinn
1986   Tammy Baltz/Brian Silk
1987   Karen Fratello/Derrick Mackie
1988   Maria Lopez/Rich Cunha
1989   Amber Bandy/Steve Bandy
1990   Terri LoCicero/Robert Harrop
1991   Wendy Lioce/Peter Lareau

AAU COUPLES JUNIOR AMERICA

1990   Molly Greathouse/
       Kevin Greathouse

IFBB MR. AMERICA

1949   Alan Stephan
1950   Jimmy Payne
1959   Chuck Sipes
1960   Gene Shuey
1962   Larry Scott
1963   Reg Lewis
1964   Harold Poole
1965   Dave Draper
1966   Chester Yorton
1967   Don Howorth
1968   Frank Zane

1969 John DeCola
1970 Mike Katz
1971 Ken Waller
1972 Ed Corney
1973 Lou Ferrigno
1974 Bob Birdsong
1975 Robby Robinson
1976 Mike Mentzer
1977 Dan Padilla

IFBB MISS AMERICANA

1963 Sheri Lewis
1967 Christine Harris
1976 Marilyn Person

UNAFFILIATED PROFESSIONAL MR. AMERICA

1947 Clarence Ross
1948 Floyd Page
1949 Armand Tanny
1951 John Farbotnik
1954 Elias Rodriquez

WBBG PROFESSIONAL MR. AMERICA

1967 Harold Poole
1968 Harold Poole
1969 Johnny Maldonado
1970 Rick Wayne
1971 Peter Caputo
1972 Bill Grant
1973 Chris Dickerson
1974 Warren Fredericks
1975 Ralph Kroger
1976 Scott Wilson
1977 Don Ross
1978 Anibal Lopez
1979 Tommy Aybar

WBBG TEENAGE MR. AMERICA

1970 Carl Greenridge

1971 Lou Ferrigno
1972 Ernesto Jiminez
1973 Dominick Meno
1974 Bob Jodkiewicz
1975 Rafet Kolenovic
1976 Scott Doring
1977 Daniel Morrow
1979 Mike Saddler

WBBG PROFESSIONAL MR. AMERICA OVER 40

1974 Elmo Santiago
1975 Bill Howard
1976 Ken Hall
1977 George Paine

WBBG PROFESSIONAL MR. AMERICA OVER 50

1977 Andrew Bostinto
1979 Ken Hall

WBBG PROFESSIONAL MR. AMERICA OVER 60

1975 Walter Podolak

YMCA MR. AMERICA

1968 Ken Waller

NBA NATURAL MR. AMERICA

1978 Tyrone Youngs (amateur)
      Dennis Tinerino (professional)
1979 Ron Mangum (amateur)
      Tyrone Youngs (professional)
1980 Charles Buser (amateur)
      Rod Koontz (professional)
1981 Eddie Love

NBA NATURAL
MR. TEENAGE AMERICA

1979   Doug Brignole
1980   Kevin McCord
1981   Weldon Baptiste

NBA OVER 40 NATURAL
MR. AMERICA

1979   Jerry Engelbert
1980   David Updyke
1981   Arthur Peacock
1982   Robert McGinty

NBA NATURAL MS. AMERICA

1980   Kathleen Cosentino
1981   Heidi Miller

NBBA NATURAL MR. AMERICA

1981   Bob Gallucci
1982   Mike Ashley

NBBA TEENAGE NATURAL
MR. AMERICA

1981   Bo Narolsky
1982   Lance Scurvin

NBBA NATURAL
MR. AMERICA OVER 40

1981   Jim Karas
1982   Reg Lewis

NBBA NATURAL
MISS AMERICA

1981   Darci Dmitrenko
1982   Debbie Bouchard

GNC NATURAL MR. AMERICA

1982   Greg Tefft

GNC NATURAL MS. AMERICA

1982   Terri Rouviere
1993   Mia Finnegan

PREFACE

1. *Muscular Development* (hereafter *MD*), October 1970, 7; B. Hoffman, *Strength and Development*.

2. Webster, *Barbells + Beefcake*.

3. Dutton, *Perfectible Body*; Klein, *Little Big Men*; Chapman, *Sandow the Magnificent*; Moore, *Building Bodies*; Fair, *Muscletown USA*.

4. Heywood, *Bodymakers*; Lowe, *Women of Steel*; Todd, *Physical Culture*.

5. Wayne, *Muscle Wars*; Fussell, *Muscle*; Minichiello, *Bodybuilders, Drugs, and Sex*; Paris, *Gorilla Suit*; Draper, *Brother Iron, Sister Steel*; Arnoldi, *Chemical Pink*; Hotten, *Muscle*; Kristin Kaye, *Iron Maidens*; Weider and Weider, *Brothers of Iron*; Lurie, *Heart of Steel*; Valentino and Jendrick, *Death, Drugs, and Muscle*.

6. Nussbaum, "Bodies That Matter," 54.

7. LaVelle, *Bodybuilding*; Tan and Brignole, *Million Dollar Muscle*.

8. Roach, *Muscle, Smoke, and Mirrors*.

9. M. Adams, *Mr. America*.

10. See Hunt, *Body Love*, and Ernst, *Weakness Is a Crime*.

INTRODUCTION

1. Bright and Geyer, "Where in the World Is America?," 64. Lawrence Samuel adds that "the American Dream," along with "Mom, apple pie, and Chevrolet," is "the purest, boldest expression of who we are as a people" (Samuel, *American Dream*, 4).

2. Tosh, *Pursuit of History*, 266.

3. Manchester, *The Glory and the Dream*, 1134–1135.

4. Toynbee, "History," 289; Dutton, *Perfectible Body*, 28–29, 16. Dutton further asserts that "the display of the muscular body as a metaphor of perfection is limited to post-Renaissance western society." James Elkins, however, contends that the twentieth century featured a breakdown in the traditional dichotomy of bodily representation in Western art (exterior) and

science (interior). In contemporary interpretations, "the inside *is* the outside" (Elkins, "What Is the Difference?," 16.

5. Dickinson, *Greek View of Life*, 144, 142, 168.

6. Livingstone, *Greek Genius*, 29–30, 32.

7. Ibid., 30, 125, 127, 128.

8. Gardner, "Lamps of Greek Art," 357, 391–392; Boardman, *Greek Art*, 158–159; Walters, *Nude Male*, 35–36.

9. E. M. Butler, *Tyranny of Greece over Germany*, 6. Frank Turner concurs: "Greek antiquity first assumed major intellectual significance in Germany. There, from approximately 1750 on, poets, literary critics, and historians of art looked to ancient Greece as an imaginative landscape on which they might discover artistic patterns, ethical values, and concepts of human nature that could displace those of Christianity and ossified French classicism" (Turner, *Greek Heritage in Victorian Britain*, 2).

10. Winckelmann, *Imitation of Greek Works*, 5.

11. Ueberhorst, *Friedrich Ludwig Jahn*, 21, 51.

12. Herder, according to E. M. Butler, after visiting Rome, regarded the Greek gods "as the highest types of humanity at its most divine" (*Tyranny of Greece over Germany*, 79).

13. See Hofmann, *American Turner Movement*, and Geldbach, "German Gymnastics in America."

14. Dutton, *Perfectible Body*, 203.

15. Beecher, *Physiology and Calisthenics*, 9; and Green, *Fit for America*, 96.

16. Like Winckelmann, Sandow was awakened to the Greeks by a visit to Italy: "I went to Italy, and there my eyes were opened. The Greek and Roman statues I saw there inspired me with envy and admiration. I became morally and mentally awakened" (*Sandow's Magazine*, January 1902, 56–58).

17. Budd, *Sculpture Machine*, 65. Maria Wyke concurs: "The rhetoric of classicism imbued the practices of bodybuilding in the 1890s and presented the cultivation of male musculature as a high and improving art at which all men should aim" (Wyke, "Herculean Muscle!," 55).

18. See Martindale and Hopkins, *Horace Made New*; Sachs, *Roman Antiquity*; Squire, *Art of the Body*; Simon Goldhill, *Victorian Culture and Classical Antiquity*; Sachs's review of Goldhill's book, *Times Literary Supplement*, February 10, 2012, 8.

19. Green, *Fit for America*, 222; Will, "Nervous Systems," 86. See also Donald Meyer, "The Discovery of the 'Nervous American,'" in *The Positive Thinkers*, 21–31.

20. Kimmel, *Manhood in America*, 120.

21. Kimmel, "Consuming Manhood," 22, 26.

22. Pope, Phillips, and Olivardia, *Adonis Complex*, 50.

23. Banner, *American Beauty*, vii.

24. Mosse, *Image of Man*, 53.

25. See Webster, *Barbells + Beefcake*; Radley, *Illustrated History of Physical Culture*; Wayne, *Muscle Wars*.

26. Bivans, *Miss America*; Riverol, *Live from Atlantic City*; Deford, *There She Is*; Banner, *American Beauty*. Also see Osborne, *Miss America*; Martin, *Miss America through the Looking Glass*; Pang, "Miss America: An American Ideal"; Watson and Martin, "The Miss America Pageant." For a broad view of beauty pageantry, see Savage, *Beauty Queens*, and Lovegrove, *Pageant*.

27. Banet-Weiser, *Most Beautiful Girl in the World*, 65, 67–68.

28. Wayne, *Muscle Wars*, 4.

29. For a broader view of the body from a photographic perspective, see Ewing, *The Body*.

30. Hupperts, "Homosexuality in Greece and Rome," 33. A slightly nuanced perspective is provided by Stephen Miller: "Profligate homosexuality was scorned and condemned. Hence, when the people of Verroia included homosexuals in the list of people banned from the gymnasion, they were forbidding perverts and prostitutes, not men who would create a caring homosexual relationship that included the erotic." Thus "homosexuality among the students in the gymnasion was . . . accepted, common, and regulated by tacit rules of conduct" (Miller, *Ancient Greek Athletics*, 193). For another aspect of Greek perceptions of the male body, see David Halperin, "The Democratic Body."

31. Dutton, *Perfectible Body*, 45, 251. Bryan Turner, taking a Foucauldian approach, views homosexuality as embedded in the power structure of ancient Greece, where "moral virtue was closely associated with the lives and values of free rational men who regulated the public sphere to the political exclusion of women, young men and slaves. . . . This pattern of relations formed the basis of homosexuality in classical Greek civilization as a norm of desirable practice between men (Turner, *Body and Society*, 11).

32. Dutton, *Perfectible Body*, 45, 251; Thomas Waugh, "Antecedents: The Physical Culture Movement of the Fin-de-Siecle," unpublished paper cited in Budd, *Sculpture Machine*, 152.

33. See Hall and Fair, "Pioneers in Protein." For a comprehensive view of the connection between nutrition and bodybuilding, see Roach, *Muscle, Smoke, and Mirrors*, vol. 1.

34. Kochakian, *How It Was*.

35. For the origins of steroid use, see Fair, "Olympic Weightlifting and Steroids," "Isometrics or Steroids?," and *Muscletown USA*, chap. 7.

36. Holt, *Sport and the British*, 100.

37. Brailsford, *British Sport*, 97–98. For other perspectives on British sporting traditions, see Wigglesworth, *Evolution of English Sport*, 85–107; Vamplew, *Pay Up and Play the Game*, 183–203; Lowerson, *Sport and the English Middle Classes*, 154–190; Birley, *Playing the Game*; MacAloon, *This Great Symbol*, 43–112; Roberts and Olson, *Winning Is the Only Thing*, 2–11.

38. Quoted in *Health and Strength*, April 19, 1962, 10.

39. Quoted in *Weightlifter and Bodybuilder*, July 1951, 14.

40. Kazin and McCartin, *Americanism*, 10–11.

41. Elliott, "Missing History," 699; Radway, "What's in a Name?," 16–17.

42. Bernal, *Cadmean Letters*, 7, and "British Utilitarians," 98; see also Bernal, *Black Athena*. Richard Jenkyns holds a similar view of the Germans in discussing the origins of Hellenism: "Like the English, they enjoyed speaking of Hellas in religious language, but in the manner less of pilgrims than of visionaries. Neither Winckelmann nor Lessing nor Goethe ever saw Greece for himself; and to the German mind Hellas became a sort of heavenly city, a shimmering fantasy on the far horizon" (Jenkyns, *Victorians and Ancient Greece*, 13).

43. F. M. Turner, *Greek Heritage in Victorian Britain*, 5, 40.

44. See Berlinerblau, *Heresy in the University*.

45. Ronald Reagan, "Remarks at the Annual Convention of the National Religious Broadcasters," January 31, 1983, http://www.reagan.utexas.edu/archives/speeches/1983/13183b.htm.

CHAPTER 1: THE GREEK IDEAL

1. Pierre de Coubertin was inspired by the young men, *ephebes*, who frequented the gymnasia of the ancient Greek city-states; see Finley and Pleket, *Olympic Games*, 1–2.

2. Guttman, *From Ritual to Record*, 20–21.

3. Dombrowski, *Contemporary Athletics and Ancient Greek Ideals*, 1–2, 20, 24.

4. Bowra, *Greek Experience*, 105–107. See also Nigel Crowther's discussion of the gymnasia and its relation to athletics in *Sport in Ancient Times*, 74–75.

5. Dutton, *Perfectible Body*, 25.

6. *New York Herald*, undated clipping in New York Public Library, c. 1902; cited in Chapman, *Sandow the Magnificent*, 139.

7. Although Ziegfeld allegedly "exploited Sandow to the limit," the famous strongman earned "an unbelievable $3,000 a week," according to Marjorie Farnsworth (*Ziegfeld Follies*, 15–16).

8. Dutton, *Perfectible Body*, 119. Allusions to the classical motifs of ancient Greece and Rome permeate Ellery Foutch's depiction of Sandow's body in her comparative study of perfectionism in the nineteenth century; see Foutch, "Arresting Beauty."

9. Webster, *Barbells + Beefcake*, 36–37.

10. *Physical Culture* (hereafter *PC*), July 1898, 80.

11. Webster, *Barbells + Beefcake*, 37.

12. Chapman, *Sandow the Magnificent*, 134.

13. In Sandow's interpretation of "the Greek 'golden mean,'" argues Budd, "the moral strictures of [Victorian] religion and mortification of the flesh were to be replaced by the physical regimen of exercise and the body's liberation." By making this "substitution of secular discipline for spiritual, he argued for the interconnectedness of body, mind and soul" (*Sculpture Machine*, 13, 67).

14. Ernst, *Weakness Is a Crime*, 214.

15. Hunt, *Body Love*, 10.

16. Webster, *Barbells + Beefcake*, 25; Chapman, *Sandow the Magnificent*, 109–110.

17. *PC*, June 1903, 537, 557.

18. Ibid., August 1903, 113.

19. Ibid., September 1903, 255.

20. Ibid., November 1903, 479.

21. Webster, *Barbells + Beefcake*, 42, 43.

22. Quoted in *PC*, March 1904, 187–189.

23. Webster, *Barbells + Beefcake*, 42; Coffin quoted in *Muscle Power* (hereafter *MP*), February 1948, 9. Likewise, David Willoughby refers to Treloar as the first Mr. America in his article "America's First Physique Contest," *Muscle Digest*, June 1980, 76.

24. Todd, "Bernarr Macfadden," 71–72.

25. *PC*, June 1905, 465–466.

26. *PC*, February 1906, 162, 164.

27. See Ernst, *Weakness Is a Crime*, 47–50; Hunt, *Body Love*, 42–44; *PC*, February 1910, 130–136.

28. Oursler, *Bernarr Macfadden*, 195.

29. *PC*, April 1908, 269.

30. Oursler recalled the purity of Macfadden's motives: "He who nearly went to jail on several occasions for offending the prudish would sicken at a foul story and shrink from an even a moderately naughty one" (Oursler, *Behold The Dreamer!*, 168).

31. *PC*, January 1909, 27.

32. Ibid., September 1911, 259–260.

33. Ibid., April 1914, 339–347.

34. Ibid., 27a; Webster, *Barbells + Beefcake*, 61–62.

35. *PC*, July 1914, 37–41; *PC*, October 1915, 14.

36. Blaikie, *How to Get Strong*; Webster, *Barbells + Beefcake*, 54.

37. *Strength*, May 1916, 3–4.

38. Ibid., July 1916, 3.

39. *PC*, May 1915, 58a.

40. Ibid., 427.

41. Ibid., April 1915, 319.

42. Ibid., 318–327, 22a.

43. Ibid., 369; September 1915, 7.

44. Ibid., June 1917, 39–42.

45. Ibid., September 1917, 7–8.

46. Ibid., April 1921, 56.

47. Butler and Gaines, *Yours in Perfect Manhood*, 57–59.

48. *Iron Man* (hereafter *IM*), September 1972, 23.

49. *PC*, October 1921, 22.

50. Ibid., November 1921, 38–39.

51. Ibid., December 1921, 38–39. According to John Barrs, a British Olympic coach in 1948, Atlas's former business partner Fred Tilney told him that "he had seen Atlas train regularly with weights" (Barrs to Hoffman, October 10, 1960, Bob Hoffman Papers [in author's possession]). Likewise, Vic Boff, who spent most of his career in New York and knew Atlas, confirms that Atlas used weights (Vic Boff, interview by the author, November 10, 1995, Fort Myers, Florida).

52. *PC*, June 1922, 51. Atlas's inspiration from the Greeks eventually became part of his legendary pitch: "My life was a misery until the day I walked into the Brooklyn Museum and saw the classical Greek statues, famous gods of strength and grace, like Hercules and Apollo" (*Health and Strength*, May 21, 1959, 17).

53. *PC*, January 1922, 18.

54. Deford, *There She Is*, 61.

55. *Atlantic City Press*, September 9, 1921.

56. Quoted in Bivans, *Miss America*, 10.

57. *IM*, September 1972, 22–23.

58. *PC*, January 1923, 37; October 1922, 66.

59. Liederman to Coulter, February 25, 1968, Coulter Papers, Stark Center, University of Texas.

60. *PC*, January 1923, 35; *Saturday Evening Post*, February 7, 1942.

61. *PC*, May 1915, 429.

CHAPTER 2: THE ATHLETIC BODY

1. Durant and Bettmann, *Pictorial History of American Sports*, 150.

2. W. Baker, *Sports in the Western World*, 215; Mrozek, "Sport in American Life," 25.

3. See Fair, "Jowett, Coulter, Willoughby."

4. Guttmann, *Olympics*, 37–52.

5. See Schodl, *Lost Past*, 42–47, 74–76.

6. See *Your Physique* (hereafter *YP*), October 1949, 32, and *Health and Life*, June 1924, 236.

7. Fair, "Father-Figure or Phony?" and "From Philadelphia to York."

8. *Strength*, January 1921, 4–5, 20–22, 24–25, 28–34, 26.

9. Ibid., March 1921, 18; September 1921, 44.

10. Ibid., July 1922, 20.

11. Ibid., October 1922, 31–32, 36.

12. *PC*, August 1923, 69.

13. Webster, *Barbells + Beefcake*, 67–68.

14. *Strength*, December 1922, 7; Butler and Gaines, *Yours in Perfect Manhood*, 59–63.

15. According to Fred Howell, Tilney ran their mail-order business from his home (which served as the "Temple of Health") until they moved it to Fifth Avenue in New York City: "Doc wrote the course, did all the ads, folders, catalogs, sales letters and managed the business for years" (*MuscleMag International* [hereafter *MMI*], Winter 1977, 95).

16. See "Muscle Pedlars," in Webster, *Barbells + Beefcake*, 59–64. It is very likely that Atlas (and Tilney) borrowed his book title and concept of dynamic tension from an earlier work by Bernarr Macfadden. In a chapter on developing shoulder muscles, for instance, the latter advises that the "antagonistic muscles are made to resist the efforts of the muscles that you are exercising"; see Macfadden, *Muscular Power and Beauty*, 53, and Atlas, *Secrets of Muscular Power and Beauty*.

17. *Strength*, December 1923, 68–69.

18. *PC*, January 1924, 19, 76–77.

19. *IM*, July, 1987, 30; Webster, *Barbells + Beefcake*, 81. See also Massey, *American Adonis*.

20. *PC*, December 1924, 90–91.

21. *Strength*, December 1924, 51.

22. Ibid., July 1925, 31; October 1927, 37. See also Jowett, *Key to Might and Muscle*, 7–9.

23. Fair, "Georgia," 26.

24. *Strength*, April 1926, 58; February 1925, 19; April 1925, 19; June 1925, 27.

25. Jowett to Ottley Coulter, February 10, 1927, Coulter Papers.

26. *Strength*, February 1924, 62–69; April 1924, 64; June 1924, 39.

27. Ibid., October 1924, 54–57; January 1926, 30–32.

28. MacMahon, however, was not out of touch with the spirit of his times. He encouraged trainees to seek "general results," adding, "I do not think a man should train just for strength, or just for shape, or just for health. He should train for all three." With all-around development, he would "be fitted for every kind of athletics" (MacMahon, *Health, Strength, and Muscular Efficiency*, 14).

29. *Strength*, April 1926, 32–35, 65; June 1926, 28–29; November 1926, 35; January 1927, 70.

30. Ibid., January 1927, 31; February 1925, 20–21.

31. Ibid., February 1926, 47.

32. See two articles from *Strength*: "Do Stage Beauties Exercise?," featuring women from "Gay Paree," the "Ziegfeld Follies," "Aloma of the South Seas," and "Chicago Artists and Models" (February 1926, 20–23), and "State Girls and Artists' Models and Posing" (November 1926, 22–25), which draws on unretouched material from Allen, *Alo Studies*, a nudist art book.

33. Quoted in Osborne, *Miss America*, 76.

34. *PC*, July 1928, 30–31, 105; June 1929, 71.

35. Ibid., July 1929, 52, 125.

36. Ibid., December 1929, 52–55, 102–103; the long quotation is on 53.

37. Ibid., 104.

38. Ibid., May 1930, 43; October 1932, 28; September 1930, 40; March 1938, 30.

39. *Strength*, October 1927, 21; July 1927, 52; April 1928, 51–53; June 1928, 49; August 1929, 53–55.

40. Ibid., August 1929, 54.

41. Ibid., September 1928, 26.

42. Ibid., 83–84.

43. Ibid., August 1928, 27.

44. Ibid., October 1929, 30.

45. Ibid., October 1928, 30, 23; January 1930, 7.

46. *PC*, September 1929, 50.

47. *Strength*, October 1929, 53.

48. Jowett to Coulter, April 17, 1931, Coulter Papers.

49. John L. Hoffman, interview by the author, Parker, Pennsylvania, January 1, 1988.

50. Hoffman, *Weight Lifting*, 37–38.

51. Fair, "From Philadelphia to York," 11–12.

52. *Strength & Health* (hereafter *SH*), December 1932, 1.

53. Ibid., December 1934, 10–11; January 1934, 10–11.

54. Hoffman, *Strength and Development*, 208–210.

55. *SH*, July 1935, 65–69; *SH*, August 1935, 62–63, 84–85; Jowett to Coulter, October 5, 1935, Coulter Papers.

56. Fair, "From Philadelphia to York," 14–15. Berry's daughter "always felt that he was heartbroken that things turned out the way they did" and claimed that Hoffman "did my father dirty" (Frances Gajkowski, interview by the author, Akron, Ohio, March 3, 2010).

57. Hoffman, *Weight Lifting*, 49, 3.

58. *SH*, August 1934, 15.

59. Ibid., September 1933, 20; November 1933, 22.

60. Ibid., August 1935, 86–87; June 1937, 28–29, 44.

61. See Edwards, "Racially Superior Athlete"; Tom Brokaw, "Black Athletes: Fact and Fiction," *NBC Evening News*, April 25, 1989, http://tvnews.vanderbilt.edu/program.pl?ID=568142; Herrnstein and Murray, *Bell Curve*; Hoberman, *Darwin's Athletes*; Entine, *Taboo*.

62. John Grimek, interview by the author, York, Pennsylvania, August 28, 1987.

63. *Arena and Strength*, August 1934, 13–16; February 1935, 33.

64. *SH*, July 1934, 27.

65. Grimek interview; *SH*, August 1936, 30; *SH*, September 1936, 30.

66. *SH*, October 1939, 5, 9.

67. Ibid., August 1935, 73; June 1936, 49.

68. *Atlantic City Press*, September 6, 1935.

69. See "Showman's Variety Jubilee," "The Great American Beauty Event," "Showmen's Show of Shows," and "Girls! Girls! Girls!," in "Miss America 20's–40's" file, Atlantic City Public Library.

70. *Atlantic City Evening Union*, September 5, 1935.

71. Osborne, *Miss America*, 86; *Atlantic City Press*, September 3, 1935.

72. Quoted in Bivans, *Miss America*, 14.

73. Osborne, *Miss America*, 86.

74. *Atlantic City Press*, September 9, 1936.

75. Osborne, *Miss America*, 86.

76. Bivans, *Miss America*, 14–16.

77. *SH*, November 1936, 49; February 1938, 26.

78. Ibid., November 1946, 26.

CHAPTER 3: THE FIRST MR. AMERICA CONTESTS

1. See the listing "AAU Mr. America Winners" in three publications: a special issue of *Muscle Training Illustrated* (hereafter *MTI*), Summer 1980, 16, 30; *Musclesearch*, August–September 1985, 2; *Musclesearch*, April–May 1988, 3–5.

2. John Hordines, interview by the author, East Branch, New York, June 22, 2003; Eliason, "All-American Johnny Hordines."

3. *Atlantic City Press*, n.d., clipping in the Hordines Papers, in author's possession.

4. John Hordines, telephone interview by the author, October 13, 2003; clipping from Hordines Papers.

5. *Body Builder Magazine*, January 1948, 6; *SH*, February 1939, 43–44.

6. *SH*, February 1939, 32–33, 42–44; March 1939, 31, 40–41.

7. Undated clipping [April 1939], *New Haven Register*, Eliason Papers.

8. Interview with Alton Eliason, Northford, Connecticut, June 24, 2003; Eliason to the author, March 19, 2008.

9. *SH*, July 1939, 39–40.

10. Osmo Kiiha clearly identifies Hordines's event as a "Mr. America" contest, thereby laying to rest other claims of precedence; see the *Iron Master*, January 1996, 7.

11. *Evening Recorder*, Amsterdam, June 10, 1939.

12. Hordines interview, June 22, 2003; publicity poster, in author's possession.

13. Publicity poster; clipping, n.d., Hordines Papers; *SH*, August 1939, 28.

14. *SH*, August 1939, 45–47, 28.

15. Joe Peters, interview by the author, Schenectady, New York, June 26, 2001. See also Thomas, "Police Chief Joe Peters."

16. *SH*, August 1939, 28; October 1939, 36; January 1940, 30–31.

17. *Iron Master*, January 1996, 5.

18. According to a later yarn spun by Liederman, Tony Terlazzo received the most points and was declared Mr. America in 1939, but the judges took a second vote because of his height (*MP*, July 1953, 72).

19. Hordines interview, June 22, 2003.

20. *SH*, July 1940, 48.

21. Ibid., August 1940, 8. It was somewhat a matter of mutual admiration for Klein, since Grimek, who first saw Klein in 1929–1930, was in awe of him and wanted to train at his gym (John Grimek, interview by the author, York, Pennsylvania, July 19, 1991).

22. *SH*, July 1940, 48.

23. Ibid., August 1940, 8.

24. Ibid., July 1940, 48.

25. Clipping from *Pic*, August 20, 1940; Howlett to Hoffman, August 18, 1940, Hoffman Papers.

26. *SH*, July 1947, 2.

27. Ibid., July 1940, 48.

28. Eliason interview; *Hardgainer*, March–April 1999, 1. In a 1993 interview, Grimek confirmed that he "only got into bodybuilding because [he] wanted to get a little heavier and stronger," adding, "That was it" (*Flex*, July 1993, 133).

29. *SH*, July 1941, 27; January 1942, 15.

30. Tommy O'Hare, interview by the author, Chalmette, Louisiana, July 13, 2002.

31. *SH*, July 1941, 26, 29.

32. Ibid., January 1942, 15.

33. Klein to John Terpak, December 18, 1941, Hoffman Papers.

34. Ibid.; Klein to Terpak, December 23, 1941, Hoffman Papers.

35. Tetrault to Hoffman, January 21, 1942, and "Hail America Program," both in Hoffman Papers.

36. Alton Eliason, interview by the author, Northford, Connecticut, November 13, 2003.

37. *SH*, August 1942, 15.

38. Ibid., July 1942, 47–48. Jules Bacon remembers Davis as a "fine man" who was "treated well" during his stay in York, noting, "Bob supported Davis" (Jules Bacon, interview by the author, York, Pennsylvania, August 30, 1988). On the other hand, after failing to make the 1955 world-championship team near the end of his career, Davis confided to Jim Murray: "I realize now . . . that it was a question of discrimination, among other things, where Bob and I were concerned" (Davis to Murray, December 21, 1955, Murray Papers, Morrisville, Pennsylvania). It is noteworthy, however, that Bob chose Jim Bradford, another African American from Washington, D.C., whose lifts approximated those of Davis, and Paul Anderson, whose lifts far exceeded either man's, as heavyweight representatives on the American team.

39. *SH*, September 1943, 18, 46–47; Hoffman to Matlin, February 9, 1945, Hoffman Papers.

40. *SH*, June 1944, 10.

41. *Mr. America* (hereafter *MA*), December 1961, 62. Dan Lurie adds that Stanko was not able to mount the platform to the boxing ring where the contest was held: "The lights went out, and he had to be carried on. He posed. The lights went out, and he was carried off" (Dan Lurie, interview by the author, Valley Stream, New York, December 16, 2003).

42. *SH*, June 1944, 10. Contrary to popular perceptions of Lurie, he expresses "no regrets" about not winning the Mr. America Contest: "There's much more to life than that—a wonderful wife, family, and home, and grandchildren. When you look at it, it's all bullshit" (Lurie interview).

43. *SH*, July 1944, 17, 40; June 1944, 15.

44. *YP*, November 1943, 21; October 1944, 13. Later in life, Weaver recollected that the Mr. Americas before 1944 "harmonized very well with the Willoughby standard of ideal proportions" published in 1933. "But after that, the deluge!" (Weaver, *Enrichment of Life*, 106). See also Willoughby, *Truth about Physical Training*, 14–17.

45. *SH*, August 1945, 17; Hoffman to Matlin, February 9, 1945.

46. *YP*, October 1945, 10; December 1945, 15. According to Grimek, Weider derived the title *Your Physique* from Mark Berry's book *Your Physique and Its Culture*. He also claimed that York Barbell "paid for it [the magazine] by taking out Ads." Grimek added that York Barbell even supported *YP*'s continuation after it ran into problems early on: "When we had so much trouble with customs into Canada, Bob wanted to give it up, and it was then the 'mighty-Joe' wrote Bob a long crying letter asking him not to cut his water but continue to carry Ads in his 30-page magazine . . . and Bob, the sucker he is at times, continued in spite of the fact that it did nothing for us but make more work" (Grimek to David Gentle, October 7, 1983, Gentle Papers, Romsey, UK).

47. *YP*, December 1945, 23; Ross to Terpak, August 20, 1945, Hoffman Papers; *SH*, October 1945, 14; *SH*, June 1946, 12–13; Lurie, *Heart of Steel*, 82–83.

48. Grimek interview, 1991; *SH*, November 1948, 26.

49. Weider and Weider, *Brothers of Iron*, 88.

50. Ibid. Lurie later admitted that the challenge was his own idea, and he "told Grimek that [they] could make money out of this challenge" (Lurie interview).

51. Roach, *Muscle, Smoke, and Mirrors*, 154; Grimek interview, 1991.

52. *YP*, August 1946, 13–14.

53. *SH*, March 1946, 5.

54. "What better," mused Slaughter, "than to have the ideal men of America run a pageant for the ideal women?" (quoted in Deford, *There She Is*, 154). No less critical in boosting the credibility of Miss America was the country's involvement in World War II, which forced women to play a more functional role in society (Savage, *Beauty Queens*, 83).

55. Bartel and Slaughter quoted in Bivans, *Miss America*, 13. Initially, New York mayor Fiorello LaGuardia, unaware of the Miss America reforms, wondered what Myerson was doing in such a disreputable affair, as she noted in her diary: "He asked me if the pageant was merely another fanny-shaking contest where I'd have to compete with a lot of empty headed females who show their legs. Made me promise I'd stick to my music and write and tell him what school I was going to attend" (quoted in Dworkin, *Miss America, 1945*, 77).

56. By way of contrast, Abbye "Pudgy" Stockton, often dubbed the "first female bodybuilder" and the nearest equivalent to Miss America, received only $1,000 for winning Bernarr Macfadden's Physical Culture Venus title in 1948, yet seemed delighted, wishing she could "receive checks like that every day" (Stockton to John Grimek, Stockton Papers, Stark Center, box 6, folder 20).

57. Osborne, *Miss America*, 158.

58. According to Henry Atkin, Stephan's poster pose featured him loading a shell into a gun, calling recruits to "Man the Guns," but "a 'dummy' shell could not be found": "Young Stephan volunteered to hold a real shell, weighing eighty-five pounds, while the artists drew the action. He held the heavy shell in a difficult bent-over position for a half hour at a time without rest" (*Vigour*, June 1947, 163).

59. *IM*, November 1946, 5.

60. Ibid., 37–38; *MP*, January 1947, 28.

61. *SH*, August 1946, 12–14, 21.

62. Ibid., July 1946, 31; September 1946, 17.

63. Whitfield to Terpak, November 21, 1946, Hoffman Papers. "Not tall but not small" was Smith's self-description. The southern strongman Bill Curry called Smith "one of the hardest workers I've ever met" (Harry Smith, interview by the author, Tampa, Florida, May 18, 2000); *St. Petersburg Times*, January 3, 1997.

64. *MP*, December 1947, 26. A postcontest interview with *Life* magazine twisted this idealistic image to fit existing stereotypes of bodybuilders. Steve's explanation that he next planned to attend college was altered to read: "When my muscles stop expanding in a couple of years, I will start expanding my brain." Steve and gym owners resented this misquotation, which made bodybuilders sound like muscle heads without brains; see LeClaire, *Steve Reeves*, 83.

65. *Steve Reeves International Society Newsletter*, 2 (July 1996): 8.

66. *IM*, October 1947, 7.

67. *YP*, September 1947, 11.

68. *IM*, October 1947, 21–24; *MP*, November 1947, 30. Dick Trusdell, an Illinois promoter for Reeves, was "praying" that his chances of capitalizing on his title went "a lot better than Al's did," since "Al had some great chances set up for him on both Coasts, and yet

somehow he didn't seem able to make them click" (Trusdell to Les Stockton, September 24, 1947, Stockton Papers, box 6, 133).

69. *IM*, 1947, 21, 36.

70. *SH*, July 1947, 23.

71. *YP*, September 1947, 11.

72. Ibid., 22; *SH*, August 1947, 12.

73. *SH*, December 1946, 24, 34; *MP*, November 1947, 19. Although he won the Professional Mr. America title in 1949, Armand Tanny regarded it as "inferior" to the Mr. USA Contest, which he won the next year (Armand Tanny, interview with the author, Canoga Park, California, June 7, 2004).

74. *SH*, October 1947, 17–19; August 1947, 12.

75. Ibid., November 1947, 19, 16; December 1947, 23.

76. Ibid., February 1947, 14, 17.

77. Rose, *Muscle Beach*, 26.

78. Tanny to Terpak, February 18, 1946, Hoffman Papers.

79. *MP*, September 1946, 34–35.

80. Ibid., August 1946, 27–28; November 1946, 14.

81. Quoted in ibid., August 1947, 13.

CHAPTER 4: THE GLORY YEARS

1. Terry Todd, interview by the author, Austin, Texas, February 6, 1993.

2. Tanny to Hoffman, June 29, 1946, Hoffman Papers; Rose, *Muscle Beach*, 37.

3. *MP*, July 1948, 43; January 1948, 17.

4. Stockton to Klein, March 23, 1948, Stockton Papers, box 6, folder 22.

5. *MP*, January 1948, 35; *SH*, May 1948, 8–11, 28; *SH*, May 1949, 24–27; *SH*, April 1948, 24.

6. E. M. Orlick, interview by the author, Brandywine, Maryland, December 14, 1993; Lurie interview; *MP*, June 1948, 16.

7. *YP*, April 1948, 21, 39–40.

8. Gene Jantzen, interview by the author, Bartelso, Illinois, December 28, 2003.

9. Orlick to Jowett, March 27, 1948, Reuben Weaver Papers, Strasburg, Virginia, cited in Roach, *Muscle, Smoke, and Mirrors*, 1:162–63. Orlick contends that he not only organized the IFBB but also was its first president (Orlick interview).

10. Lurie, *Heart of Steel*, 66–67; Roach, *Muscle, Smoke, and Mirrors*, 1:162.

11. *MP*, June 1948, 14; *YP*, February 1948, 24–25.

12. Weider and Weider, *Brothers of Iron*, 70.

13. See, for example, *Flex*, October 1986, 84, and *Muscle & Fitness* (hereafter *MF*), July 1999, 220.

14. *SH*, February 1947, 47; Smith to Dennis Weis, July 26, 1987, Weis Papers, http://www.dennisbweis.com/letters/letters.pdf.

15. *YP*, May 1948, 26–27, 30–32.

16. *SH*, February 1948, 11, 47–48.

17. *IM*, January 1949, 28; September 1949, 12, August 1950, 30.

18. *MP*, May 1948, 16–17, 38.

19. *YP*, August 1948, 39; November 1948, 16.

20. Ibid., February 1949, 10, 18, 36; August 1949, 10, 38.

21. *IM*, July 1948, 8; Jim Murray, interview by the author, Morrisville, Pennsylvania, December 15, 2003.

22. *SH*, June–July 1949, 12–13, 47–48; *IM*, July 1949, 38; *SH*, August 1948, 13.

23. See *SH*, December 1947, 30; *SH*, February 1949, 32; LeClaire, *Steve Reeves*, 66–67.

24. *IM*, March 1949, 5.

25. Paschall, *Muscle Moulding*, 31–32.

26. *SH*, January 1948, 13; June–July 1948, 13.

27. *YP*, August 1948, 12.

28. Ibid., 30, 32.

29. *IM*, March 1949, 5.

30. Ibid., May 1950, 5; September 1949, 5, 34.

31. Jimmy Payne, interview by the author, June 6, 2004; *YP*, October 1948, 44.

32. Payne interview.

33. *Healdsburg Tribune*, February 18 and 19, 2004; see the *Santa Rosa Press Democrat*, March 20, 2011, for an update.

34. Payne interview. Photographs of Payne with the winner (Floyd Page) and the runner-up (Norman Marks) in the 1948 contest appear in *Body Moderne*, January 1949, 41; photographs of Payne with the winner (Armand Tanny) and the runner-up (Bob McCune) in the 1949 contest appear in *YP*, March 1950, 13.

35. *MP*, February 1950, 47.

36. Payne interview; Payne, conversation with the author, March 24, 2011.

37. *MP*, July 1950, 5, 23.

38. Ibid., April 1950, 28; June 1950, 26–27.

39. Weider to the author, May 8, 2008 (in author's possession).

40. *YP*, October 1948, 45.

41. *Muscle Builder* (hereafter *MB*), July 1962, 9, 49.

42. Payne interview; *Junior Mr. & Miss America Club Exercise Booklet* (in Payne scrapbook). "LaLanne was smarter," Payne admits. "He hit the women's market. I did kids." Yet he has no regrets.

43. See *MB*, March 1966, 70–77, and *MTI*, Summer 1980 (special edition), 5. According to Ben Weider, "Tony is very precise and has all of the information about the IFBB since its inception (Weider to the author and Blinn to the author, May 5, 2008; in author's possession).

44. *MP*, July 1949, 23.

45. *YP*, January 1950, 16–17.

46. Ibid., 39.

47. Ibid., 14–15; *MP*, January 1950, 5; *MP*, May 1950, 7.

48. *MP*, July 1950, 46.

49. *MP*, October 1950, 43.

50. *YP*, March 1950, 6, 8.

51. *MP*, May 1950, 28; *MP*, December 1949, 23; *IM*, February 1951, 5; *SH*, December 1949, 26.

52. *SH*, August 1949, 19; *YP*, February 1950, 24–25, 34–35.

53. *SH*, March 1950, 15.

54. Orlick interview.

55. *MP*, September 1950, 28–29; Orlick interview. Charles Smith, who worked for Weider for eight years, concurs that he "didn't see ANYTHING initiated by Joe against Hoffman"

(Smith to Joe Roark, July 17, 1985, quoted in *Iron History*, August 16–September 5, 2002, cyberpump.com [donation required]). It seemed to be the other way around.

56. Eiferman to Hoffman, July 3, 1948, Hoffman Papers.

57. *YP*, December 1950, 29–30.

58. *SH*, January 1950, 29.

59. *MP*, November 1950, 11.

60. *SH*, December 1950, 7.

61. Ibid., 18, 47.

62. *YP*, March 1951, 36–37.

63. *SH*, April 1951, 9.

64. *MP*, April 1951, 29; *SH*, July 1951, 9.

65. The first version of *Mr. America*, a continuation of *Your Physique*, ran from August to November 1952. The latter appeared from January 1958 to March 1973.

66. See *MP*, September 1951, 7; *MP*, March 1952, 17; *MB*, May 1954, 13; *MB*, August 1955, 26; *MB*, July 1958, 26.

67. *YP*, April 1952, 5, 44.

68. *MB*, August 1954, 3. Joe even showed respect for Hoffman: "I always understood Hoffman and I admired his tenacity as a businessman, he said what he meant, advertise[d] what he sold, and no matter what he said of he [me], he said it in self-survival. He was forward and honest" (Weider to Rader, March 17, 1953, Rader Papers).

69. *YP*, March 1951, 36; Peters interview. Bob Bendel, who served on the judging panel, thought that Wells "should have won" because he "looked like he had five times as many muscles as Farbotnik," with one exception: "Only his calves seemed wanting" (Bendel, interview by the author, Moorestown, New Jersey, July 10, 2001). Likewise, the physique model and photographer Bob Delmontique thought Wells "had a better body than Farbotnik, but he didn't have calves" (Delmontique, interview by the author, Woodland Hills, California, June 3, 2004).

70. *YP*, March 1949, 38; *YP*, August 1950, 8; *MP*, October 1950, 42–43.

71. *SH*, April 1951, 9.

72. *YP*, August 1951, 43; *MP*, August 1951, 37.

73. *MP*, November 1951, 49; *IM*, October 1951, 17.

74. *IM*, October 1951, 10, 27; *SH*, September 1951, 9.

75. *MP*, October 1951, 40–41; *SH*, December 1951, 30.

76. *SH*, February 1951, 27.

77. Ibid., February 1949, 13.

78. Ibid., 31–32.

79. Ibid.

80. *MP*, August 1950, 5; Ian McQueen, interview by the author, Martinsburg, West Virginia, December 14, 2003.

81. Bivans, *Miss America*, 20–25; *Atlantic City Press*, September 13, 1953.

82. *IM*, August 1952, 12–13, 33.

83. *MA*, November 1952, 26.

84. *MP*, November 1952, 27.

85. *SH*, January 1953, 39, 60–61.

86. Ibid., November 1952, 27.

87. *MP*, December 1952, 65; Murray interview. For Park's view, see *SH*, April 1953, 28.

88. *American Manhood*, December 1952, 15, 59.

89. *MP*, December 1952, 56.

90. *MP*, March 1953, 18–21, 50; Tom Manfre, interview by the author, Land O' Lakes, Florida, June 1, 2010.

91. *SH*, September 1954, 29. Park, however, left York frustrated that he had "won everything there was to win" and that "Bob never promoted physique contests as he should have" (Jim Park, interview by the author, Ripley, West Virginia, December 22, 1990). Otherwise, Weider would not have gained a foothold.

92. *MP*, November 1951, 11; August 1952, 21; September 1952, 37; January 1953, 22.

93. Ibid., June 1951, 50.

94. *SH*, March 1952, 20.

95. *IM*, February 1953, 6–7.

96. *SH*, June 1953, 22.

97. Len Bosland, interview by the author, Glen Rock, New Jersey, January 28, 2004.

98. *SH*, February 1953, 37.

99. Ibid., September 1953, 34, 19.

100. *IM*, August 1953, 19.

101. *MP*, October 1953, 80; Murray interview. Pearl remembers the incident and his ride to the Indianapolis contest in Grimek's 1953 Packard. About halfway there, Grimek surprised him: "He opened up the glove box, and he pulled out two great big Hershey chocolate bars. It must have been two-pound chocolate bars each, and he asked if I wanted a chocolate bar, and I said, 'No, John, I'm competing in the contest.' He said, 'The damn thing's not going to kill you. Eat it.' So here I am . . . eating a two-pound Hershey chocolate bar, trying to compete in the most major physique contest I ever thought I'd enter. Fortunately I won" (Bill Pearl, interview by the author, Phoenix, Oregon, July 30, 2010).

102. *MP*, February 1953, 60.

103. Ibid., June 1953, 80; October 1953, 61.

104. *SH*, October 1954, 46.

105. Ibid., November 1954, 30, 49.

106. *MP*, September 1954, 46, 48, 62.

107. LeClaire, *Steve Reeves*, 158–60; *MP*, November 1954, 63–64.

108. *MP*, January 1955, 65; December 1954, 57–58; September 1954, 62.

109. Ibid., September 1954, 10, 55, 57; December 1954, 58; March 1954, 59; Hoffman to Schusterich, November 18, 1954, Hoffman Papers; *MP*, December 1954, 42.

110. *IM*, September 1954, 42.

111. Ibid., September 1955, 11.

112. *SH*, September 1955, 22.

113. Steve Klisanin, interview by the author, Seal Beach, California, March 18, 2005.

114. *IM*, September 1955, 8, 47.

115. *MP*, June 1955, 60; *MB*, May 1955, 59.

116. Hordines interview, June 22, 2003.

117. *SH*, August 1955, 57.

118. *MB*, May 1955, 32; November 1955, 62.

CHAPTER 5: MULTIPLE MR. AMERICAS

1. Gitlin, *Sixties*, 1, 18.

2. *MP*, May 1956, 57; *IM*, June 1956, 19.

3. *Weightlifting, 1965–1966 Official Rules*, 121–122; *IM*, October 1955, 7.

4. *IM*, April 1956, 46, 25.

5. According to Valentine Hooven, Weider's magazines, following a precedent set by Bob Mizer's controversial *Physique Pictorial*, were the first to offer color photographs and to be printed in a larger format. They were part of a 1950s genre that sought to avoid governmental repression while appealing to gay men "starved for visual stimulation": "Without presenting anything overtly homosexual, each issue was so clearly designed by and for gay men it was obvious to even the youngest and most inexperienced of them" (Hooven, *Beefcake*, 64, 72).

6. *SH*, June 1957, 17, 56. No doubt Paschall's list of "dirty little books" would have included *Tomorrow's Man*, published by Rheo Blair from 1952 to 1971, which included photographs of many leading bodybuilders.

7. Hunter McLean to Hoffman, January 25, 1957, Hoffman Papers. Hoffman lived with a common-law wife and had numerous girlfriends with questionable reputations. For more information, see the full discussion in Fair, *Muscletown USA*.

8. *SH*, June 1956, 26; June 1957, 8–9.

9. *MP*, April 1956, 49–50.

10. *MB*, January 1956, 9, 64; March 1956, 11.

11. *IM*, May 1956, 47; September 1956, 22–25.

12. Ibid., September 1956, 52–53; Bill Colonna, interview by the author, Chesapeake, Virginia, August 2, 2005.

13. Klisanin's victory and the controversy apparently had little impact on him. His sister-in-law commented that she "never heard him brag to anybody about being a Mr. America or Mr. Universe" (Joan Klisanin, interview by the author, Long Beach, California, October 9, 2005).

14. *MB*, October 1956, 22–25, 46; Hoffman's remarks to the newspaper were quoted in the magazine.

15. *SH*, October 1956, 28.

16. Ibid., June 1957, 10. After coaching lifting teams in Iran and Mexico and running health clubs in Florida and Kansas, Klisanin became a CIA operative (Steve Klisanin interview). According to his sister-in-law, Steve "was involved with the Bay of Pigs invasion" and other covert activities: "Everything was secretive and he would disappear from his wife and family for months with no phone or address. Off to Baltimore. A very hidden and secret life and a reason for the breakup of his first marriage. He received two Social Security checks because he had two identities in the CIA" (Joan Klisanin interview).

17. *MB*, March 1957, 53; May 1957, 45.

18. Ibid., February 1957, 49; June 1957, 18; July 1957, 36. According to Horvath, Daniel Ferris, the AAU's secretary-treasurer, refused to examine the evidence of Hoffman's misconduct. Whether Johnson also refused is uncertain, but he did acknowledge Horvath's protest (Horvath to Johnson, July 26, 1956, and August 15, 1956, Rader Papers).

19. Bob Crist, interview by the author, August 3, 2005, Hampton, Virginia; Colonna interview. The speculations of Charles Smith go even further than Colonna's: "There wasn't —to my limited knowledge—a SINGLE MR. A contest that Boob [sic] didn't try to influence to HIS advantage. And of course, looking at it cold bloodedly, he would have been a business ninny—old time for nerd—if he hadn't." (Smith to Joe Roark, August 22, 1985, quoted in *Iron History*, September 5, 2002).

20. *MB*, March 1957, 9.

21. Ibid., October 1957, 5, 38.

22. Ibid., March 1958, 9.

23. Ibid., December 1957, 31, 61.

24. Crist interview, 2005; Colonna interview.

25. *SH*, May 1957, 26; December 1957, 26.

26. Ibid., September 1957, 49; *IM*, January 1958, 37.

27. *MB*, December 1957, 21–22, 56–57. The true scenario was worse than the Weiders suspected. Hoffman confessed that postal inspectors had traced the "wrong kind" of letters, with unadorned photos, to league correspondence, leading the U.S. district attorney to rant about that "Slimy Salacious Strength and Health," which encouraged readers "to exchange unnatural sex letters and pictures." Faced with $10,000 in legal fees and possible imprisonment, Hoffman abandoned the league (*SH*, April 1947, 5).

28. *SH*, April 1958, 61. Indeed, Valentine Hooven distinguishes between depictions of physiques in *Strength & Health* and those in Weider magazines, which "threw the old-style bodybuilding world into a homophobic panic" (*Beefcake*, 64–66). That distinction is less clear to Vince Aletti: "Like all commercial artists, physique photographers were operating in the busy, contested territory between art and commerce, which put them at a distinct disadvantage. No matter how tastefully executed their work, when it appeared on a newsstand it was perceived by many (including its grateful buyers) as homosexual pornography. It didn't help that, for all intents and purposes, that's what it was. Gay men were certainly among the buyers of mainstream bodybuilder magazines like *Strength & Health* and *Muscle Power*, even if they had no interest in weight lifting[;] weight lifters, many of whom posed in the nude during the 1930s and 1940s, were definitely hunky and had the distinct advantage of being the only game in town." But gay men were the target audience, argues Aletti, of the "friskier, funkier little magazines that sprang up in the postwar years," including *Adonis* and *Body Beautiful*; see Massengill, *Male Ideal*, 8. David Chapman and Brett Josef Grubisic likewise blur the distinction between male physique artistry and erotica in *American Hunks*.

29. *MA*, January 1958, 28–29; February 1958, 33, 52–54; May 1958, 16–17.

30. *SH*, June 1958, 3.

31. Ibid., 6.

32. *MB*, June 1958, 19.

33. Weider and Weider, *Brothers of Iron*, 115.

34. Johnson, "Physique Pioneers," 867; Wyke, "Herculean Muscle!," 60.

35. Hooven, however, confirms that these magazines sold in huge numbers during the repressed 1950s (*Beefcake*, 72).

36. Orlick interview. Jowett questioned whether the money was worth the legal hassles that Joe endured. "1962 was a bad year for Joe," he confided to Ottley Coulter. "He had several Federal inditements [*sic*] against him particularly on his pornographic mags, 'M'Sieur,' 'Gem' & 'After Dark.' They were banned from the newsstands. He claimed he sold [the] titles. I see 'Gem' & 'M'Sieur' out sometimes, but another firm. That homo P.C. pocket mag 'Adonis' was also indited. He carries it on (claims sold) by a guy who fronts for him" (Jowett to Coulter, December 29, 1962, Coulter Papers).

37. Orlick to Rader, November 24, 1964, Rader Papers. Likewise, Dian Hanson, a historian of erotica, questions why Joe Weider chose to "jeopardize his status in the body building market . . . by producing gay titles." She concludes the effects of the gay magazines were offset by those featuring cheesecake, through which his future wife, Betty Brosmer, became an icon: "Supporters and detractors alike agree Weider seldom left any avenue unexplored in the effort to turn a profit." Hence, he validated his growing beefcake business by linking it with heterosexuality. It was "during the critical empire-building decades of the 50s and

60s," when "Joe so thoroughly exploited both homoerotic interest in hardbody hunks, and hetero-male interest in Betty's delectable face and form, that in significant part his fitness empire can fairly be described as a solid-brick building built by beautiful boys and Betty Brosmer's bosom"; see Hanson, *History of Men's Magazines*, 2:349–358. For other magazines in which Betty appeared in the 1950s, see *Weider World Fanzine* #59 (January–February 1991), 2, 7.

38. See *SH*, November 1958, 22; *SH*, January 1958, 3; *MP*, May 1957, 16; *MB*, July 1958, 18.

39. *IM*, January 1957, 14; September 1957, 43–45.

40. *MA*, June 1958, 11–13, 19–21; *MB*, January 1957, 10–11; *MP*, June 1956, 33.

41. *MB*, 9 (October 1957), 18–19 and 54.

42. Ibid., June 1958, 36; December 1958, 7, 9, 33.

43. Ibid., October 1958, 9–11, 43; *SH*, November 1958, 34–37; *IM*, September 1958, 8–10.

44. *IM*, November 1958, 42; January 1959, 56.

45. Johnson, an employee of Lockheed Aircraft, also worked part-time as a bouncer at Hank and Jerry's Hideaway in Atlanta. Byron Cohen, the club's former owner, recalls, "Having Johnson as a bouncer was like having the fastest gun in the West. Seldom a night passed without some drunk or insecure bully wanting to prove he could whip Mr. America. But no one ever did" (quoted in *Georgia Trend* 14 [November 1999], 70).

46. *IM*, October 1959, 9–10; July 1959, 13.

47. Harry Johnson, interview by the author, Auburn, Georgia, July 24, 2001. Likewise, Santiago could not understand why he placed only sixth after winning the Junior Mr. America Contest (Elmo Santiago, interview by the author, New York City, April 16, 2004).

48. Jubinville to Hoffman, March 18, 1958; Hoffman to Jubinville, March 20, 1958; both in Hoffman Papers.

49. *SH*, July 1959, 22–23, 47–48.

50. Riverol, *Live from Atlantic City*, 82; *Atlantic City Press*, September 8 and 6, 1959.

51. *Wall Street Journal*, September 10, 1965; Neva Fickling, interview by the author, Macon, Georgia, November 23, 2009.

52. *SH*, February 1960, 7–8.

53. *MB*, August 1959, 10–13.

54. Ibid., July 1960, 48.

55. Ibid., October 1960, 52.

56. Ibid., March 1961, 50.

57. Lerille says he wanted to be Mr. America from age eight and "always knew he would open a gym." Although he does not "see where the Mr. America Contest has helped [him] in this business," he has created one of the world's largest and best-equipped gyms, covering more than two hundred thousand square feet on twenty acres with around nine thousand members; see Lloyd Lerille, interview by the author, Lafayette, Louisiana, May 31, 2007, and *Club Industry* 7 (September 2011): 22–41.

58. *IM*, August 1960, 18; *SH*, October 1960, 14.

59. *MA*, February 1960, 20–21; *MB*, February 1960, 48.

60. *MB*, March 1961, 52.

61. Ibid., April 1961, 46.

62. Ibid., May 1961, 52.

63. *MA*, March 1961, 12.

64. Ibid., 14.

65. *IM*, September 1961, 8, 33.

66. *SH*, November 1961, 56; January 1962, 48.

67. *MA*, November 1961, 37, 63–64.

68. Ibid., January 1962, 27, 61; September 1961, 29–33.

69. *SH*, March 1962, 46–47; May 1962, 7.

70. *MB*, October 1962, 51, 78; *SH*, November 1960, 24; Liederman to Hoffman, March 12, 1959, Hoffman Papers.

71. *MA*, November 1962, 80, 83; *IM*, August 1962, 15.

72. Fair, *Muscletown USA*, 195; Pearl, *Getting Stronger*, 405; see also *MF*, June 1987, 68, and a 2006 interview with Ray Markunas cited in Roach, *Muscle, Smoke, and Mirrors*, 337. Charles Kochakian, who developed steroids as a University of Rochester graduate student, explains that they were first used "to ameliorate clinical cases of impairment in growth and deficiency in protein synthesis" and were used during the war to improve bone healing and recovery from battle wounds. He never anticipated their use "in the enhancement of performance by bodybuilders or athletes," calling his steroids "innocent victims of misuse" (Kochakian to the author, August 10, 1994); see also *Birmingham News*, March 20, 1989, and Kochakian, *How It Was*, 33.

73. Joe Abbenda, interview by the author, Garden City, New York, June 20, 2005; Vern Weaver, interview by the author, Dover, Pennsylvania, July 3, 1992. According to Pearl, he learned about the effects of steroids in 1957 from a veterinarian who was treating horses and cows—"beautiful animals"—at a clinic opposite his gym in Pasadena. He learned more when he went to Florida to work on a film with Arthur Jones (Pearl interview).

74. L. Scott, *Loaded Guns*, 27.

75. Abbenda interview; *SH*, September 1962, 17.

76. *MB*, November 1961, 48; *MA*, November 1961, 66; *MB*, June 1962, 30; *MB*, October 1962, 47.

77. *MA*, January 1963, 39–40, 97.

78. L. Scott, *Loaded Guns*, 2, 5, 26–28, 36.

79. *IM*, January 1961, 7, 40; *IM*, August 1962, 14–15; *SH*, May 1961, 47.

80. *MB*, December 1962, 15. As a reserve officer with the U.S. Air Force in England, Schusterich was able to confer with Oscar Heidenstam at the 1963 Mr. Universe Contest (Schusterich to Rader, October 25, 1963, Hoffman Papers).

81. Schusterich to Hoffman, February 21 and March 2, 1964; Schusterich to Sablo, March 11, 1964; all in Hoffman Papers.

CHAPTER 6: WINDS OF CHANGE

1. Macmillan, *Pointing the Way*, 156.

2. Hoffman to Jubinville, March 20, 1958, Hoffman Papers.

3. *IM*, September 1961, 12.

4. *SH*, October 1963, 63. Al Antuck reported the reaction: "The audience almost rioted. The boos, hisses, and catcalls were loud and long. Weaver accepted the Mr. America trophy with surprise and embarrassment" (*Muscle Digest*, August 1979, 6).

5. Neil B. Allison to Rader, November 4, 1963, and Fred Hofmeister to Rader, July 16, 1963, Rader Papers. Another correspondent insisted that Weaver was a professional and should not have competed: "Weaver appeared for months in the Show, Little Abner, has been an extra in the movies and done night club and T.V. work. He is more a professional than Degni or Scott ever were!" (Jose Escobar to Rader, [1963], Rader Papers).

6. *SH*, November 1963, 11; December 1963, 11.

7. *MMI*, July 2008, 258.

8. *IM*, September 1963, 14, 60; Wayne, *Muscle Wars*, 4.

9. *SH*, December 1963, 10–11; Rudy Sablo, interview by the author, New York City, July 7, 2001.

10. *IM*, April 1963, 11; *IM*, October 1963, 60; Bob Crist, interview by the author, Hampton, Virginia, July 9, 2001; Bendel interview; Val Vasilieff, interview by the author, Sewell, New Jersey, June 16, 1992.

11. *IM*, October 1963, 30; August 1963, 29.

12. Ibid., December 1963, 28–29.

13. Weaver to Rader, January 1, 1964, Rader Papers.

14. Weaver interview; Dick Smith, interview by the author, Hanover, Pennsylvania, May 20, 2008.

15. *MB*, March 1964, 12–19; Gene Mozee, interview by the author, Hollywood, California, June 3, 2004.

16. *MB*, March 1964, 69–70.

17. Ibid., April 1964, 9, 70. An independent observer, however, believed that the Weider show was only "a moderate success" that played to an "enthusiastic but half-capacity crowd" (George Cohen to Rader, October 31, 1963, Rader Papers).

18. *MB*, April 1964, 55–56.

19. Ibid., August 1963, 46–47. Ken Sprague believes that it was Gene Mozee, later the editor of *Muscle Builder*, who "really put Joe on the map," since Mozee "came up with bombing and blitzing and the master blaster" (Sprague, interview by the author, Marietta, Georgia, September 25, 2004).

20. See Fair, *Muscletown USA*, 195–202; *MB*, May 1963, 13.

21. *MA*, February 1964, 5, 7, 38.

22. *Young Mr. America*, July 1964, 7, 13.

23. *MA*, July 1963, 64; *MB*, April 1964, 66–67.

24. *SH*, December 1964, 22; *SH*, July, 1966, 39; *MD*, February 1968, 26–27; *MTI*, January 1968, 59.

25. *IM*, August 1963, 27.

26. Ibid., September 1964, 7, 59, 64; Richard Cavaler, interview by the author, Southfield, Michigan, June 24, 2007; and Roach, *Muscle, Smoke, and Mirrors*, 2:264.

27. *MB*, January 1965, 65.

28. Ibid., July 1964, 68.

29. Ibid., October 1964, 77.

30. According to David Gentle, "Heidenstam and State really hated each other" Gentle, interview by the author, Romsey, UK, July 3, 2004.

31. State to Rader, November 18, 1962, and Hasse to Rader, January 24, 1963, Rader Papers. The FIHC (Fédération Internationale Haltérophile et Culturiste), the successor to the FIH, encompassed bodybuilding as well as weightlifting. Hasse could not understand Hoffman's continued support of the FIHC: "Hoff can't seem to get it through his skull that Weider owns Oscar State lock stock and barrel, and he seems to think that because he's on the FIHC physical culture committee that he can keep State on the straight and narrow. What a laugh" (Hasse to Rader, April 19, 1963).

32. Weider and Weider, *Brothers of Iron*, 72.

33. *MB*, January 1965, 67; *MA*, March 1961, 43.

NOTES TO PAGES 168–176

34. *MA*, April 1961, 18–20; *MB*, May 1961, 17.

35. *MB*, July 1964, 55.

36. Ibid., January 1963, 58.

37. Ibid., March 1963, 31; *MA*, January 1963, 97.

38. *MB*, March 1964, 69; November 1964, 71.

39. Howard Bovell, a weightlifter who emigrated from Guyana to the United States in the 1960s, attributes the success of Caribbean strength athletes to a "can't afford to fail" attitude. He thinks the social mobility in their less segregated homelands helped inspire African Americans (Bovell, interview by the author, Washington, D.C., April 8, 2004).

40. *IM*, December 1964, 34.

41. *MB*, February 1965, 88–90.

42. Ibid., January 1966, 68–77; Dave Draper, interview by the author, Aptos, California, May 30, 2004; *MA*, January 1966, 89. Chester Yorton, however, called Draper's victory "a farce": "It was a total fix. Weider wanted him as Mr. America to sell to all the young blond surfer kids" (Yorton, interview by the author, Woodland Hills, California, June 4, 2011).

43. Draper interview; *MA*, January 1966, 5, 123.

44. Twichell to Rader, September 17, 1964; Ben Weider to Rader, August 3, 1964; Valentine to Rader, August 31, 1963; all in Rader Papers.

45. *IM*, September 1964, 11; *SH*, September 1964, 76.

46. *IM*, September 1964, 13–14, 35; John DeCola, interview by the author, Hagerstown, Maryland, June 21, 2003.

47. *IM*, December 1965, 32; *IM*, August 1964, 12; John Balik, interview by the author, Santa Monica, California, June 2, 2004.

48. *MD*, November 1965, 25.

49. Rader to Twichell, July 9, 1965, Rader Papers.

50. *SH*, October 1965, 63.

51. Balik interview; Balik reported Gajda as having said this.

52. Sablo interview; Crist interview; *Muscle Builder/Power* (hereafter *MBP*), April 1968, 19, 23.

53. *MBP*, December 1966, 17; April 1968, 19, 23.

54. Wayne, *Muscle Wars*, 98.

55. Oliva, *Sergio Oliva*, 35.

56. Ken "Leo" Rosa, interview by the author, New York City, April 7, 2004. Likewise, Elmo Santiago, who won the Junior Mr. America Contest in 1959, thinks of himself as Puerto Rican "rather than white or black" (Santiago interview).

57. *MA*, April 1965, 82; *MB*, March 1965, 67; *MB*, September 1965, 89.

58. *MB*, October 1965, 19; Wayne, *Muscle Wars*, 11, 13.

59. Interviews with Lurie, 2004–2007, cited in Roach, *Muscle, Smoke, and Mirrors*, 361. E. M. Orlick claims that he organized the WBBG and *Muscle Training Illustrated*: "All of the names on the masthead were me" (Orlick interview).

60. *MTI*, November 1965, 16; September 1967, 26.

61. Ibid., October 1968, 40. According to Bill Pearl—and with all due respect to some top bodybuilders, including Chris Dickerson, who won the WBBG Mr. America title— "Dan picked up all the bottom feeders" (Pearl interview).

62. *MTI*, February 1969, 5. A decade later, Peary Rader was still struggling with whether to feature the newly crowned Mr. Olympia, Chris Dickerson, on a magazine cover. As he explained to Garry Bartlett: "We've been getting a lot of flack recently for using black men on

the cover. . . . I don't mind this so much personally and they do have outstanding physiques . . . but the readers opinion must be considered if we are to continue publishing *Iron Man*" (Rader to Bartlett, November 30, 1982, Rader Papers). Blacks had been working out at Leo Stern's gym in San Diego since 1948, but the only discrimination that Stern encountered was "on the covers of magazines" (Stern, interview by the author, San Diego, June 6, 2004.

63. *MTI*, October 1968, 16, 36.

64. Ibid., November 1969, 18–27.

65. Ibid., January 1971, 26–29.

66. *MA*, April 1968, 23–25, 7.

67. Don Howorth, interview by the author, Los Angeles, June 4, 2004. According to one report, "drugs became a habit with him, starting out with the growth drugs and graduating to others." His conviction for trafficking came from being "caught visiting the home of a Hell's Angel leader, being raided at the time, and he was carrying a briefcase with enough heroin and cocaine to supply thirty thousand addicts . . . a million dollars worth of dangerous drugs" (*IM*, July 1972, 32). See also Roach, *Muscle, Smoke, and Mirrors*, 2:267–268.

68. Howorth interview.

69. *MA*, July 1968, 48.

70. *MBP*, December 1968, 42–45.

71. *MB*, November 1966, 10, 54–55.

72. Ibid., January 1968, 65.

73. *MBP*, April 1970, 61–62.

74. DeCola interview; Jerry Daniels, interview by the author, Chattanooga, Tennessee, September 27, 2000.

75. *MTI*, February 1971, 45.

76. Ibid., 53.

77. Weider and Weider, *Brothers of Iron*, 177.

78. Wayne, *Bodymen*, 44; Oliva, *Sergio Oliva*, 40, 320.

79. *MD*, April 1971, 7; Michael Katz v. Strength & Health Publishing Co., October 20–21 and 26–28, 1977, Superior Court, New Haven County, Connecticut, trial transcript; David Reif to John Terpak, November 7, 1977, and Reif to John Boddington, July 25, 1979, Terpak Papers.

80. *Philadelphia Inquirer*, October 15, 1967.

81. *Atlantic City Press*, September 11, 1968.

82. Bivans, *Miss America*, 25–26.

83. *IM*, September 1966, 32; *SH*, September 1967, 15.

84. *MTI*, November 1967, 59; *IM*, October 1967, 14, 77.

85. *SH*, September 1967, 21.

86. Ibid., October 1967, 41, 77.

87. *MMI*, January 2007, 198–199.

88. *MD*, September 1968, 32, 57; *IM*, September 1968, 38. Boyer, who won virtually every body part award and was named most muscular, was frustrated at always placing second to Haislop; see *California Bodybuilding-Powerlifting News* 1 (July 1977): 12.

89. *IM*, September 1969, 12. Len Bosland points out that he started announcing Mr. America contests in 1965 and then, after much soul searching, moved to the IFBB in 1976. He emceed six Mr. Olympia and two Ms. Olympia events (Bosland, interview with the author, Glen Rock, New Jersey, July 24, 2002).

90. Ken Rosa recalls a strong association with Bosland: "[When I was young] we didn't

have TV and listened to the radio. My hero was the Lone Ranger, the greatest voice I've ever heard. I wanted to sound like that. Every time I see Len Bosland, I call him the Lone Ranger." (Rosa interview).

91. *MBP*, April 1979, 61.

92. Coe to the author, August 22, 2007 (in author's possession).

93. Ibid.; Frank Zane, telephone interview by the author, La Mesa, California, June 6, 2007; *Reps!*, Summer 2006, 116.

94. *IM*, May 1965, 5; May 1969, 48. In 1968, yet another offshoot appeared, YMCA Mr. America, staged by Bob Gajda in Chicago and won by Ken Waller, of Kentucky; see *IM*, July 1968, 16, and Jeff Preston, "Waller, Catching Up with the 'Freckled Heckler,'" available through the Internet Archive's Wayback Machine: http://web.archive.org /web/20080624092145/http://www.ironage.us/articles/preston-waller.html.

95. *MBP*, August 1969, 7, 50. At the 1969 contest, the weightlifting coach Louis De-Marco observed that "people at the Mr. America felt like second cousins to the weightlifters, and because of the explosion of bodybuilding and the Weiders you could see the division between the two." DeMarco, interview by the author, Vienna, Ohio, March 27, 2007. Weightlifting, often called Olympic lifting, is performed in two overhead movements—the snatch, and the clean and jerk—that require a high degree of strength, speed, agility, and athleticism. Powerlifting, which consists of the squat, bench press, and dead lift, is chiefly a test of strength.

96. *IM*, May 1965, 62–63.

97. *SH*, November 1968, 56, 63.

98. See, for example, ibid., June 1965, 26; May 1967, 50.

99. *Atlantic City Press*, August 25 and 26, 1967.

100. *Philadelphia Bulletin*, September 15, 1968.

101. Clipping titled "Along with Miss America, There's Now Miss Black America," September 9, 1969, in the "Miss America 66–69" file, Atlantic City Public Library.

102. Chris Dickerson, interview by the author, Fort Lauderdale, Florida, November 9, 2006; Dickerson to the author, December 1, 2006 (in author's possession).

103. Wayne, *Muscle Wars*, 88; *SH*, December 1970, 31.

104. *SH*, July 1971, 42, 75.

105. Pearl interview. Pearl contrasted his trainees with three other blacks—Sergio Oliva, Harold Poole, and Robbie Robinson—who failed to meet AAU criteria: "Robbie had a gold tooth up front. Long hair and stuff. They didn't like that."

106. *SH*, October 1971, 20–21.

107. Wayne, *Muscle Wars*, 199. A decade later, Dickerson, by then a convert to the IFBB, was more frank about racial matters: "I had always been aware of what was going on in the AAU, that many worthy Mr. America contenders had been eliminated because of the color of their skin" (*MF*, October 1981, 52, 172).

CHAPTER 7: THE ARNOLD ERA

1. Quoted in I. Halperin, *Governator*, 168.

2. According to Bob Kennedy, "Arnold first went to Hoffman, who told him he didn't hire pro bodybuilders. Reg Park told him to go to Weider. Joe gave him a car, a yellow Volkswagen that didn't fit him. 'You're German,' said Joe, 'I thought you would like it.' Joe

paid him $200 per week, but Arnold had to chase him down for it every Friday" (Kennedy, interview by the author, Mississauga, Ontario, March 28, 2007).

3. *MA*, March 1969, 5.

4. Ibid., June 1969, 7, 19; August 1969, 46; April 1970, 19; June 1970, 37; May 1971, 28; July 1971, 19, 41.

5. Ibid., August 1969, 20–21; April 1970, 61.

6. Ibid., July 1971, 92.

7. Draper interview.

8. Draper, *Brother Iron, Sister Steel*, 24–27.

9. *MA*, August 1969, 34–35, 63.

10. *MBP*, December 1971, 90; February 1972, 58.

11. *MA*, October 1970, 76. Rick Wayne, the editor of *Muscle Builder/Power*, noted that *Mr. America* was outselling his magazine "two-and-a-half to one" and that he was "sick, sick, sick of the situation" (*MBP*, December 1970, 7; September 1973, 33).

12. *MBP*, March 1970, 87.

13. B. Baker, *Arnold and Me*, 51, 205. For other Schwarzenegger accounts, see Leigh, *Arnold*; G. Butler, *Arnold Schwarzenegger*; Andrews, *True Myths*; Leamer, *Fantastic*; Krasniewicz and Blitz, *Arnold Schwarzenegger*; Mathews, *People's Machine*; Weintraub, *Party of One*; I. Halperin, *Governator*. See also Minichiello, *Bodybuilders, Drugs, and Sex*, a novel in which Arnold serves as model for the protagonist; Arnold's first autobiography, *Arnold*; and his *Total Recall*.

14. *MA*, April 1970, 56.

15. *MBP*, March 1971, 7.

16. Ibid., December 1971, 75–82; *IM*, January 1972, 18–19.

17. *MBP*, June 1970, 15; December 1971, 59.

18. *SH*, September 1970, 9; *SH*, July 1971, 9; *MD*, February 1971, 7.

19. *SH*, September 1971, 21, 84.

20. Parker to Rader [1974], with enclosures, Rader Papers.

21. *SH*, October 1970, 18, 76–77; *IM*, September 1970, 13; *IM*, September 1971, 12.

22. *MD*, October 1971, 27; *IM*, September 1971, 29.

23. *MBP*, September 1971, 96.

24. *MD*, April 1971, 6.

25. Ibid., February 1971, 53.

26. *IM*, September 1972, 15.

27. *MTI*, October 1972, 29.

28. *MMI*, October 2003, 247–248.

29. *IM*, September 1972, 34.

30. *MD*, September 1972, 19, 50. When Tom Sansone, Mr. America 1958, died of cancer in 1974, there was much discussion over whether steroids were responsible; see *MD*, January 1975, 7, 25, and May 1975, 7.

31. *IM*, September 1972, 16–17.

32. Michalik, *Atomic Fitness*, 292–294.

33. Steve Michalik, interview by the author, Easley, South Carolina, July 26, 2011. Apparently, Michalik's account of his drug abuse is telescoped into a single time frame, whereas Paul Solotaroff's account, which pertains to his bout with liver cysts and death, relates to the latter part of his competitive career, in the early 1980s; see Paul Solotaroff, "The Power and the Gory," *Village Voice*, October 29, 1991. For more on Michalik's accident and recovery, see *Mr. and Ms. Jones Beach USA*, August 24, 2008.

34. Michalik interview.

35. Pearl interview.

36. Michalik interview.

37. Kim Wood, interview by the author, Cincinnati, Ohio, March 24, 2007.

38. *IM*, September 1972, 14.

39. *MD*, September 1973, 12, 63.

40. *IM*, September 1973, 12, 84; recollections of the author.

41. *MBP*, August 1978, 82.

42. Recollections of the author.

43. Placement is a purely subjective rendering in which each judge ranks all the contestants and then the judges' rankings are combined to come up with the final placements.

44. *SH*, October 1971, 58; *IM*, November 1973, 9; *IM*, January 1974, 38.

45. But see, for instance, "Weight Training among the Ancient Greeks," *IM*, July 1972, 27, and "Ancient Greek Athletes," *MD*, May 1975, 8.

46. *IM*, November 1973, 9; September 1973, 11.

47. *SH*, January 1972, 9.

48. Bivans, *Miss America*, 27.

49. Deford, *There She Is*, 251.

50. Ibid., 254 (this is from the 1978 revision of Deford's 1971 book). Although there was never a Black Mr. America Contest, a lively debate occurred over racial exclusiveness. George Wilkie, of New York, believed that "if blacks have the right to put on all black Miss America contests and whites are not allowed to enter, then what's wrong with white Americans being able to put on [an] all white Mr. America contest and do the same thing" (letter to the editor, *SH*, April 1971, 8).

51. *New York Sunday News*, September 6, 1970.

52. Ibid.; Deford, *There She Is*, 255.

53. Quoted in Deford, *There She Is*, 256.

54. Riverol, *Live from Atlantic City*, 93; Passarelli quoted in Bivans, *Miss America*, 28.

55. Jim Lorimer, interview by the author, Columbus, Ohio, June 29, 2006. For broader coverage of Lorimer's role in the sport, see Murray, "Jim Lorimer," and Richter and Todd, "Jim Lorimer's Unexpected Path."

56. *SH*, January 1971, 88.

57. Schwarzenegger quoted in Lorimer interview; *MD*, December 1970, 8–9, 67–68.

58. Schwarzenegger, *Arnold*, 94–95. As the NABBA official Norman Hibbert observed, "Arnold didn't have the best physique, but he had something special. . . . Arnold really brought bodybuilding to the masses. . . . You've got to hand it to Weider because he was a ruthless businessman. Oscar [Heidenstam] was an amateur" (Norman and Sylvia Hibbert, interview by the author, London, July 2004).

59. Radley and Gentle, *Classic Muscle Art*, 132; *Natural Body and Fitness*, February 1989, 53.

60. Joe Weider, however, begrudged the attention lavished on Arnold: "Never forget, if it weren't for the Weider organization, *Muscle Builder* magazine and its outgrowth, and the IFBB, there wouldn't have been an Arnold, nor TV exposure, nor the international recognition which the sport boasts today" (*MF*, April 1979, 107).

61. *MD*, September 1971, 30; *MD*, February 1972, 9; *IM*, March 1972, 17.

62. Weider to Terpak, December 2, 1971, Rader Papers.

63. *IM*, January 1973, 37; *MD*, February 1973, 10.

64. *MD*, February 1974, 22–23; *MTI*, January 1974, 62.

65. For the significance of Johnson's loss of the IWF presidency to the York-Weider power struggle, see *SH*, January 1973, 55, and *MBP*, October 1973, 30–31.

66. *Official Minutes, I.F.B.B. International Congress*, Baghdad, Iraq, November 20, 1972, 3–4; *Report to All National Federations* 5 (Montreal): 1–3.

67. Weider virtually admits State's responsibility for the IFBB's membership, noting after his election as general secretary that he "has always been the guiding light of the IFBB and due to his vast experience the IFBB has been able to learn, grow, and take its rightful place in international amateur sports" (*MBP*, March 1973, 85). A more emphatic recognition of State's role appeared several decades later in the chapter "Oscar's Golden Key" in Weider and Weider, *Brothers of Iron*, 205–233. York's cynical view was that State had, "for a fee, connived membership in GAIF for the IFBB" (*MD*, May 1976, 69).

68. Unable to pry the IFBB from its privileged position, he secured NABBA's affiliation with the International Federation of Physical Culture and Sport (IFPCS), which had been hastily formed by the French Federation of Physical Culture and Sport to counter Weider's moves in Europe. Bodybuilding associations in Belgium, Switzerland, and Luxembourg soon joined the federation, and Oscar became its president (Heidenstam to Terpak, February 15, April 7, and May 18, 1972, Hoffman Papers).

69. *MBP*, June 1972, 28–29.

70. *IM*, March 1972, 34–35. Terpak claimed that he had been misquoted. What he said was that "eventually IFBB members may be permitted to enter A.A.U. sanctioned meets if and when the IFBB becomes an Allied member of the AAU" (Terpak to Rader, January 19, 1972, Hoffman Papers; *IM*, May 1972, 37).

71. Kelly hinted at forthcoming changes in AAU policies just after his election as president at the 1970 annual meeting in San Francisco. "Let us not waste energy homesteading the status quo," he stated. "The status quo is for the tired and timid"; see *Honolulu Sunday Star Bulletin and Advertiser*, December 6, 1970, and Kelly to Weider, June 17, 1971, Hoffman Papers.

72. *IM*, May 1972, 37, 59. In a letter to Rader, Bob Hise explained what happened: "IFBB belongs to the same organization that the FHI[C] does, General Assembly of the International Sports Federations. To quote Jack Kelly, 'It is the most prestigious Sports Organization in the entire world, even stronger than the I.O.C.' . . . One thing certain Ben made fools out of Terpak and Sablo. Dave Mayor and Pete Miller, Jack King and I had little to say. Sablo did most of the talking and Ben answered and tripped him up on every turn" (Hise to Rader, November 21, 1971, Rader Papers).

73. "Since the use of the Mr. America name is offensive to you," Weider later told Terpak, he had "authorized our American Organizing Committee not to use this name in 1972, and instead they will organise the American Bodybuilding Championships" (Weider to Terpak, November 25, 1971, Rader Papers). This change occurred several years later, when it was forced on the IFBB.

74. Terpak later told Murray Levin that he had received "some vicious letters from Ben, only because I have taken [a] 'Rock of Gibralter' stand against IFBB affiliation with the A.A.U." Chagrined that Weider appeared to have "Jack Kelly's blessing," he concluded, "You can't win a pissing match with a skunk" (Terpak to Levin, December 23, 1971, Hoffman Papers). For the Weider version of the meeting, which stresses the international leverage of the IFBB, see *MB*, May 1973, 12, 62–63, 69, 76–77. While admitting that he was "no fan of Weider or the Weider Publications," Clarence Bass advised Bob Crist, the newly elected

AAU chairman, that he saw "no point to continuing the argument in apartments with only a few people present." Instead, "let's bring it out in the open and try to do something about it" (Bass to Crist, January 11, 1972, Rader Papers).

75. *MBP*, November 1972, 53, 82.

76. Ibid., March 1973, 26, 85, 88; May 1973, 24. Weider addressed the 1973 GAISF meeting in Oklahoma, to which the AAU executives, meeting in the same hotel, were also invited. "Hoffman, Sablo, Terpak, Matlin and Crist were all there," he reported to Rader, "and I can assure you, that they were very unhappy" (Weider to Rader, May 28, 1973, Rader Papers).

77. *MBP*, May 1973, 62–63; August 1973, 31, 77; March 1973, 77. To reinforce the niche of the AABA and IFBB in the GAISF and to parry the influence of Hoffman in another sport, Weider even joined the short-lived United States Amateur Athletic Federation, created by Don Porter, vice president of the International Softball Federation; see *MBP*, July 1974, 40.

78. *United States Olympic Committee News Letter* 8 (August 1973): 1; *MBP*, January 1974, 7, 53, 57, 78, 85; *MBP*, May 1974, 49, 62–63. Upon the failure of the 1973 Amateur Athletic Act, Weider lent his support to an amateur sports bill sponsored by Congressman Bob Mathias of California, which called for compulsory arbitration of all disputes between sports organizations seeking U.S. recognition in a specific sport; see *MBP*, October 1974, 42–43, 52.

79. *MD*, April 1974, 69; *MTI*, May 1975, 58.

80. *MTI*, February 1971, 27; January 1971, 17–18.

81. Ibid., January 1973, 55–56.

82. Bill Grant, interview by the author, Orange, New Jersey, March 24, 2003.

83. Lurie, *Heart of Steel*, 150–156.

84. *MTI*, January 1974, 5, 32, 61.

85. Warren Frederick, interview by the author, Tampa, Florida, May 6, 2004. Chris Dickerson, who eventually joined the IFBB and won the Mr. Olympia Contest in 1982, harbors similar resentments against the Weiders: "Joe Weider never liked me, and I never liked him, but went only because of Bill Pearl. I was a thorn in their side. They cheated everyone. Everyone hated them. Everyone will be happy when they die. They are the kind of Jews that good Jews are ashamed of" (Dickerson interview). Pearl harbors similar resentments, sans the ethnic bite: "The Weiders exploited everybody. I can't name one person in the magazines they didn't get to" (Pearl interview).

86. *MTI*, March 1975, 22–27.

87. Lurie, *Heart of Steel*, 167–168; Lurie interview.

88. *MTI*, November 1975, 5.

89. Lurie interview; Weider and Weider, *Brothers of Iron*, 160, 89. According to Lurie's gossip column, Joe Weider had been sued more than two hundred times in the previous thirty years, and Dave Draper was suing him for breach of contract (*MTI*, May 1975, 13).

90. *MTI*, January 1976, 31; January 1977, 31; November 1975, 30–31.

91. Kennedy's explanation of his magazine's origin appeared in *MMI*, September 2009, 138–148.

92. Ibid., Fall 1974, 9, 34, 89, 100–101; Winter 1975, 3, 8–9, 93; Winter 1976, 9–11, 28–29.

93. Ibid., Summer 1975, 9, 25, 77–78, 101. Kennedy also takes credit for being the first to feature women in thongs (*MMI*, September 2009, 146).

94. *IM*, November 1974, 12–13; January 1975, 15; September 1974, 35–36, 51.

95. *MD*, September 1975, 32, 57, 59.

96. Dale Adrian, interview by the author, Simi Valley, California, June 7, 2004; *IM*, March 1976, 15–16.

97. *MD*, September 1976, 34–36; *MMI*, Winter 1976, 14.

98. *MTI*, January 1977, 37; *MBP*, November 1976, 23, 92.

99. *IM*, March 1976, 34. As Randy Roach points out, athletes and spectators were "tiring of the pageant style of judging" (*Muscle, Smoke, and Mirrors*, 2:113).

100. *MBP*, May 1974, 7, 13, 28; June 1975, 20, 96.

101. *MF*, July 1981, 48; *IM*, September 1976, 37.

102. The change resulted from a 1974 court order restricting Ben Weider from using the Mr. America title but allowing "Mr. Americas"; see Edward Colbert to Clarence Bass, December 31, 1974, and Bass to Peary Rader, January 7, 1975, both in Rader Papers. See also Amateur Athletic Union of the United States v. New York University and International Federation of Body Builders, Joseph Weider and Bud Parker, U.S. District Court, Southern District of New York, Civil Action No. 70, April 21, 1975, copy in Rieger Papers, Stark Center, University of Texas.

103. *MBP*, April 1976, 38, 47, 55.

104. The AAU promoter Cliff Sawyer recalls Arnold saying after a 1969 contest in Brooklyn: "There are four things I wanna do. I wanna be the best bodybuilder of all times. I wanna be a millionaire. I wanna go into movies. And I wanna go into politics" (Sawyer, interview by the author, Worcester, Massachusetts, May 22, 2008).

105. Krasniewicz and Blitz, *Arnold Schwarzenegger*, 60; *MMI*, January 1979, 11, 66; Leamer, *Fantastic*, 106.

106. Krasniewicz and Blitz, *Arnold Schwarzenegger*, 56–57; see also "The Genesis of 'Pumping Iron,'" *MBP*, March 1977, 14–17.

107. Ferrigno quoted in *MMI*, Summer 1976, 8–9.

108. Wayne DeMilia, interview by the author, New York City, December 17, 2010.

109. *MMI*, Summer 1976, 63–71.

110. Ibid.

111. Much of the public, argued a 1975 article, were put off by the sport: "A lot of people consider the idea of body building a little weird, if not downright sick, an obsession with exaggerated masculinity at a time when traditional concepts of masculinity are under heavy assault. Popular stereotypes depict the body builder as homosexual and narcissistic, a muscle-bound clown who functions as the male equivalent of the female 'dumb-blonde' sex object" (Vicki Goldberg, *New York Times Magazine*, November 30, 1975).

112. Draper interview.

113. *MBP*, April 1976, 28, 30, 27, 2, 66.

114. *MMI*, Summer 1976, 7, 11.

115. Roach, *Muscle, Smoke, and Mirrors*, 2:248.

116. *MBP*, August 1973, 57; *IM*, May 1976, 36; *MBP*, November 1976, 6.

CHAPTER 8: THE SPRAGUE REVOLUTION

1. Marvin Jones, "Ken Sprague, aka Dakota," *In Touch* (1974), available from the Internet Archive's Wayback Machine, http://web.archive.org/web/20020806202708/liunkvidco.com/library/Dakota; Wood interview.

2. Jones, "Ken Sprague."

3. Ibid.

4. Ibid.; Wood interview.

5. Carter, *Iron Game*, 29, 38, 98.

6. Jones, "Ken Sprague."

7. Ken Sprague, interview by the author, Marietta, Georgia, October 13, 2009.

8. Carter, *Iron Game*, 48, 74.

9. Baker, *Arnold and Me*, 121–122.

10. Sprague interview, 2009.

11. Carter, *Iron Game*, 44–45. While Joe Weider, despite putting out several "picture magazines" targeting gay men in the 1950s, eagerly distanced himself from gays in his autobiography, he did admit that his publications "sold big to gays"; see Weider and Weider, *Brothers of Iron*, 115.

12. Sprague interview, 2009.

13. Klein, *Little Big Men*, 156, 57, 198–199. Much the same scenario shows up in Fussell, *Muscle*, 139–41, 147; and Arnoldi, *Chemical Pink*, 65–68.

14. Jones, "Ken Sprague"; Carter, *Iron Game*, 96, 112, 124–126.

15. Mike Graham, interview by the author, Lockhart, Texas, March 15, 2012.

16. Sprague interview, 2009. Dan Howard recalls the "Missing Link" as a "strong sucker": "Whew! Pound for pound . . . that sucker probably could deadlift more than anybody even close at his bodyweight. . . . I remember one time he was deadlifting, and Arnold and Franco came in. And Franco was a hell of a deadlifter, and Arnold started in on Franco. He says, 'You can't do as much as the Link does.' And Franco like to killed himself, you know. And I think he finally did pick it up. And then Beckman [Carter] went on and put on another fifty pounds and did more. Yeah, he was an animal" (Howard, interview by the author, Riverside, California, June 6, 2011).

17. Carter, *Iron Game*, 216–217.

18. Sprague interview, 2004; Ken Sprague, interview by the author, Marietta, Georgia, January 13, 2005. For further details about the purchase, see Roach, *Muscle, Smoke, and Mirrors*, 2:41.

19. Jones, "Ken Sprague"; Sprague interview, 2009.

20. Howard interview; Sprague interview, 2004; Carter, *Iron Game*, 93.

21. *MMI*, Spring 1977, 58.

22. *MTI*, June 1978, 62.

23. *MBP*, July 1978, 12, 128.

24. Sprague interview, 2004.

25. "Ken Sprague," LongandStrong.com, April 24, 2008, http://www.longandstrong .com/Interviews/sprague.html; *MBP*, January 1978, 81.

26. Sprague interview, 2004.

27. Jones, "Ken Sprague."

28. Pearl interview.

29. Sprague interview, 2004; Howard interview.

30. Carter, *Iron Game*, 132, 99, 58–59.

31. Pearl interview.

32. Jones, "Ken Sprague."

33. The breakup occurred on November 8, 1978, with passage of the Amateur Sports Act of 1978.

34. To this end, an exploratory meeting was held in February 1976 between members of the AAU and IFBB, including Crist and Ben Weider, to discuss affiliation. "The meeting

was considered productive," reported Crist, and it was agreed to pursue further exploratory measures (Crist, memorandum to National Physique Committee, February 9, 1976, Hoffman Papers).

35. *MBP*, August 1977, 87; AAU Notice #76-70, November 30, 1975; AAU Notice #76-51, January–February, 1976, Countryman Papers, San Francisco, California.

36. AAU Notice #76-89, May 1976; AAU Notice #76-101, July 1, 1976, Countryman Papers.

37. AAU Notice #76-112, August 1, 1976, and AAU Notice #76–121, September 9, 1976, both in Countryman Papers; Sprague interview, 2004.

38. AAU Notice #76-150, November 9, 1976, and AAU Notice #77-7, January 25, 1977, both in Countryman Papers; *MBP*, May 1977), 96.

39. AAU Notice #77-44, April 22, 1977, Countryman Papers; *Muscle Digest*, November 1977, 27.

40. *IM*, September 1977, 40; AAU Notice #77-98, August 10, 1977, and Countryman to Weider, July 27, 1977, both in Countryman Papers. The dissidents included the former Weider associates Ed Jubinville, Serge Nubret, and Ludwig Shusterich [*sic*]; the last, disbelieving that Olympic aspirations were the Weiders' motive for affiliation, concluded it was "just a stab at acquiring more power!" (*MD*, December 1977, 62).

41. Bass to Countryman, July 19, 1977, Countryman Papers.

42. Hurley to Weis, August 18, 1977; Weis to Hurley, September 15, 1977, both in Countryman Papers.

43. *MBP*, August 1977, 17.

44. Ibid., May 1978, 86; AAU Notice #77-135, October 25, 1977; AAU Notice #78-33, February 23, 1978, both notices in Countryman Papers.

45. For a voting breakdown, see Ed Jubinville to Rader, n.d., Rader Papers. Only Mike Katz abstained. "As you can see we had no chance," Ed told Peary. Clarence Bass believed that with affiliation, "the AAU Mr. America title can regain its status as the true national championship of physique" (Bass to Rader, February 8, 1978, Rader Papers).

46. *MTI*, January 1980, 9. Manion called it "a free-for-all": "They got completely off the track, and it became York against Weider, Weider against Lurie, and so on" (*Bodybuilding World*, January 1978, 11–12). Bill Reynolds called it "comedy of the highest order," with Lurie "hollering that Ben had once lied on a witness stand when he allegedly said his brother Joe had set a world weightlifting record in his bedroom" (*Bodybuilding World*, February 1978, 3). According to Sprague, he greeted members of the AAU who had critical things to say about Gold's Gym with lawsuits as they walked through the door, which set the tone for the meeting: "They sat through the whole meeting like church mice. They didn't say a thing" (Sprague interview, 2009).

47. Jan Dellinger, interview by the author, Red Lion, Pennsylvania, December 14, 1992. That recently crowned Tony Pearson was not selected to represent the United States no doubt signified the lessening importance of Mr. America in the Weider pantheon of physique titles; see *MF*, February 1979, 27.

48. *MD*, September 1976, 33; *MMI*, Spring 1977, 16–18.

49. *MBP*, October 1977, 74.

50. Ibid., 104, 108.

51. Ibid., 77–81.

52. *IM*, September 1977, 36–37.

53. Bill Reynolds expressed delight that "the thousands who attended the Mr. America

were there for the Mr. America," which "was no longer being used to draw people to the lifting" (*Bodybuilding World*, January 1977, 13).

54. *MD*, October 1977, 21; *IM*, September 1977, 36–37; *MTI*, March 1978, 8; *MBP*, October 1977, 117, 123; *MBP*, December 1977, 58.

55. Sprague interview, 2009.

56. *MBP*, May 1978, 52–53.

57. *MTI*, February 1979, 17. Dan Howard takes credit for the first Gold's Classic. As he puts it, "We did some real fun stuff," including a revolving platform: "A guy would get on the front of it and revolve into the lights. And another guy would be getting off and another one getting on, and we had about five or six really good bodybuilders." He calls it "one of the best bodybuilding shows [he had] ever seen." Howard similarly takes credit for organizing the 1977 Mr. America Contest and parade for Sprague: "Kenny wasn't around" (Howard interview).

58. *MBP*, September 1978, 133; *IM*, November 1978, 28–29.

59. Sprague interview, 2004; *MBP*, February 1979, 132; *MD*, December 1978, 30–34; *IM*, January 1979, 12, 15.

60. *MBP*, December 1978, 60; August 1978, 63, 111. Donald Wong, the editor, criticized Sprague not only for wielding dictatorial power but also for turning physique contests into "cheap P. T. Barnum imitations" (*Muscle Digest*, December 1978, 2).

61. *IM*, January 1979, 44; AAU Notice #78-149, November 8, 1978, Countryman Papers; *MTI*, January 1980, 9–10.

62. Sprague interview, 2004.

63. *MTI*, May 1979, 62–63; AAU Notice #79-5, Countryman Papers.

64. Sprague interview, 2009.

65. DeMilia interview, 2010; Roach, *Muscle, Smoke, and Mirrors*, 198; Graham interview.

66. *MTI*, January 1980, 9.

67. *MBP*, June 1978, 97; January 1977, 48–63; October 1977, 82–84.

68. Ibid., September 1977, 74–76; Wayne, *Bodymen*, 39.

69. *MTI*, June 1978, 11; March 1980, 63.

70. Ibid., March 1980, 14. By the end of 1980, the SPA, still headed by Barrilleaux, had changed its name to the American Federation of Women Bodybuilders and received a ringing endorsement from the curmudgeonly Vince Gironda, who called women's bodybuilding "a new art form" (*SPA News* 2 [January 1981]: 3–4).

71. Minichiello to Rader, March 16, 1978, and Ben Weider to AFAB Officials, March 1978, Rader Papers. The AFAB, refusing to die, staged a final comeback in 1980; see *Natural Bodybuilder*, Fall 1980, 24.

72. *MD*, August 1978, 25; *IM*, November 1980, 38; Heidenstam to Terpak, February 2, 1976, Hoffman Papers; *MD*, June 1978, 22–23, 56; *IM*, May 1982, 29.

73. AAU Notice #79-80, July 17, 1979, Countryman Papers. According to a complaint filed by the committee member Ira Hurley, nude photographs of Pearson that appeared in *Honcho* magazine not only violated his amateur status but also compromised the moral standards of the AAU: "You may call it art—I call it Pornography" (Hurley to Robert H. Helmick, November 13, 1978, Rader Papers).

74. *MTI*, January 1980, 63.

75. Ibid., April 1980, 41–42, 63. In November 1979, the AAU established a women's physique organization, chaired by Lisa Lyon, to parallel the NPC. The previous June, Lyon had won the first Women's World Bodybuilding Championship, which was held with the Junior Mr. America Contest sponsored by Gold's Gym in Los Angeles; see *IM*, May 1980, 31, and November 1979, 35.

76. NPC 1980 Newsletters #3 and #4, July 14 and November 1, 1980; Jerome Weis to Members of Board of Governors, January 12, 1981, Countryman Papers.

77. Josh Henson, interview by the author, Falls Church, Virginia, July 31, 2011. For Crist's account of these transactions, see *MD*, June 1982, 33.

78. "I will always remember November 31 [*sic*], 1980," Henson later recalled to Crist, "when you came to my suite in Miami and I asked you to chair the Mr. America Committee. You were the only one I knew to turn to, and in my opinion, you did a hell of a good job" (Henson to Crist, November 4, 1983, Rieger Papers).

79. Henson to Manion, February 6, 1981, Hoffman Papers. Robert Paul, a legal adviser for Crist's committee, employed the services of Sheppard and Woolslair, a Florida legal firm, and O'Brien and Jacobson, a patent attorney firm in Washington, to certify with the U.S. Patent Office on June 11, 1968, that "the AAU as the Principal Register of the Service Mark 'Mr. America'" had "the exclusive right to conduct an annual contest to select a Mr. America." As a follow-up to this legal sanction, AAU attorneys advised affiliates to register all relevant trademarks with both state and federal governments to ensure further protection. See Paul to Crist, April 16, 1973, attached to a letter from Achilles Kallos, April 12, 1973, in the Hoffman Papers; see also *AAU Physique News* 1 (May 1982): 4.

80. Bass to Crist, January 23, 1981, and Bass to Rader, February 18, 1981, Rader Papers. Bass's perception of the AAU was likely based in part on the decline of its weightlifting sector. As the USWF president Murray Levin observed, participation at the local level was declining: "Where formerly there was tremendous activity," as in New York and Philadelphia, "now there is none." He added apocalyptically, "*WHAT WE ARE ACTUALLY SEEING IS THE DEATH OF WEIGHTLIFTING*" (Levin to Athletes, Coaches, and Officials, September 22, 1981, Rader Papers).

81. Bass to Manion, December 1, 1981, Countryman Papers; *Muscle Digest*, March 1982, 16.

82. *MD*, December 1979, 29–30; *IM*, November 1979, 28.

83. *MD*, December 1980, 44; *IM*, November 1980, 35. Sprague took a firm hand with this contest partly because of how Grymkowski had conducted the previous year's Junior Mr. America Contest. As Bill Reynolds reported, "The current ownership can't even carry Sprague's jock when it comes to putting on a bodybuilding show!" The clincher was Grymkowski's "lewd and lascivious" conduct while presenting trophies to the top five women. Pete allegedly "set women's bodybuilding back 50 years" (*MF*, October 1979, 62).

84. *MD*, February 1981, 29–32, 66; *MF*, December 1980, 136; *MMI*, January 1981, 22.

85. *MMI*, January 1981, 21, 38; *MTI*, January 1981, 6.

86. Boyer Coe attributes Belknap's muscularity partly to his taking insulin (for diabetes) before bodybuilders realized it was the "greatest anabolic of all." The hormone makes "everything grow": "And that's why those guys develop these huge abdominal areas. Even though they have excellent abdominal development, it shoves everything forward because their intestines are enlarged and pushes everything out" (Coe, interview by the author, Huntingdon Beach, California, June 3, 2011).

87. *MD*, December 1981, 27; *MD*, February 1982, 36–37; *MMI*, March 1982, 53; *MF*, January 1982, 22.

88. *MD*, February 1982, 32–33, 24; *MF*, March 1982, 56.

89. The escalation of drug use by the early 1980s was evident from Bill Reynolds's estimate in 1977, after polling "several top men," that the average dosage was only 5–10 mg of Dianabol daily and a weekly Primobolan shot before a contest; see *California Bodybuilding-Powerlifting*, July 1977, 13. It was obvious to Jack King, winner of the short class at the 1977

Masters Mr. America, that some contestants were using drugs, including Kent Kuehn, the winner, who "even talked openly about taking them" (King, interview by the author, Chesapeake, Virginia, July 19, 2011).

90. *MBP*, September 1977, 6, 95; October 1977, 28, 94; August 1978, 82, 106.

91. *MMI*, March 1979, 7.

92. Sprague quoted in Goldman, *Death in the Locker Room*, 150–151.

93. *MTI*, October 1982, 72. On hearing that Casey Viator had died three times from "his drug habit" and had needed to be resuscitated in the hospital, Peary Rader queried, "Why do people keep on doing this? It is beyond comprehension that they would prefer to die rather than lose a little bit of their muscle tissue that they have gained through the use of drugs"; see Bruce Page to Rader, September 7, 1980, and Rader to Page, September 25, 1980, Rader Papers.

94. *MTI*, October 1980, 5, 23, 45.

95. *IM*, July 1981, 39.

96. Quoted in *MF*, July 1982, 223.

97. *IM*, July 1978, 14–15.

98. *MTI*, October 1978, 20, 32.

99. *IM*, May 1979, 41; *IM*, March 1980, 20–21.

100. *Natural Bodybuilder*, Spring 1981, 1; *MD*, June 1981, 70; *IM*, January 1982, 15.

101. *Natural Bodybuilding*, April 1982, i, 28–39, 54–57. Peary Rader expressed frustration over the many "splinter groups of physique committees," of which he counted nine internationally. "Too bad they can't get together in one organization and really do something for the sport," he argued to Franklin Page, but all seemed interested in "'the almighty dollar'" (Rader to Page, February 5, 1981, Rader Papers).

102. *MF*, January 1980, 5, 105; *MF*, February 1981, 4–5; Mozee interview.

103. *MMI*, July 1980, 24–25; *MTI*, August 1982, 7–9.

104. Josh Henson, interview by the author, Arlington, Virginia, August 8, 2005;

105. Sprague interview, 2004.

CHAPTER 9: PROFESSIONALIZING AMATEURISM

1. *AAU Physique News*, May 1982, 1–2; *MF*, November 1982, 211; *MF*, January 1983, 211.

2. *MF*, December 1982, 203.

3. For details of the settlement, see Carl J. Morelli to Board of Governors of the National Physique Committee, February 3, 1983; National Physique Committee and International Federation of Bodybuilders v. The Amateur Athletic Union, U.S. District Court, Southern District of New York, 82 Civ. 4535; both in Rader Papers.

4. The Amateur Athletic Union v. The National Physique Committee et al., U.S. District Court for the Eastern District of Tennessee, Civil Action No. 1-82-83, and John Carl Mese v. Stan Morey and Florida Association of AAU, Appeal from the U.S. District Court for the Middle District of Florida in the United States Court of Appeals for the Eleventh Circuit, No. 84–3287; copies of both in Rieger Papers. For the final settlement of the Florida case, see *AAU Physique News*, Spring 1984, 1.

5. *AAU Physique News*, November 1982, 18; *MF*, February 1983, 221.

6. DeMilia interview, 2010.

7. Ibid.

8. Ibid.; *IM*, January 1979, 21, 85.

9. DeMilia interview, 2010.

10. Mozee interview. "Let's face it," DeMilia later boasted. "I'm the most prominent promoter in the history of the IFBB." See "Wayne DeMilia, April 13, 2006," available from the Internet Archive's Wayback Machine: https://web.archive.org/web/20130509131434/http://getbig.com/iview/demilia060413.htm.

11. DeMilia claims that he rescued Manion when Doc Neeley appeared to have enough votes to replace Manion as NPC chairman; DeMilia impersonated Neeley in threatening telephone calls to Manion's wife (DeMilia interview, 2010).

12. DeMilia interview, 2010.

13. Ibid.

14. The emerging dilemma of ascendance was evident as early as 1980 to Gary Leonard just after he won the Mr. America title: "Mr. Universe is a big title, but it's not the Mr. America! There's one Mr. America and four Mr. Universes. Mr. Universe can qualify me for the Olympia. That's the best in the world. That's why I have to win the Mr. Universe this year" (*Muscle Digest*, April 1981, 84).

15. *AAU Physique News*, May 1982, 3–4, 8–10; Dellinger interview.

16. *MD*, August 1982, 62; *MD*, October 1982, 36; *IM*, November 1982, 14–15.

17. *IM*, November 1982, 43–45.

18. Sawyer interview.

19. *AAU Physique News*, November 1982, 6–7; *MD*, February 1983, 6–7; *Muscle Digest*, March 1982, 28–31.

20. *MTI*, June 1982, 9.

21. *MF*, September 1982, 179; *IM*, November 1982, 52c.

22. *IM*, January 1983, 16–17; March 1983, 18. Peary Rader, who attended both contests, deemed the AAU version "much better organized" (Rader to Franklin Page, November 30, 1982, Rader Papers).

23. *MF*, March 1983, 46, 49, 163; February 1983, 221.

24. "Ben wants three things in life," observes Kennedy, "appreciation, awards, and, most of all, money. Ben paid me to give him an award from *MuscleMag* in appreciation. Ben put on a surprise. Ben loves money and prestige" (Kennedy interview).

25. *MF*, November 1982, 115, 156, 209; Weider and Weider, *Brothers of Iron*, 254–283. According to Jon Rieger, the rumor was that IOC officials considered Ben "a four-flusher and a con man and his IFBB a joke" (Jon Rieger, interview by the author, Louisville, Kentucky, February 29, 2012). Rather chillingly, Coe described Ben Weider as "one of the most successful and skillful manipulators of people I have ever come up against" (*MMI*, January 1984, 31).

26. *Physique News*, Summer 1983, 3, 11; Spring 1984, 1, 6, 9.

27. *Flex*, April 1983, 4, 68.

28. *MD*, August 1983, 7.

29. *IM*, January 1984, 34, 36.

30. Ibid., 78; Dellinger interview; Jeff King, interview by Steve Colescott, *Peak Training Journal* 2, available at RxMuscle.com, http://www.rxmuscle.com/articles/latest-news/1014.

31. Jeff King interview.

32. Fred Yale, interview by the author, Tucson, Arizona, June 24, 2007; *MTI*, June 1986, 6. Jon Rieger considered King "an educated young man who was passing through bodybuilding and ended up in something real": "When Jeff King got off drugs, you wouldn't recognize him" (Jon Rieger, interview by the author, Louisville, Kentucky, March 22, 2007).

33. Lending his "full support" to the NPC, Arnold Schwarzenegger, by then a national icon, told Jim Manion that he was even willing to lend his "business expertise" to raise funds for the organization; see *Flex*, January 1984, 75.

34. *MF*, March 1984, 86, 96, 256. Another Weider icon was Frank Zane, an IFBB Mr. America and three-time Mr. Olympia who, according to Steve Wright, was "a Greek statue in the flesh" and "every man's ideal"; see *IM*, January 1985, 12.

35. *IM*, December 1984, 70; *MD*, December 1984, 40; *MD*, December 1985, 20–21; *Physique News*, Winter 1985, 1, 7; *IM*, March 1985, 103; *IM*, January 198), 37, 39. The increased muscularity of female entrants sometimes led to awkward moments of gender confusion, as in the 1983 Ms. America Contest when Faye King, one of the judges, placed one of the contestants last for looking more like a man than a woman. The woman's husband and other officials told her she was judging improperly. According to Faye, she had "learned how to judge contestants" by the following year. It was for King "a critical point for change in the direction of women's bodybuilding" (Faye King, interview by the author, Chesapeake, Virginia, August 2, 2005). In another instance, Ted Karnezis, observing a bodybuilder doing push-ups, said, "Hey, buddy, get up. We're doing men." But it was a woman, Cathy Butler, who became the 1988 Ms. America. "She made some sort of smart retort," Karnezis recalled (Ted Karnezis, interview by the author, Washington, D.C., August 8, 2005).

36. Gaines and Butler, *Pumping Iron II*, 9.

37. Ibid., 162.

38. *MD*, November 1985, 49. For an analysis of the conundrum of muscularity and femininity, see Mansfield and McGinn, "Pumping Irony."

39. *MD*, June 1984, 7; *MD*, August 1984, 7; *Flex*, February 1985, 9.

40. *MF*, January 1985, 45–46, 167. The 80 percent figure for "chemical users" among competitive bodybuilders is also cited by Dr. Carlos DeJesus (*IM*, September 1984, 11).

41. Goldman, *Death in the Locker Room*, 56.

42. *MF*, August 1984, 49, 66–67, 102–105; *Flex*, October 1984, 13.

43. *MD*, February 1983, 46–47, 72–73; *IM*, January 1983, 32–33, 103; *MMI*, January 1984, 47. Natural bodybuilders experienced intimidation from drug users and dealers according to Jack O'Bleness, a promoter of drug-free training. After O'Bleness's truck was burned outside his home in Redondo Beach, California, he was accompanied to a drug-free contest by a black biker gang; O'Bleness, interview by the author, Apple Valley, California, June 5, 2011. See also *Apple Valley Daily Press*, August 20, 2010.

44. *MF*, September 1984, 5, 156, 158, 79–94; January 1985, 200.

45. *MD*, February 1985, 43.

46. "Miss America 1980s" file, Atlantic City Public Library; Watson and Martin, "Miss America Pageant," 112, 115.

47. Osborne, *Miss America*, 122; *Atlantic City Press*, September 6, 1981; Bivans, *Miss America*, 37.

48. *Flex*, May 1983, 50, 79; *MF*, May 1984, 156; *MD*, December 1985, 24.

49. *Muscle Up*, February 1984, 30, 34–35; *MD*, November 1985, 20.

50. Andrew Sullivan, "Muscleheads: Bodybuilding's Bottom Line," *New Republic*, September 15, 1986, 25.

51. *Physique News*, September 1985, 1, 3. Of the twenty-four notable figures initially proposed for the Bodybuilding Hall of Fame, only Joe and Ben Weider were deleted; see Minutes of the AAU America Committee, June 23, 1985, Memphis, Tennessee, Rieger Papers.

52. *MF*, April 1984, 43, 140, 166, 171; March 1985, 56, 65, 116.

53. Paris, *Gorilla Suit*, 216–217.

54. *MF*, April 1985, 40.

55. Additionally, the NABBA Universe was struggling to such an extent that Franklin Page, an *Iron Game* reporter, declined to write about the 1980 contest. "It was pretty terrible," he confided to Peary Rader, and "seems to be on the skids"; Page to Rader, January 29, 1981, Rader Papers.

56. Heidenstam to Terpak, February 2, 1976, Hoffman Papers; *Bodybuilding World*, September 1977, 5–7; *Health and Strength* 108, no. 8 (1979): 7.

57. Heidenstam to Grimek, December 21, 1983; Oscar Heidenstam, "Resignation from W.A.B.B.A.—Great Britain," December 15, 1983, Hoffman Papers; Malcolm Whyatt, interview by the author, July 2, 2004, Hereford, UK. According to the NABBA official Ian McQueen, Oscar opposed Nubret not only "on grounds of his taking drugs but selling them" (McQueen interview).

58. Heidenstam to Grimek, February 17, 1984, and Sawyer to Nubret, December 28, 1983, Hoffman Papers.

59. Sawyer to Heidenstam, December 28, 1984, and Heidenstam to Sawyer, January 23, 1985, Hoffman Papers.

60. *MMI*, June 1986, 32–39; long quotation on 35.

61. *MD*, March 1986, 39, 66–68.

62. *MTI*, February 1986, 57, 60, 62, 53–54.

63. *MMI*, June 1986, 39; *MD*, March 1986, 67.

64. Dellinger added, "I'm giving serious thought to packing it in because these people from 'lip service society' (AAU) quite honestly can't seem to be able to pour piss out of a boot if the directions were on the heel" (Dellinger to Rieger, n.d. [1986; rec'd August 16, 1986], Rieger Papers).

65. Hallum to Rieger, September 23, 1986, Rieger Papers. Pete Miller, Chairman of the Potomac Valley AAU, admitted, "The NPC has beaten us very badly on the p.r." (*Mostly Muscle*, October 1986, 1).

66. *IM*, November 1985, 16 18; *IM*, September 1986, 44; *MD*, February 1987, 39; *MD*, May 1987, 58–61; *MD*, January 1988, 70.

67. *IM*, January 1987, 101; *MTI*, January 1986, 10, 13; *MD*, January 1987, 23.

68. Dellinger to Rieger, [January 1987], Rieger Papers. Included in the agenda was a vertical progression for physique competitions leading from the state level to Mr. America (AAU/MAC) to the Pan American Games (PAPF) to Mr. Universe (IAPF/NABBA) to a World Games (GAISF) to the Olympic Games (IOC) to a Mr. World professional contest sanctioned by a World Professional Physique Association; see "AAU America Corporate Planning Conference" January 10, 1987, Rieger Papers.

69. *MTI*, May 1987, 52. Though the PAPF championship was not drug-tested at first, Miller felt that "the road to success leading to the Olympic Games was in establishing a hemispheral championship" (*Mostly Muscle*, October 1986, 6).

70. The need for a firm stand against drug use by athletes was first raised by former president Henson at a 1983 physique committee meeting; see "1983 AAU Convention Minutes, Physique Committee, September 10, Washington, DC," Rader Papers.

71. Sawyer to Harkins, [rec'd January 31, 1987], Rieger Papers; *AAU Physique Sport Chairman's Newsletter* 87-2 (March 2, 1987), 1; *AAU Physique Sport Chairman's Newsletter* 87-4 (June 1987), 1.

72. Sawyer to AAU Association Physique Chairmen and AAU America Committee, July

7, 1987, Rieger Papers; Rieger, *Official Physique Manual*.

73. Minutes from National Convention, September 8 and 9, 1988, and *Chairman's Newsletter*, November 7, 1988, both in Rieger Papers. For a survey on the development of drug testing before the mid-1980s, see *Natural Bodybuilder*, May 1985, 4–5.

74. *MTI*, May 1987, 52; see also *AAU Physique Sport Chairman's Newsletter* 87–2 (March 2, 1987), 1.

75. Indicative of disillusionment was the resignation of Stan Morey of Tampa from the executive committee. On leaving Knoxville, he was "elated that the AAU physique program looked as if it was going to move forward—what actually occurred was absolutely nothing. I have put my heart and soul plus my families' [*sic*] finances on the line for the AAU—but, this has to end" (Morey to Committee Members, June 26, 1987, Rieger Papers).

76. *MD*, December 1988, 9. For examples of the change in *Muscular Development* policy, see *MD*, November 1986, 5; February 1987, 8–9, 58–59; August 1987, 7; February 1988, 58. Leading up to this change, Dellinger confided to Rieger, "We have unofficial ground rules between MD and the NPC (at the top). A certain amount of info comes via third parties or if Jim wishes he can write me direct" (Dellinger to Rieger, January 1987, Rieger Papers).

77. Bob Bonham, interview by the author, East Rutherford, New Jersey, July 29, 2011.

78. *MD*, April 1986, 38–39; November 1986, 64, 69.

79. Ibid., January 1987, 17; *MTI*, August 1987, 95; *IM*, September 1988, 15; *MTI*, November 1989, 8.

80. *MTI*, August 1987, 95.

81. *MD*, February 1989, 42; *MF*, February 1987, 86; *MMI*, March 1988, 9;

82. *MTI*, April 1988, 67.

83. *Flex*, December 1989, 88.

84. *IM*, January 1990, 58. Similar sentiments were expressed by Phil Hill, who defected to the NPC in 1987: "My final word on the AAU from experience is it offers you no room for growth. You compete to a certain point—the Mr. America contest—and then you plateau off and the only place left to go is down" (*NPC News*, November 1989, 65).

85. *MF*, January 1986, 53; *MD*, August 1987, 7.

86. *International Congress and 41st World Bodybuilding Championships* (Montreal, 1987), 26.

87. *Flex*, August 1988, 139; *MF*, July 1986, 53.

88. *Flex*, November 1989, 145. If Parees's estimates are accurate, NPC registrations increased dramatically in the late 1980s. Data from the independent American Sports Management indicate slow growth before then, from 5,307 in 1979 to 6,792 in 1983—an average annual increase of around 6.4 percent; see NPC Print Out, American Sports Management, Rieger Papers.

89. DeMilia interview, 2010. The *Los Angeles Times* (March 2, 1989) estimated that the Weider commercial empire boasted "2,000 employees worldwide and gross revenues of more than $250 million a year. . . . In the relatively small, little-known world of bodybuilding, Weider is an unchallenged Goliath."

90. According to DeMilia, though he supplied a lot of information to Mike Steere, who assisted the Weiders with their autobiography, Steere later called him with bad news: "I don't know how to tell you this," but "they took you out all the way because, you know, the differences" (Wayne DeMilia, interview by the author, Ridgefield, New Jersey, July 30, 2011).

91. "Bodybuilding changed in September 1988," argues DeMilia, "That's the turning point. When Ben Johnson got caught, steroids were no longer a secret. It was on the front page of every newspaper in the world" (DeMilia interview, 2010).

92. *MMI*, April 1988, 32.

93. *MF*, August 1985, 5; September 1986, 41.

94. Ibid., December 1986, 37; *Flex*, August 1987, 11; *MF*, March 1988, 62; *Flex*, September 1988, 75. The heading for a picture of IFBB executives, dubbed "The Drug Fighters," on the report of the 1987 IFBB Madrid Congress is "First Totally Drug Free 'World Championships'" (*International Congress*, 1).

95. *MD*, November 1989, 8.

96. *MMI*, March 1988, 69.

97. *MF*, October 1988, 147; Coe interview.

98. *MMI*, December 1988, 128–29.

99. Ibid., November 1989, 64–66.

100. *MD*, November 1989, 24.

101. *IM*, January 1989, 11. Crist was unsuccessful in finding sponsorship for a national drug-tested contest for 1991, but remained committed to the cause; see *AAU Sport of Physique Newsletter and Directory*, March 16, 1990, and May 18, 1991, Rieger Papers.

102. *MMI*, July 1989, 58.

103. *MF*, December 1987, 96.

104. *Flex*, September 1989, 17, 37, 54, 59, 76–78, 112.

105. *MMI*, July 1989, 27.

106. *MD*, January 1988, 70.

107. *IM*, September 1988, 71.

108. *Flex*, April 1987, 64.

109. *MF*, August 1985, 7.

110. Ibid., November 1986, 98.

111. *IM*, May 1989, 7.

112. *MF*, January 1990, 53.

113. *MMI*, April 1988, 33–35, 38. However much he admired the idealism of Zulak, the newly appointed editor of *MuscleMag*, Joe Roark rightly reckoned that "there will be no uniformity on this matter," which "will remain a Zulag archipelago" (*Musclesearch*, April–May 1988, 1).

114. *MMI*, April 1988, 35; November 1989, 66.

115. Coe to the author, August 22, 2007; Coe interview; Dellinger interview; *IM*, February 1990, 71.

CHAPTER 10: ECLIPSE OF AN ICON

1. *MMI*, April 1990, 60; *MTI*, February 1990, 157.

2. *MMI*, January 1991, 100; October 1990, 9; November 1990, 13, 149. Cliff Sawyer confirms that "DuFresne got caught for dealing with steroids through the mail" (Sawyer interview).

3. *MTI*, June 1990, 85.

4. *MD*, February 1991, 35–36.

5. *MMI*, March 1991, 40; *MD*, May 1991, 9. Miller was available for posing, seminars, exhibitions, and endorsements for $400–$1,200 an appearance plus expenses (Miller to Rieger, December 18, 1990, Rieger Papers).

6. *MTI*, January 1991, 100; *MD*, September 1991, 61; *MMI*, April 1991, 150.

7. *MMI*, February 1992, 131–32.

8. *MD*, November 1991, 62.

9. *MMI*, May 1992, 103.

10. Joe Tete, interview by the author, Medford, New Jersey, July 29, 2011. Tete added that his expenses were low. The casinos never charged him to use facilities because he was attracting people. It also helped that the casino president's wife was a former Miss New Jersey.

11. *MD*, May 1992, 123.

12. *IM*, October 1996, 98.

13. *MMI*, May 1993, 90.

14. Ibid., September 1993, 18; Anderson, *World's Strongest Man*.

15. *MMI*, September 1993, 22.

16. Mark Donald, "Even Former Mr. America Mike Scarcella Wasn't Strong Enough to Beat the Horrors of GHB Addiction," *Mario Strong's Natural Muscle News*, May 20, 2008, http://www.mariostrong.blogspot.com/2008/05/even-former-mr-america-mike-scarcella .html.

17. At that time, according to public relations agent Joel Parker, his firm was representing both McMahon's WWF and Weider's Mr. Olympia and "served them both well" by providing a communication link between the organizations; Charlotte and Joel Parker, interview by the author, Los Angeles, June 7, 2011.

18. *MD*, February 1991, 9; *MMI*, April 1991, 11; *MD*, July 1991, 9; *IM*, May 1991, 18.

19. *MD*, October 1991, 41–42, 148, 150.

20. Gary Strydom earned $100,000 for first place, and runner-up Mike Christian received $75,000; see *Bodybuilding Lifestyles*, September 1991, 21–22.

21. See Rieger to Larry Thomas, January 31, 1987; Scott V. Kissinger to Jim Manion, February 10, 1988; "Physique Committee Minutes," September 29, 1989; Crist to Executive Board Members and Representatives, September 5, 1990; and *AAU Sport of Physique, 1990, Newsletter and Directory*, December 1, 1990; all in Rieger Papers.

22. Crist to National Officers, December 18, 1991, Rieger Papers. Pete Miller was more blunt. "Linda said, 'We'll have to pick the winner, of course,' and Bob said, 'The conversation is over'" (Pete Miller, interview by the author, Arlington, Virginia, August 8, 2005). What sustained AAU physique, Jon Rieger told Hooley, was its set of published rules, autonomy, amateur ideals, and democratic procedures. McMahon wanted "total domination" with "a business objective, i.e., that of producing spectacles that will maximize profit, and the nature of that business is such that 'honest competition' is a superfluous and quite meaningless concept" (Rieger to Hooley, January 10, 1992, Rieger Papers).

23. *MD*, October 1992, 57; *MD*, November 1991, 9; *MMI*, July 1992, 167; *IM*, July 1992, 18.

24. Coe interview.

25. *MMI*, September 1992, 143; April 1993, 136.

26. *Muscle Media 2000*, Summer 1992, 38.

27. *MD*, November 1992, 132; *Muscle Media 2000*, Summer 1992, 36–38.

28. Dellinger interview.

29. Coe interview.

30. Mauro Di Pasquale, interview by the author, Montreal, August 10, 2011.

31. *Muscle Media 2000*, Summer 1992, 36–38.

32. *MTI*, February 1990, 88; January 1991, 72.

33. *MMI*, November 1991, 150.

34. *MTI*, January 1991, 12. After moving to Venice in the mid-1980s, Dan Duchaine became the main supplier of American and European steroids to retail steroid dealers in Gold's

Gym. He recalled:"I must have had six or maybe nine steroid dealers buying from me.They almost had to wait next to my door to get their stuff in turn.And some of the names I could tell you—you'd be shocked at who they were" (*Muscle Media 2000*, July 1996, 134).

35. *MMI*, June 1992, 175.

36. Di Pasquale interview.

37. Ibid. Designer steroids, the natural-physique promoter Matt Shepley explains, are engineered from a compound for which a test already exists: "They do a little tweak to make it a little different. It will still have anabolic effects on you, but it's not something that gets picked up by the test. . . . So now you have to factor in a way to screen for that.Testers are always behind because people are always creating stuff, and then it takes a while for the authorities, organizations, or drug-testing labs to catch on to it" (Shepley, interview by the author, Surprise,Arizona, June 7, 2011).

38. Hurley to Crist, January 8, 1993; Crist to Dodd, February 11, 1993; Hurley to Dodd, March 4, 1993; all in Rieger Papers. Hurley also cites the *AAU Physique Handbook*, part 5.

39. Pete Miller to Dodd, March 29, 1993; Crist to Ray Mozingo, March 12, 1993; both in Rieger Papers.

40. Crist to Dodd, March 26, 1993; Crist to Mozingo, April 14, 1993; and "Meeting of the Executive Committee of Physique," March 27, 1993; all in Rieger Papers.

41. Karnezis interview; Karnezis to Mozingo, April 12, 1993; Paul Watkins to AAU Official [rec'd September 7, 1993]; "Physique Chairman's Report," *1993 Convention Book, Amateur Athletic Union*, 47, Rieger Papers.

42. *MD*, December 1991, 8; Karnezis interview.

43. Bonham interview; DeMilia interview, 2011; Karnezis interview.

44. Karnezis interview; *MD*, March 1993, 7; October 1993, 184.

45. *MMI*, July 1994, 73, 77, 80; Karnezis interview. "We had been, in my opinion, deceived and kept in the dark," Karnezis confided to Harry Silas, a committee member.

46. Yale interview; *MMI*, July 1994, 73, 77, 80; Karnezis interview. Afterward, Yale reflected that "with the outcome of this past Ms America, many, including myself, feel adjustments are due": "It is one thing to have a female on drugs, but not a female with 'male' bodyparts. . . .To 'hit the nail on the head,' when the overall trophy was being presented, Bob Kennedy remarked, 'That's a giant step backwards'" (Yale to Rieger, November 11, 1993, Rieger Papers).

47. Yale interview; *MMI*, April 1995, 10.

48. *MD*, March 1994, 189.

49. *MMI*, October 1995, 130, 132, 134–135; Yale interview.

50. Miller to America Committee Members, January 6, 1994, and Karnezis to AAU America Committee, January 25, 1994, Rieger Papers. Don Ross, however, viewed drug testing as contrary to restoring greatness to the Mr. America title. He wrote to Karnezis: "Bodybuilding fans pay to see FREAKS, not a posedown between a line-up of good little girls and boys.Very few freaks are drug-free. . . . If you drug test, these guys and gals will have no place to go, and it's producing SUPERSTARS that will put you on the map again!" (Ross to Karnezis, January 26, 1995, Rieger Papers).

51. *MMI*, October 1995, 136; *MD*, September 1995, 222; Karnezis to America Committee Members, April 11, 1995, all in Rieger Papers; Fairfax Hackley, interview by the author, Falls Church,Virginia, August 7, 2011.

52. *MD*, October 1995, 230.

53. *MMI*, April 1995, 54, 56.

54. Offering consolation, Don Ross told Karnezis that the AAU remained a "perfect alternative to those who are tired of the 'Weider Intercourse System'" (Manion to Karnezis, November 9, 1994, and Ross to Karnezis, November 8, 1994, Rieger Papers).

55. Hackley to AAU State Chairpersons, April 21, 1995; Hackley interview; Karnezis to America Committee Members, April 24, 1995; Crist to Karnezis, May 16, 1995; Crist to Rieger, May 16, 1995; all correspondence in Rieger Papers.

56. Karnezis to America Committee Members, June 15, 1995; Physique Committee, Official Meeting Minutes, September 8, 1995; AAU Physique Committee Report, September 6–9, 1995; Karnezis to America Committee Members, September 15, 1995; all in Rieger Papers.

57. *MD*, May 1996, 59.

58. David Chapman contrasts Hackley with Karnezis: "[Karnezis was] this perfectly nice guy; scruffy; he wore loud ties that were out of fashion. Fairfax came in dressed to the nines. It was clear what they saw in him. They saw that here is a way to tap into the world of glamour and glitz. . . . So we're going to use this vehicle to acquire that stuff, and it didn't work out quite the way they thought. Because along with the glitter, glitz, and glamour you get a lot of other baggage that comes along with it—like the drugs" (Chapman, interview by the author, Seattle, Washington, July 28, 2010).

59. George Helmer's "Mr./Ms. America" report is focused almost entirely on Reeves, including the signing of his recently published book, *Building the Classic Physique*, and the many honors that Hackley bestowed on him, but virtually nothing on the contest; see *Steve Reeves International Society Newsletter*, 2 (October 1996): 7–9.

60. Chapman interview.

61. Ibid.; Hackley interview. Terry Hairston, however, recalled things differently: "The night show was full. It was a packed house" (Hairston, interview by the author, Huntington Beach, California, June 17, 2011).

62. Chapman interview. Wayne DeMilia elaborates on this lack of appeal: "You look at all these guys. There's this mass of muscle. This thickness, but there's not the excitement no more when they flex and pose. . . . Nothing pops no more. . . . It just stays the same because the tendons are getting thicker, and you just become one muscular slab. . . . So by taking all this stuff, they're ruining not only the beauty of the physique . . . they're also ruining the entertainment factor" (DeMilia interview, 2010).

63. *Washington City Paper*, September 27, 1996.

64. Chapman interview.

65. Pearl interview; Chapman interview.

66. Crist to Karnezis, November 19, 1995, and Karnezis to America Committee Members, December 7, 1995, Rieger Papers.

67. Hackley interview; Hairston interview; Hairston to the author, June 17, 2011, and July 12, 2011. According to Crist, Hairston, who was "found positive for a controlled substance . . . circled his wagons, called in his attorneys and was crowned the 1995 MR AMERICA" (*Steele Jungle*, December 1999, 17). Max Furek, who was also present, confirms this: "Hairston definitely tested positive. Harry Silas said, 'Let him go—he's just a kid.' The others were concerned with the legal ramifications and costs" (Furek, interview by the author, Mocanaqua, Pennsylvania, March 26, 2013).

68. Karnezis to America Committee Members, April 16, 1996, and July 15, 1996, Rieger Papers.

69. Yale to Karnezis, July 9, 1996, and Crist to Karnezis, July 9, 1996, Rieger Papers.

70. Karnezis to Physique Chairs and National Judges, August 8, 1996, Rieger Papers;

Hackley to Chapman, January 18, 1996, Chapman Papers, Seattle, Washington; and "Minutes of the Mid-Year AAU Physique Committee Meeting, June 30, 1996, Petersburg, Virginia," Rieger Papers.

71. Undated, unidentified clipping [*Washington City Paper?*], Rieger Papers.

72. Hackley interview. Karnezis later justified his actions to Max Furek, the editor of *Steele Jungle*: "After all the committee could barely afford to pay for the tests let alone someone to independently administer them. Not one individual stepped forward to perform the collection process, everyone knew it carried a clear and daunting liability" (Karnezis to Furek, n.d., Karnezis Papers, in author's possession).

73. Crist to Karnezis, January 4, 1997, Rieger Papers.

74. *MD*, March 1997, 195; *MD*, April 1997, 64–81; Karnezis interview.

75. *MMI*, September 1993, 16.

76. *MD*, January 1997, 191.

77. *MMI*, May 1997, 55.

78. *New York Times Magazine*, September 19, 1965.

79. Deford, *There She Is*, 11; *Atlantic City Press*, September 8, 1981.

80. Banet-Weiser, *Most Beautiful Girl*, 32.

81. Bivans, *Miss America*, 72.

82. *MMI*, March 1994, 184.

83. Thesander, *Feminine Ideal*; Pearlman, *Pretty Smart*, 1, 7.

84. *MMI*, November 1993, 166; *MD*, April 1994, 187; *MMI*, March 1991, 129.

85. *MD*, December 1990, 10.

86. *IM*, November 1992, 24.

87. *MMI*, September 1992, 17; November 1992, 166.

88. Pearl interview.

89. *MD*, November 1993, 94; *MD*, May 1996, 124; *MMI*, October 1995, 235; *MMI*, November 1996, 257.

90. *MD*, March 1994, 96; *MMI*, October 1994, 152.

91. *IM*, December 1999, 12.

92. *MD*, March 2000, 170.

93. *MMI*, March 1996, 30; April 2000, 226. What transpired, as Wayne DeMilia explains, was the emergence of a series of fitness spin-offs: "Bikini is for girls not taking drugs, figure for those taking some drugs, women's physique for women taking a little more drugs, and women's bodybuilding for women taking a lot of drugs" (DeMilia interview, 2010).

94. *IM*, September 1993, 14; *MD*, February 1994, 108; Hotten, *Muscle*, 54. Rick Wayne, never one to mince words, called Yates "the ugliest thing in bodybuilding today. . . . A hundred years from now, people will say, 'What the hell was that?'" (*Muscle Media 2000*, February 1994, 125).

95. *MMI*, September 1995, 207; *MD*, September 1994, 185; *MMI*, August 1995, 136, 138; *MD*, May 1996, 64; *MMI*, February 2000, 263.

96. *MMI*, July 1997, 15.

97. *MD*, March 1997, 12.

98. *MMI*, November 1998, 196.

99. *MD*, April 1997, 12.

100. *MMI*, January 2000, 143; *Reps!*, Summer 2006, 117–118.

101. Paris, *Gorilla Suit*, 118.

102. DeMilia interview, 2011. DeMilia makes the point that bodybuilding is losing some

of its core clientele. A fan once told him: "Ronnie Coleman and Jay Cutler are not a gay man's fantasy. And if the gay men are turned off, I'm sure the women are turned off too. They're grotesque" (DeMilia interview, 2010).

103. *MMI*, November 1992, 109; *MMI*, December 1992, 12; *Birmingham Post-Herald*, July 15, 1994; *Muscle Media 2000*, October 1994, 40; *MMI*, June 1996, 196.

104. *Flex*, July 1996, 84; Zabo Kozewski, interview by the author, Los Angeles, June 2, 2004; *IM*, July 1997, 132.

105. *IM*, December 1993, 14; *MMI*, March 1994, 214.

106. *IM*, December 1994, 16; July 1995, 13; December 1995, 8; April 1997, 10.

107. *MMI*, March 1994, 147; *MMI*, April 1994, 235; *MD*, February 1997, 107.

108. Balik to Weider, March 18, 1996, Chapman Papers.

109. *MMI*, April 1997, 184.

110. *MD*, February 1993, 159; Assael, *Steroid Nation*, 38; Paris, *Gorilla Suit*, 84.

111. *IM*, July 1997, 160; Hotten, *Muscle*, 12, 165–166.

112. *IM*, February 1997, 156–162.

113. Ibid., March 1994, 14.

114. Ibid., July 1997, 136, 160.

115. *MMI*, April 1998, 143; Wheeler, *Flex Ability*, 187.

116. *MMI*, December 1997, 185.

117. For details on the AAU alliance with Disney, see "Bobby Dodd to All AAU Family Members," August 2, 1995, Rieger Papers.

118. *MD*, January 1997, 191.

119. *Mr. and Ms. America*, October 11, 1997, 1, 3.

120. Pearl interview; Dellinger interview; Yale interview; Chapman interview.

121. Rieger interview, 2007; Kennedy interview; Dellinger interview; Miller interview; Crist interview; *MD*, August 1999, 183.

122. Yale interview; *Steele Jungle*, December 1998, 4.

123. Karnezis interview.

124. Yale interview.

125. *Steele Jungle*, March 2002, 10.

126. As Josh Henson explains, Bobby Dodd was a "practical guy" with whom it was possible to sit down and "work out a deal," but "all the America guys to their dying day were like purists": "Ted Karnezis wanted to drug test. Bobby the practical guy didn't want lawsuits. Ted and Bobby got into fights, and Ted was unwilling to compromise" (Henson interview, 2011).

127. Karnezis interview; Crist interview; Karnezis to Max Furek, n.d., Karnezis Papers. Karnezis argued that all of the AAU's revenue went into its general fund and "not one penny" to support its doping policy; see Karnezis to Bill Hybl, January 28, 2000, Karnezis Papers.

128. Rieger interview, 2007; Henson interview, 2005; Yale interview; *MMI*, April 1998, 126.

EPILOGUE AND CONCLUSION

1. Yale interview; Crist interview, 2005; *Steele Jungle*, March 2002, 10. Even over a decade later, the AAU remained bitter. When approached by the New York promoter Dave Davis about restoring the organization's sponsorship of physique, President Louis Stout wanted nothing to do with it, "mainly because of drugs" (Davis, interview by the author, Amherst, New York, April 12, 2012).

2. World Bodybuilding and Fitness Association brochure and "2004 WBFA Sanctioned Mr./Ms. America Official Entry Form," in the author's possession; *MMI*, October 2005, 34; Kelvin Fountano, interview by the author, Sacramento, California, May 31, 2004.

3. Bonham interview. Trademarkia indicates that Bonham filed for a U.S. trademark on the name "Mr. America" on December 1, 2009, and that it was formally registered on September 6, 2011 (77883831); see http://www.trademarkia.com/mr-america-77883831.html.

4. DeMilia interview, 2011.

5. With such a minimal expenditure, Bonham "thought [the contest] was going to make money, which it didn't," but he at least "pretty much broke even" (Bonham interview).

6. Ibid.

7. Ibid.; Lori Braun, "2011 Mr. America and Women's Championship Results," Fema leMuscle.com, http://femalemuscle.com/2011-mr-america-and-womens-championship -results.

8. Klein, "Pumping Irony"; Klein, *Little Big Men*, 214.

9. Luciano, *Looking Good*, 153, 208.

10. Pope, Phillips, and Olivardia, *Adonis Complex*, 31.

11. H. Mansfield, *Manliness*, 23; Pope, Phillips, and Olivardia, *Adonis Complex*, 25. Threatened male hegemony is also the theme of Gillett and White, "Male Bodybuilding and Hegemonic Masculinity."

12. Tom Mortensen, "Women Outnumber Men among College Graduates," interview by Steve Inskeep, *Morning Edition*, NPR, May 17, 2005, http://www.npr.org/templates/story/story.php?storyId=4654635.

13. Pope, Phillips, and Olivardia, *Adonis Complex*, 47–48. John Kasson argues that the Adonis complex is hardly new, that men in the late nineteenth and early twentieth centuries displayed similar concerns with their bodies; see Kasson, *Houdini, Tarzan, and the Perfect Man*.

14. Faludi, *Stiffed*, 9, 35, 298, 598–599, 602. Another body of scholarship challenges the notion of a crisis in masculinity and of bodybuilding's cult of muscularity being associated with it; see Richardson and Shaw, *The Body in Qualitative Research*, 27. 53.

15. Lee, *Talking Tough*, ix, 143; Mosse, *Image of Man*, 193. What Brian Caldwell sees is not a new masculinity so much as men resorting to "compensatory masculinities" as stopgaps to the crisis; see Caldwell, "Muscling In on the Movies," 139.

16. Mosse, *Image of Man*, 192; Klein, *Little Big Men*, 22, 246–247, 251. Christopher Forth concurs: "In a society where extreme muscular development has scant functional value in everyday life, the look and feel of strength may be attractive for the aura of control and invulnerability it seems to confer. Muscles have become male fashion accessories in the cult of appearances" (Forth, *Masculinity in the Modern West*, 220).

17. *MMI*, December 1999, 98, 122.

18. Pope, Phillips, and Olivardia, *Adonis Complex*, 35, 67, 72, 84–85, 107; Klein, "Life's Too Short to Die Small," 109.

19. Bordo, *Male Body*, 221.

20. Mauro Di Pasquale, "Performance Enhancement: Drugs in Sports," June 23, 2011, MauroMD.com, www.mauromd.com/det-articles-60-Performance-Enhancement-Drugs -in-Sports.php; Pope, Phillips, and Olivardia, *Adonis Complex*, 60.

21. Di Pasquale, "Performance Enhancement"; see also Nieminen et al., "Serious Cardiovascular Side Effects"; Santora et al., "Coronary Calcification in Body Builders"; Fanton et al., "Heart Lesions Associated with Anabolic Steroid Abuse"; Vanberg and Atar, "Androgenic Anabolic Steroid Abuse."

22. These data were drawn largely from the compilations of Joe Roark in IronHistory .com. Joe Tete notes that Joe DeAngelis, who won the 1991 contest and became Mr. Universe, had two massive heart attacks in his late thirties. Tete was told by DeAngelis: "It was from steroids . . . drugs, cholesterol, heart racing" (Tete, interview by the author, Medford, New Jersey, July 29, 2011).

23. Gordon LaVelle provides a longer list of bodybuilders for whom drugs either "precipitated or aggravated" medical conditions leading to premature deaths; see LaVelle, *Bodybuilding*, 203.

24. Klein, *Little Big Men*, 153.

25. Pearl interview; *MMI*, January 2011, 240.

26. *MMI*, September 1995, 230.

27. *Louisville Courier-Journal*, September 13, 1973.

28. Henson interviews, 2011 and 2005; Michalik interview.

29. *MMI*, April 1997, 182.

30. Tommy Suggs, interview by the author, Freeport, Texas, February 3, 1993; *Musclesearch*, April–May 1988, 1.

31. David Webster, interview by the author, Irvine, UK, July 23, 2004.

32. By 2010, NABBA's top professional prize money was only $2,000, compared to $200,000 for the Mr. Olympia; see *MMI*, November 2011, 299.

33. Weider and Weider, *Brothers of Iron*, 135.

34. Bill Starr, interview by the author, Bel Air, Maryland, July 20, 1991; Adrian interview; Thirer and Greer, "Competitive Bodybuilding," 187; Yale interview; Rieger interview, 2007.

35. Radley and Gentle, *Classic Muscle Art*, 132; Butler, *Arnold Schwarzenegger*, 38.

36. James, *Fame in the Twentieth Century*, 236. However, Arnold's public relations agent, Charlotte Parker, claims credit for transforming his image from bodybuilder to businessman and actor and for making him a national and international name. She notes: "I would say that I was very instrumental in helping Arnold become a very big star. . . . Together we were an incredible team" (Parker interview).

37. Sprague interview, 2009; Sprague to Roach, e-mails, 2006–2011, cited in Roach, *Muscle, Smoke, and Mirrors*, 2:184, 41.

38. Weiss, *Sport*, 209; DeMilia interviews, 2010 and 2011.

39. Roach, *Muscle, Smoke, and Mirrors*, 2:171; LaVelle, *Bodybuilding*, 105, 196–197, 204, 211.

40. Hodgson, *America in Our Time*, 67–68, 492–494; Cantril, *Pattern of Human Concerns*.

41. Graham interview. Kim Wood concurs that "the game couldn't have survived without homosexuality" (Wood interview).

42. J. Scott, "Women's History," 58; Mosse, *Image of Man*, 168–169; Hitler, *Mein Kampf*, 614.

43. Bendel interview; Bosland interview; Crist interview.

44. Michael Budd makes this point by contrasting the physique of a Zulu tribesman, "the finest type of all the black races," with his white counterpart during the Sandow era: "His lean frame was clearly at another extreme from the Greek-inspired ideal seen in most physical culture representations of white European men" (Budd, *Sculpture Machine*, 90).

45. *IM*, June 2003, 219; Grant interview. The female superstar Cory Everson concurs with Robinson: "I believe that physiques should always have long, graceful lines and appear functional—not so stocky or squatty that the person can barely move. . . . When the muscular development becomes overbearing, it's gone overboard" (*IM*, August 2004, 284).

46. One elite bodybuilder, David Dearth, expressed a desire in the 1990s for shows,

similar to women's fitness competitions, in which bodybuilders could prove that they are athletes: "It's kind of hard to get a crowd that's not a bodybuilding crowd hyped up for guys just standing around in their underwear" (*Muscle Media 2000*, June 1993, 16).

47. Wyke, "Herculean Muscle!," 70.

48. Goldstein, *Male Body*, ix.

49. Dombrowski, *Contemporary Athletics*, 92. "I'm not sure there was a Greek ideal other than our looking back and saying they had a Greek ideal," says Mike Graham, drawing perceptions full circle to Winkelmann's creation (Graham interview).

50. Klein, *Little Big Men*, 215; Fussell, "Bodybuilder Americanus," 55–56.

51. See Fair, "The USA vs. the World."

52. *Fit and Firm Magazine*, April 2012, 138; "Fitness with Style: An Interview with WBFF Founder Paul Dillett," Dustin Lapray, Bodybuilding.com, July 30, 2013, http://www.body building.com/fun/fitness-with-style-an-interview-with-wbff-founder-paul-dillett.html.

53. DeMilia interview, 2011; Wayne DeMilia, interview by the author, New York City, August 14, 2013.

54. Tete interview.

55. CrossFit Instructor Manual, 1–2, http://www.slideshare.net/leeshouse/crossfit -instructor-manual-v4.

CrossFit can be traced back to the 1970s, when the former gymnast Greg Glassman initiated the exercises in a garage gym in Santa Cruz, California. But it was not until after 2000 that the concept mushroomed. From 2005 to 2013, the number of CrossFit gyms grew from 18 to over 6,000 worldwide. The top prize for individual champions in 2013 was $275,000. Reebok, the corporate sponsor, has increased the total purse to $1,000,000. For the history of CrossFit, see "Ever Wondered about the History of CrossFit?," CrossFit Zone, http://www.crossfitzone.ca/ever-wondered-about-the-history-of-crossfit; "Greg Glassman, Founder and CEO, CrossFit, March 13, 2013, Full Talk," http://www.youtube.com /watch?v=kPAXQtDNLQ0.

56. "Performance Enhancing Drugs (PEDs) Prohibited for CrossFit Games Participants," CrossFit Games 2010, http://games2010.crossfit.com/drugpolicy; Jeff "Garddawg" Martin, *CrossFit Brand X*, March 21, 2009, http://forum.crossfitbrandx.com/index.php/forums /viewthread/6436/P15.

57. Big Dawg, *CrossFit Brand X*, August 10, 2009, http://forum.crossfitbrandx.com /index.php/forums/viewthread/7674; Russell Berger, "Form Follows Function," *Cross-Fit Journal*, December 29, 2009, http://journal.crossfit.com/2009/12 /form-follows-function.tpl.

58. David Lee Nall, interview by the author, Austin, Texas, April 20, 2012.

59. Graham interview.

60. *Sullivan County Democrat*, September 28, 2004; Hordines interview, June 2003.

61. Michalik interview.

62. On October 22, 2013, Bob Bonham informed prospective contestants that the 2014 Mr. America Contest had been canceled (personal communication to the author). In its place he established a "Gay Mr. America and Women's Extravaganza Championships, LGBT," which was to take place on April 11, 2014, but that event also had to be canceled "due to lack of support by the competitors." Bonham to the author, May 9, 2014.

ARCHIVAL AND MANUSCRIPT SOURCES

David Chapman Papers, Seattle, Washington
Ralph Countryman Papers, San Francisco, California
Ottley Coulter Papers, University of Texas
Bob Crist Papers, author's possession
Alton Eliason Papers, author's possession
David Gentle Papers, Romsey, UK
Bob Hoffman Papers, author's possession
John Hordines Papers, author's possession
Ted Karnezis Papers, author's possession
Earle Liederman File, University of Texas
Miss America Papers, Atlantic City Public Library
Jim Murray Papers, Morrisville, Pennsylvania
Jimmy Payne scrapbook, Healdsburg, California
Peary and Mabel Rader Papers, University of Texas
Jon Rieger Papers, University of Texas
Abbye and Les Stockton Papers, University of Texas
John Terpak Papers, author's possession
Reuben Weaver Papers, Strasburg, Virginia

INTERVIEWS

Joe Abbenda, Garden City, New York, June 20, 2005
Dale Adrian, Simi Valley, California, June 7, 2004
Jules Bacon, York, Pennsylvania, August 30, 1988
John Balik, Santa Monica, California, June 2, 2004
Clarence Bass, Albuquerque, New Mexico, June 8, 2011
Bob Bendel, Moorestown, New Jersey, July 10, 2001

Vic Boff, Fort Myers, Florida, November 10, 1995

Bob Bonham, East Rutherford, New Jersey, July 29, 2011

Len Bosland, Glen Rock, New Jersey, July 24, 2002; January 28, 2004

Howard Bovell, Washington, D.C., April 8, 2004

Richard Cavaler, Southfield, Michigan, June 24, 2007

David Chapman, Seattle, Washington, July 28, 2010

Boyer Coe, Huntington Beach, California, June 3, 2011

Bill Colonna, Chesapeake, Virginia, August 2, 2005

Bob Crist, Hampton, Virginia, July 9, 2001; August 3, 2005

Jerry Daniels, Chattanooga, Tennessee, September 27, 2000

Dave Davis, Amherst, New York, April 12, 2012

John DeCola, Hagerstown, Maryland, June 21, 2003

Jan Dellinger, Red Lion, Pennsylvania, December 14, 1992

Bob Delmontique, Woodland Hills, California, June 3, 2004

Louis DeMarco, Vienna, Ohio, March 27, 2007

Wayne DeMilia, New York, New York, December 17, 2010; New Jersey, July 30, 2011; August 14, 2013

Chris Dickerson, Fort Lauderdale, Florida, November 9, 2006

Mauro Di Pasquale, Montreal, Quebec, August 10, 2011

Dave Draper, Aptos, California, May 30, 2004

Alton Eliason, Northford, Connecticut, June 24, 2003; November 13, 2003

Neva Fickling, Macon, Georgia, November 23, 2009

Kelvin Fountano, Sacramento, California, May 31, 2004

Warren Frederick, Tampa, Florida, May 6, 2004

Max Furek, Mocanaqua, Pennsylvania, March 26, 2013

Frances Gajkowski, Akron, Ohio, March 2, 2010

David Gentle, Romsey, UK, July 3, 2004

Mike Graham, Lockhart, Texas, March 15, 2012

Bill Grant, Orange, New Jersey, March 24, 2003

John Grimek, York, Pennsylvania, August 28, 1987; July 19, 1991

Fairfax Hackley, Falls Church, Virginia, August 7, 2011

Terry Hairston, Huntington Beach, California, June 17, 2011

Josh Henson, Falls Church, Virginia, August 8, 2005; July 21, 2011

Norman and Sylvia Hibbert, London, UK, July 2004

John L. Hoffman, Parker, Pennsylvania, January 1, 1988

John Hordines, East Branch, New York, June 22, 2003; telephone interview, October 13, 2003

Dan Howard, Riverside, California, June 6, 2011

Don Howorth, Los Angeles, California, June 6, 2004

Gene Jantzen, Bartelso, Illinois, December 28, 2003

Harry Johnson, Auburn, Georgia, July 24, 2001

Ted Karnezis, Washington, D.C., August 8, 2005

Bob Kennedy, Mississauga, Ontario, March 28, 2007

Faye King, Chesapeake, Virginia, August 21, 2005

Jack King, Chesapeake, Virginia, July 19, 2011

Joan Klisanin, Long Beach, California, August 9, 2005

Steve Klisanin, Seal Beach, California, March 18, 2005

Charles Kochakian, Birmingham, Alabama, June 25, 1994

Zabo Kozewski, Los Angeles, California, June 2, 2004

Lloyd "Red" Lerille, Lafayette, Louisiana, May 31, 2007

Jim Lorimer, Columbus, Ohio, June 29, 2006

Dan Lurie, Valley Stream, New York, December 16, 2003

Ian McQueen, Martinsburg, West Virginia, December 14, 2003

Tom Manfre, Land O' Lakes, Florida, June 1, 2010

Steve Michalik, Easley, South Carolina, July 26, 2011

Pete Miller, Arlington, Virginia, August 8, 2005

Gene Mozee, Hollywood, California, June 3, 2004

Jim Murray, Morrisville, Pennsylvania, December 15, 2003

David Lee Nall, Austin, Texas, April 20, 2012

Jack O'Bleness, Apple Valley, California, June 5, 2011

Tommy O'Hare, Chalmette, Louisiana, July 13, 2002

E. M. Orlick, Brandywine, Maryland, December 14, 1993

Jim Park, Ripley, West Virginia, December 22, 1996

Charlotte and Joel Parker, Los Angeles, California, June 7, 2011

Jimmy Payne, Healdsburg, California, June 6, 2004

Bill Pearl, Phoenix, Oregon, July 30, 2010

Joe Peters, Schenectady, New York, June 26, 2001

Jon Rieger, Louisville, Kentucky, March 22, 2007; March 29, 2012

Ken "Leo" Rosa, New York, New York, April 7, 2004

Rudy Sablo, New York, New York, July 7, 2001

Elmo Santiago, New York, New York, April 16, 2004

Cliff Sawyer, Worcester, Massachusetts, May 22, 2008

Matt Shepley, Surprise, Arizona, June 7, 2011

Dick Smith, Hanover, Pennsylvania, May 20, 2008

Harry Smith, Tampa, Florida, May 18, 2000

Ken Sprague, Marietta, Georgia, September 25, 2004; January 13, 2005; October 13, 2009

Bill Starr, Bel Air, Maryland, July 20, 1991

Leo Stern, San Diego, California, June 6, 2004

Tommy Suggs, Freeport, Texas, February 3, 1993

Armand Tanny, Canoga Park, California, June 7, 2004

John Terpak, York, Pennsylvania, July 25, 1991

Joe Tete, Medford, New Jersey, July 29, 2011

Terry Todd, Austin, Texas, February 6, 1993

Val Vasilieff, Sewell, New Jersey, June 6, 2002

Vern Weaver, Dover, Pennsylvania, July 3, 1992

David Webster, Irvine, UK, July 23, 2004

Malcolm Whyatt, Hereford, UK, July 2, 2004

Kim Wood, Cincinnati, Ohio, March 24, 2007

Fred Yale, Tucson, Arizona, June 24, 2007

Chet Yorton, Woodland Hills, California, June 4, 2011

Frank Zane, La Mesa, California, June 6, 2007 (by telephone)

BOOKS AND ARTICLES

Adams, Mark. *Mr. America: How Muscular Millionaire Bernarr Macfadden Transformed the Nation through Sex, Salad, and the Ultimate Starvation Diet*. New York: HarperCollins, 2009.

Adams, Rachel, and David Savran, eds. *The Masculinity Studies Reader*. Oxford: Blackwell, 2002.

Allen, Albert Arthur. *Alo Studies*. Oakland, Calif.: Allen Art Studios, 1920.

Aldrich, Robert, ed. *Gay Life and Culture: A World History*. New York: Universe, 2006.

Anderson, Paul. *The World's Strongest Man*. Wheaton, Ill.: Victor, 1975.

Andrews, Nigel. *True Myths: The Life and Times of Arnold Schwarzenegger*. Secaucus, N.J.: Birch Lane, 1996.

Armstrong, Tim, ed. *American Bodies: Cultural Histories of the Physique*. New York: New York University Press, 1996.

Arnoldi, Katie. *Chemical Pink: A Novel of Obsession*. New York: Doherty, 2001.

Assael, Shaun. *Steroid Nation*. New York: ESPN Books, 2007.

Atlas, Charles. *Secrets of Muscular Power and Beauty*. New York, 1924.

Baker, Barbara Outland. *Arnold and Me: In the Shadow of the Austrian Oak*. Bloomington, Ind.: AuthorHouse, 2006.

Baker, William. *Sports in the Western World*. Totowa, N.J.: Rowman and Littlefield, 1982.

Banet-Weiser, Sarah. *The Most Beautiful Girl in the World: Beauty Pageants and National Identity*. Berkeley and Los Angeles: University of California Press, 1999.

Banner, Lois W. *American Beauty*. New York: Knopf, 1983.

Beecher, Catharine. *Physiology and Calisthenics for Schools and Families*. New York: Harper and Brothers, 1856.

Bender, Thomas, ed. *Rethinking American History in a Global Age*. Berkeley and Los Angeles: University of California Press, 2002.

Berlinerblau, Jacques. *Heresy in the University: The "Black Athena" Controversy and the Responsibilities of American Intellectuals*. New Brunswick, N.J.: Rutgers University Press, 1999.

Bernal, Martin. *Black Athena: The Afroasiatic Roots of Classical Civilization*. New Brunswick, N.J.: Rutgers University Press, 1987.

———. "The British Utilitarians, Imperialism and the Fall of the Ancient Model." *Culture and History* 3 (1988): 98–127.

———. *Cadmean Letters: The Transmission of the Alphabet to the Aegean and Further West before 1400 B.C.* Winona Lake, Ind.: Eisenbrauns, 1990.

Birley, Derek. *Playing the Game, Sport and British Society, 1910–45*. Manchester: Manchester University Press, 1995.

Bivans, Ann-Marie. *Miss America: In Pursuit of the Crown*. New York: Mastermedia, 1991.

Blaikie, William. *How to Get Strong and How to Stay So*. New York: Harper and Brothers, 1883.

Boardman, John. *Greek Art*. 4th ed. London: Thames and Hudson, 1996.

Bordo, Susan. *The Male Body: A New Look at Men in Public and in Private*. New York: Farrar, Straus, and Giroux, 1999.

Bowra, C. M. *The Greek Experience*. New York: World, 1957.

Brailsford, Dennis. *British Sport: A Social History*. Cambridge: Lutterworth, 1992.

Bright, Charles, and Michael Geyer. "Where in the World Is America?" In Bender, *Rethinking American History in a Global Age*, 63–100.

Budd, Michael Anton. *The Sculpture Machine: Physical Culture and Body Politics in the Age of Empire*. New York: New York University Press, 1997.

Burke, Peter, ed. *New Perspectives on Historical Writing*. University Park: Penn State University Press, 2001.

Butler, E. M. *The Tyranny of Greece over Germany: A Study of the Influence Exercised by Greek Art and Poetry over the Great German Writers of the Eighteenth, Nineteenth, and Twentieth Centuries*. Boston: Beacon, 1958.

Butler, George. *Arnold Schwarzenegger: A Portrait*. New York: Simon and Schuster, 1990.

Butler, George, and Charles Gaines. *Yours in Perfect Manhood, Charles Atlas*. New York: Simon and Schuster, 1982.

Caldwell, Brian. "Muscling In on the Movies: Excess and the Representation of the Male Body in Films of the 1980s and 1990s." In Armstrong, *American Bodies,* 133–140.

Cantril, Hadley. *The Pattern of Human Concerns*. New Brunswick, N.J.: Rutgers University Press, 1965.

Carter, David. *The Iron Game*. Venice, Calif., 1976.

Chapman, David L. *Sandow the Magnificent: Eugen Sandow and the Beginnings of Bodybuilding*. Urbana: University of Illinois Press, 1994.

Chapman, David L., and Brett Josef Grubisic. *American Hunks: The Muscular Male Body in Popular Culture, 1860–1970*. Vancouver: Arsenal Pulp, 2009.

Crowther, Nigel B. *Sport in Ancient Times*. London: Praeger, 2007.

Deford, Frank. *There She Is: The Life and Times of Miss America*. New York: Viking, 1971; rev. ed., New York: Penguin, 1978.

Dickinson, G. Lowes. *The Greek View of Life*. London: Methuen, 1896. Reprint, Westport, Conn.: Greenwood, 1979.

Dombrowski, Daniel. *Contemporary Athletics and Ancient Greek Ideals*. Chicago: University of Chicago Press, 2009.

Draper, Dave. *Brother Iron, Sister Steel: A Bodybuilder's Book*. Aptos, Calif.: On Target, 2001.

Durant, John, and Otto Bettmann. *Pictorial History of American Sports from Colonial Times to the Present*. New York: Barnes, 1952.

Dutton, Kenneth. *The Perfectible Body: The Western Ideal of Male Physical Development*. New York: Continuum, 1995.

Dworkin, Susan. *Miss America, 1945: Bess Myerson's Own Story*. New York: Newmarket, 1987.

Edwards, Harry. "The Myth of the Racially Superior Athlete." *Intellectual Digest* 2 (March 1972): 58–60.

Eliason, Alton. "All-American Johnny Hordines: Originator of the Mr. America Contest." *Body Builder Magazine,* January 1948, 4–5.

Elkins, James. "What Is the Difference between the Body's Inside and Its Outside?" In Shigehisa, *Imagination of the Body,* 9–16.

Elliott, J. H. "The Missing History: A Symposium." *Times Literary Supplement*, June 23, 1989, 699.

Entine, Jon. *Taboo: Why Black Athletes Dominate Sports and Why We're Afraid to Talk about It*. New York: Public Affairs, 2000.

Ernst, Robert. *Weakness Is a Crime: The Life of Bernarr Macfadden*. Syracuse, N.Y.: Syracuse University Press, 1991.

Ewing, William A. *The Body: Photographs of the Human Form*. San Francisco: Chronicle, 1994.

Fair, John D. "Father-Figure or Phony? George Jowett, the ACWLA and the Milo Barbell Company, 1924–1927." *Iron Game History* 3 (December 1994).

———. "From Philadelphia to York: George Jowett, Mark Berry, Bob Hoffman, and the Rebirth of American Weightlifting, 1927–1936." *Iron Game History* 4 (April 1996).

———. "George Jowett, Ottley Coulter, David Willoughby and the Organization of American Weightlifting, 1911–1924." *Iron Game History* 2 (May 1993).

———. "Georgia: 'Cradle' of Southern Strongmen in the Twentieth Century." *Atlanta History* 45, no. 3 (Summer 2002): 25–45.

———. "Isometrics or Steroids? Exploring New Frontiers in Strength in the Early 1960s" *Journal of Sport History* 20 (Spring 1993): 1–24.

———. *Muscletown USA: Bob Hoffman and the Manly Culture of York Barbell.* University Park: Pennsylvania State University Press, 1999.

———. "Olympic Weightlifting and the Introduction of Steroids: A Statistical Analysis of World Championship Results, 1948–1972." *International Journal on the History of Sport* 5 (Spring 1988): 96–114.

———. "The USA vs. the World: A Statistical Analysis of American, World, and Olympic Weightlifting Results, 1970–1992." *Iron Game History* 12 (August 2013): 19–25.

Faludi, Susan. *Stiffed: The Betrayal of the American Man.* New York: Putnam, 1999.

Fanton, L., D. Belhani, F. Vaillant, A. Tabib, L. Gomez, J. Descotesk, L. Dehina, B. Bui-Xuan, D. Malicier, and Q. Timour. "Heart Lesions Associated with Anabolic Steroid Abuse: Comparison of Post-mortem Findings of Athletes and Norethandrolone-induced Lesions in Rabbits." *Experimental Toxicology Pathology* 61 (July 2009): 317–323.

Farnsworth, Marjorie. *The Ziegfeld Follies.* London: Davies, 1956.

Finley, M. I., and H. W. Pleket. *The Olympic Games: The First Thousand Years.* London: Chatto and Windus, 1976.

Forth, Christopher E. *Masculinity in the Modern West: Gender, Civilization, and the Body.* New York: Palgrave Macmillan, 2008.

Foutch, Ellery. "Arresting Beauty: The Perfectionist Impulse in Peale's Butterflies, Heade's Hummingbirds, Blaschka's Flowers, and Sandow's Body." PhD diss., University of Pennsylvania, 2011.

Fussell, Samuel Wilson. "Bodybuilder Americanus." In Goldstein, *The Male Body*, 43–60.

———. *Muscle: Confessions of an Unlikely Bodybuilder.* New York: Poseidon, 1991.

Gaines, Charles, and George Butler. *Pumping Iron II: The Unprecedented Woman.* New York: Simon and Schuster, 1984.

Gardner, Percy. "The Lamps of Greek Art." In Livingstone, *Legacy of Greece*, 353–396.

Geldbach, Erich. "The Beginning of German Gymnastics in America." *Journal of Sport History* 3 (Winter 1976): 236–272.

Gillett, James, and Philip G. White. "Male Bodybuilding and the Reassertion of Hegemonic Masculinity: A Critical Feminist Perpsective." *Play and Culture* 5 (1992): 358–369.

Gitlin, Todd. *The Sixties: Years of Hope, Days of Rage.* New York: Bantam, 1987.

Goldhill, Simon. *Victorian Culture and Classical Antiquity.* Princeton, N.J.: Princeton University Press, 2011.

Goldman, Bob. *Death in the Locker Room: Steroids and Sports.* South Bend, Ind.: Icarus, 1984.

Goldstein, Laurence, ed. *The Male Body: Features, Destinies, Exposures.* Ann Arbor: University of Michigan Press, 1994.

Green, Harvey. *Fit for America: Health, Fitness, Sport and American Society.* New York: Pantheon, 1986.

Grover, Kathryn, ed. *Fitness in American Culture: Images of Health, Sport, and the Body, 1830–1940.* Amherst: University of Massachusetts Press, 1989.

Guttmann, Allen. *From Ritual to Record: The Nature of Modern Sports*. New York: Columbia University Press, 1978.

———. *The Olympics: A History of the Modern Games*. Urbana: University of Illinois Press, 1992.

Hall, Daniel T., and John D. Fair. "The Pioneers of Protein." *Iron Game History* 8 (May–June 2004): 23–34.

Hall, Douglas Kent. *Arnold: The Education of a Bodybuilder*. New York: Simon and Schuster, 1977.

Halperin, David. "The Democratic Body: Prostitution and Citizenship in Classical Athens." *South Atlantic Quarterly* 88 (Winter 1989): 149–160.

Halperin, Ian. *The Governator: From Muscle Beach to his Quest for the White House, the Improbable Rise of Arnold Schwarzenegger*. New York: HarperCollins, 2010.

Hanson, Dian. *The History of Men's Magazines*. Vol. 2, *Post-war to 1959*. Cologne: Taschen, 2004.

Herrnstein, Richard J., and Charles Murray. *The Bell Curve: Intelligence and Class Structure in American Life*. New York: Free Press, 1994.

Heywood, Leslie. *Bodymakers: A Cultural Anatomy of Women's Body Building*. New Brunswick, N.J.: Rutgers University Press, 1998.

Hitler, Adolf. *Mein Kampf*. New York: Reynal and Hitchcock, 1939.

Hoberman, John. *Darwin's Athletes: How Sports Has Damaged Black America and Preserved the Myth of Race*. Boston: Houghton Mifflin, 1997.

Hodgson, Godfrey. *America in Our Time*. Garden City, N.Y.: Doubleday, 1976.

Hofmann, Annette. *The American Turner Movement: A History from Its Beginnings to 2000*. Indianapolis: Max Kade German-American Center, Indiana University–Purdue University Indianapolis, 2010.

Hoffman, Bob. *Secrets of Strength and Development*. York, Pa.: Strength and Health, 1940.

———. *Weight Lifting*. York, Pa.: Strength and Health, 1939.

Holt, Richard. *Sport and the British: A Modern History*. Oxford: Oxford University Press, 1989.

Hooven, F. Valentine, III. *Beefcake: The Muscle Magazines of America 1950–1970*. Cologne: Taschen, 1995.

Hotten, Jon. *Muscle: A Writer's Trip through a Sport with No Boundaries*. London: Yellow Jersey, 2004.

Hunt, William R. *Body Love: The Amazing Career of Bernarr Macfadden*. Bowling Green, Ohio: Bowling Green State University Popular Press, 1989.

Hupperts, Charles. "Homosexuality in Greece and Rome." In Robert Aldrich, *Gay Life and Culture*, 29–56.

James, Clive. *Fame in the Twentieth Century*. New York: Random House, 1993.

Jenkyns, Richard. *The Victorians and Ancient Greece*. Cambridge, Mass.: Harvard University Press, 1980.

Johnson, David K. "Physique Pioneers: The Politics of the 1960s Gay Consumer Culture." *Journal of Social History* 43 (Summer 2010): 867–892.

Jowett, George F. *Key to Might and Muscle*. Philadelphia: Milo, 1926.

Kasson, John F. *Houdini, Tarzan, and the Perfect Man: The White Male Body and the Challenge of Modernity in America*. New York: Hill and Wang, 2001.

Kaye, Kristin. *Iron Maidens: The Celebration of the Most Awesome Female Muscle in the World*. New York: Running Press, 2005.

Kazin, Michael, and Joseph A. McCartin, eds. *Americanism: New Perspectives on the History of an Ideal*. Chapel Hill: University of North Carolina Press, 2006.

Kimmel, Michael. "Consuming Manhood: The Feminization of American Culture and the Recreation of the Male Body, 1832–1920." In Goldstein, *The Male Body*, 12–41.

———. *Manhood in America: A Cultural History*. New York: Free Press, 1996.

Klein, Alan M. "Life's Too Short to Die Small: Steroid Use among Male Bodybuilders." In Sabo and Gordon, *Men's Health and Illness*, 105–121.

———. *Little Big Men: Bodybuilding Subculture and Gender Construction*. Albany: State University of New York Press, 1993.

———. "Pumping Irony: Crisis and Contradiction in Bodybuilding." *Sport Sociology Journal* 3 (1986): 112–133.

Kochakian, Charles D. *How It Was: Anabolic Action of Steroids and Remembrances*. Birmingham: University of Alabama School of Medicine, 1984.

Krasniewicz, Louise, and Michael Blitz. *Arnold Schwarzenegger: A Biography*. Westport, Conn.: Greenwood, 2006.

Kuriyama, Shigehisa. *The Expressiveness of the Body and the Divergence of Greek and Chinese Medicine*. New York: Zone, 1999.

Kuriyama, Shigehisa, ed. *The Imagination of the Body and the History of Bodily Experience*. Kyoto: International Research Center for Japanese Studies, 2001.

Lasch, Christopher. "The Baby Boomers: Here Today, Gone Tomorrow." *New Oxford Review* 60 (September 1993): 7–8, 10.

LaVelle, Gordon. *Bodybuilding: Tracing the Evolution of the Ultimate Physique*. Romanart Books, 2011.

Leamer, Laurence. *Fantastic: The Life of Arnold Schwarzenegger*. New York: St. Martin's, 2005.

LeClaire, Chris. *Steve Reeves: Worlds to Conquer; An Authorized Biography*. South Chatham, Mass.: Monomoy, 1999.

Lee, Carol. *Talking Tough: The Fight for Masculinity*. London: Arrow, 1993.

Leigh, Wendy. *Arnold: An Unauthorized Biography*. Chicago: Congdon and Weed, 1990.

Livingstone, R. W. *The Greek Genius and Its Meaning to Us*. Oxford: Clarendon Press, 1912.

———, ed. *The Legacy of Greece*. Oxford: Clarendon Press, 1921.

Lovegrove, Keith. *Pageant: The Beauty Contest*. London: Laurence King, 2002.

Lowe, Maria R. *Women of Steel: Female Body Builders and the Struggle for Self-Definition*. New York: New York University Press, 1998.

Lowerson, John. *Sport and the English Middle Classes, 1870–1914*. Manchester: Manchester University Press, 1993.

Luciano, Lynne. *Looking Good: Male Body Image in Modern America*. New York: Hill and Wang, 2001.

Lurie, Dan. *Heart of Steel: The Dan Lurie Story*. Bloomington, Ind.: AuthorHouse, 2009.

MacAloon, John. *This Great Symbol: Pierre de Coubertin and the Origins of the Modern Olympic Games*. Chicago: University of Chicago Press, 1981.

Macfadden, Bernarr. *Muscular Power and Beauty*. New York: Physical Culture, 1906.

MacMahon, Charles. *Health, Strength and Muscular Efficiency*. Philadelphia, 1926.

Macmillan, Harold. *Pointing the Way, 1959–1961*. London: Macmillan, 1972.

Manchester, William. *The Glory and the Dream: A Narrative History of America, 1932–1972*. Boston: Little, Brown, 1973.

Mansfield, Alan, and Barbara McGinn. "Pumping Irony: The Muscular and the Feminine." In Scott and Morgan, *Body Matters*, 49–68.

Mansfield, Harvey C. *Manliness*. New Haven, Conn.: Yale University Press, 2006.

Martin, Nancie. *Miss America through the Looking Glass: The Story behind the Scenes*. New York: Messner, 1985.

Martindale, Charles, and David Hopkins. *Horace Made New: Horatian Influences on British Writing*. Cambridge: Cambridge University Press, 2009.

Marwick, Arthur. *Beauty in History: Society, Politics and Personal Appearance, c. 1500 to the Present*. London: Thames and Hudson, 1988.

Massengill, Reed. *The Male Ideal: Lon of New York and the Masculine Physique*. New York: Universe, 2003.

Massey, John. *American Adonis: Tony Sansone, the First Male Physique Icon*. New York: Universe, 2004.

Mathews, Joe. *The People's Machine: Arnold Schwarzenegger and the Rise of Blockbuster Democracy*. New York: PublicAffairs, 2006.

Meyer, Donald. *The Positive Thinkers: A Study of the American Quest for Health, Wealth, and Personal Power from Mary Baker Eddy to Norman Vincent Peale*. Garden City, N.Y.: Doubleday, 1965.

Michalik, Steve. *Atomic Fitness: The Alternative to Drugs, Steroids, Wacky Diets, and Everything Else That's Failed*. Laguna Beach, Calif.: Basic Health, 2006.

Miller, Stephen G. *Ancient Greek Athletics*. New Haven, Conn.: Yale University Press, 2004.

Minichiello, Tom. *Bodybuilders, Drugs, and Sex*. Fort Myers, Fla.: Mid-City, 1997.

Moore, Pamela L. *Building Bodies*. New Brunswick, N.J.: Rutgers University Press, 1997.

Mosse, George L. *The Image of Man: The Creation of Modern Masculinity*. New York: Oxford University Press, 1996.

Mrozek, Donald. "Sport in American Life: From National Health to Personal Fulfillment, 1890–1940." In Grover, *Fitness in American Culture*, 18–46.

Murray, Jim. "Jim Lorimer: The Iron Game's Greatest Promoter." *Iron Game History* 5 (December 1998): 4–7.

Nieminen, M. S., M. P. Ramo, M. Viitasalo, P. Heikkila, J. Karjalainen, M. Mantysaari, and J. Heikkila. "Serious Cardiovascular Side Effects of Large Doses of Anabolic Steroids in Weight Lifters." *European Heart Journal* 17 (October 1996): 1576–1583.

Nussbaum, Emily. "Bodies That Matter." *Lingua Franca*, October 1998.

Oliva, Sergio. *Sergio Oliva: The Myth*. Miami: Gras, 2007.

Osborne, Angela Salino. *Miss America: The Dream Lives On*. Dallas: Taylor, 1995.

Oursler, Fulton. *Behold the Dreamer! An Autobiography*. Boston: Little, Brown, 1964.

———. *The True Story of Bernarr Macfadden*. New York: Bernarr MacFadden Foundation, 1930.

Pang, Henry. "Miss America: An American Ideal." *Journal of Popular Culture* 3 (Spring 1969): 687–696.

Paris, Bob. *Gorilla Suit: My Adventures in Bodybuilding*. New York: St. Martin's, 1997.

Paschall, Harry. *Muscle Moulding: A Bosco Book for Advanced Body-Builders*. London: Vigour Press, 1950. Reprint, Farmington, Mich.: Hinbern, 1976.

Pearl, Bill. *Getting Stronger*. Bolinas, Calif.: Shelter, 1986.

Pearlman, Penny. *Pretty Smart: Lessons from Our Miss Americas*. Bloomington, Ind.: AuthorHouse, 2008.

Plato. *The Republic*. Translated by Francis Macdonald Cornford. New York, 1963.

Pope, Harrison G., Jr., Katharine A. Phillips, and Roberto Olivardia. *The Adonis Complex: The Secret Crisis of Male Body Obsession*. New York: Free Press, 2000.

Radley, Alan. *The Illustrated History of Physical Culture*. Preston, UK: Snape, 2001.

Radley, Alan, and David Gentle. *Classic Muscle Art: Muscular Ideals and Inspirations*. Blackpool, UK: Radley, 2011.

Radway, Janice A. "What's in a Name?" *American Quarterly* 51 (March 1999): 1–32.

Reeves, Steve. *Building the Classic Physique the Natural Way.* Calabasas, Calif.: Little-Wolff Group, 1996.

Richardson, John, and Alison Shaw. *The Body in Qualitative Research.* Aldershot, UK: Ashgate, 1998.

Richter, Kat, and Jan Todd. "Jim Lorimer's Unexpected Path: From the Ohio Track Club to the Arnold Sports Festival." *Iron Game History* 11 (June 2011): 19–32.

Rieger, Jon H., ed. *Official Physique Manual: AAU Official Rules for Amateur Physique Competition.* Indianapolis: Amateur Athletic Union of the United States, 1987.

Riverol, A. R. *Live from Atlantic City: The History of the Miss America Pageant before, after, and in spite of Television.* Bowling Green, Ohio: Bowling Green State University Popular Press, 1992.

Roach, Randy. *Muscle, Smoke, and Mirrors.* 2 vols. Bloomington, Ind.: AuthorHouse, 2008, 2011.

Roberts, Randy, and James Olson. *Winning Is the Only Thing: Sports in America since 1945.* Baltimore: Johns Hopkins University Press, 1989.

Rose, Marla Matzer. *Muscle Beach: Where the Best Bodies in the World Started a Fitness Revolution.* New York: LA Weekly Books, 2001.

Sabo, Donald, and David Frederick Gordon, eds. *Men's Health and Illness: Gender, Power, and the Body.* Thousand Oaks, Calif.: Sage 1995.

Sachs, Jonathan. "Empire-themed." *Times Literary Supplement,* February 10, 2012.

———. *Roman Antiquity: Rome in the British Imagination, 1789–1832.* Oxford: Oxford University Press, 2009.

Samuel, Lawrence R. *The American Dream: A Cultural History.* Syracuse, N.Y.: Syracuse University Press 2012.

Santora, L. J., J. Marin, J. Vangrow, C. Minegar, M. Robinson, J. Mora, and G. Friede. "Coronary Calcification in Body Builders Using Anabolic Steroids." *Preventive Cardiology* 9 (Fall 2006): 198–201.

Savage, Candace. *Beauty Queens: A Playful History.* New York: Abbeville, 1998.

Schodl, Gottfried. *The Lost Past: A Story of the International Weightlifting Federation.* Budapest: International Weightlifting Federation, 1992.

Schwarzenegger, Arnold. *Arnold: The Education of a Bodybuilder.* New York: Simon and Schuster, 1977.

———. *Total Recall: My Unbelievably True Life Story.* New York: Simon and Schuster, 2012.

Scott, Joan. "Women's History." In Burke, *New Perspectives on Historical Writing,* 42–66.

Scott, Larry. *Loaded Guns.* Salt Lake City: Scott and Associates, 1991.

Scott, Sue, and David Morgan. *Body Matters: Essays on the Sociology of the Body.* London: Falmer, 1993.

Squire, Michael. *The Art of the Body: Antiquity and Its Legacy.* London: Tauris, 2011.

Sullivan, Andrew. "Muscleheads: Bodybuilding's Bottom Line." *New Republic,* September 15, 1986.

Tan, Adrian James, and Doug Brignole. *Million Dollar Muscle: A Historical and Sociological Perspective of the Fitness Industry.* San Diego: Cognella Academic, 2012.

Thesander, Marianne. *The Feminine Ideal.* London: Reaktion, 1997.

Thirer, Joel, and Donald L. Greer. "Competitive Bodybuilding: Sport, Art, or Exhibitionism?" *Journal of Sport Behavior* 1 (1978): 186–194.

Thomas, Al. "Police Chief Joe Peters: Lawman as Strongman." *Iron Game History,* April 1992, 18–19.

Todd, Jan. "Bernarr Macfadden: Reformer of Feminine Form." *Journal of Sport History* 14 (Spring 1987): 61–75.

———. *Physical Culture and the Body Beautiful.* Macon, Ga.: Mercer University Press, 1999.

Tosh, John. *The Pursuit of History: Aims, Methods and New Directions in the Study of Modern History.* Harlow, UK: Longman, 2010.

Toynbee, Arnold. "History." In Livingstone, *Legacy of Greece,* 289–320.

Turner, Bryan S. *The Body and Society: Explorations in Social Theory.* 2nd ed. London: Sage, 1996.

Turner, Frank M. *The Greek Heritage in Victorian Britain.* New Haven, Conn.: Yale University Press, 1981.

Ueberhorst, Horst. *Friedrich Ludwig Jahn and His Time, 1778–1852.* Munich: Moos, 1978.

Valentino, Gregg, and Nathan Jendrick. *Death, Drugs, and Muscle.* Toronto: ECW, 2010.

Vamplew, Wray. *Pay Up and Play the Game: Professional Sport in Britain, 1875–1914.* Cambridge: Cambridge University Press, 1988.

Vanberg, P., and D. Atar. "Androgenic Anabolic Steroid Abuse and the Cardiovascular System." *Handbook of Experimental Pharmacology* 195 (2010): 411–457.

Walters, Margaret. *The Nude Male: A New Perspective.* New York: Paddington, 1978.

Watson, Elwood, and Darcy Martin. "The Miss America Pageant: Pluralism, Femininity, and Cinderella All in One." *Journal of Popular Culture* 34 (Summer 2000): 105–126.

Wayne, Rick. *The Bodymen.* St. Lucia: Star, 1978.

———. *Muscle Wars.* New York: St. Martin's, 1985.

Weaver, George Russell. *The Enrichment of Life: Fourteen Keys That Reveal Some Secrets of Sports, Health, Sex, Mental Development, the Enjoyment of Art, and a Liberal Self-Education.* Buffalo, N.Y.: Prometheus, 1986.

Webster, David. *Barbells + Beefcake: An Illustrated History of Bodybuilding.* Irvine, UK: published by the author, 1979.

Weider, Joe, and Ben Weider. *Brothers of Iron.* Champaign, Ill.: Sports Publishing, 2006.

Weintraub, Daniel. *Party of One: Arnold Schwarzenegger and the Rise of the Independent Voter.* Sausalito, Calif.: PoliPoint, 2007.

Weiss, Paul. *Sport: A Philosophic Inquiry.* Carbondale: Southern Illinois University Press, 1969.

Wheeler, Flex. *Flex Ability: A Story of Strength and Survival.* Carlsbad, Calif.: Hay House, 2003.

Wigglesworth, Neil. *The Evolution of English Sport.* London: Cass, 1996.

Will, Barbara. "Nervous Systems, 1880–1915." In Armstrong, *American Bodies,* 86–100.

Willoughby, David P. *The Truth about Physical Training.* Santa Barbara, Calif., 1933.

Winckelmann, Johann. *Reflections on the Imitation of Greek Works in Painting and Sculpture.* Translated by Elfriede Heyer and Roger C. Norton. 1755. La Salle, Ill.: Open Court, 1987.

Wyke, Maria. "Herculean Muscle! The Classicizing Rhetoric of Bodybuilding." *Arion* 4 (1996): 51–79.

INDEX

Fox, Bertil, 214, 302
Fox, Jim, 254
Francis, Beverley, 281
Franco-Prussian War, 52
Fratello, Karen, 375
Frederick, Warren, 176, 219, 220, 289, 376, 404n85
Freeman, Patricia, 189
Fritsche, John, 110
Furek, Max, 316, 418n67
Fury, Ed, 148
Fussell, Samuel, 365

Gaines, Charles, 32, 227–229, 280, 359
Gajda, Bob, 174, 371
Gajkowski, Frances, 385n56
Gallasch, Wayne, 271, 291
Gallucci, Bob, 262–263, 282, 373, 377
Gallucci, Joseph, 205
Galton, Francis, 31
Ganakes, Nick, 308
Gardner, Carroll "Pink," 68, 70
Gardner, Percy, 4–5
Gaspari, Rich, 280, 297, 338
Gaubert, James, 275
Gaudreau, Leo, 99
Gay, Arthur, 32, 37
General Assembly of International Sports Federations (GAISF), 215–218, 241–242, 268, 276, 322, 358, 404nn76–77
General Electric Company, 72
General Motors, 145
Gentle, David, 213, 359
George, Zelma, 189, 210
Georgetown University, 324
Geyer, Michael, 1
Giambologna (Jean Boulogne), 23
Giello, Tony, 374
Gilchrist, Elliot, 176
Gironda, Vince, 103, 178
Gitlin, Todd, 127
Giuliani, Ed, 238, 252, 260
Glassman, Greg, 423n55
Gleneicki, John, 328
Glossbrenner, Herb, 214
Gneisenau, August von, 6
Godbout, Germain, 141, 147

Goethe, Johann Wolfgang von, 4, 13
Going Down (film), 235
Gold, Joe, 123, 213, 237
Goldberg, Abe, 106
Goldhill, Simon, 380n18
Goldman, Bob, 262, 282, 300, 315
Gold's Classic, 245, 247, 408n57
Gold's Gym, 212, 225, 232, 235, 237–241, 243, 245–251, 258–260, 315, 331, 359
Goldstein, Laurence, 364
Goll, Mike, 373
Gompers, Samuel, 36
Goodrich, Bert, 67, 69, 71–72, 78, 91, 94–95, 98, 123, 246, 354, 371
Goodwin, Budd, 43
Gorman, Margaret, 35
Gosch, Robert, 373
Gourgott, John, 159, 165, 372–373
Grafas, Paul, 309, 373
Graham, Mike, 236, 251, 362, 367, 423n49
Graham, Paul, 269
Grandjean, Ann, 262
Grandmasters Mr. America: AAU over 50, 374; AAU over 60, 374; AAU over 70, 374
Grannis, Lori, 335
Grant, Bill, 188, 202, 203, 219, 223, 245, 247, 308, 364, 376
Grant, Paul, 214, 216
Greathouse, Kevin, 375
Greathouse, Molly, 375
Greeks, ancient, xi, 1–7, 9–12, 17–18, 20–24, 26–33, 35, 37–39, 41–43, 45, 52–54, 58, 60–61, 63, 68–69, 72, 74, 80, 84, 86–89, 92, 94–95, 99–101, 107–118, 114–115, 120, 123, 125, 128–129, 139, 144, 147, 165, 178–180, 183, 186–187, 191, 202–203, 220, 222–223, 229–230, 237, 239, 254, 258, 263–265, 279–280, 282–283, 302, 304–307, 311, 331, 341, 347, 351, 355, 357, 359–360, 362–365, 367–369, 380n9, 380n16, 381n31, 382n8, 383n52, 412n34, 423n49
Green, Harvey, 6–7
Green, Rawle, 350, 372
Greenfield, George, 131, 133
Greenough, Horatio, 6